Garfield
FAT CAT 3-PACK
VOLUME 17

Garfield
FAT CAT 3-PACK
VOLUME 17

BY
JIM DAVIS

BALLANTINE BOOKS TRADE PAPERBACKS · NEW YORK

2014 Ballantine Books Trade Paperback Edition

Published in the United States by Ballantine Books, an imprint of Random House,
a division of Penguin Random House LLC, New York.

BALLANTINE and the HOUSE colophon are registered trademarks of Random House LLC.

NICKELODEON is a Trademark of Viacom International, Inc.

ISBN 978-0-345-52603-8

Printed in China on acid-free paper

randomhousebooks.com

10

Garfield

WEIGHS HIS OPTIONS

BY JIM DAVIS

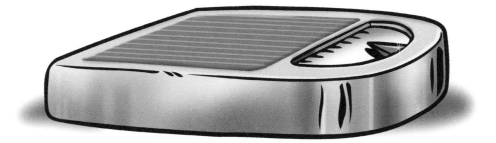

Ballantine Books Trade Paperbacks • New York

GARFIELD FROM THE TRASH BIN

One cat's trash is another cat's treasure, and in the all-new Ballantine book, Garfield creator Jim Davis has collected the best of the worst: never-before-seen rejected comic strips, questionable covers, silly sketches, and over-the-top outtakes sure to amuse—or offend—just about everyone. So hold your nose and dive in!

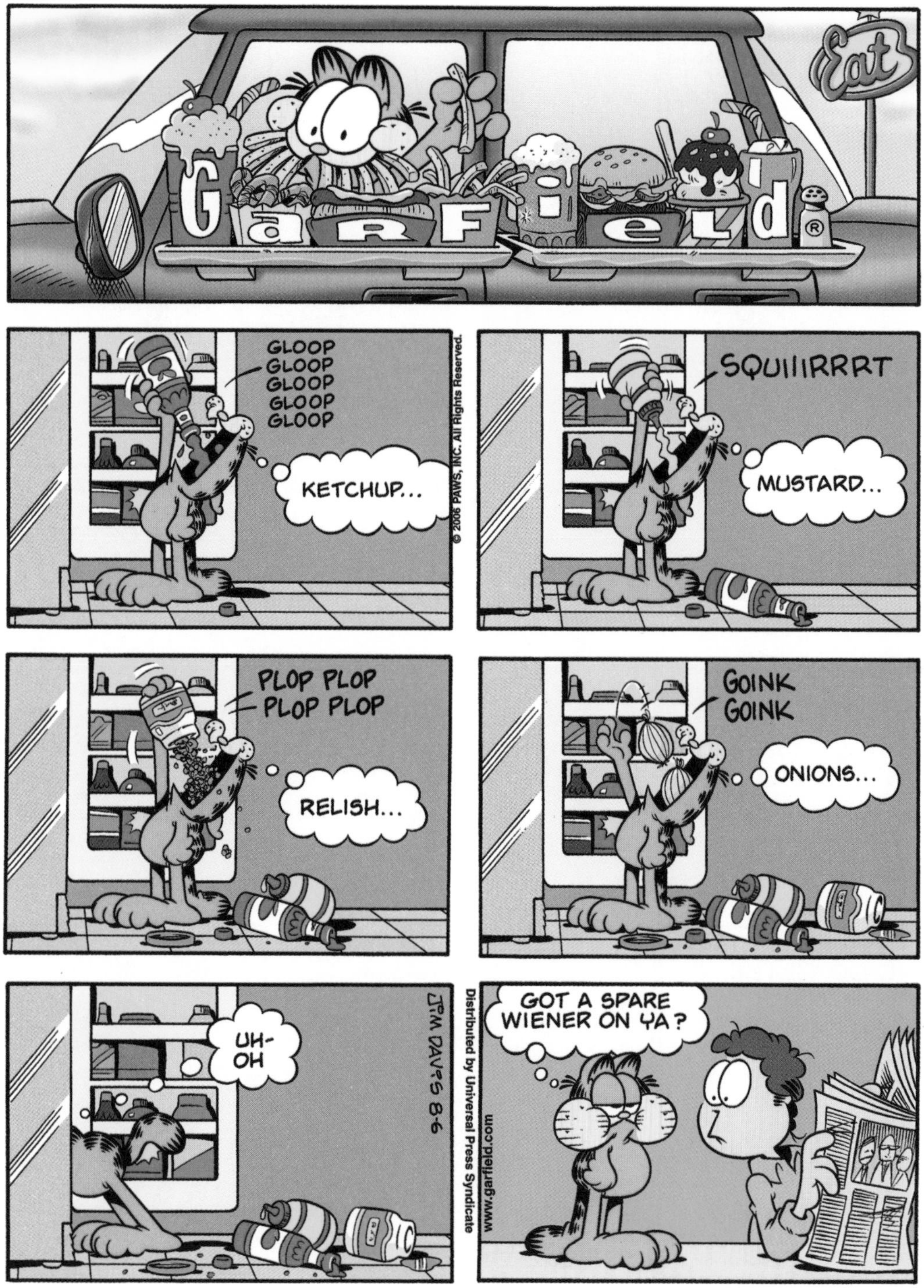
Eat
Garfield®
GLOOP GLOOP GLOOP GLOOP GLOOP
KETCHUP...
© 2006 PAWS, INC. All Rights Reserved.
SQUIIIRRRT
MUSTARD...
PLOP PLOP PLOP PLOP
RELISH...
GOINK GOINK
ONIONS...
UH-OH
JIM DAVIS 8-6
Distributed by Universal Press Syndicate
www.garfield.com
GOT A SPARE WIENER ON YA?

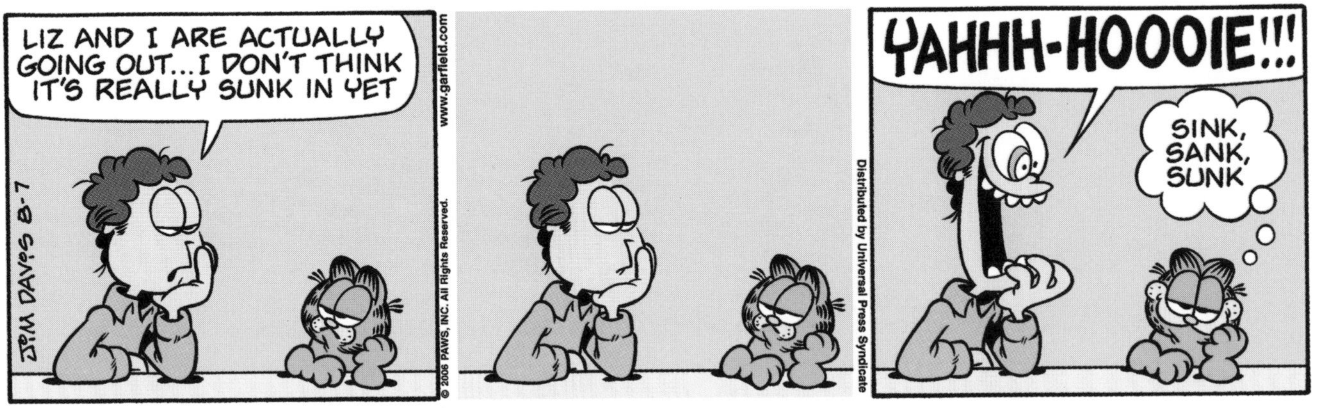
LIZ AND I ARE ACTUALLY GOING OUT... I DON'T THINK IT'S REALLY SUNK IN YET
JIM DAVIS 8-7
© 2006 PAWS, INC. All Rights Reserved. www.garfield.com
Distributed by Universal Press Syndicate
YAHHH-HOOOIE!!!
SINK, SANK, SUNK

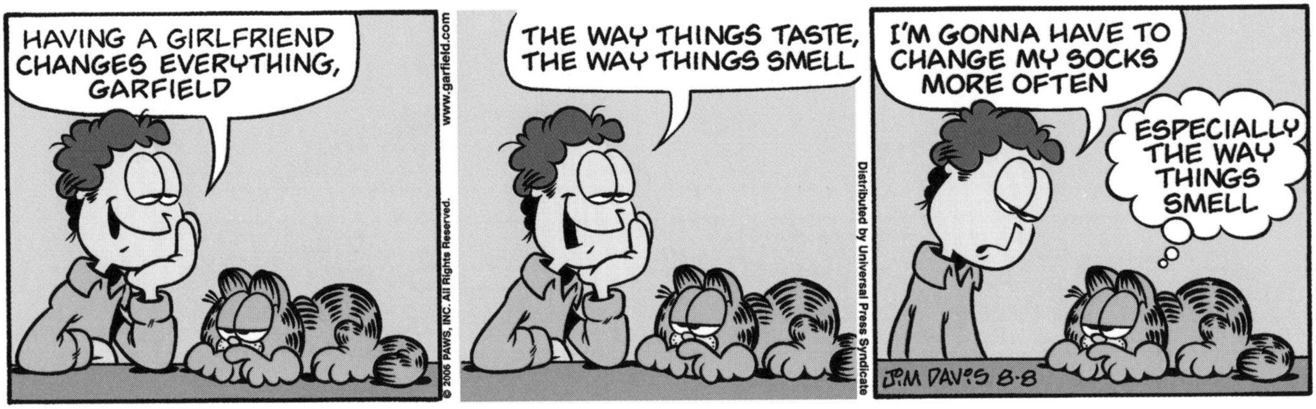
HAVING A GIRLFRIEND CHANGES EVERYTHING, GARFIELD
© 2006 PAWS, INC. All Rights Reserved. www.garfield.com
THE WAY THINGS TASTE, THE WAY THINGS SMELL
Distributed by Universal Press Syndicate
I'M GONNA HAVE TO CHANGE MY SOCKS MORE OFTEN
ESPECIALLY THE WAY THINGS SMELL
JIM DAVIS 8-8

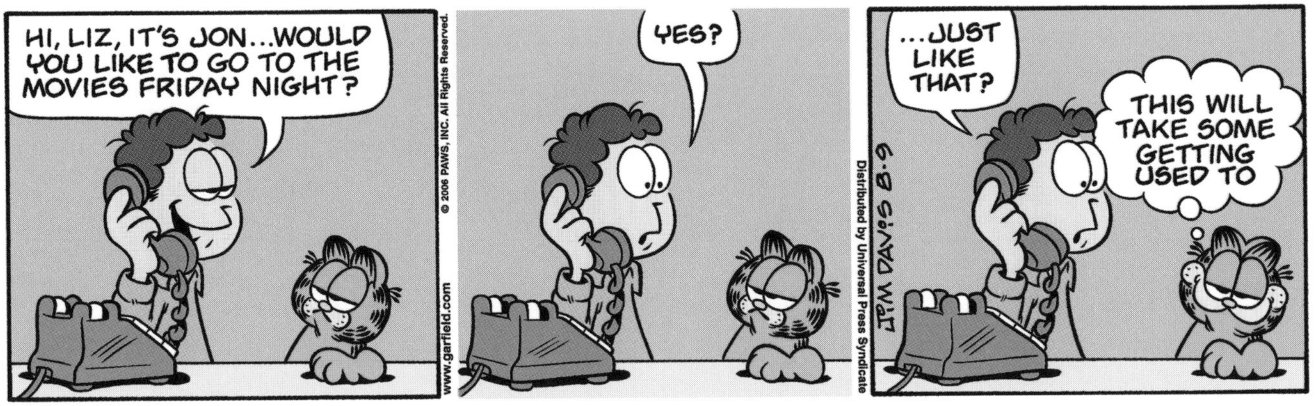
HI, LIZ, IT'S JON... WOULD YOU LIKE TO GO TO THE MOVIES FRIDAY NIGHT?
© 2006 PAWS, INC. All Rights Reserved. www.garfield.com
YES?
Distributed by Universal Press Syndicate
JIM DAVIS 8-9
...JUST LIKE THAT?
THIS WILL TAKE SOME GETTING USED TO

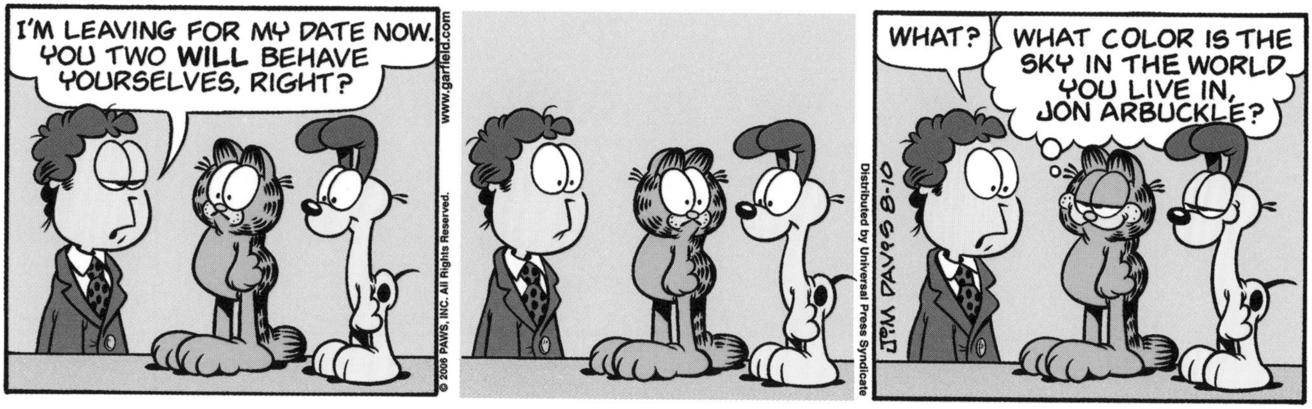
I'M LEAVING FOR MY DATE NOW. YOU TWO WILL BEHAVE YOURSELVES, RIGHT?
WHAT?
WHAT COLOR IS THE SKY IN THE WORLD YOU LIVE IN, JON ARBUCKLE?
© 2006 PAWS, INC. All Rights Reserved.
www.garfield.com
Distributed by Universal Press Syndicate
JIM DAVIS 8-10

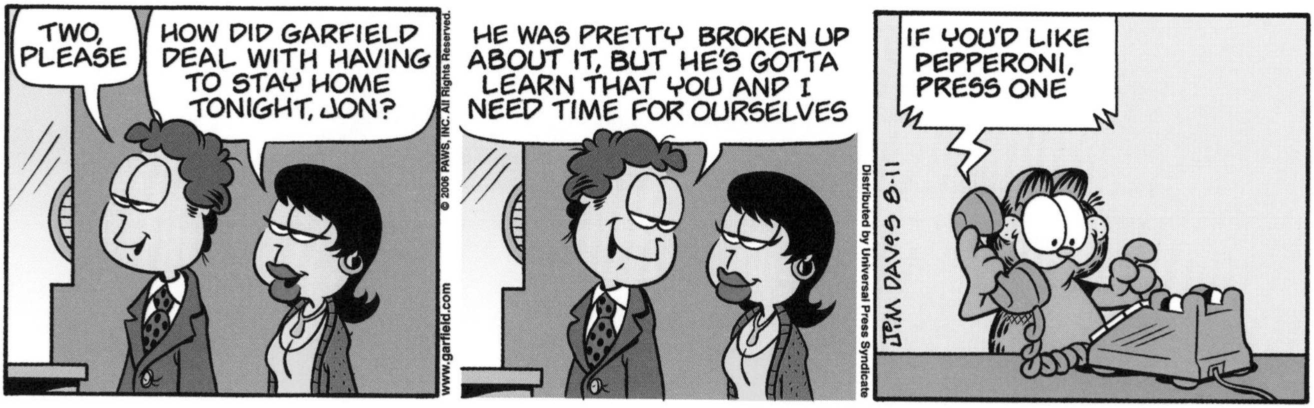
TWO, PLEASE
HOW DID GARFIELD DEAL WITH HAVING TO STAY HOME TONIGHT, JON?
HE WAS PRETTY BROKEN UP ABOUT IT, BUT HE'S GOTTA LEARN THAT YOU AND I NEED TIME FOR OURSELVES
IF YOU'D LIKE PEPPERONI, PRESS ONE
© 2006 PAWS, INC. All Rights Reserved.
www.garfield.com
Distributed by Universal Press Syndicate
JIM DAVIS 8-11

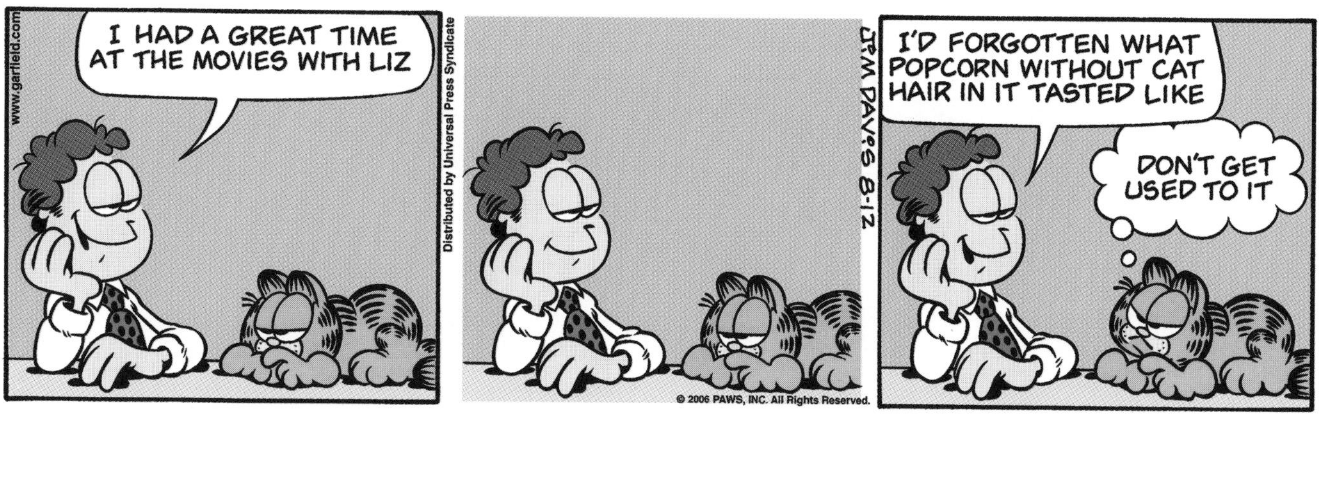
I HAD A GREAT TIME AT THE MOVIES WITH LIZ
I'D FORGOTTEN WHAT POPCORN WITHOUT CAT HAIR IN IT TASTED LIKE
DON'T GET USED TO IT
www.garfield.com
Distributed by Universal Press Syndicate
JIM DAVIS 8-12
© 2006 PAWS, INC. All Rights Reserved.

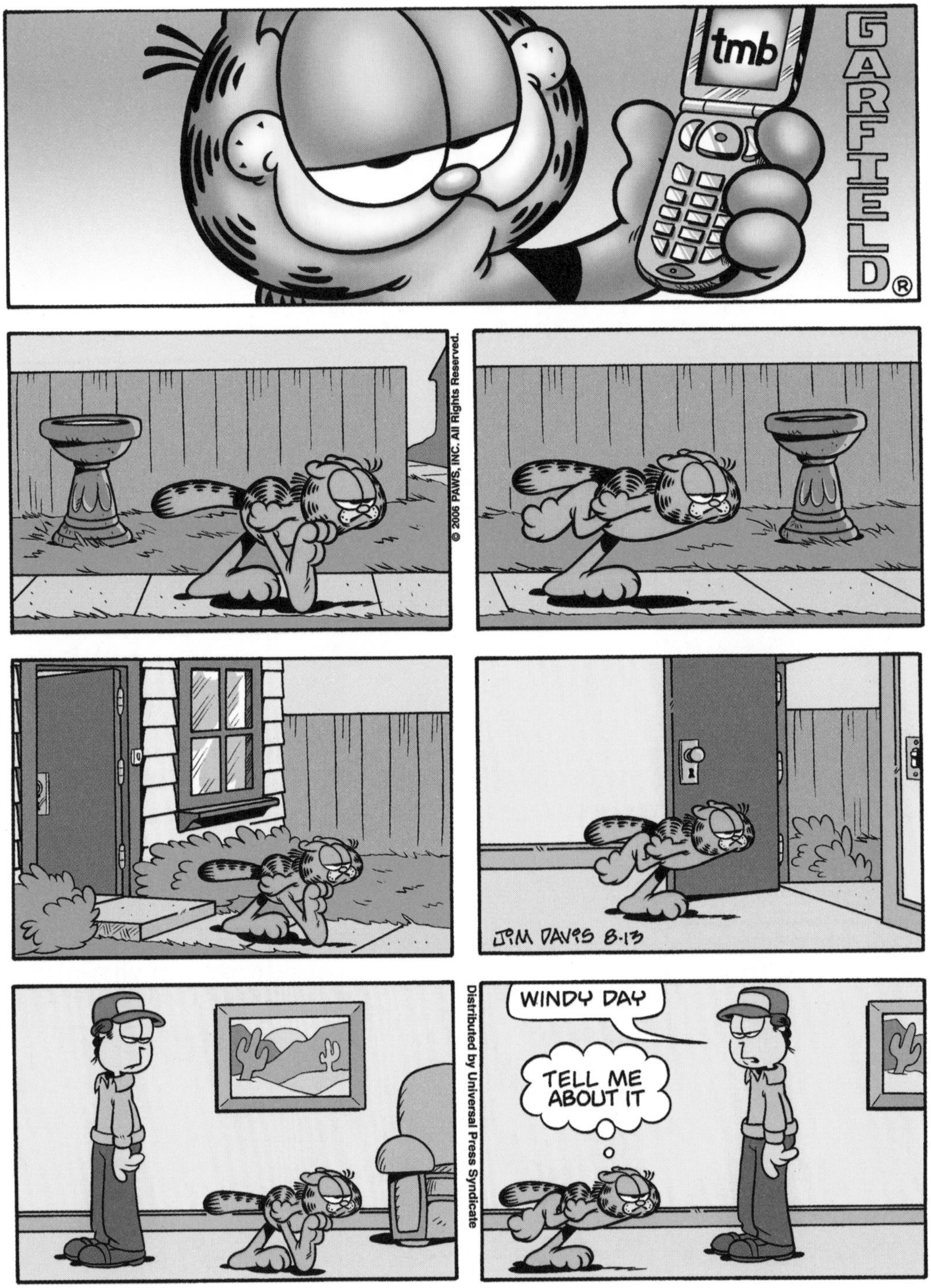
GARFIELD®
tmb
© 2006 PAWS, INC. All Rights Reserved.
JIM DAVIS 8-13
Distributed by Universal Press Syndicate
WINDY DAY
TELL ME ABOUT IT

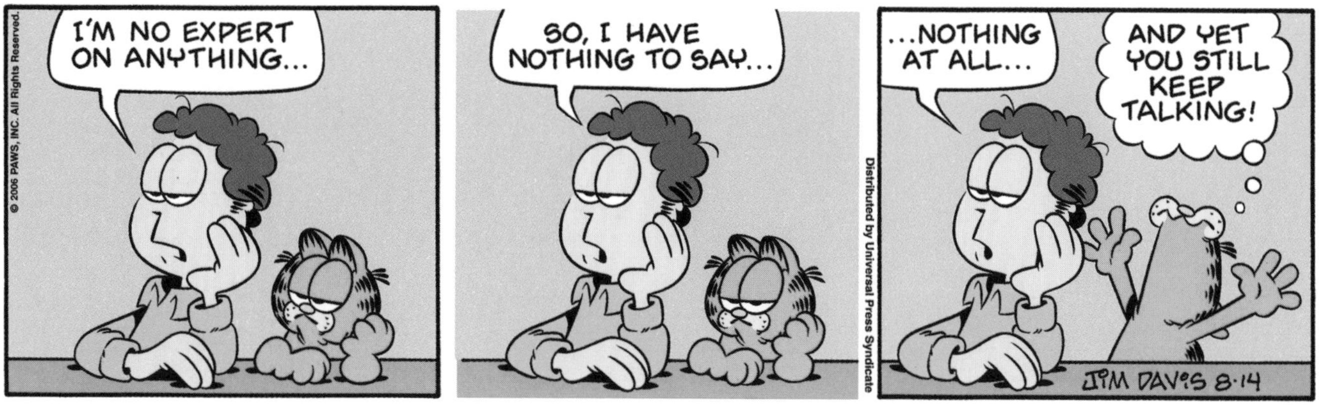
I'M NO EXPERT ON ANYTHING...
SO, I HAVE NOTHING TO SAY...
...NOTHING AT ALL...
AND YET YOU STILL KEEP TALKING!
JIM DAVIS 8·14
© 2006 PAWS, INC. All Rights Reserved.
Distributed by Universal Press Syndicate

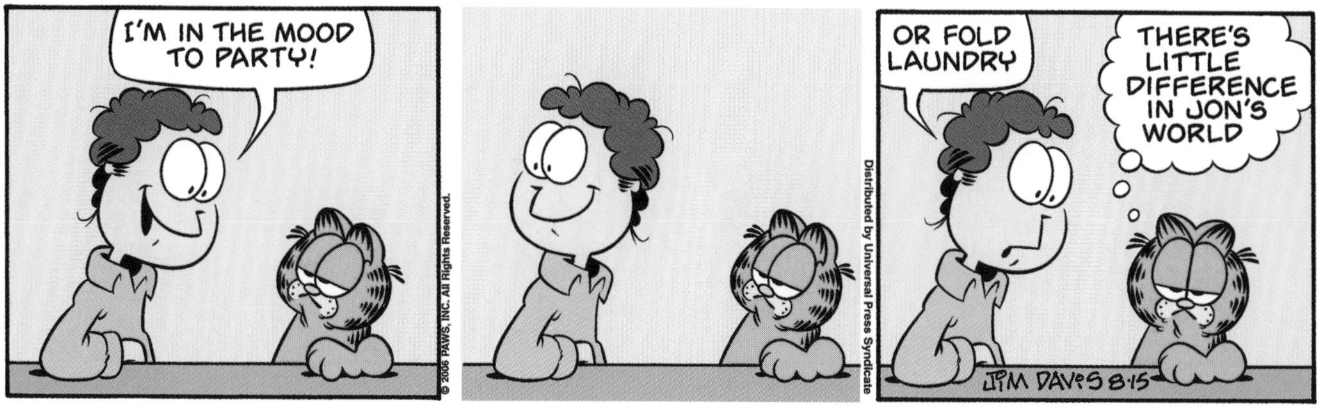
I'M IN THE MOOD TO PARTY!
OR FOLD LAUNDRY
THERE'S LITTLE DIFFERENCE IN JON'S WORLD
JIM DAVIS 8·15
© 2006 PAWS, INC. All Rights Reserved.
Distributed by Universal Press Syndicate

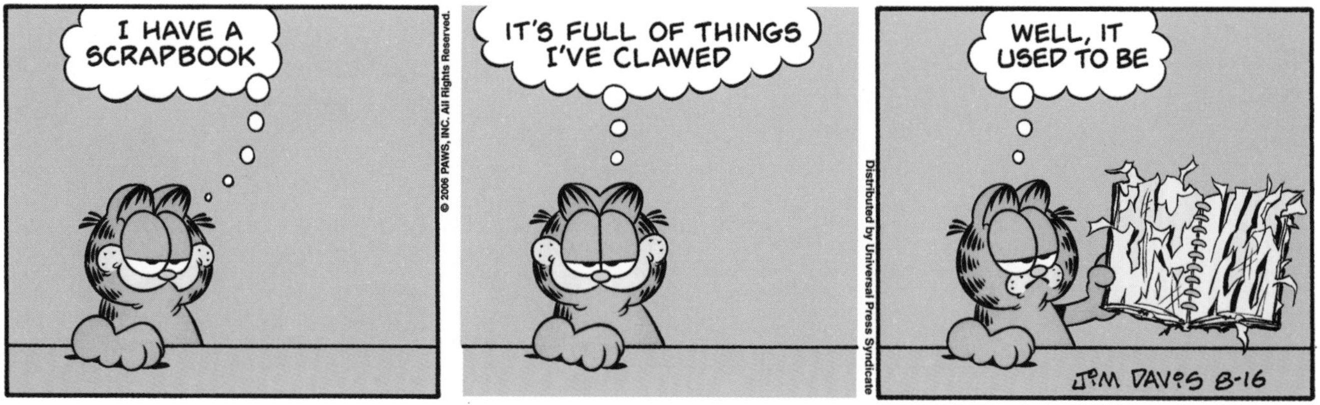
I HAVE A SCRAPBOOK
IT'S FULL OF THINGS I'VE CLAWED
WELL, IT USED TO BE
JIM DAVIS 8-16
© 2006 PAWS, INC. All Rights Reserved.
Distributed by Universal Press Syndicate

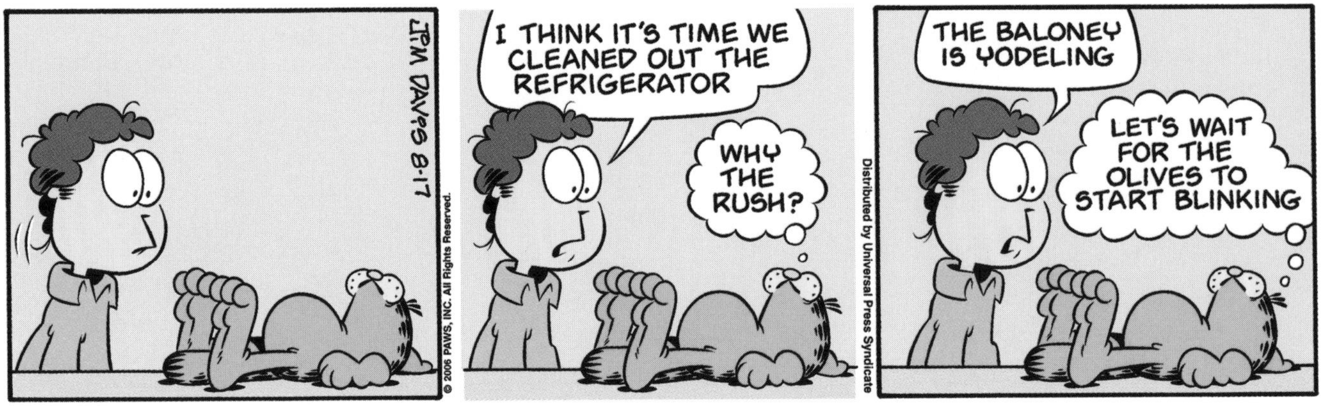
JIM DAVIS 8-17
© 2006 PAWS, INC. All Rights Reserved.
I THINK IT'S TIME WE CLEANED OUT THE REFRIGERATOR
WHY THE RUSH?
Distributed by Universal Press Syndicate
THE BALONEY IS YODELING
LET'S WAIT FOR THE OLIVES TO START BLINKING

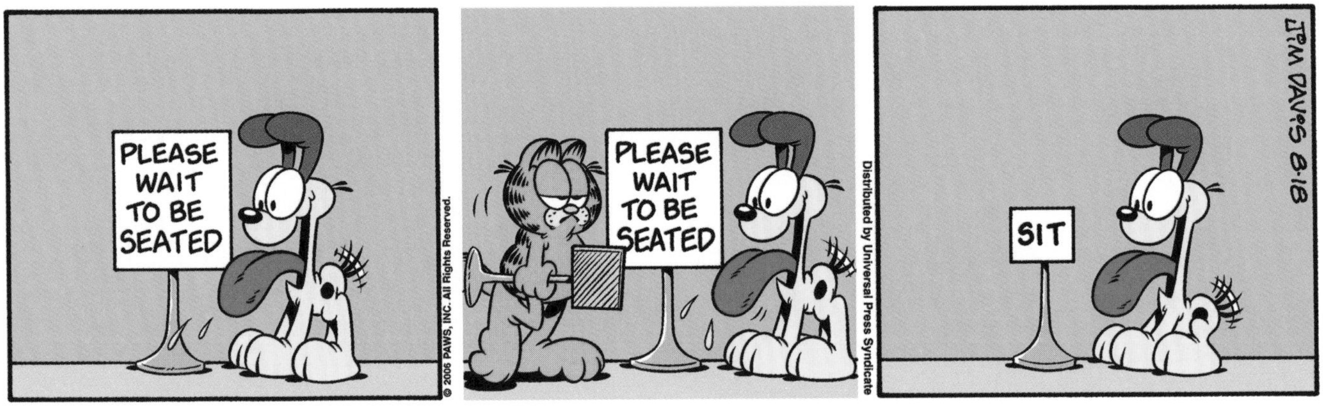
PLEASE WAIT TO BE SEATED
© 2006 PAWS, INC. All Rights Reserved.
PLEASE WAIT TO BE SEATED
Distributed by Universal Press Syndicate
SIT
JIM DAVIS 8-18

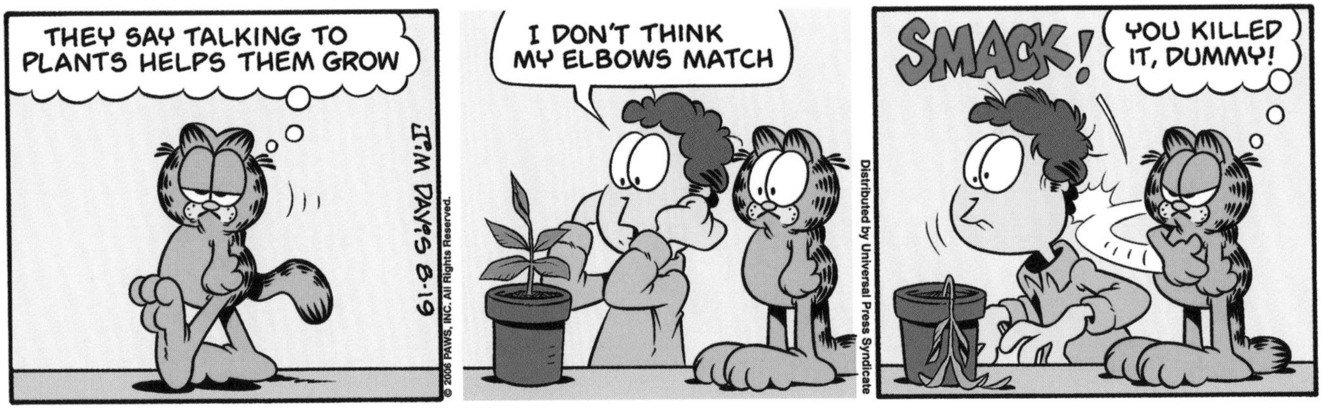
THEY SAY TALKING TO PLANTS HELPS THEM GROW
JIM DAVIS 8-19
© 2006 PAWS, INC. All Rights Reserved.
I DON'T THINK MY ELBOWS MATCH
Distributed by Universal Press Syndicate
SMACK!
YOU KILLED IT, DUMMY!

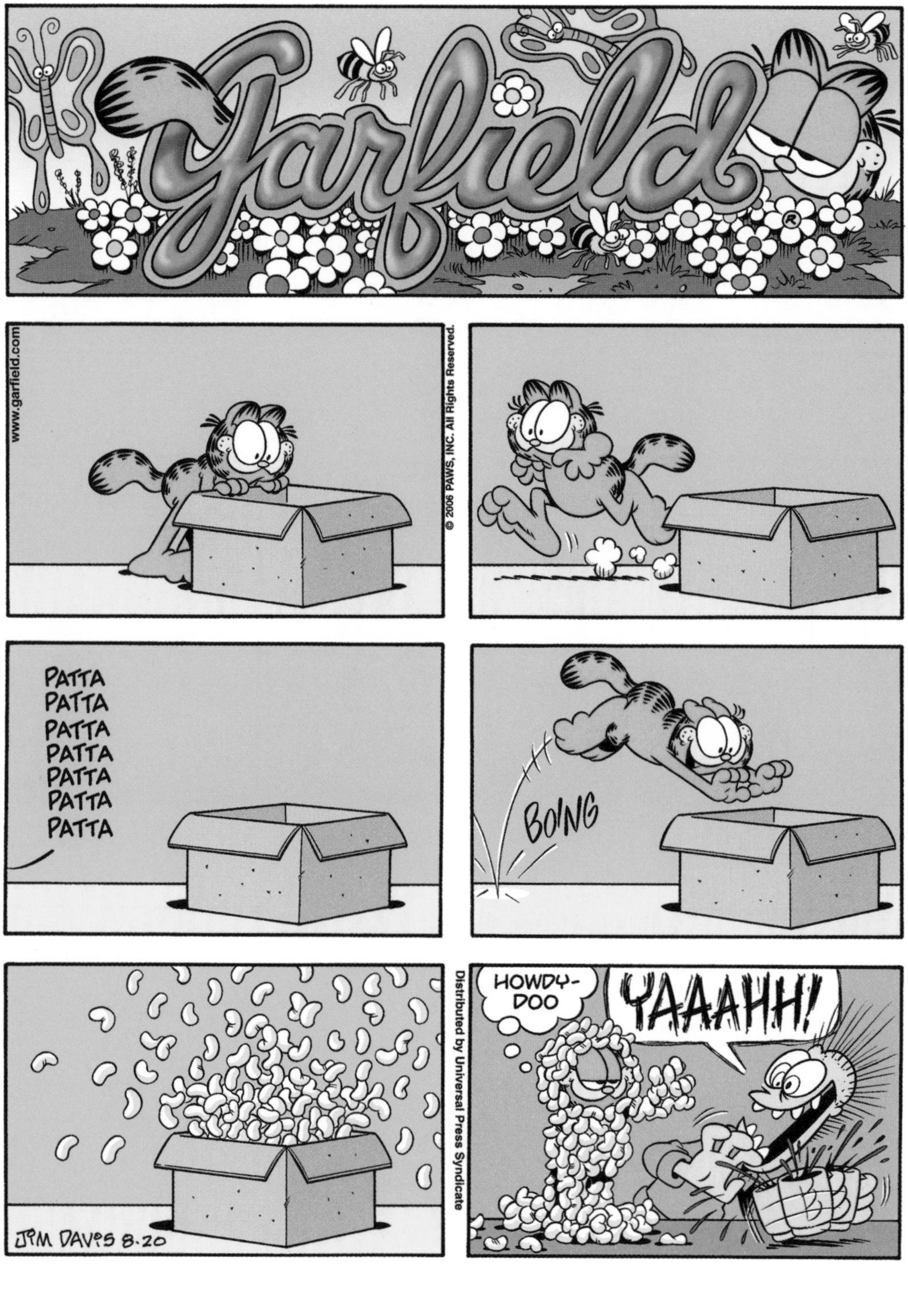
Garfield
www.garfield.com
© 2006 PAWS, INC. All Rights Reserved.
PATTA PATTA PATTA PATTA PATTA PATTA PATTA
BOING
JIM DAVIS 8-20
Distributed by Universal Press Syndicate
HOWDY-DOO
YAAAHH!

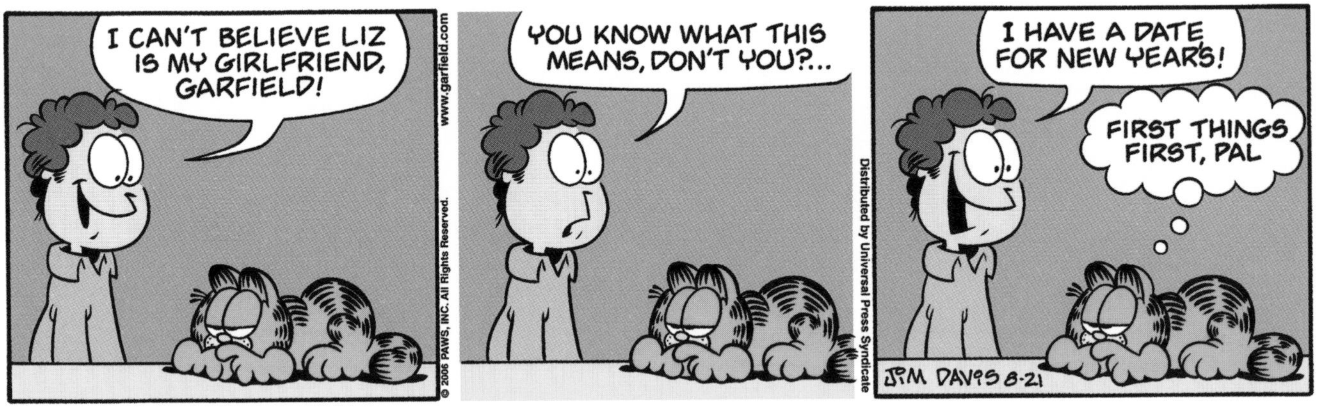
I CAN'T BELIEVE LIZ IS MY GIRLFRIEND, GARFIELD!
YOU KNOW WHAT THIS MEANS, DON'T YOU?...
I HAVE A DATE FOR NEW YEAR'S!
FIRST THINGS FIRST, PAL
JIM DAVIS 8-21
© 2006 PAWS, INC. All Rights Reserved. www.garfield.com
Distributed by Universal Press Syndicate

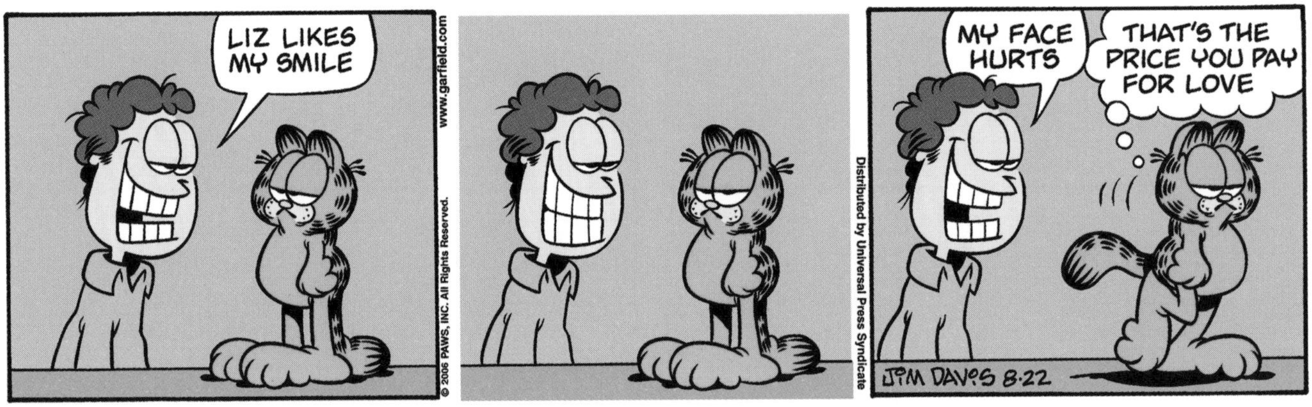
LIZ LIKES MY SMILE
MY FACE HURTS
THAT'S THE PRICE YOU PAY FOR LOVE
JIM DAVIS 8-22
© 2006 PAWS, INC. All Rights Reserved. www.garfield.com
Distributed by Universal Press Syndicate

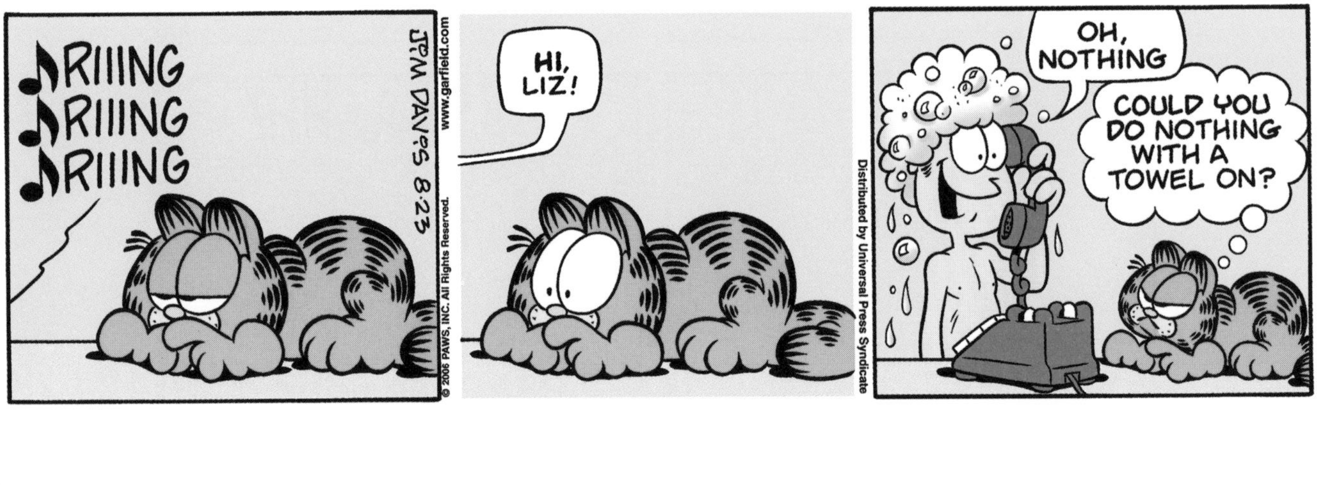
RIIING
RIIING
RIIING
JIM DAVIS 8-23
HI, LIZ!
OH, NOTHING
COULD YOU DO NOTHING WITH A TOWEL ON?
© 2006 PAWS, INC. All Rights Reserved. www.garfield.com
Distributed by Universal Press Syndicate

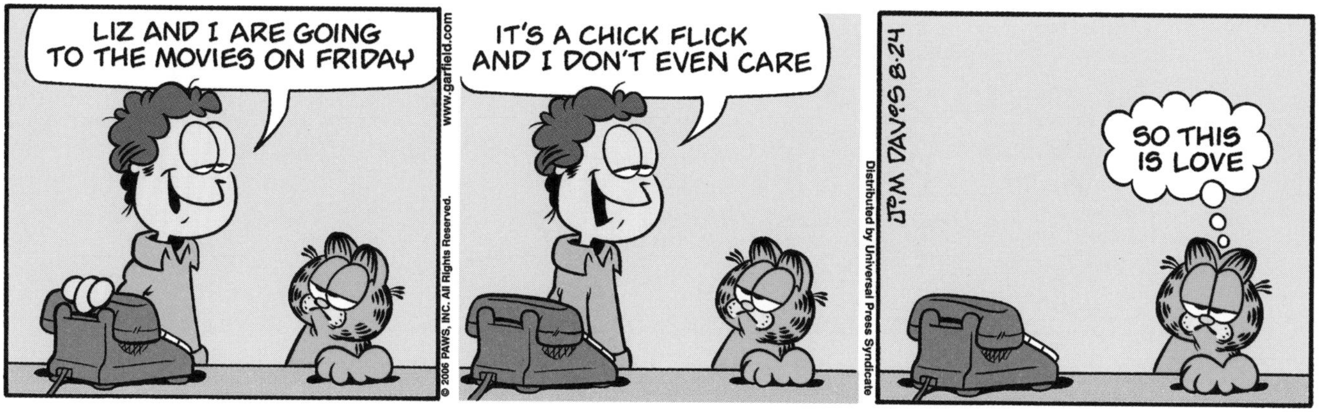
LIZ AND I ARE GOING TO THE MOVIES ON FRIDAY
IT'S A CHICK FLICK AND I DON'T EVEN CARE
SO THIS IS LOVE
www.garfield.com
© 2006 PAWS, INC. All Rights Reserved.
Distributed by Universal Press Syndicate
JIM DAVIS 8·24

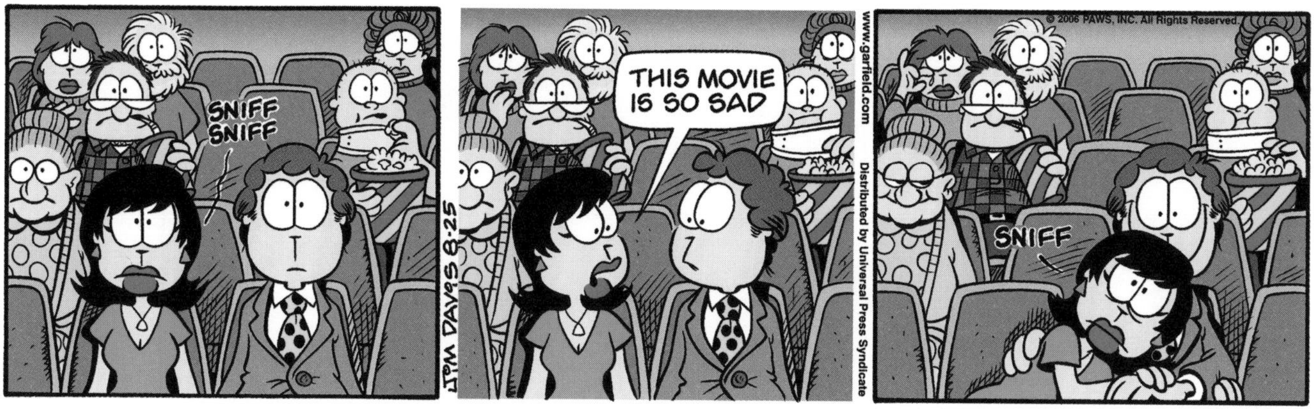
SNIFF SNIFF
THIS MOVIE IS SO SAD
SNIFF
JIM DAVIS 8·25
www.garfield.com
Distributed by Universal Press Syndicate
© 2006 PAWS, INC. All Rights Reserved.

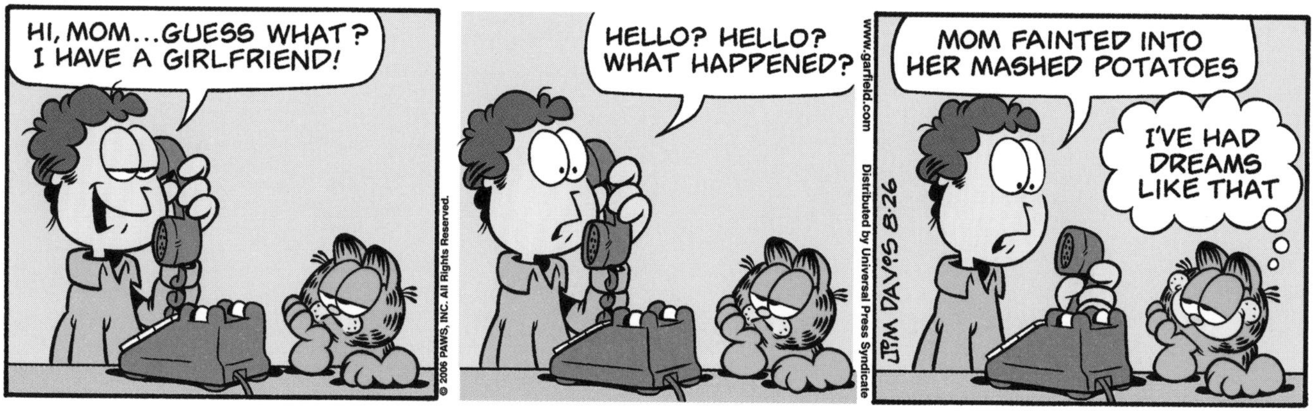
HI, MOM...GUESS WHAT? I HAVE A GIRLFRIEND!
HELLO? HELLO? WHAT HAPPENED?
MOM FAINTED INTO HER MASHED POTATOES
I'VE HAD DREAMS LIKE THAT
© 2006 PAWS, INC. All Rights Reserved.
www.garfield.com
Distributed by Universal Press Syndicate
JIM DAVIS 8·26

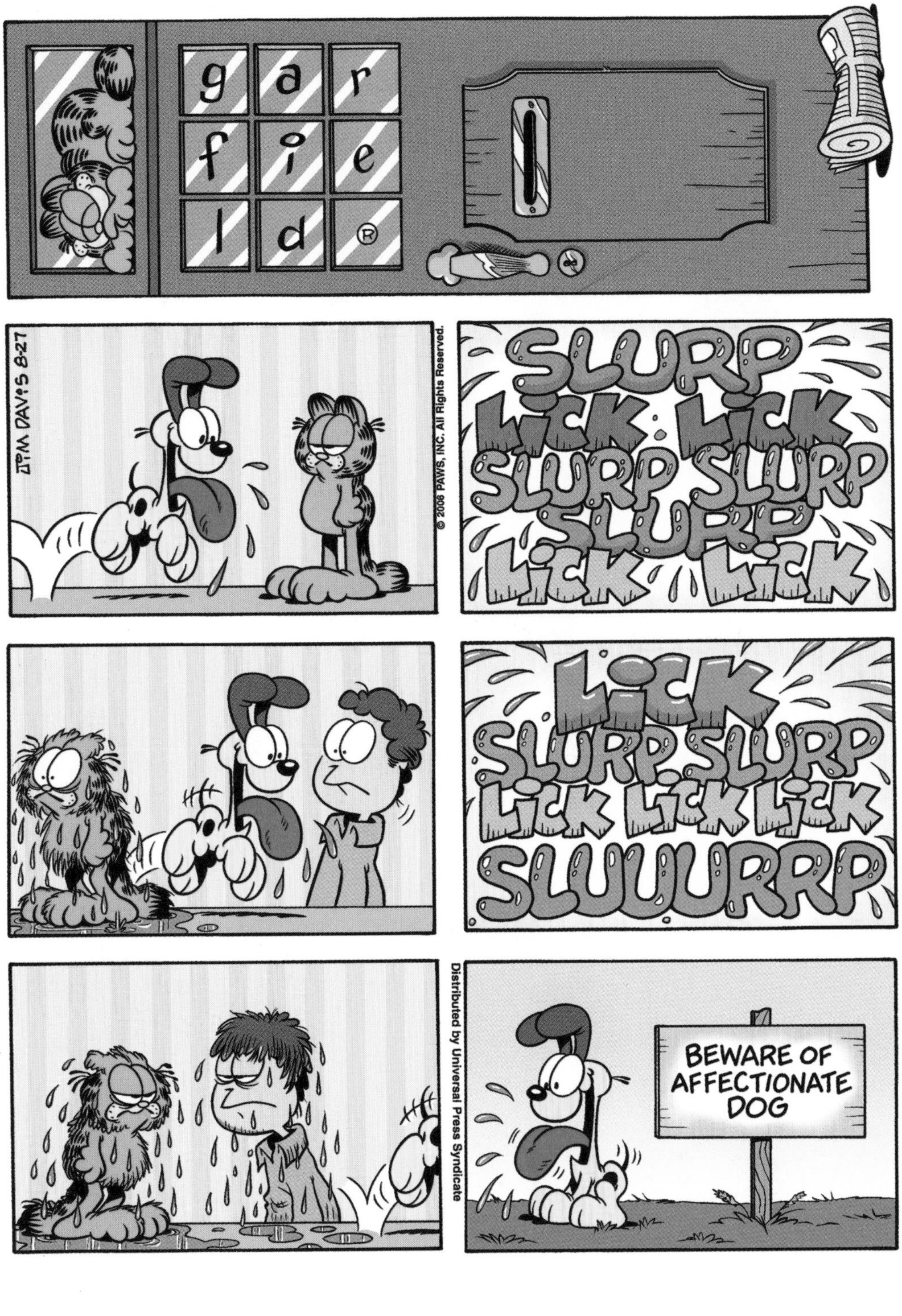
garfield®
JIM DAVIS 8-27
© 2008 PAWS, INC. All Rights Reserved.
SLURP
LICK LICK
SLURP SLURP
SLURP
LICK LICK
LICK
SLURP SLURP
LICK LICK LICK
SLUUURRP
Distributed by Universal Press Syndicate
BEWARE OF AFFECTIONATE DOG

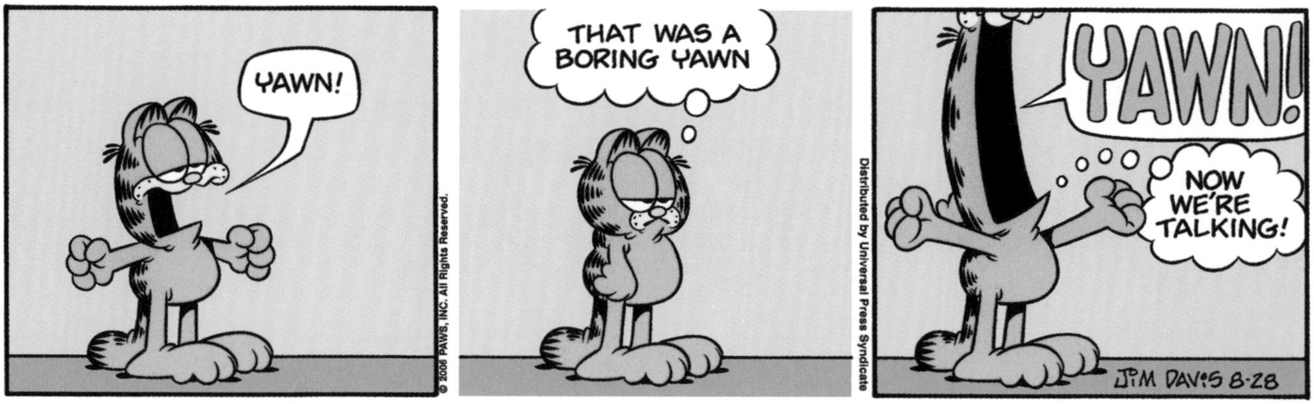
YAWN!
THAT WAS A BORING YAWN
YAWN!
NOW WE'RE TALKING!
JIM DAVIS 8-28
© 2006 PAWS, INC. All Rights Reserved.
Distributed by Universal Press Syndicate

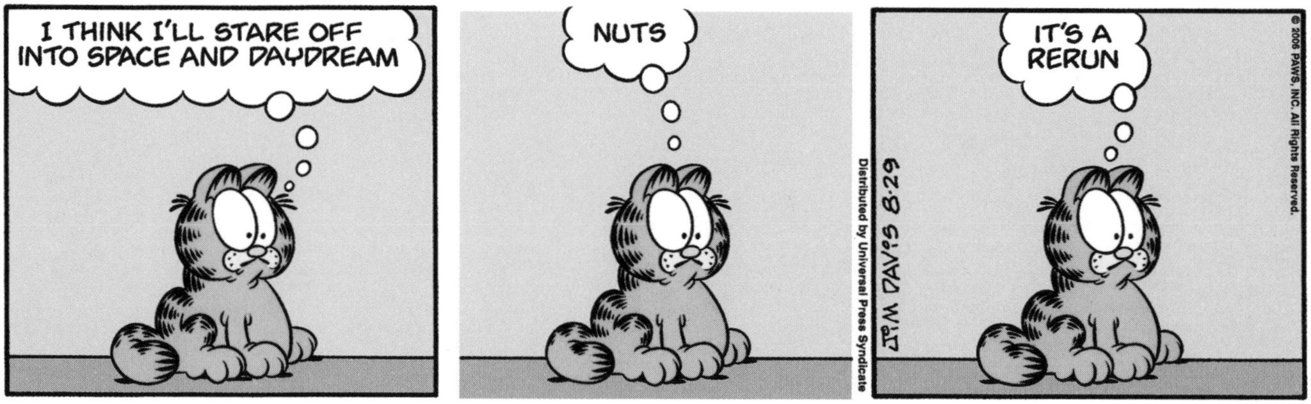
I THINK I'LL STARE OFF INTO SPACE AND DAYDREAM
NUTS
IT'S A RERUN
JIM DAVIS 8-29
Distributed by Universal Press Syndicate
© 2006 PAWS, INC. All Rights Reserved.

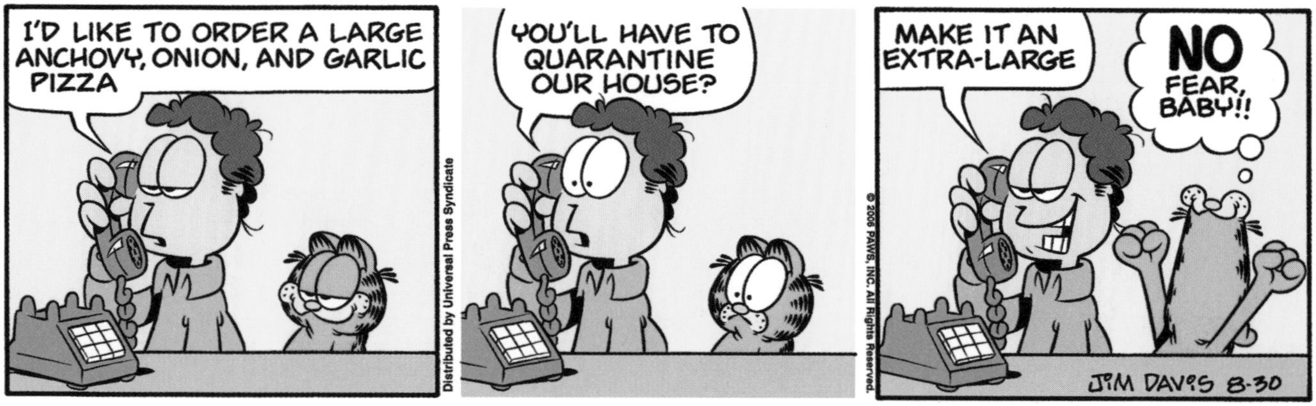
I'D LIKE TO ORDER A LARGE ANCHOVY, ONION, AND GARLIC PIZZA
YOU'LL HAVE TO QUARANTINE OUR HOUSE?
MAKE IT AN EXTRA-LARGE
NO FEAR, BABY!!
JIM DAVIS 8-30
Distributed by Universal Press Syndicate
© 2006 PAWS, INC. All Rights Reserved.

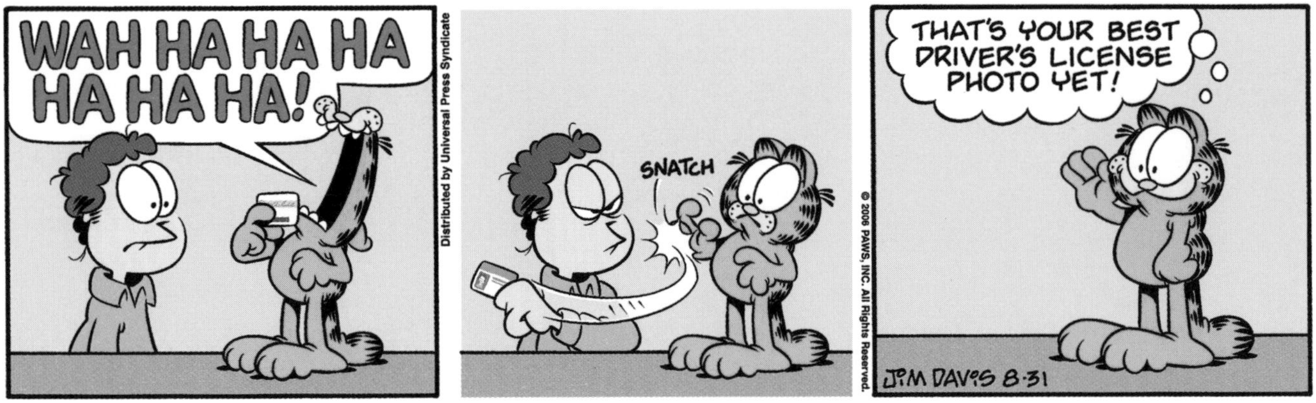
WAH HA HA HA HA HA HA!
Distributed by Universal Press Syndicate
SNATCH
© 2006 PAWS, INC. All Rights Reserved.
THAT'S YOUR BEST DRIVER'S LICENSE PHOTO YET!
JIM DAVIS 8-31

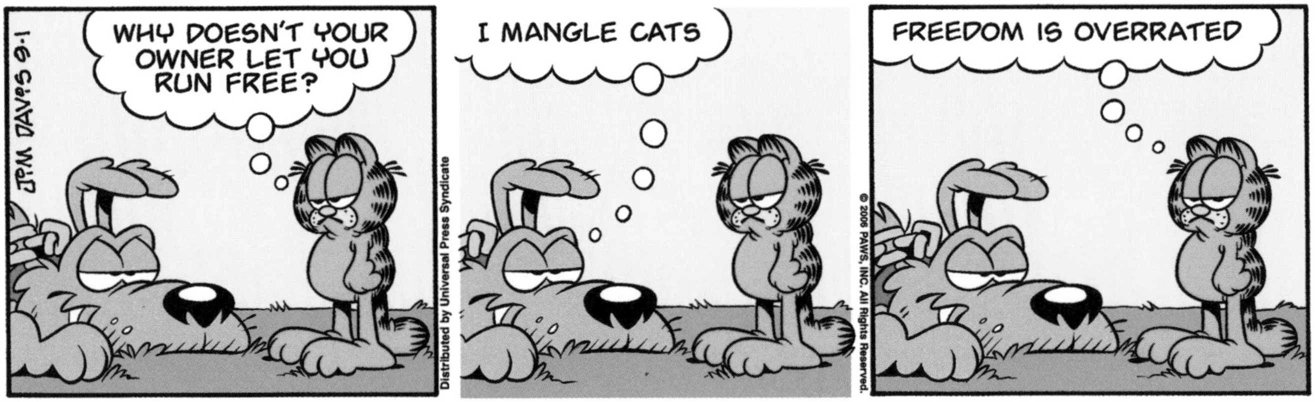
JIM DAVIS 9-1
WHY DOESN'T YOUR OWNER LET YOU RUN FREE?
Distributed by Universal Press Syndicate
I MANGLE CATS
© 2006 PAWS, INC. All Rights Reserved.
FREEDOM IS OVERRATED

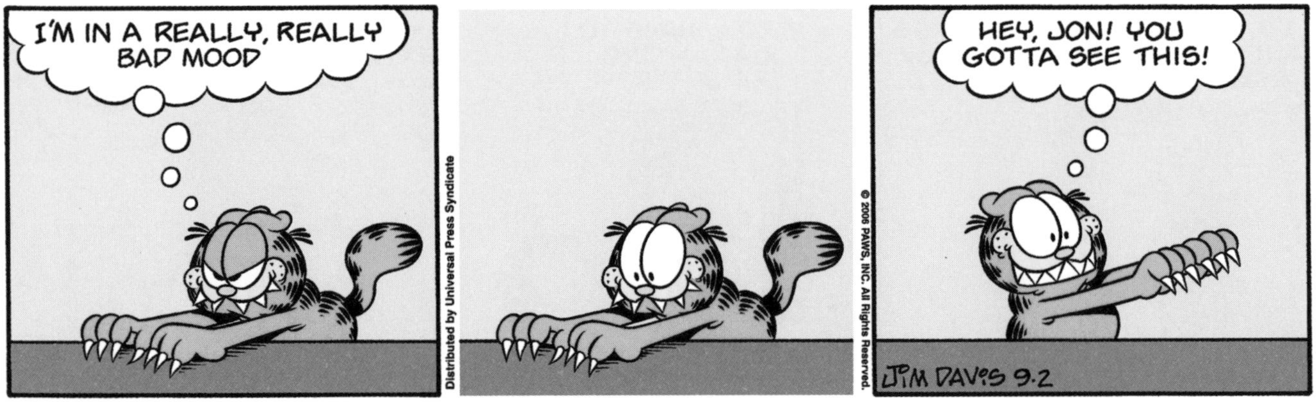
I'M IN A REALLY, REALLY BAD MOOD
Distributed by Universal Press Syndicate
© 2006 PAWS, INC. All Rights Reserved.
HEY, JON! YOU GOTTA SEE THIS!
JIM DAVIS 9-2

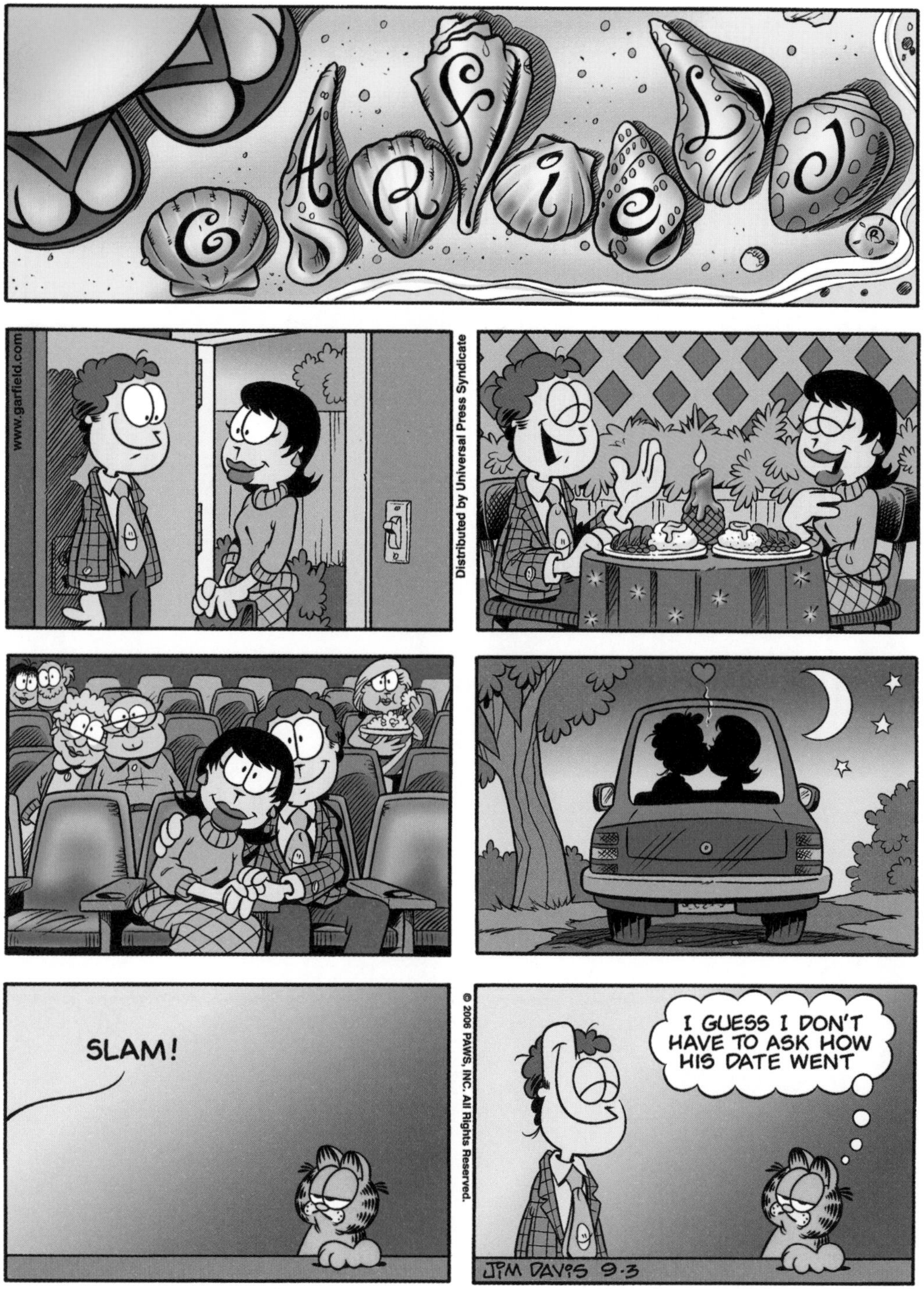
GARFIELD
www.garfield.com
Distributed by Universal Press Syndicate
© 2006 PAWS, INC. All Rights Reserved.
SLAM!
I GUESS I DON'T HAVE TO ASK HOW HIS DATE WENT
JIM DAVIS 9-3

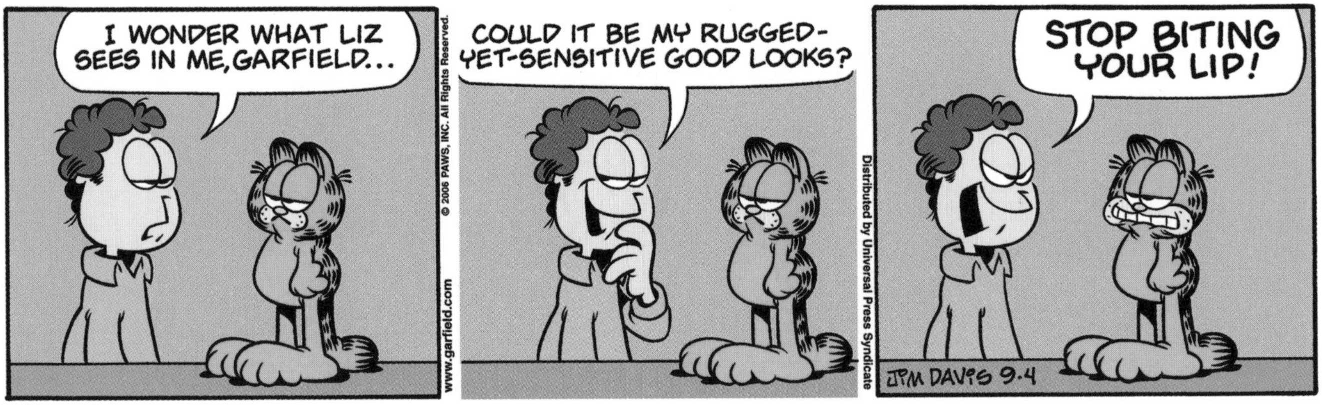
I WONDER WHAT LIZ SEES IN ME, GARFIELD...
COULD IT BE MY RUGGED-YET-SENSITIVE GOOD LOOKS?
STOP BITING YOUR LIP!
JIM DAVIS 9.4
© 2006 PAWS, INC. All Rights Reserved.
www.garfield.com
Distributed by Universal Press Syndicate

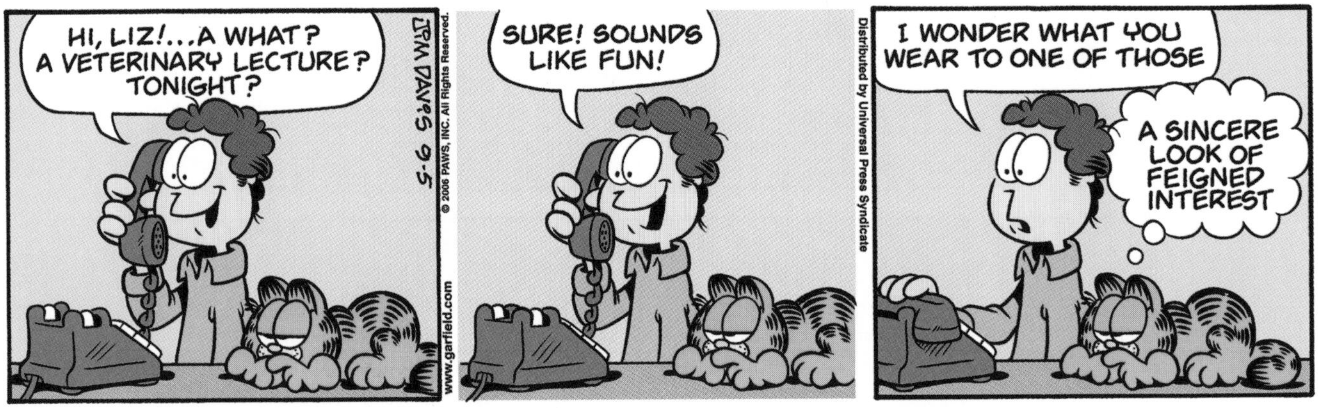
HI, LIZ!...A WHAT? A VETERINARY LECTURE? TONIGHT?
JIM DAVIS 9-5
SURE! SOUNDS LIKE FUN!
I WONDER WHAT YOU WEAR TO ONE OF THOSE
A SINCERE LOOK OF FEIGNED INTEREST
© 2006 PAWS, INC. All Rights Reserved.
www.garfield.com
Distributed by Universal Press Syndicate

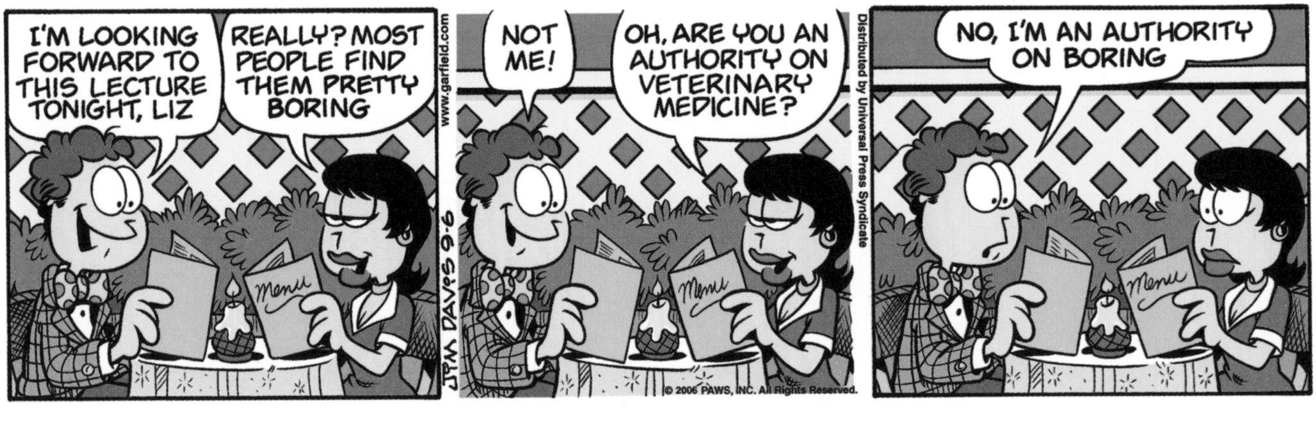
I'M LOOKING FORWARD TO THIS LECTURE TONIGHT, LIZ
REALLY? MOST PEOPLE FIND THEM PRETTY BORING
Menu
JIM DAVIS 9-6
NOT ME!
OH, ARE YOU AN AUTHORITY ON VETERINARY MEDICINE?
NO, I'M AN AUTHORITY ON BORING
www.garfield.com
© 2006 PAWS, INC. All Rights Reserved.
Distributed by Universal Press Syndicate

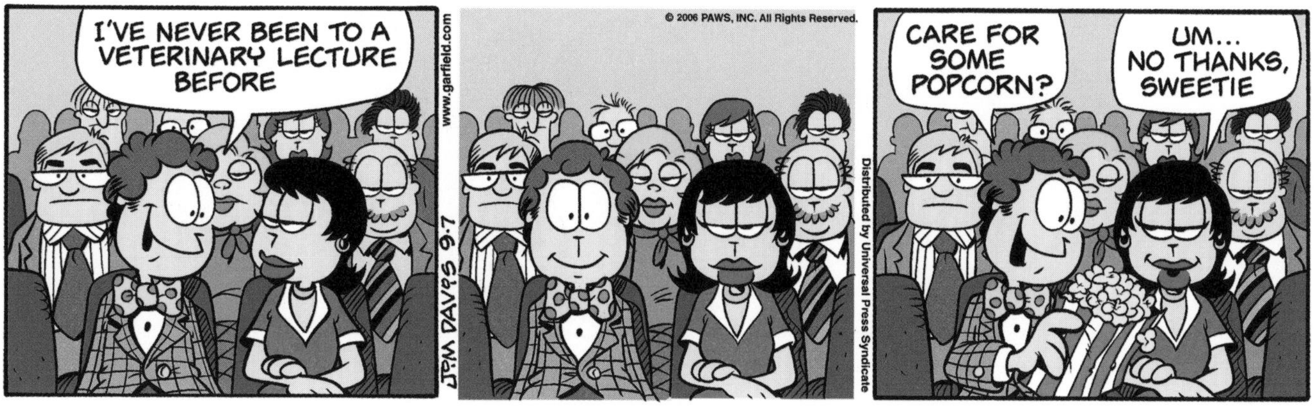
I'VE NEVER BEEN TO A VETERINARY LECTURE BEFORE
www.garfield.com
JIM DAVIS 9-7
© 2006 PAWS, INC. All Rights Reserved.
Distributed by Universal Press Syndicate
CARE FOR SOME POPCORN?
UM... NO THANKS, SWEETIE

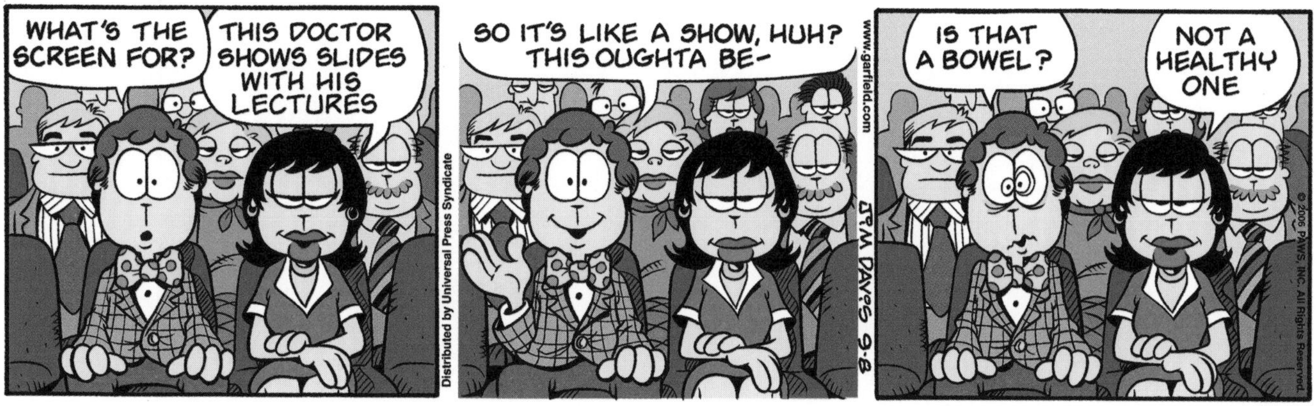
WHAT'S THE SCREEN FOR?
THIS DOCTOR SHOWS SLIDES WITH HIS LECTURES
Distributed by Universal Press Syndicate
SO IT'S LIKE A SHOW, HUH? THIS OUGHTA BE-
www.garfield.com
JIM DAVIS 9-8
IS THAT A BOWEL?
NOT A HEALTHY ONE
© 2006 PAWS, INC. All Rights Reserved.

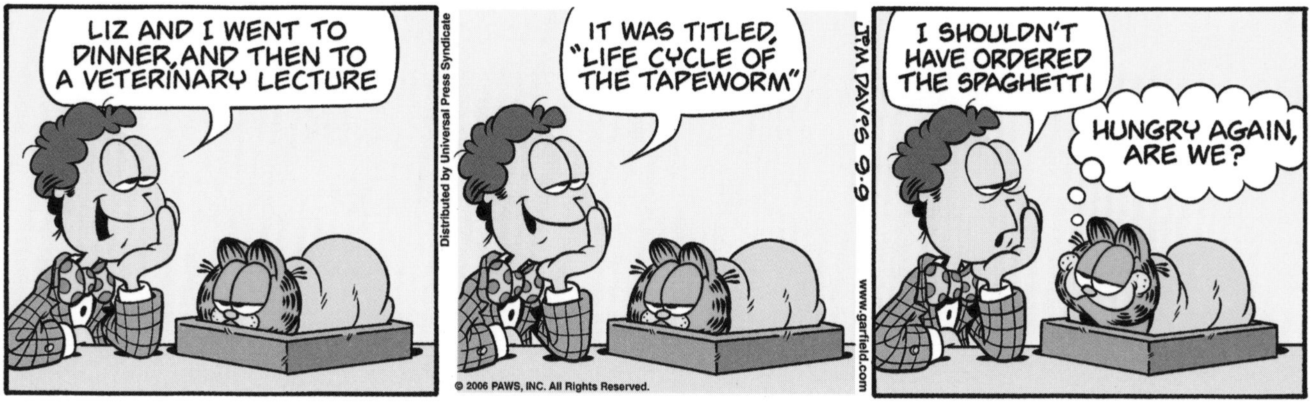
LIZ AND I WENT TO DINNER, AND THEN TO A VETERINARY LECTURE
Distributed by Universal Press Syndicate
IT WAS TITLED, "LIFE CYCLE OF THE TAPEWORM"
© 2006 PAWS, INC. All Rights Reserved.
JIM DAVIS 9-9
www.garfield.com
I SHOULDN'T HAVE ORDERED THE SPAGHETTI
HUNGRY AGAIN, ARE WE?

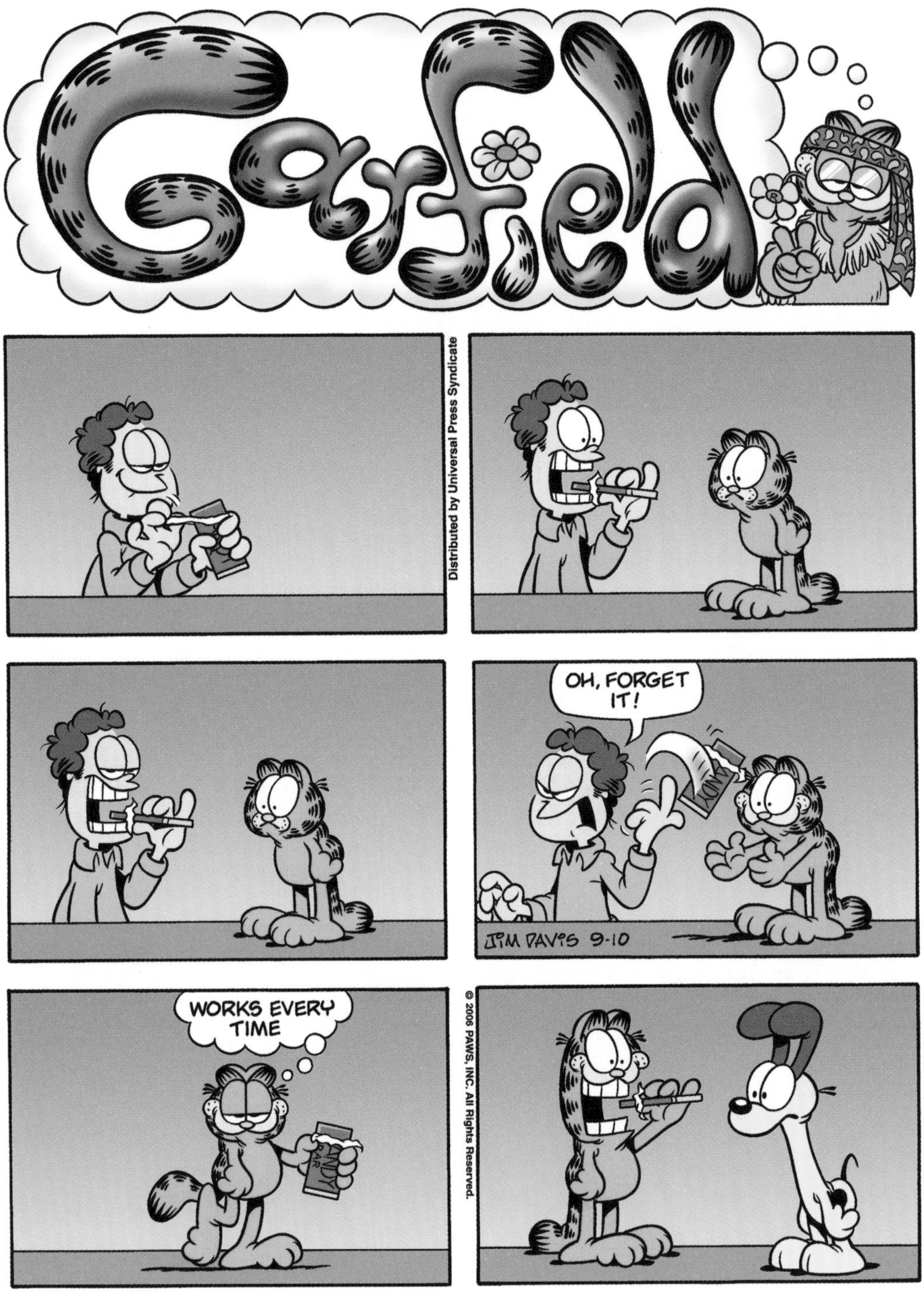
Garfield
OH, FORGET IT!
JIM DAVIS 9-10
WORKS EVERY TIME
Distributed by Universal Press Syndicate
© 2006 PAWS, INC. All Rights Reserved.

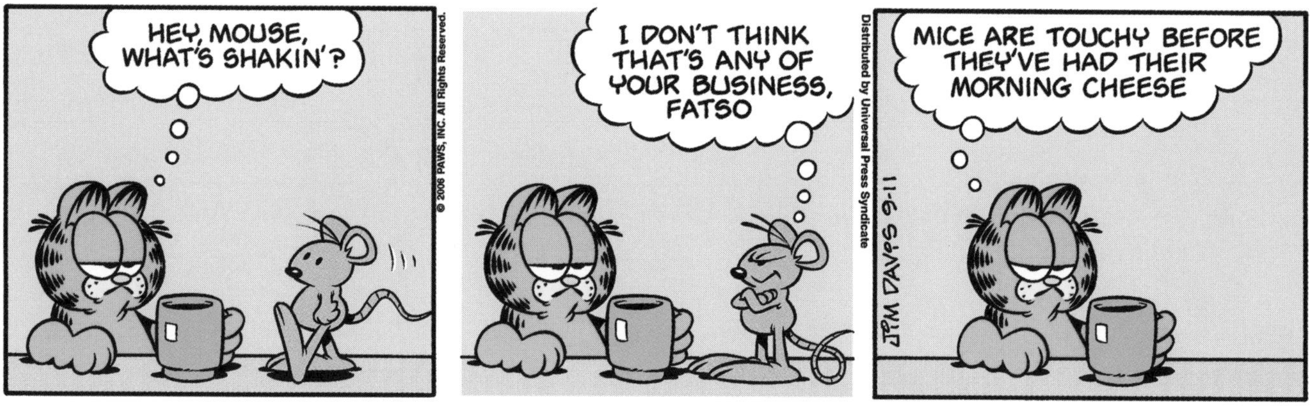
HEY, MOUSE, WHAT'S SHAKIN'?
I DON'T THINK THAT'S ANY OF YOUR BUSINESS, FATSO
MICE ARE TOUCHY BEFORE THEY'VE HAD THEIR MORNING CHEESE
JPM DAVPS 9-11

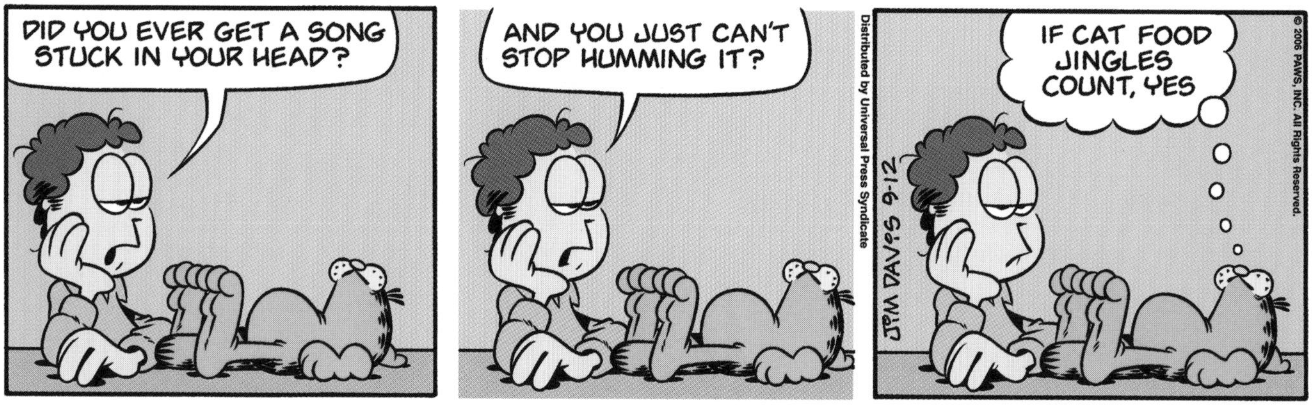
DID YOU EVER GET A SONG STUCK IN YOUR HEAD?
AND YOU JUST CAN'T STOP HUMMING IT?
IF CAT FOOD JINGLES COUNT, YES
JPM DAVPS 9-12

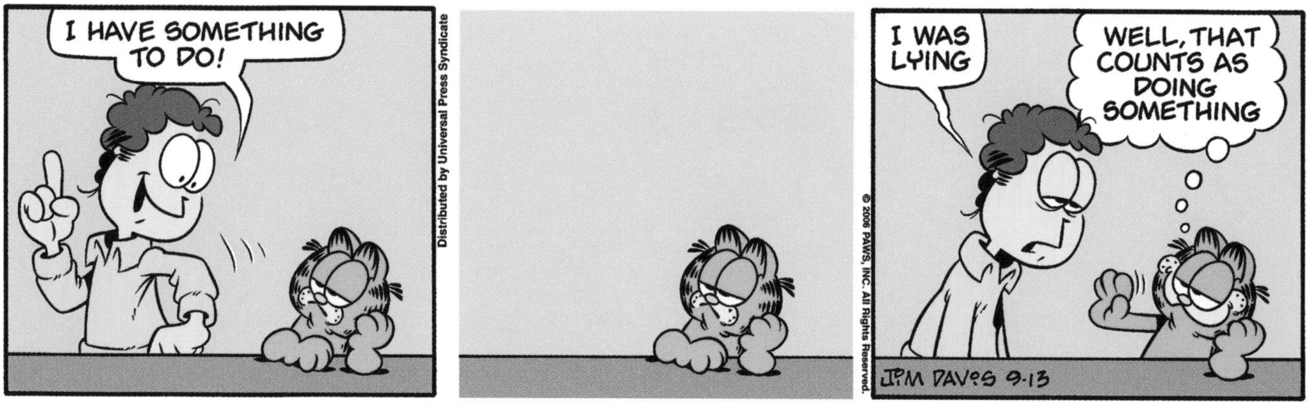
I HAVE SOMETHING TO DO!
I WAS LYING
WELL, THAT COUNTS AS DOING SOMETHING
JPM DAVPS 9-13

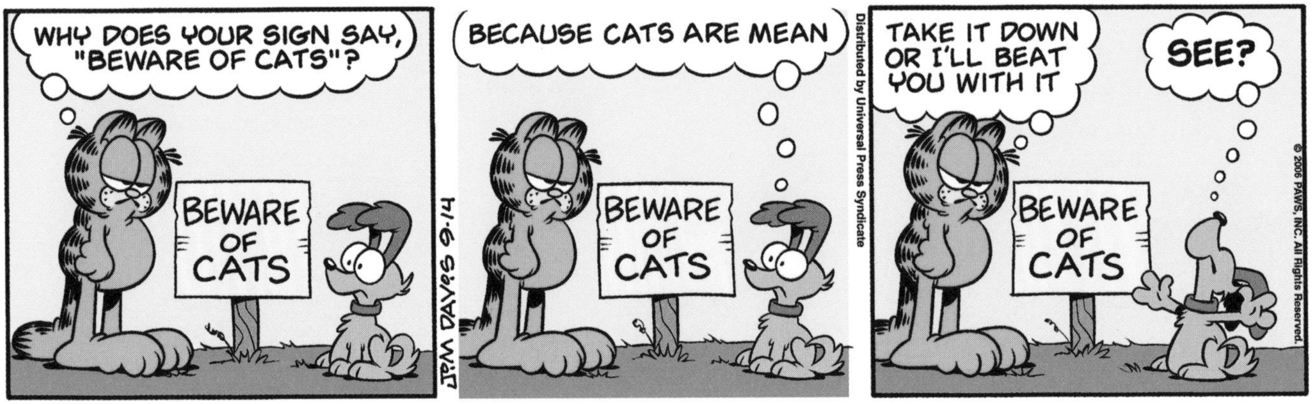
WHY DOES YOUR SIGN SAY, "BEWARE OF CATS"?
BEWARE OF CATS
JIM DAVIS 9-14
BECAUSE CATS ARE MEAN
Distributed by Universal Press Syndicate
TAKE IT DOWN OR I'LL BEAT YOU WITH IT
SEE?
© 2006 PAWS, INC. All Rights Reserved.

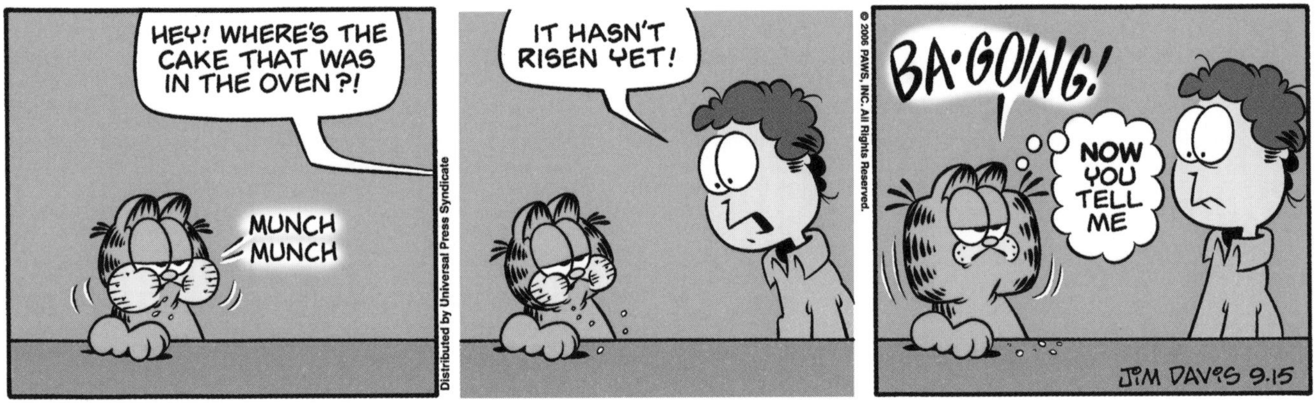
HEY! WHERE'S THE CAKE THAT WAS IN THE OVEN?!
MUNCH MUNCH
Distributed by Universal Press Syndicate
IT HASN'T RISEN YET!
© 2006 PAWS, INC. All Rights Reserved.
BA·GOING!
NOW YOU TELL ME
JIM DAVIS 9-15

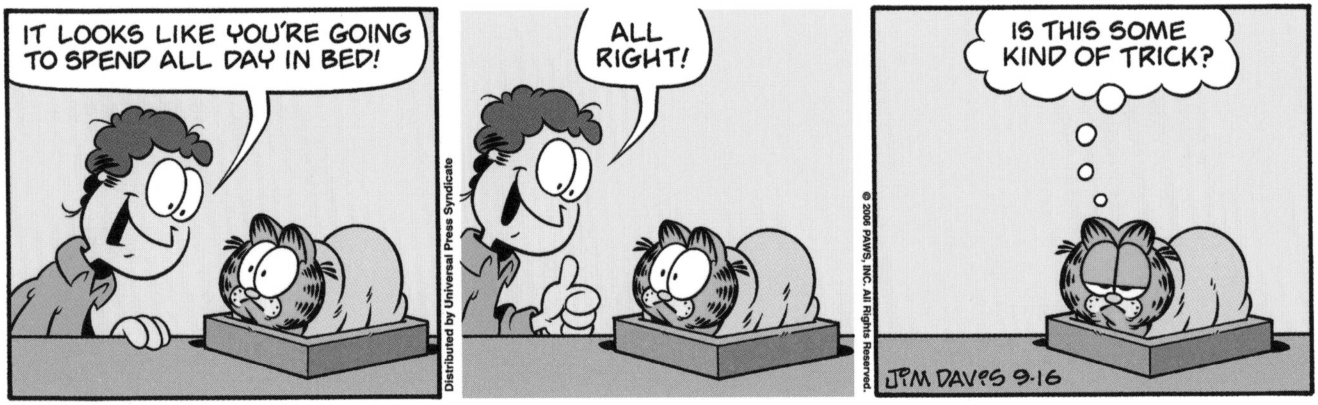
IT LOOKS LIKE YOU'RE GOING TO SPEND ALL DAY IN BED!
Distributed by Universal Press Syndicate
ALL RIGHT!
© 2006 PAWS, INC. All Rights Reserved.
IS THIS SOME KIND OF TRICK?
JIM DAVIS 9-16

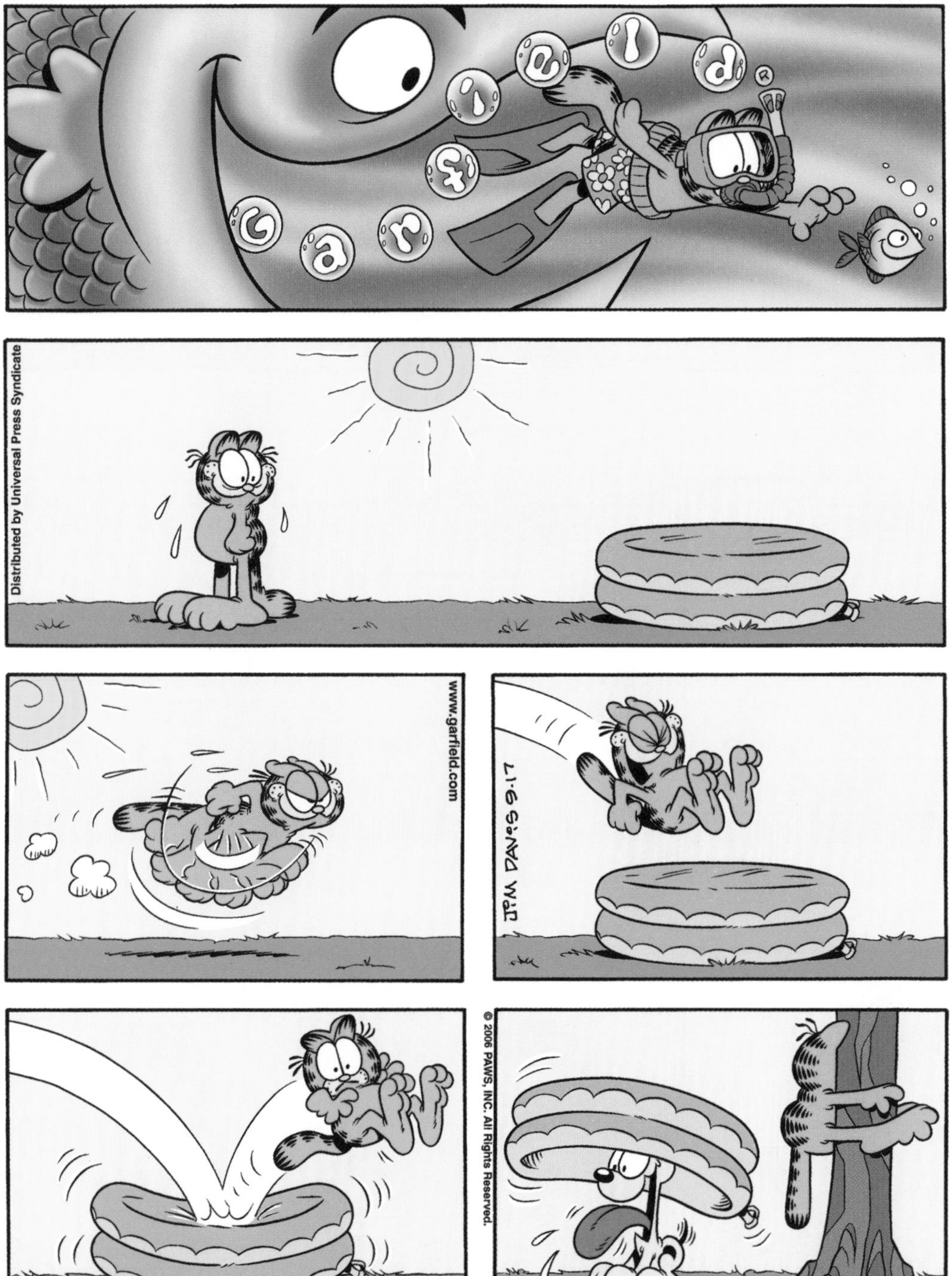
garfield®
Distributed by Universal Press Syndicate
www.garfield.com
JPM DAVIS 9-17
© 2006 PAWS, INC. All Rights Reserved.

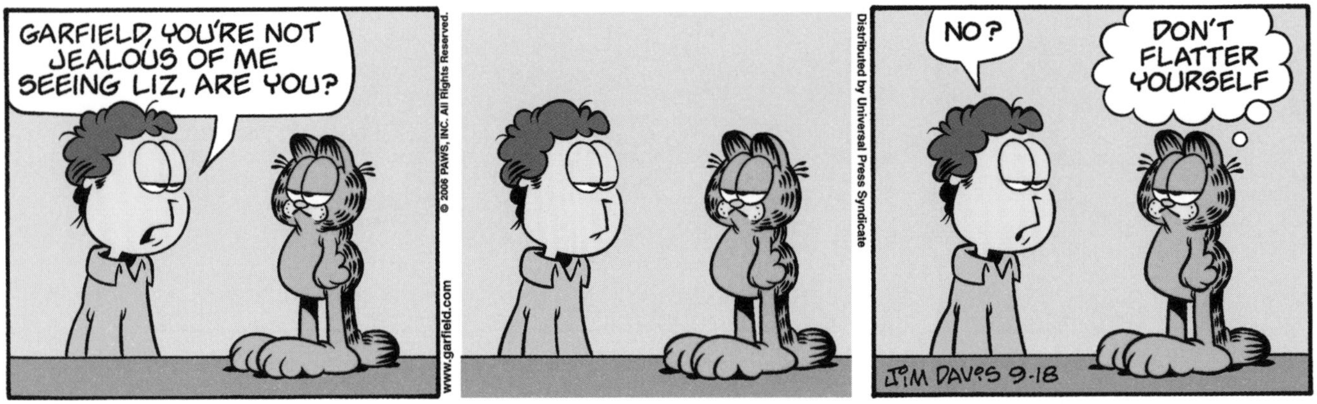
GARFIELD, YOU'RE NOT JEALOUS OF ME SEEING LIZ, ARE YOU?
© 2006 PAWS, INC. All Rights Reserved.
www.garfield.com
Distributed by Universal Press Syndicate
NO?
DON'T FLATTER YOURSELF
JIM DAVIS 9-18

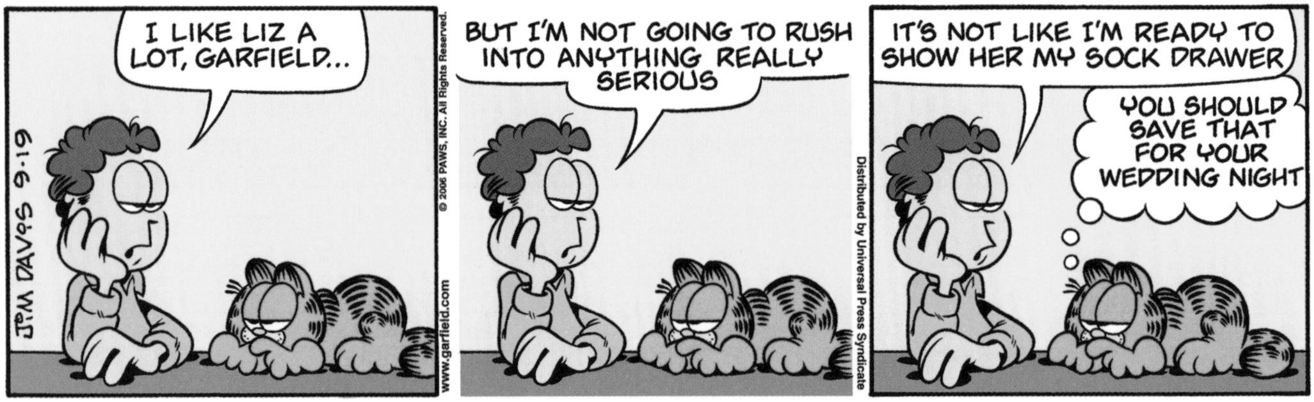
JIM DAVIS 9-19
I LIKE LIZ A LOT, GARFIELD...
© 2006 PAWS, INC. All Rights Reserved.
www.garfield.com
BUT I'M NOT GOING TO RUSH INTO ANYTHING REALLY SERIOUS
Distributed by Universal Press Syndicate
IT'S NOT LIKE I'M READY TO SHOW HER MY SOCK DRAWER
YOU SHOULD SAVE THAT FOR YOUR WEDDING NIGHT

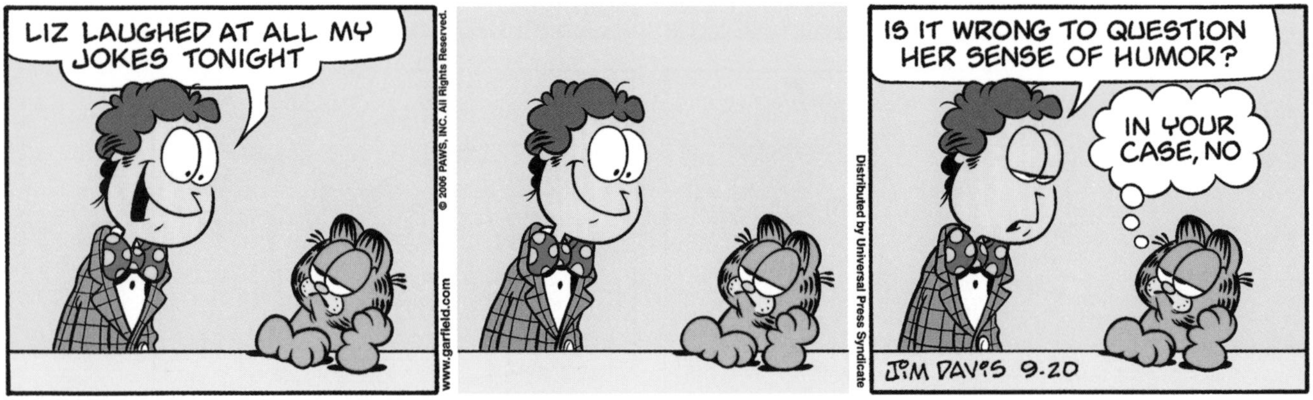
LIZ LAUGHED AT ALL MY JOKES TONIGHT
© 2006 PAWS, INC. All Rights Reserved.
www.garfield.com
Distributed by Universal Press Syndicate
IS IT WRONG TO QUESTION HER SENSE OF HUMOR?
IN YOUR CASE, NO
JIM DAVIS 9-20

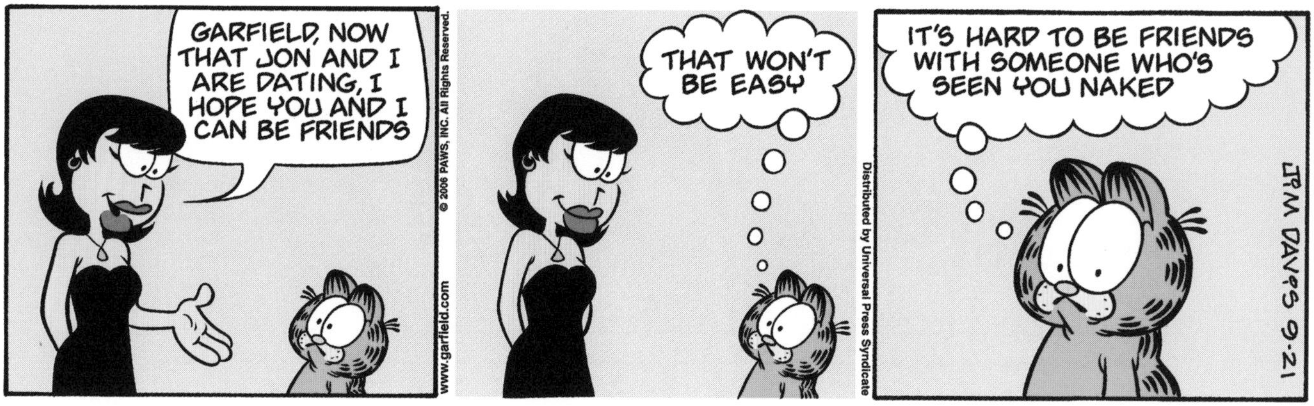
GARFIELD, NOW THAT JON AND I ARE DATING, I HOPE YOU AND I CAN BE FRIENDS
© 2006 PAWS, INC. All Rights Reserved.
www.garfield.com
THAT WON'T BE EASY
Distributed by Universal Press Syndicate
IT'S HARD TO BE FRIENDS WITH SOMEONE WHO'S SEEN YOU NAKED
JIM DAVIS 9-21

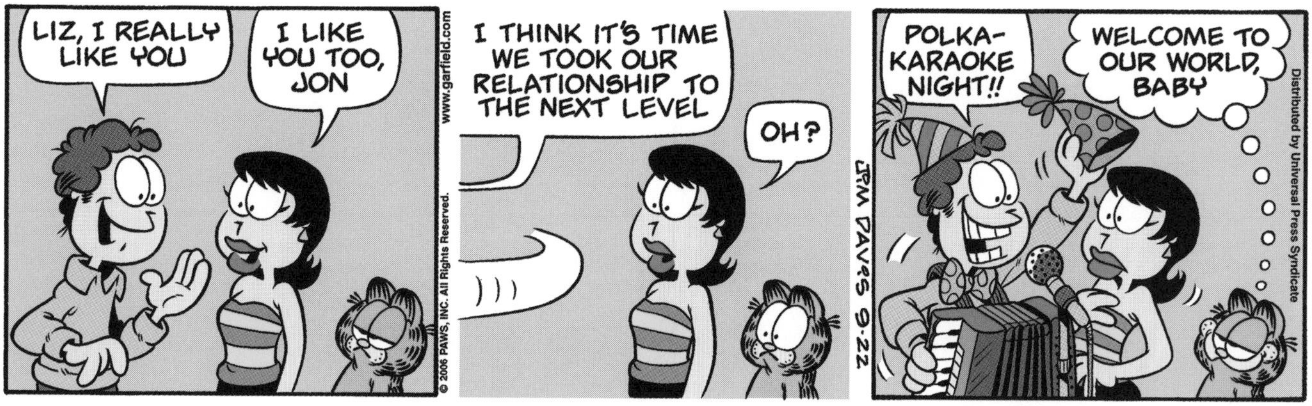
LIZ, I REALLY LIKE YOU
I LIKE YOU TOO, JON
© 2006 PAWS, INC. All Rights Reserved.
www.garfield.com
I THINK IT'S TIME WE TOOK OUR RELATIONSHIP TO THE NEXT LEVEL
OH?
JIM DAVIS 9-22
POLKA-KARAOKE NIGHT!!
WELCOME TO OUR WORLD, BABY
Distributed by Universal Press Syndicate

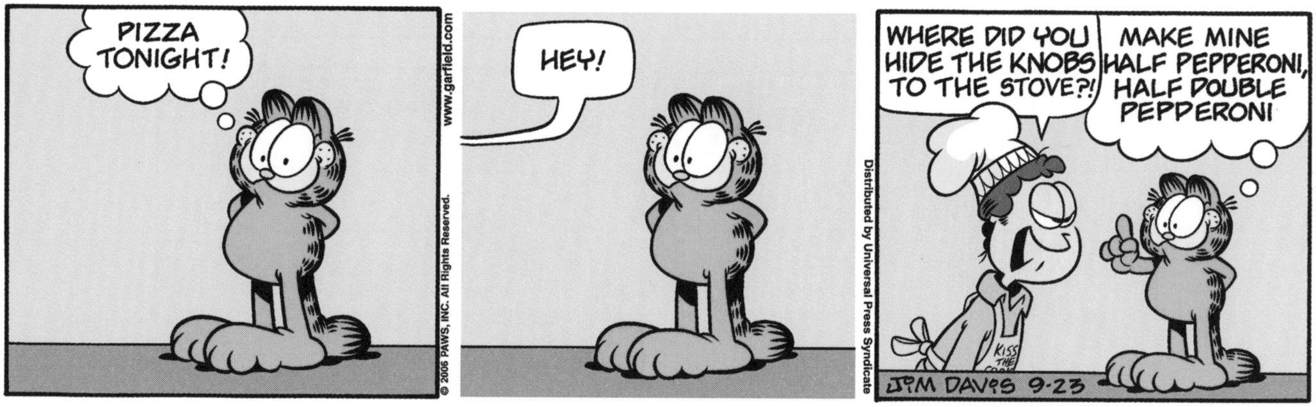
PIZZA TONIGHT!
© 2006 PAWS, INC. All Rights Reserved.
www.garfield.com
HEY!
Distributed by Universal Press Syndicate
WHERE DID YOU HIDE THE KNOBS TO THE STOVE?!
MAKE MINE HALF PEPPERONI, HALF DOUBLE PEPPERONI
JIM DAVIS 9-23

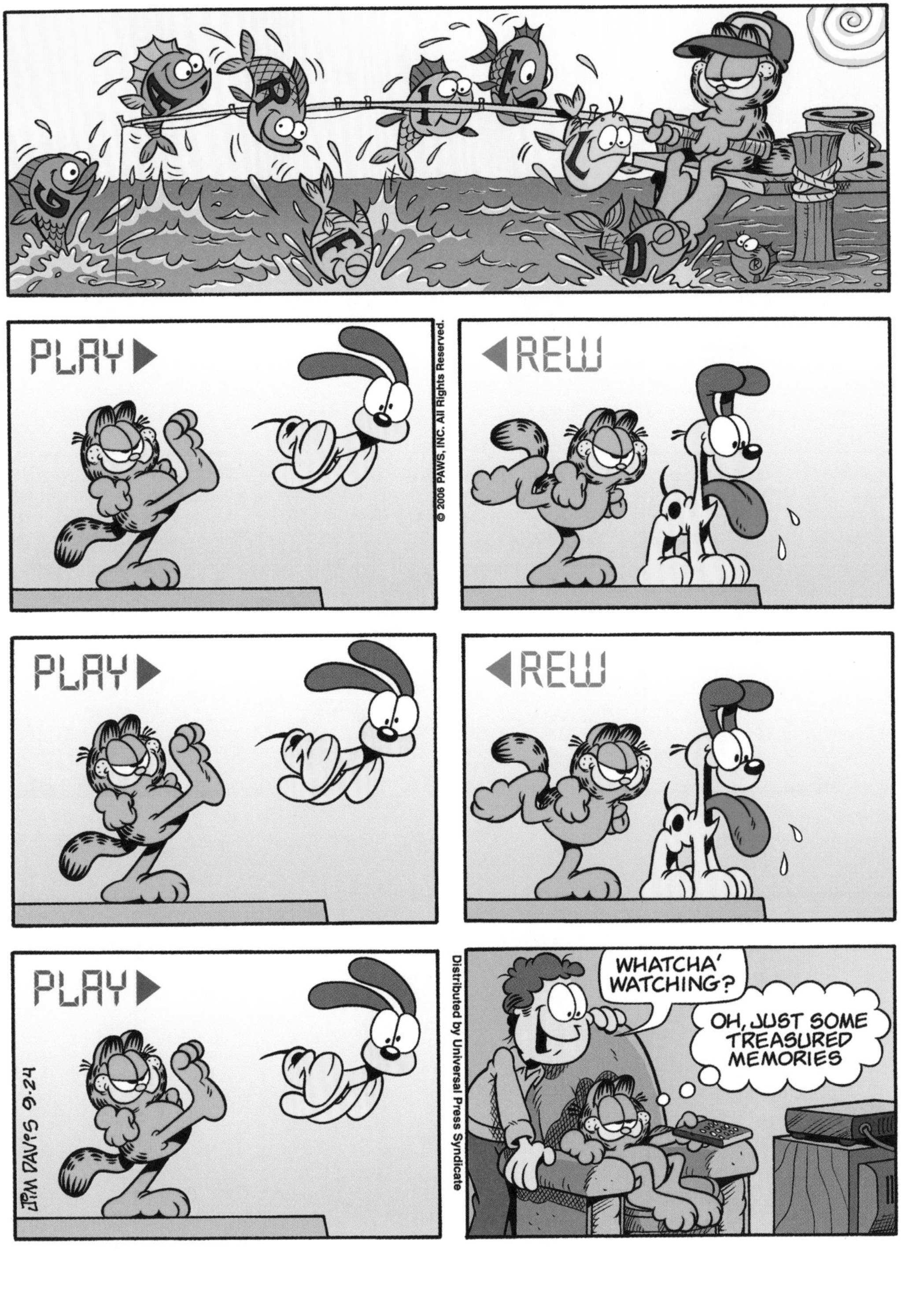
GARFIELD
PLAY ▶
◀REW
PLAY ▶
◀REW
PLAY ▶
JPM DAVIS 9·24
WHATCHA' WATCHING?
OH, JUST SOME TREASURED MEMORIES

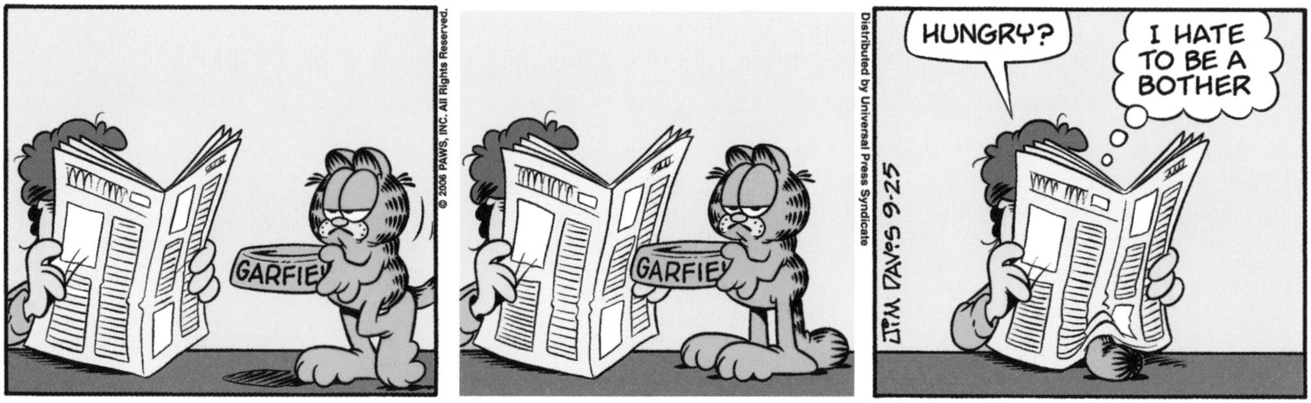
GARFIELD
© 2006 PAWS, INC. All Rights Reserved.
GARFIELD
Distributed by Universal Press Syndicate
JIM DAVIS 9-25
HUNGRY?
I HATE TO BE A BOTHER

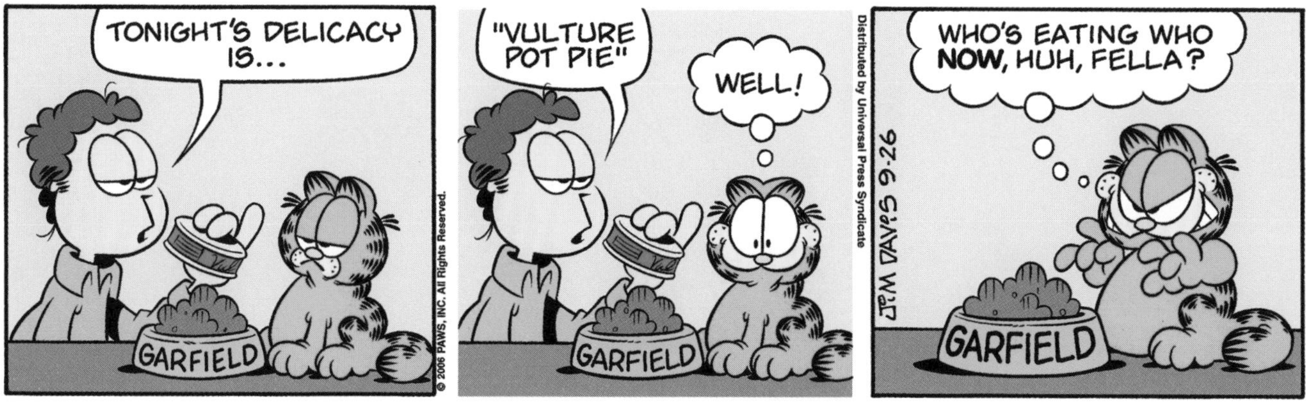
TONIGHT'S DELICACY IS...
GARFIELD
© 2006 PAWS, INC. All Rights Reserved.
"VULTURE POT PIE"
WELL!
GARFIELD
Distributed by Universal Press Syndicate
JIM DAVIS 9-26
WHO'S EATING WHO **NOW**, HUH, FELLA?
GARFIELD

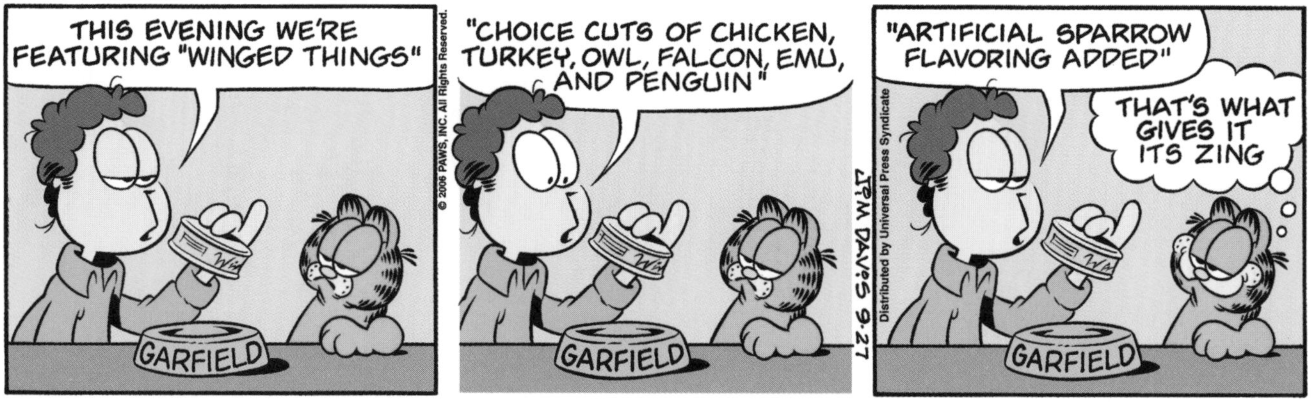
THIS EVENING WE'RE FEATURING "WINGED THINGS"
GARFIELD
© 2006 PAWS, INC. All Rights Reserved.
"CHOICE CUTS OF CHICKEN, TURKEY, OWL, FALCON, EMU, AND PENGUIN"
GARFIELD
JIM DAVIS 9-27
Distributed by Universal Press Syndicate
"ARTIFICIAL SPARROW FLAVORING ADDED"
THAT'S WHAT GIVES IT ITS ZING
GARFIELD

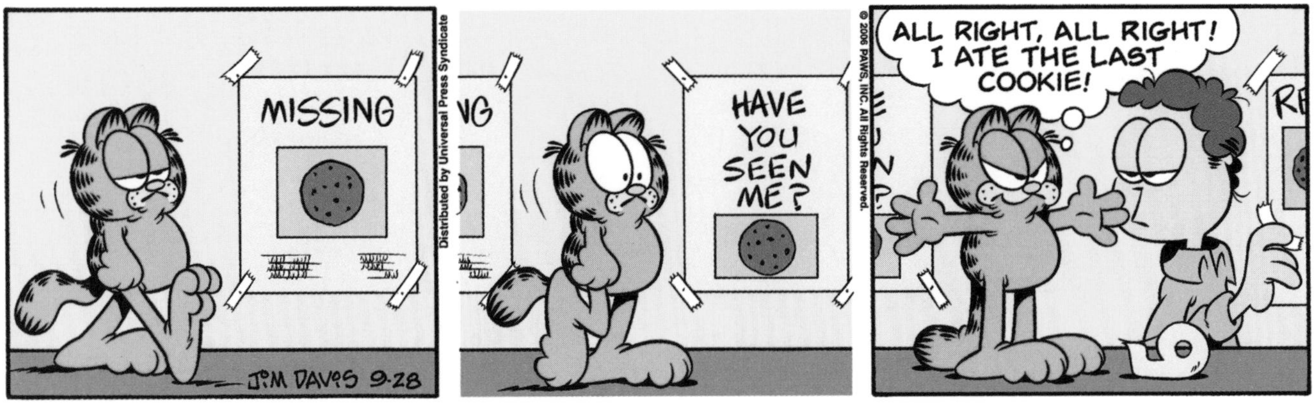
MISSING
JIM DAVIS 9-28
Distributed by Universal Press Syndicate
HAVE YOU SEEN ME?
© 2006 PAWS, INC. All Rights Reserved.
ALL RIGHT, ALL RIGHT! I ATE THE LAST COOKIE!

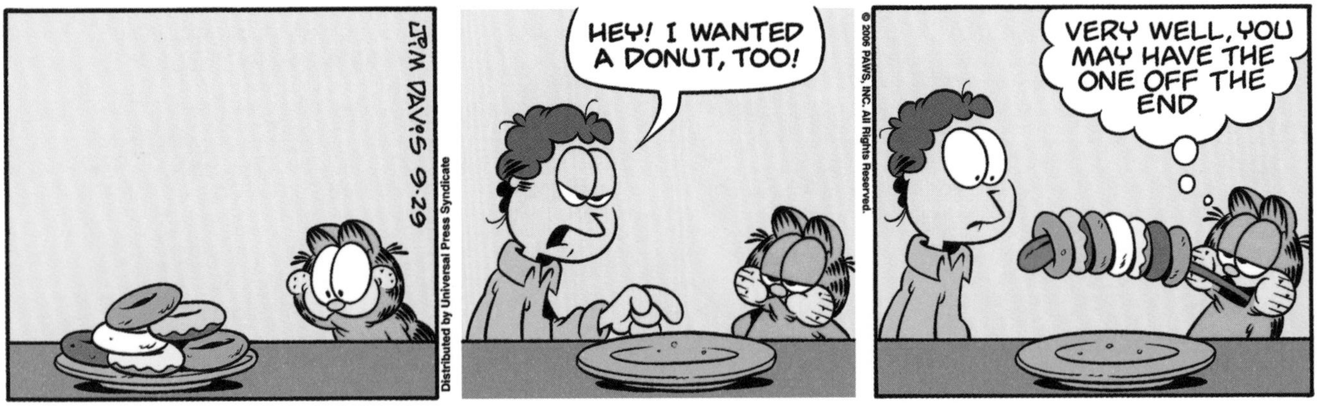
JIM DAVIS 9-29
Distributed by Universal Press Syndicate
HEY! I WANTED A DONUT, TOO!
© 2006 PAWS, INC. All Rights Reserved.
VERY WELL, YOU MAY HAVE THE ONE OFF THE END

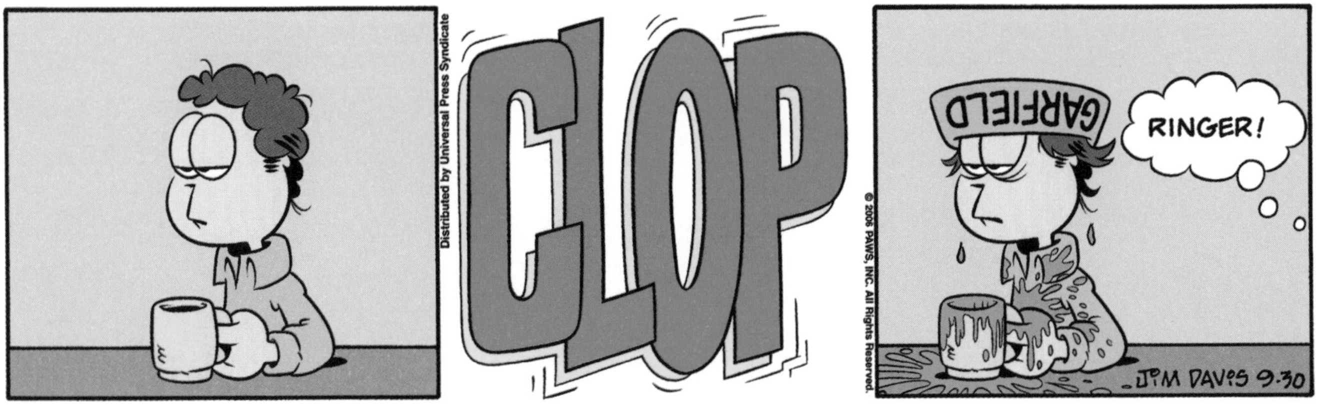
Distributed by Universal Press Syndicate
CLOP
© 2006 PAWS, INC. All Rights Reserved.
GARFIELD
RINGER!
JIM DAVIS 9-30

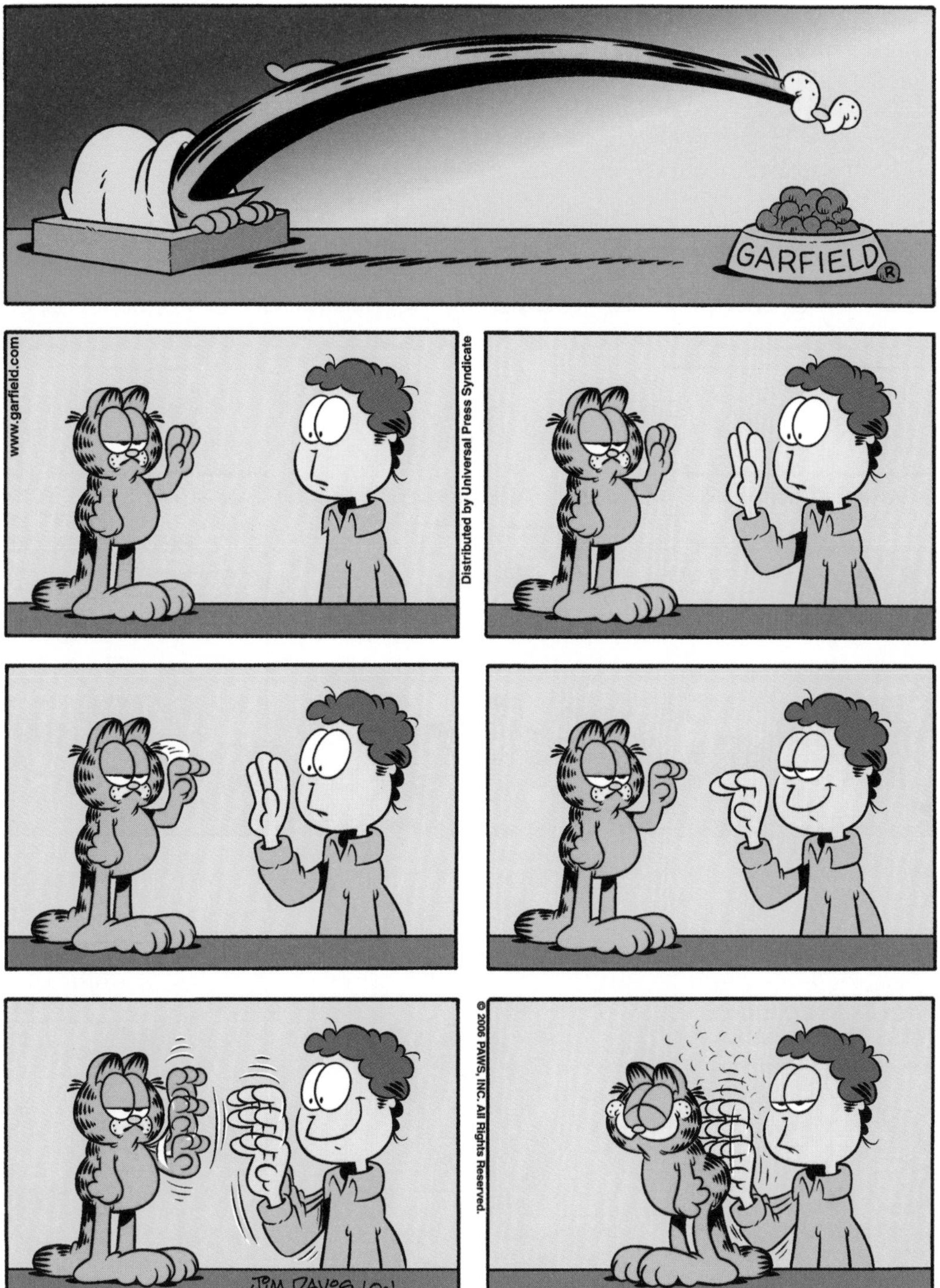
GARFIELD
www.garfield.com
Distributed by Universal Press Syndicate
© 2006 PAWS, INC. All Rights Reserved.
JIM DAVIS 10-1

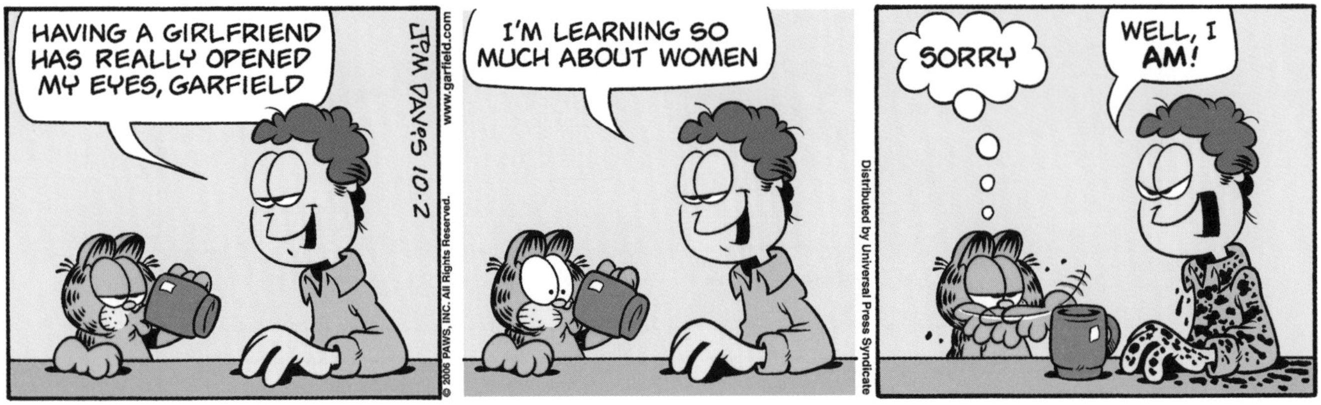
HAVING A GIRLFRIEND HAS REALLY OPENED MY EYES, GARFIELD
JIM DAVIS 10-2
© 2006 PAWS, INC. All Rights Reserved.
www.garfield.com
I'M LEARNING SO MUCH ABOUT WOMEN
Distributed by Universal Press Syndicate
SORRY
WELL, I **AM**!

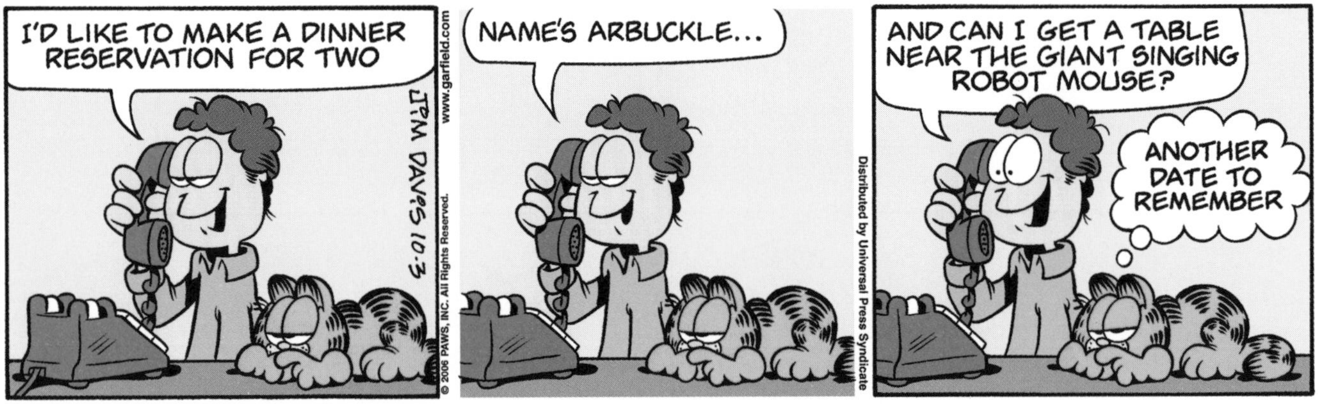
I'D LIKE TO MAKE A DINNER RESERVATION FOR TWO
JIM DAVIS 10-3
© 2006 PAWS, INC. All Rights Reserved.
www.garfield.com
NAME'S ARBUCKLE...
Distributed by Universal Press Syndicate
AND CAN I GET A TABLE NEAR THE GIANT SINGING ROBOT MOUSE?
ANOTHER DATE TO REMEMBER

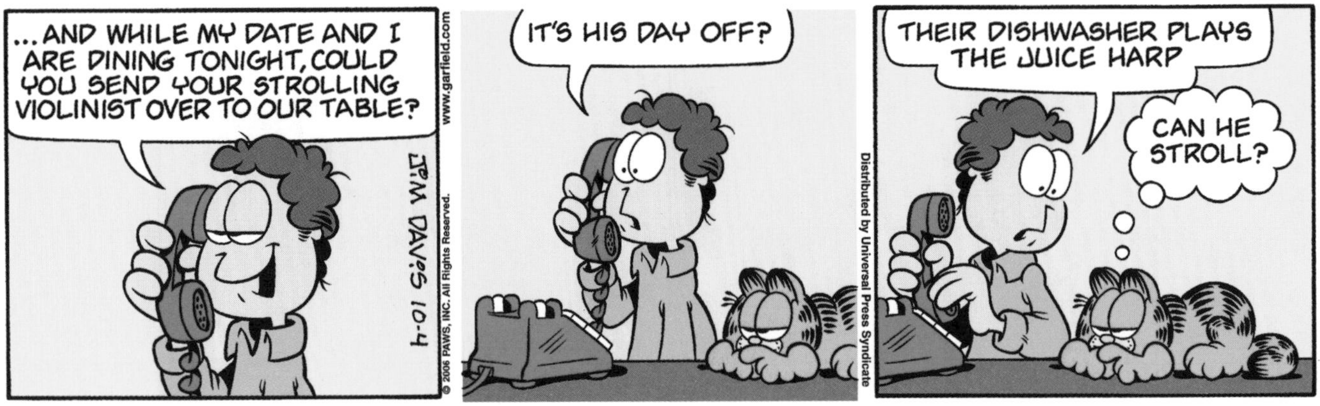
...AND WHILE MY DATE AND I ARE DINING TONIGHT, COULD YOU SEND YOUR STROLLING VIOLINIST OVER TO OUR TABLE?
JIM DAVIS 10-4
© 2006 PAWS, INC. All Rights Reserved.
www.garfield.com
IT'S HIS DAY OFF?
Distributed by Universal Press Syndicate
THEIR DISHWASHER PLAYS THE JUICE HARP
CAN HE STROLL?

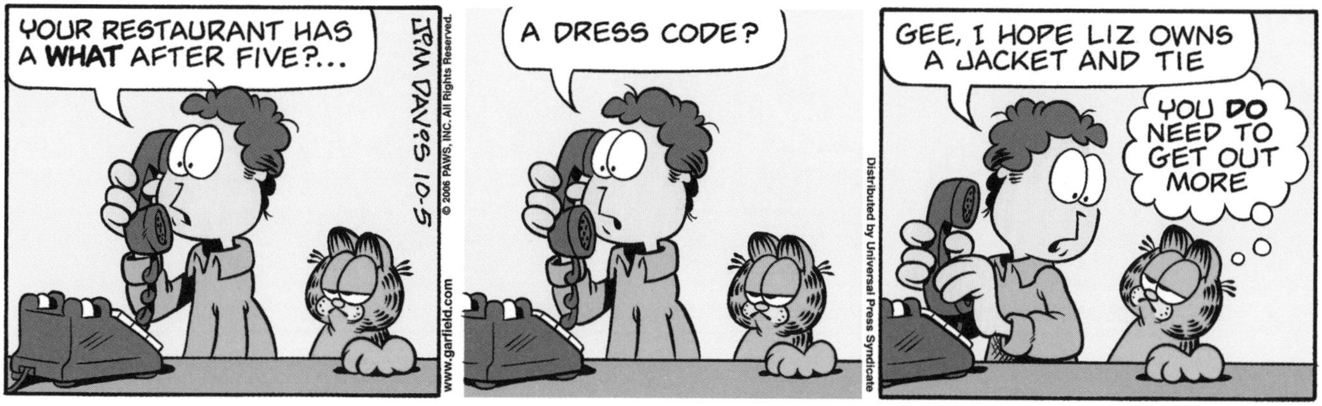
JIM DAVIS 10-5
© 2006 PAWS, INC. All Rights Reserved.
www.garfield.com
YOUR RESTAURANT HAS A **WHAT** AFTER FIVE?...
A DRESS CODE?
Distributed by Universal Press Syndicate
GEE, I HOPE LIZ OWNS A JACKET AND TIE
YOU **DO** NEED TO GET OUT MORE

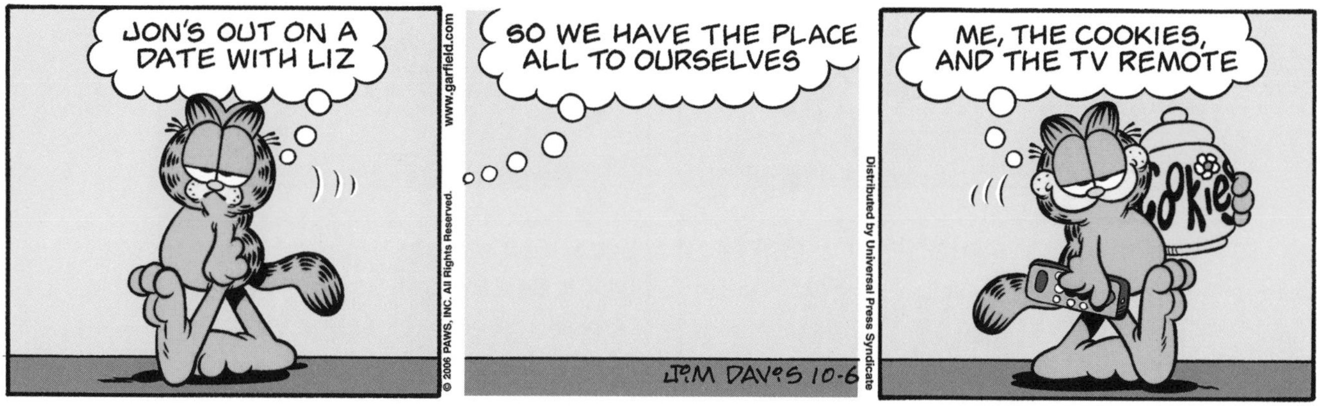
www.garfield.com
© 2006 PAWS, INC. All Rights Reserved.
JON'S OUT ON A DATE WITH LIZ
SO WE HAVE THE PLACE ALL TO OURSELVES
JIM DAVIS 10-6
Distributed by Universal Press Syndicate
ME, THE COOKIES, AND THE TV REMOTE
COOKIES

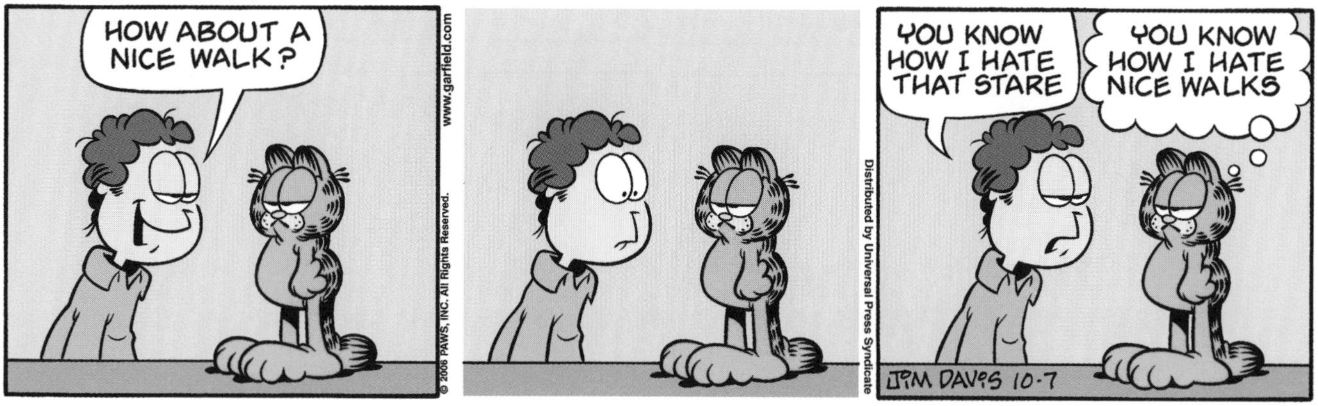
www.garfield.com
© 2006 PAWS, INC. All Rights Reserved.
HOW ABOUT A NICE WALK?
Distributed by Universal Press Syndicate
YOU KNOW HOW I HATE THAT STARE
YOU KNOW HOW I HATE NICE WALKS
JIM DAVIS 10-7

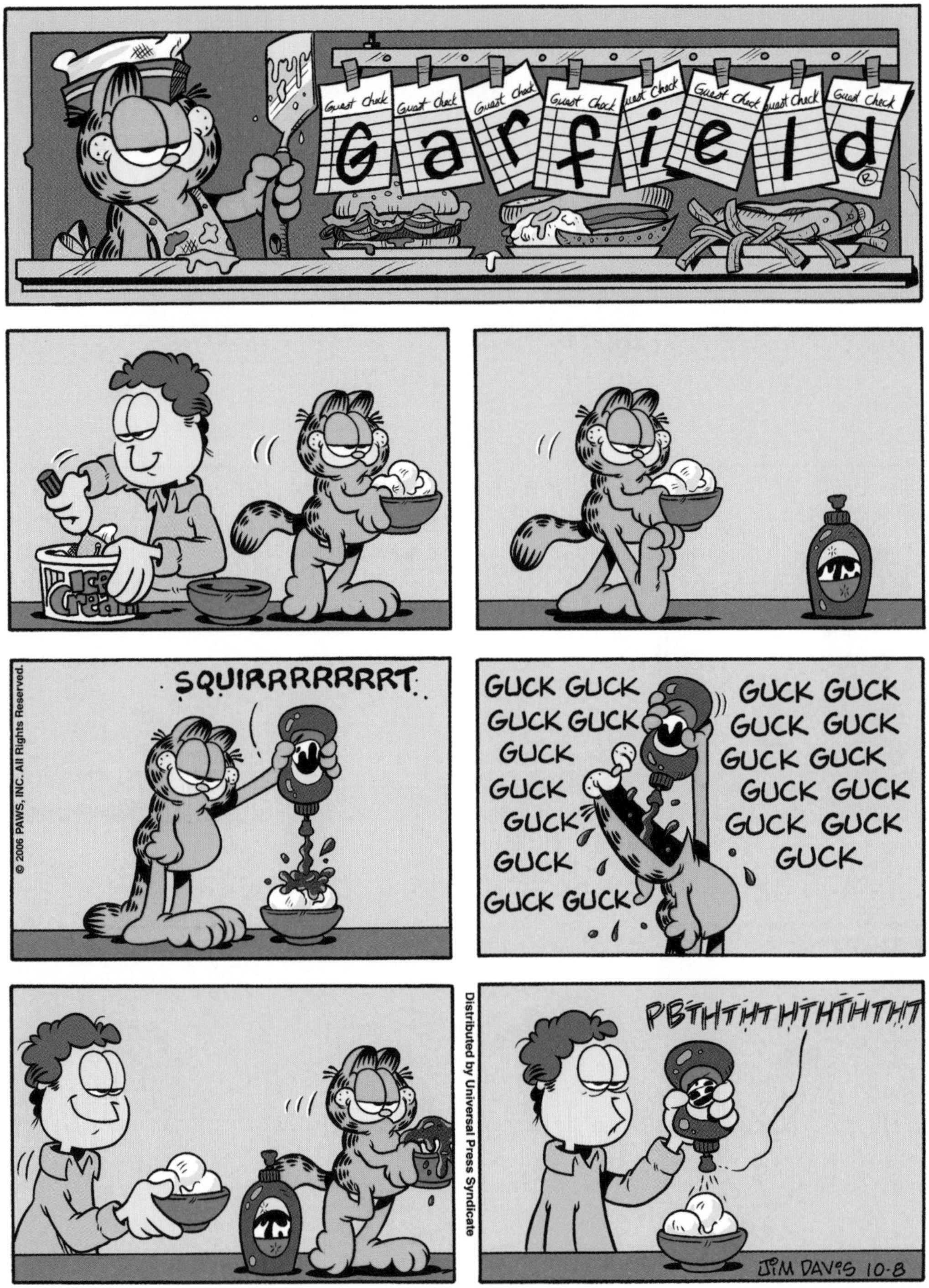
Garfield
Guest Check
SQUIRRRRRRRRT
GUCK GUCK
GUCK GUCK
GUCK
GUCK
GUCK
GUCK
GUCK GUCK
GUCK GUCK
GUCK GUCK
GUCK GUCK
GUCK GUCK
GUCK GUCK
GUCK
PBTHTHTHTHTHTHT
JIM DAVIS 10-8
© 2006 PAWS, INC. All Rights Reserved.
Distributed by Universal Press Syndicate

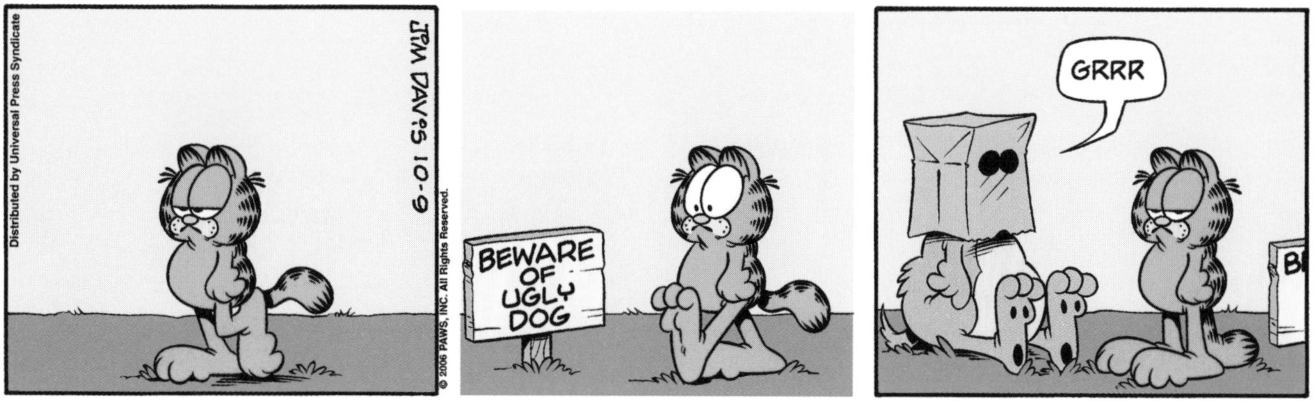
Distributed by Universal Press Syndicate
JIM DAVIS 10-9
© 2006 PAWS, INC. All Rights Reserved.
BEWARE OF UGLY DOG
GRRR

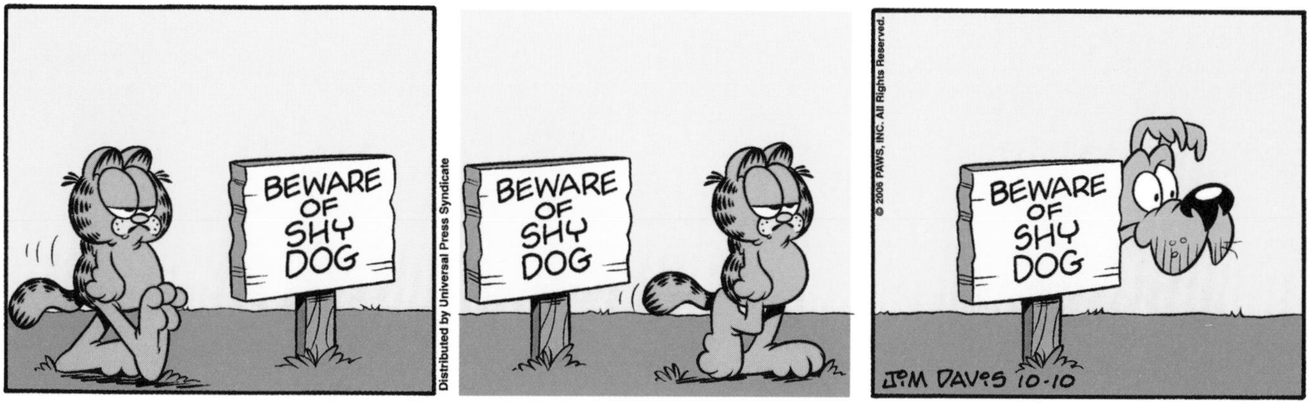
BEWARE OF SHY DOG
Distributed by Universal Press Syndicate
BEWARE OF SHY DOG
© 2006 PAWS, INC. All Rights Reserved.
BEWARE OF SHY DOG
JIM DAVIS 10-10

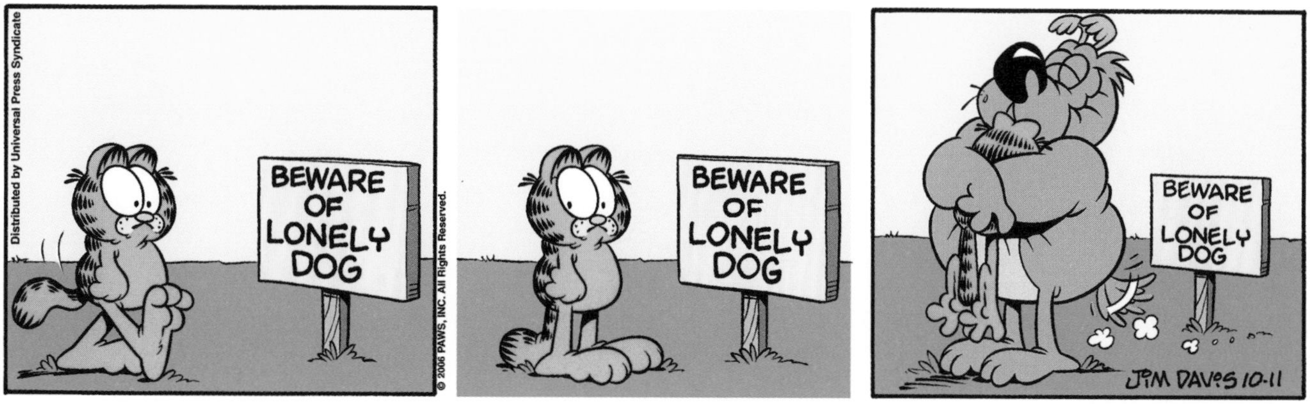
Distributed by Universal Press Syndicate
BEWARE OF LONELY DOG
© 2006 PAWS, INC. All Rights Reserved.
BEWARE OF LONELY DOG
BEWARE OF LONELY DOG
JIM DAVIS 10-11

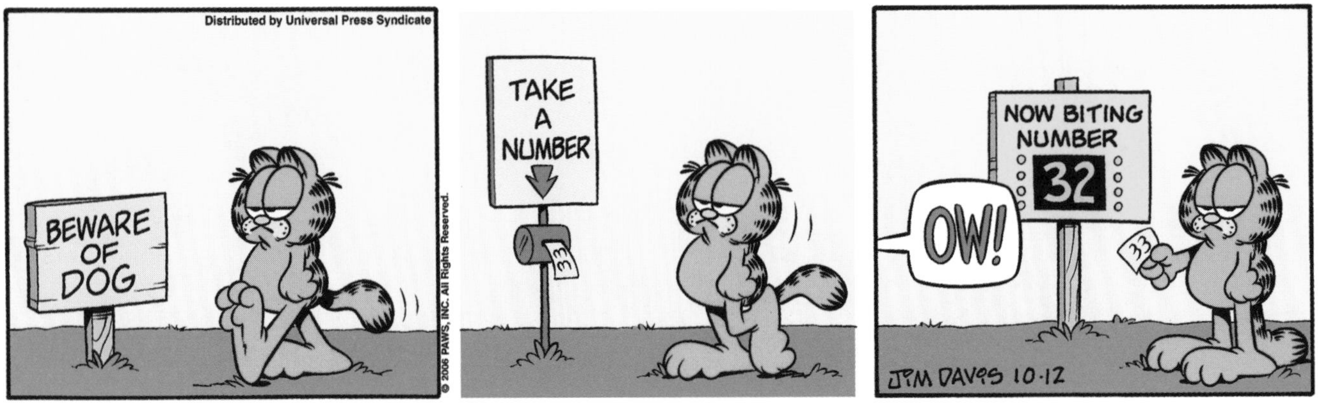
Distributed by Universal Press Syndicate
BEWARE OF DOG
© 2006 PAWS, INC. All Rights Reserved.
TAKE A NUMBER
33
NOW BITING NUMBER
32
OW!
33
JIM DAVIS 10-12

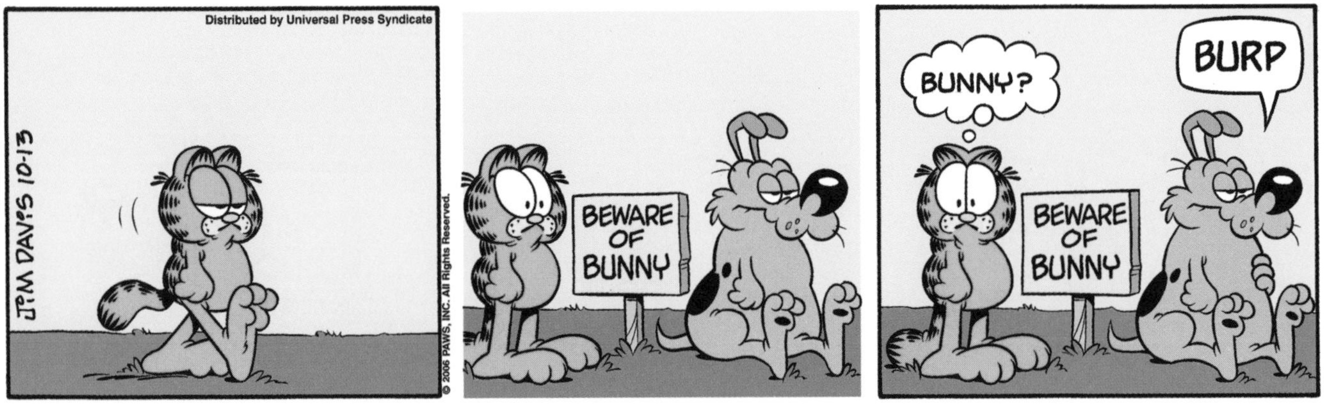
Distributed by Universal Press Syndicate
JIM DAVIS 10-13
© 2006 PAWS, INC. All Rights Reserved.
BEWARE OF BUNNY
BUNNY?
BURP
BEWARE OF BUNNY

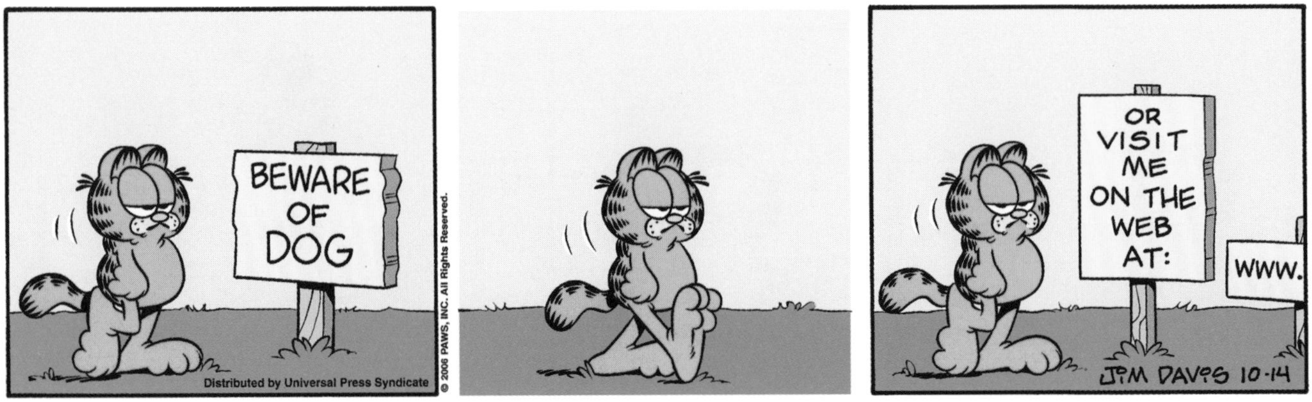
BEWARE OF DOG
Distributed by Universal Press Syndicate
© 2006 PAWS, INC. All Rights Reserved.
OR VISIT ME ON THE WEB AT:
WWW.
JIM DAVIS 10-14

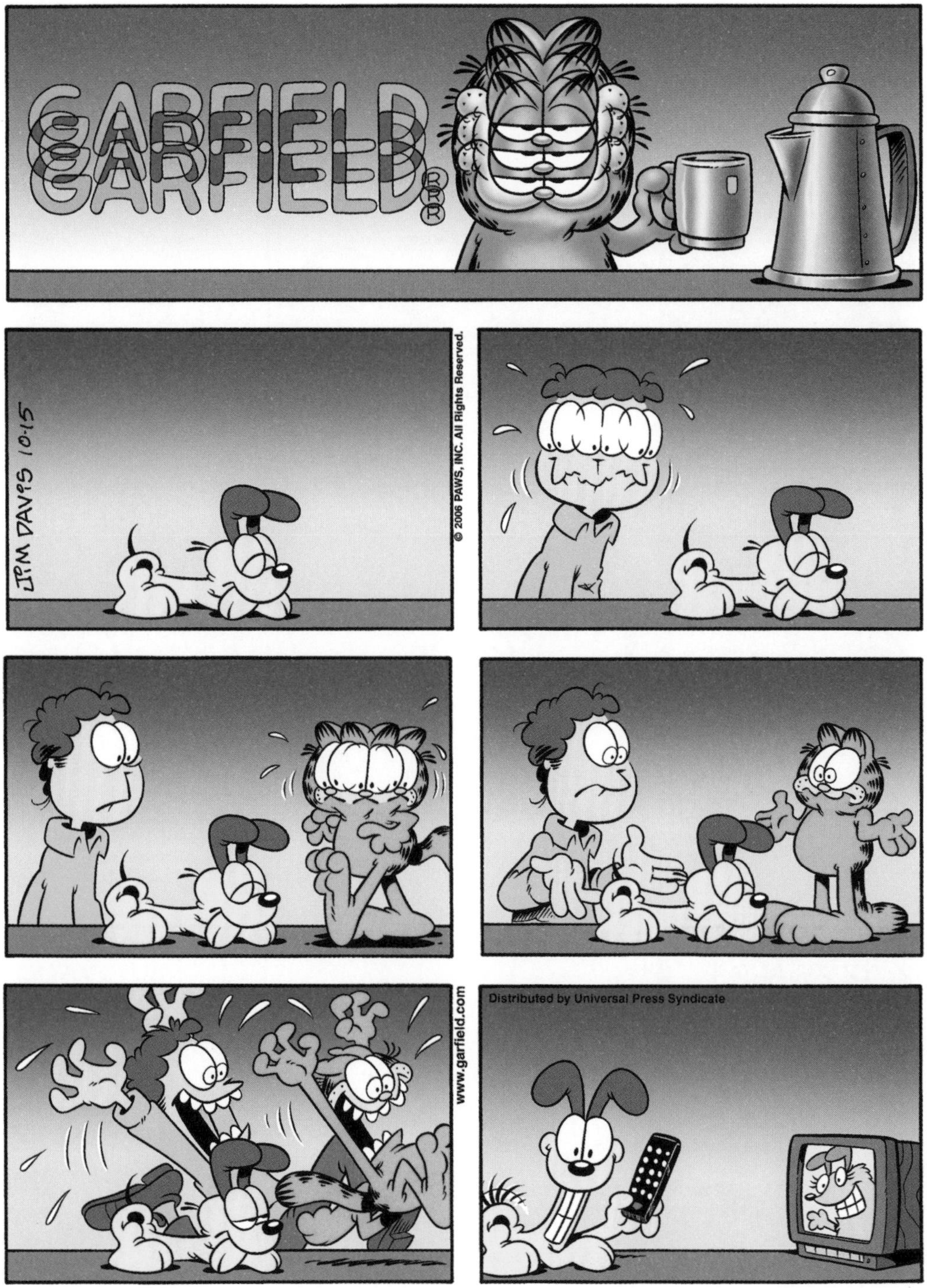
GARFIELD
JIM DAVIS 10-15
© 2006 PAWS, INC. All Rights Reserved.
www.garfield.com
Distributed by Universal Press Syndicate

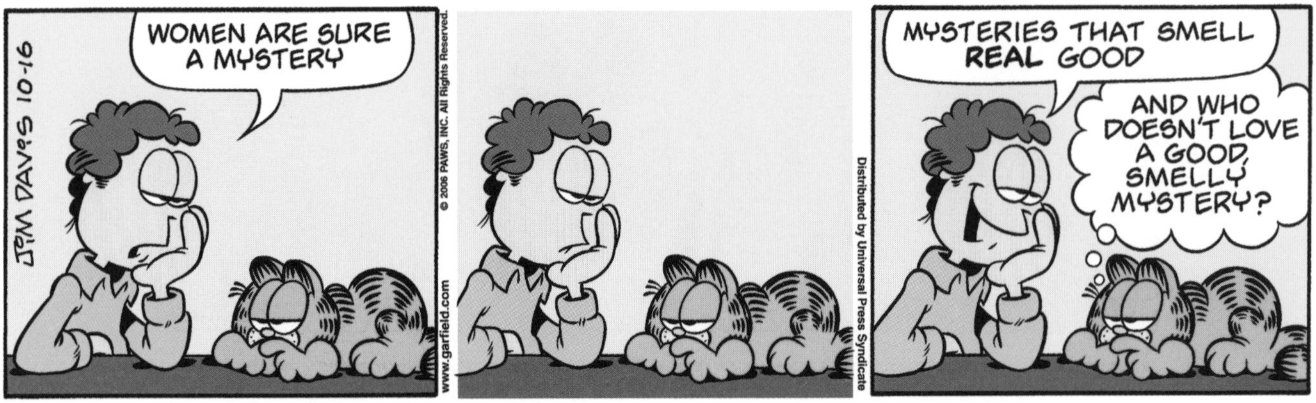
JIM DAVIS 10-16
WOMEN ARE SURE A MYSTERY
© 2006 PAWS, INC. All Rights Reserved.
www.garfield.com
Distributed by Universal Press Syndicate
MYSTERIES THAT SMELL REAL GOOD
AND WHO DOESN'T LOVE A GOOD, SMELLY MYSTERY?

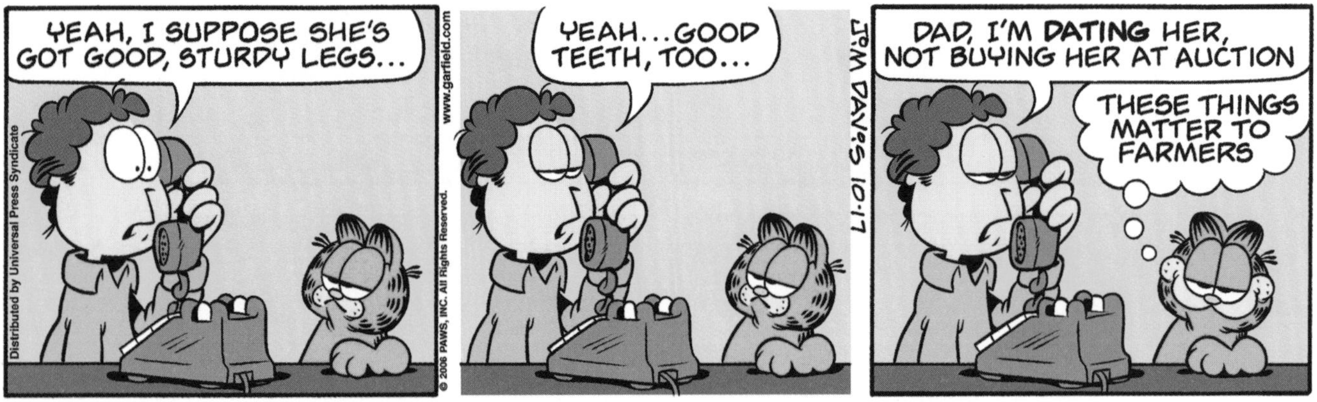
YEAH, I SUPPOSE SHE'S GOT GOOD, STURDY LEGS...
Distributed by Universal Press Syndicate
www.garfield.com
© 2006 PAWS, INC. All Rights Reserved.
YEAH...GOOD TEETH, TOO...
JIM DAVIS 10-17
DAD, I'M DATING HER, NOT BUYING HER AT AUCTION
THESE THINGS MATTER TO FARMERS

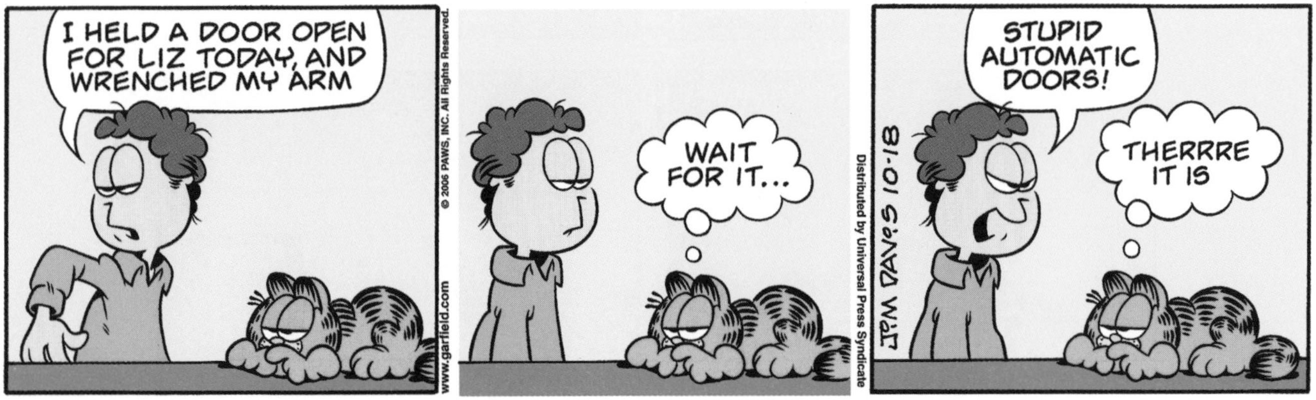
I HELD A DOOR OPEN FOR LIZ TODAY, AND WRENCHED MY ARM
© 2006 PAWS, INC. All Rights Reserved.
www.garfield.com
WAIT FOR IT...
Distributed by Universal Press Syndicate
JIM DAVIS 10-18
STUPID AUTOMATIC DOORS!
THERRRE IT IS

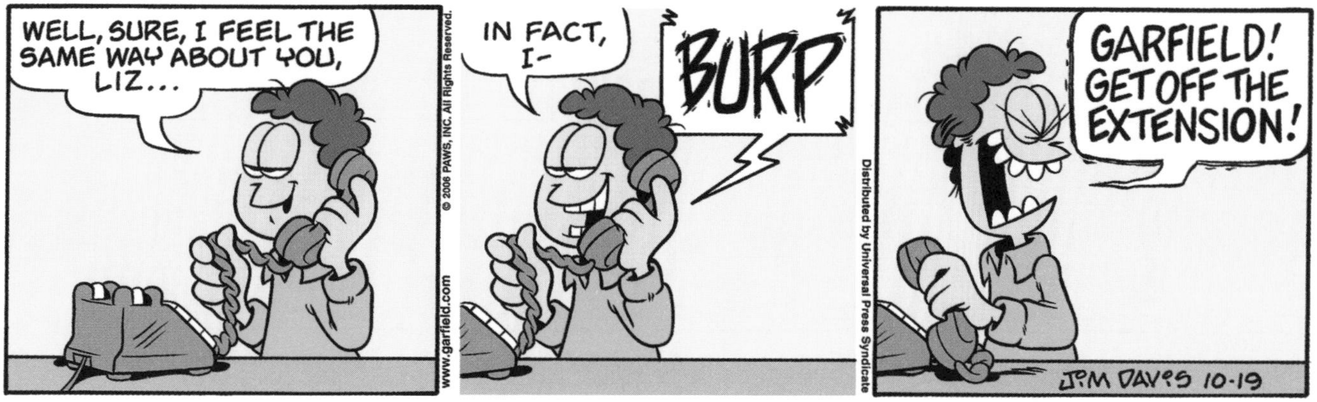
WELL, SURE, I FEEL THE SAME WAY ABOUT YOU, LIZ...
© 2006 PAWS, INC. All Rights Reserved. www.garfield.com
IN FACT, I-
BURP
Distributed by Universal Press Syndicate
GARFIELD! GET OFF THE EXTENSION!
JIM DAVIS 10-19

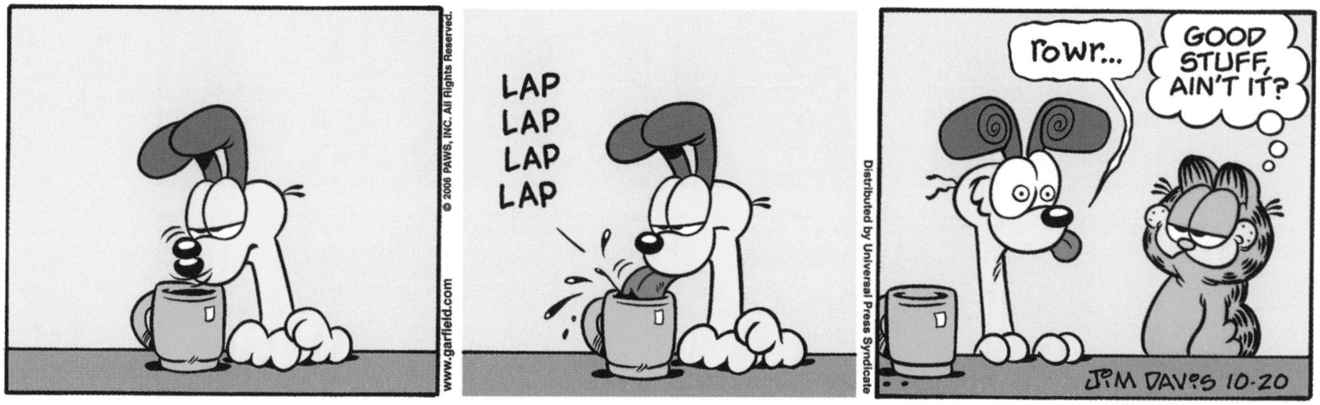
© 2006 PAWS, INC. All Rights Reserved. www.garfield.com
LAP LAP LAP LAP
Distributed by Universal Press Syndicate
rowr...
GOOD STUFF, AIN'T IT?
JIM DAVIS 10-20

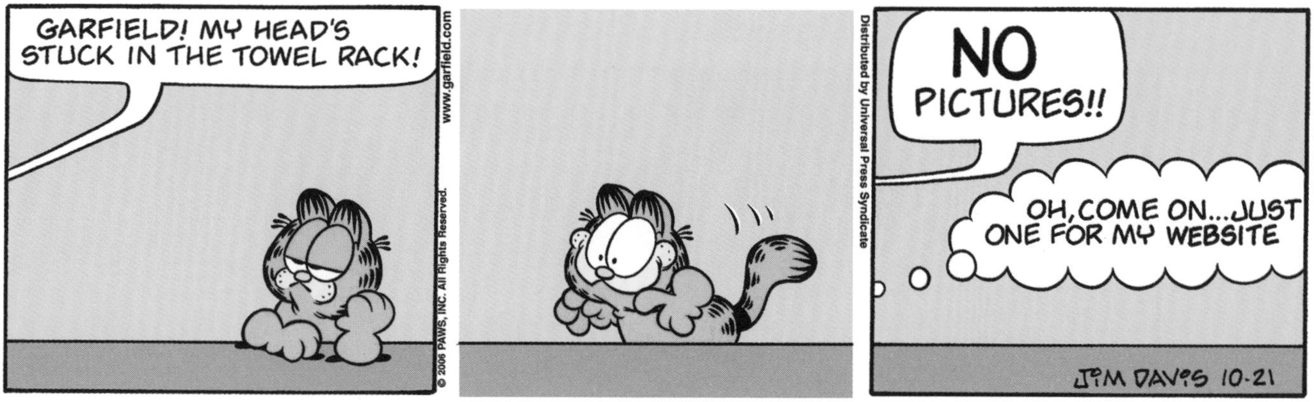
GARFIELD! MY HEAD'S STUCK IN THE TOWEL RACK!
www.garfield.com © 2006 PAWS, INC. All Rights Reserved.
Distributed by Universal Press Syndicate
NO PICTURES!!
OH, COME ON...JUST ONE FOR MY WEBSITE
JIM DAVIS 10-21

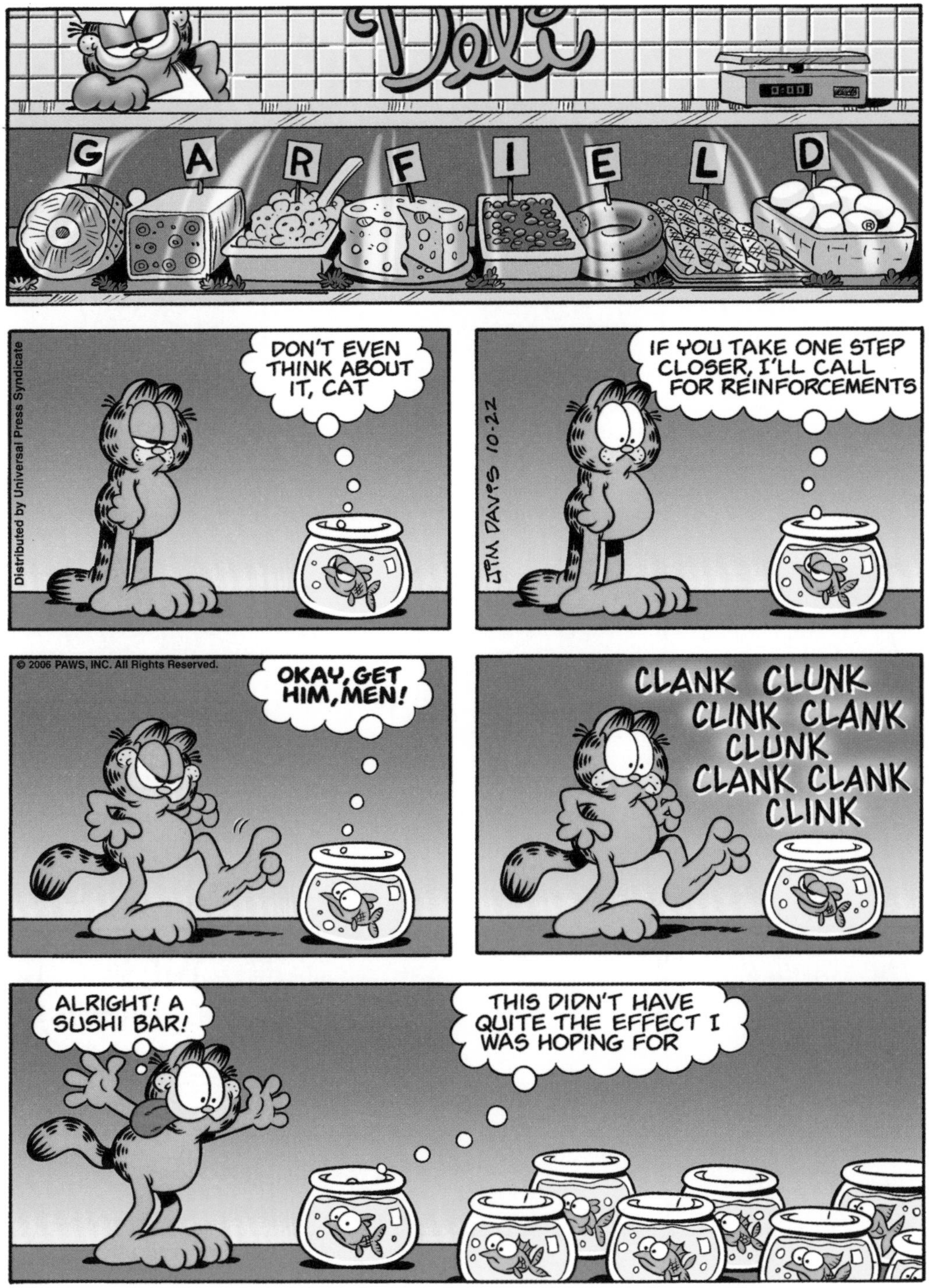
Deli
G A R F I E L D
DON'T EVEN THINK ABOUT IT, CAT
Distributed by Universal Press Syndicate
JIM DAVIS 10-22
IF YOU TAKE ONE STEP CLOSER, I'LL CALL FOR REINFORCEMENTS
© 2006 PAWS, INC. All Rights Reserved.
OKAY, GET HIM, MEN!
CLANK CLUNK
CLINK CLANK
CLUNK
CLANK CLANK
CLINK
ALRIGHT! A SUSHI BAR!
THIS DIDN'T HAVE QUITE THE EFFECT I WAS HOPING FOR

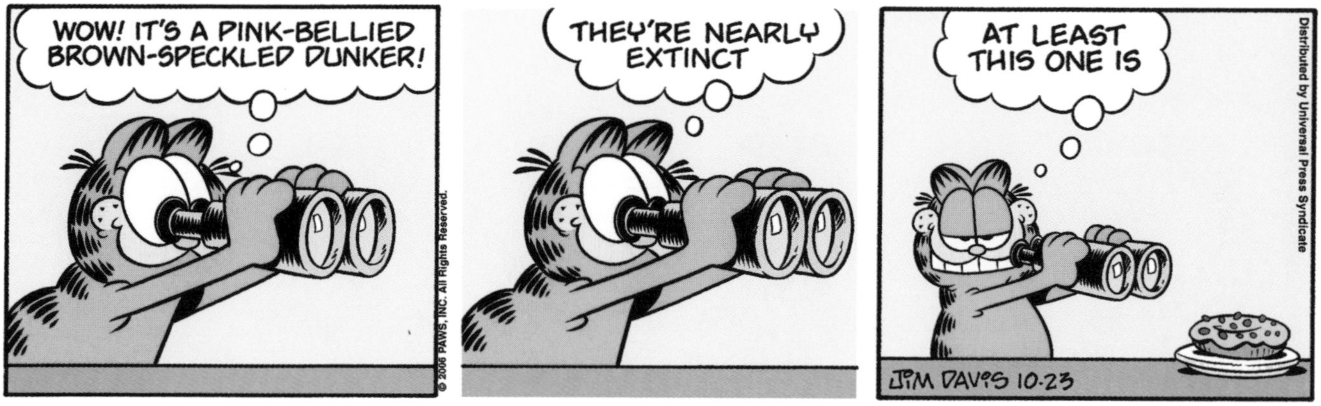
WOW! IT'S A PINK-BELLIED BROWN-SPECKLED DUNKER!
THEY'RE NEARLY EXTINCT
AT LEAST THIS ONE IS
JIM DAVIS 10-23
© 2006 PAWS, INC. All Rights Reserved.
Distributed by Universal Press Syndicate

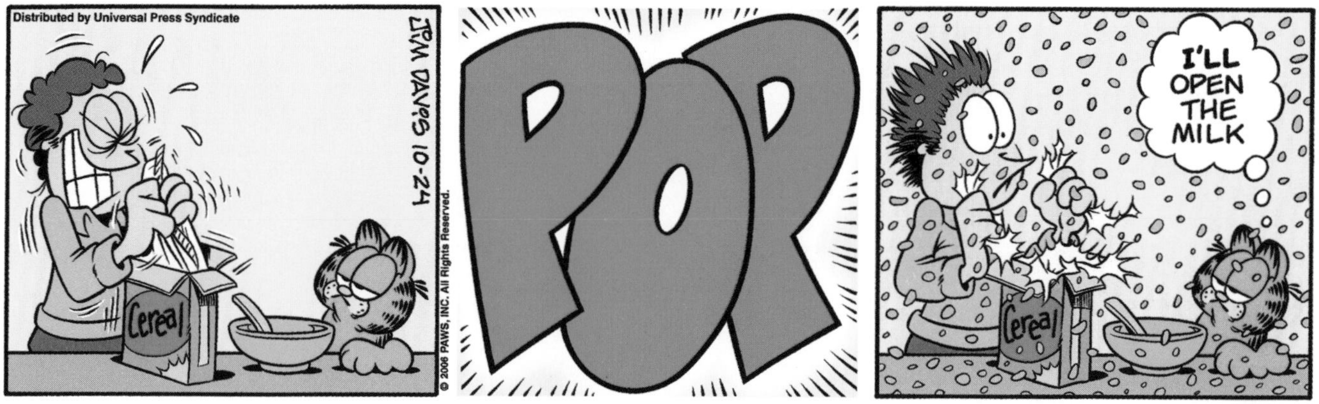
Distributed by Universal Press Syndicate
JIM DAVIS 10-24
Cereal
© 2006 PAWS, INC. All Rights Reserved.
POP
I'LL OPEN THE MILK
Cereal

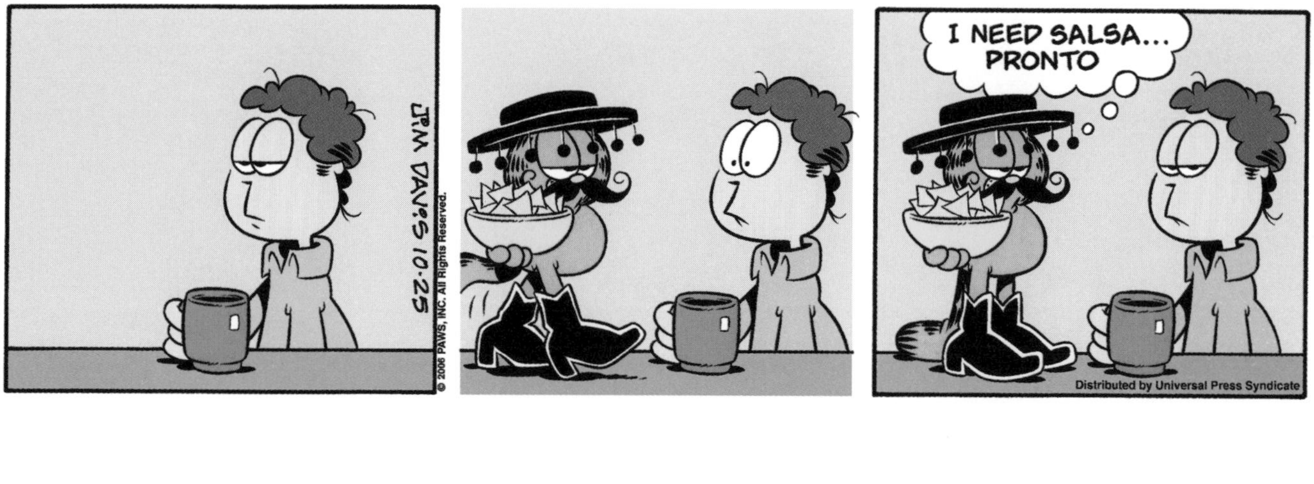
JIM DAVIS 10-25
© 2006 PAWS, INC. All Rights Reserved.
I NEED SALSA... PRONTO
Distributed by Universal Press Syndicate

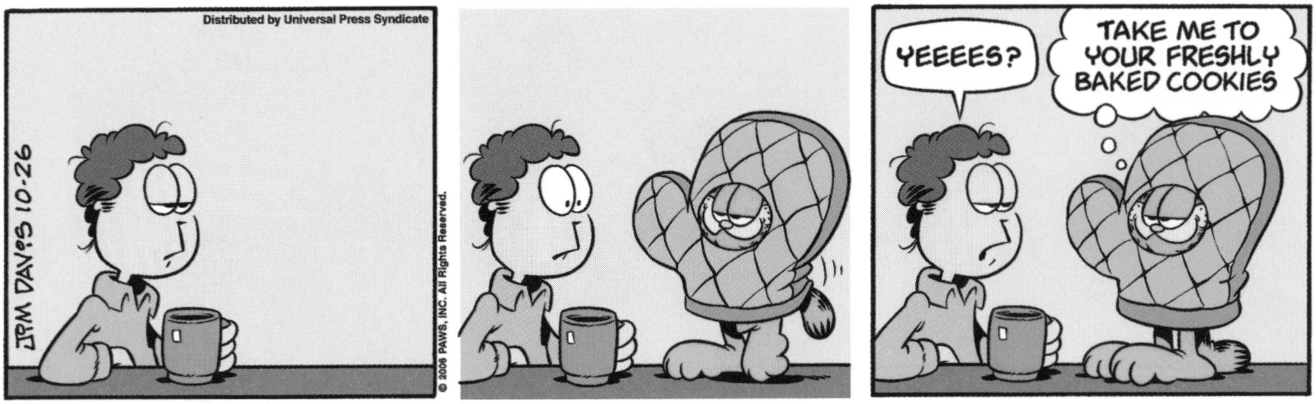
Distributed by Universal Press Syndicate
JIM DAVIS 10-26
© 2006 PAWS, INC. All Rights Reserved.
YEEEES?
TAKE ME TO YOUR FRESHLY BAKED COOKIES

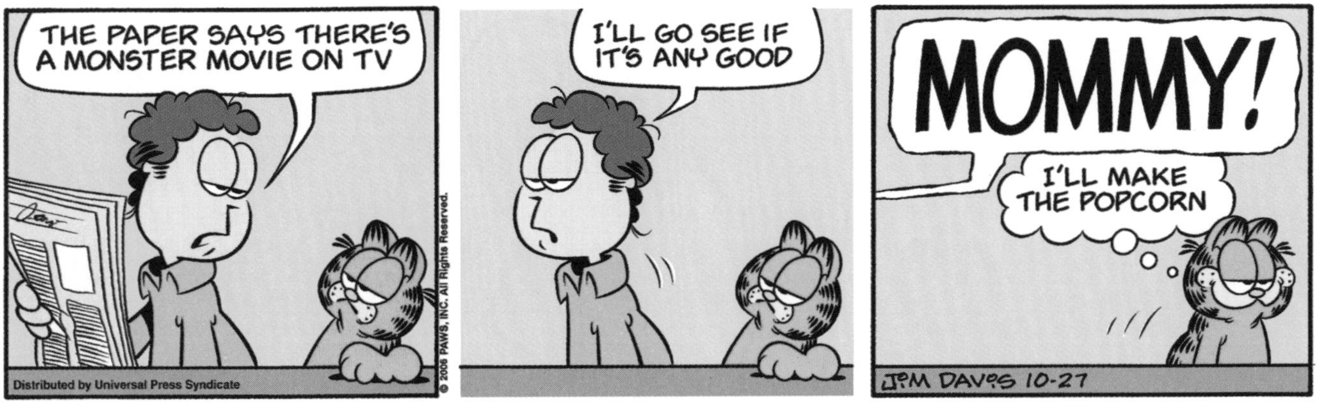
THE PAPER SAYS THERE'S A MONSTER MOVIE ON TV
Distributed by Universal Press Syndicate
© 2006 PAWS, INC. All Rights Reserved.
I'LL GO SEE IF IT'S ANY GOOD
MOMMY!
I'LL MAKE THE POPCORN
JIM DAVIS 10-27

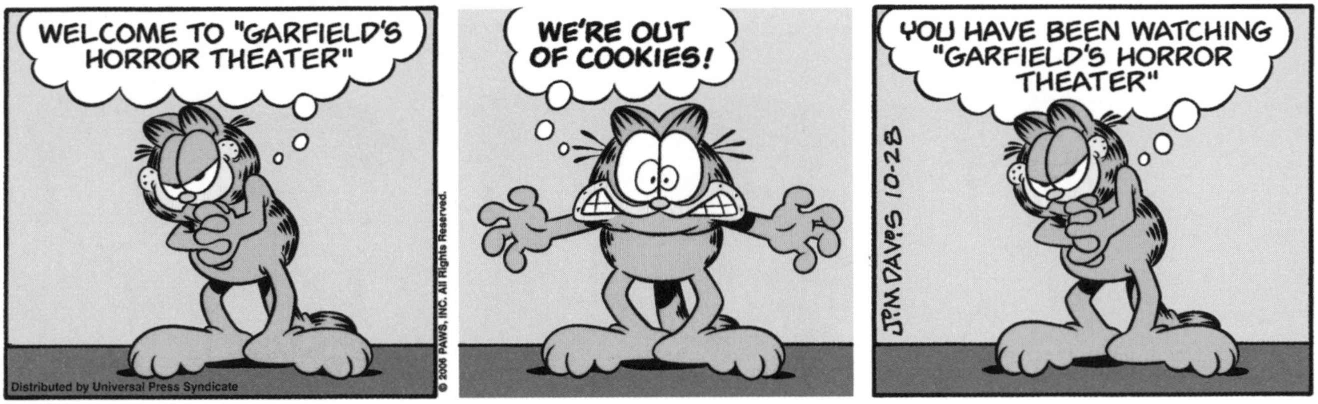
WELCOME TO "GARFIELD'S HORROR THEATER"
Distributed by Universal Press Syndicate
© 2006 PAWS, INC. All Rights Reserved.
WE'RE OUT OF COOKIES!
JIM DAVIS 10-28
YOU HAVE BEEN WATCHING "GARFIELD'S HORROR THEATER"

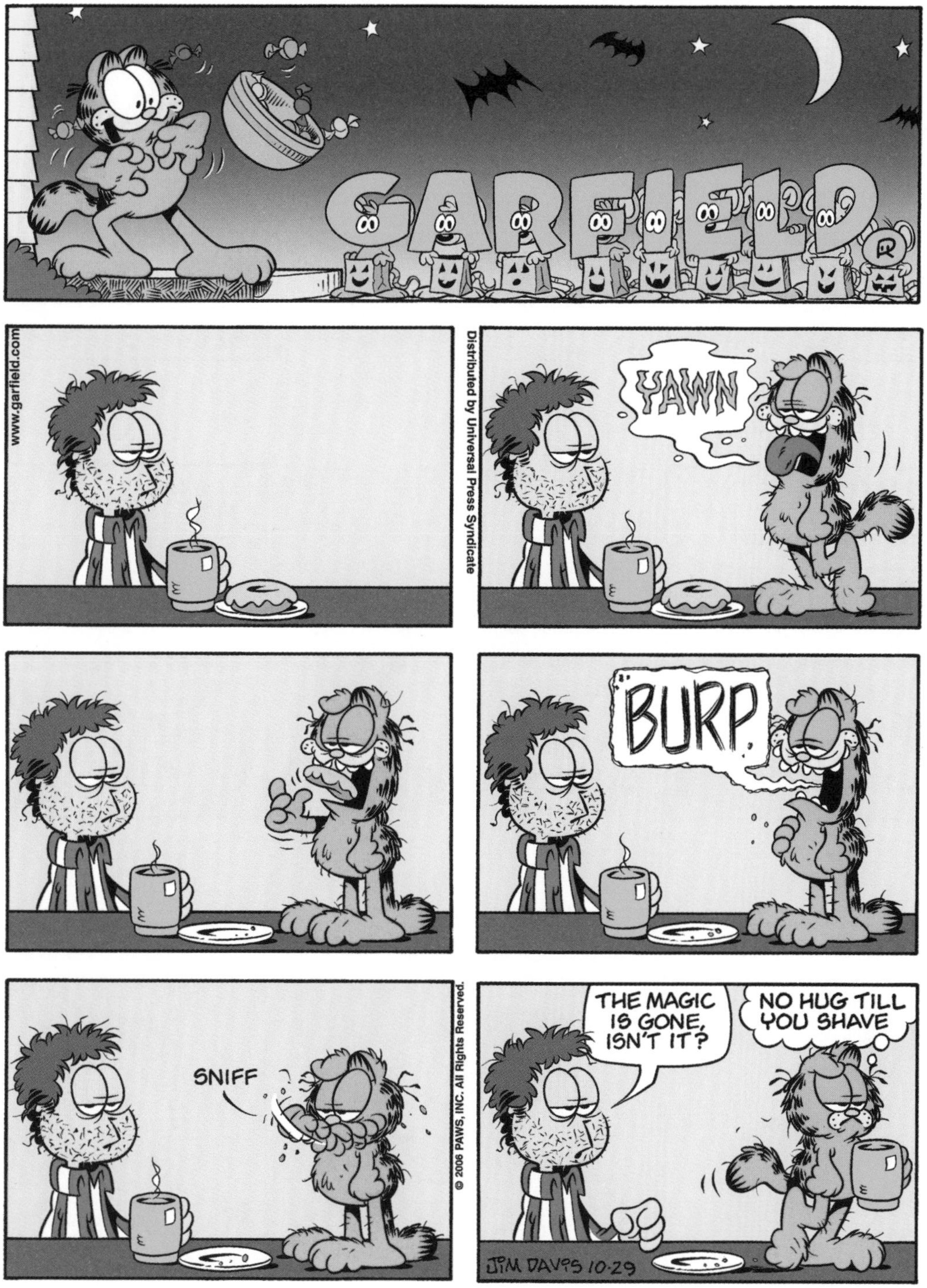
GARFIELD
www.garfield.com
Distributed by Universal Press Syndicate
YAWN
BURP
SNIFF
© 2006 PAWS, INC. All Rights Reserved.
THE MAGIC IS GONE, ISN'T IT?
NO HUG TILL YOU SHAVE
JIM DAVIS 10-29

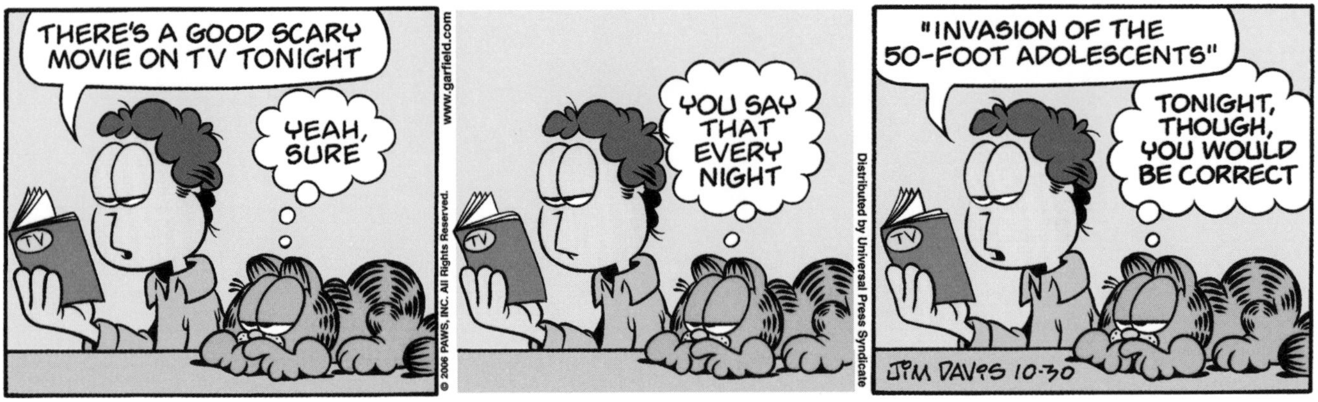
THERE'S A GOOD SCARY MOVIE ON TV TONIGHT
YEAH, SURE
© 2006 PAWS, INC. All Rights Reserved. www.garfield.com
YOU SAY THAT EVERY NIGHT
Distributed by Universal Press Syndicate
"INVASION OF THE 50-FOOT ADOLESCENTS"
TONIGHT, THOUGH, YOU WOULD BE CORRECT
JIM DAVIS 10-30

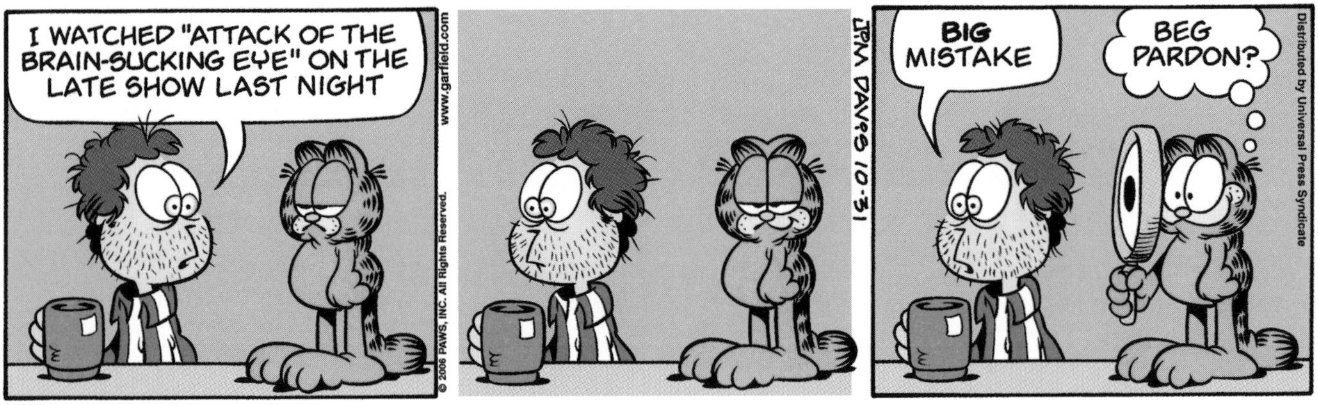
I WATCHED "ATTACK OF THE BRAIN-SUCKING EYE" ON THE LATE SHOW LAST NIGHT
© 2006 PAWS, INC. All Rights Reserved. www.garfield.com
JIM DAVIS 10-31
BIG MISTAKE
BEG PARDON?
Distributed by Universal Press Syndicate

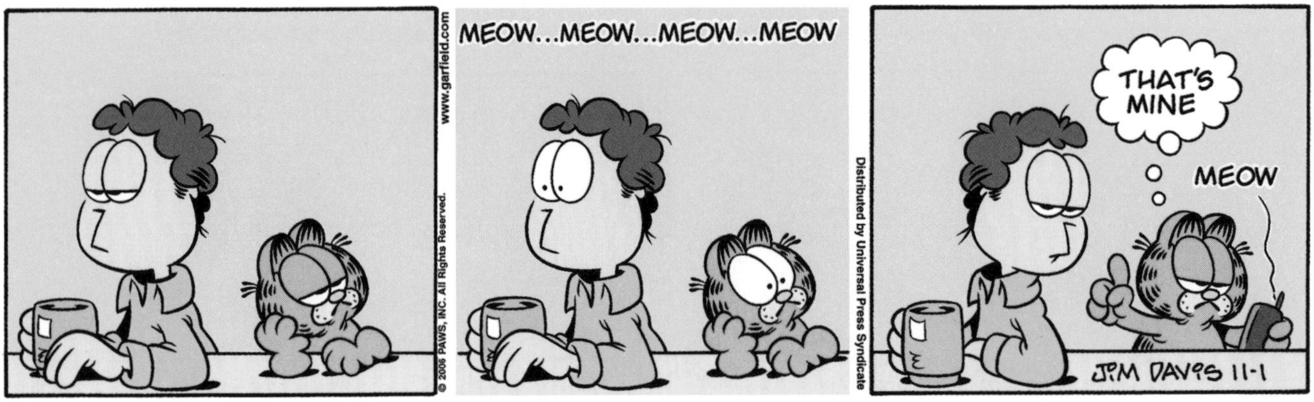
© 2006 PAWS, INC. All Rights Reserved. www.garfield.com
MEOW...MEOW...MEOW...MEOW
Distributed by Universal Press Syndicate
THAT'S MINE
MEOW
JIM DAVIS 11-1

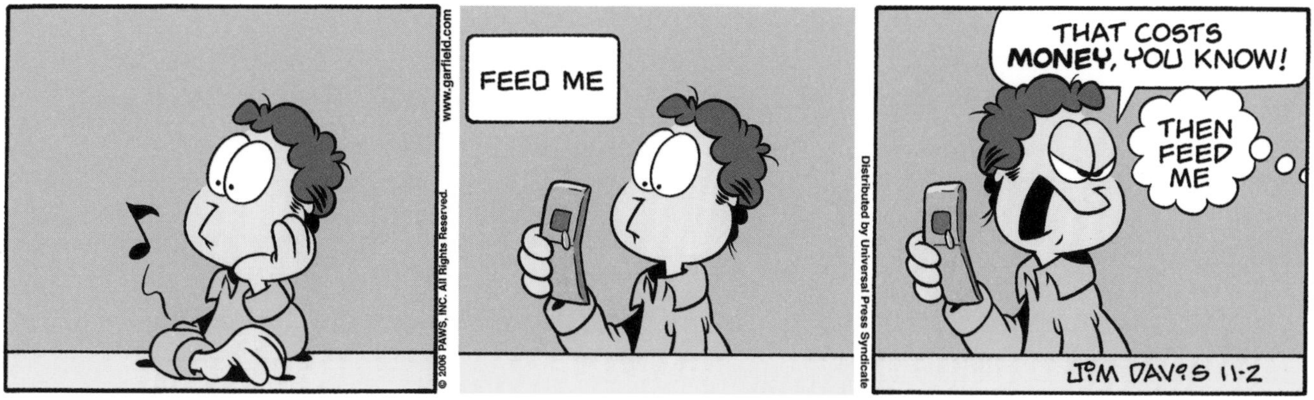
© 2006 PAWS, INC. All Rights Reserved. www.garfield.com
FEED ME
THAT COSTS MONEY, YOU KNOW!
THEN FEED ME
Distributed by Universal Press Syndicate
JIM DAVIS 11-2

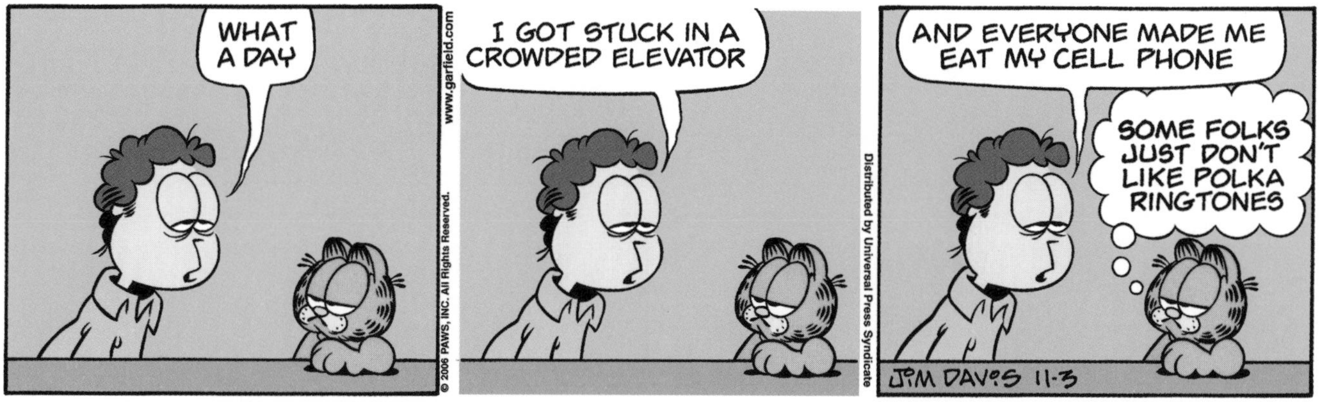
© 2006 PAWS, INC. All Rights Reserved. www.garfield.com
WHAT A DAY
I GOT STUCK IN A CROWDED ELEVATOR
AND EVERYONE MADE ME EAT MY CELL PHONE
SOME FOLKS JUST DON'T LIKE POLKA RINGTONES
Distributed by Universal Press Syndicate
JIM DAVIS 11-3

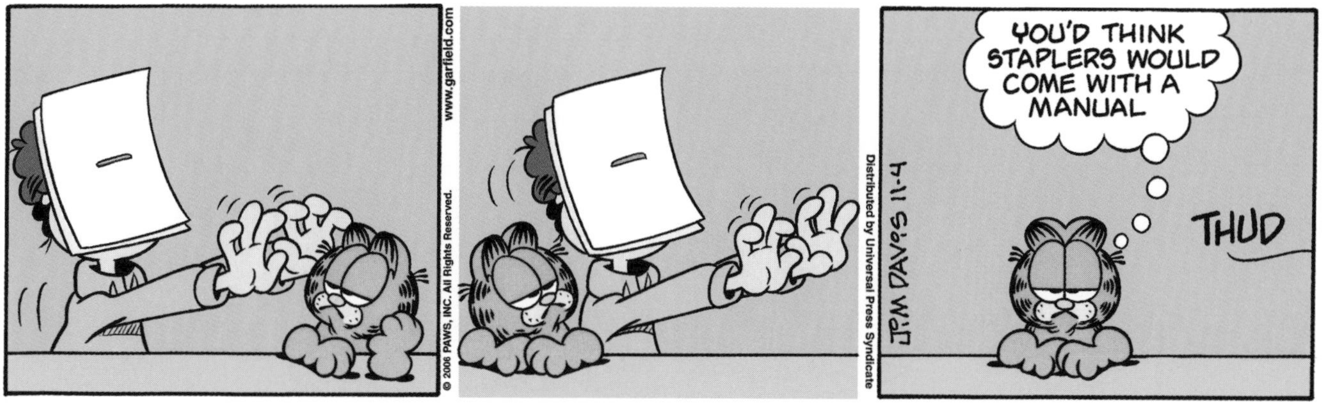
© 2006 PAWS, INC. All Rights Reserved. www.garfield.com
Distributed by Universal Press Syndicate
JIM DAVIS 11-4
YOU'D THINK STAPLERS WOULD COME WITH A MANUAL
THUD

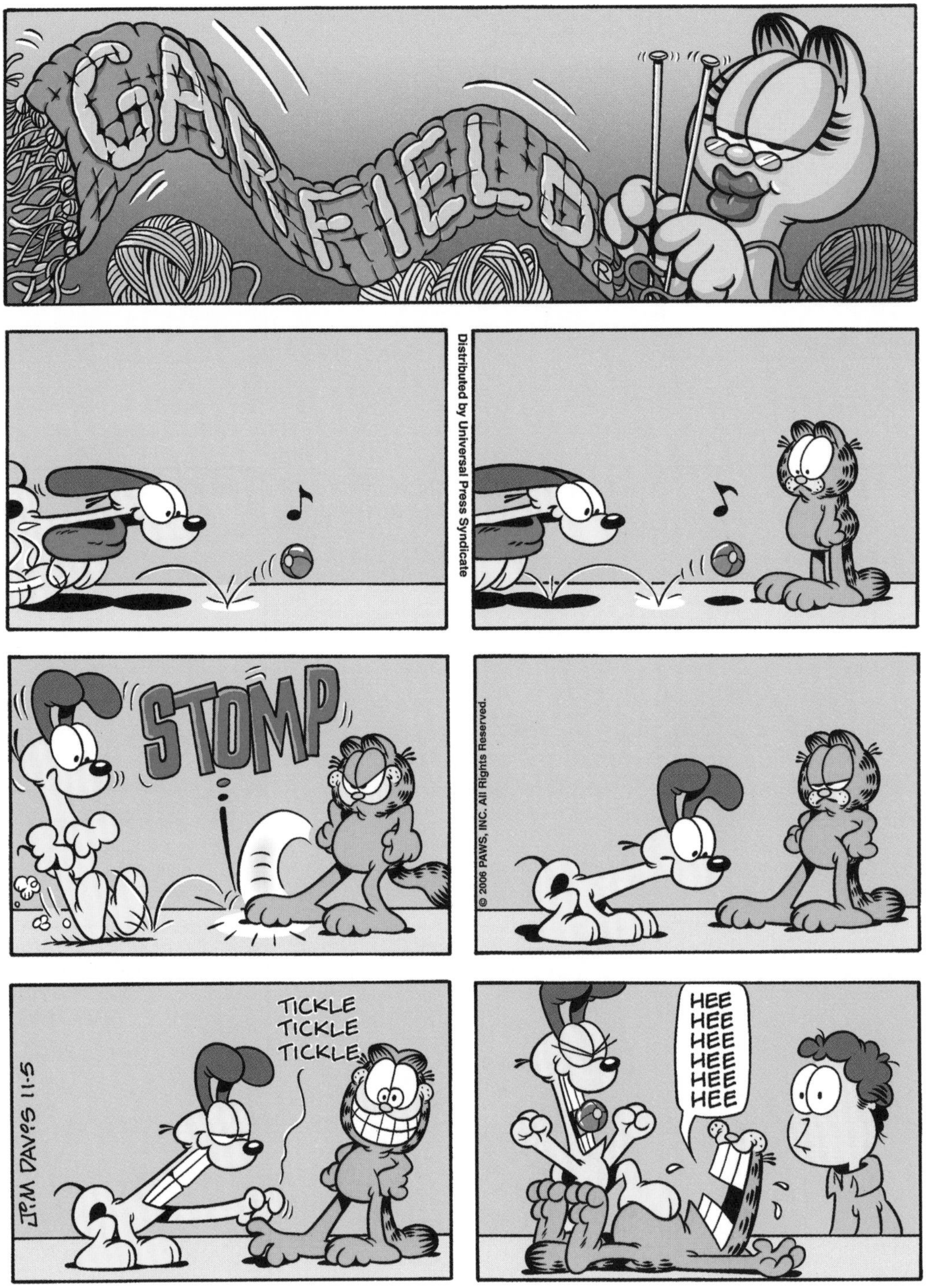
GARFIELD
Distributed by Universal Press Syndicate
STOMP
© 2006 PAWS, INC. All Rights Reserved.
JIM DAVIS 11-5
TICKLE
TICKLE
TICKLE
HEE
HEE
HEE
HEE
HEE
HEE

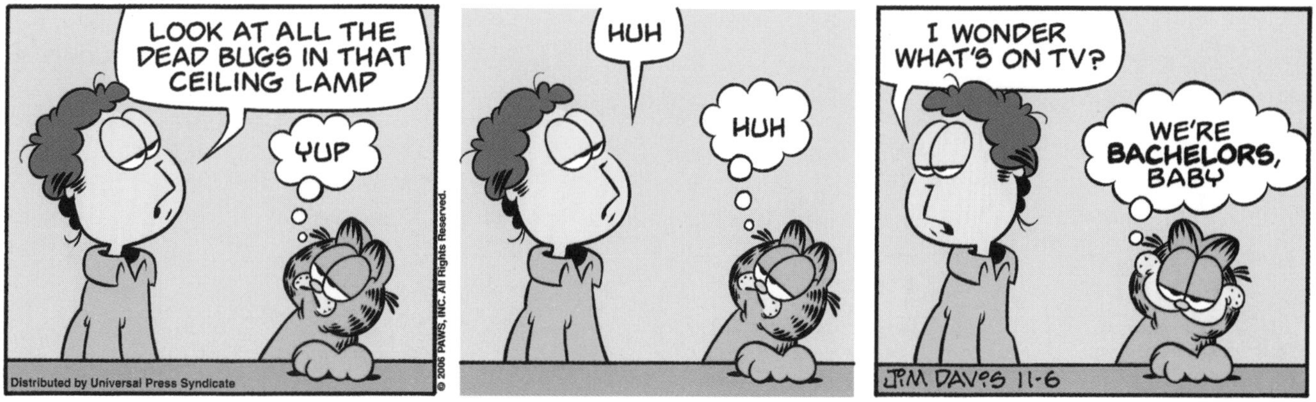
LOOK AT ALL THE DEAD BUGS IN THAT CEILING LAMP
YUP
Distributed by Universal Press Syndicate
© 2006 PAWS, INC. All Rights Reserved.
HUH
HUH
I WONDER WHAT'S ON TV?
WE'RE **BACHELORS,** BABY
JIM DAVIS 11-6

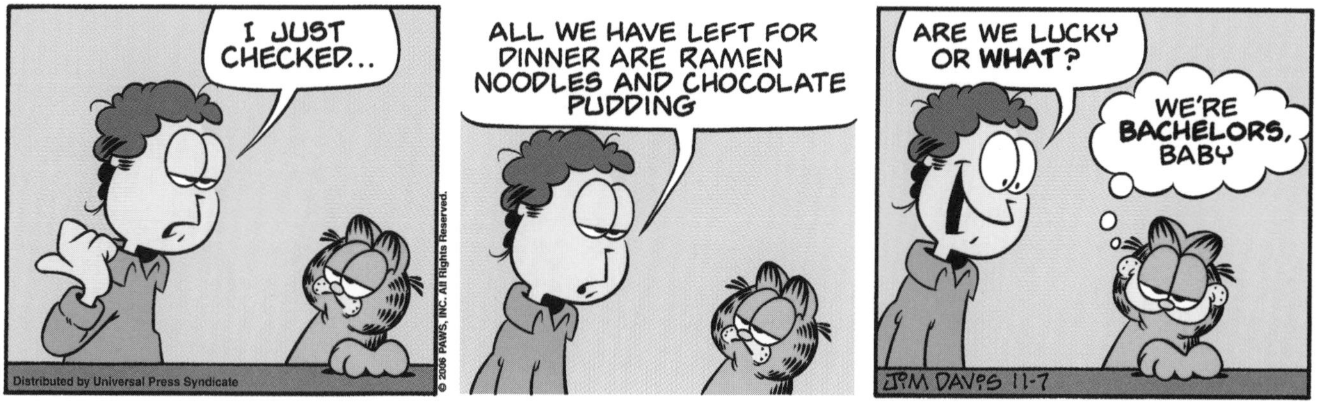
I JUST CHECKED...
Distributed by Universal Press Syndicate
© 2006 PAWS, INC. All Rights Reserved.
ALL WE HAVE LEFT FOR DINNER ARE RAMEN NOODLES AND CHOCOLATE PUDDING
ARE WE LUCKY OR **WHAT**?
WE'RE **BACHELORS,** BABY
JIM DAVIS 11-7

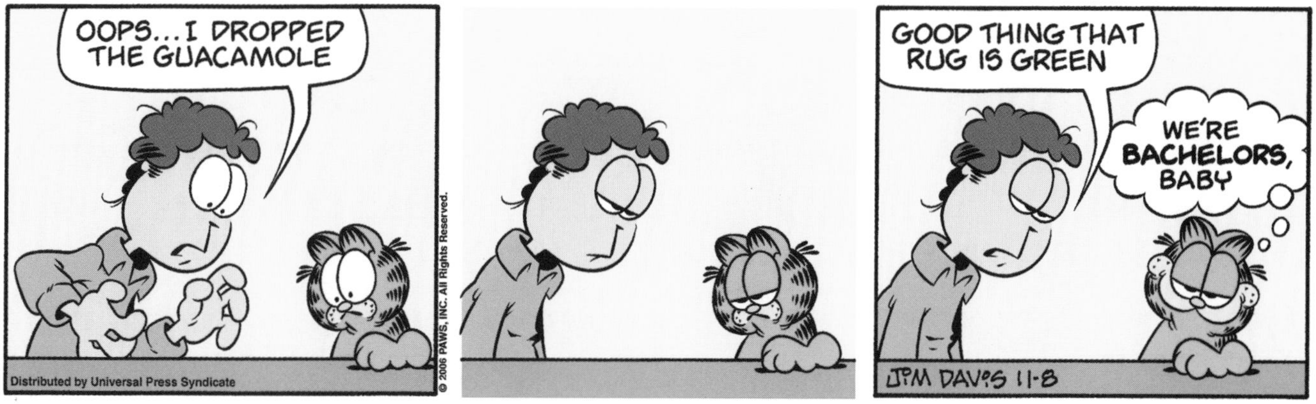
OOPS... I DROPPED THE GUACAMOLE
Distributed by Universal Press Syndicate
© 2006 PAWS, INC. All Rights Reserved.
GOOD THING THAT RUG IS GREEN
WE'RE **BACHELORS,** BABY
JIM DAVIS 11-8

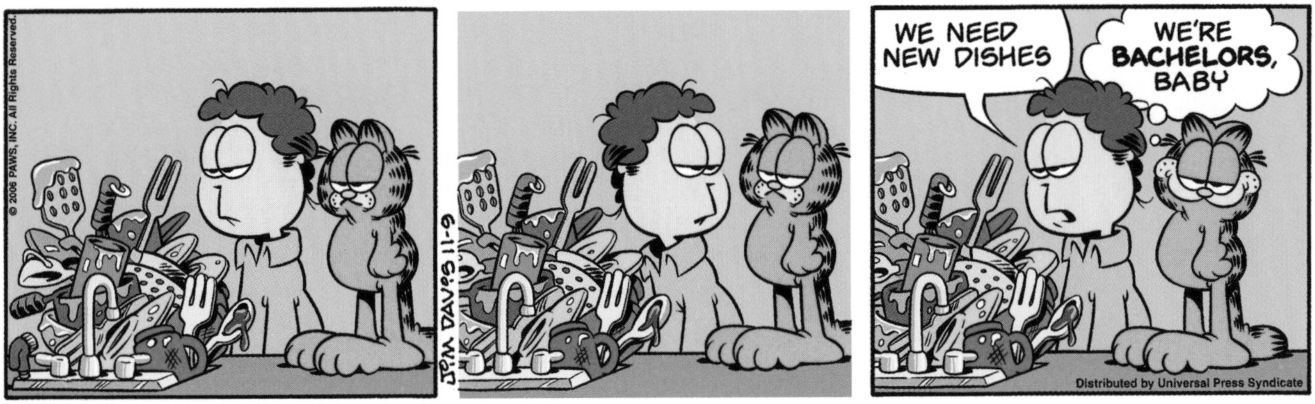
© 2006 PAWS, INC. All Rights Reserved.
JIM DAVIS 11-9
WE NEED NEW DISHES
WE'RE **BACHELORS,** BABY
Distributed by Universal Press Syndicate

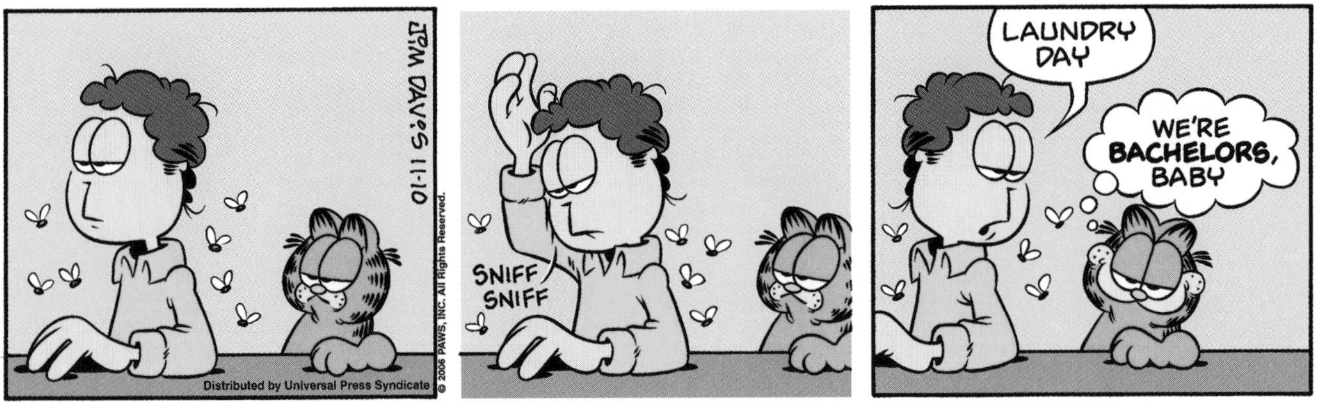
JIM DAVIS 11-10
Distributed by Universal Press Syndicate
© 2006 PAWS, INC. All Rights Reserved.
SNIFF SNIFF
LAUNDRY DAY
WE'RE **BACHELORS,** BABY

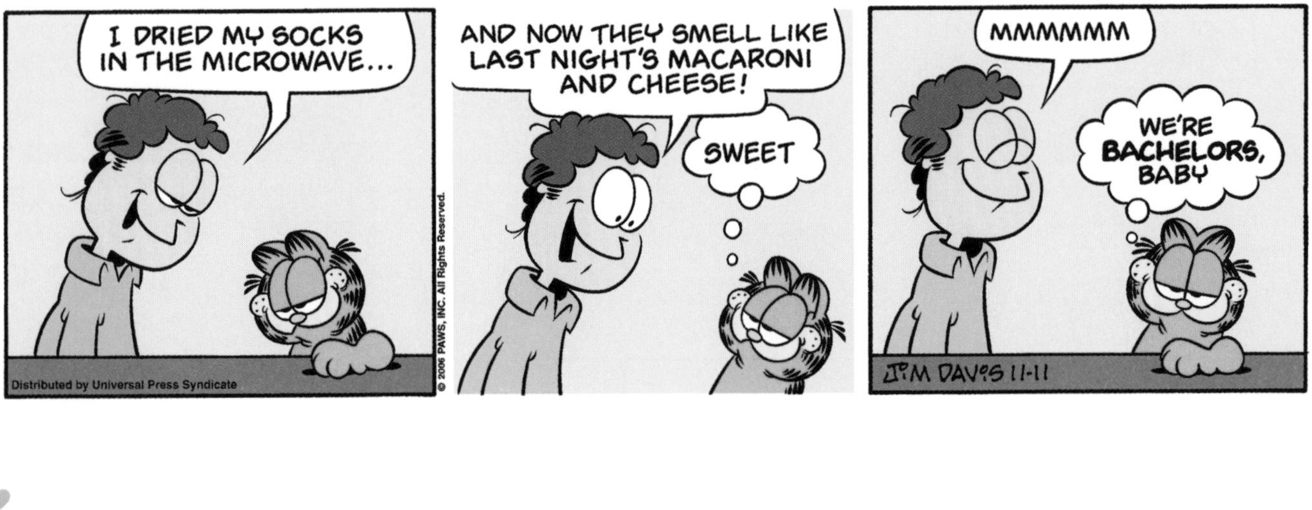
I DRIED MY SOCKS IN THE MICROWAVE...
Distributed by Universal Press Syndicate
© 2006 PAWS, INC. All Rights Reserved.
AND NOW THEY SMELL LIKE LAST NIGHT'S MACARONI AND CHEESE!
SWEET
MMMMMM
WE'RE **BACHELORS,** BABY
JIM DAVIS 11-11

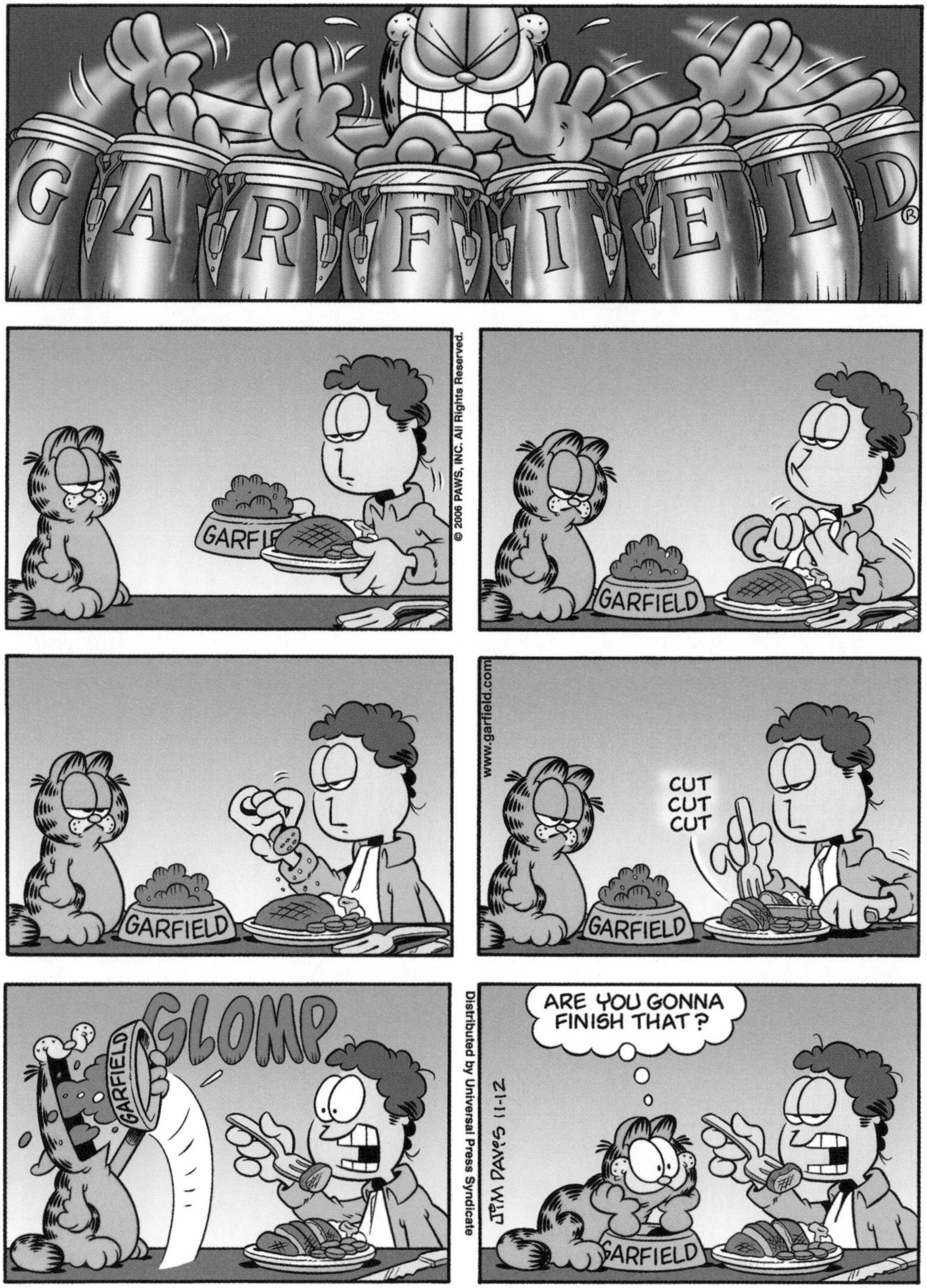
GARFIELD®
© 2006 PAWS, INC. All Rights Reserved.
GARFIELD
GARFIELD
www.garfield.com
GARFIELD
CUT
CUT
CUT
GARFIELD
GLOMP
GARFIELD
Distributed by Universal Press Syndicate
JIM DAVIS 11-12
ARE YOU GONNA FINISH THAT?
GARFIELD

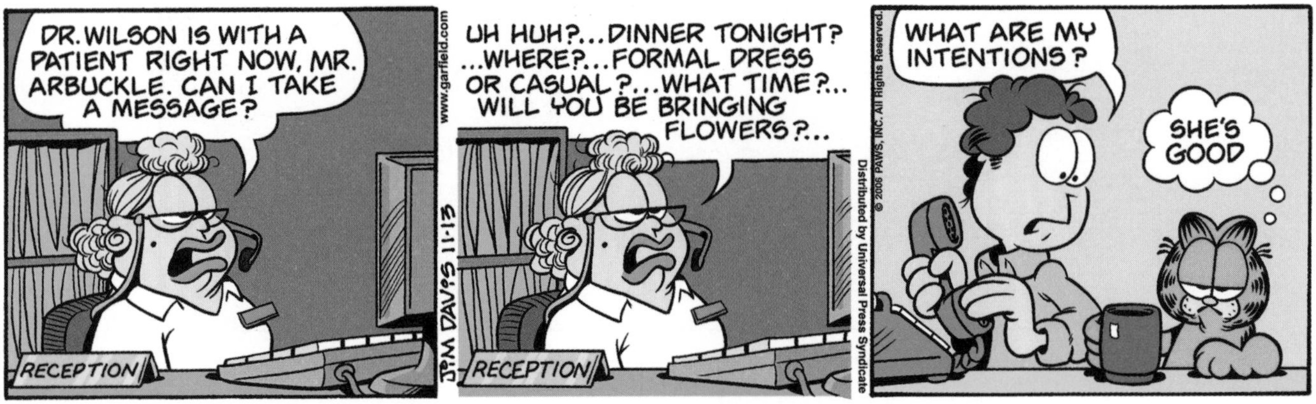
DR. WILSON IS WITH A PATIENT RIGHT NOW, MR. ARBUCKLE. CAN I TAKE A MESSAGE?
RECEPTION
UH HUH?... DINNER TONIGHT? ...WHERE?... FORMAL DRESS OR CASUAL?... WHAT TIME?... WILL YOU BE BRINGING FLOWERS?...
RECEPTION
WHAT ARE MY INTENTIONS?
SHE'S GOOD
JPM DAVIS 11-13
www.garfield.com
© 2006 PAWS, INC. All Rights Reserved. Distributed by Universal Press Syndicate

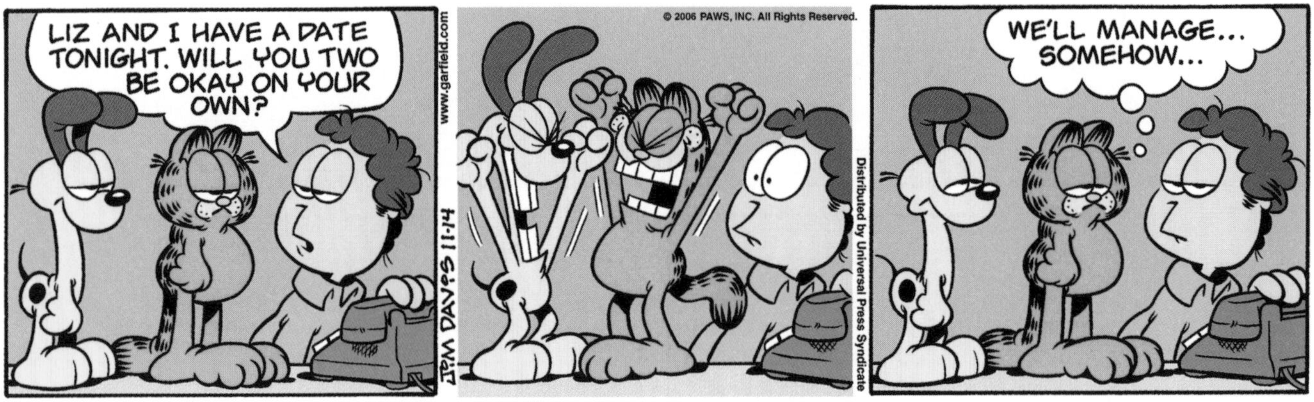
LIZ AND I HAVE A DATE TONIGHT. WILL YOU TWO BE OKAY ON YOUR OWN?
WE'LL MANAGE... SOMEHOW...
JPM DAVIS 11-14
www.garfield.com
© 2006 PAWS, INC. All Rights Reserved.
Distributed by Universal Press Syndicate

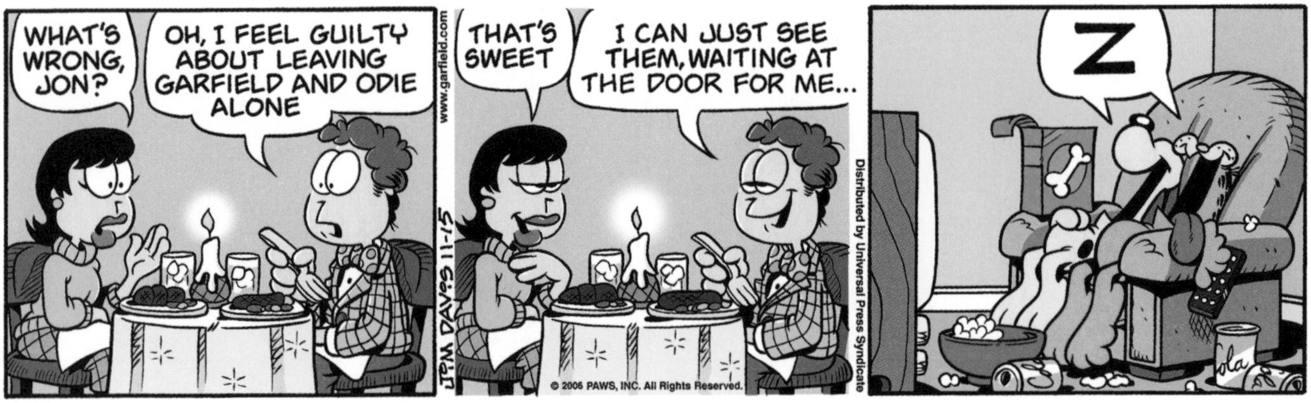
WHAT'S WRONG, JON?
OH, I FEEL GUILTY ABOUT LEAVING GARFIELD AND ODIE ALONE
THAT'S SWEET
I CAN JUST SEE THEM, WAITING AT THE DOOR FOR ME...
Z
Cola
JPM DAVIS 11-15
www.garfield.com
© 2006 PAWS, INC. All Rights Reserved.
Distributed by Universal Press Syndicate

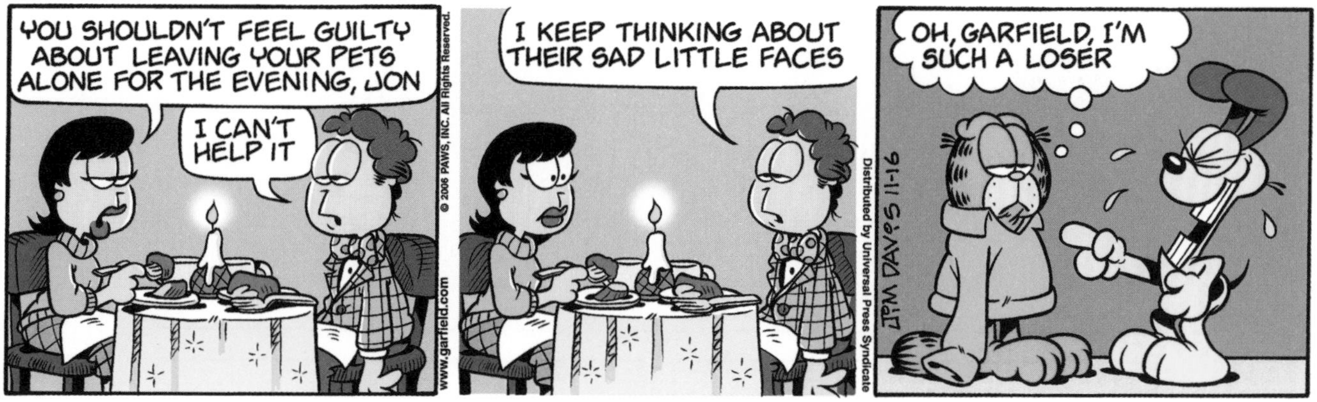
YOU SHOULDN'T FEEL GUILTY ABOUT LEAVING YOUR PETS ALONE FOR THE EVENING, JON
I CAN'T HELP IT
© 2006 PAWS, INC. All Rights Reserved.
www.garfield.com
I KEEP THINKING ABOUT THEIR SAD LITTLE FACES
Distributed by Universal Press Syndicate
JIM DAVIS 11-16
OH, GARFIELD, I'M SUCH A LOSER

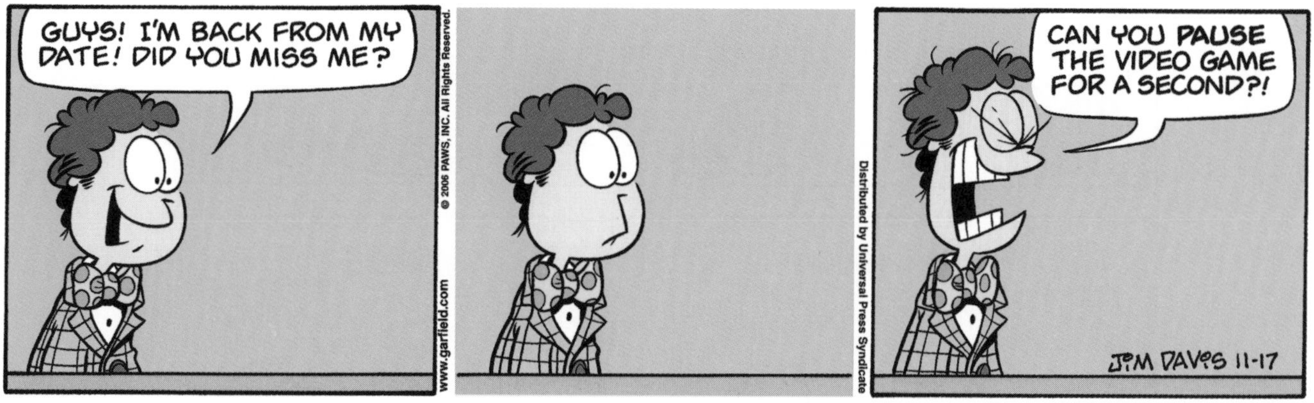
GUYS! I'M BACK FROM MY DATE! DID YOU MISS ME?
© 2006 PAWS, INC. All Rights Reserved.
www.garfield.com
Distributed by Universal Press Syndicate
CAN YOU PAUSE THE VIDEO GAME FOR A SECOND?!
JIM DAVIS 11-17

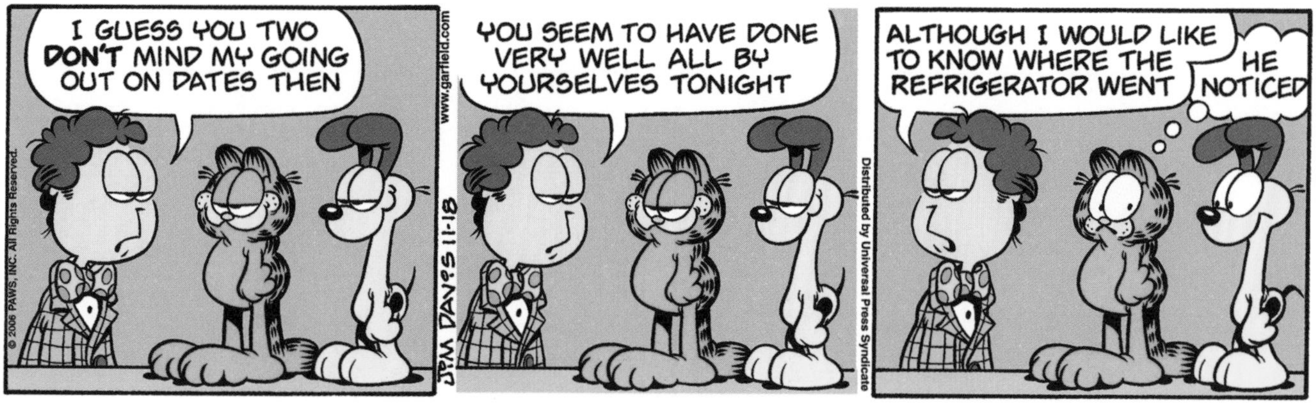
I GUESS YOU TWO DON'T MIND MY GOING OUT ON DATES THEN
© 2006 PAWS, INC. All Rights Reserved.
www.garfield.com
JIM DAVIS 11-18
YOU SEEM TO HAVE DONE VERY WELL ALL BY YOURSELVES TONIGHT
Distributed by Universal Press Syndicate
ALTHOUGH I WOULD LIKE TO KNOW WHERE THE REFRIGERATOR WENT
HE NOTICED

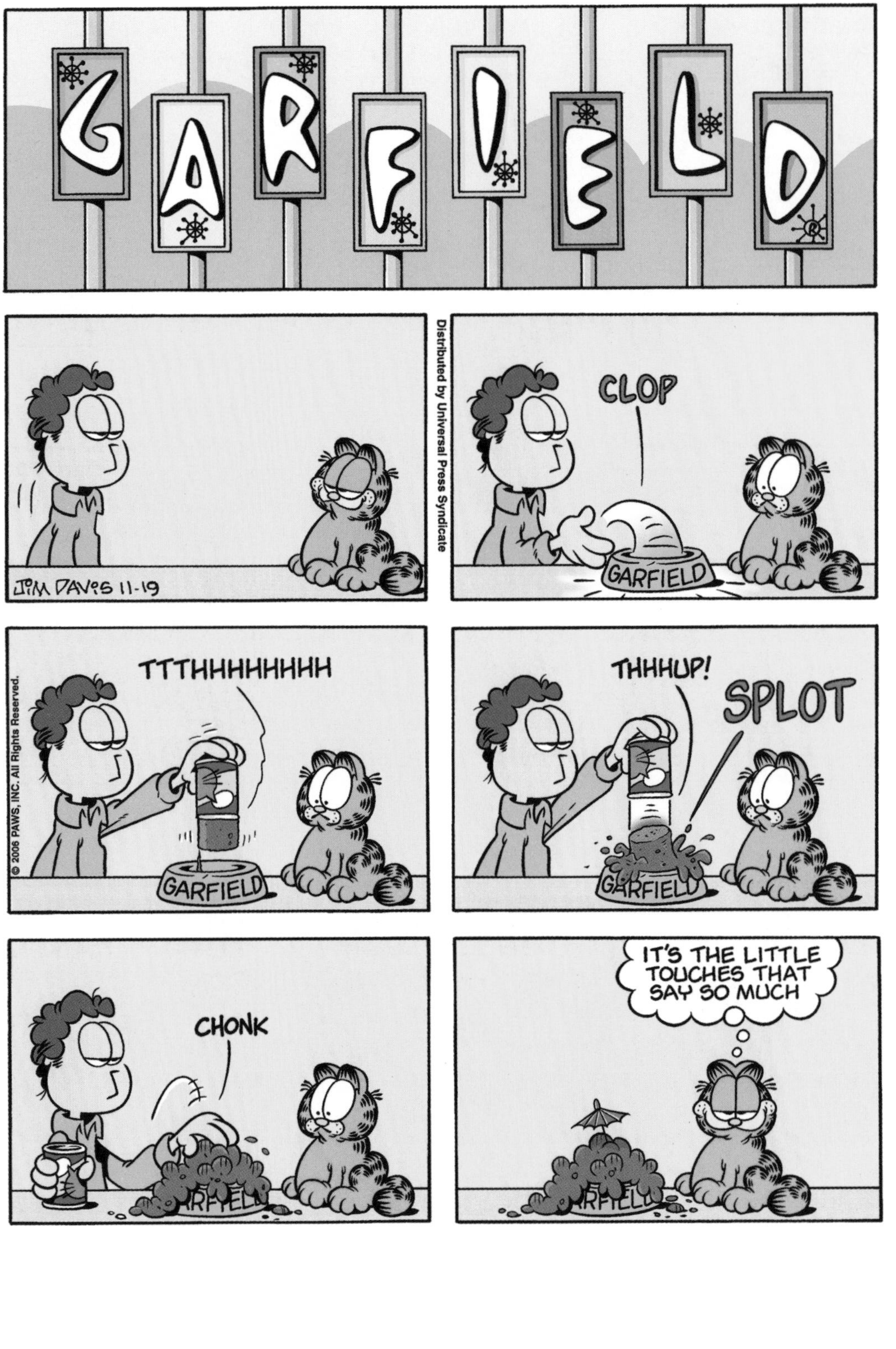
GARFIELD
JIM DAVIS 11-19
Distributed by Universal Press Syndicate
CLOP
GARFIELD
© 2006 PAWS, INC. All Rights Reserved.
TTTHHHHHHHH
GARFIELD
THHHUP!
SPLOT
GARFIELD
CHONK
IT'S THE LITTLE TOUCHES THAT SAY SO MUCH

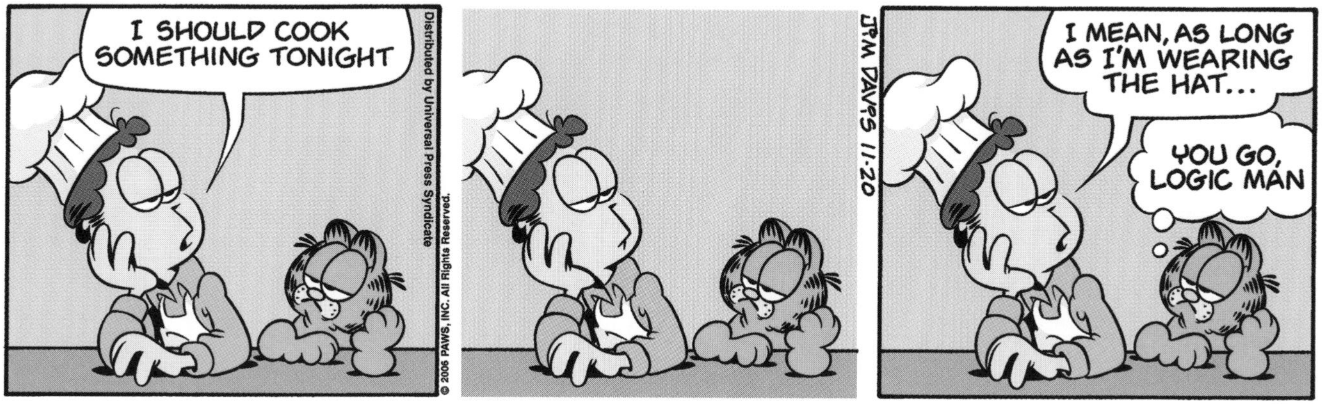
I SHOULD COOK SOMETHING TONIGHT
Distributed by Universal Press Syndicate
© 2006 PAWS, INC. All Rights Reserved.
JIM DAVIS 11-20
I MEAN, AS LONG AS I'M WEARING THE HAT...
YOU GO, LOGIC MAN

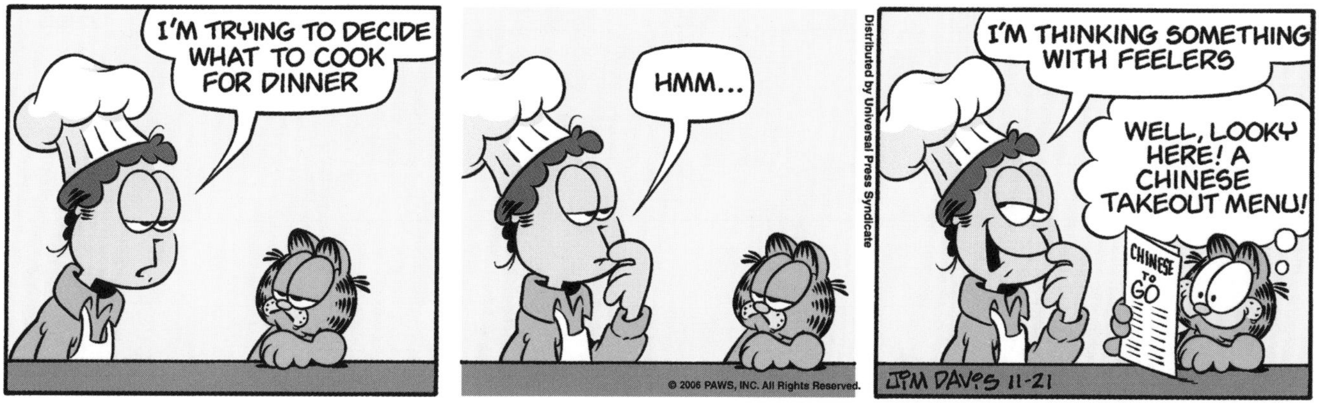
I'M TRYING TO DECIDE WHAT TO COOK FOR DINNER
HMM...
© 2006 PAWS, INC. All Rights Reserved.
Distributed by Universal Press Syndicate
I'M THINKING SOMETHING WITH FEELERS
WELL, LOOKY HERE! A CHINESE TAKEOUT MENU!
CHINESE TO GO
JIM DAVIS 11-21

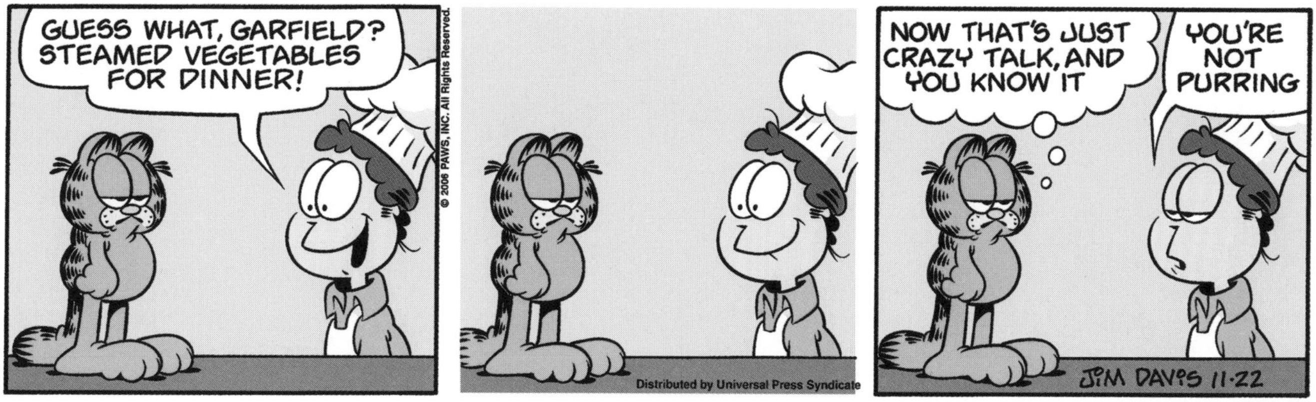
GUESS WHAT, GARFIELD? STEAMED VEGETABLES FOR DINNER!
© 2006 PAWS, INC. All Rights Reserved.
Distributed by Universal Press Syndicate
NOW THAT'S JUST CRAZY TALK, AND YOU KNOW IT
YOU'RE NOT PURRING
JIM DAVIS 11-22

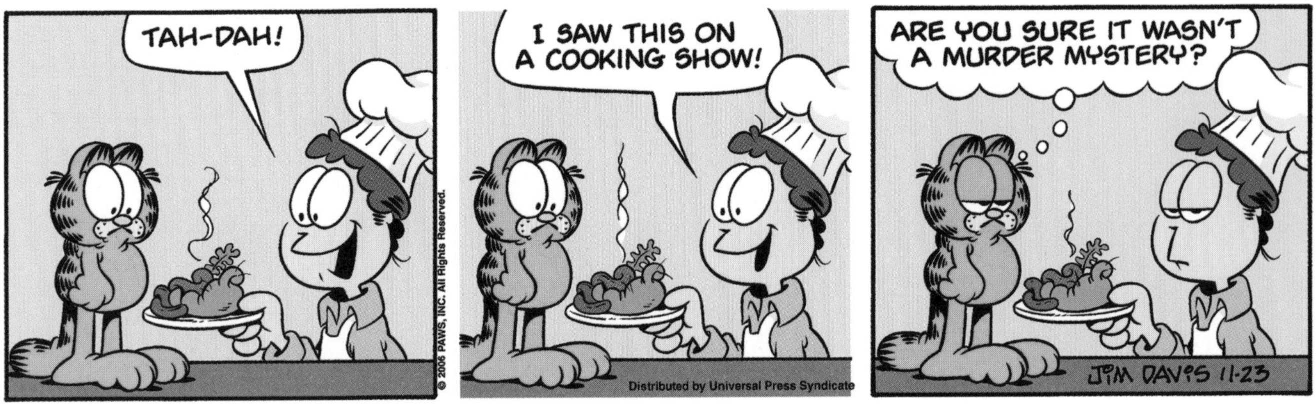
TAH-DAH!
I SAW THIS ON A COOKING SHOW!
ARE YOU SURE IT WASN'T A MURDER MYSTERY?
JIM DAVIS 11-23
© 2006 PAWS, INC. All Rights Reserved.
Distributed by Universal Press Syndicate

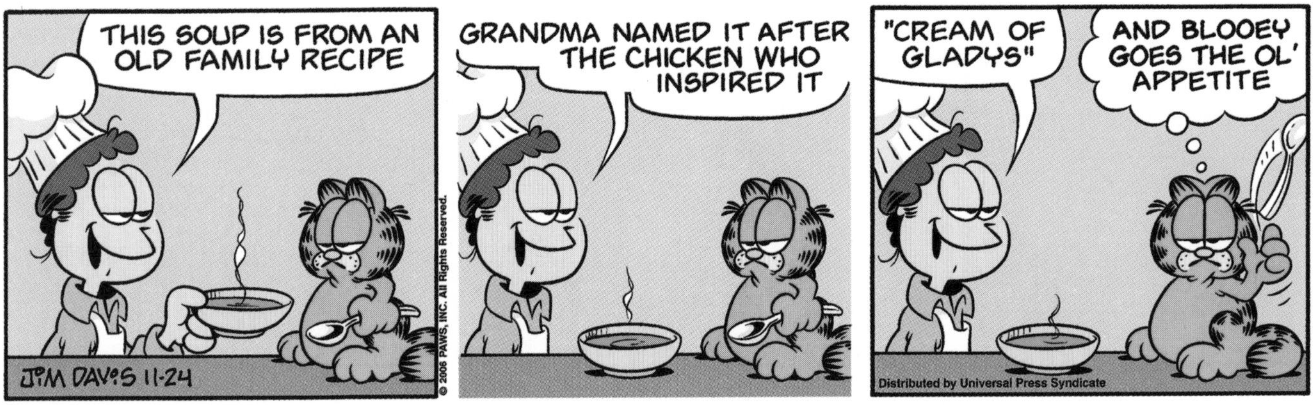
THIS SOUP IS FROM AN OLD FAMILY RECIPE
GRANDMA NAMED IT AFTER THE CHICKEN WHO INSPIRED IT
"CREAM OF GLADYS"
AND BLOOEY GOES THE OL' APPETITE
JIM DAVIS 11-24
© 2006 PAWS, INC. All Rights Reserved.
Distributed by Universal Press Syndicate

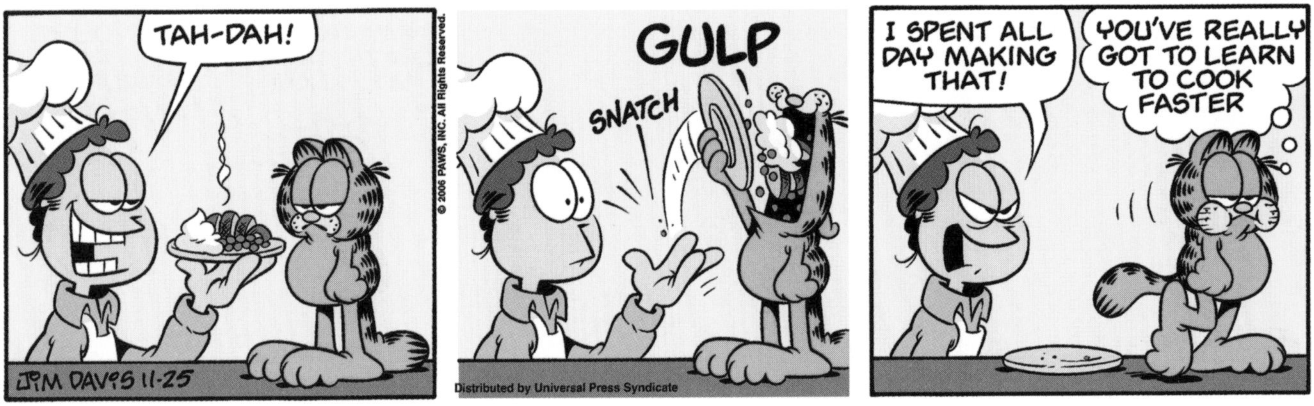
TAH-DAH!
SNATCH
GULP
I SPENT ALL DAY MAKING THAT!
YOU'VE REALLY GOT TO LEARN TO COOK FASTER
JIM DAVIS 11-25
© 2006 PAWS, INC. All Rights Reserved.
Distributed by Universal Press Syndicate

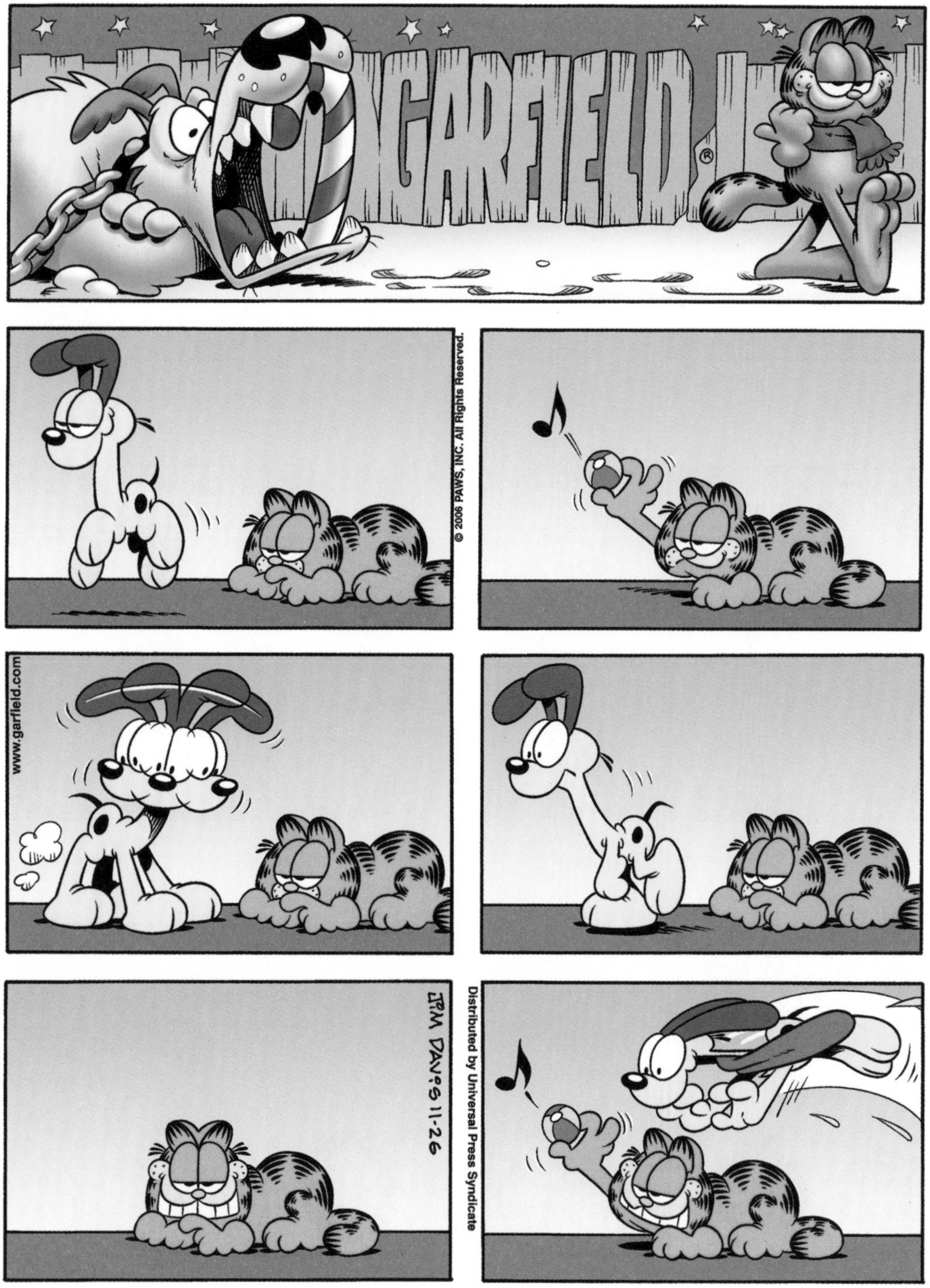
GARFIELD
© 2006 PAWS, INC. All Rights Reserved.
www.garfield.com
JPM DAVIS 11-26
Distributed by Universal Press Syndicate

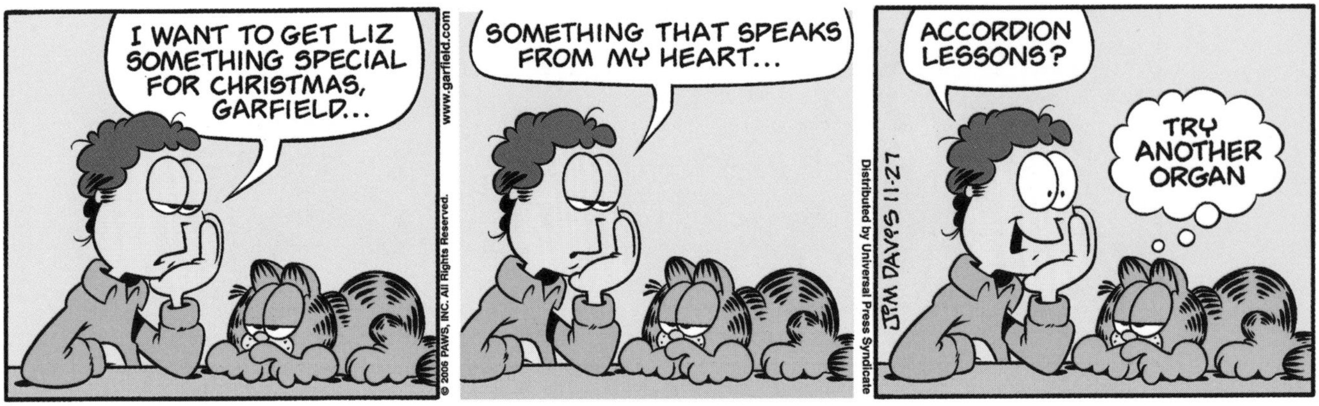
I WANT TO GET LIZ SOMETHING SPECIAL FOR CHRISTMAS, GARFIELD...
SOMETHING THAT SPEAKS FROM MY HEART...
ACCORDION LESSONS?
TRY ANOTHER ORGAN
© 2006 PAWS, INC. All Rights Reserved. www.garfield.com
Distributed by Universal Press Syndicate

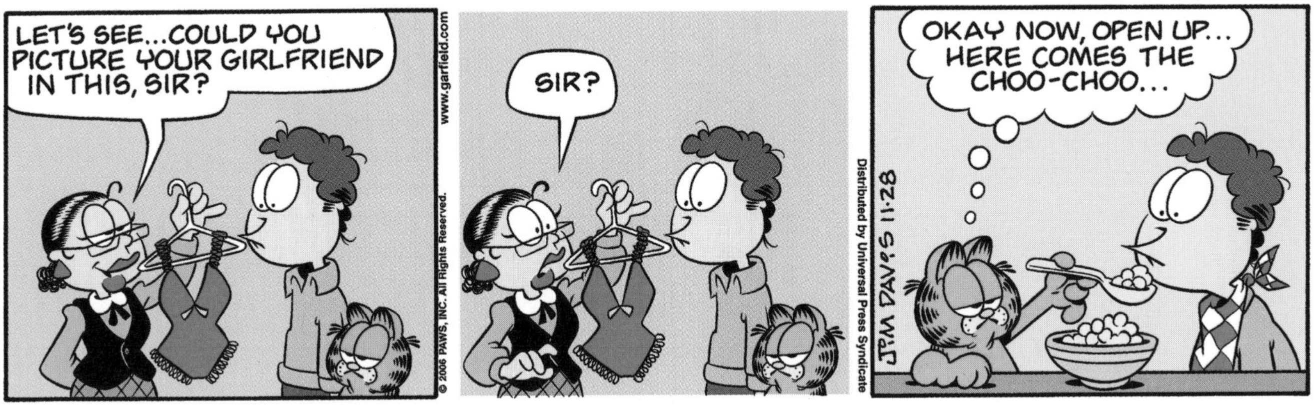
LET'S SEE...COULD YOU PICTURE YOUR GIRLFRIEND IN THIS, SIR?
SIR?
OKAY NOW, OPEN UP... HERE COMES THE CHOO-CHOO...
© 2006 PAWS, INC. All Rights Reserved. www.garfield.com
Distributed by Universal Press Syndicate

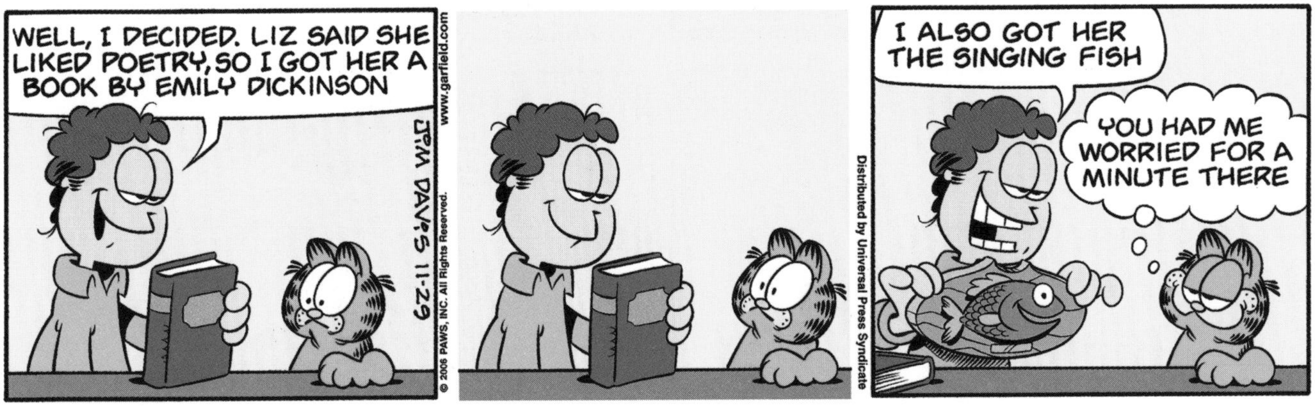
WELL, I DECIDED. LIZ SAID SHE LIKED POETRY, SO I GOT HER A BOOK BY EMILY DICKINSON
I ALSO GOT HER THE SINGING FISH
YOU HAD ME WORRIED FOR A MINUTE THERE
© 2006 PAWS, INC. All Rights Reserved. www.garfield.com
Distributed by Universal Press Syndicate

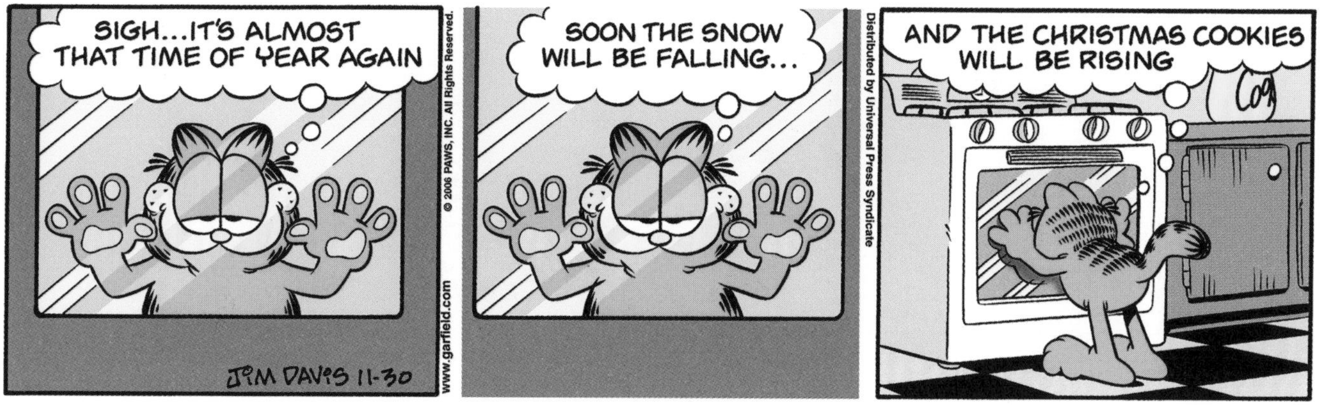
SIGH...IT'S ALMOST THAT TIME OF YEAR AGAIN
JIM DAVIS 11-30
© 2006 PAWS, INC. All Rights Reserved.
www.garfield.com
SOON THE SNOW WILL BE FALLING...
Distributed by Universal Press Syndicate
AND THE CHRISTMAS COOKIES WILL BE RISING

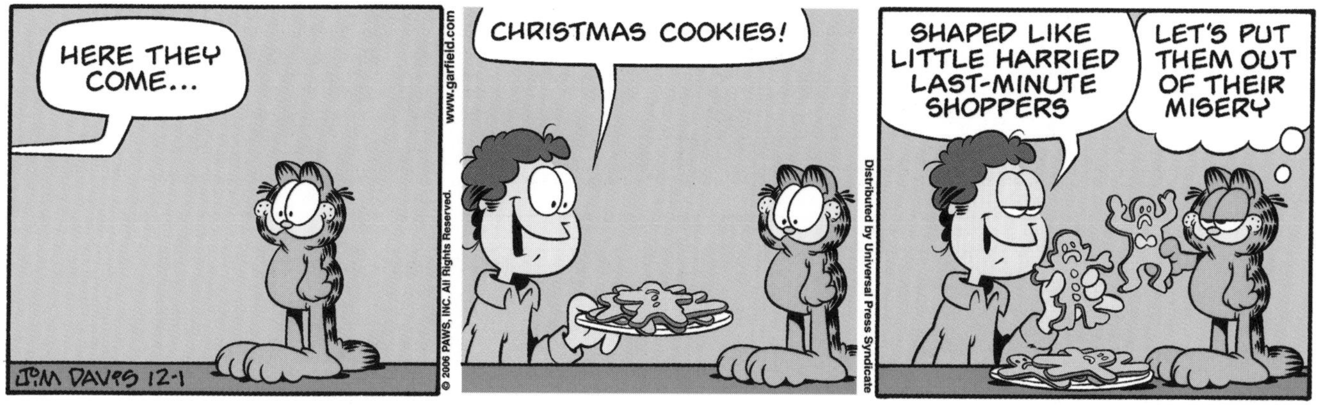
HERE THEY COME...
JIM DAVIS 12-1
© 2006 PAWS, INC. All Rights Reserved.
www.garfield.com
CHRISTMAS COOKIES!
Distributed by Universal Press Syndicate
SHAPED LIKE LITTLE HARRIED LAST-MINUTE SHOPPERS
LET'S PUT THEM OUT OF THEIR MISERY

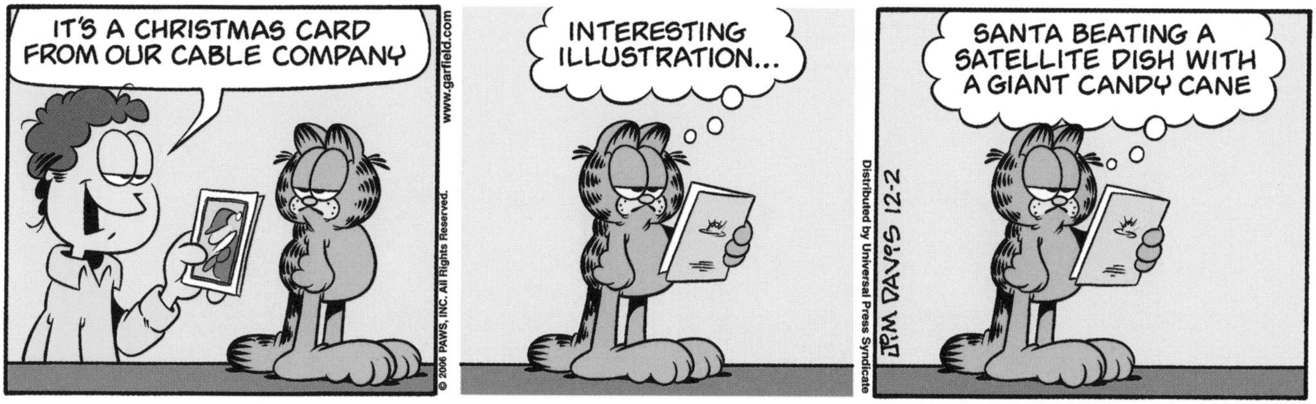
IT'S A CHRISTMAS CARD FROM OUR CABLE COMPANY
© 2006 PAWS, INC. All Rights Reserved.
www.garfield.com
INTERESTING ILLUSTRATION...
Distributed by Universal Press Syndicate
JIM DAVIS 12-2
SANTA BEATING A SATELLITE DISH WITH A GIANT CANDY CANE

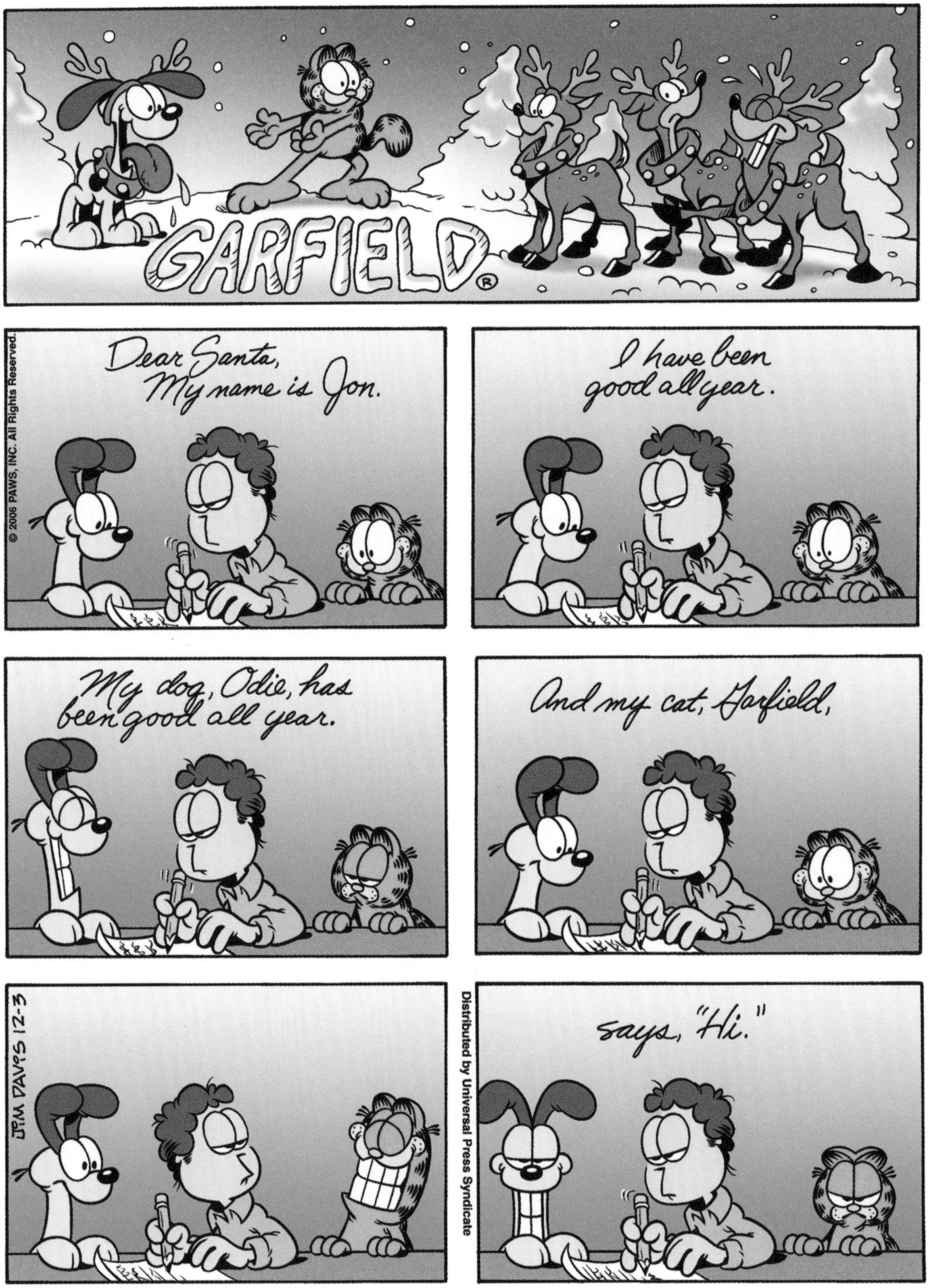
GARFIELD®
© 2006 PAWS, INC. All Rights Reserved.
Dear Santa,
My name is Jon.
I have been
good all year.
My dog, Odie, has
been good all year.
And my cat, Garfield,
JPM DAVIS 12-3
Distributed by Universal Press Syndicate
says, "Hi."

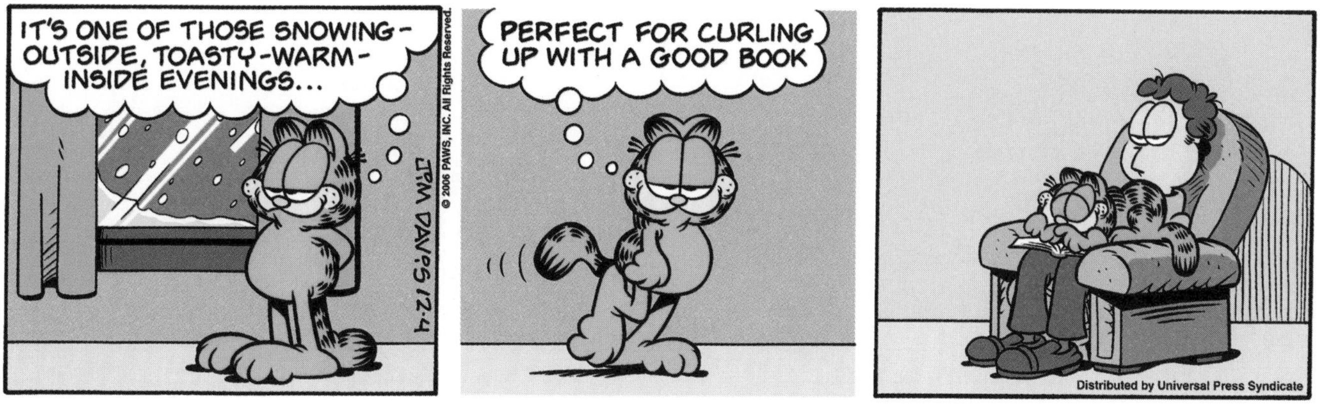
IT'S ONE OF THOSE SNOWING-OUTSIDE, TOASTY-WARM-INSIDE EVENINGS...
JPM DAVPS 12-4
© 2006 PAWS, INC. All Rights Reserved.
PERFECT FOR CURLING UP WITH A GOOD BOOK
Distributed by Universal Press Syndicate

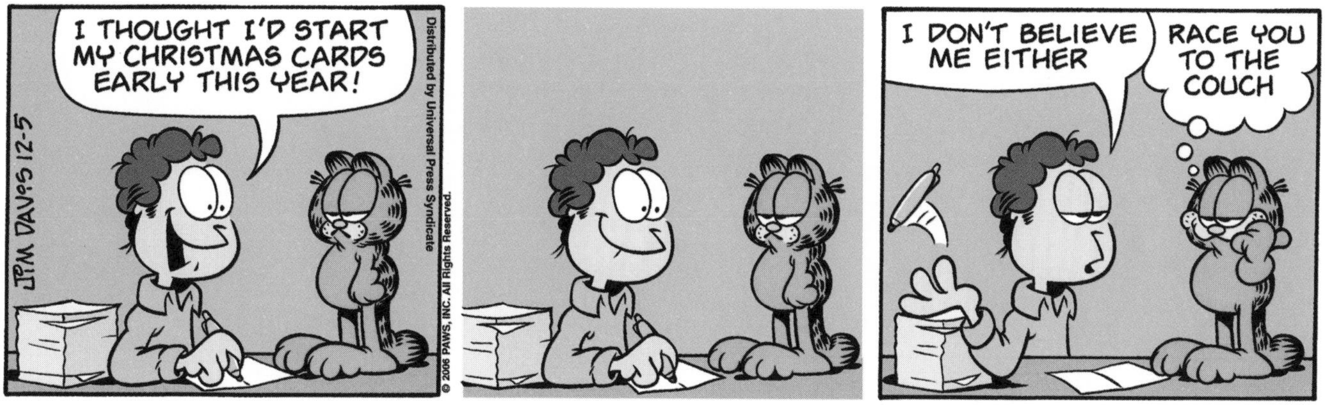
I THOUGHT I'D START MY CHRISTMAS CARDS EARLY THIS YEAR!
JPM DAVPS 12-5
Distributed by Universal Press Syndicate
© 2006 PAWS, INC. All Rights Reserved.
I DON'T BELIEVE ME EITHER
RACE YOU TO THE COUCH

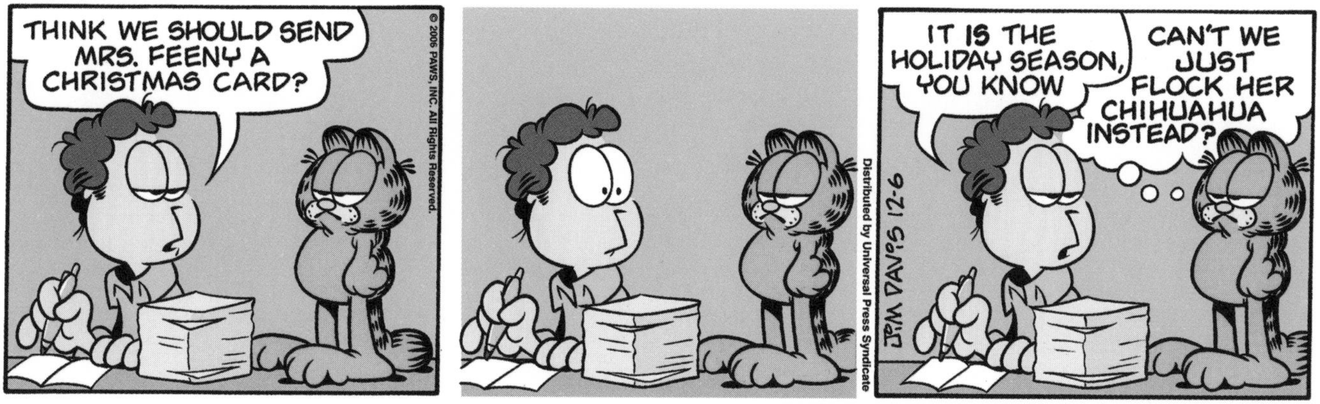
THINK WE SHOULD SEND MRS. FEENY A CHRISTMAS CARD?
© 2006 PAWS, INC. All Rights Reserved.
Distributed by Universal Press Syndicate
JPM DAVPS 12-6
IT IS THE HOLIDAY SEASON, YOU KNOW
CAN'T WE JUST FLOCK HER CHIHUAHUA INSTEAD?

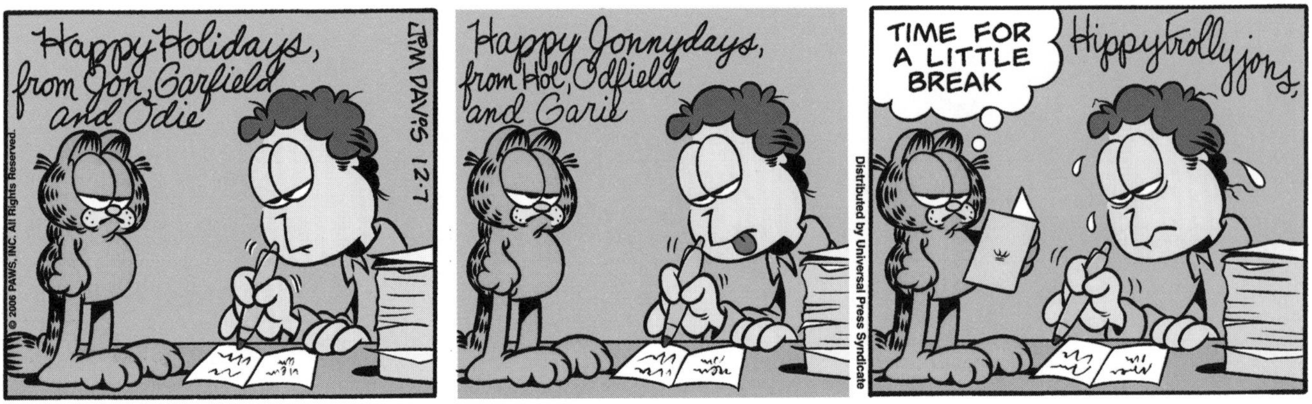
Happy Holidays, from Jon, Garfield and Odie
JIM DAVIS 12-7
© 2006 PAWS, INC. All Rights Reserved.
Happy Jonnydays, from Hol, Odfield and Garie
Distributed by Universal Press Syndicate
TIME FOR A LITTLE BREAK
HippyTrollyjons,

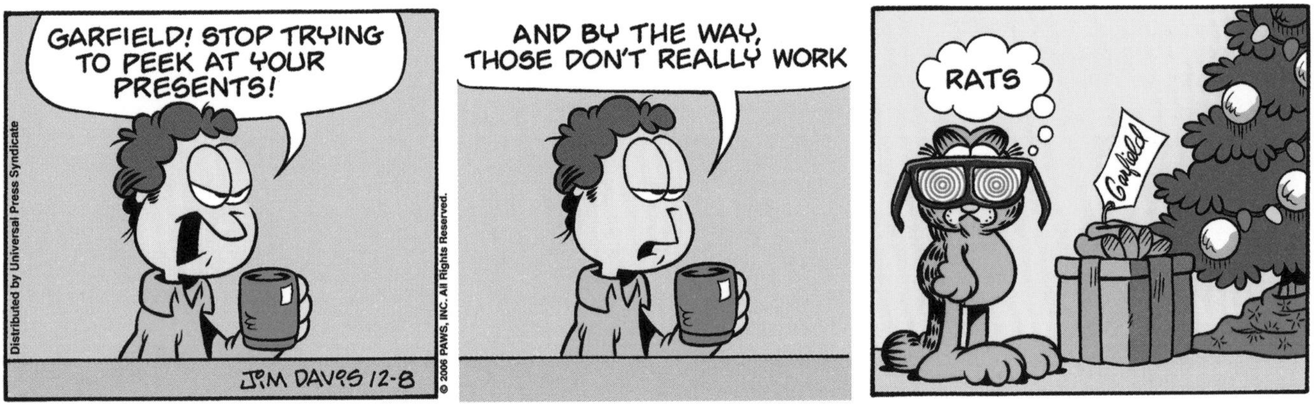
GARFIELD! STOP TRYING TO PEEK AT YOUR PRESENTS!
Distributed by Universal Press Syndicate
JIM DAVIS 12-8
AND BY THE WAY, THOSE DON'T REALLY WORK
© 2006 PAWS, INC. All Rights Reserved.
RATS
Garfield

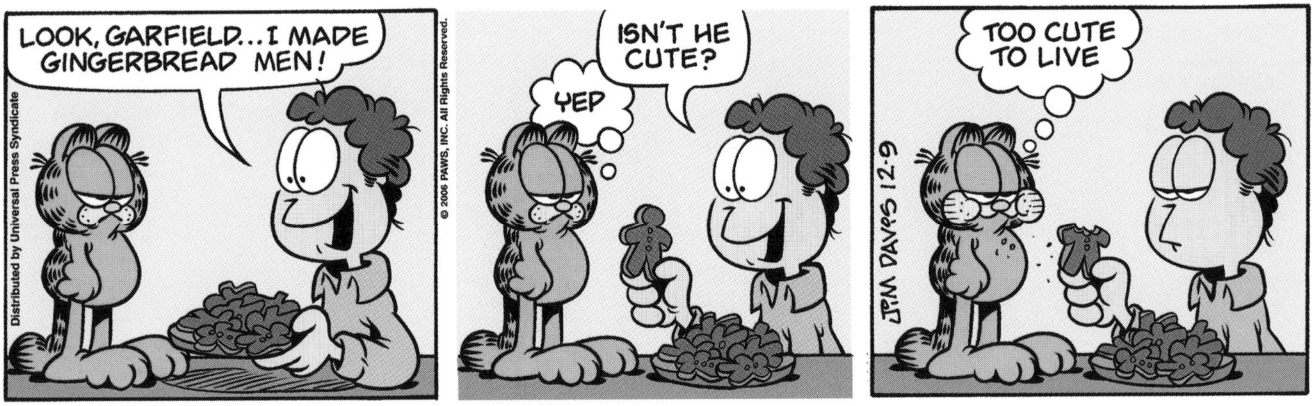
LOOK, GARFIELD... I MADE GINGERBREAD MEN!
Distributed by Universal Press Syndicate
© 2006 PAWS, INC. All Rights Reserved.
ISN'T HE CUTE?
YEP
JIM DAVIS 12-9
TOO CUTE TO LIVE

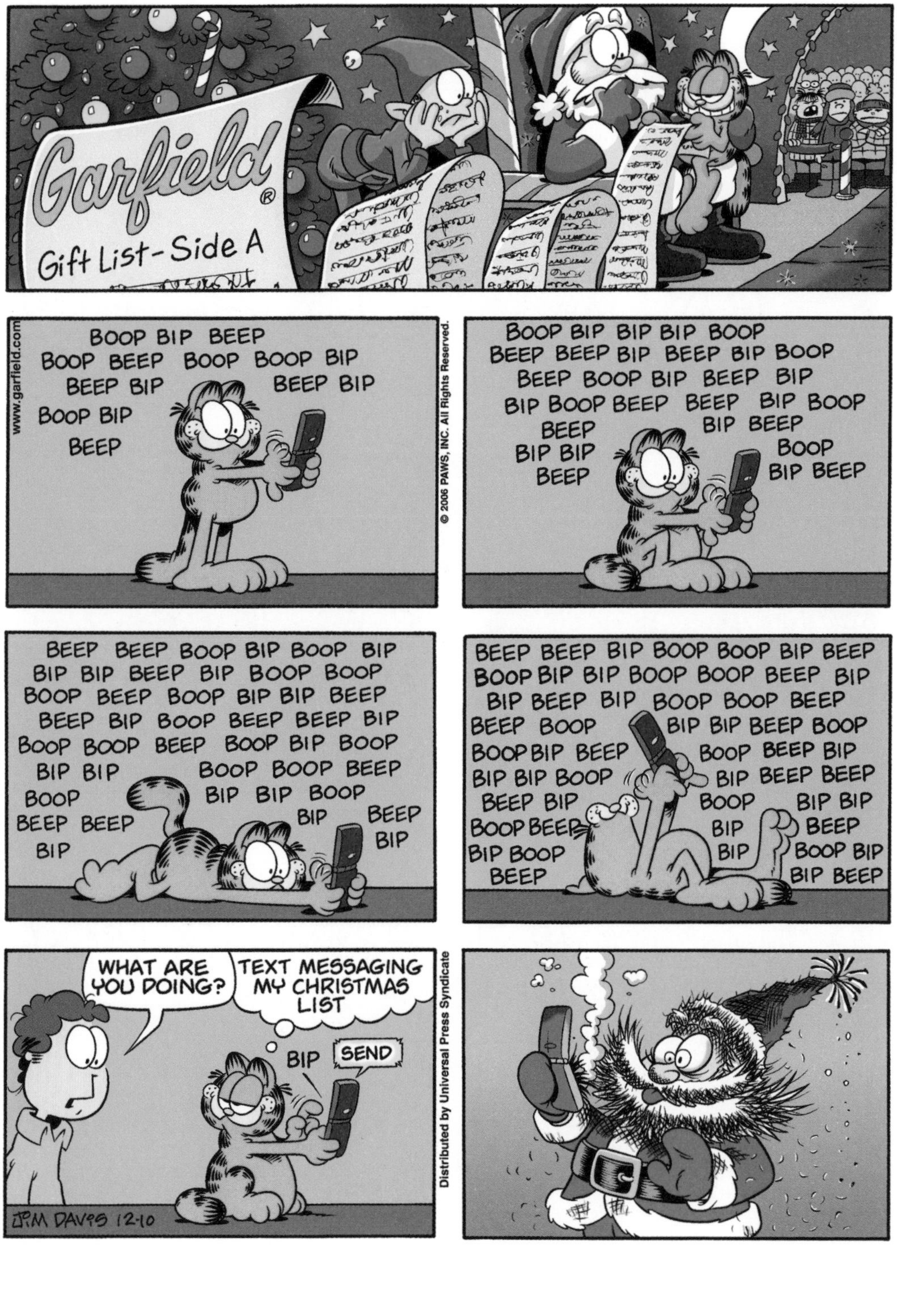
Garfield®
Gift List - Side A
www.garfield.com
BOOP BIP BEEP
BOOP BEEP BOOP BOOP BIP
BEEP BIP BEEP BIP
BOOP BIP
BEEP
© 2006 PAWS, INC. All Rights Reserved.
BOOP BIP BIP BIP BOOP
BEEP BEEP BIP BEEP BIP BOOP
BEEP BOOP BIP BEEP BIP
BIP BOOP BEEP BEEP BIP BOOP
BEEP
BIP BEEP
BIP BIP
BOOP
BEEP
BIP BEEP
BEEP BEEP BOOP BIP BOOP BIP
BIP BIP BEEP BIP BOOP BOOP
BOOP BEEP BOOP BIP BIP BEEP
BEEP BIP BOOP BEEP BEEP BIP
BOOP BOOP BEEP BOOP BIP BOOP
BIP BIP BOOP BOOP BEEP
BOOP BIP BIP BOOP
BEEP BEEP BIP BEEP
BIP BIP
BEEP BEEP BIP BOOP BOOP BIP BEEP
BOOP BIP BIP BOOP BOOP BEEP BIP
BIP BEEP BIP BOOP BOOP BEEP
BEEP BOOP BIP BIP BEEP BOOP
BOOP BIP BEEP BOOP BEEP BIP
BIP BIP BOOP BIP BEEP BEEP
BEEP BIP BOOP BIP BIP
BOOP BEEP BIP BEEP
BIP BOOP BIP BOOP BIP
BEEP BIP BEEP
WHAT ARE YOU DOING?
TEXT MESSAGING MY CHRISTMAS LIST
BIP
SEND
JIM DAVIS 12-10
Distributed by Universal Press Syndicate

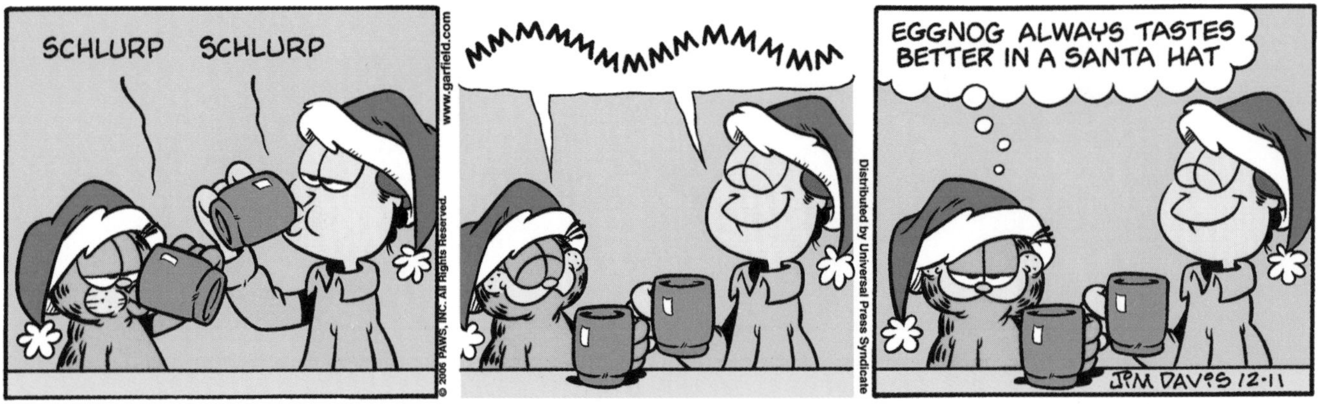
SCHLURP SCHLURP
© 2006 PAWS, INC. All Rights Reserved. www.garfield.com
MMMMMMMMMMMMMMMMM
Distributed by Universal Press Syndicate
EGGNOG ALWAYS TASTES BETTER IN A SANTA HAT
JIM DAVIS 12-11

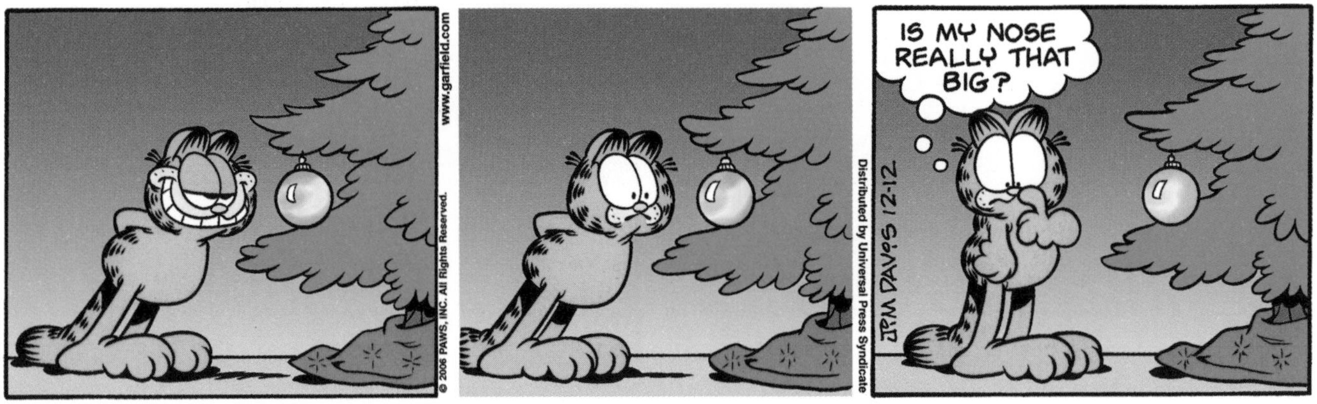
© 2006 PAWS, INC. All Rights Reserved. www.garfield.com
Distributed by Universal Press Syndicate
IS MY NOSE REALLY THAT BIG?
JIM DAVIS 12-12

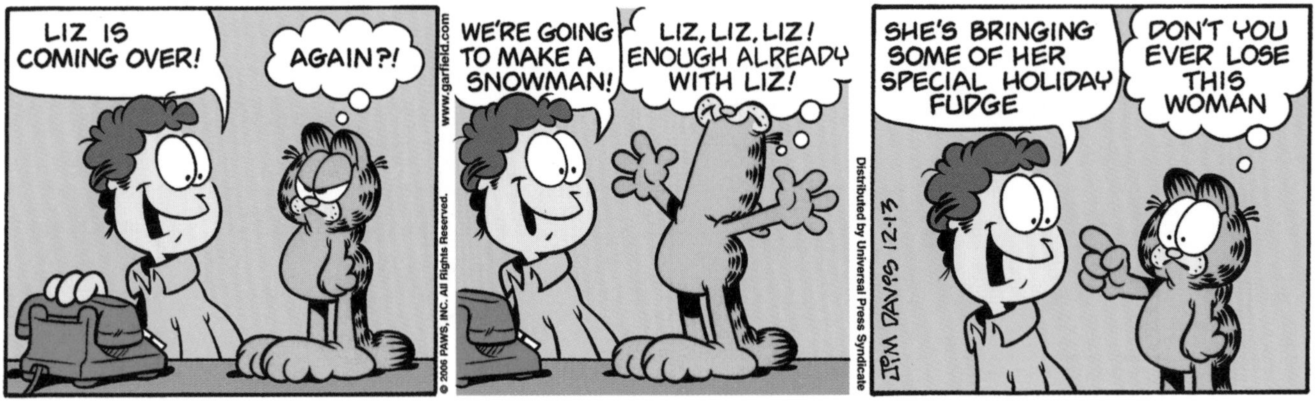
LIZ IS COMING OVER!
AGAIN?!
© 2006 PAWS, INC. All Rights Reserved. www.garfield.com
WE'RE GOING TO MAKE A SNOWMAN!
LIZ, LIZ, LIZ! ENOUGH ALREADY WITH LIZ!
Distributed by Universal Press Syndicate
SHE'S BRINGING SOME OF HER SPECIAL HOLIDAY FUDGE
DON'T YOU EVER LOSE THIS WOMAN
JIM DAVIS 12-13

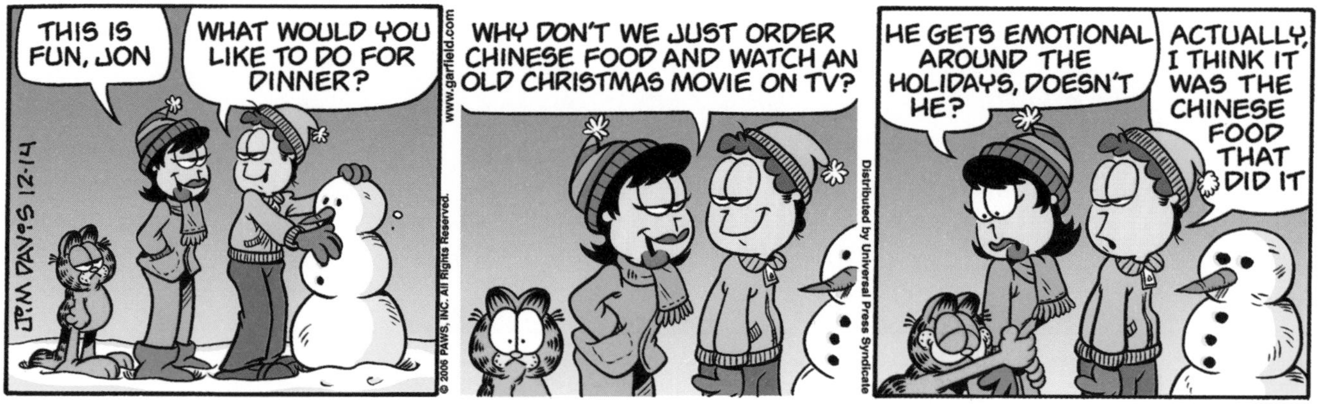
THIS IS FUN, JON
WHAT WOULD YOU LIKE TO DO FOR DINNER?
JIM DAVIS 12·14
www.garfield.com
© 2006 PAWS, INC. All Rights Reserved.
WHY DON'T WE JUST ORDER CHINESE FOOD AND WATCH AN OLD CHRISTMAS MOVIE ON TV?
Distributed by Universal Press Syndicate
HE GETS EMOTIONAL AROUND THE HOLIDAYS, DOESN'T HE?
ACTUALLY, I THINK IT WAS THE CHINESE FOOD THAT DID IT

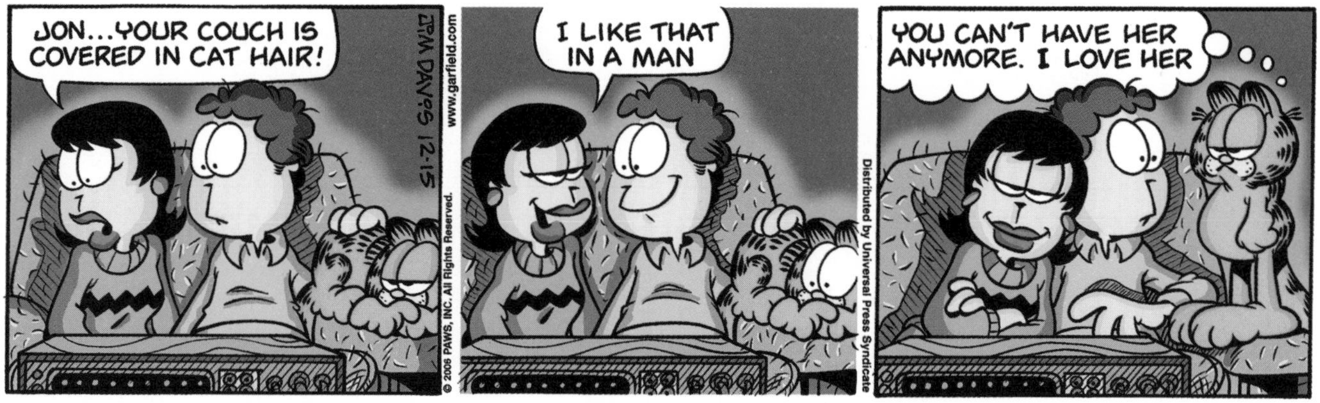
JON...YOUR COUCH IS COVERED IN CAT HAIR!
JIM DAVIS 12·15
www.garfield.com
© 2006 PAWS, INC. All Rights Reserved.
I LIKE THAT IN A MAN
Distributed by Universal Press Syndicate
YOU CAN'T HAVE HER ANYMORE. I LOVE HER

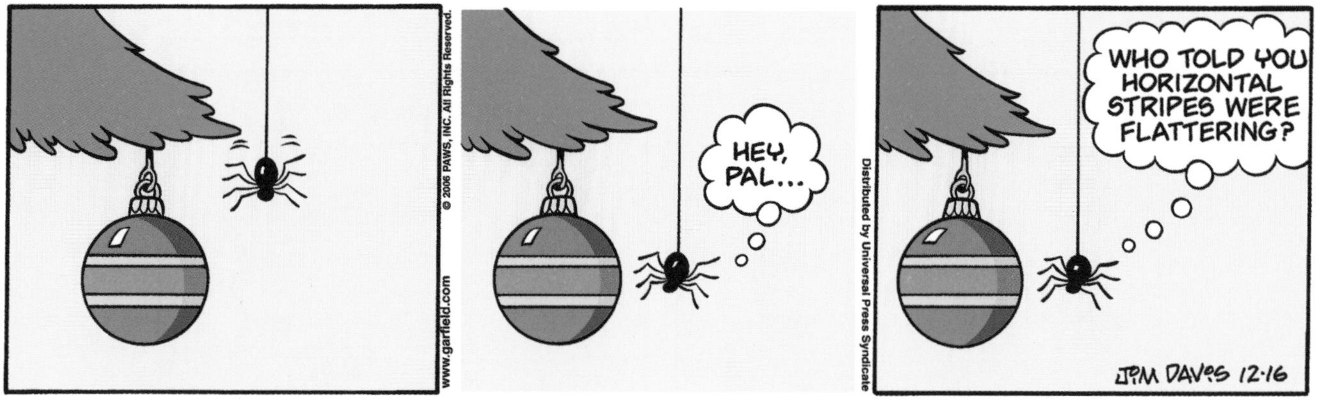
© 2006 PAWS, INC. All Rights Reserved.
www.garfield.com
HEY, PAL...
Distributed by Universal Press Syndicate
WHO TOLD YOU HORIZONTAL STRIPES WERE FLATTERING?
JIM DAVIS 12·16

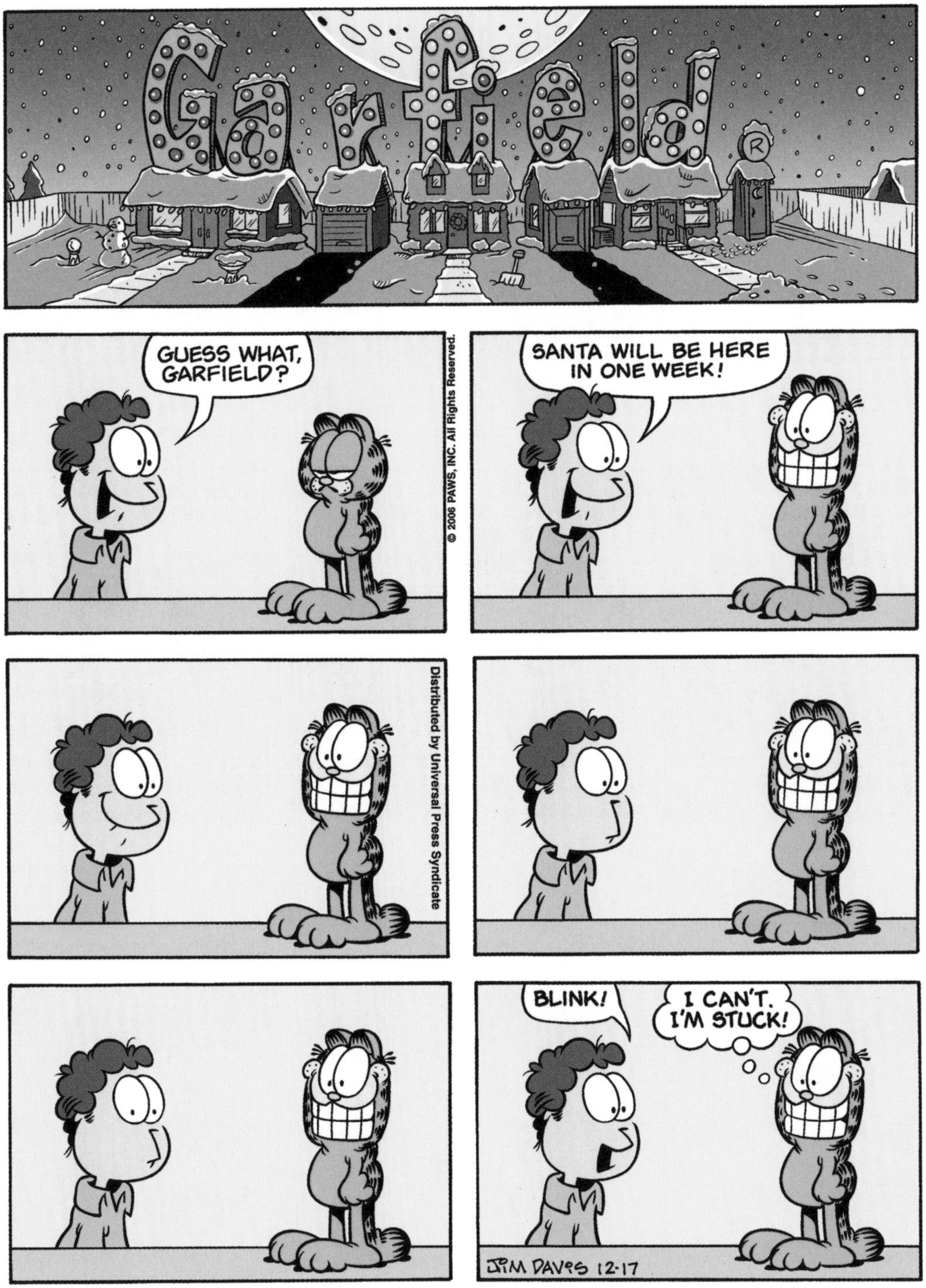
Garfield®
GUESS WHAT, GARFIELD?
SANTA WILL BE HERE IN ONE WEEK!
BLINK!
I CAN'T. I'M STUCK!
© 2006 PAWS, INC. All Rights Reserved.
Distributed by Universal Press Syndicate
JIM DAVIS 12-17

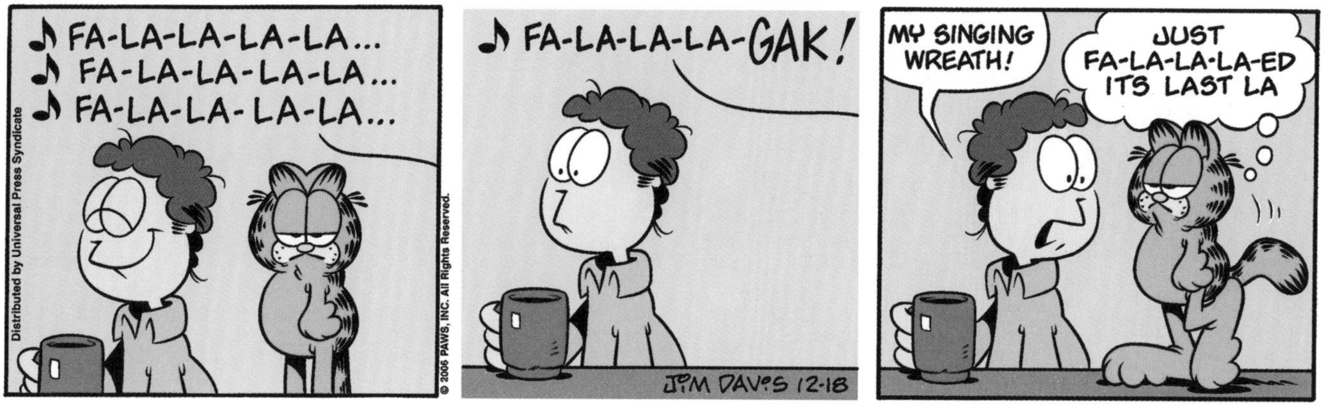
♪ FA-LA-LA-LA-LA...
♪ FA-LA-LA-LA-LA...
♪ FA-LA-LA-LA-LA...
♪ FA-LA-LA-LA-GAK!
MY SINGING WREATH!
JUST FA-LA-LA-LA-ED ITS LAST LA
JIM DAVIS 12-18
Distributed by Universal Press Syndicate
© 2006 PAWS, INC. All Rights Reserved.

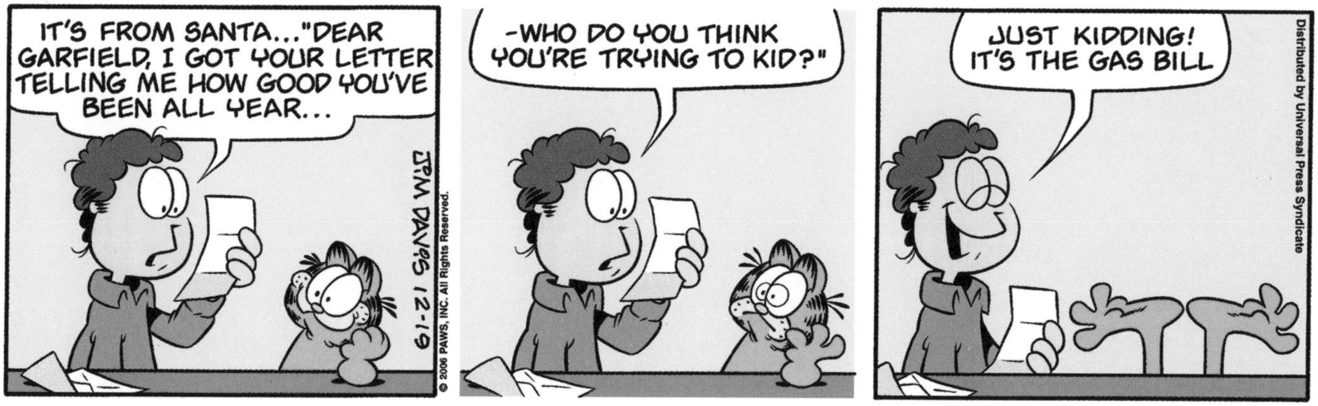
IT'S FROM SANTA..."DEAR GARFIELD, I GOT YOUR LETTER TELLING ME HOW GOOD YOU'VE BEEN ALL YEAR...
-WHO DO YOU THINK YOU'RE TRYING TO KID?"
JUST KIDDING! IT'S THE GAS BILL
JIM DAVIS 12-19
© 2006 PAWS, INC. All Rights Reserved.
Distributed by Universal Press Syndicate

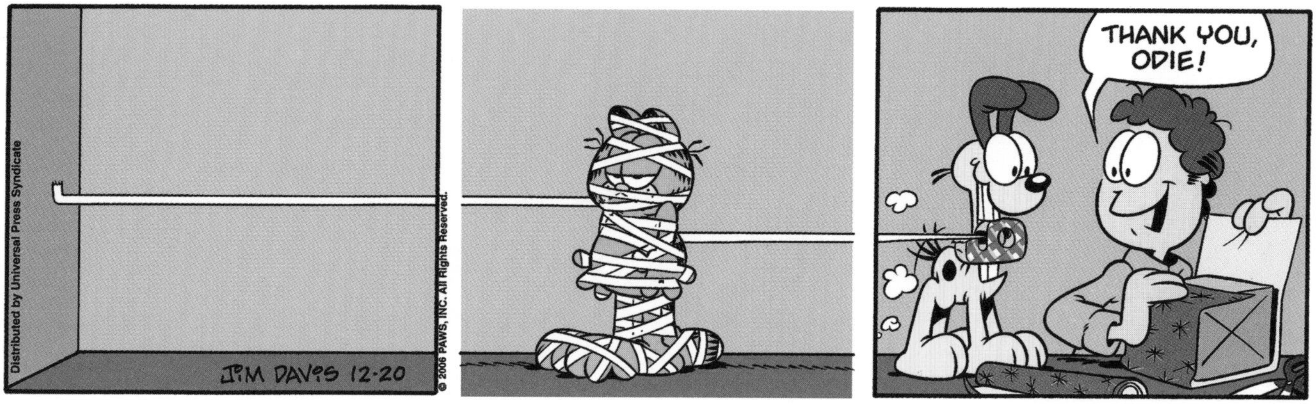
THANK YOU, ODIE!
JIM DAVIS 12-20
Distributed by Universal Press Syndicate
© 2006 PAWS, INC. All Rights Reserved.

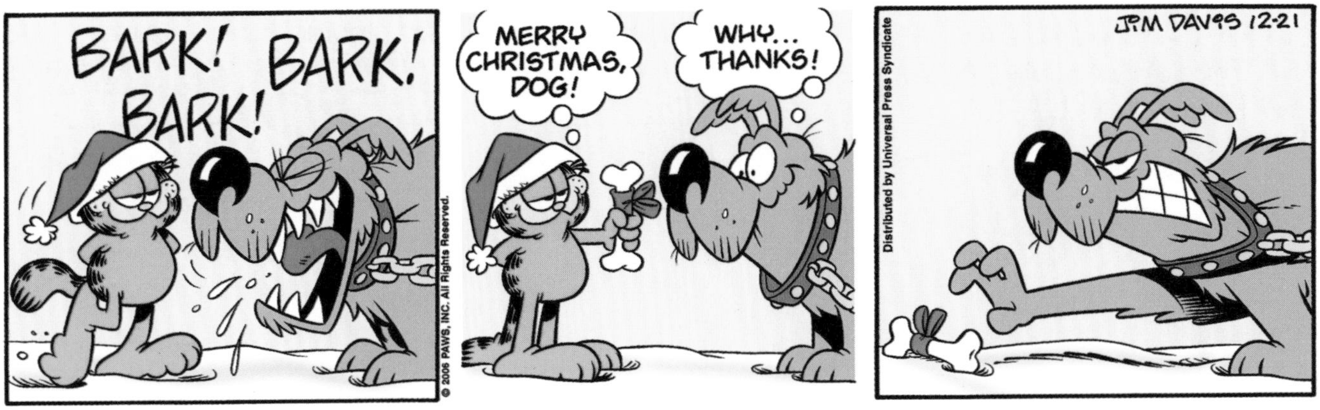
BARK! BARK! BARK!
MERRY CHRISTMAS, DOG!
WHY... THANKS!
JIM DAVIS 12-21
© 2006 PAWS, INC. All Rights Reserved.
Distributed by Universal Press Syndicate

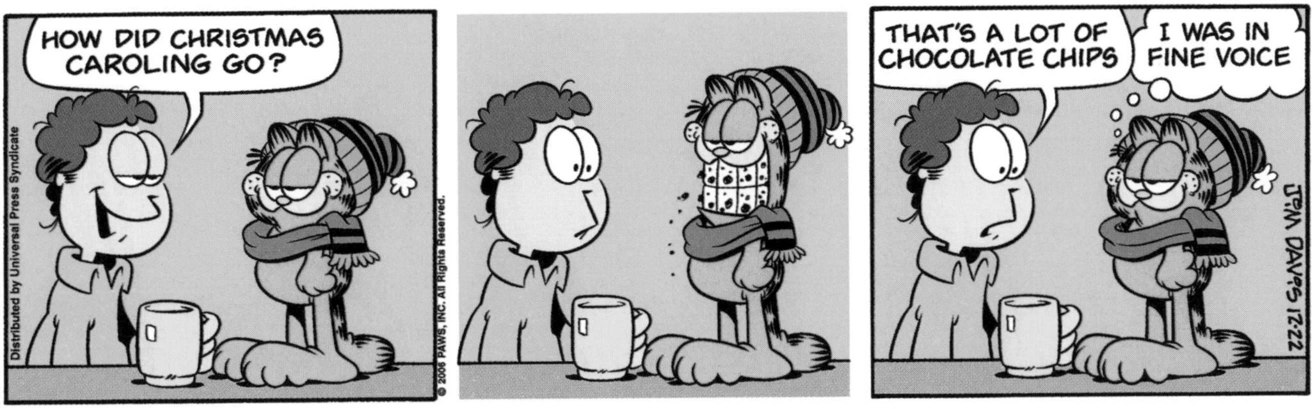
HOW DID CHRISTMAS CAROLING GO?
THAT'S A LOT OF CHOCOLATE CHIPS
I WAS IN FINE VOICE
JIM DAVIS 12-22
Distributed by Universal Press Syndicate
© 2006 PAWS, INC. All Rights Reserved.

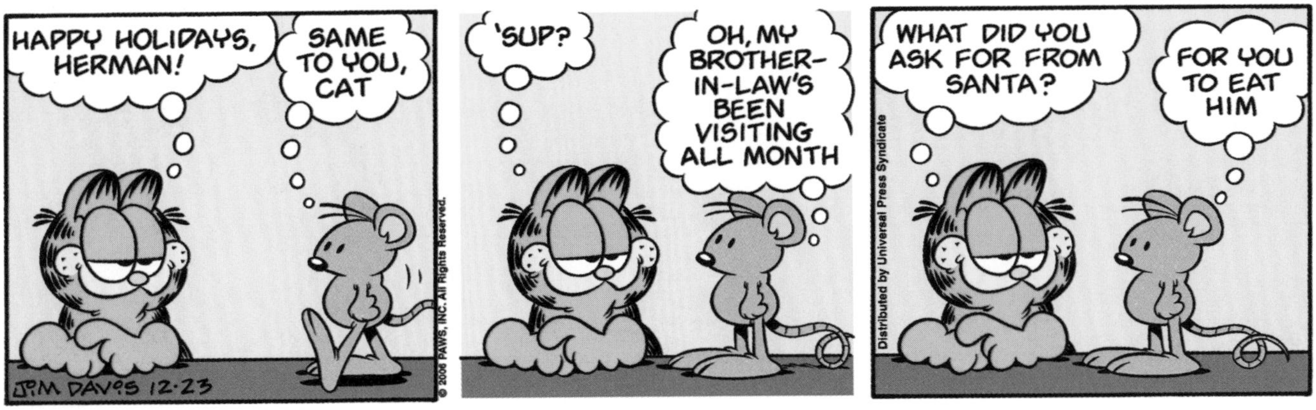
HAPPY HOLIDAYS, HERMAN!
SAME TO YOU, CAT
'SUP?
OH, MY BROTHER-IN-LAW'S BEEN VISITING ALL MONTH
WHAT DID YOU ASK FOR FROM SANTA?
FOR YOU TO EAT HIM
JIM DAVIS 12-23
© 2006 PAWS, INC. All Rights Reserved.
Distributed by Universal Press Syndicate

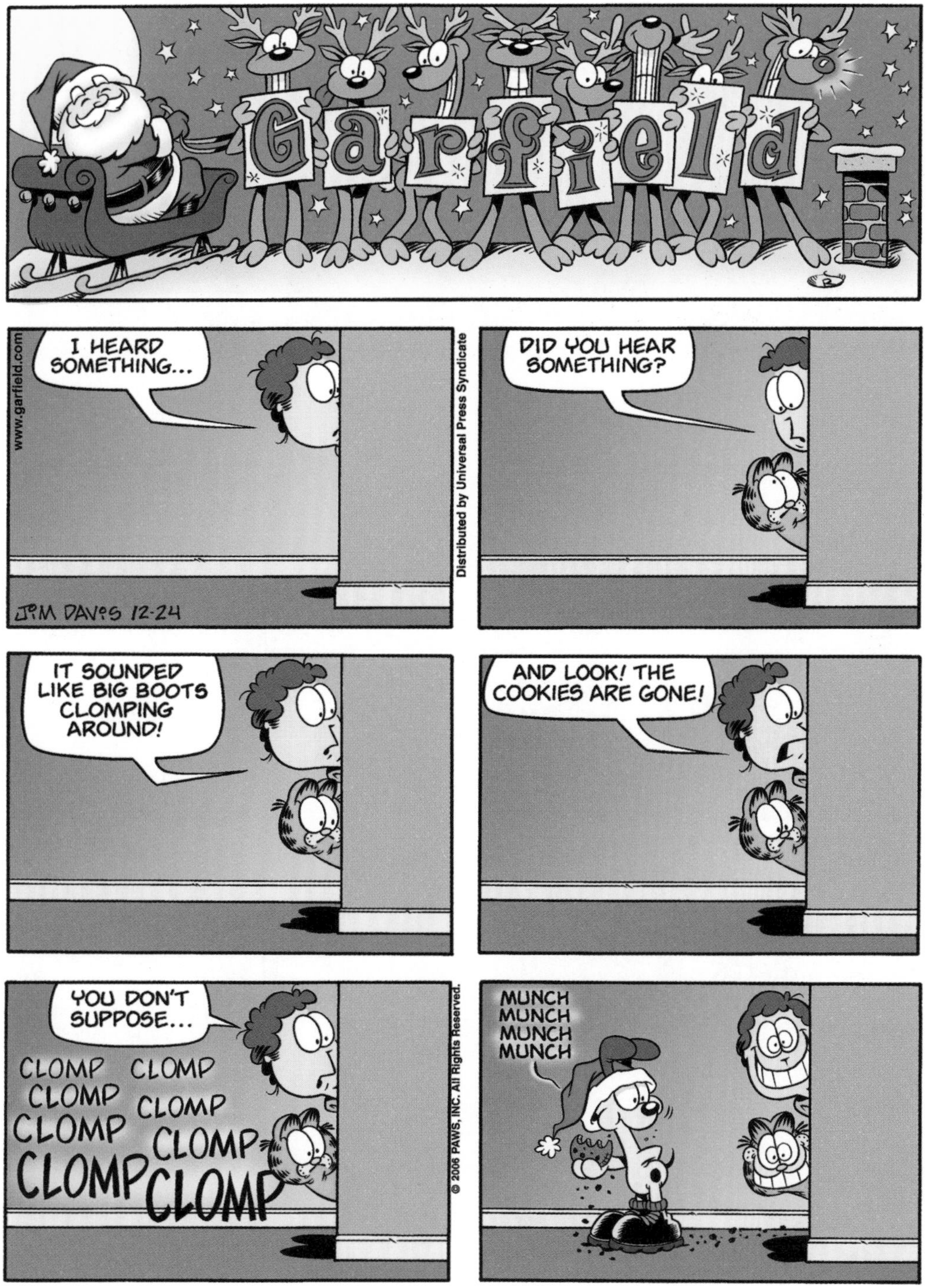
Garfield
www.garfield.com
I HEARD SOMETHING...
JIM DAVIS 12-24
Distributed by Universal Press Syndicate
DID YOU HEAR SOMETHING?
IT SOUNDED LIKE BIG BOOTS CLOMPING AROUND!
AND LOOK! THE COOKIES ARE GONE!
YOU DON'T SUPPOSE...
CLOMP CLOMP CLOMP CLOMP CLOMP CLOMP CLOMP CLOMP
© 2006 PAWS, INC. All Rights Reserved.
MUNCH MUNCH MUNCH MUNCH

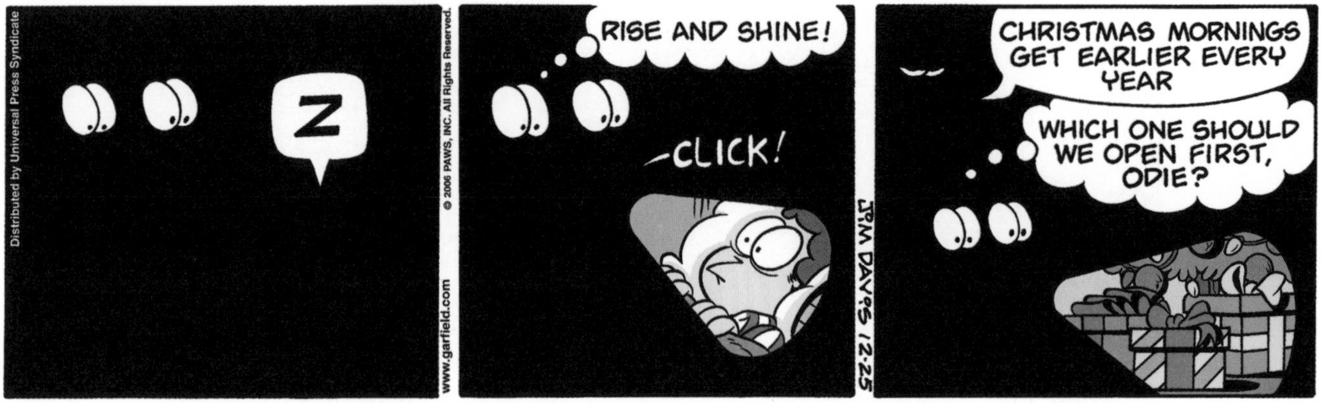
Distributed by Universal Press Syndicate
Z
© 2006 PAWS, INC. All Rights Reserved.
www.garfield.com
RISE AND SHINE!
-CLICK!
JIM DAVIS 12-25
CHRISTMAS MORNINGS GET EARLIER EVERY YEAR
WHICH ONE SHOULD WE OPEN FIRST, ODIE?

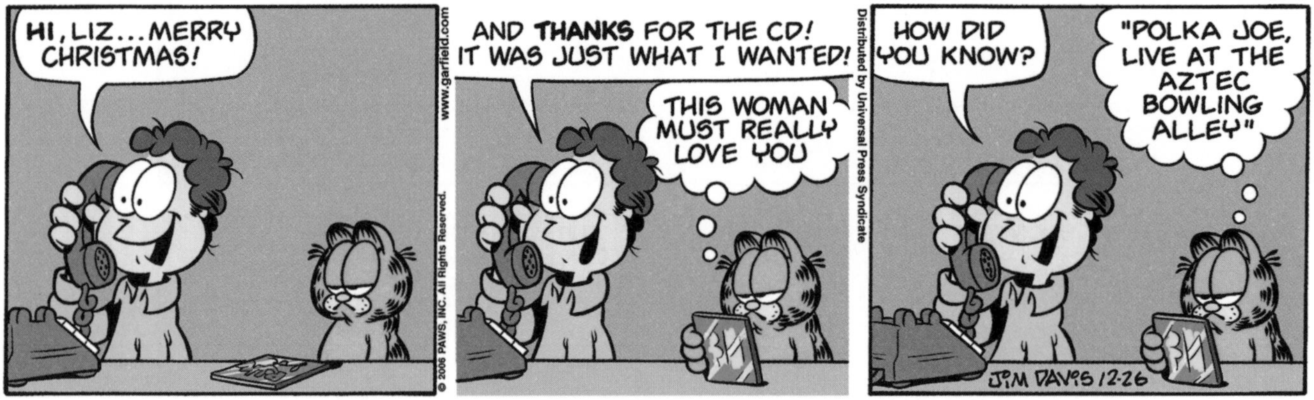
HI, LIZ...MERRY CHRISTMAS!
www.garfield.com
© 2006 PAWS, INC. All Rights Reserved.
AND THANKS FOR THE CD! IT WAS JUST WHAT I WANTED!
THIS WOMAN MUST REALLY LOVE YOU
Distributed by Universal Press Syndicate
HOW DID YOU KNOW?
"POLKA JOE, LIVE AT THE AZTEC BOWLING ALLEY"
JIM DAVIS 12-26

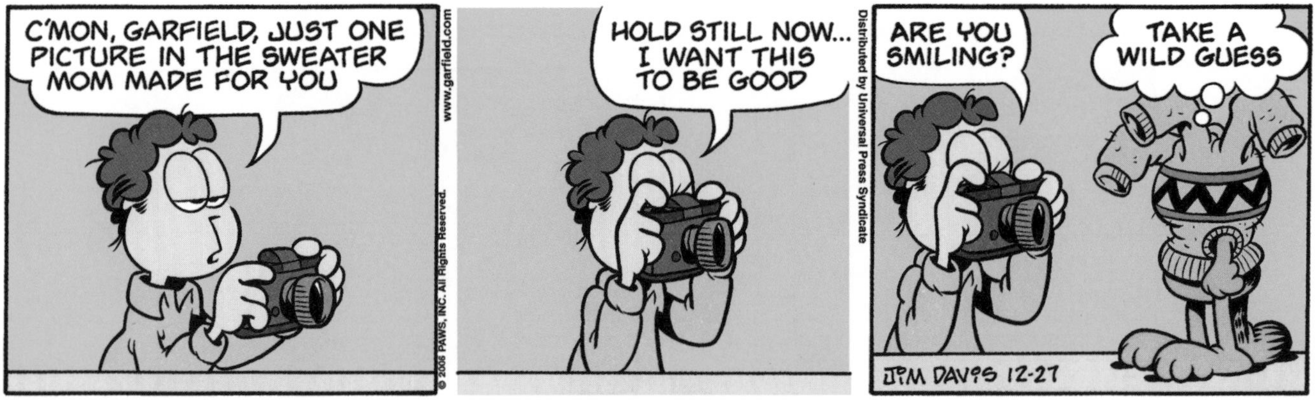
C'MON, GARFIELD, JUST ONE PICTURE IN THE SWEATER MOM MADE FOR YOU
www.garfield.com
© 2006 PAWS, INC. All Rights Reserved.
HOLD STILL NOW... I WANT THIS TO BE GOOD
Distributed by Universal Press Syndicate
ARE YOU SMILING?
TAKE A WILD GUESS
JIM DAVIS 12-27

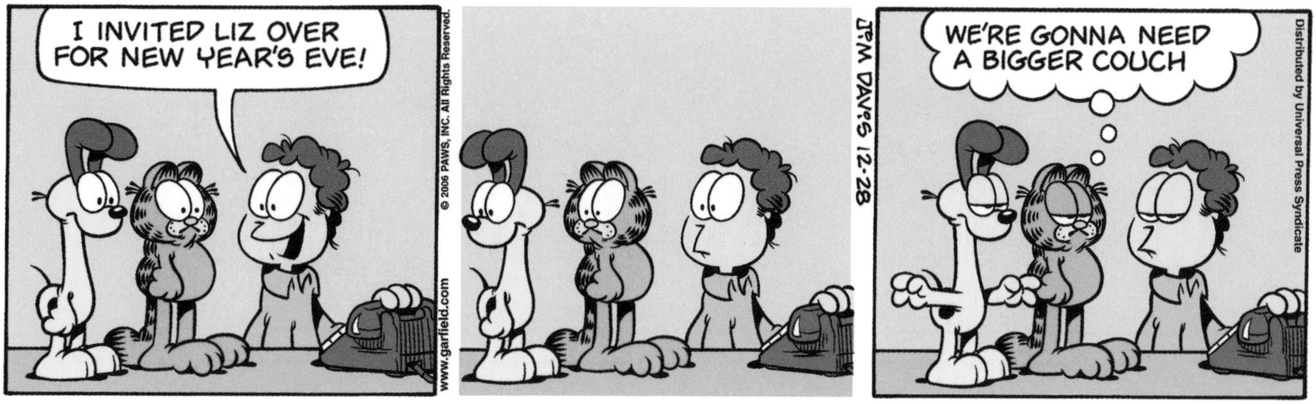
I INVITED LIZ OVER FOR NEW YEAR'S EVE!
WE'RE GONNA NEED A BIGGER COUCH
JIM DAVIS 12-28
© 2006 PAWS, INC. All Rights Reserved.
www.garfield.com
Distributed by Universal Press Syndicate

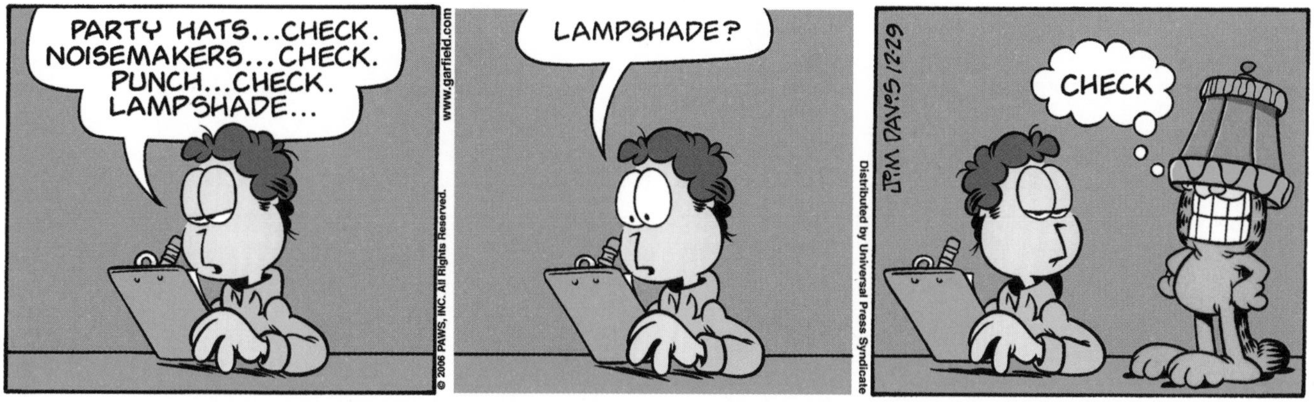
PARTY HATS...CHECK. NOISEMAKERS...CHECK. PUNCH...CHECK. LAMPSHADE...
LAMPSHADE?
CHECK
JIM DAVIS 12-29
© 2006 PAWS, INC. All Rights Reserved.
www.garfield.com
Distributed by Universal Press Syndicate

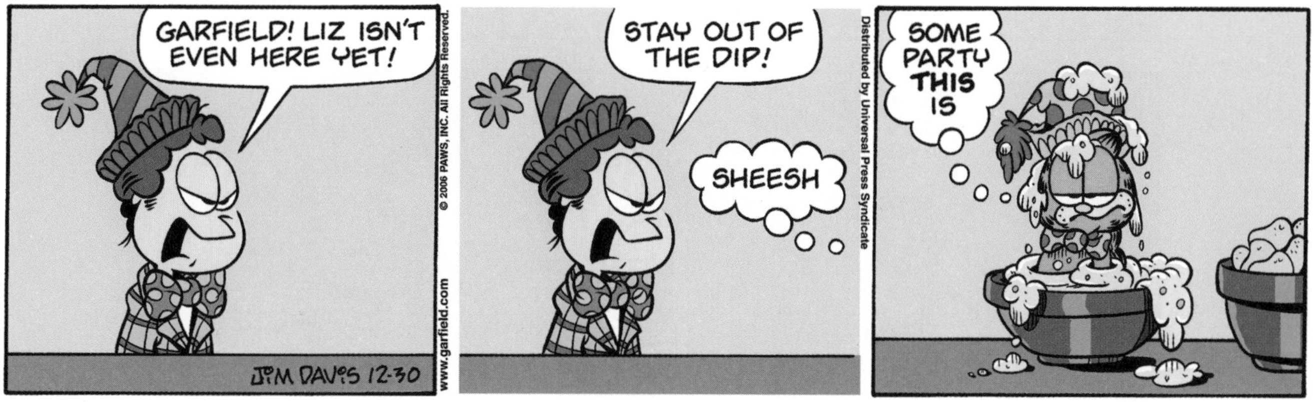
GARFIELD! LIZ ISN'T EVEN HERE YET!
STAY OUT OF THE DIP!
SHEESH
SOME PARTY THIS IS
JIM DAVIS 12-30
© 2006 PAWS, INC. All Rights Reserved.
www.garfield.com
Distributed by Universal Press Syndicate

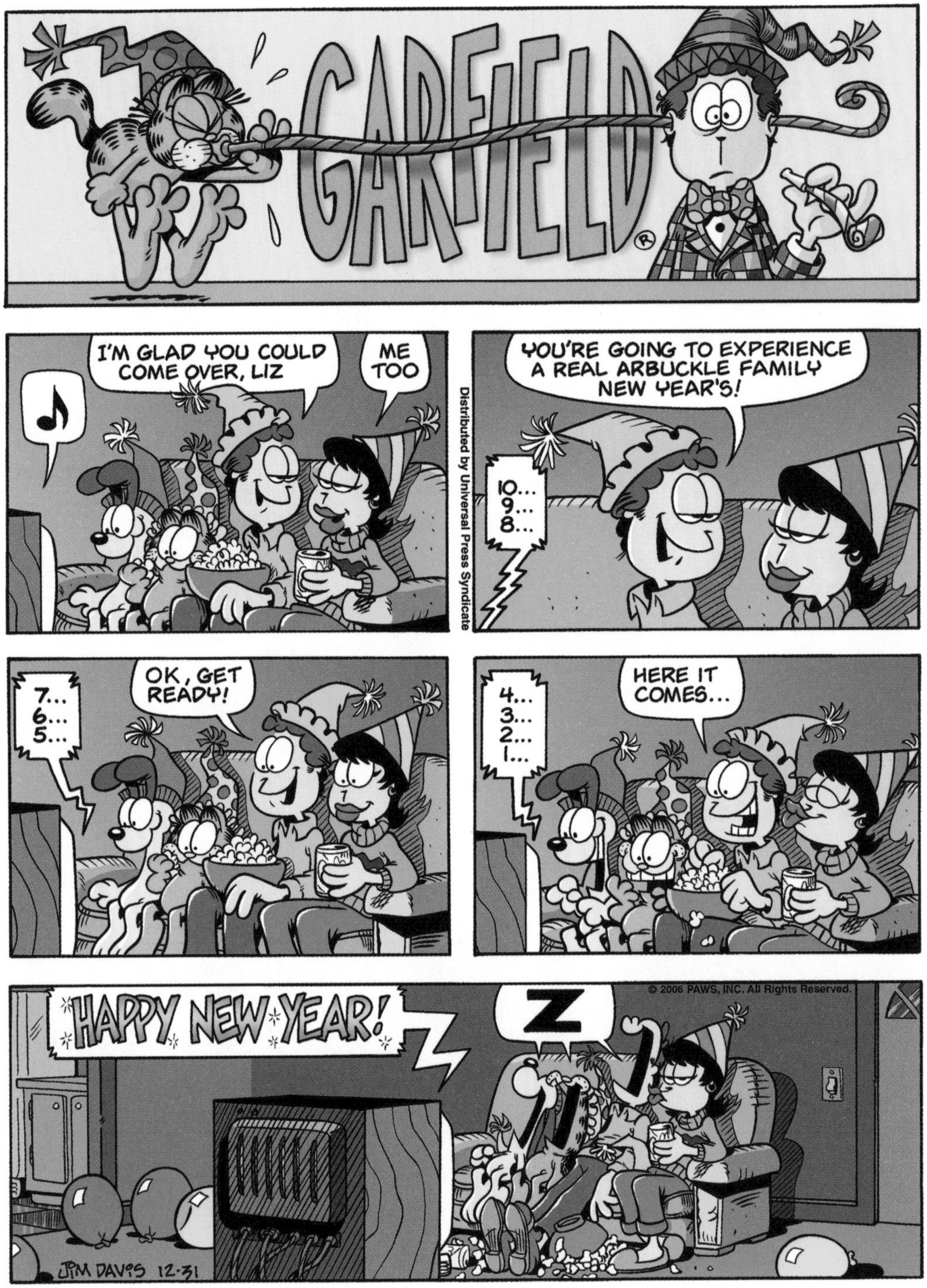
GARFIELD®
♪
I'M GLAD YOU COULD COME OVER, LIZ
ME TOO
Distributed by Universal Press Syndicate
YOU'RE GOING TO EXPERIENCE A REAL ARBUCKLE FAMILY NEW YEAR'S!
10... 9... 8...
7... 6... 5...
OK, GET READY!
4... 3... 2... 1...
HERE IT COMES...
HAPPY NEW YEAR!
Z
© 2006 PAWS, INC. All Rights Reserved.
JIM DAVIS 12-31

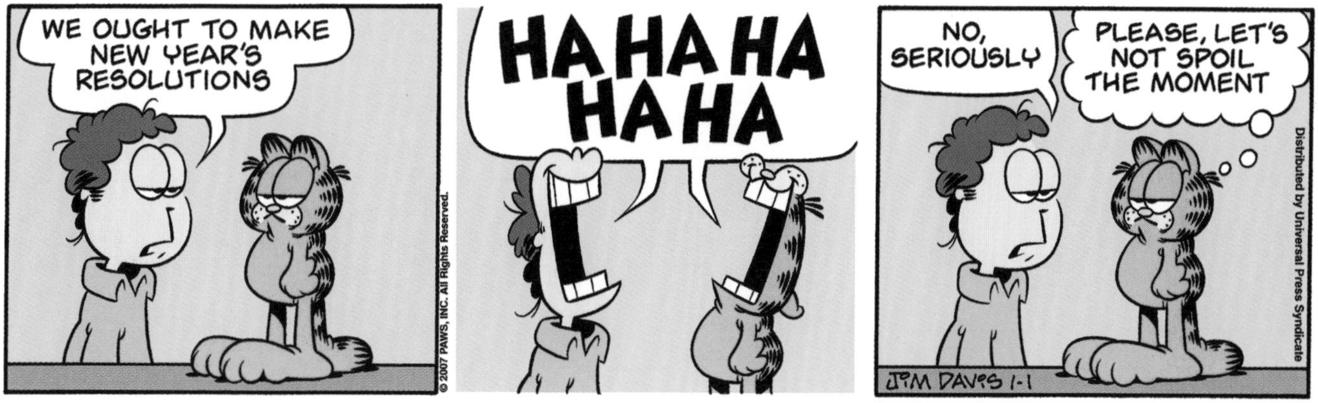
WE OUGHT TO MAKE NEW YEAR'S RESOLUTIONS
© 2007 PAWS, INC. All Rights Reserved.
HAHAHA HAHA
NO, SERIOUSLY
PLEASE, LET'S NOT SPOIL THE MOMENT
JIM DAVIS 1-1
Distributed by Universal Press Syndicate

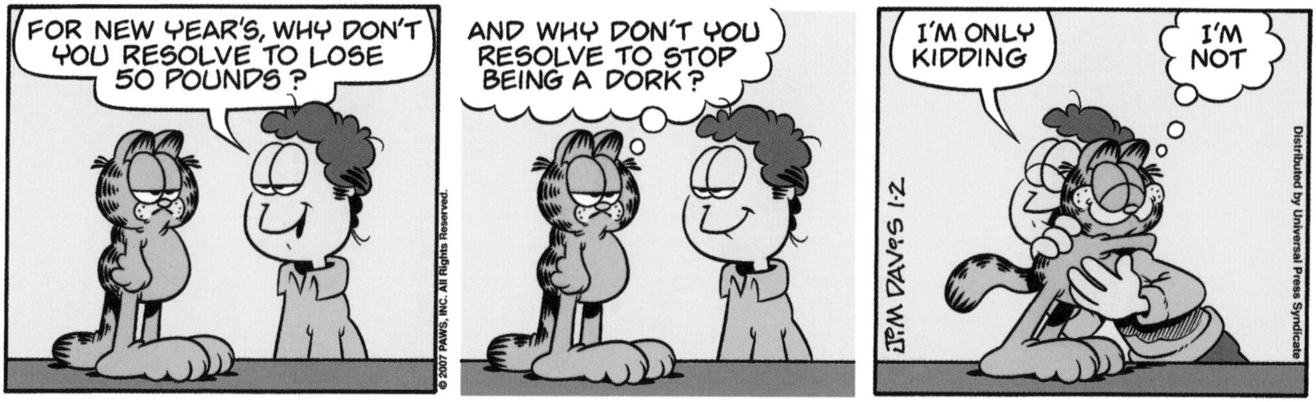
FOR NEW YEAR'S, WHY DON'T YOU RESOLVE TO LOSE 50 POUNDS?
© 2007 PAWS, INC. All Rights Reserved.
AND WHY DON'T YOU RESOLVE TO STOP BEING A DORK?
I'M ONLY KIDDING
I'M NOT
JIM DAVIS 1-2
Distributed by Universal Press Syndicate

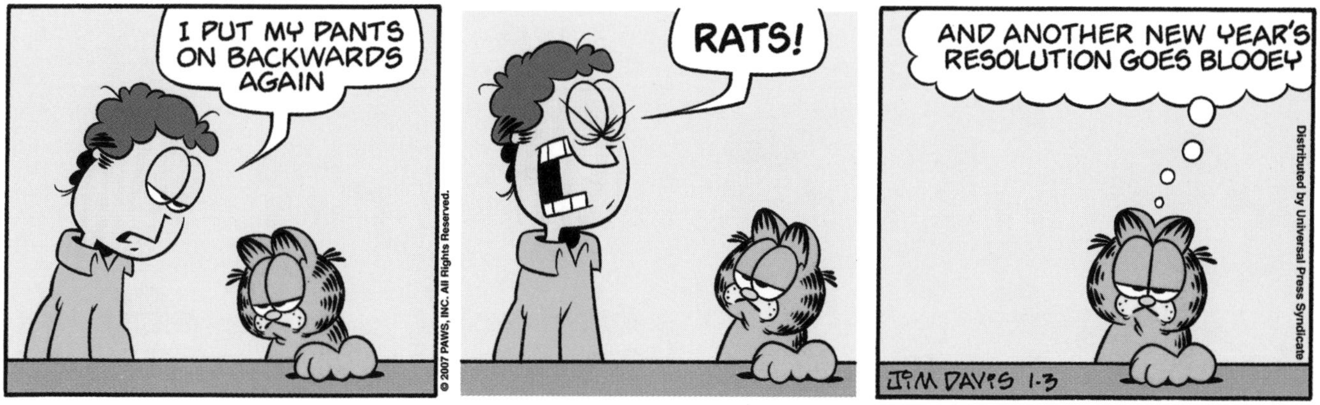
I PUT MY PANTS ON BACKWARDS AGAIN
© 2007 PAWS, INC. All Rights Reserved.
RATS!
AND ANOTHER NEW YEAR'S RESOLUTION GOES BLOOEY
JIM DAVIS 1-3
Distributed by Universal Press Syndicate

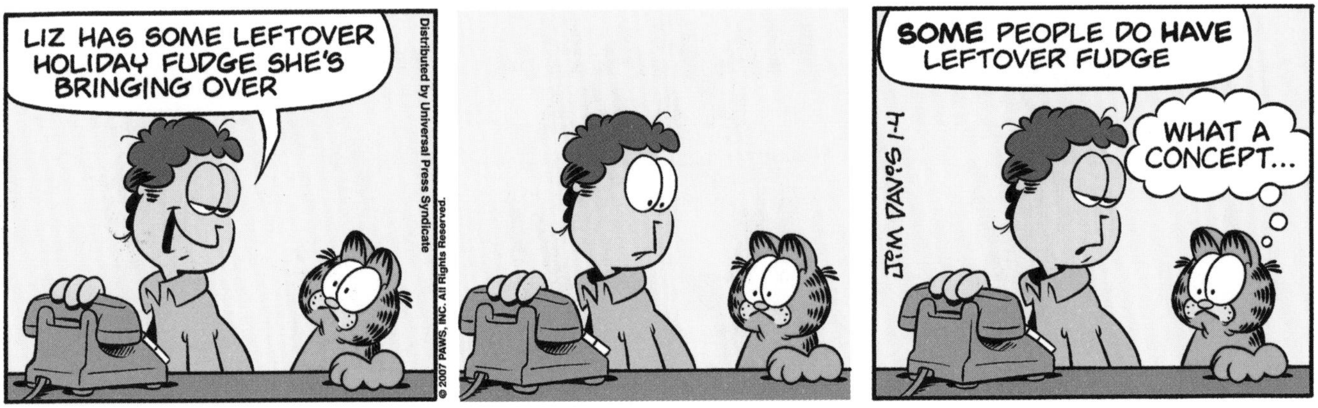
LIZ HAS SOME LEFTOVER HOLIDAY FUDGE SHE'S BRINGING OVER
© 2007 PAWS, INC. All Rights Reserved.
Distributed by Universal Press Syndicate
SOME PEOPLE DO HAVE LEFTOVER FUDGE
WHAT A CONCEPT...
JIM DAVIS 1-4

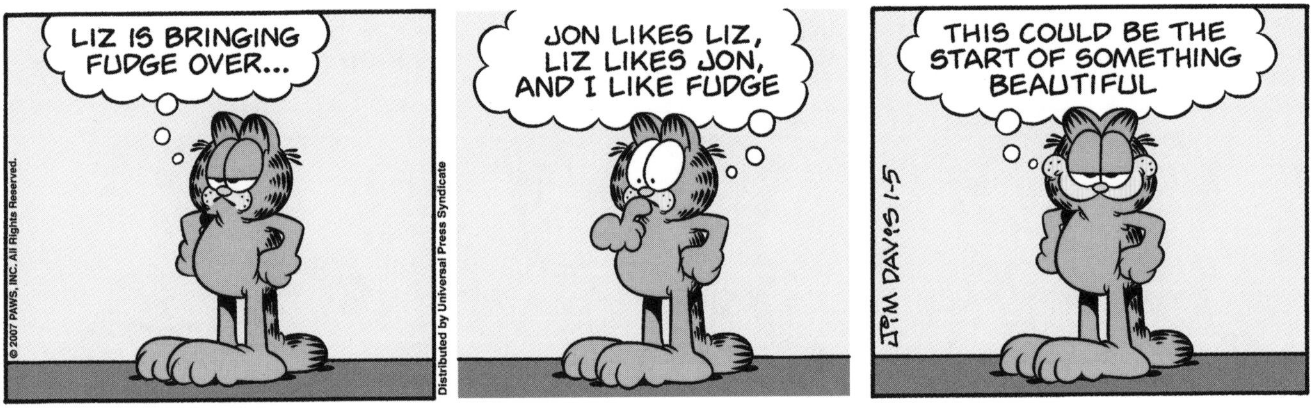
LIZ IS BRINGING FUDGE OVER...
© 2007 PAWS, INC. All Rights Reserved.
Distributed by Universal Press Syndicate
JON LIKES LIZ, LIZ LIKES JON, AND I LIKE FUDGE
THIS COULD BE THE START OF SOMETHING BEAUTIFUL
JIM DAVIS 1-5

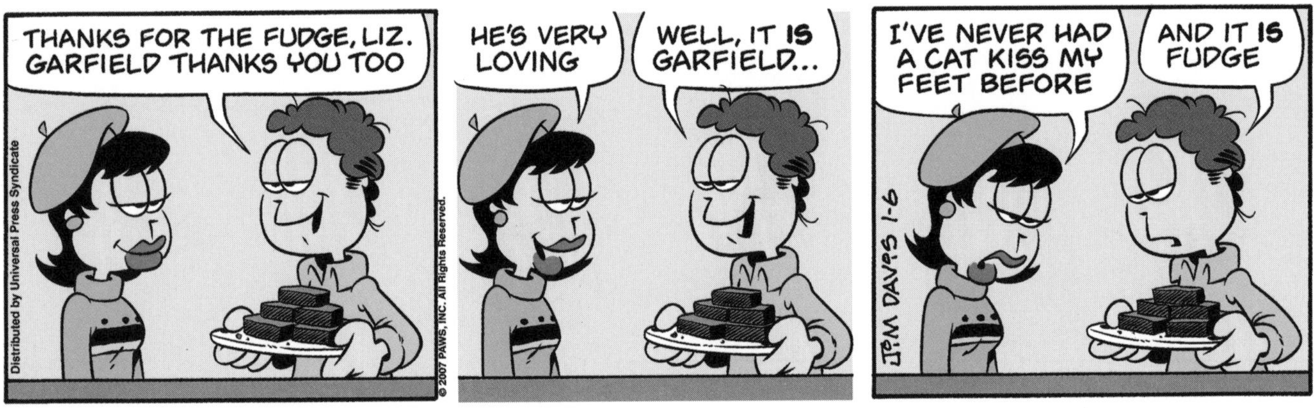
THANKS FOR THE FUDGE, LIZ. GARFIELD THANKS YOU TOO
Distributed by Universal Press Syndicate
© 2007 PAWS, INC. All Rights Reserved.
HE'S VERY LOVING
WELL, IT IS GARFIELD...
I'VE NEVER HAD A CAT KISS MY FEET BEFORE
AND IT IS FUDGE
JIM DAVIS 1-6

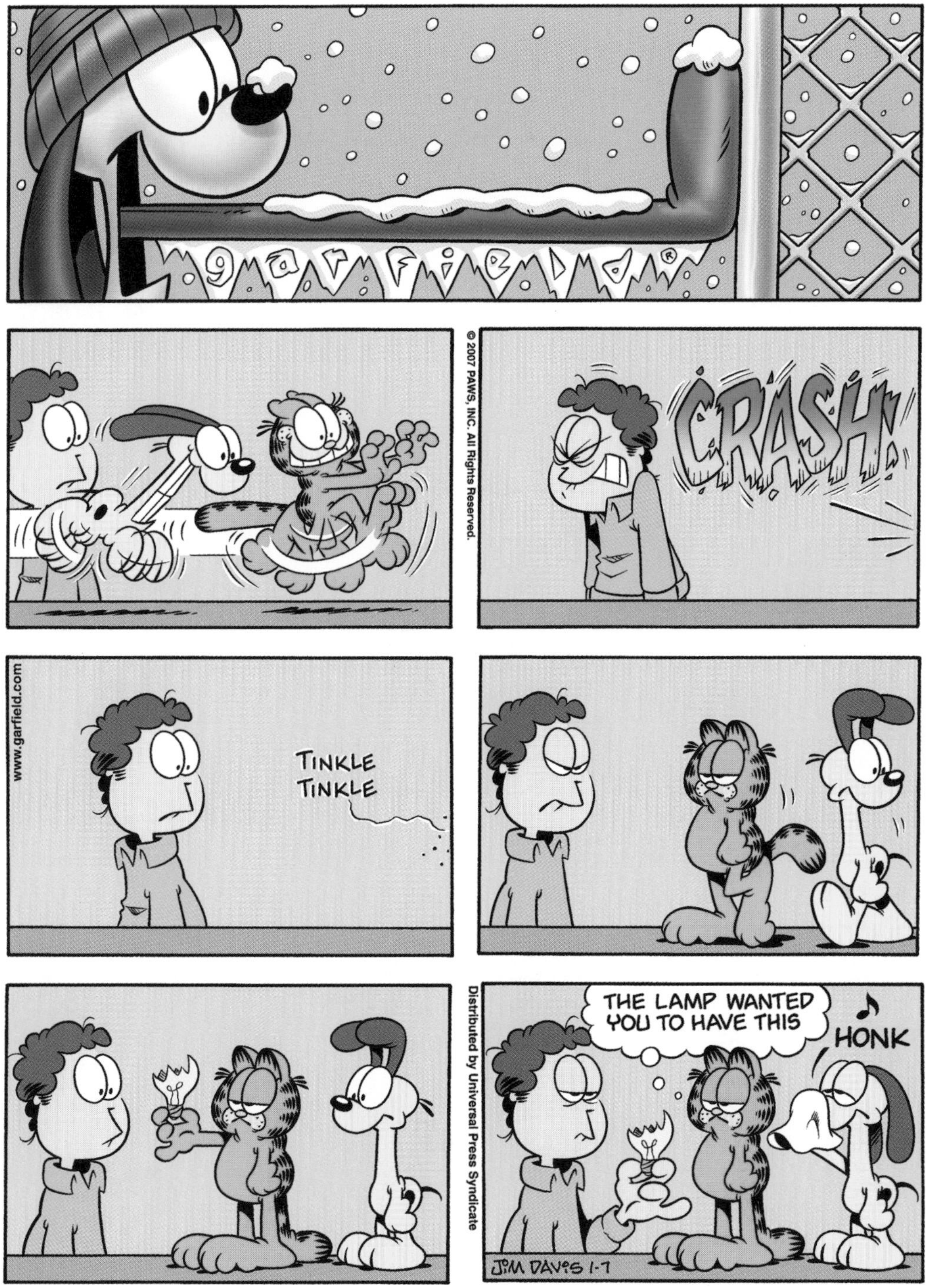
garfield®
© 2007 PAWS, INC. All Rights Reserved.
CRASH!
www.garfield.com
TINKLE
TINKLE
THE LAMP WANTED YOU TO HAVE THIS
HONK
Distributed by Universal Press Syndicate
JIM DAVIS 1-7

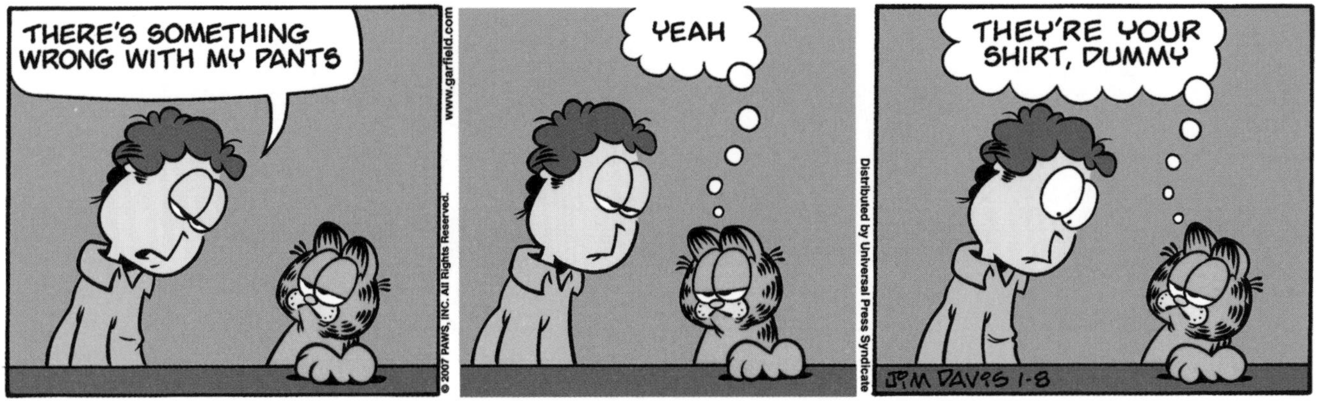
THERE'S SOMETHING WRONG WITH MY PANTS
YEAH
THEY'RE YOUR SHIRT, DUMMY
© 2007 PAWS, INC. All Rights Reserved. www.garfield.com
Distributed by Universal Press Syndicate
JIM DAVIS 1-8

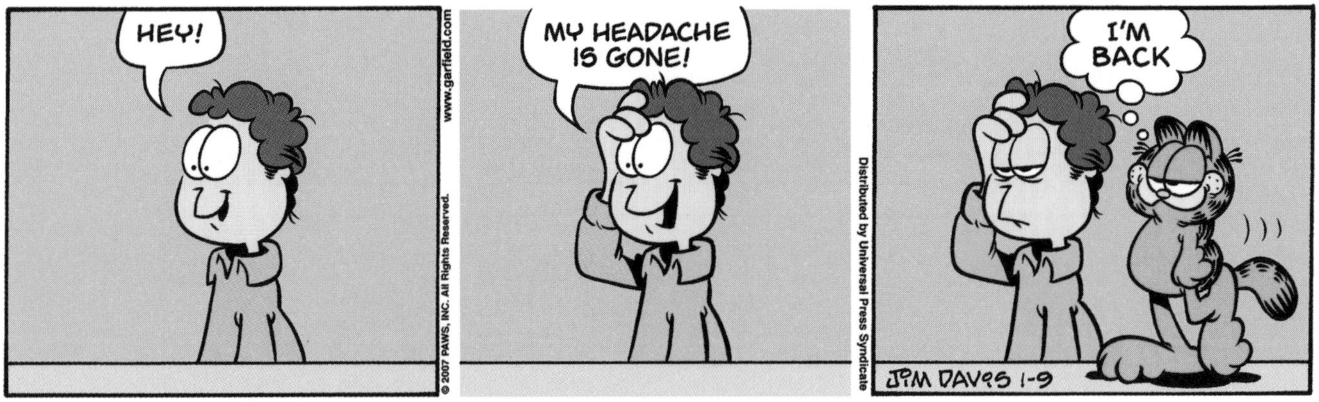
HEY!
MY HEADACHE IS GONE!
I'M BACK
© 2007 PAWS, INC. All Rights Reserved. www.garfield.com
Distributed by Universal Press Syndicate
JIM DAVIS 1-9

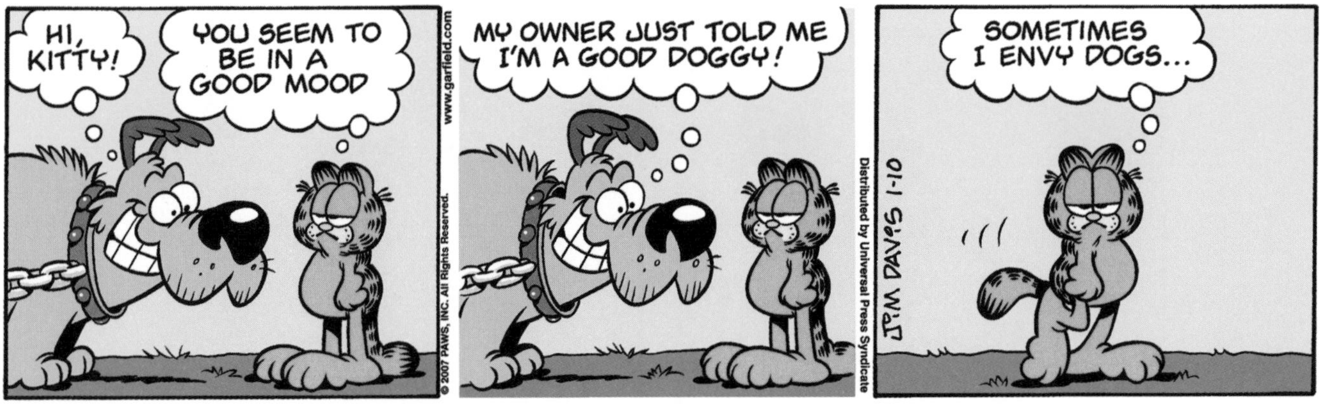
HI, KITTY!
YOU SEEM TO BE IN A GOOD MOOD
MY OWNER JUST TOLD ME I'M A GOOD DOGGY!
SOMETIMES I ENVY DOGS...
© 2007 PAWS, INC. All Rights Reserved. www.garfield.com
Distributed by Universal Press Syndicate
JIM DAVIS 1-10

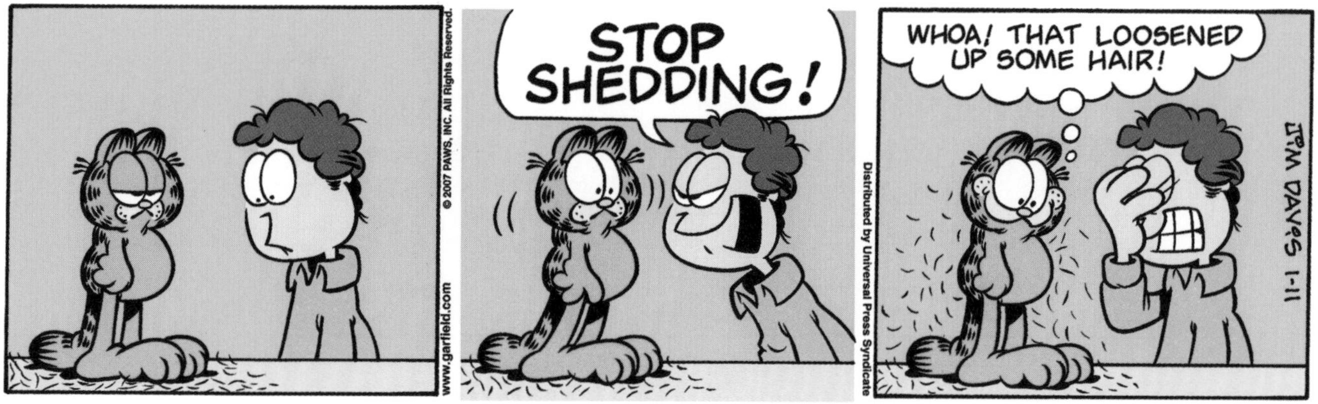
© 2007 PAWS, INC. All Rights Reserved. www.garfield.com
STOP SHEDDING!
Distributed by Universal Press Syndicate
WHOA! THAT LOOSENED UP SOME HAIR!
JIM DAVIS 1-11

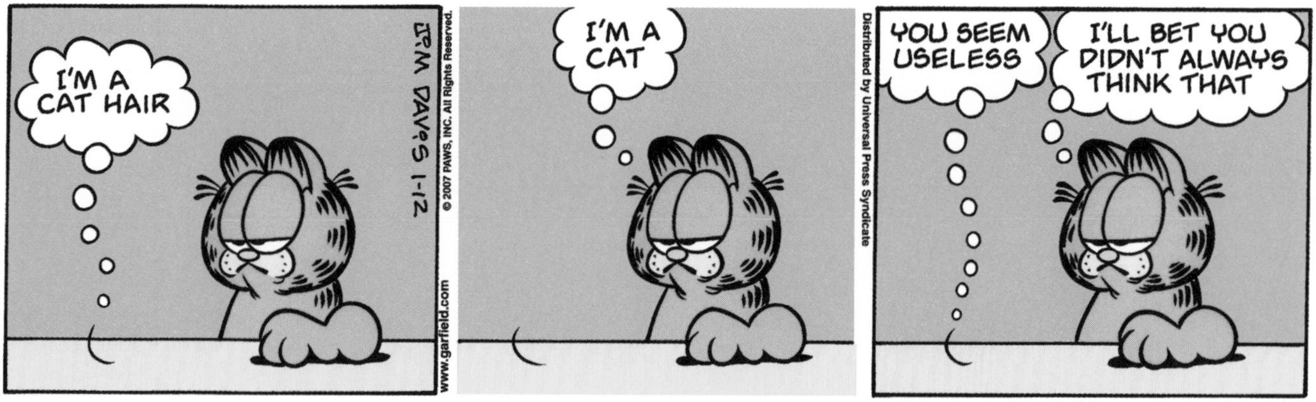
I'M A CAT HAIR
JIM DAVIS 1-12
© 2007 PAWS, INC. All Rights Reserved. www.garfield.com
I'M A CAT
Distributed by Universal Press Syndicate
YOU SEEM USELESS
I'LL BET YOU DIDN'T ALWAYS THINK THAT

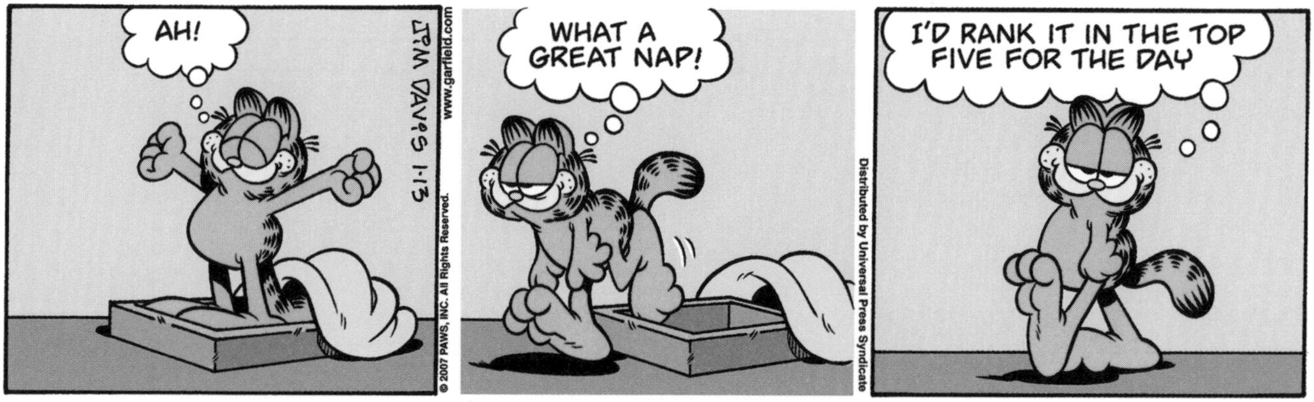
AH!
JIM DAVIS 1-13
© 2007 PAWS, INC. All Rights Reserved. www.garfield.com
WHAT A GREAT NAP!
Distributed by Universal Press Syndicate
I'D RANK IT IN THE TOP FIVE FOR THE DAY

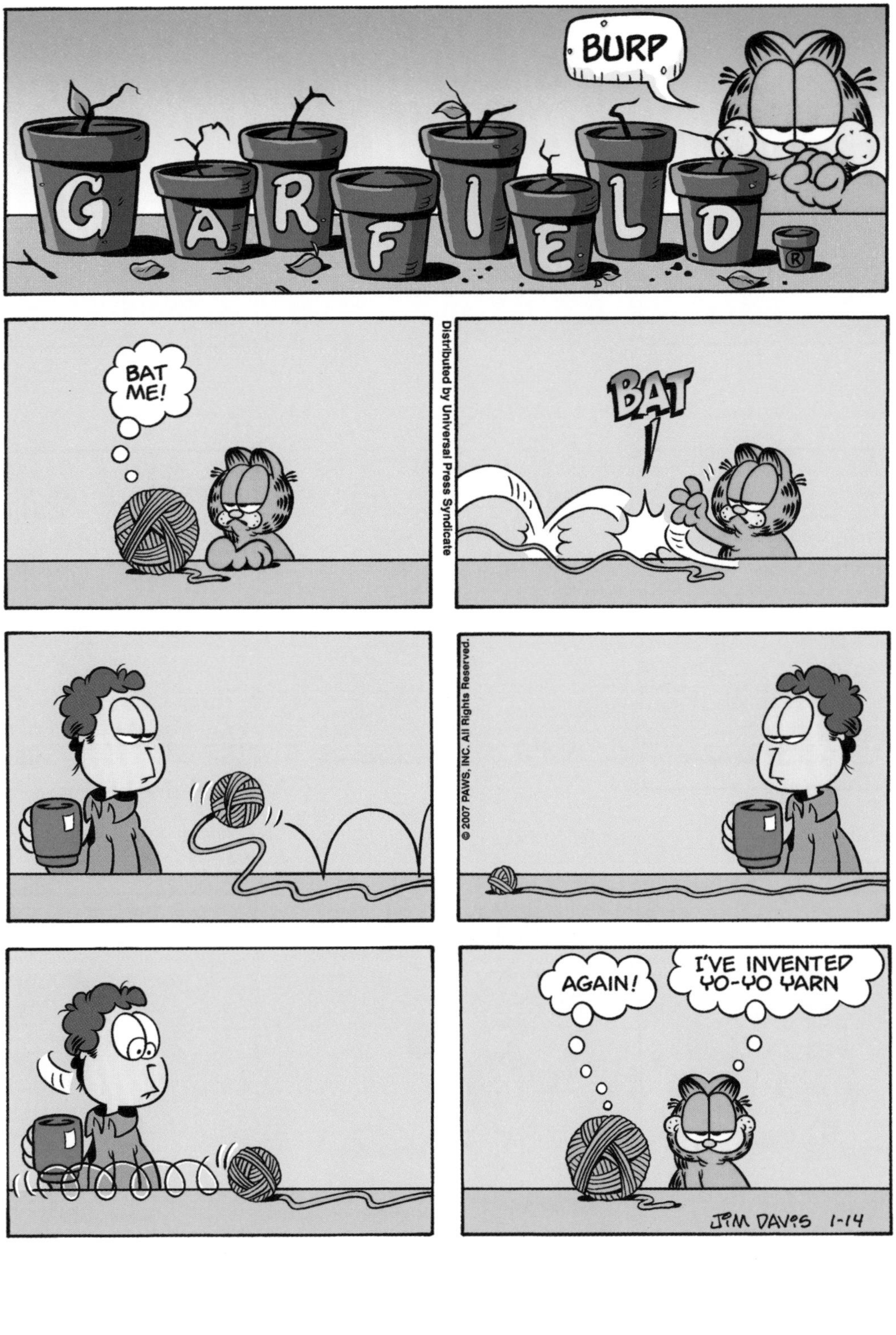

BURP
GARFIELD®
Distributed by Universal Press Syndicate
BAT ME!
BAT
© 2007 PAWS, INC. All Rights Reserved.
AGAIN!
I'VE INVENTED YO-YO YARN
JIM DAVIS 1-14

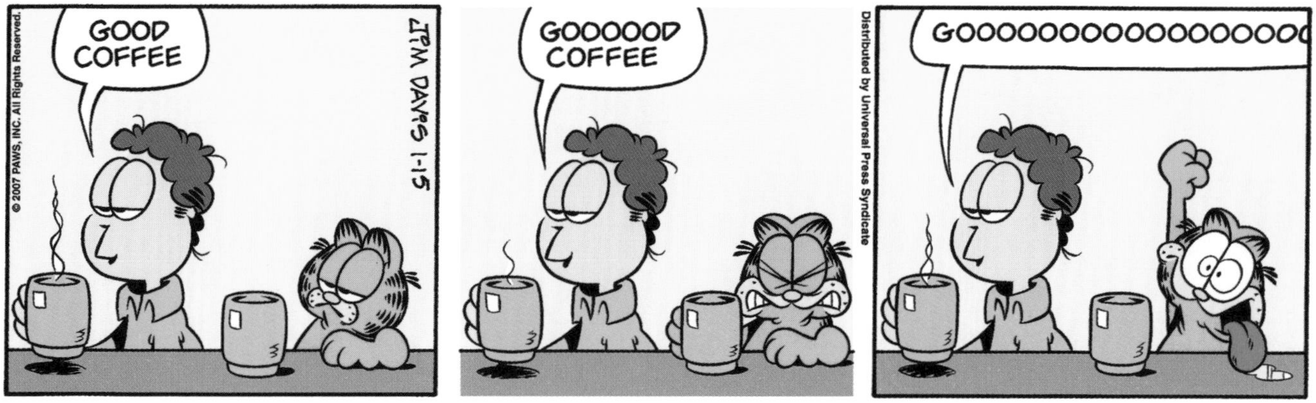
GOOD COFFEE
JIM DAVIS 1-15
© 2007 PAWS, INC. All Rights Reserved.
GOOOOOD COFFEE
Distributed by Universal Press Syndicate
GOOOOOOOOOOOOOOOOOOO

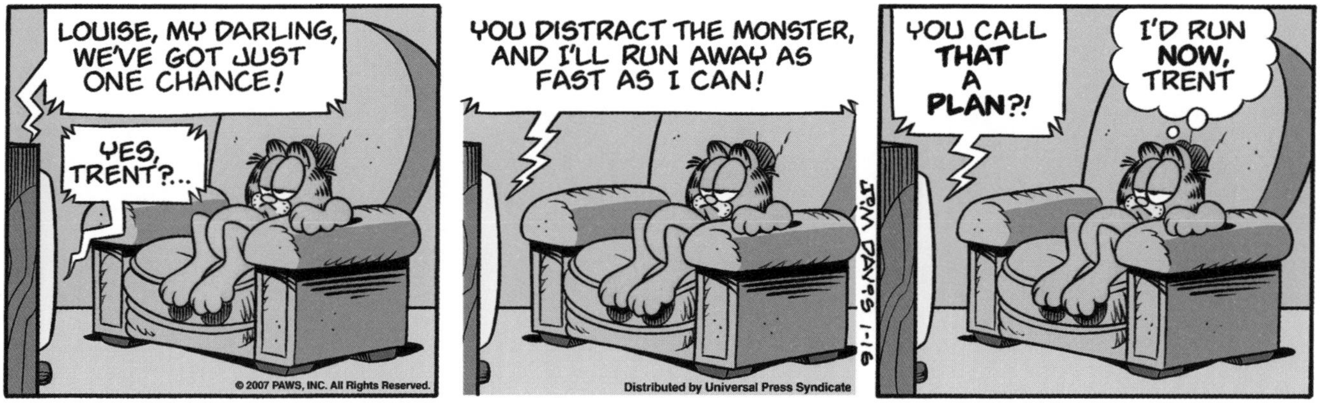
LOUISE, MY DARLING, WE'VE GOT JUST ONE CHANCE!
YES, TRENT?...
© 2007 PAWS, INC. All Rights Reserved.
YOU DISTRACT THE MONSTER, AND I'LL RUN AWAY AS FAST AS I CAN!
JIM DAVIS 1-16
Distributed by Universal Press Syndicate
YOU CALL THAT A PLAN?!
I'D RUN NOW, TRENT

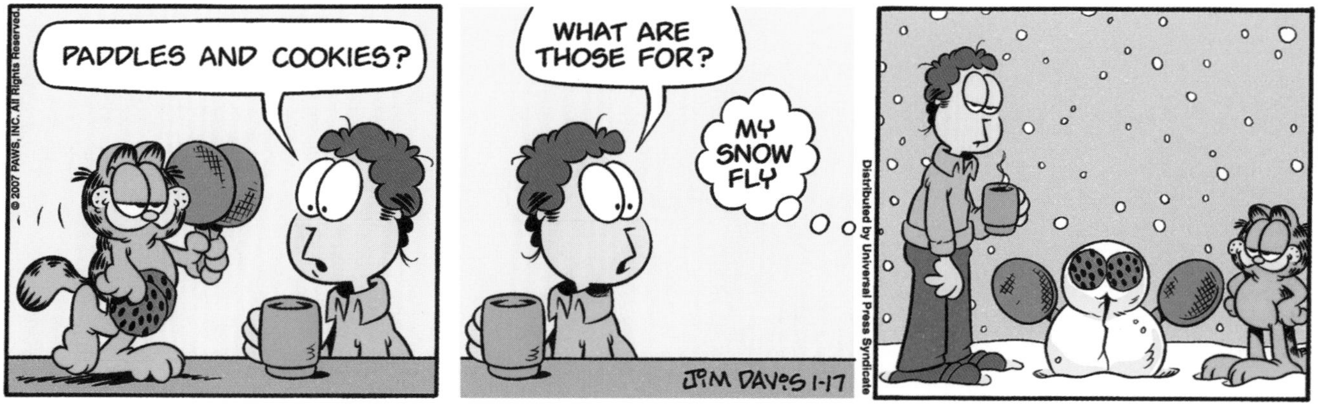
PADDLES AND COOKIES?
© 2007 PAWS, INC. All Rights Reserved.
WHAT ARE THOSE FOR?
MY SNOW FLY
JIM DAVIS 1-17
Distributed by Universal Press Syndicate

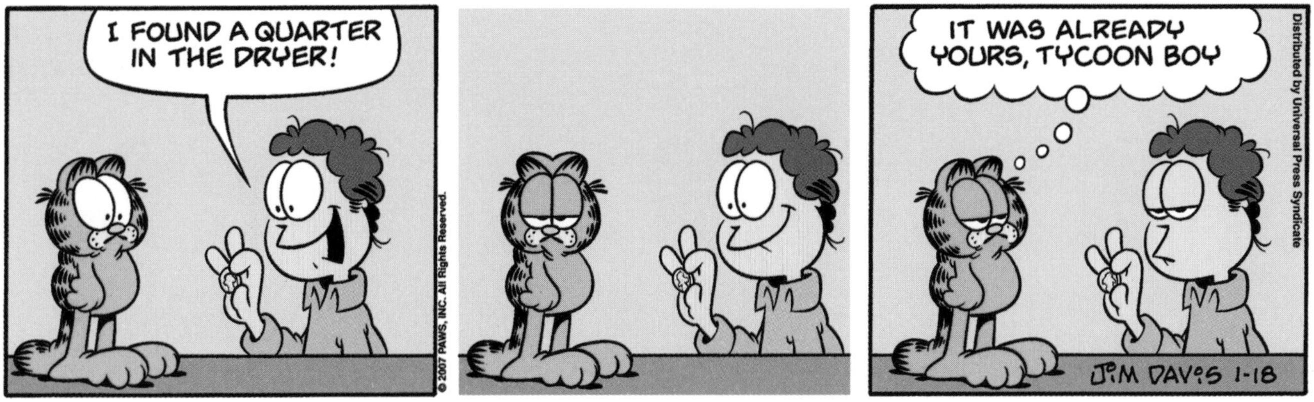
I FOUND A QUARTER IN THE DRYER!
© 2007 PAWS, INC. All Rights Reserved.
IT WAS ALREADY YOURS, TYCOON BOY
Distributed by Universal Press Syndicate
JIM DAVIS 1-18

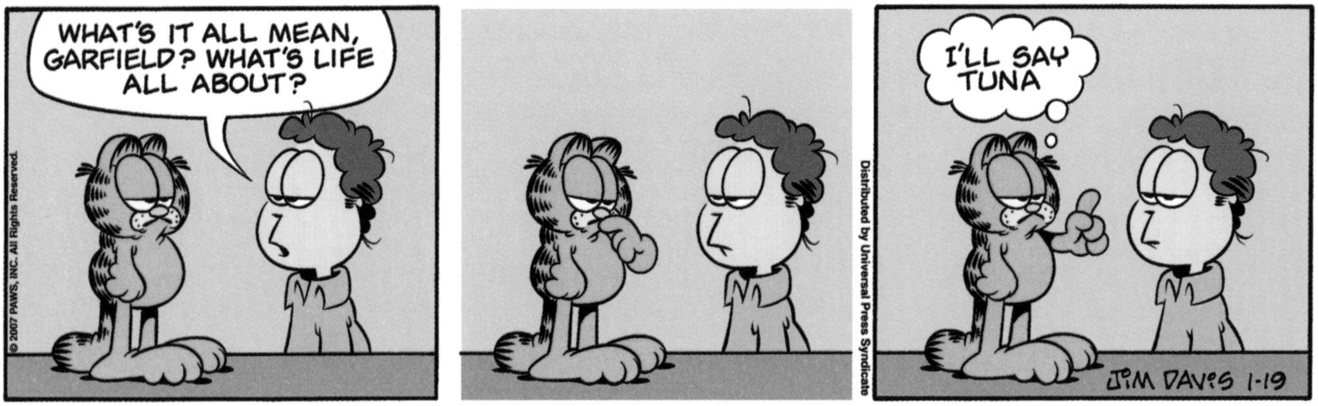
WHAT'S IT ALL MEAN, GARFIELD? WHAT'S LIFE ALL ABOUT?
© 2007 PAWS, INC. All Rights Reserved.
Distributed by Universal Press Syndicate
I'LL SAY TUNA
JIM DAVIS 1-19

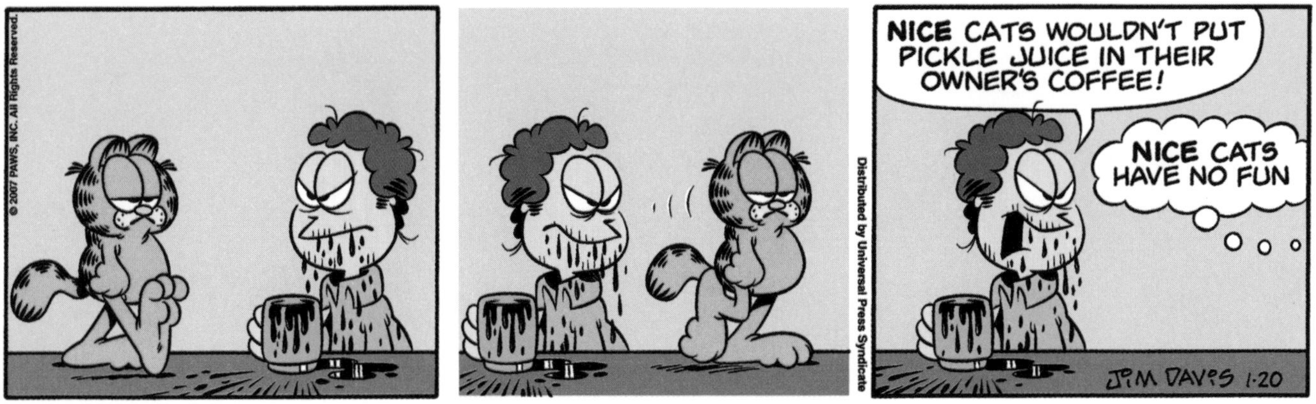
© 2007 PAWS, INC. All Rights Reserved.
Distributed by Universal Press Syndicate
NICE CATS WOULDN'T PUT PICKLE JUICE IN THEIR OWNER'S COFFEE!
NICE CATS HAVE NO FUN
JIM DAVIS 1-20

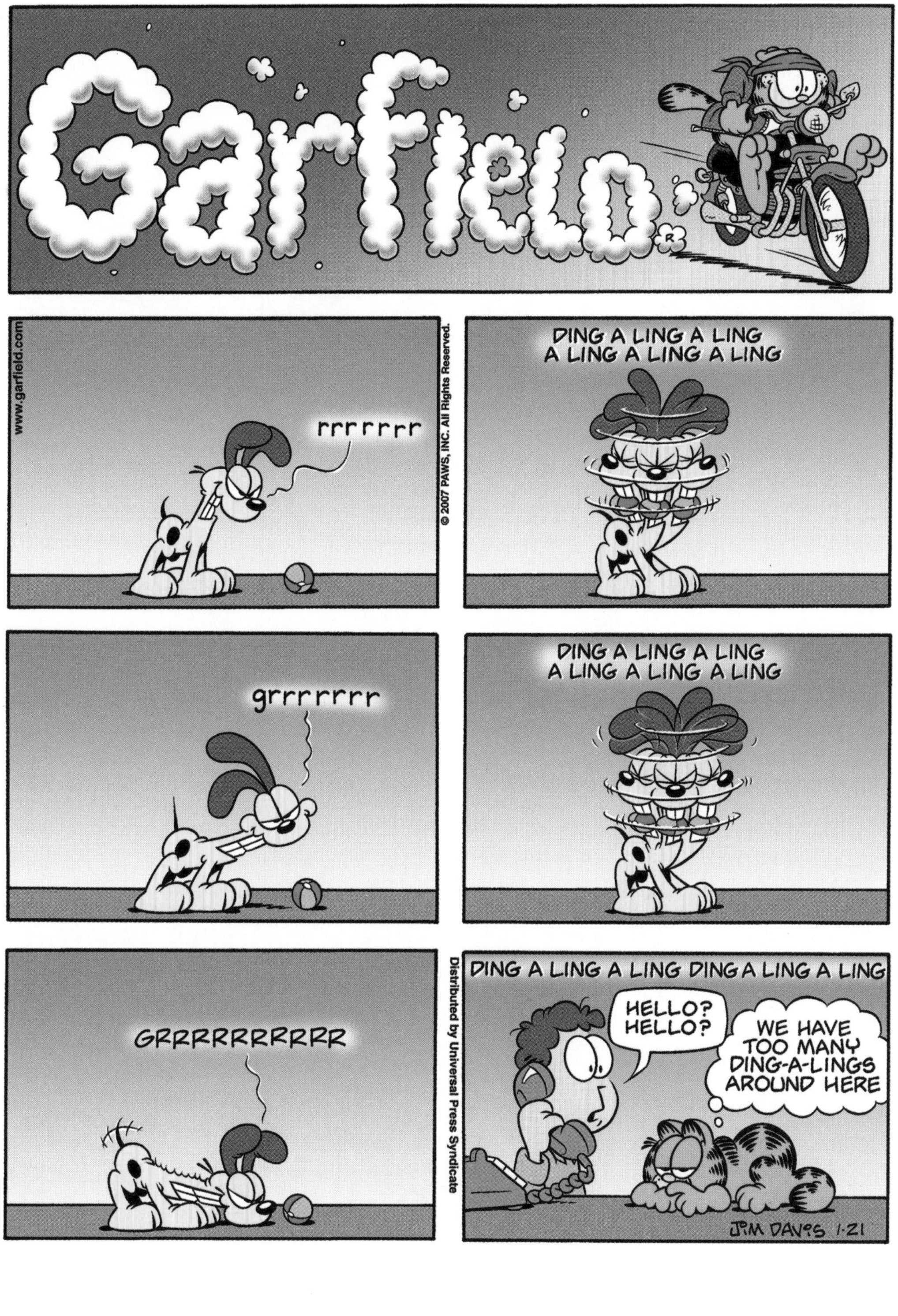
Garfield
www.garfield.com
© 2007 PAWS, INC. All Rights Reserved.
rrrrrrr
DING A LING A LING A LING A LING A LING
grrrrrrr
DING A LING A LING A LING A LING A LING
GRRRRRRRRRR
Distributed by Universal Press Syndicate
DING A LING A LING DING A LING A LING
HELLO? HELLO?
WE HAVE TOO MANY DING-A-LINGS AROUND HERE
JIM DAVIS 1-21

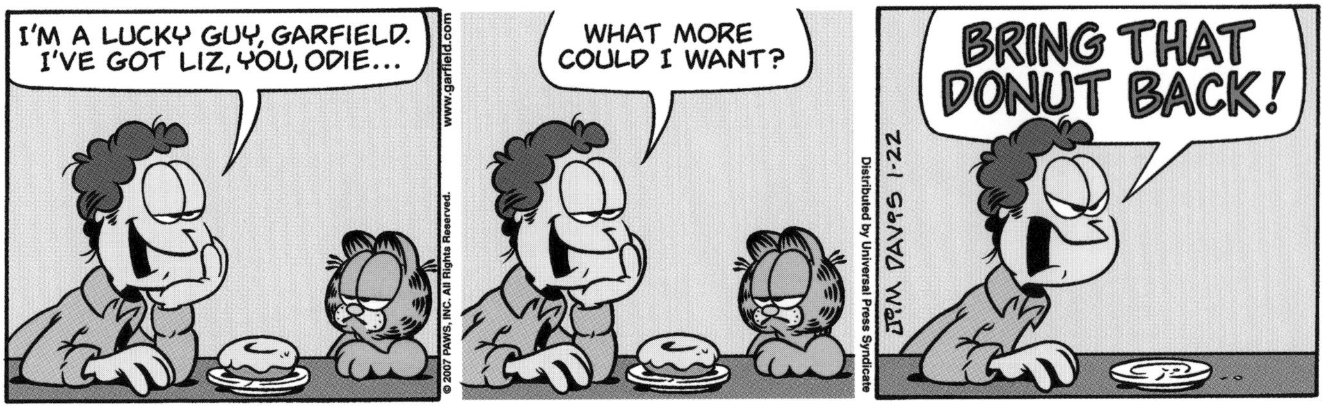
I'M A LUCKY GUY, GARFIELD. I'VE GOT LIZ, YOU, ODIE...
WHAT MORE COULD I WANT?
BRING THAT DONUT BACK!
© 2007 PAWS, INC. All Rights Reserved. www.garfield.com
Distributed by Universal Press Syndicate
JIM DAVIS 1-22

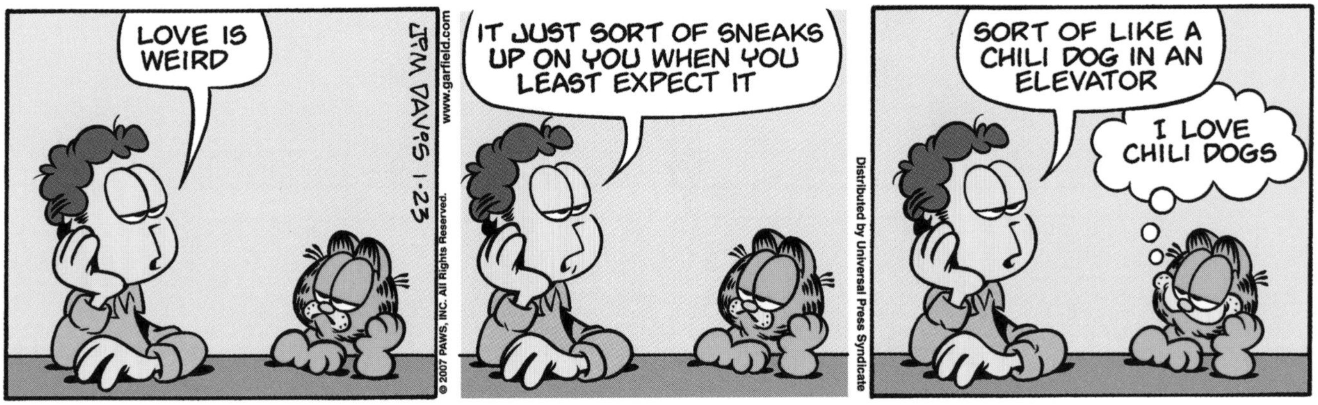
LOVE IS WEIRD
IT JUST SORT OF SNEAKS UP ON YOU WHEN YOU LEAST EXPECT IT
SORT OF LIKE A CHILI DOG IN AN ELEVATOR
I LOVE CHILI DOGS
JIM DAVIS 1-23
© 2007 PAWS, INC. All Rights Reserved. www.garfield.com
Distributed by Universal Press Syndicate

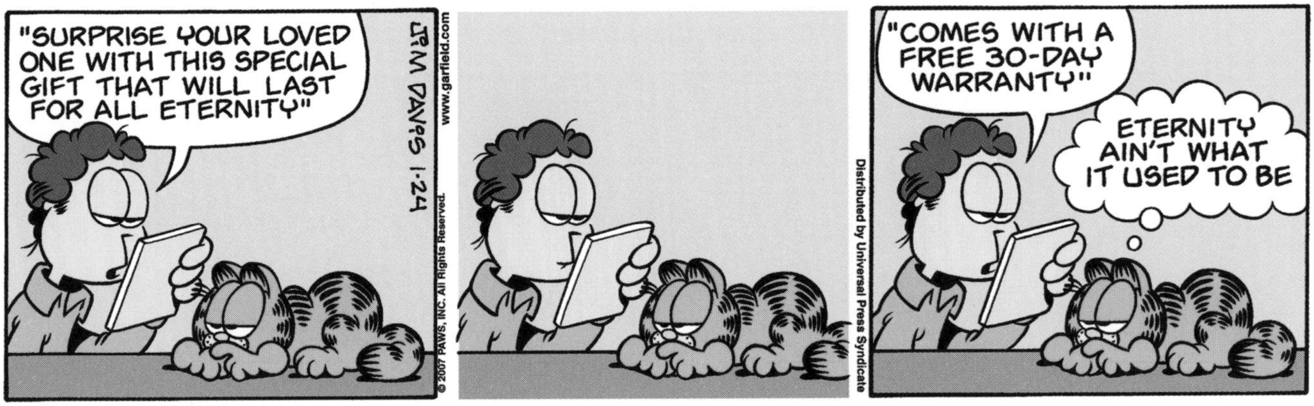
"SURPRISE YOUR LOVED ONE WITH THIS SPECIAL GIFT THAT WILL LAST FOR ALL ETERNITY"
"COMES WITH A FREE 30-DAY WARRANTY"
ETERNITY AIN'T WHAT IT USED TO BE
JIM DAVIS 1-24
© 2007 PAWS, INC. All Rights Reserved. www.garfield.com
Distributed by Universal Press Syndicate

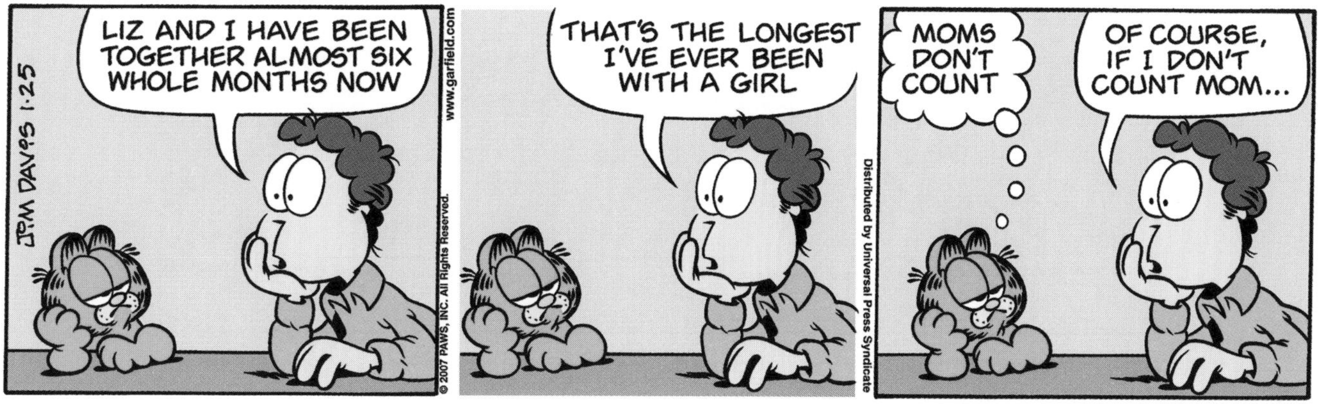
JIM DAVIS 1·25
LIZ AND I HAVE BEEN TOGETHER ALMOST SIX WHOLE MONTHS NOW
www.garfield.com
© 2007 PAWS, INC. All Rights Reserved.
THAT'S THE LONGEST I'VE EVER BEEN WITH A GIRL
Distributed by Universal Press Syndicate
MOMS DON'T COUNT
OF COURSE, IF I DON'T COUNT MOM...

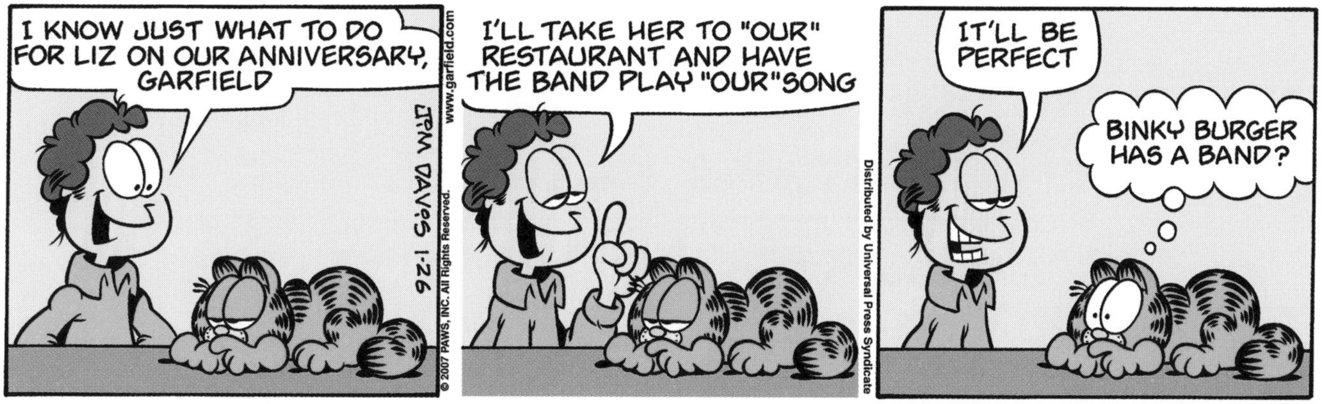
I KNOW JUST WHAT TO DO FOR LIZ ON OUR ANNIVERSARY, GARFIELD
JIM DAVIS 1·26
www.garfield.com
© 2007 PAWS, INC. All Rights Reserved.
I'LL TAKE HER TO "OUR" RESTAURANT AND HAVE THE BAND PLAY "OUR" SONG
Distributed by Universal Press Syndicate
IT'LL BE PERFECT
BINKY BURGER HAS A BAND?

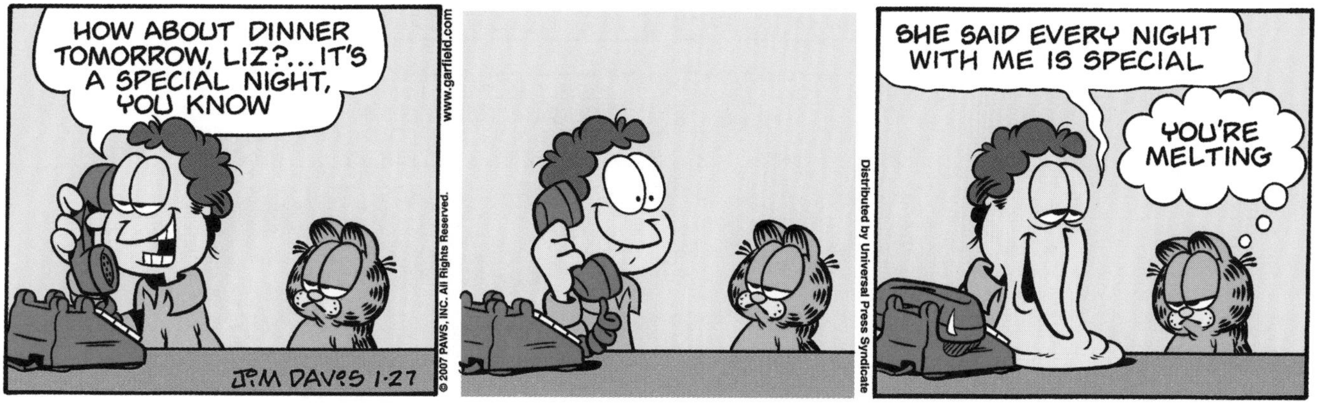
HOW ABOUT DINNER TOMORROW, LIZ?... IT'S A SPECIAL NIGHT, YOU KNOW
JIM DAVIS 1·27
www.garfield.com
© 2007 PAWS, INC. All Rights Reserved.
Distributed by Universal Press Syndicate
SHE SAID EVERY NIGHT WITH ME IS SPECIAL
YOU'RE MELTING

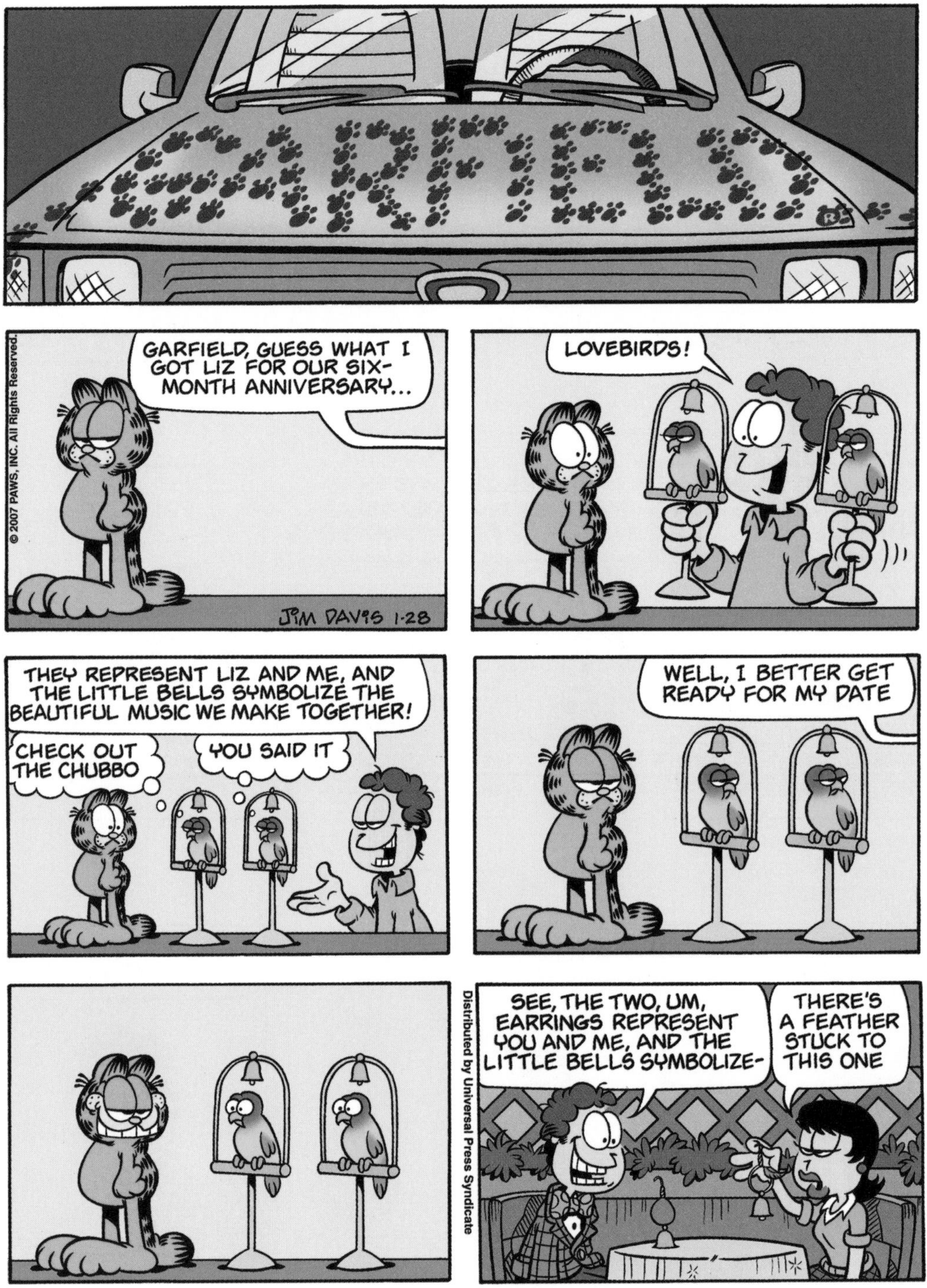
GARFIELD
© 2007 PAWS, INC. All Rights Reserved.
GARFIELD, GUESS WHAT I GOT LIZ FOR OUR SIX-MONTH ANNIVERSARY...
JIM DAVIS 1-28
LOVEBIRDS!
THEY REPRESENT LIZ AND ME, AND THE LITTLE BELLS SYMBOLIZE THE BEAUTIFUL MUSIC WE MAKE TOGETHER!
CHECK OUT THE CHUBBO
YOU SAID IT
WELL, I BETTER GET READY FOR MY DATE
Distributed by Universal Press Syndicate
SEE, THE TWO, UM, EARRINGS REPRESENT YOU AND ME, AND THE LITTLE BELLS SYMBOLIZE-
THERE'S A FEATHER STUCK TO THIS ONE

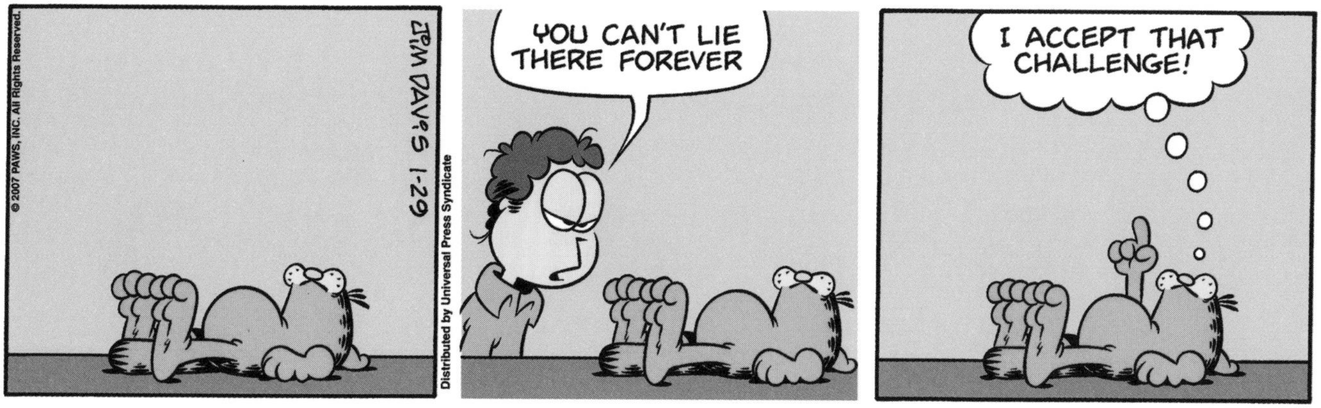
© 2007 PAWS, INC. All Rights Reserved.
JIM DAVIS 1-29
Distributed by Universal Press Syndicate
YOU CAN'T LIE THERE FOREVER
I ACCEPT THAT CHALLENGE!

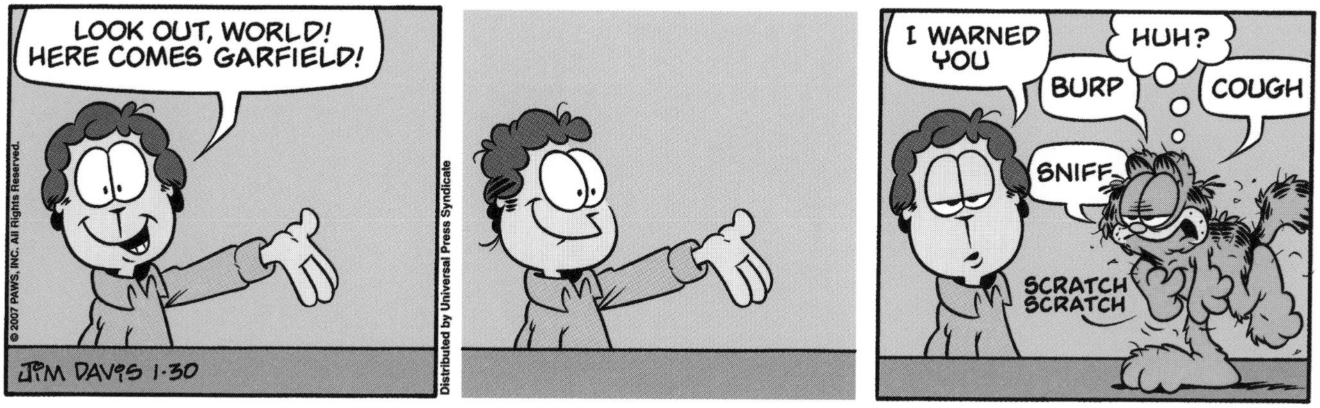
© 2007 PAWS, INC. All Rights Reserved.
LOOK OUT, WORLD! HERE COMES GARFIELD!
JIM DAVIS 1-30
Distributed by Universal Press Syndicate
I WARNED YOU
HUH?
BURP
COUGH
SNIFF
SCRATCH SCRATCH

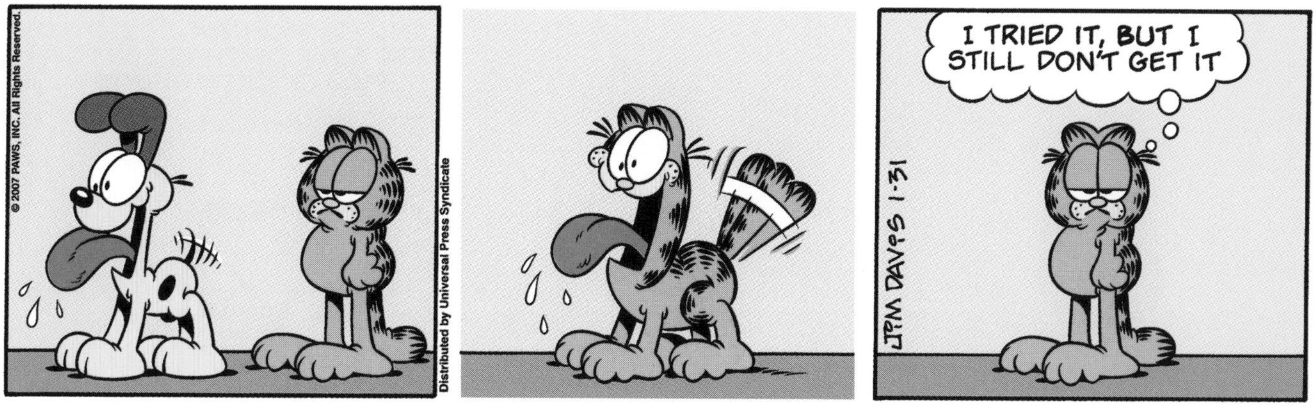
© 2007 PAWS, INC. All Rights Reserved.
Distributed by Universal Press Syndicate
JIM DAVIS 1-31
I TRIED IT, BUT I STILL DON'T GET IT

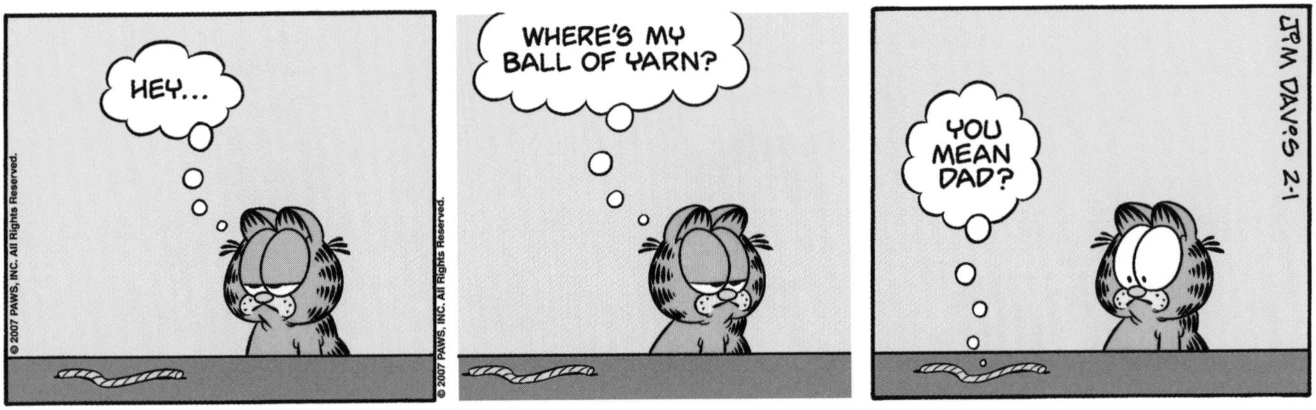
HEY...
WHERE'S MY BALL OF YARN?
YOU MEAN DAD?
JIM DAVIS 2-1
© 2007 PAWS, INC. All Rights Reserved.

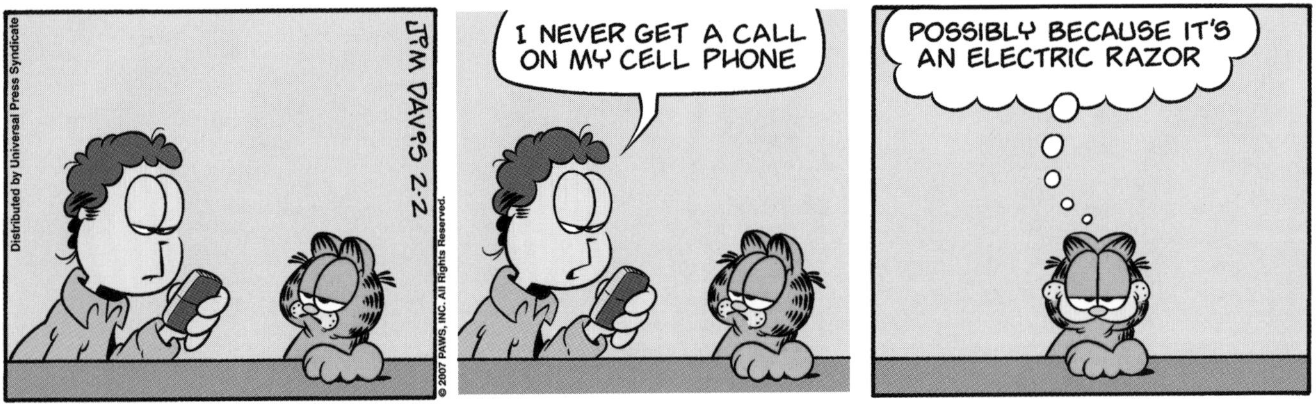
I NEVER GET A CALL ON MY CELL PHONE
POSSIBLY BECAUSE IT'S AN ELECTRIC RAZOR
JIM DAVIS 2-2
Distributed by Universal Press Syndicate
© 2007 PAWS, INC. All Rights Reserved.

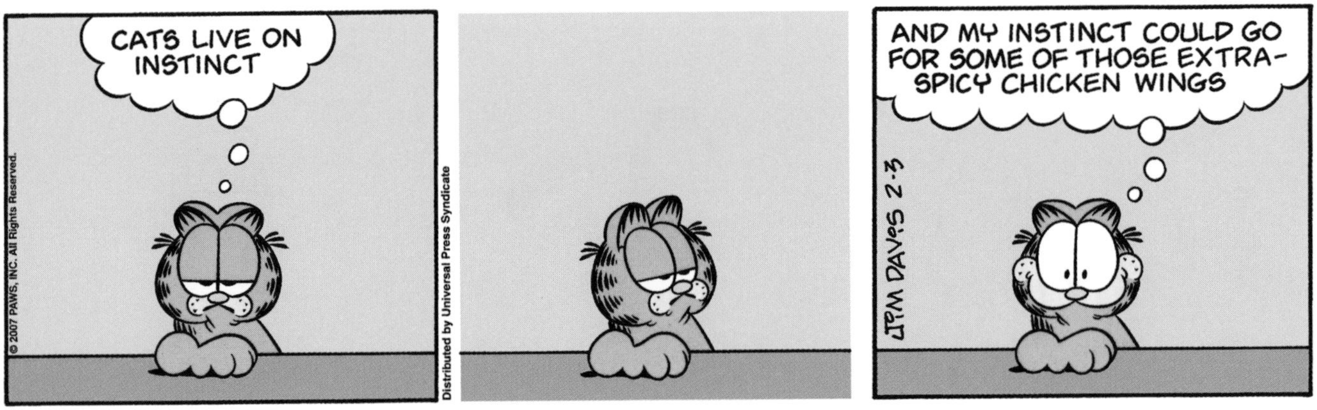
CATS LIVE ON INSTINCT
AND MY INSTINCT COULD GO FOR SOME OF THOSE EXTRA-SPICY CHICKEN WINGS
JIM DAVIS 2-3
© 2007 PAWS, INC. All Rights Reserved.
Distributed by Universal Press Syndicate

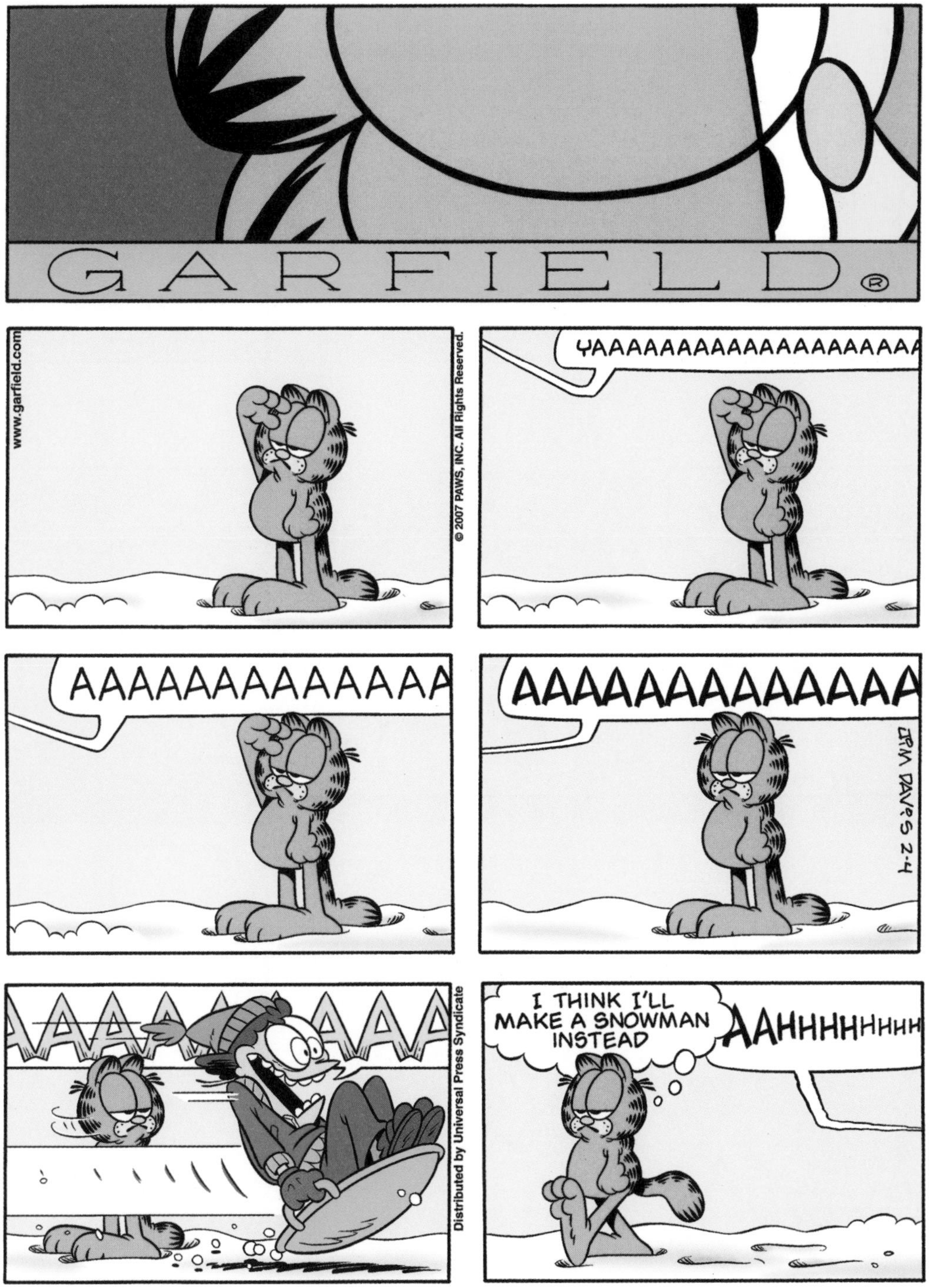
GARFIELD®
www.garfield.com
© 2007 PAWS, INC. All Rights Reserved.
YAAAAAAAAAAAAAAAAAAA
AAAAAAAAAAAAAA
AAAAAAAAAAAAAA
JPM DAVIS 2-4
AAAAAAAAA
Distributed by Universal Press Syndicate
I THINK I'LL MAKE A SNOWMAN INSTEAD
AAHHHHHHHH

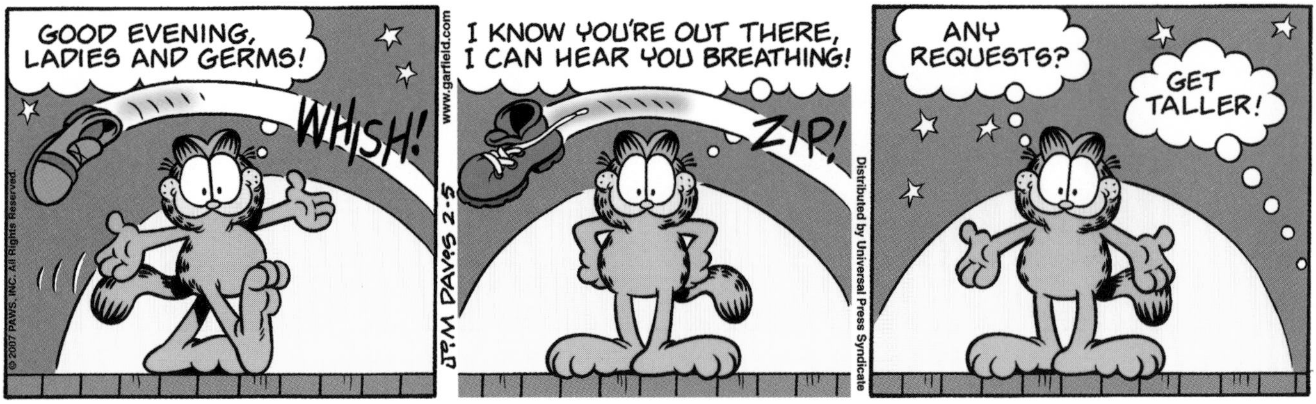
GOOD EVENING, LADIES AND GERMS!
WHISH!
© 2007 PAWS, INC. All Rights Reserved
www.garfield.com
JIM DAVIS 2-5
I KNOW YOU'RE OUT THERE, I CAN HEAR YOU BREATHING!
ZIP!
Distributed by Universal Press Syndicate
ANY REQUESTS?
GET TALLER!

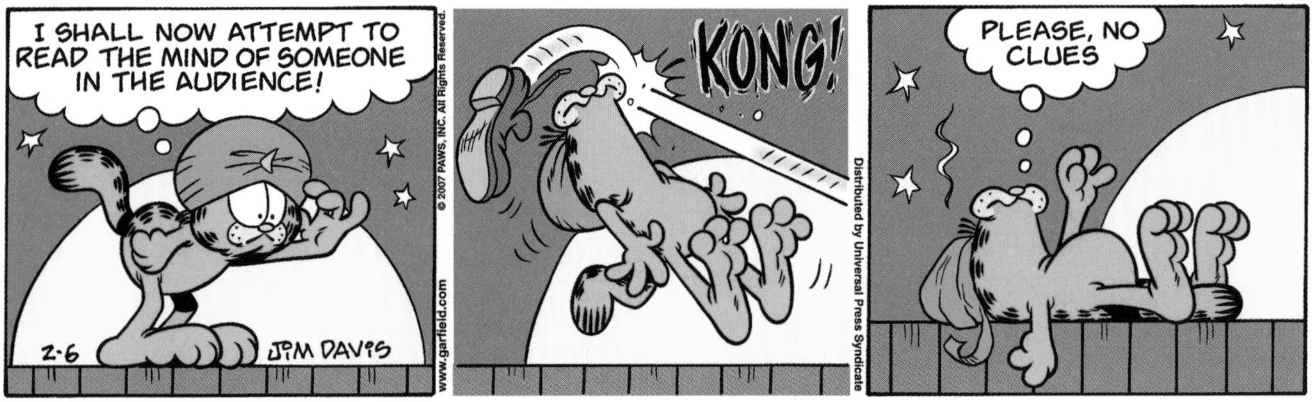
I SHALL NOW ATTEMPT TO READ THE MIND OF SOMEONE IN THE AUDIENCE!
2-6
JIM DAVIS
© 2007 PAWS, INC. All Rights Reserved
www.garfield.com
KONG!
Distributed by Universal Press Syndicate
PLEASE, NO CLUES

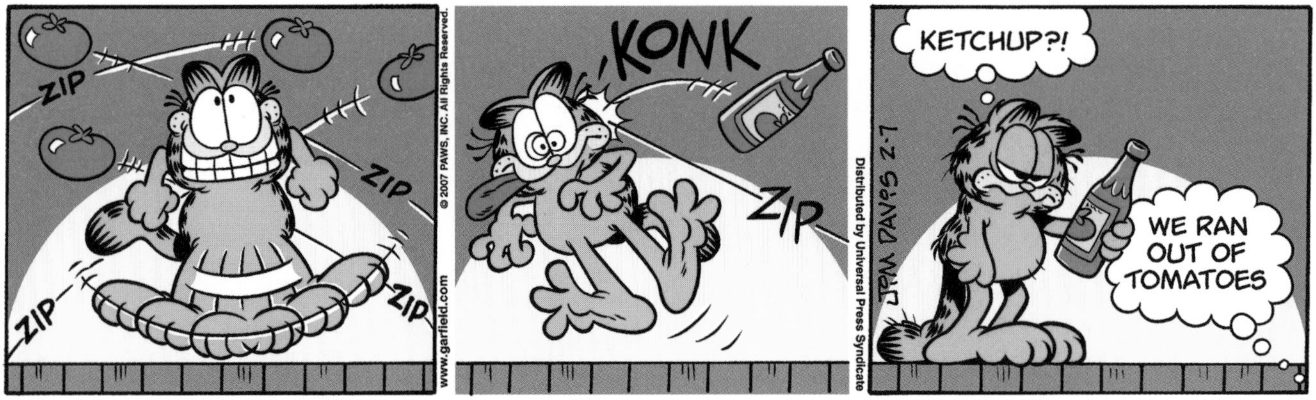
ZIP
ZIP
ZIP
ZIP
© 2007 PAWS, INC. All Rights Reserved
www.garfield.com
KONK
ZIP
Distributed by Universal Press Syndicate
JIM DAVIS 2-7
KETCHUP?!
WE RAN OUT OF TOMATOES

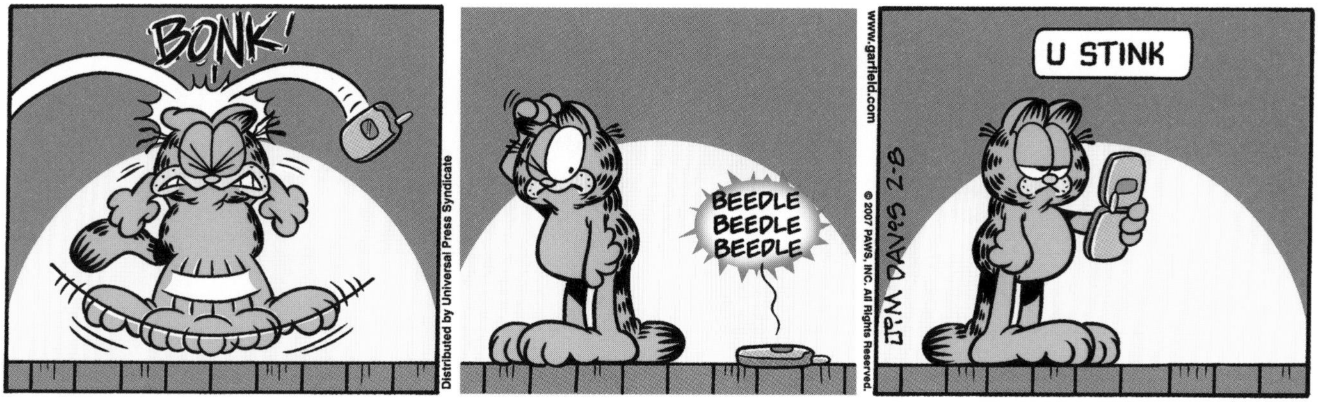
BONK!
Distributed by Universal Press Syndicate
BEEDLE BEEDLE BEEDLE
www.garfield.com
© 2007 PAWS, INC. All Rights Reserved.
JIM DAVIS 2-8
U STINK

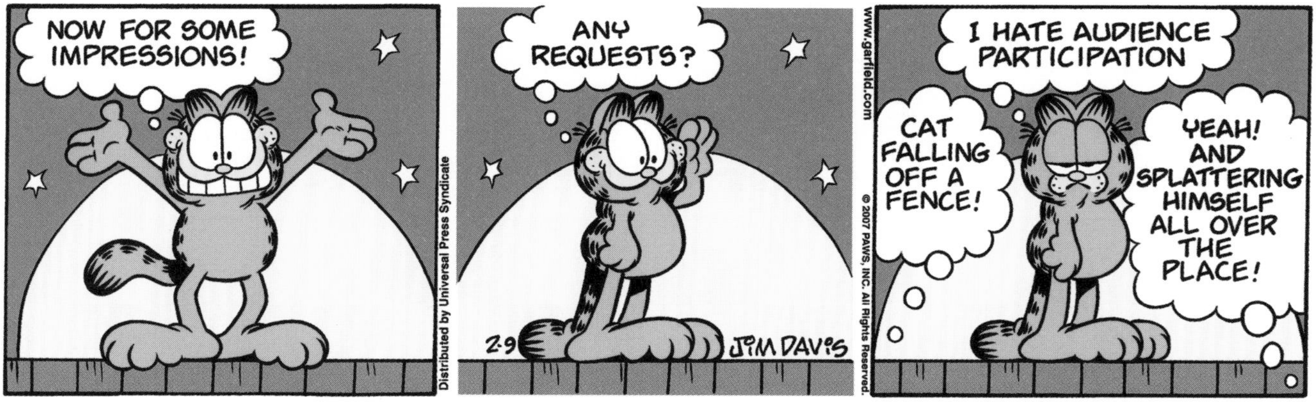
NOW FOR SOME IMPRESSIONS!
Distributed by Universal Press Syndicate
ANY REQUESTS?
2-9
JIM DAVIS
www.garfield.com
© 2007 PAWS, INC. All Rights Reserved.
I HATE AUDIENCE PARTICIPATION
CAT FALLING OFF A FENCE!
YEAH! AND SPLATTERING HIMSELF ALL OVER THE PLACE!

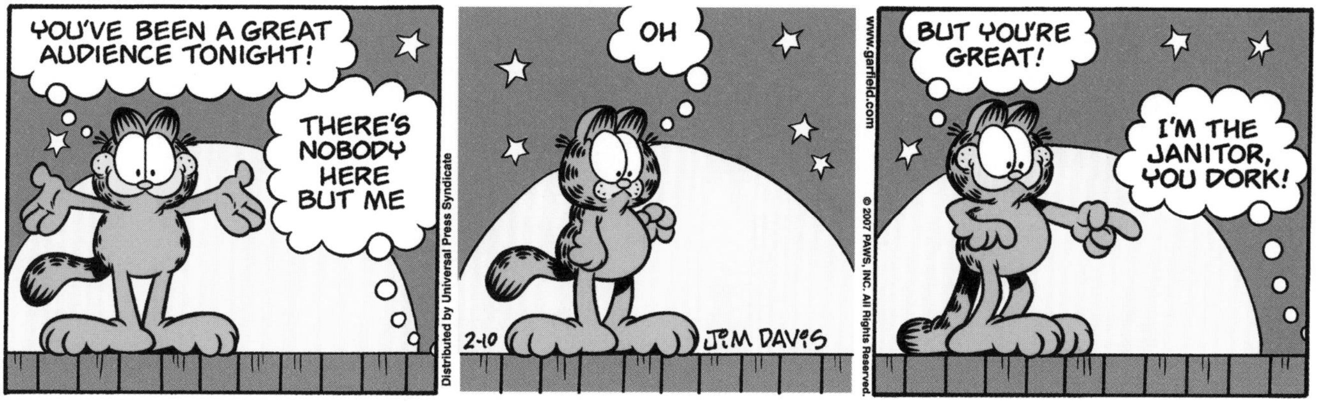
YOU'VE BEEN A GREAT AUDIENCE TONIGHT!
THERE'S NOBODY HERE BUT ME
Distributed by Universal Press Syndicate
OH
2-10
JIM DAVIS
www.garfield.com
© 2007 PAWS, INC. All Rights Reserved.
BUT YOU'RE GREAT!
I'M THE JANITOR, YOU DORK!

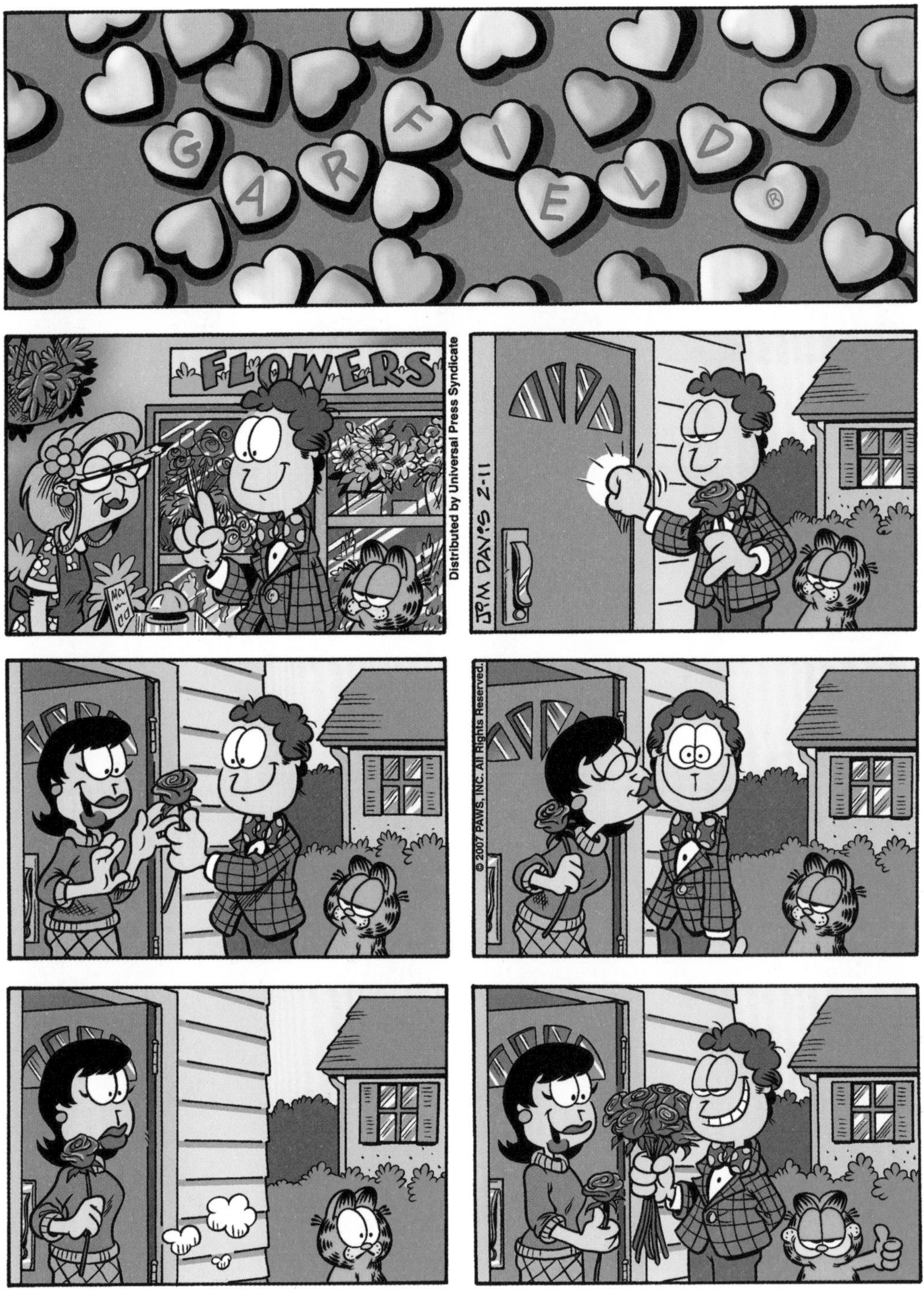
GARFIELD®
FLOWERS
Distributed by Universal Press Syndicate
JIM DAVIS 2-11
© 2007 PAWS, INC. All Rights Reserved.

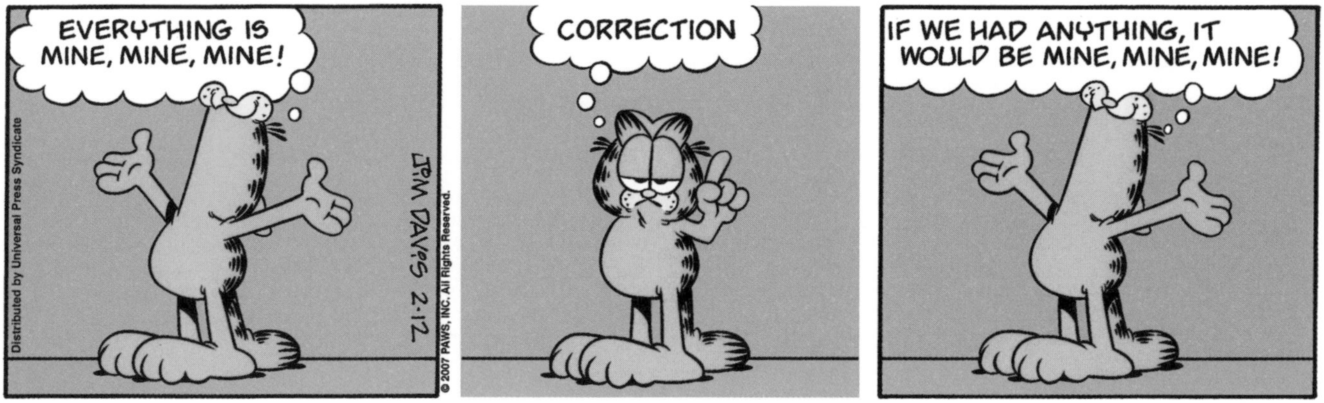
EVERYTHING IS MINE, MINE, MINE!
CORRECTION
IF WE HAD ANYTHING, IT WOULD BE MINE, MINE, MINE!
JIM DAVIS 2-12
© 2007 PAWS, INC. All Rights Reserved.
Distributed by Universal Press Syndicate

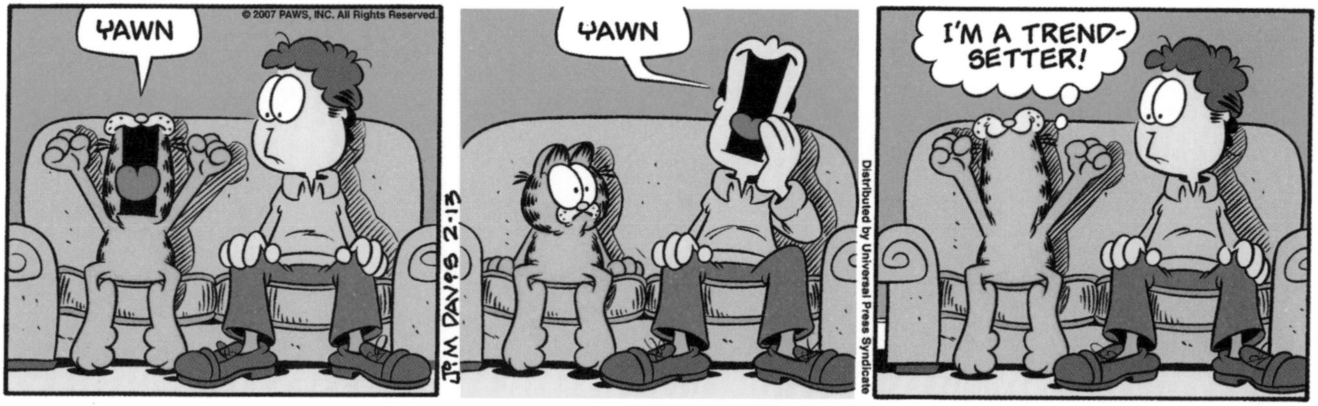
YAWN
YAWN
I'M A TREND-SETTER!
JIM DAVIS 2-13
© 2007 PAWS, INC. All Rights Reserved.
Distributed by Universal Press Syndicate

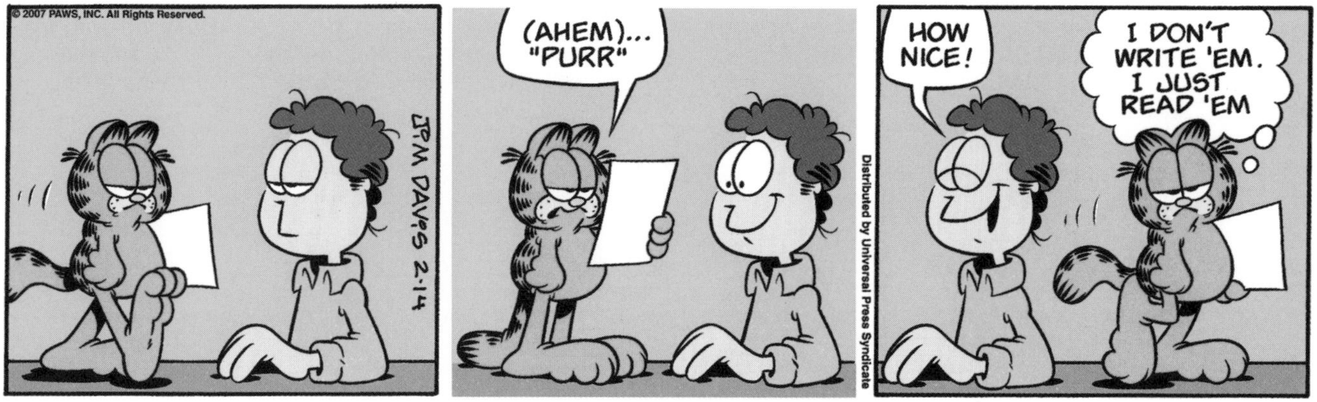
(AHEM)... "PURR"
HOW NICE!
I DON'T WRITE 'EM. I JUST READ 'EM
JIM DAVIS 2-14
© 2007 PAWS, INC. All Rights Reserved.
Distributed by Universal Press Syndicate

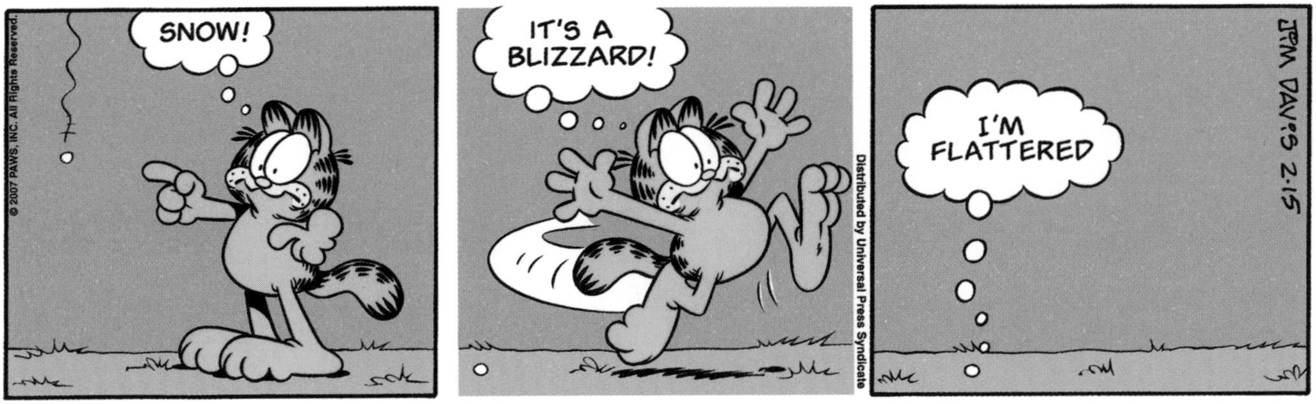
© 2007 PAWS, INC. All Rights Reserved.
SNOW!
IT'S A BLIZZARD!
Distributed by Universal Press Syndicate
I'M FLATTERED
JIM DAVIS 2-15

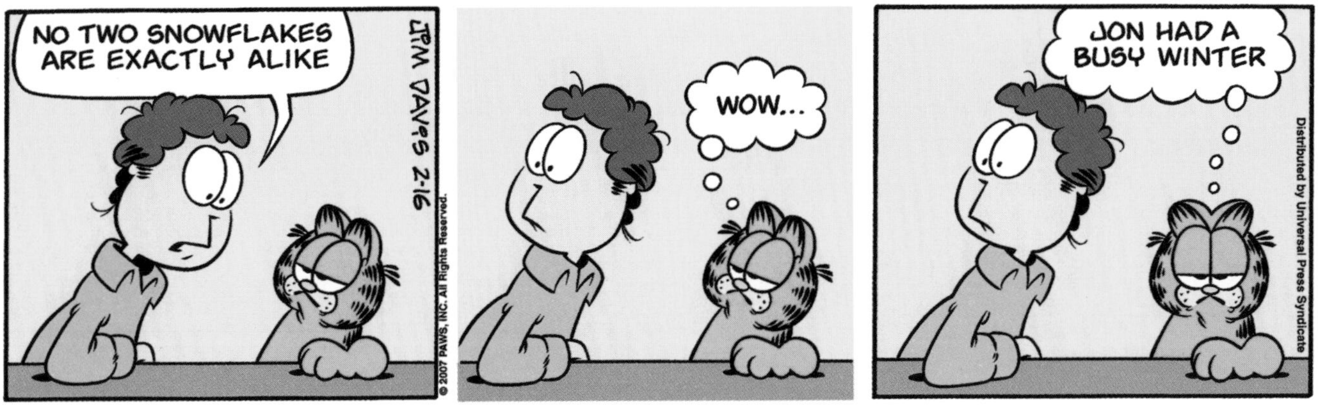
NO TWO SNOWFLAKES ARE EXACTLY ALIKE
JIM DAVIS 2-16
© 2007 PAWS, INC. All Rights Reserved.
WOW...
JON HAD A BUSY WINTER
Distributed by Universal Press Syndicate

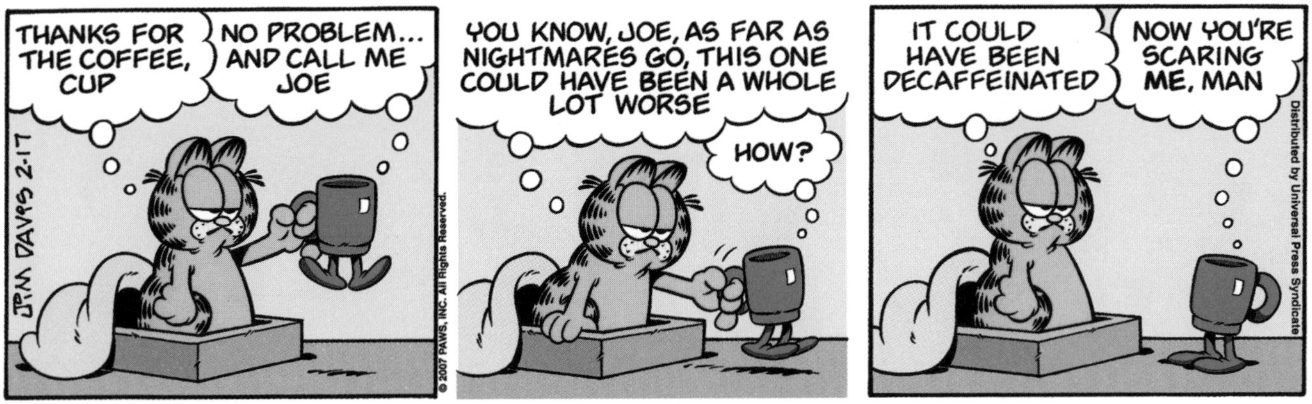
THANKS FOR THE COFFEE, CUP
NO PROBLEM... AND CALL ME JOE
JIM DAVIS 2-17
© 2007 PAWS, INC. All Rights Reserved.
YOU KNOW, JOE, AS FAR AS NIGHTMARES GO, THIS ONE COULD HAVE BEEN A WHOLE LOT WORSE
HOW?
IT COULD HAVE BEEN DECAFFEINATED
NOW YOU'RE SCARING ME, MAN
Distributed by Universal Press Syndicate

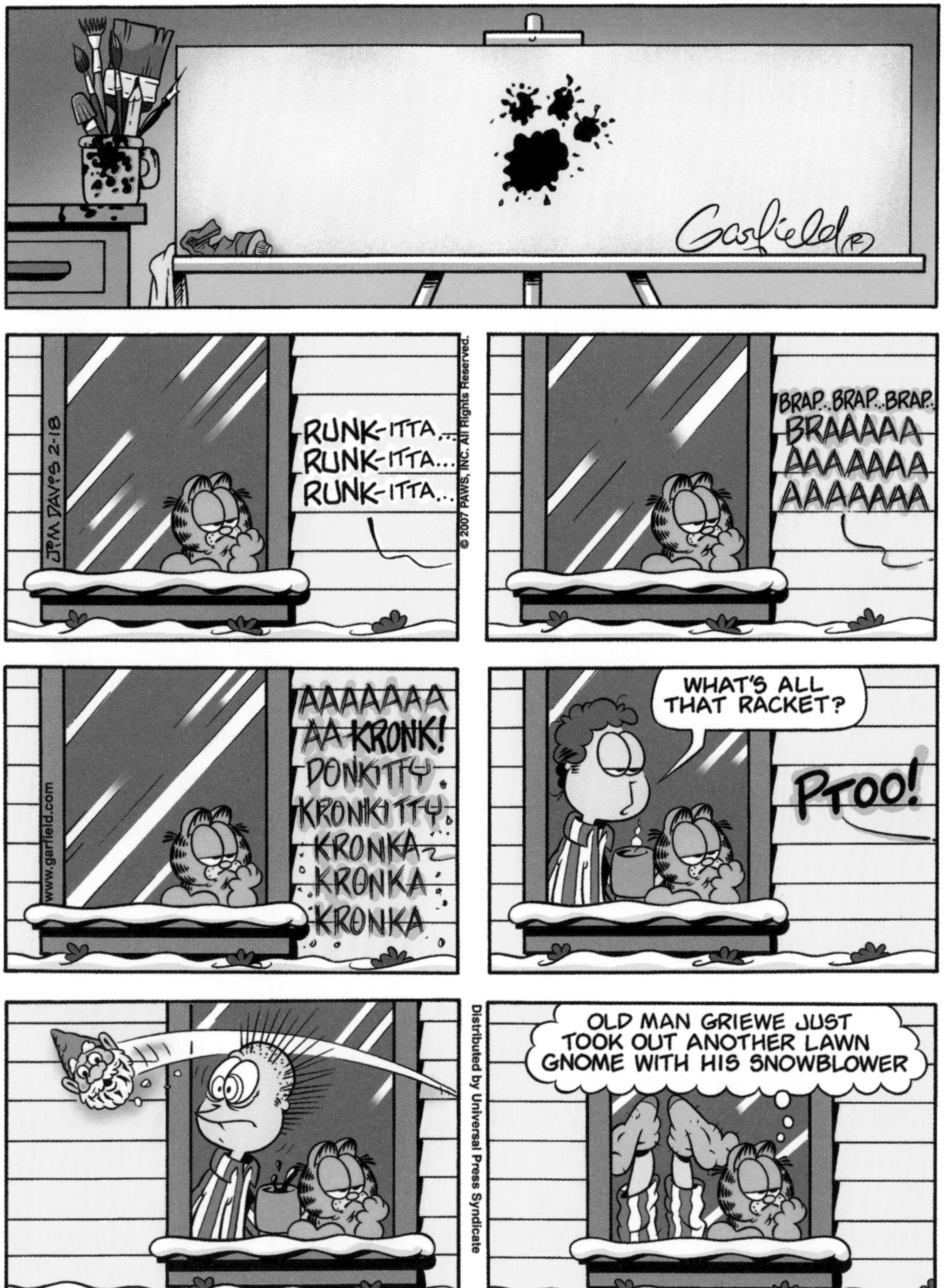
Garfield®
JIM DAVIS 2-18
© 2007 PAWS, INC. All Rights Reserved.
RUNK-ITTA...
RUNK-ITTA...
RUNK-ITTA...
BRAP..BRAP..BRAP..
BRAAAAA
AAAAAAA
AAAAAAA
www.garfield.com
AAAAAAA
AA KRONK!
DONKITTY
KRONKITTY
KRONKA
KRONKA
KRONKA
WHAT'S ALL THAT RACKET?
PTOO!
Distributed by Universal Press Syndicate
OLD MAN GRIEWE JUST TOOK OUT ANOTHER LAWN GNOME WITH HIS SNOWBLOWER

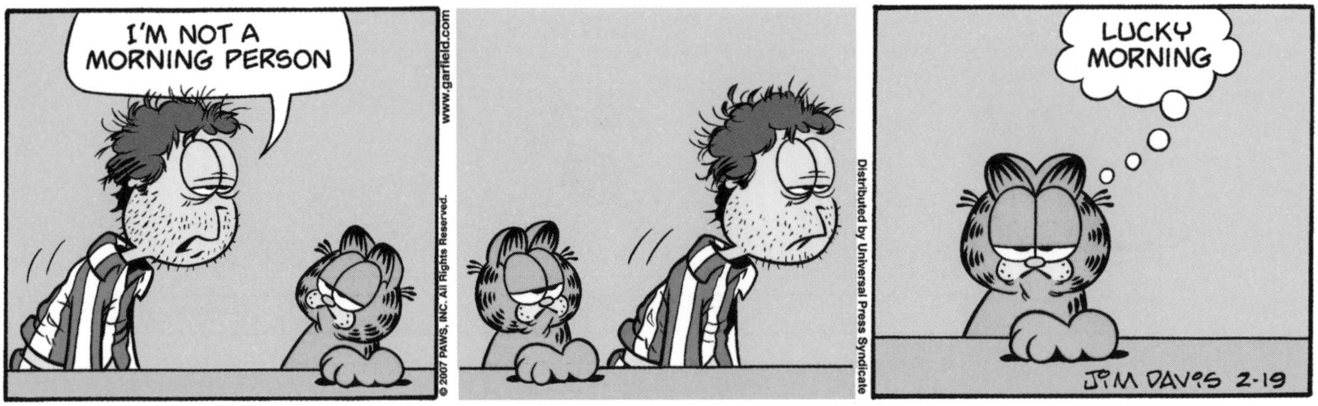
I'M NOT A MORNING PERSON
© 2007 PAWS, INC. All Rights Reserved. www.garfield.com
Distributed by Universal Press Syndicate
LUCKY MORNING
JIM DAVIS 2-19

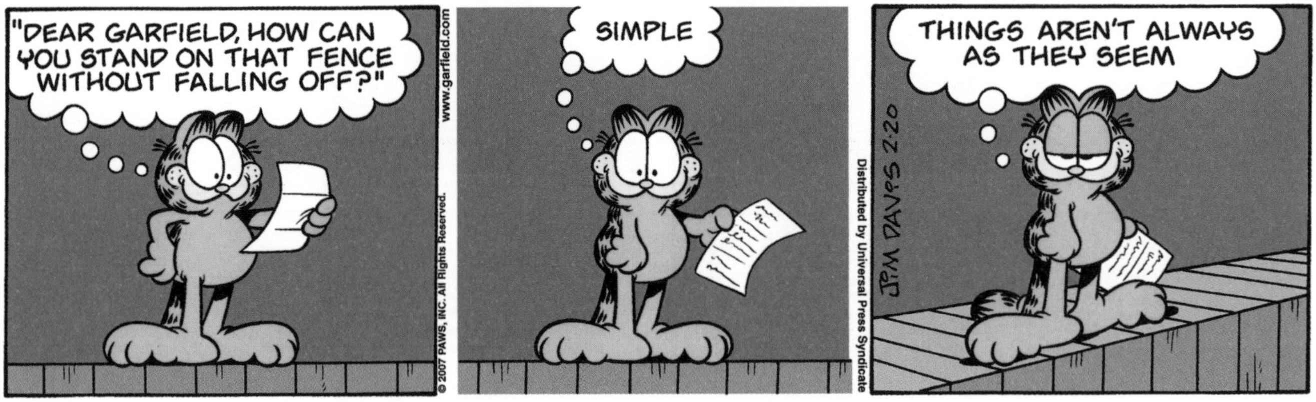
"DEAR GARFIELD, HOW CAN YOU STAND ON THAT FENCE WITHOUT FALLING OFF?"
© 2007 PAWS, INC. All Rights Reserved. www.garfield.com
SIMPLE
Distributed by Universal Press Syndicate
JIM DAVIS 2-20
THINGS AREN'T ALWAYS AS THEY SEEM

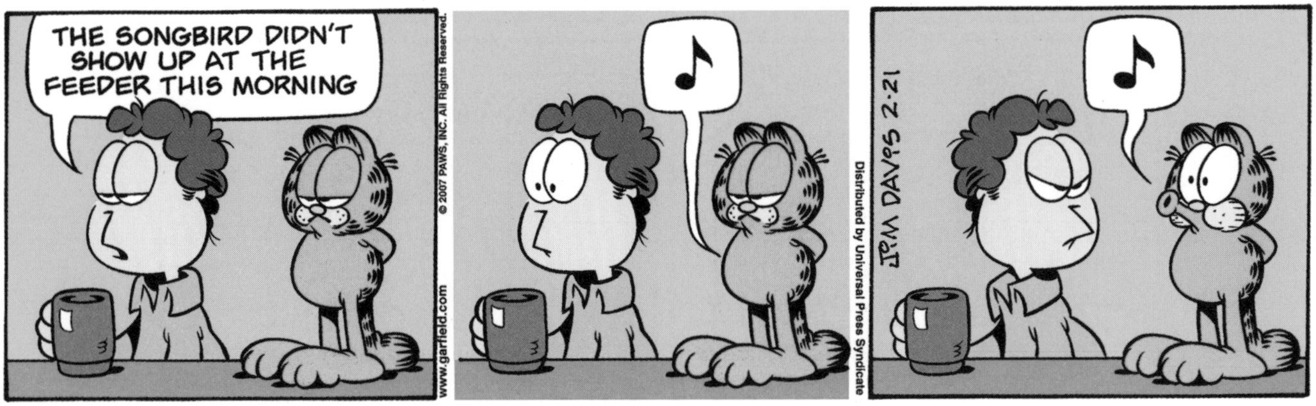
THE SONGBIRD DIDN'T SHOW UP AT THE FEEDER THIS MORNING
© 2007 PAWS, INC. All Rights Reserved. www.garfield.com
Distributed by Universal Press Syndicate
JIM DAVIS 2-21

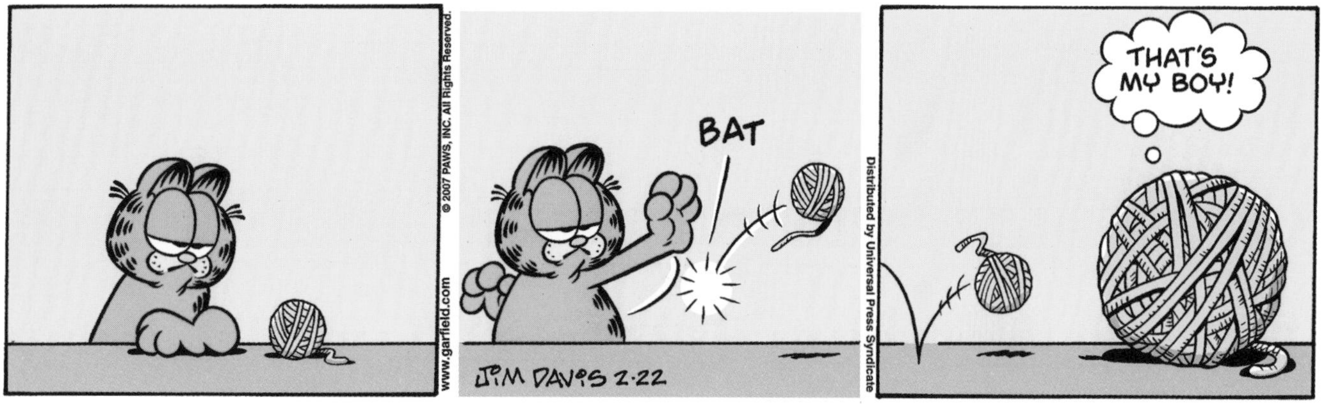
BAT
JIM DAVIS 2-22
THAT'S MY BOY!

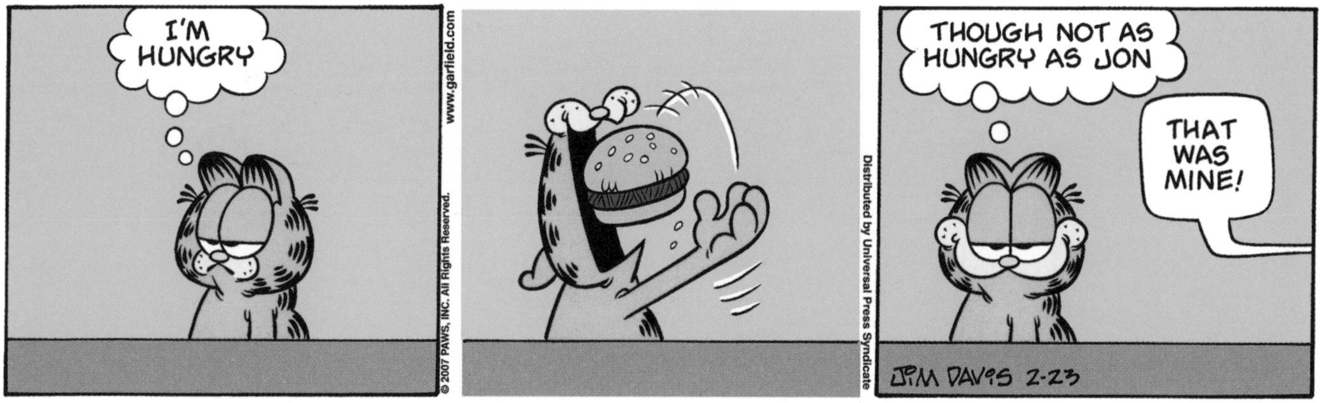
I'M HUNGRY
THOUGH NOT AS HUNGRY AS JON
THAT WAS MINE!
JIM DAVIS 2-23

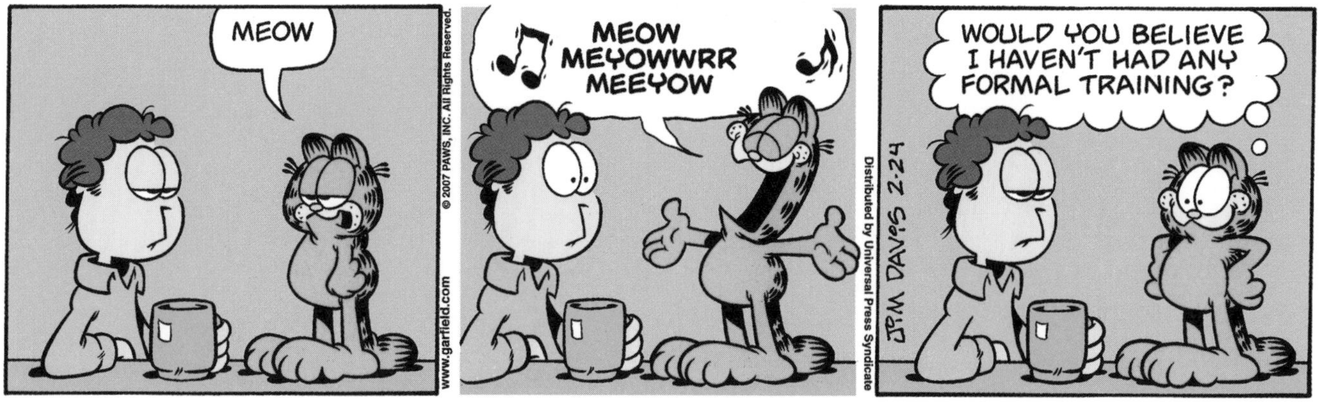
MEOW
MEOW MEYOWWRR MEEYOW
JIM DAVIS 2-24
WOULD YOU BELIEVE I HAVEN'T HAD ANY FORMAL TRAINING?

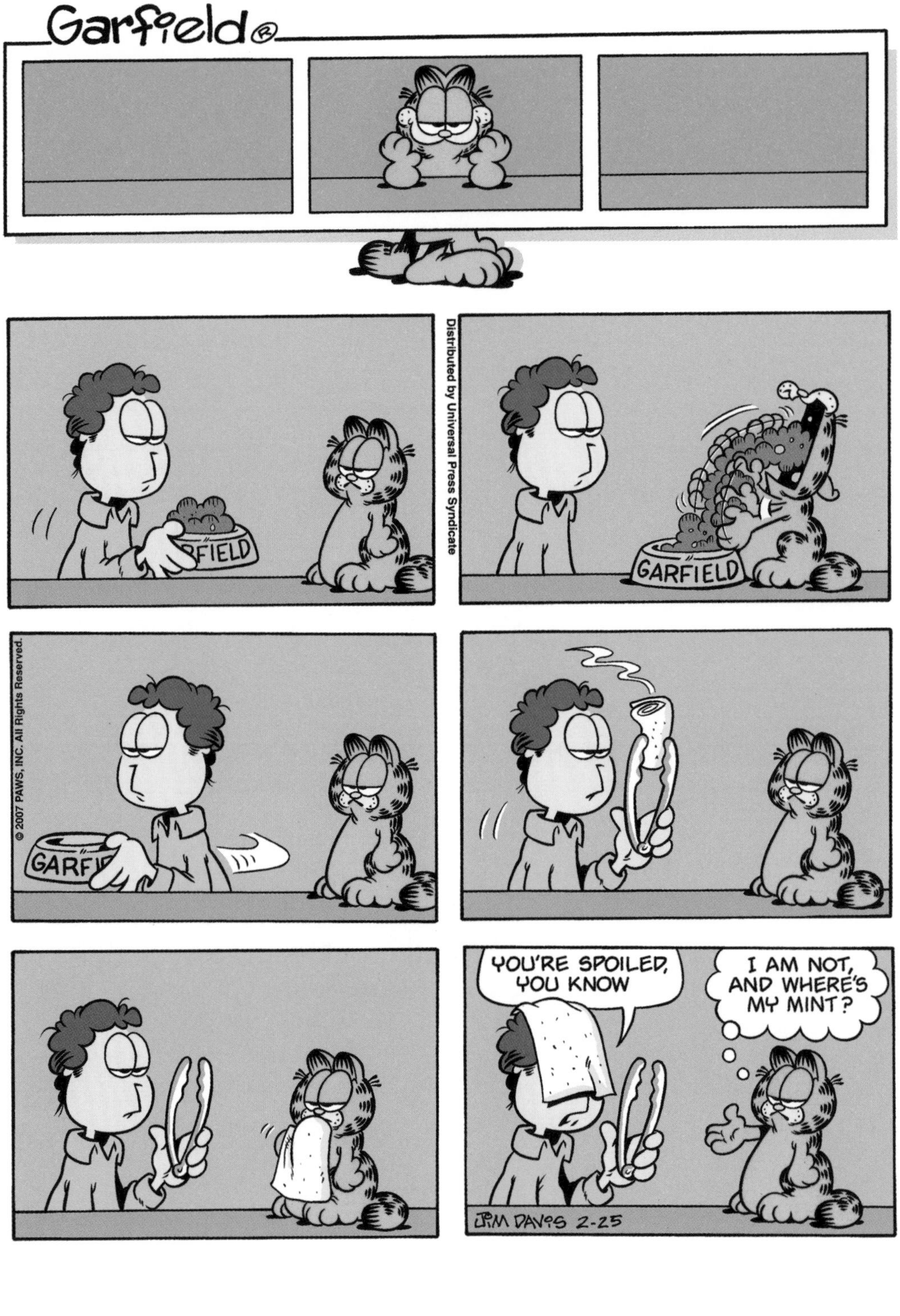
Garfield®
RFIELD
Distributed by Universal Press Syndicate
GARFIELD
© 2007 PAWS, INC. All Rights Reserved.
GARFI
YOU'RE SPOILED, YOU KNOW
I AM NOT, AND WHERE'S MY MINT?
JIM DAVIS 2-25

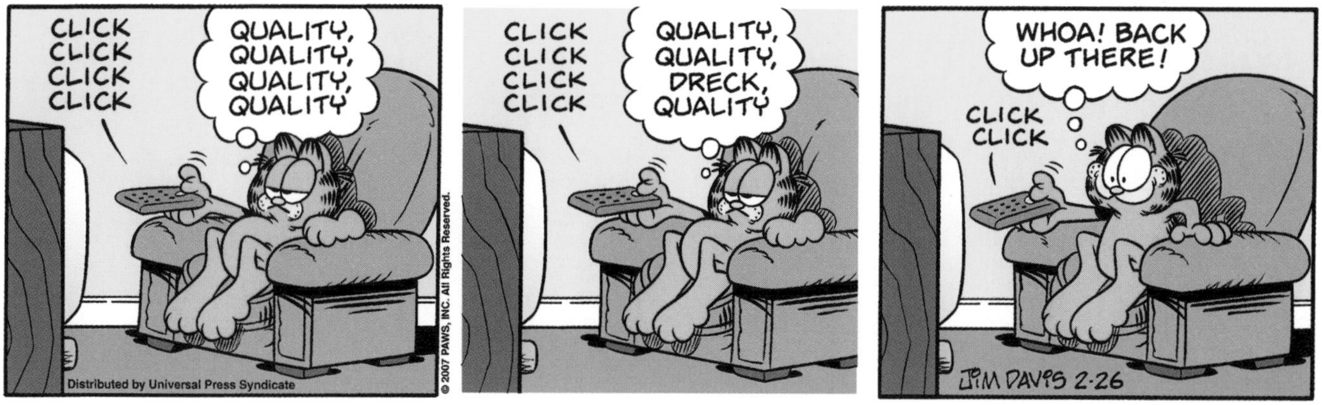
CLICK CLICK CLICK CLICK
QUALITY, QUALITY, QUALITY, QUALITY
CLICK CLICK CLICK CLICK
QUALITY, QUALITY, DRECK, QUALITY
WHOA! BACK UP THERE!
CLICK CLICK
JIM DAVIS 2-26
Distributed by Universal Press Syndicate
© 2007 PAWS, INC. All Rights Reserved.

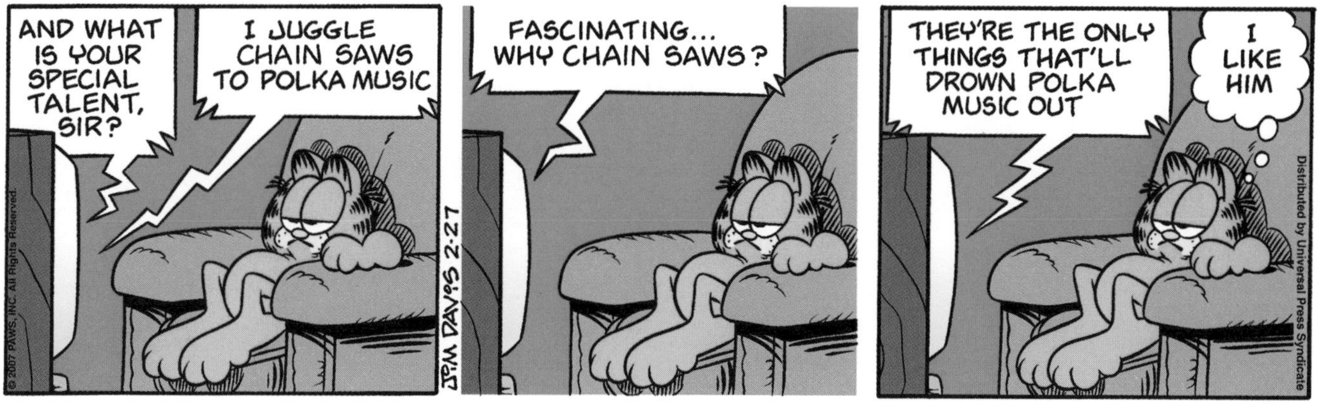
AND WHAT IS YOUR SPECIAL TALENT, SIR?
I JUGGLE CHAIN SAWS TO POLKA MUSIC
FASCINATING... WHY CHAIN SAWS?
THEY'RE THE ONLY THINGS THAT'LL DROWN POLKA MUSIC OUT
I LIKE HIM
JIM DAVIS 2-27
© 2007 PAWS, INC. All Rights Reserved.
Distributed by Universal Press Syndicate

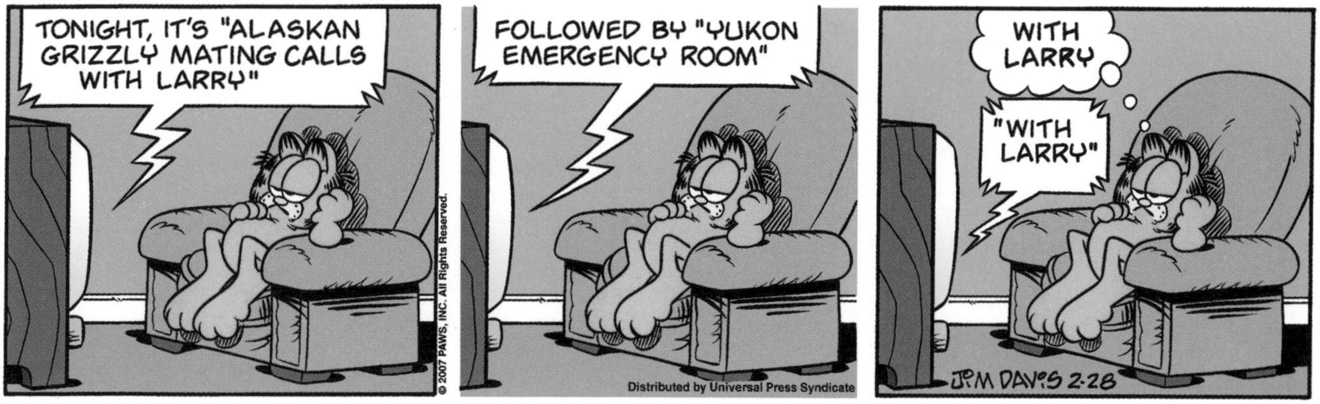
TONIGHT, IT'S "ALASKAN GRIZZLY MATING CALLS WITH LARRY"
FOLLOWED BY "YUKON EMERGENCY ROOM"
WITH LARRY
"WITH LARRY"
JIM DAVIS 2-28
© 2007 PAWS, INC. All Rights Reserved.
Distributed by Universal Press Syndicate

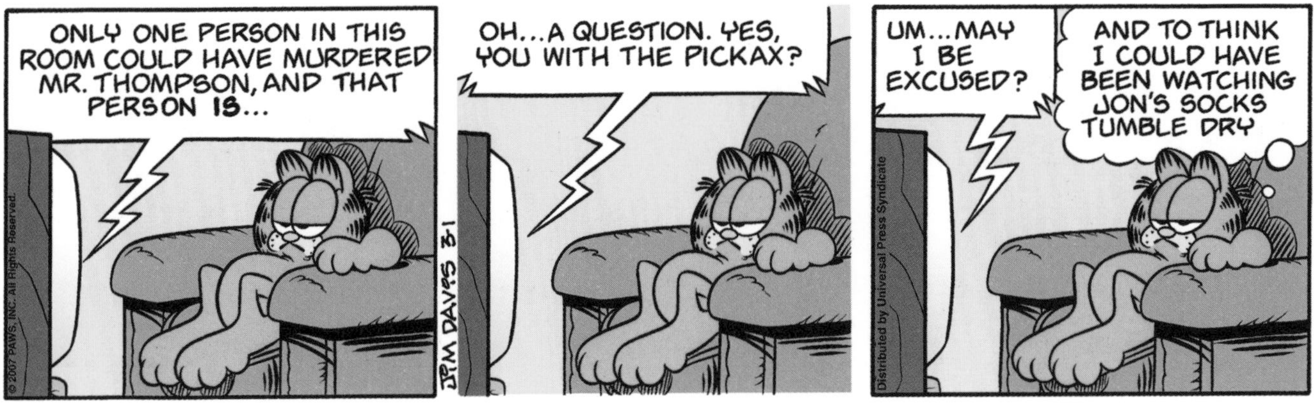
ONLY ONE PERSON IN THIS ROOM COULD HAVE MURDERED MR. THOMPSON, AND THAT PERSON IS...
OH...A QUESTION. YES, YOU WITH THE PICKAX?
UM...MAY I BE EXCUSED?
AND TO THINK I COULD HAVE BEEN WATCHING JON'S SOCKS TUMBLE DRY
© 2007 PAWS, INC. All Rights Reserved.
Distributed by Universal Press Syndicate

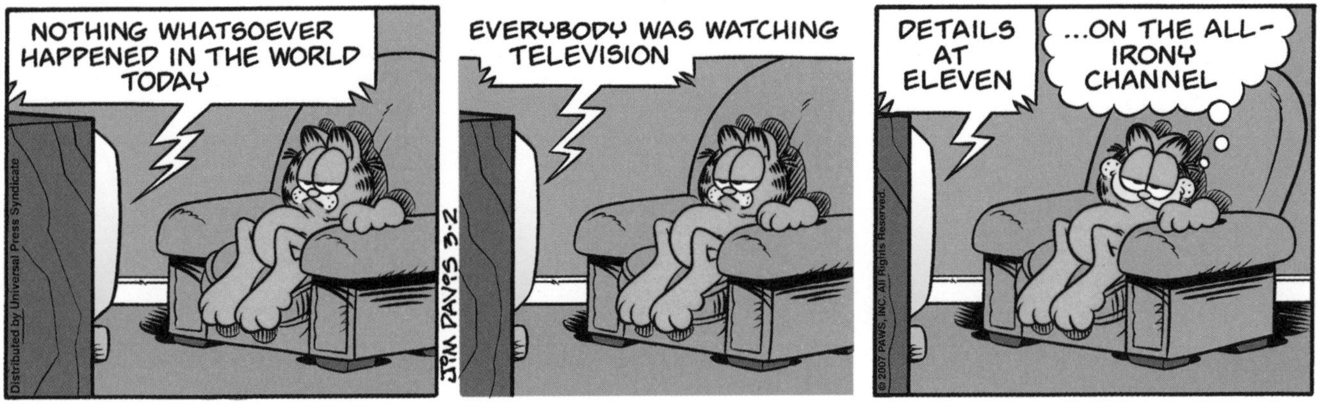
NOTHING WHATSOEVER HAPPENED IN THE WORLD TODAY
EVERYBODY WAS WATCHING TELEVISION
DETAILS AT ELEVEN
...ON THE ALL-IRONY CHANNEL
Distributed by Universal Press Syndicate
© 2007 PAWS, INC. All Rights Reserved.

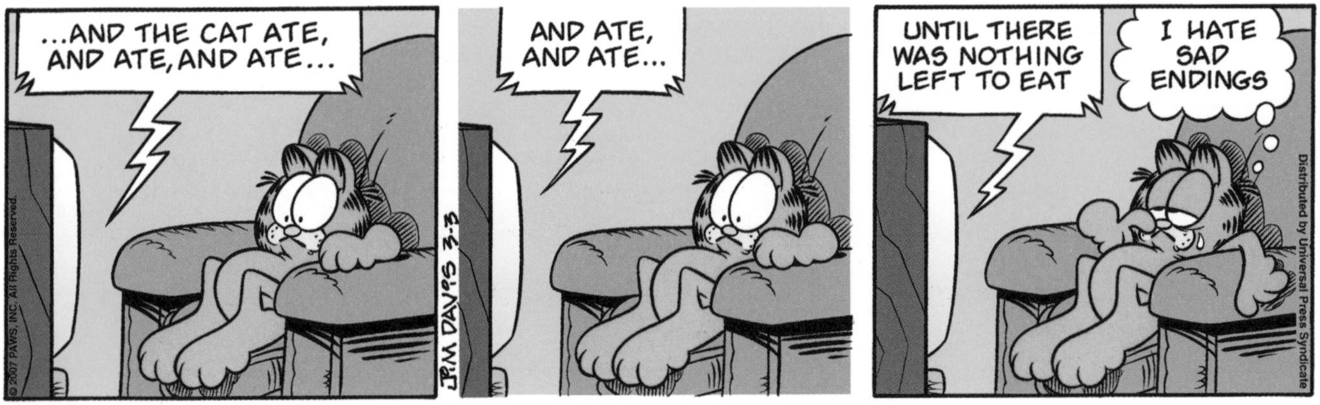
...AND THE CAT ATE, AND ATE, AND ATE...
AND ATE, AND ATE...
UNTIL THERE WAS NOTHING LEFT TO EAT
I HATE SAD ENDINGS
© 2007 PAWS, INC. All Rights Reserved.
Distributed by Universal Press Syndicate

GARFIELD FROM THE TRASH BIN

WARNING!

This page contains gross gags, crass cartoons, sick sketches, and truly tasteless trash that may cause brain damage, liver damage, foot fungus, painful earwax buildup, multiple personalities, bulging eyes, decreased night vision, dizziness, confusion, atypical facial pain, itching without a rash, itching with a rash, splotchy complexion, excessive thirst, insomnia, bloating, and really, really bad breath.

READ AT YOUR OWN RISK!

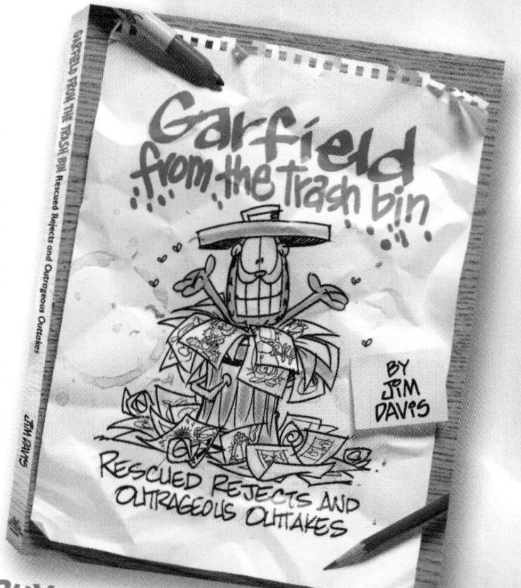
GARFIELD FROM THE TRASH BIN Rescued Rejects and Outrageous Outtakes
JIM DAVIS
Garfield from the Trash bin
BY JIM DAVIS
RESCUED REJECTS AND OUTRAGEOUS OUTTAKES

BUY THE BOOK FEBRUARY 2010!

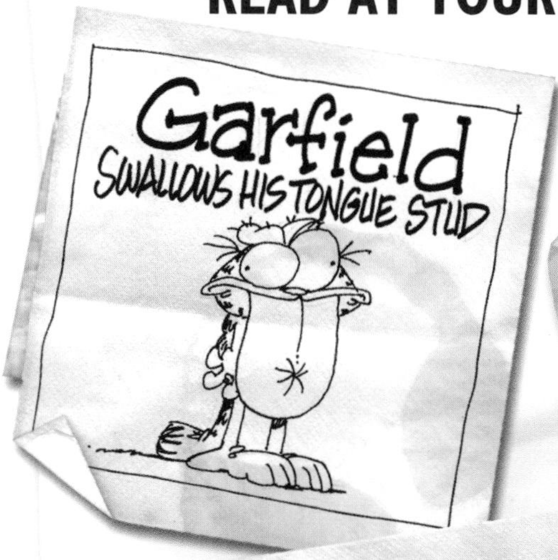
Garfield
SWALLOWS HIS TONGUE STUD

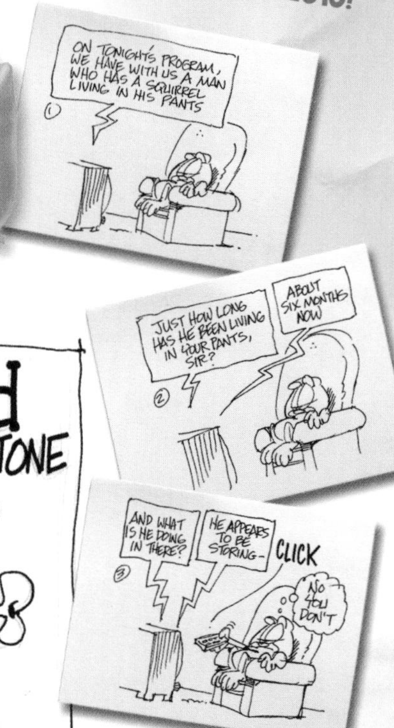
ON TONIGHT'S PROGRAM, WE HAVE WITH US A MAN WHO HAS A SQUIRREL LIVING IN HIS PANTS
JUST HOW LONG HAS HE BEEN LIVING IN YOUR PANTS, SIR?
ABOUT SIX MONTHS NOW
AND WHAT IS HE DOING IN THERE?
HE APPEARS TO BE STORING-
CLICK
NO YOU DON'T

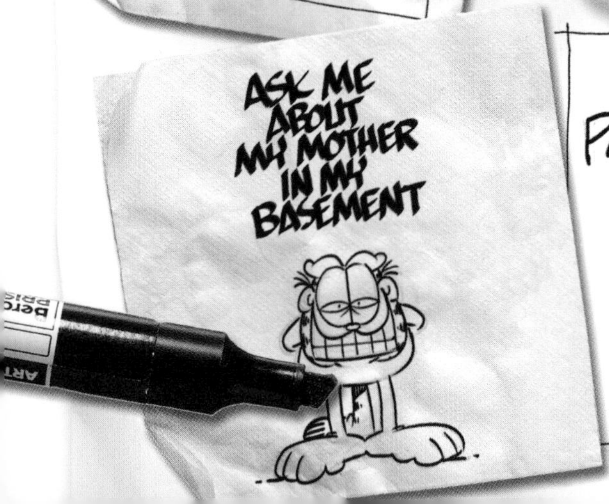
ASK ME ABOUT MY MOTHER IN MY BASEMENT

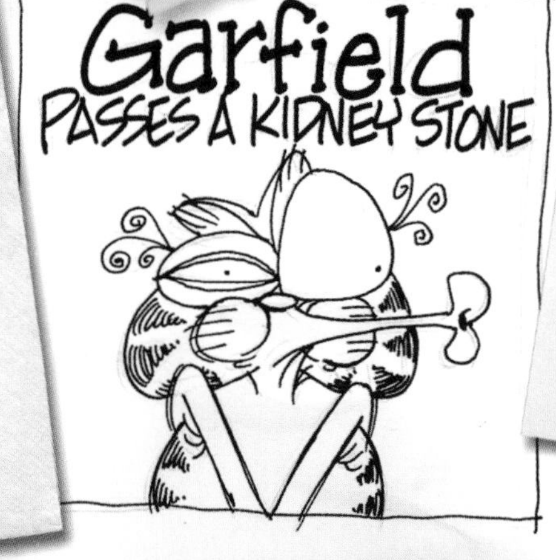
Garfield
PASSES A KIDNEY STONE

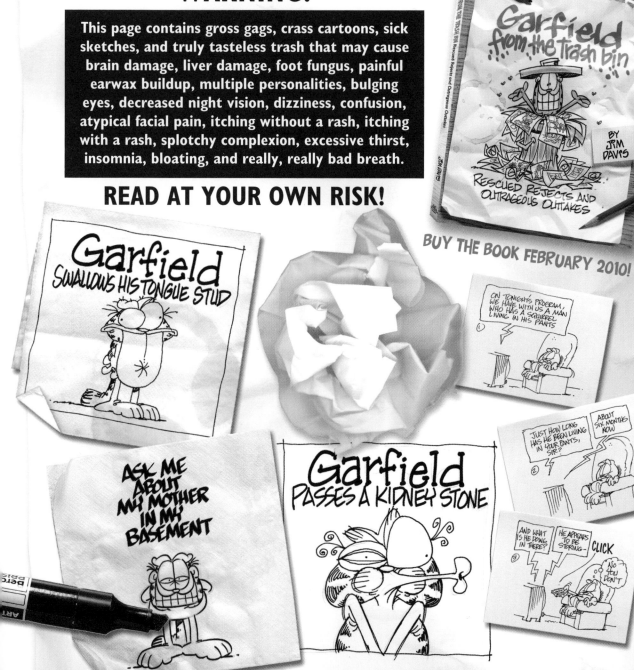

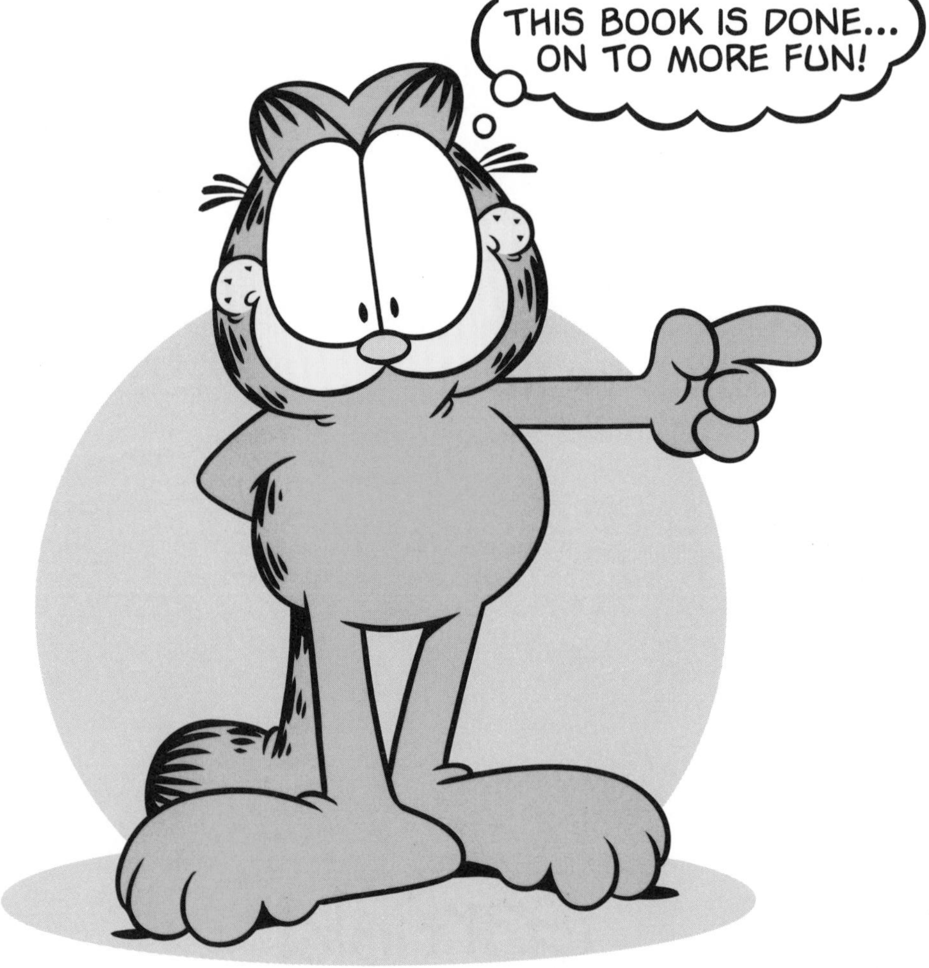
THIS BOOK IS DONE...
ON TO MORE FUN!

Garfield
POTBELLY OF GOLD

BY JIM DAVIS

ATTENTION PARTY ANIMALS!
Check out the TOP 50 REASONS TO PARTY! on page 144

Ballantine Books Trade Paperbacks • New York

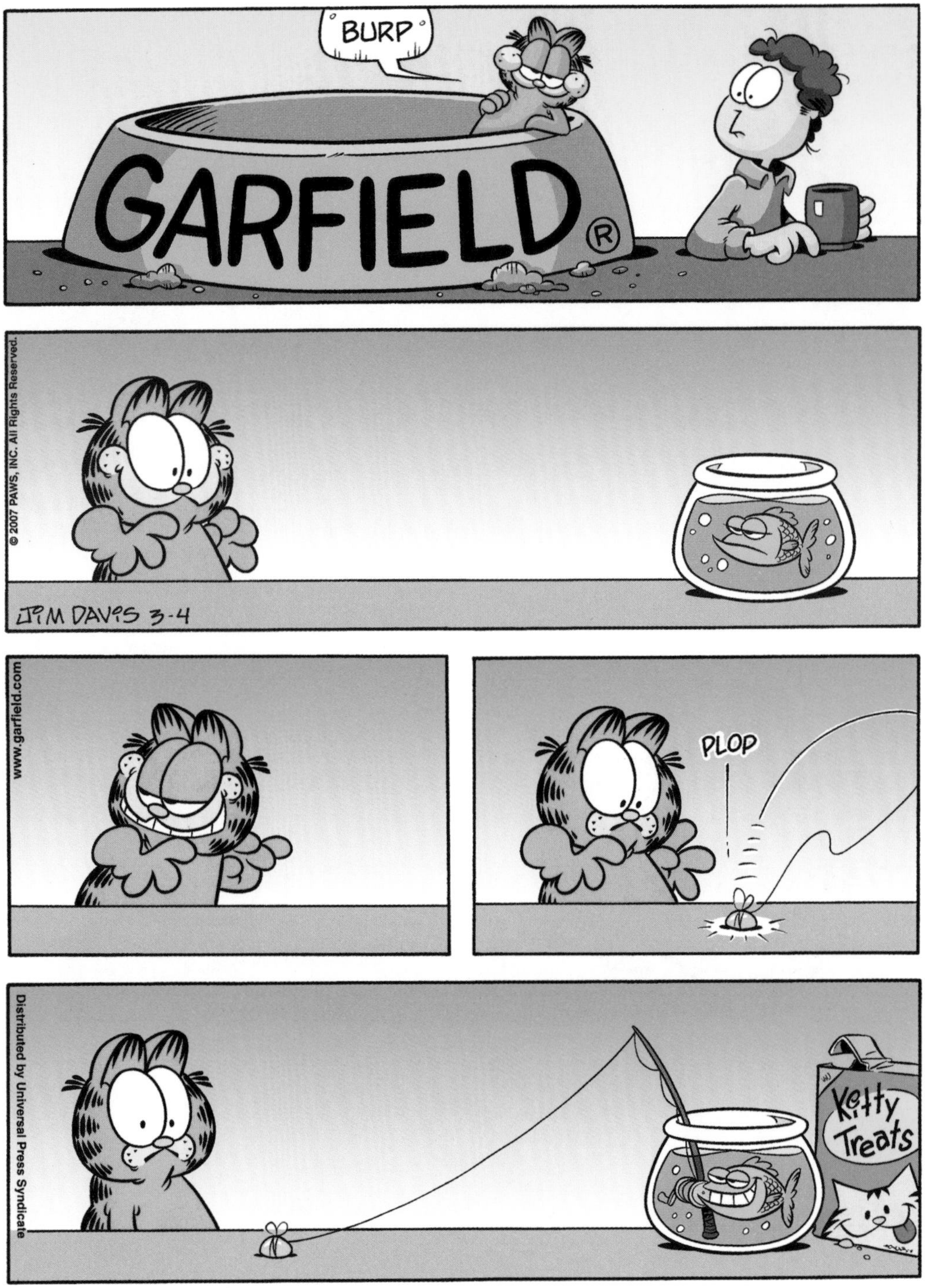
BURP
GARFIELD®
© 2007 PAWS, INC. All Rights Reserved.
JIM DAVIS 3-4
www.garfield.com
PLOP
Distributed by Universal Press Syndicate
Kitty Treats

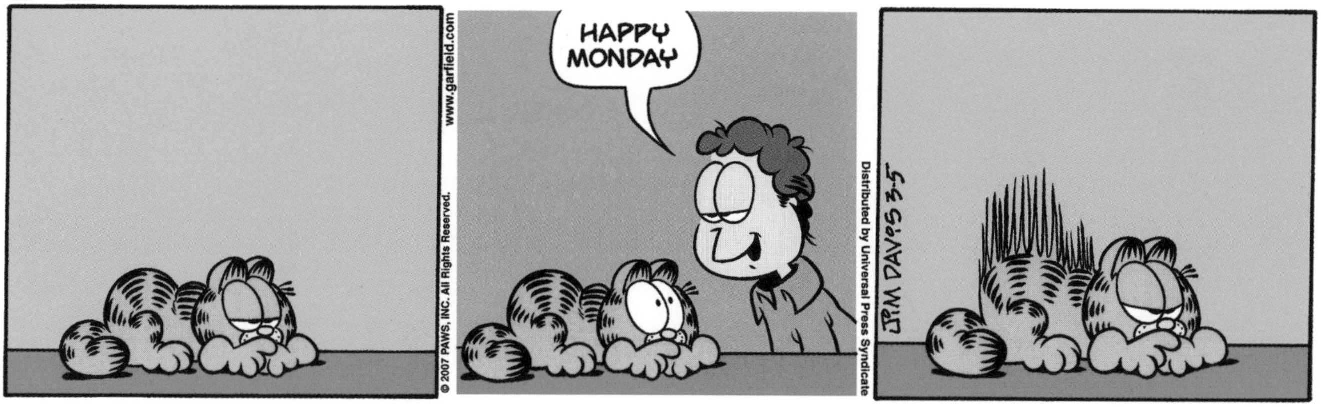
© 2007 PAWS, INC. All Rights Reserved.
www.garfield.com
HAPPY MONDAY
Distributed by Universal Press Syndicate
JIM DAVIS 3-5

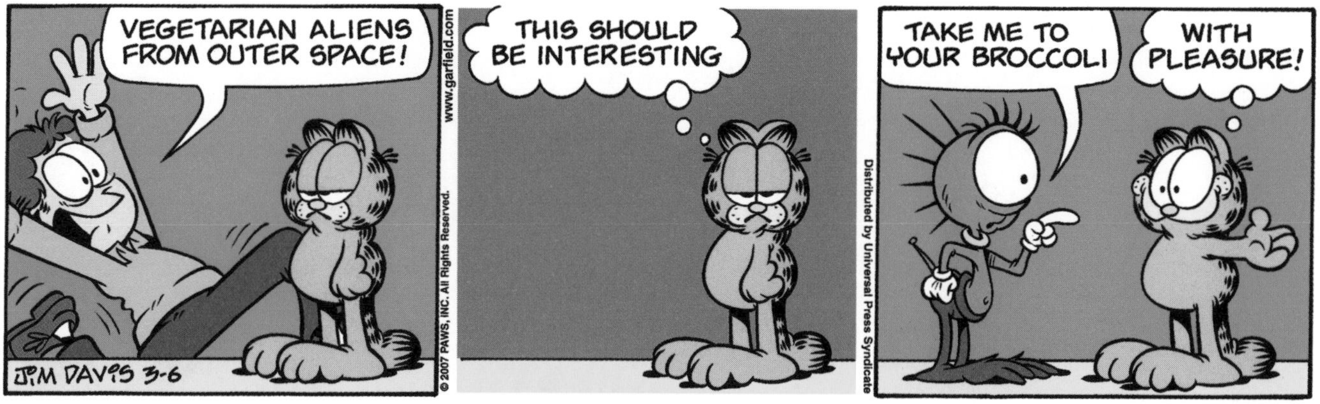
VEGETARIAN ALIENS FROM OUTER SPACE!
JIM DAVIS 3-6
© 2007 PAWS, INC. All Rights Reserved.
www.garfield.com
THIS SHOULD BE INTERESTING
Distributed by Universal Press Syndicate
TAKE ME TO YOUR BROCCOLI
WITH PLEASURE!

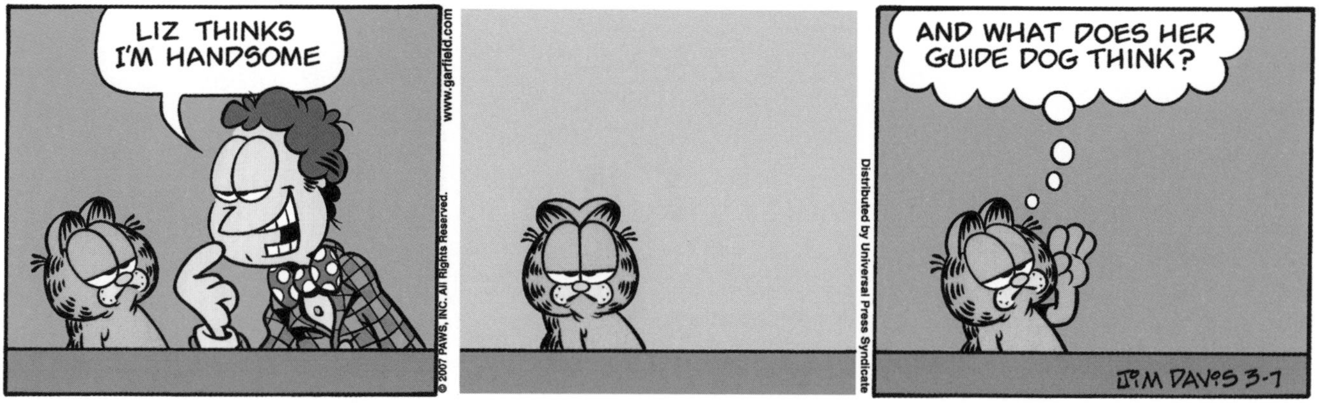
LIZ THINKS I'M HANDSOME
© 2007 PAWS, INC. All Rights Reserved.
www.garfield.com
Distributed by Universal Press Syndicate
AND WHAT DOES HER GUIDE DOG THINK?
JIM DAVIS 3-7

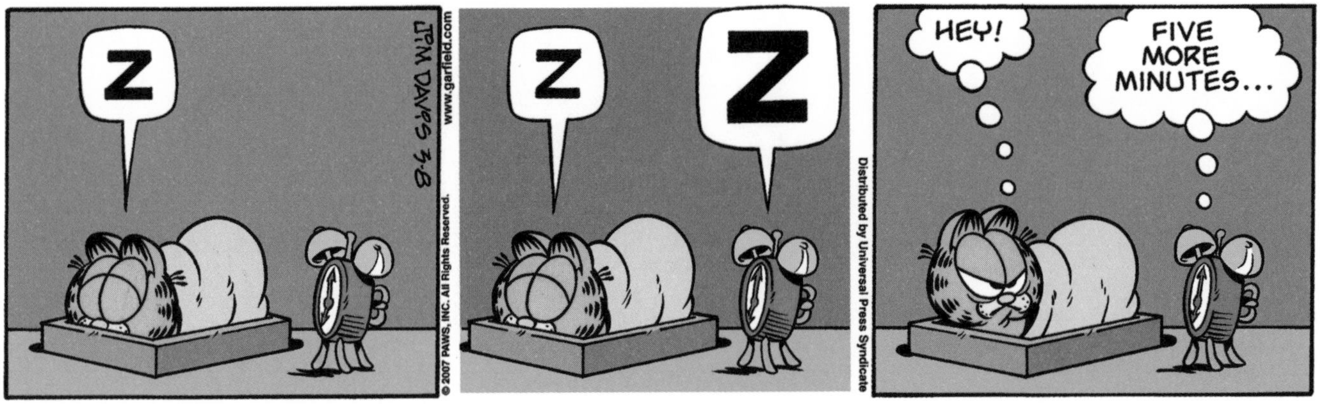
JIM DAVIS 3-8
www.garfield.com
© 2007 PAWS, INC. All Rights Reserved.
Distributed by Universal Press Syndicate
Z
Z
Z
HEY!
FIVE MORE MINUTES...

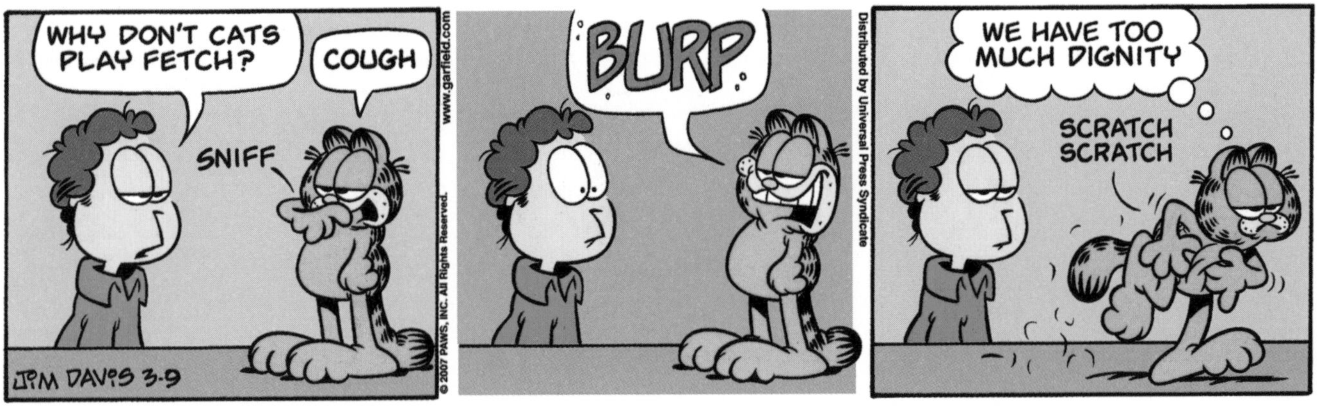
WHY DON'T CATS PLAY FETCH?
COUGH
SNIFF
JIM DAVIS 3-9
www.garfield.com
© 2007 PAWS, INC. All Rights Reserved.
BURP
Distributed by Universal Press Syndicate
WE HAVE TOO MUCH DIGNITY
SCRATCH SCRATCH

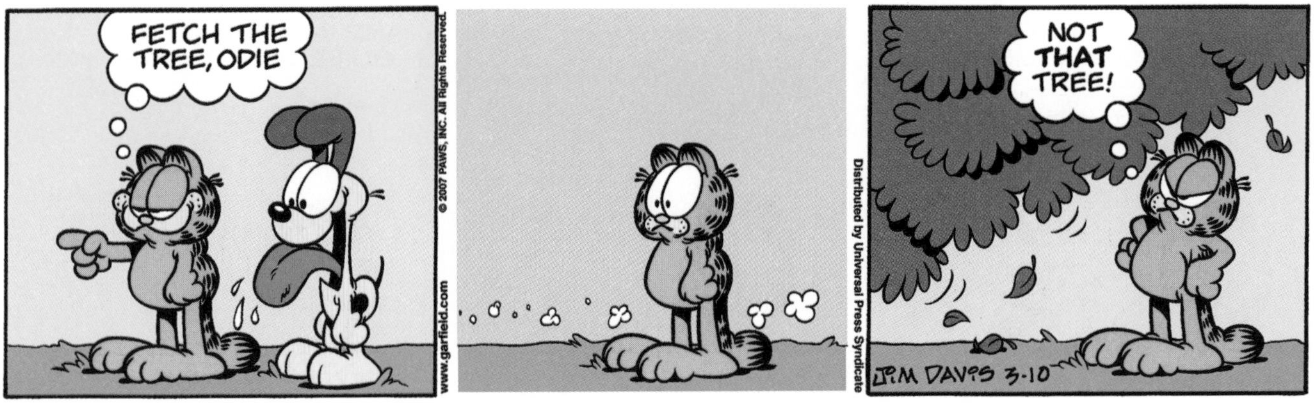
FETCH THE TREE, ODIE
© 2007 PAWS, INC. All Rights Reserved.
www.garfield.com
Distributed by Universal Press Syndicate
NOT THAT TREE!
JIM DAVIS 3-10

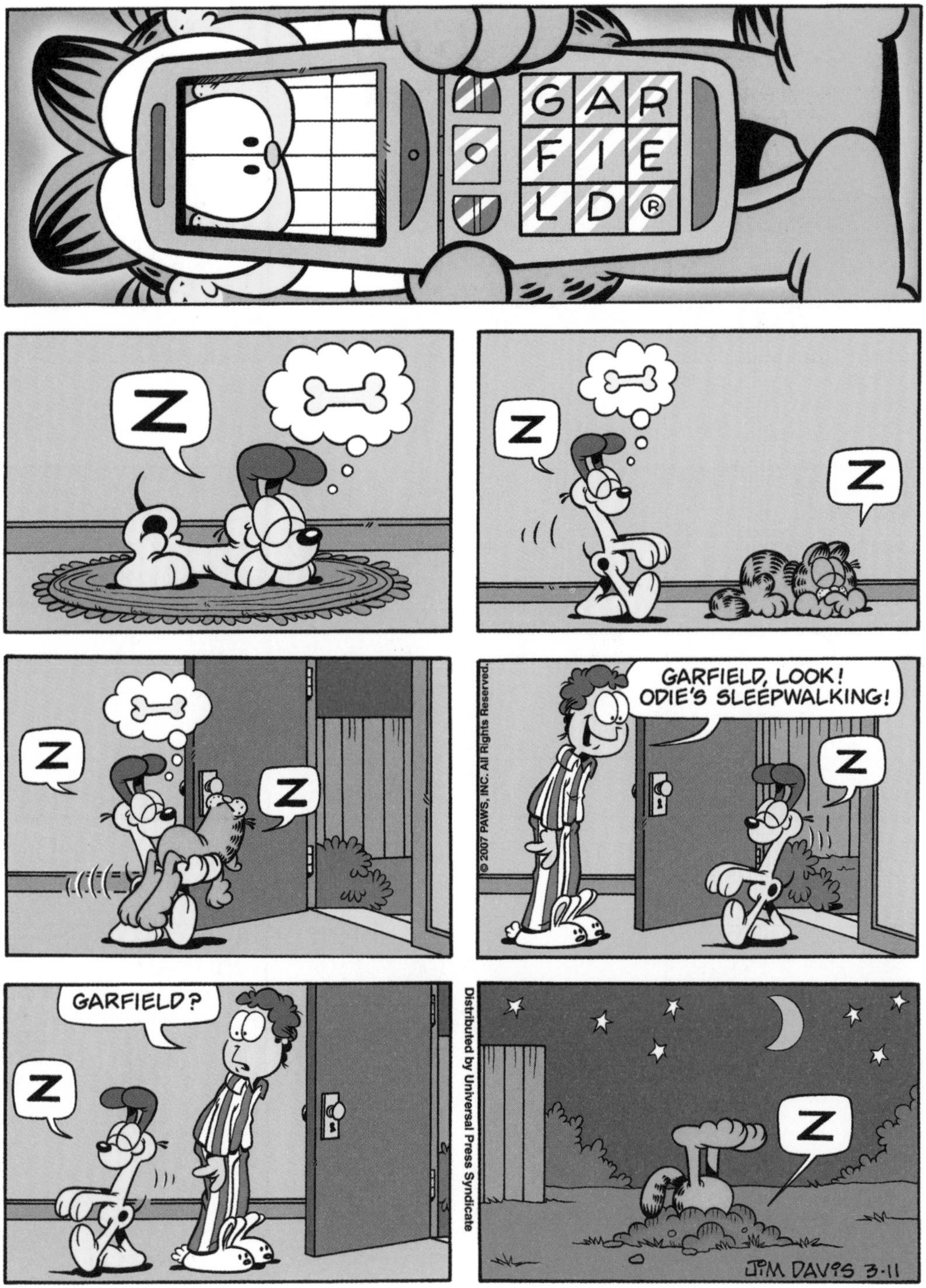
GAR
FIE
LD®
Z
Z
Z
Z
Z
© 2007 PAWS, INC. All Rights Reserved.
GARFIELD, LOOK! ODIE'S SLEEPWALKING!
Z
GARFIELD?
Z
Distributed by Universal Press Syndicate
Z
JIM DAVIS 3-11

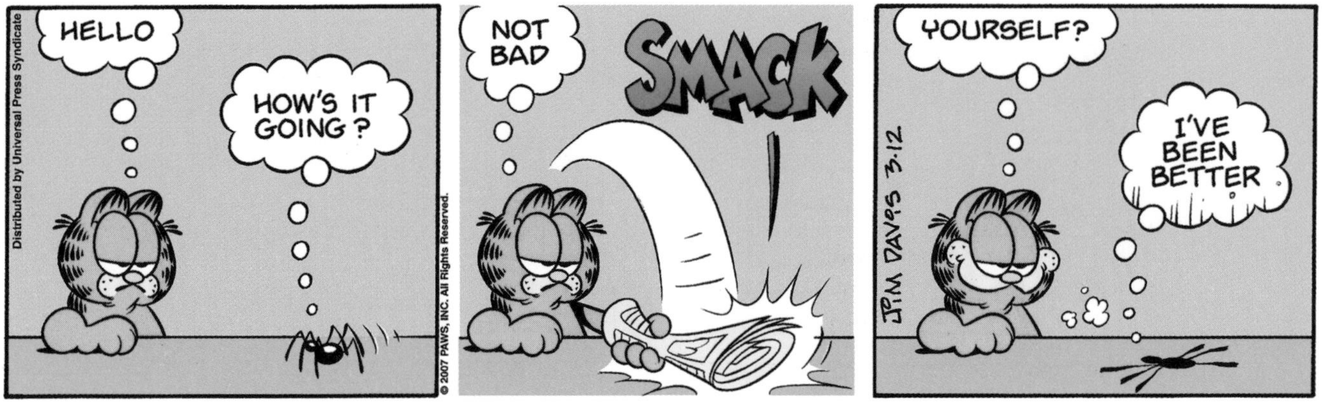
HELLO
HOW'S IT GOING?
NOT BAD
SMACK
YOURSELF?
I'VE BEEN BETTER
JIM DAVIS 3.12
Distributed by Universal Press Syndicate
© 2007 PAWS, INC. All Rights Reserved.

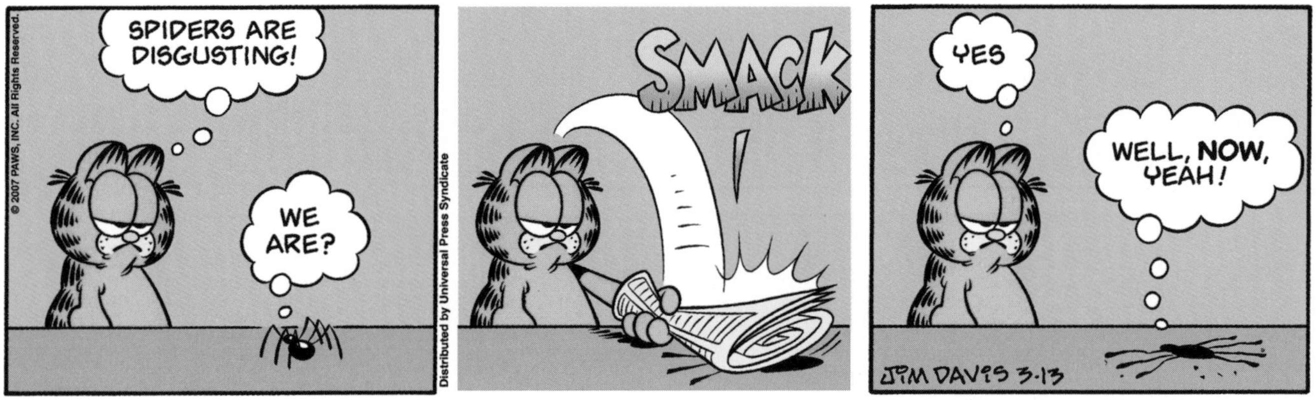
SPIDERS ARE DISGUSTING!
WE ARE?
SMACK
YES
WELL, NOW, YEAH!
JIM DAVIS 3-13
© 2007 PAWS, INC. All Rights Reserved.
Distributed by Universal Press Syndicate

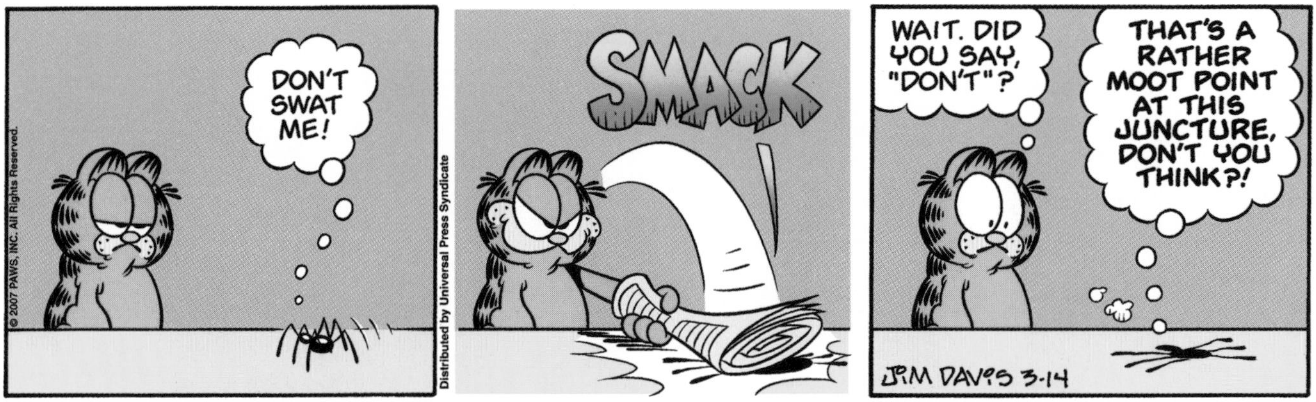
DON'T SWAT ME!
SMACK
WAIT. DID YOU SAY, "DON'T"?
THAT'S A RATHER MOOT POINT AT THIS JUNCTURE, DON'T YOU THINK?!
JIM DAVIS 3-14
© 2007 PAWS, INC. All Rights Reserved.
Distributed by Universal Press Syndicate

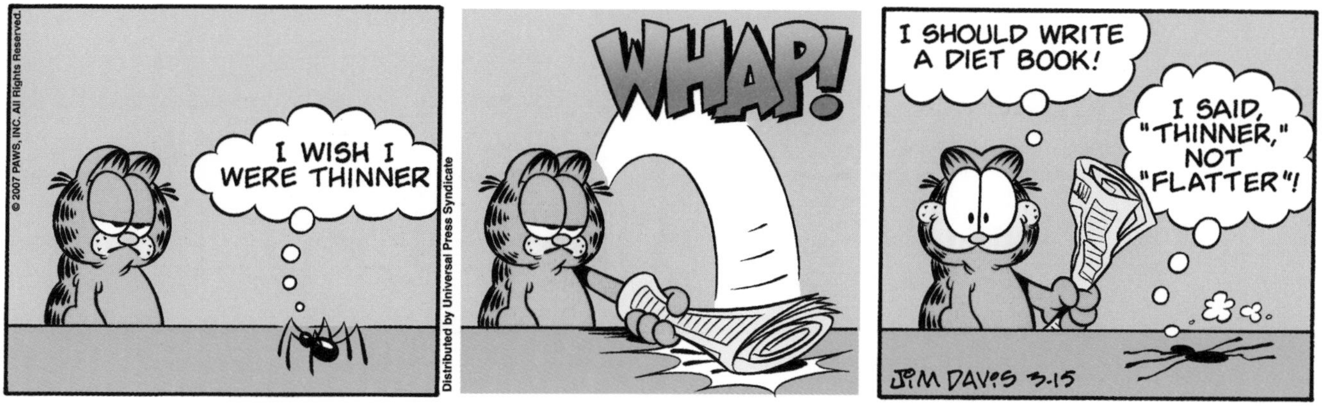
© 2007 PAWS, INC. All Rights Reserved.
I WISH I WERE THINNER
Distributed by Universal Press Syndicate
WHAP!
I SHOULD WRITE A DIET BOOK!
I SAID, "THINNER," NOT "FLATTER"!
JIM DAVIS 3-15

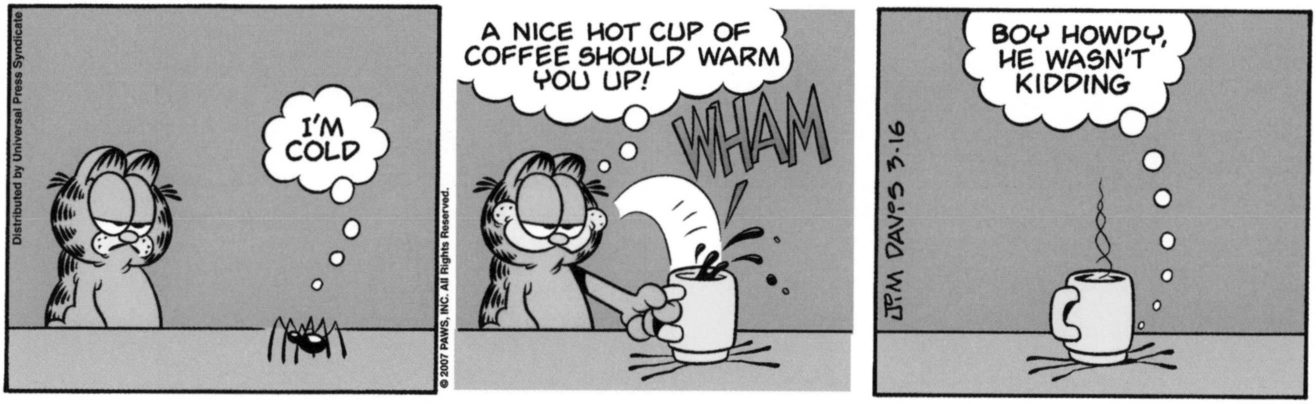
Distributed by Universal Press Syndicate
I'M COLD
© 2007 PAWS, INC. All Rights Reserved.
A NICE HOT CUP OF COFFEE SHOULD WARM YOU UP!
WHAM
BOY HOWDY, HE WASN'T KIDDING
JIM DAVIS 3-16

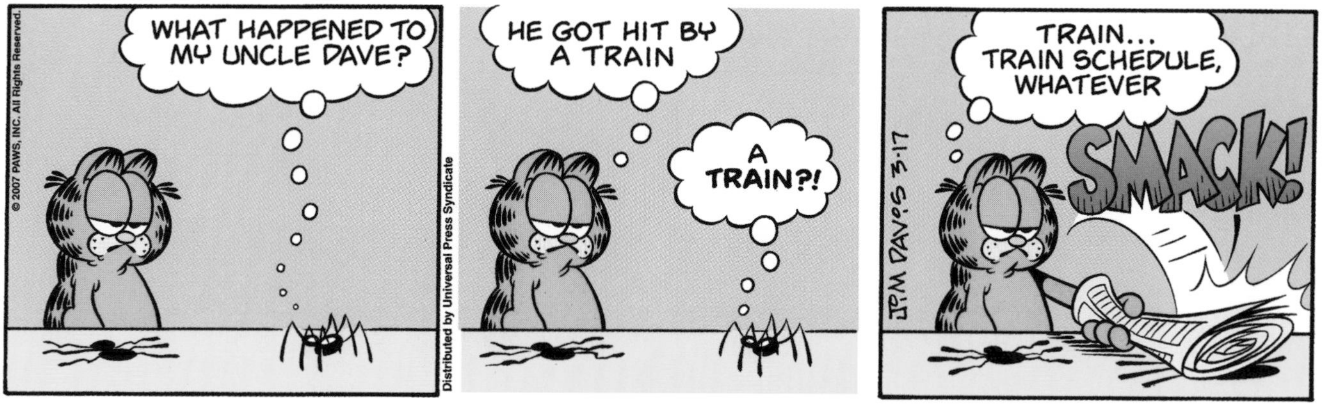
© 2007 PAWS, INC. All Rights Reserved.
WHAT HAPPENED TO MY UNCLE DAVE?
Distributed by Universal Press Syndicate
HE GOT HIT BY A TRAIN
A TRAIN?!
TRAIN... TRAIN SCHEDULE, WHATEVER
SMACK!
JIM DAVIS 3-17

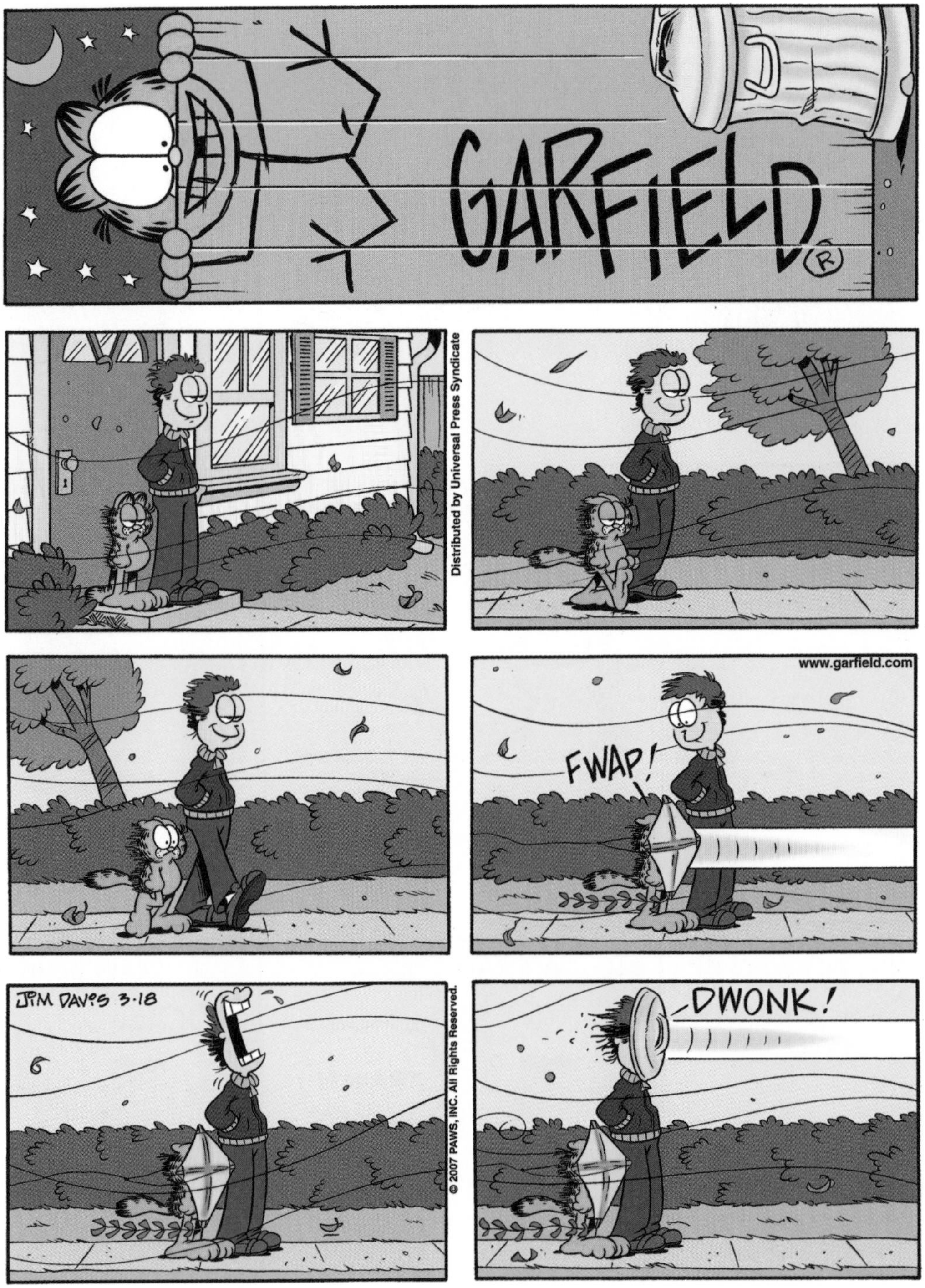
GARFIELD®
Distributed by Universal Press Syndicate
www.garfield.com
FWAP!
JIM DAVIS 3-18
© 2007 PAWS, INC. All Rights Reserved.
DWONK!

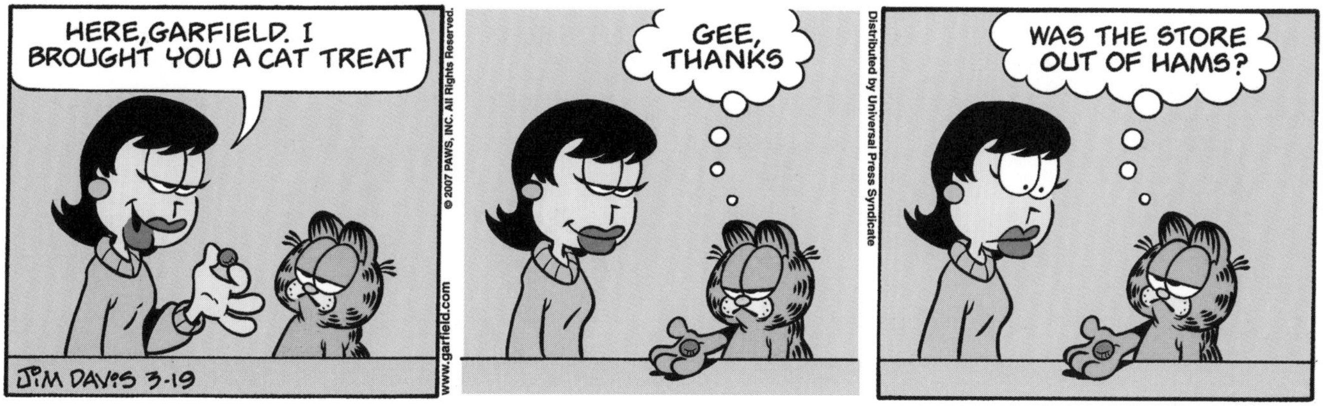
HERE, GARFIELD. I BROUGHT YOU A CAT TREAT
JIM DAVIS 3-19
© 2007 PAWS, INC. All Rights Reserved.
www.garfield.com
GEE, THANKS
Distributed by Universal Press Syndicate
WAS THE STORE OUT OF HAMS?

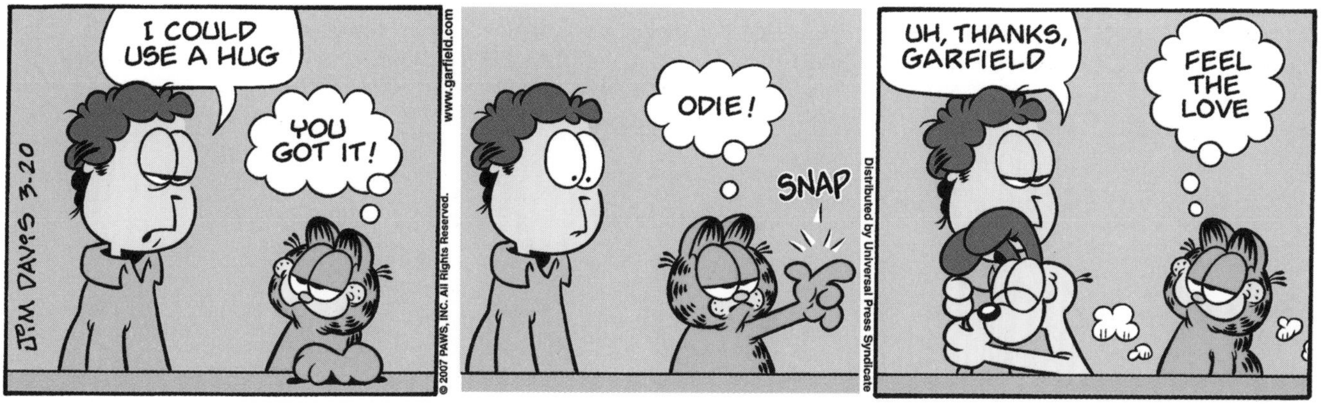
I COULD USE A HUG
YOU GOT IT!
JIM DAVIS 3-20
www.garfield.com
© 2007 PAWS, INC. All Rights Reserved.
ODIE!
SNAP
Distributed by Universal Press Syndicate
UH, THANKS, GARFIELD
FEEL THE LOVE

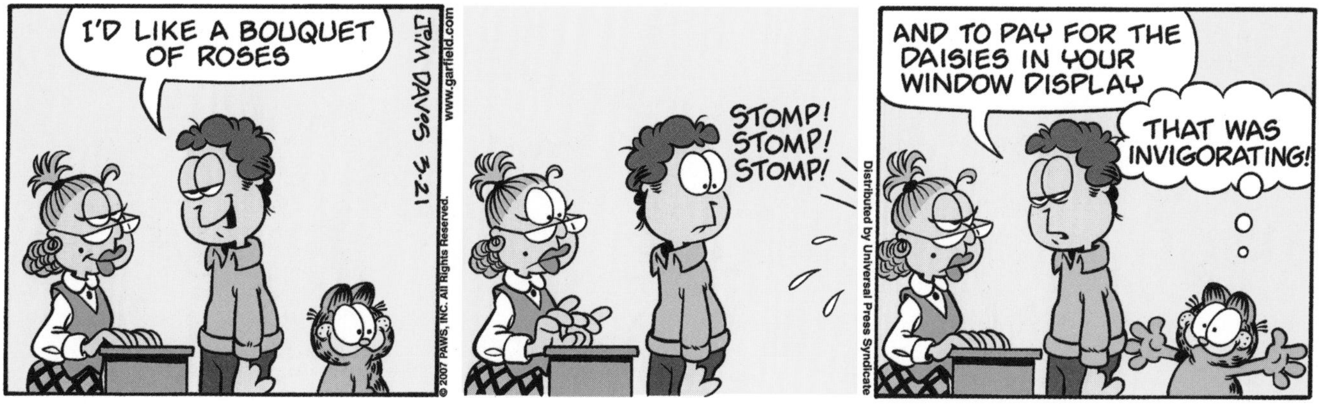
I'D LIKE A BOUQUET OF ROSES
JIM DAVIS 3-21
www.garfield.com
© 2007 PAWS, INC. All Rights Reserved.
STOMP! STOMP! STOMP!
Distributed by Universal Press Syndicate
AND TO PAY FOR THE DAISIES IN YOUR WINDOW DISPLAY
THAT WAS INVIGORATING!

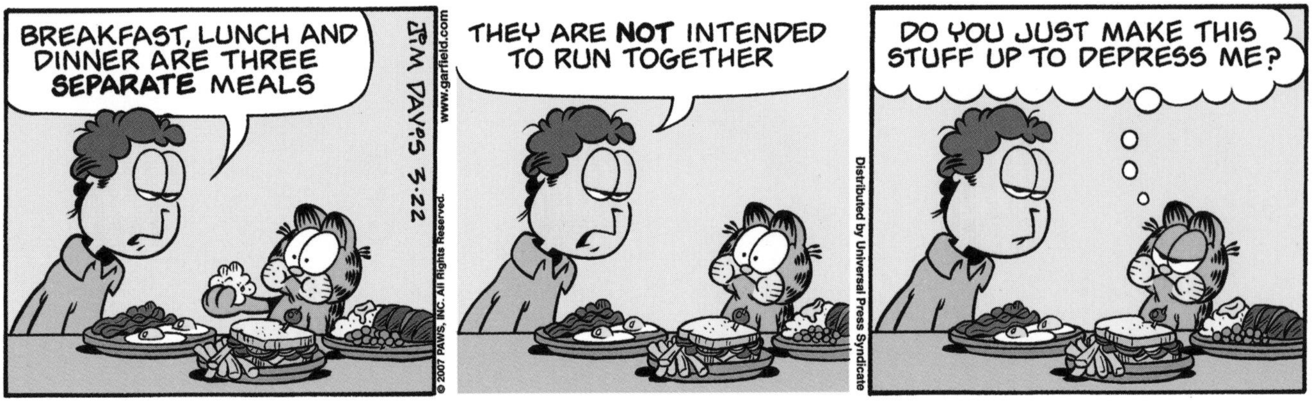
BREAKFAST, LUNCH AND DINNER ARE THREE **SEPARATE** MEALS
JIM DAVIS 3-22
www.garfield.com
© 2007 PAWS, INC. All Rights Reserved.
THEY ARE **NOT** INTENDED TO RUN TOGETHER
Distributed by Universal Press Syndicate
DO YOU JUST MAKE THIS STUFF UP TO DEPRESS ME?

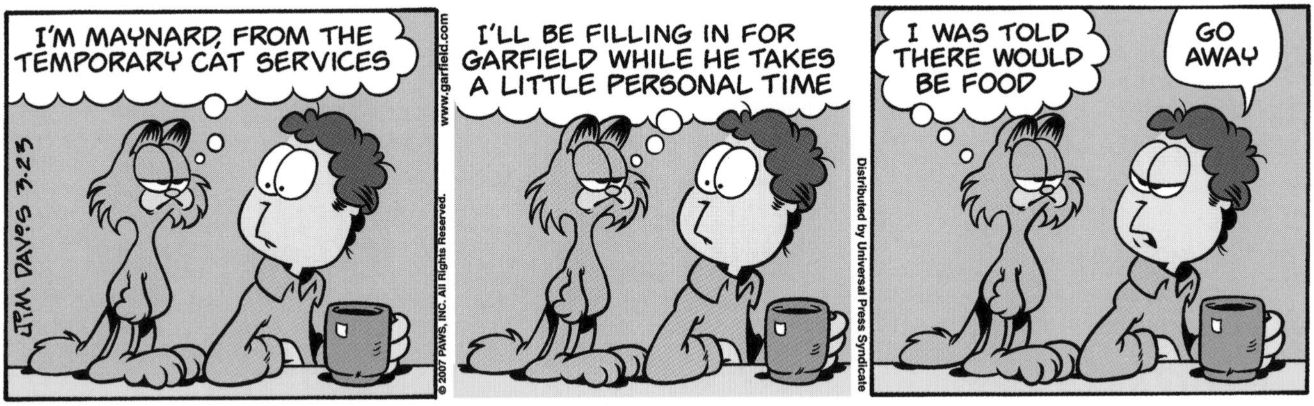
I'M MAYNARD, FROM THE TEMPORARY CAT SERVICES
JIM DAVIS 3-23
www.garfield.com
© 2007 PAWS, INC. All Rights Reserved.
I'LL BE FILLING IN FOR GARFIELD WHILE HE TAKES A LITTLE PERSONAL TIME
Distributed by Universal Press Syndicate
I WAS TOLD THERE WOULD BE FOOD
GO AWAY

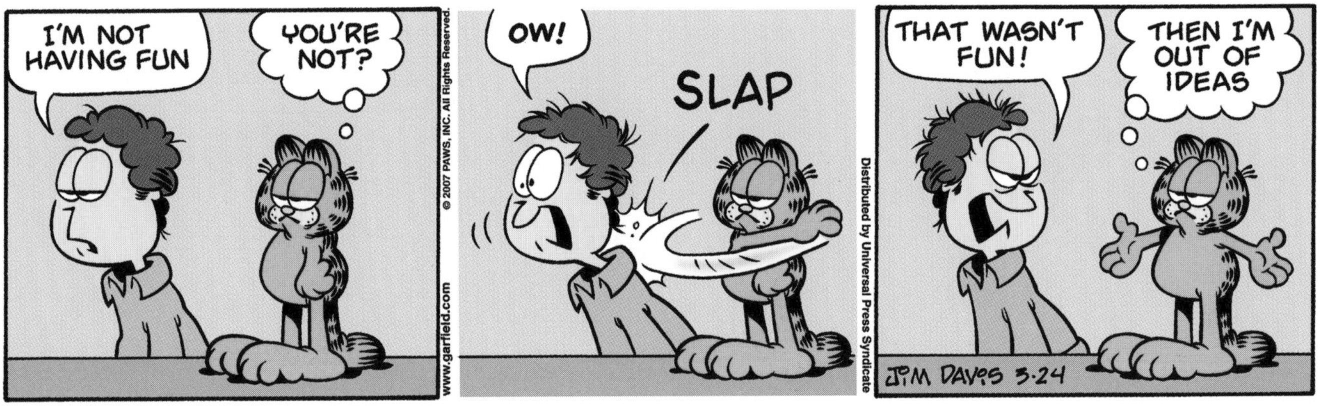
I'M NOT HAVING FUN
YOU'RE NOT?
© 2007 PAWS, INC. All Rights Reserved.
www.garfield.com
OW!
SLAP
Distributed by Universal Press Syndicate
THAT WASN'T FUN!
THEN I'M OUT OF IDEAS
JIM DAVIS 3-24

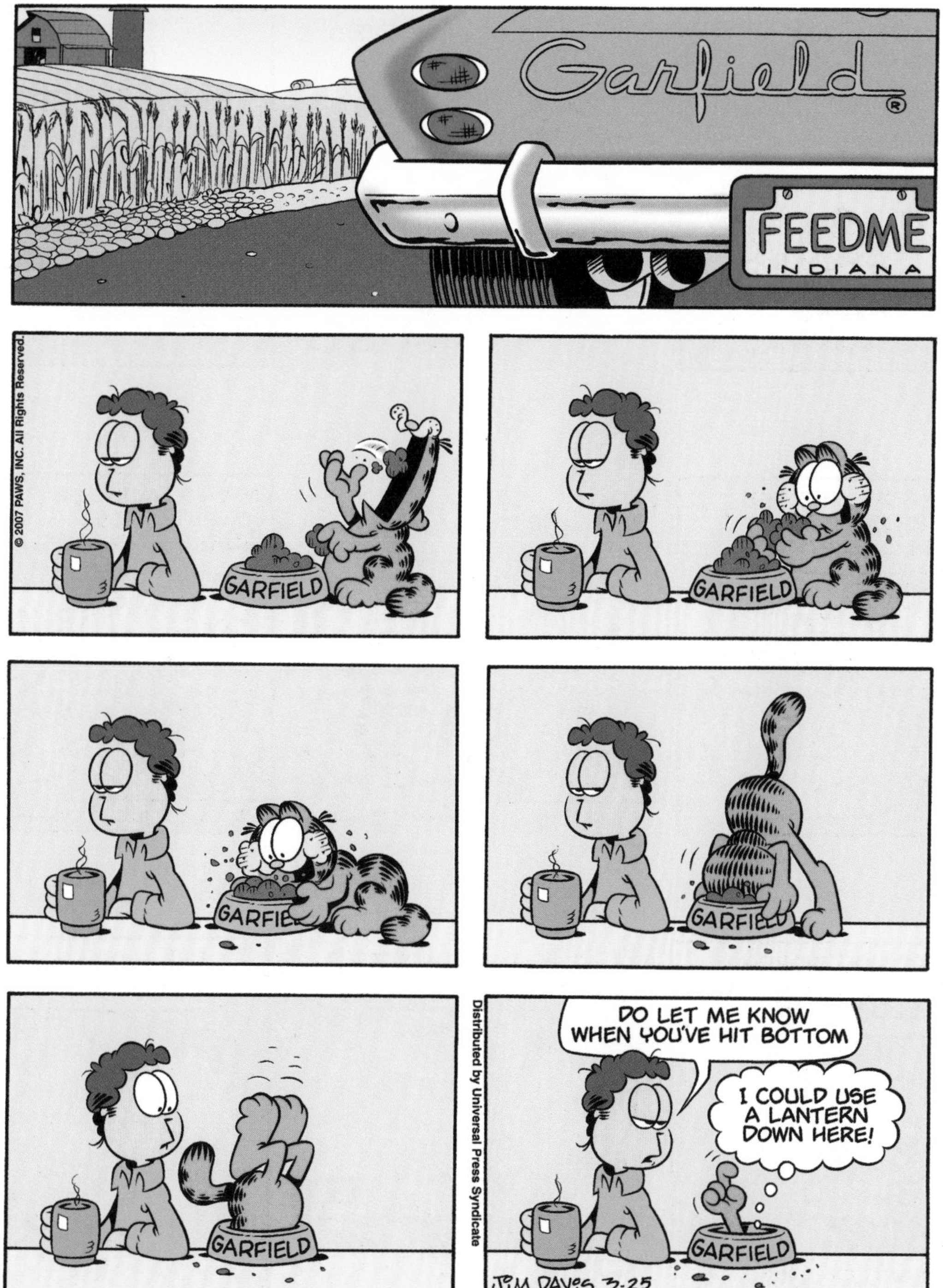
Garfield®
FEEDME
INDIANA
© 2007 PAWS, INC. All Rights Reserved.
GARFIELD
GARFIELD
GARFIE
GARFIE
Distributed by Universal Press Syndicate
GARFIELD
DO LET ME KNOW WHEN YOU'VE HIT BOTTOM
I COULD USE A LANTERN DOWN HERE!
GARFIELD
JIM DAVIS 3-25

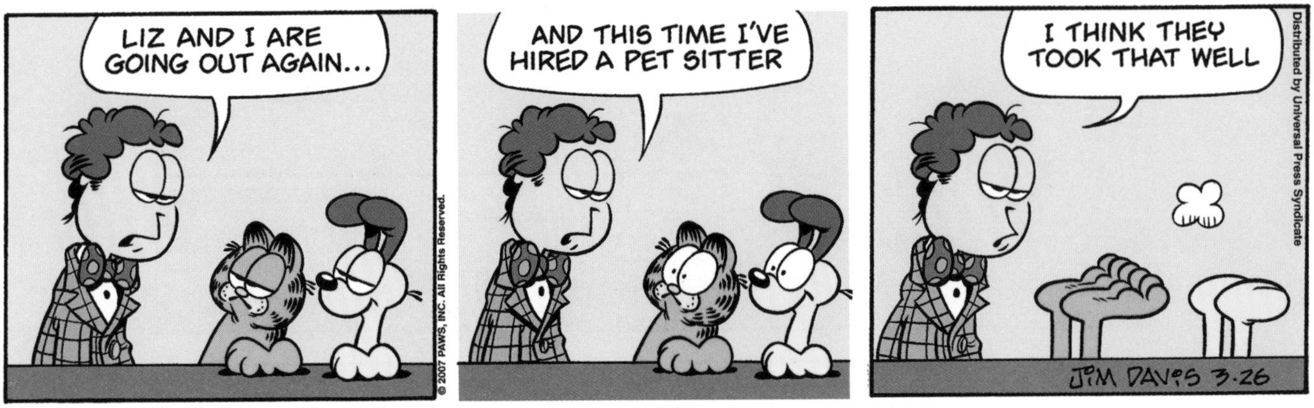
LIZ AND I ARE GOING OUT AGAIN...
© 2007 PAWS, INC. All Rights Reserved.
AND THIS TIME I'VE HIRED A PET SITTER
I THINK THEY TOOK THAT WELL
Distributed by Universal Press Syndicate
JIM DAVIS 3-26

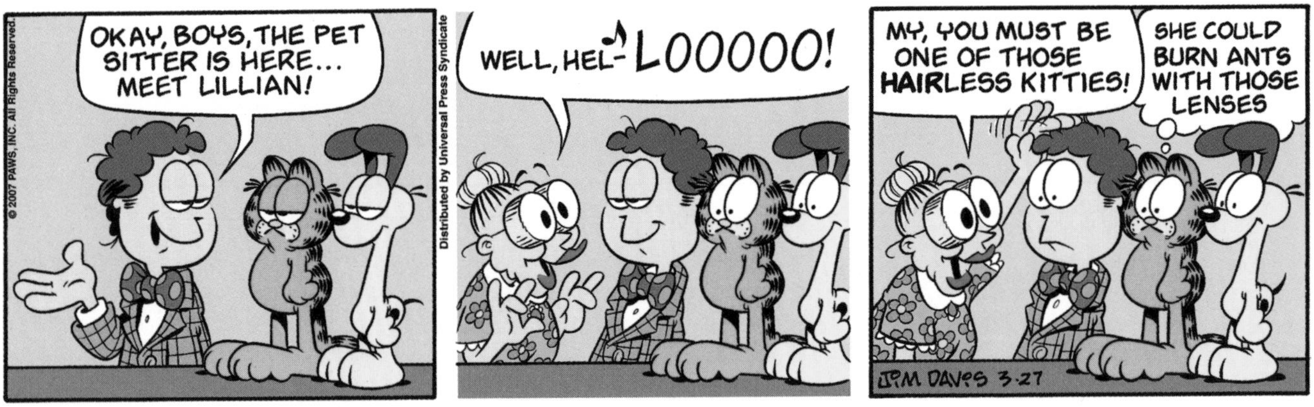
© 2007 PAWS, INC. All Rights Reserved.
OKAY, BOYS, THE PET SITTER IS HERE... MEET LILLIAN!
Distributed by Universal Press Syndicate
WELL, HEL-LOOOOO!
MY, YOU MUST BE ONE OF THOSE HAIRLESS KITTIES!
SHE COULD BURN ANTS WITH THOSE LENSES
JIM DAVIS 3-27

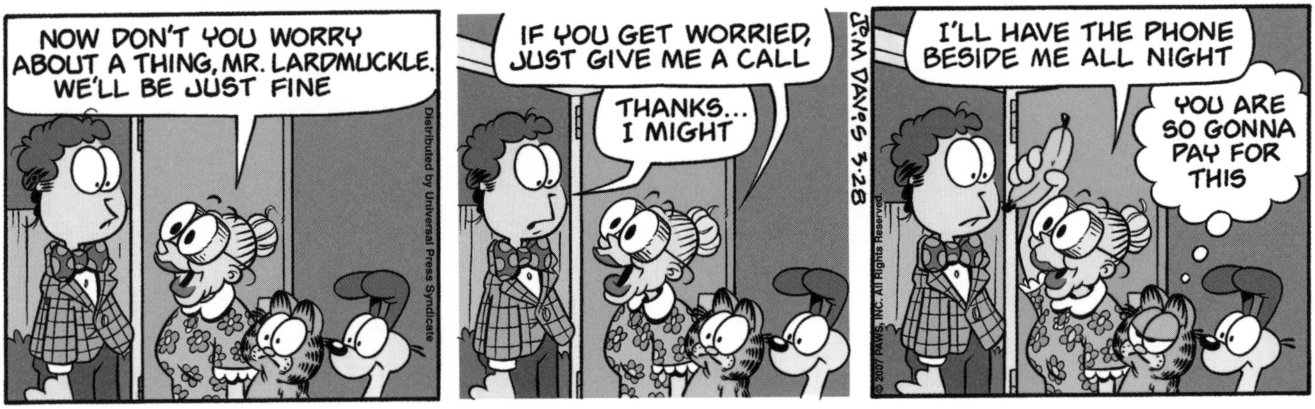
NOW DON'T YOU WORRY ABOUT A THING, MR. LARDMUCKLE. WE'LL BE JUST FINE
Distributed by Universal Press Syndicate
IF YOU GET WORRIED, JUST GIVE ME A CALL
THANKS... I MIGHT
JIM DAVIS 3-28
© 2007 PAWS, INC. All Rights Reserved.
I'LL HAVE THE PHONE BESIDE ME ALL NIGHT
YOU ARE SO GONNA PAY FOR THIS

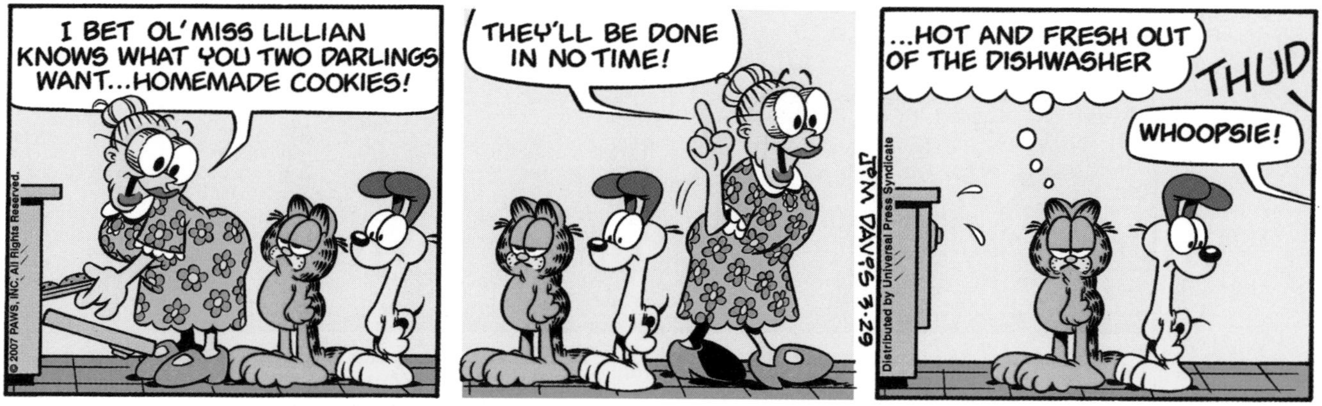
I BET OL' MISS LILLIAN KNOWS WHAT YOU TWO DARLINGS WANT...HOMEMADE COOKIES!
© 2007 PAWS, INC. All Rights Reserved.
THEY'LL BE DONE IN NO TIME!
JIM DAVIS 3.29
Distributed by Universal Press Syndicate
...HOT AND FRESH OUT OF THE DISHWASHER
THUD
WHOOPSIE!

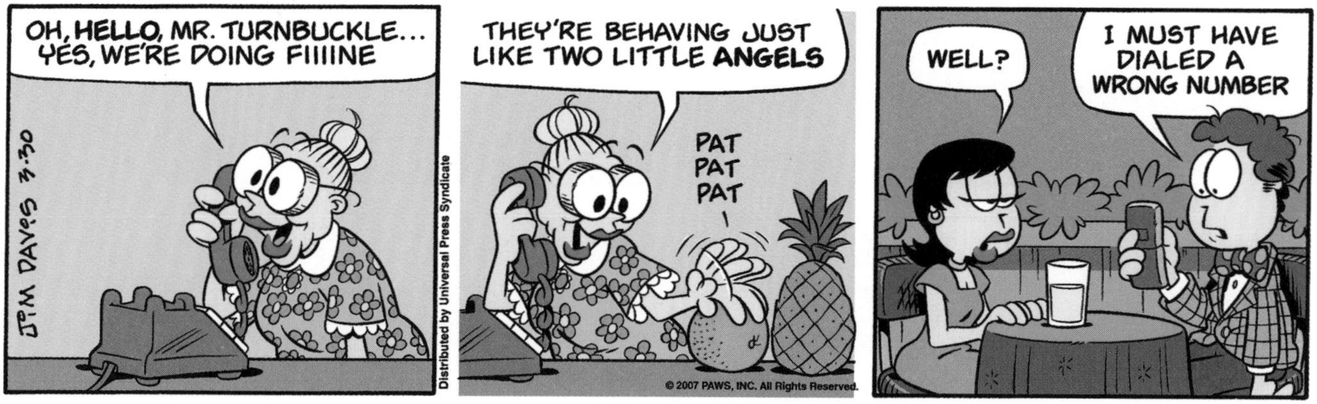
OH, HELLO, MR. TURNBUCKLE... YES, WE'RE DOING FIIIINE
JIM DAVIS 3.30
Distributed by Universal Press Syndicate
THEY'RE BEHAVING JUST LIKE TWO LITTLE ANGELS
PAT PAT PAT
© 2007 PAWS, INC. All Rights Reserved.
WELL?
I MUST HAVE DIALED A WRONG NUMBER

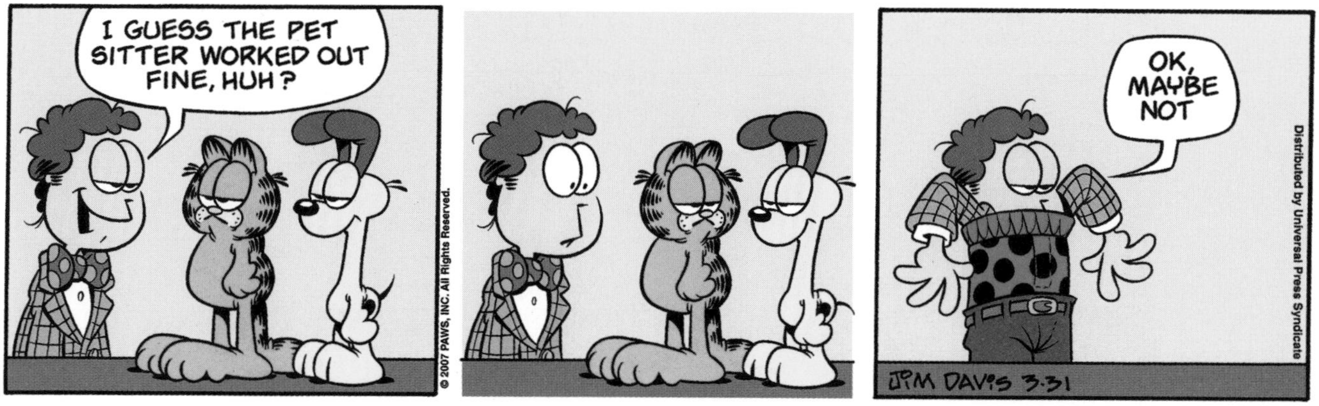
I GUESS THE PET SITTER WORKED OUT FINE, HUH?
© 2007 PAWS, INC. All Rights Reserved.
OK, MAYBE NOT
JIM DAVIS 3.31
Distributed by Universal Press Syndicate

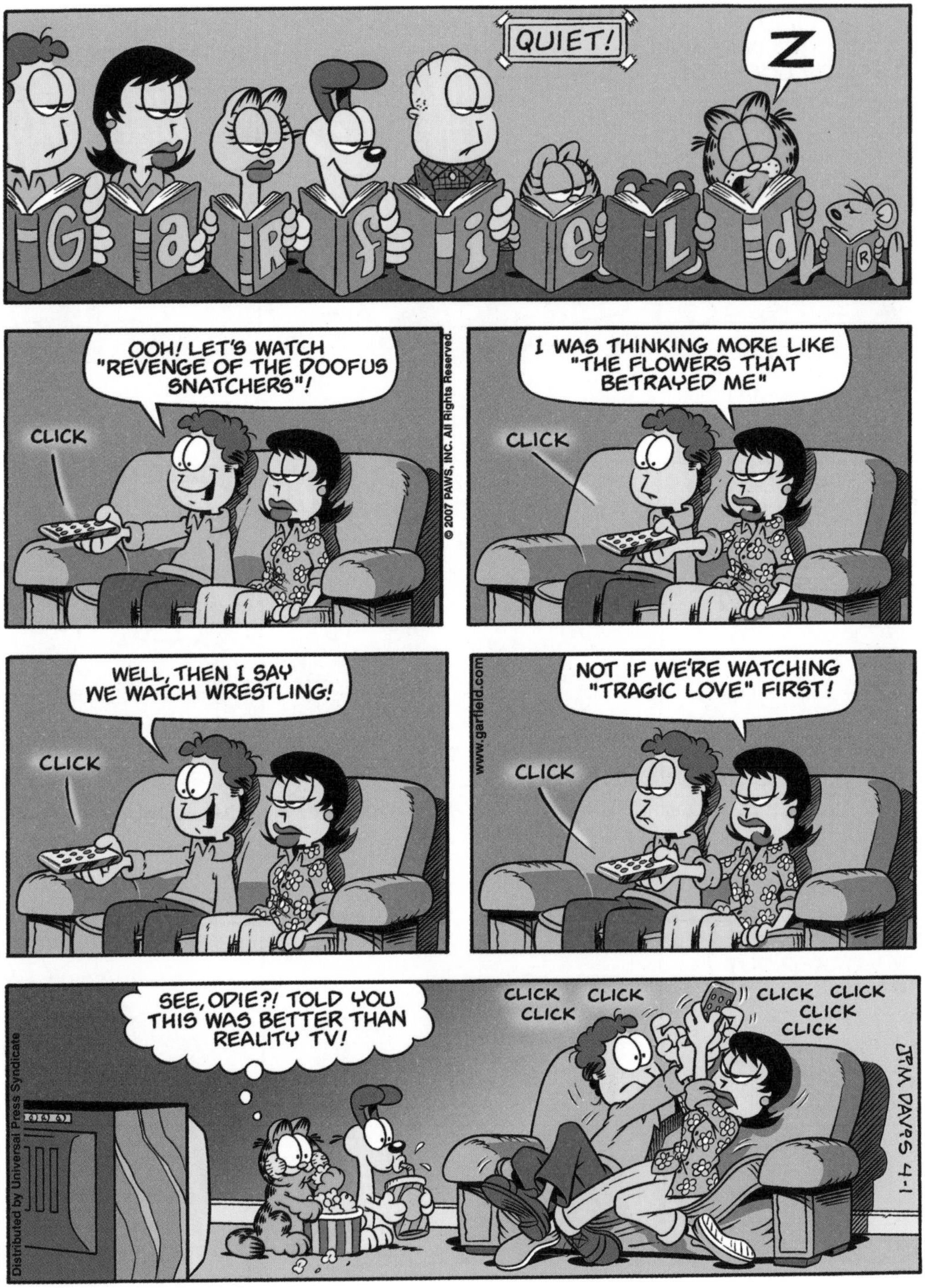

QUIET!
Z
GaRfieLd
OOH! LET'S WATCH "REVENGE OF THE DOOFUS SNATCHERS"!
CLICK
© 2007 PAWS, INC. All Rights Reserved.
I WAS THINKING MORE LIKE "THE FLOWERS THAT BETRAYED ME"
CLICK
WELL, THEN I SAY WE WATCH WRESTLING!
CLICK
www.garfield.com
NOT IF WE'RE WATCHING "TRAGIC LOVE" FIRST!
CLICK
SEE, ODIE?! TOLD YOU THIS WAS BETTER THAN REALITY TV!
CLICK CLICK CLICK
CLICK CLICK CLICK CLICK
Distributed by Universal Press Syndicate
JIM DAVIS 4-1

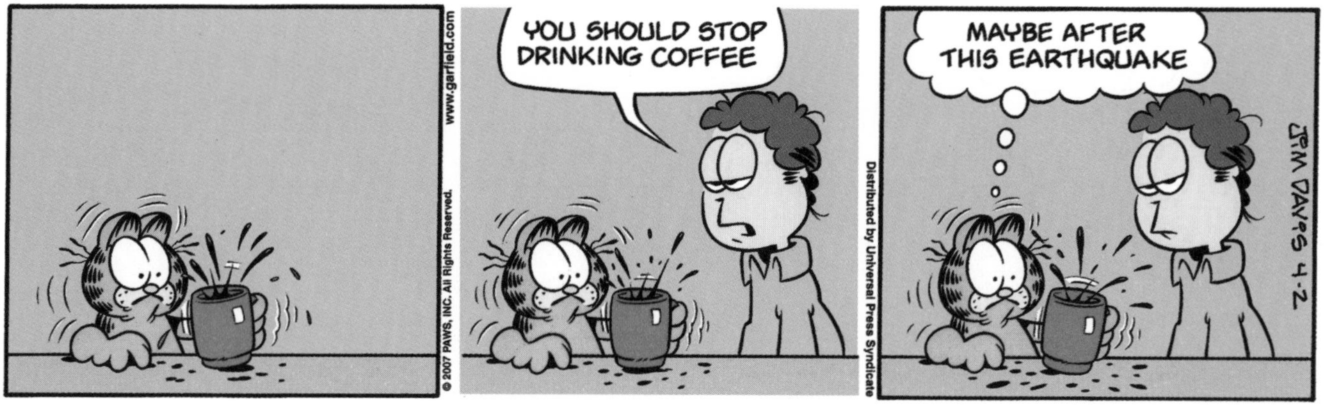
www.garfield.com
© 2007 PAWS, INC. All Rights Reserved.
YOU SHOULD STOP DRINKING COFFEE
Distributed by Universal Press Syndicate
MAYBE AFTER THIS EARTHQUAKE
JPM DAVPS 4-2

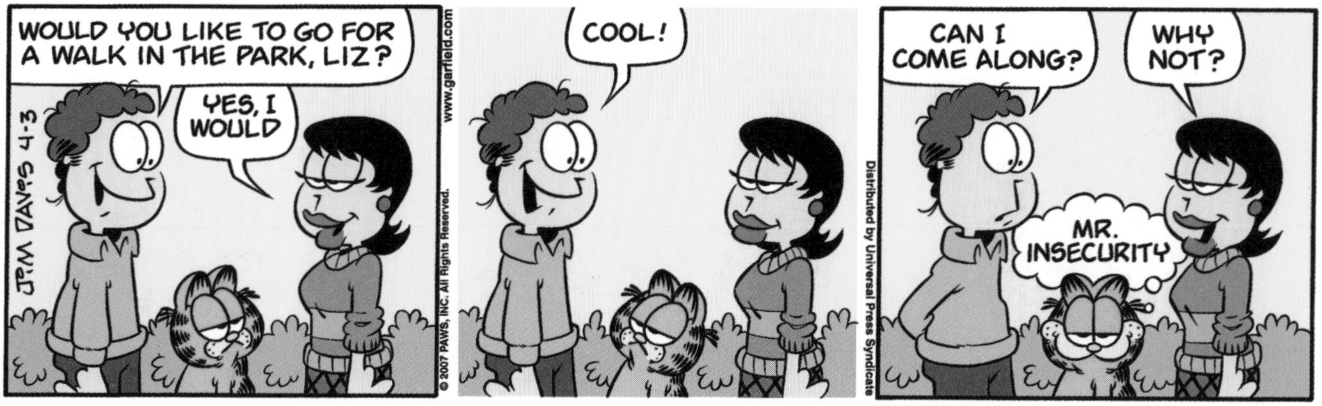
WOULD YOU LIKE TO GO FOR A WALK IN THE PARK, LIZ?
YES, I WOULD
JPM DAVPS 4-3
www.garfield.com
© 2007 PAWS, INC. All Rights Reserved.
COOL!
Distributed by Universal Press Syndicate
CAN I COME ALONG?
WHY NOT?
MR. INSECURITY

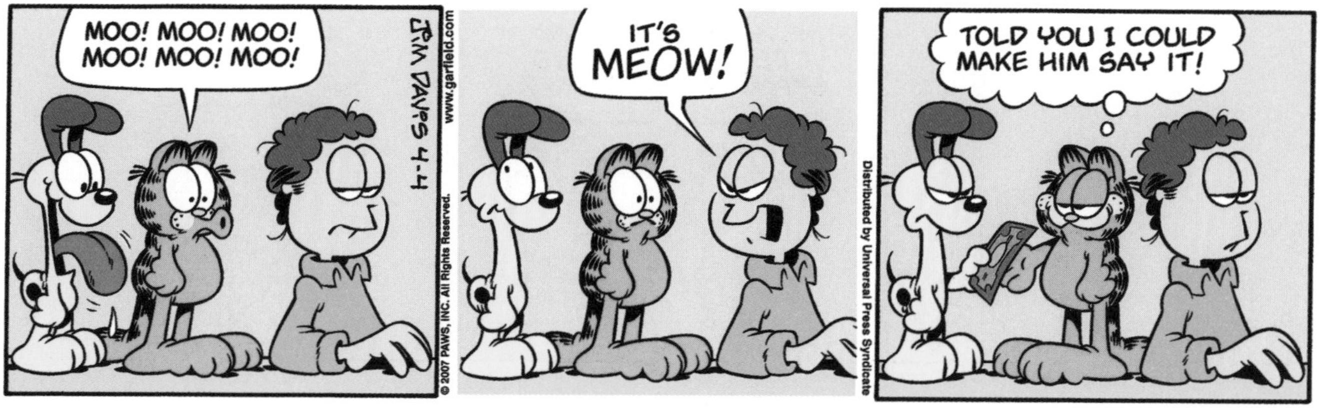
MOO! MOO! MOO! MOO! MOO! MOO!
JPM DAVPS 4-4
www.garfield.com
© 2007 PAWS, INC. All Rights Reserved.
IT'S MEOW!
Distributed by Universal Press Syndicate
TOLD YOU I COULD MAKE HIM SAY IT!

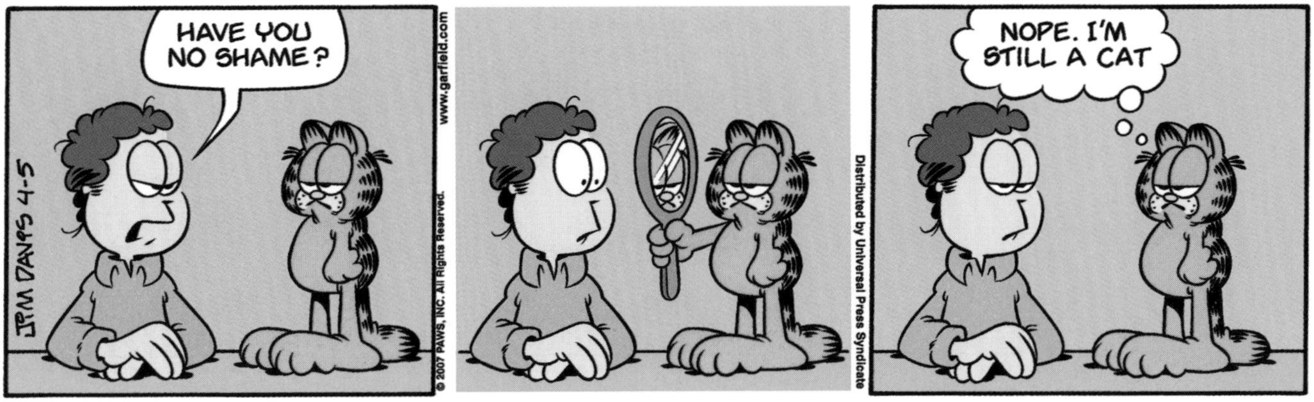
HAVE YOU NO SHAME?
NOPE. I'M STILL A CAT
JIM DAVIS 4-5
© 2007 PAWS, INC. All Rights Reserved.
www.garfield.com
Distributed by Universal Press Syndicate

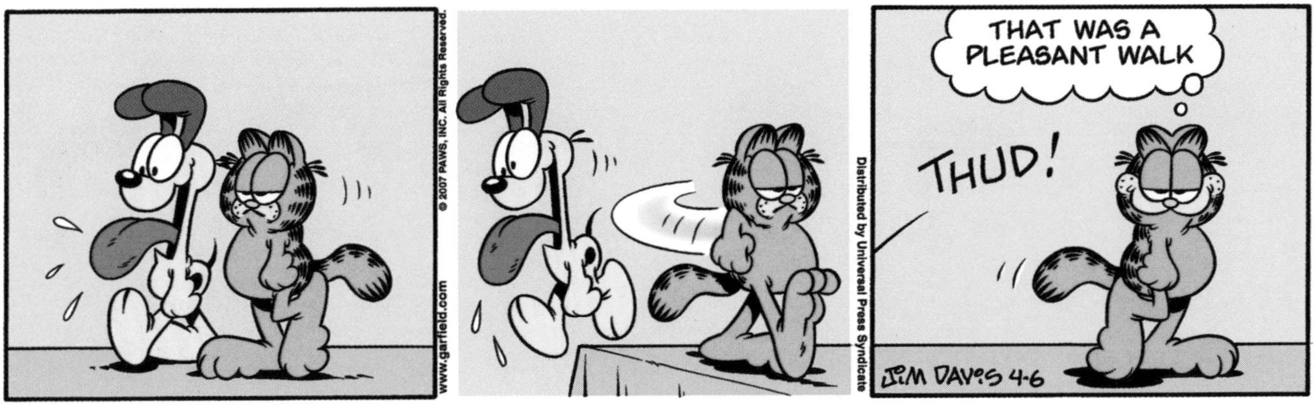
THUD!
THAT WAS A PLEASANT WALK
JIM DAVIS 4-6
© 2007 PAWS, INC. All Rights Reserved.
www.garfield.com
Distributed by Universal Press Syndicate

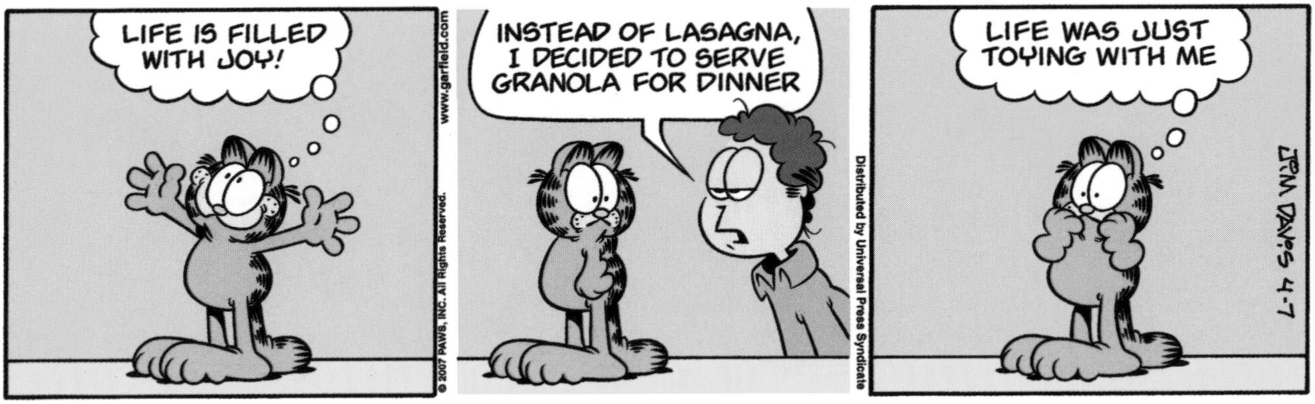
LIFE IS FILLED WITH JOY!
INSTEAD OF LASAGNA, I DECIDED TO SERVE GRANOLA FOR DINNER
LIFE WAS JUST TOYING WITH ME
JIM DAVIS 4-7
© 2007 PAWS, INC. All Rights Reserved.
www.garfield.com
Distributed by Universal Press Syndicate

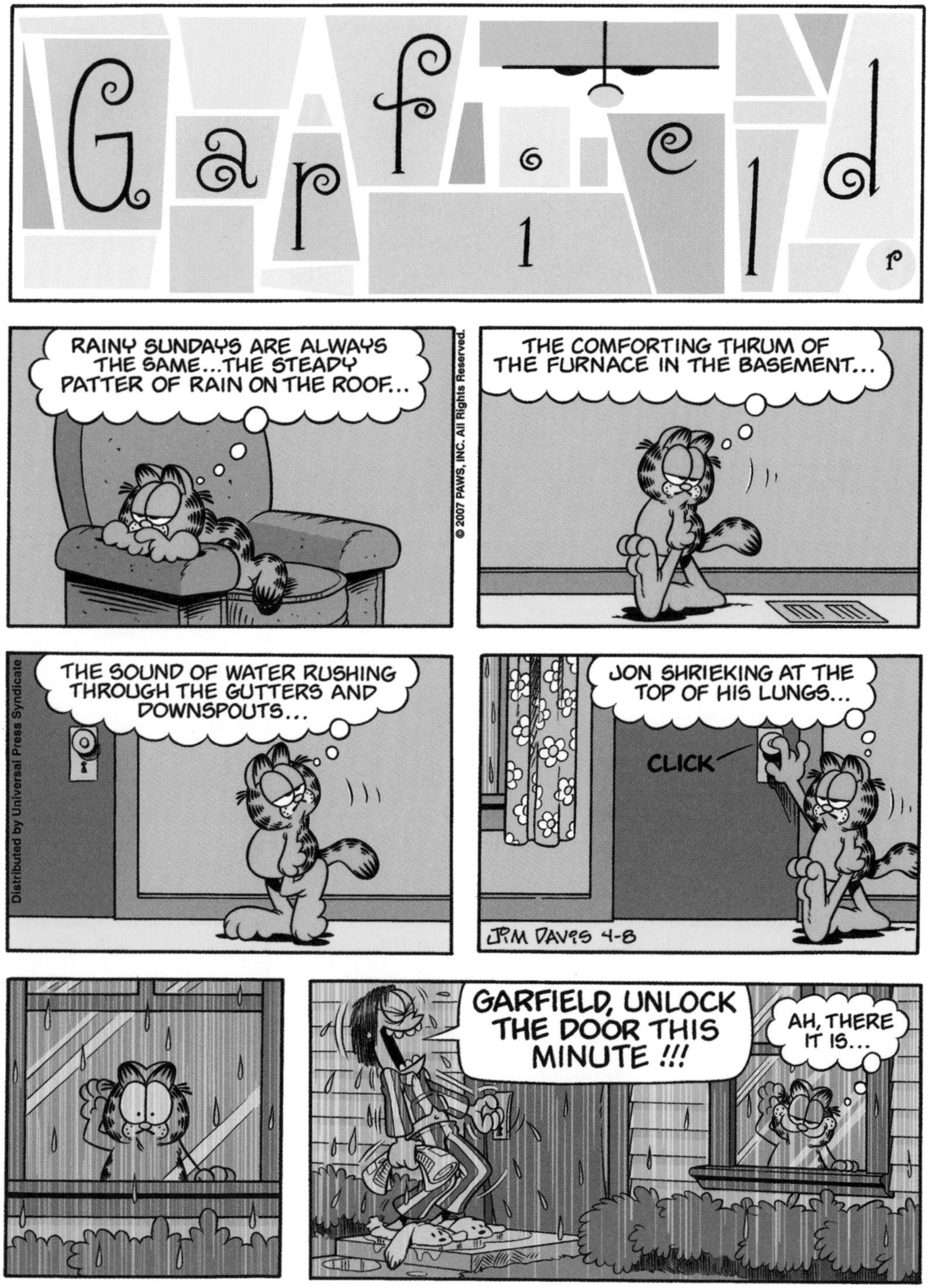
Garfield
RAINY SUNDAYS ARE ALWAYS THE SAME...THE STEADY PATTER OF RAIN ON THE ROOF...
© 2007 PAWS, INC. All Rights Reserved.
THE COMFORTING THRUM OF THE FURNACE IN THE BASEMENT...
Distributed by Universal Press Syndicate
THE SOUND OF WATER RUSHING THROUGH THE GUTTERS AND DOWNSPOUTS...
JON SHRIEKING AT THE TOP OF HIS LUNGS...
CLICK
JIM DAVIS 4-8
GARFIELD, UNLOCK THE DOOR THIS MINUTE !!!
AH, THERE IT IS...

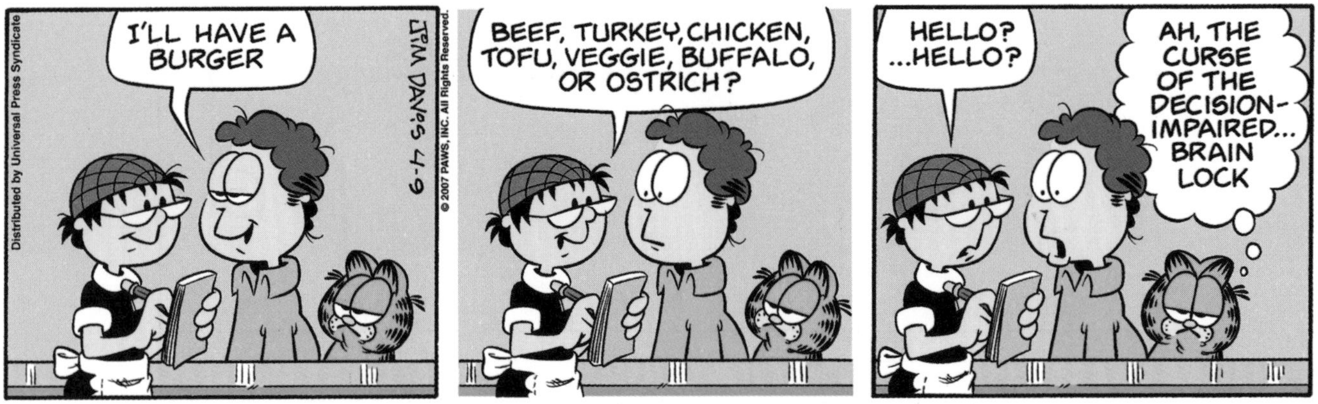
Distributed by Universal Press Syndicate
I'LL HAVE A BURGER
JIM DAVIS 4-9
© 2007 PAWS, INC. All Rights Reserved.
BEEF, TURKEY, CHICKEN, TOFU, VEGGIE, BUFFALO, OR OSTRICH?
HELLO? ...HELLO?
AH, THE CURSE OF THE DECISION-IMPAIRED... BRAIN LOCK

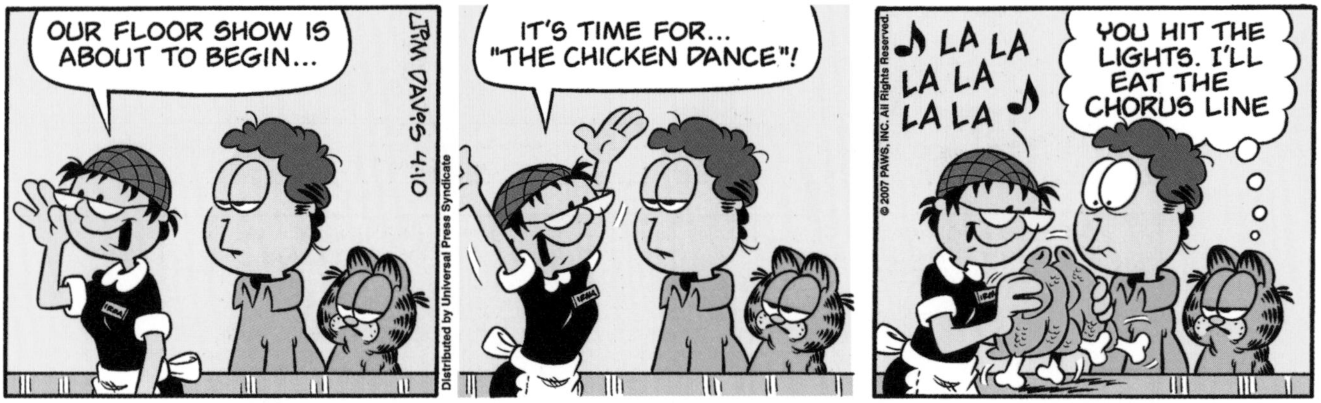
OUR FLOOR SHOW IS ABOUT TO BEGIN...
JIM DAVIS 4-10
Distributed by Universal Press Syndicate
IT'S TIME FOR... "THE CHICKEN DANCE"!
© 2007 PAWS, INC. All Rights Reserved.
♪ LA LA LA LA LA LA LA ♪
YOU HIT THE LIGHTS. I'LL EAT THE CHORUS LINE

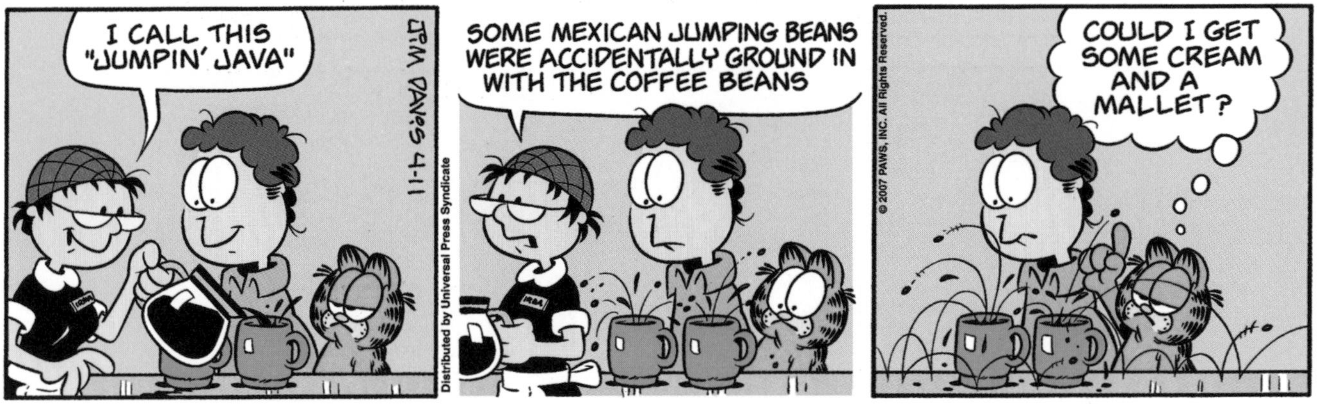
I CALL THIS "JUMPIN' JAVA"
JIM DAVIS 4-11
Distributed by Universal Press Syndicate
SOME MEXICAN JUMPING BEANS WERE ACCIDENTALLY GROUND IN WITH THE COFFEE BEANS
© 2007 PAWS, INC. All Rights Reserved.
COULD I GET SOME CREAM AND A MALLET?

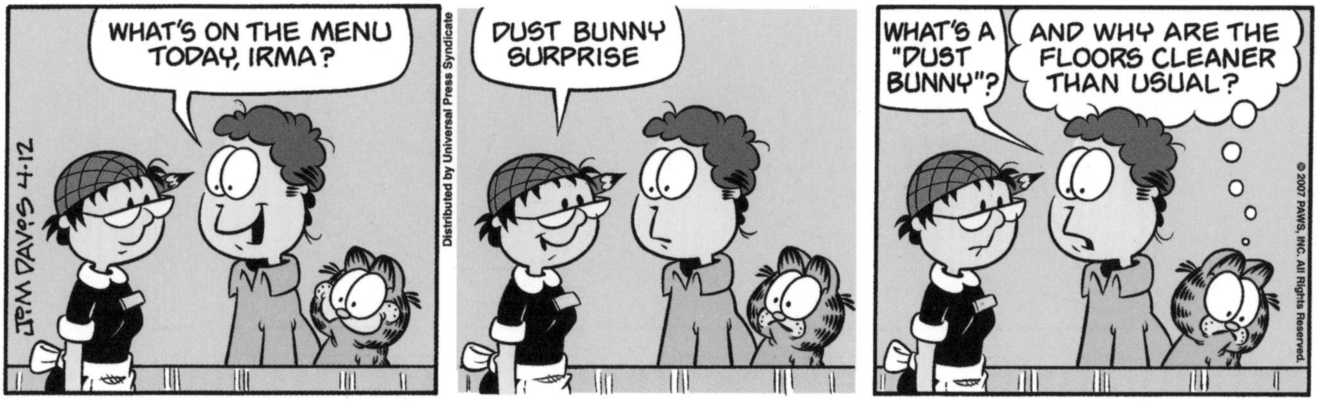
JIM DAVIS 4-12
WHAT'S ON THE MENU TODAY, IRMA?
Distributed by Universal Press Syndicate
DUST BUNNY SURPRISE
WHAT'S A "DUST BUNNY"?
AND WHY ARE THE FLOORS CLEANER THAN USUAL?
© 2007 PAWS, INC. All Rights Reserved.

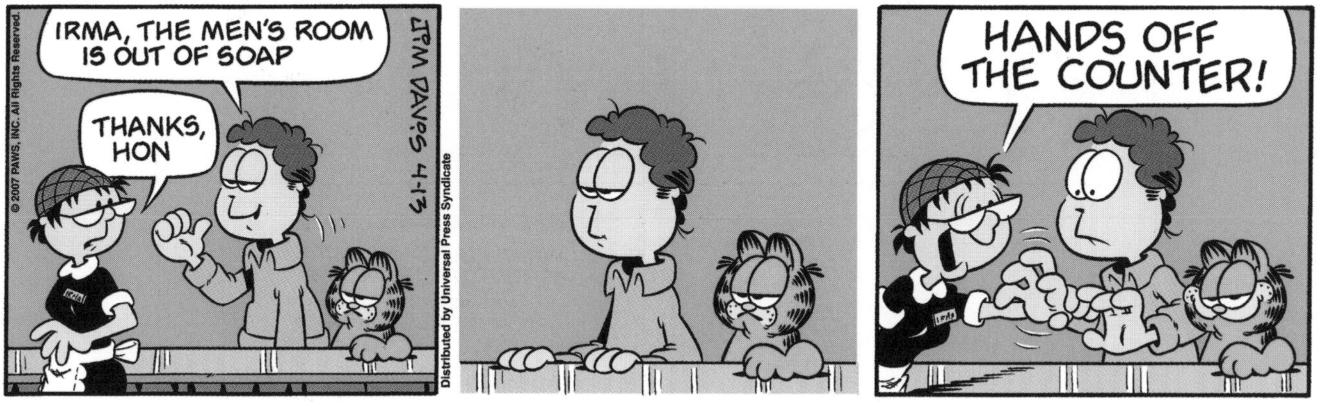
© 2007 PAWS, INC. All Rights Reserved.
IRMA, THE MEN'S ROOM IS OUT OF SOAP
THANKS, HON
JIM DAVIS 4-13
Distributed by Universal Press Syndicate
HANDS OFF THE COUNTER!

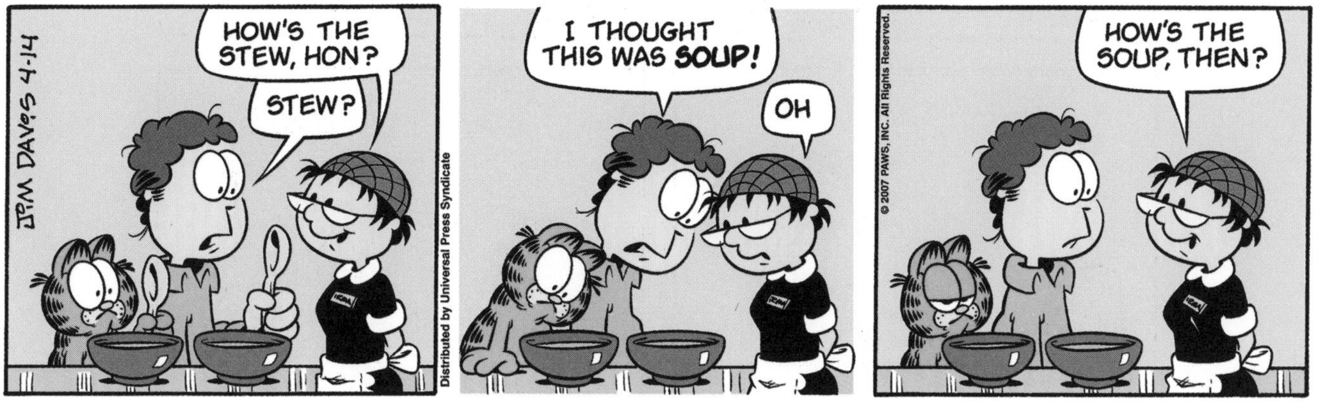
JIM DAVIS 4-14
HOW'S THE STEW, HON?
STEW?
Distributed by Universal Press Syndicate
I THOUGHT THIS WAS SOUP!
OH
© 2007 PAWS, INC. All Rights Reserved.
HOW'S THE SOUP, THEN?

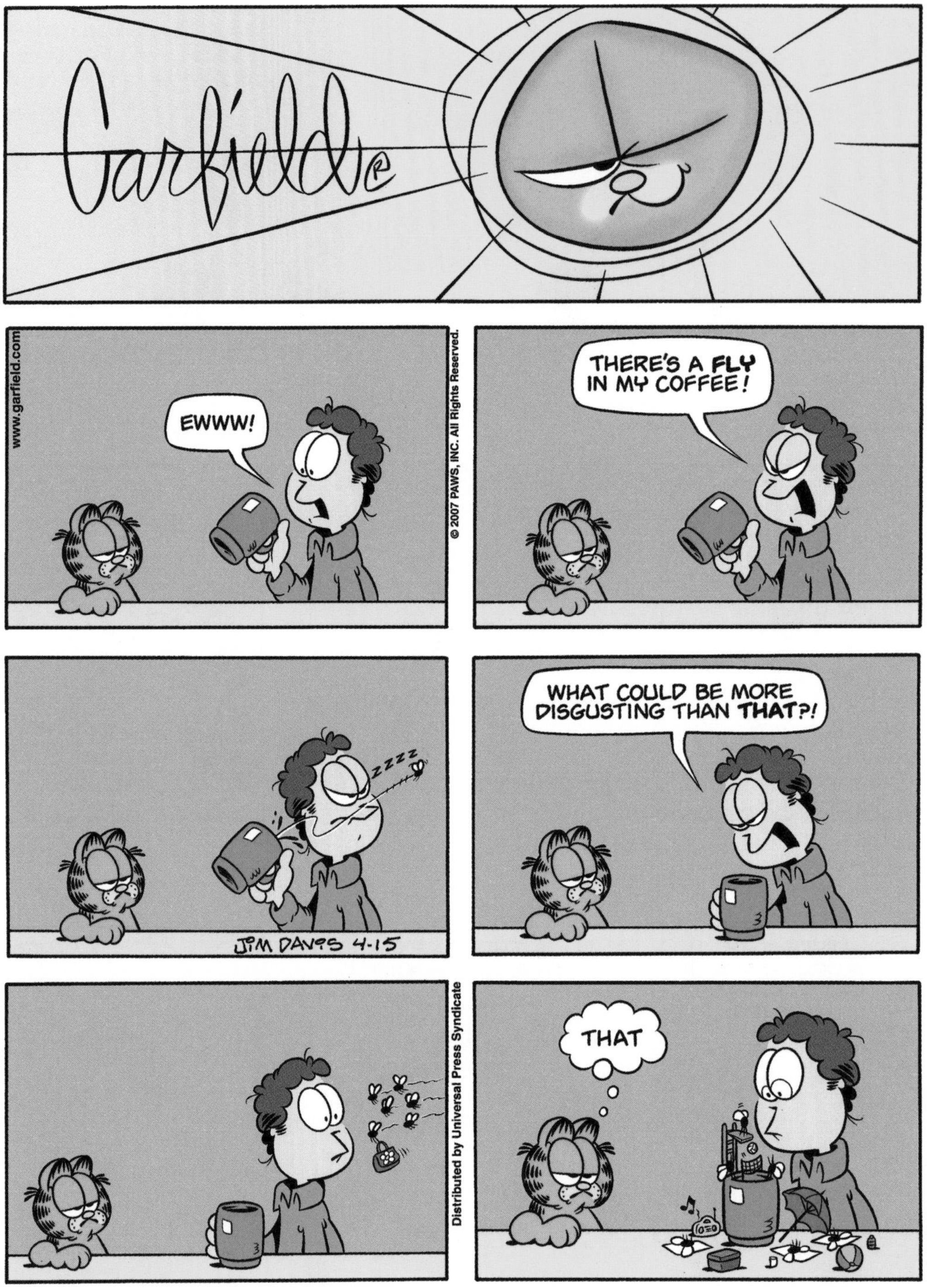
Garfield®
www.garfield.com
© 2007 PAWS, INC. All Rights Reserved.
EWWW!
THERE'S A FLY IN MY COFFEE!
ZZZZ
JIM DAVIS 4-15
WHAT COULD BE MORE DISGUSTING THAN THAT?!
Distributed by Universal Press Syndicate
THAT

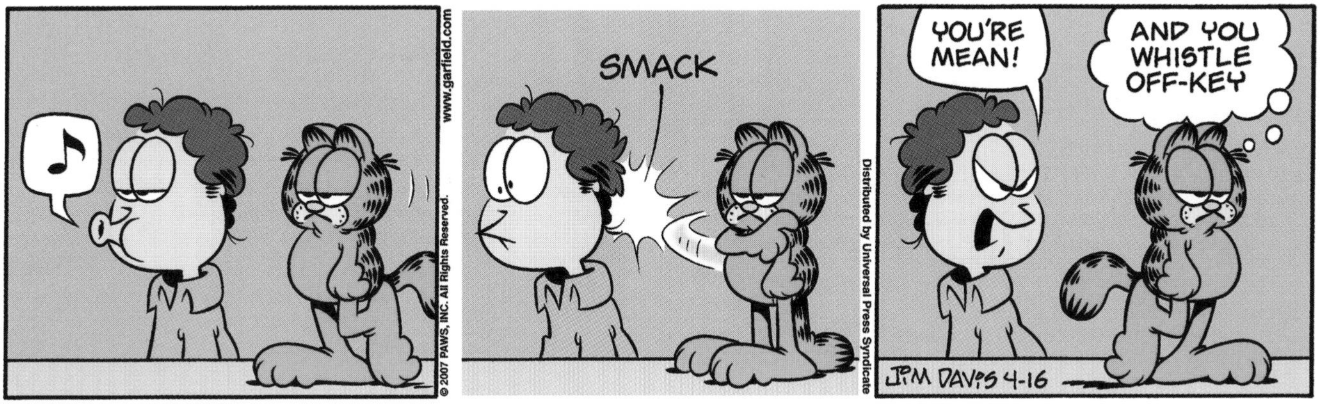
♪
SMACK
YOU'RE MEAN!
AND YOU WHISTLE OFF-KEY
© 2007 PAWS, INC. All Rights Reserved. www.garfield.com
Distributed by Universal Press Syndicate
JIM DAVIS 4-16

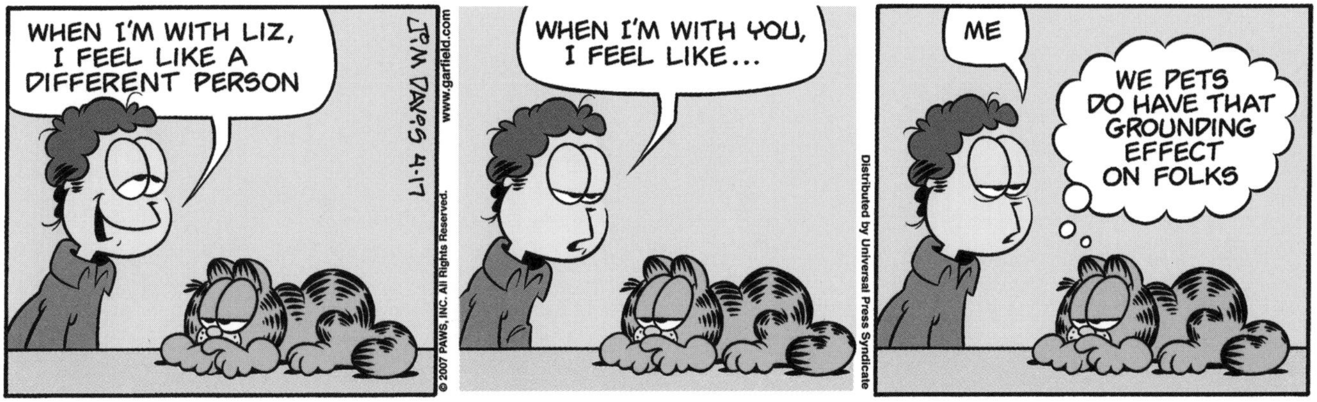
WHEN I'M WITH LIZ, I FEEL LIKE A DIFFERENT PERSON
WHEN I'M WITH YOU, I FEEL LIKE...
ME
WE PETS DO HAVE THAT GROUNDING EFFECT ON FOLKS
JIM DAVIS 4-17
© 2007 PAWS, INC. All Rights Reserved. www.garfield.com
Distributed by Universal Press Syndicate

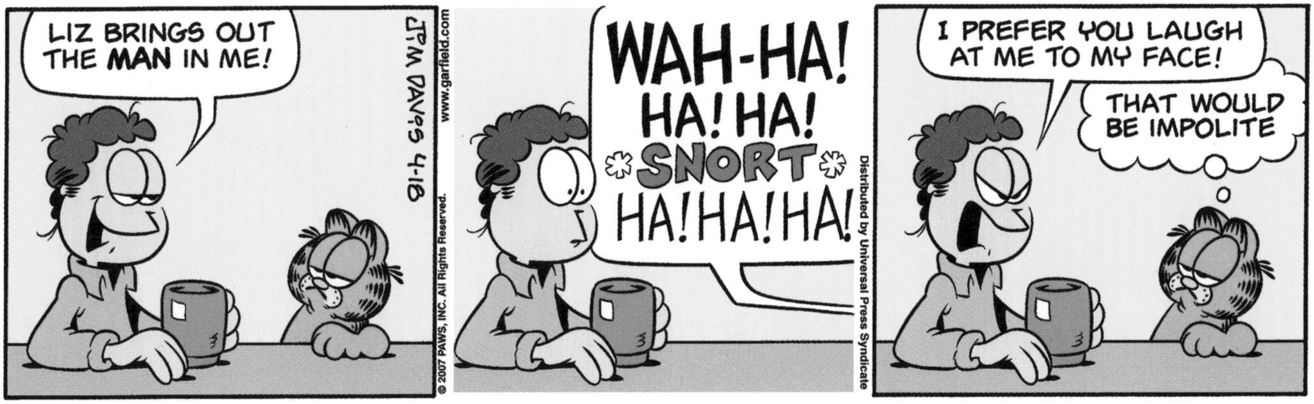
LIZ BRINGS OUT THE **MAN** IN ME!
WAH-HA! HA! HA! *SNORT* HA! HA! HA!
I PREFER YOU LAUGH AT ME TO MY FACE!
THAT WOULD BE IMPOLITE
JIM DAVIS 4-18
© 2007 PAWS, INC. All Rights Reserved. www.garfield.com
Distributed by Universal Press Syndicate

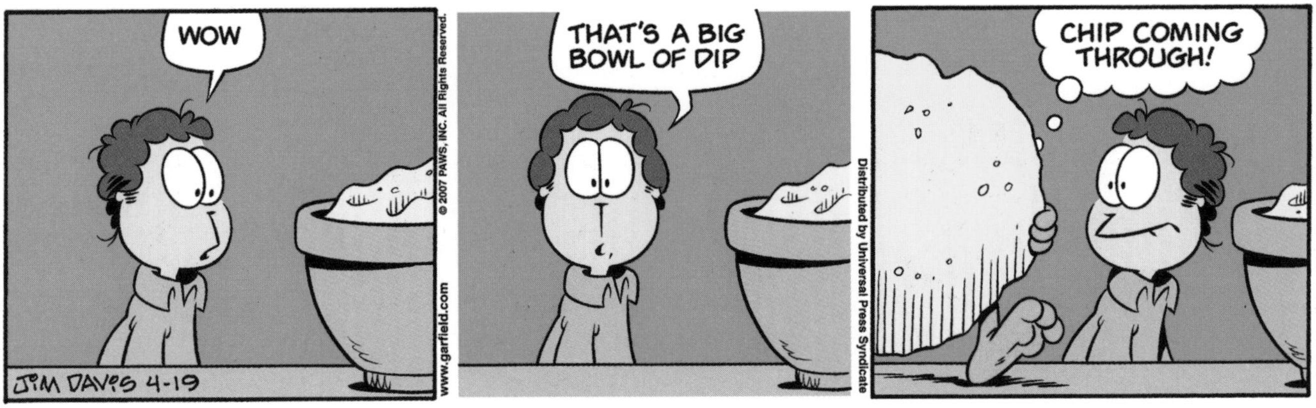
WOW
JIM DAVIS 4-19
THAT'S A BIG BOWL OF DIP
CHIP COMING THROUGH!
© 2007 PAWS, INC. All Rights Reserved.
www.garfield.com
Distributed by Universal Press Syndicate

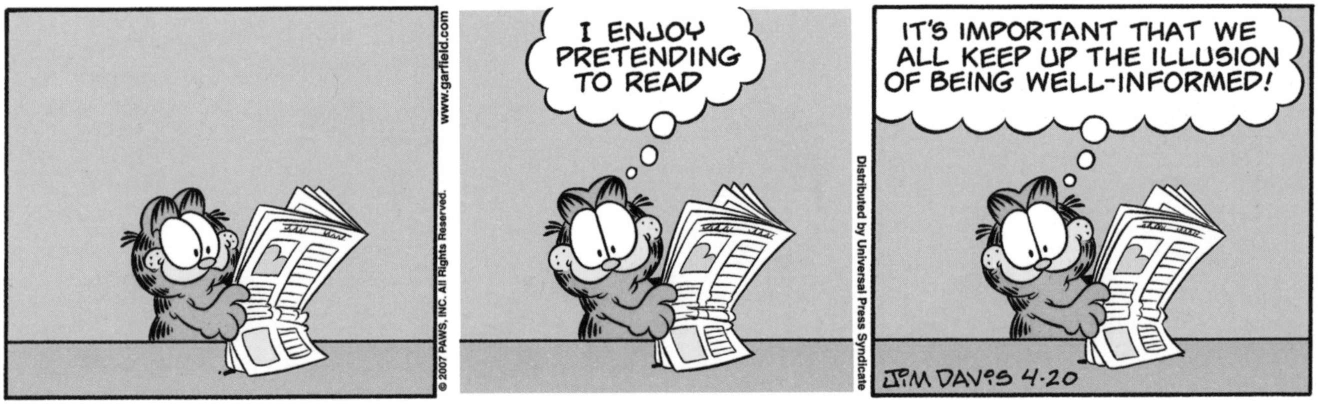
I ENJOY PRETENDING TO READ
IT'S IMPORTANT THAT WE ALL KEEP UP THE ILLUSION OF BEING WELL-INFORMED!
JIM DAVIS 4-20
© 2007 PAWS, INC. All Rights Reserved.
www.garfield.com
Distributed by Universal Press Syndicate

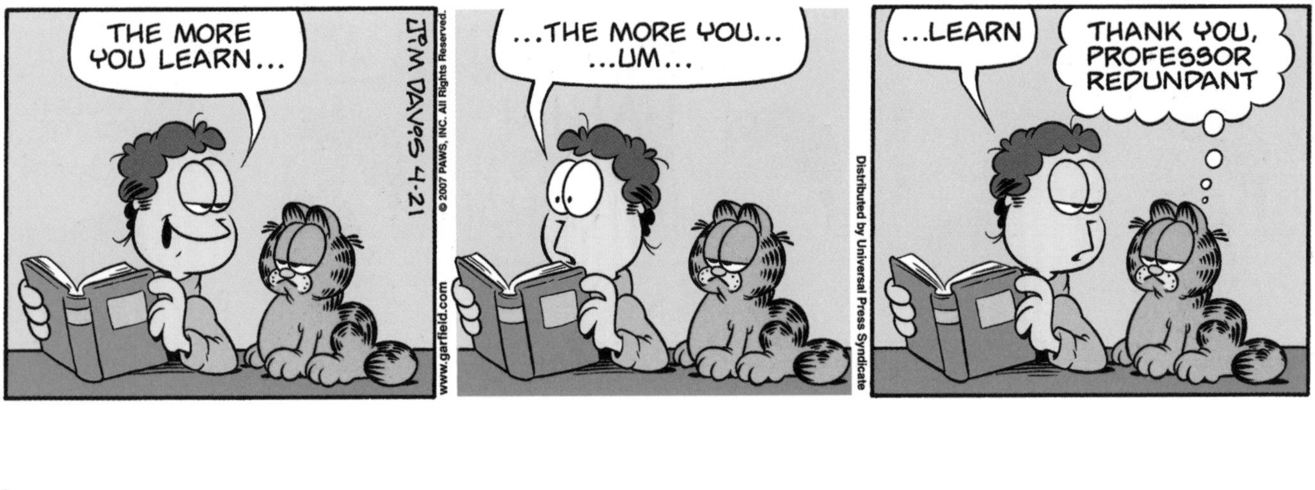
THE MORE YOU LEARN...
JIM DAVIS 4-21
...THE MORE YOU... ...UM...
...LEARN
THANK YOU, PROFESSOR REDUNDANT
© 2007 PAWS, INC. All Rights Reserved.
www.garfield.com
Distributed by Universal Press Syndicate

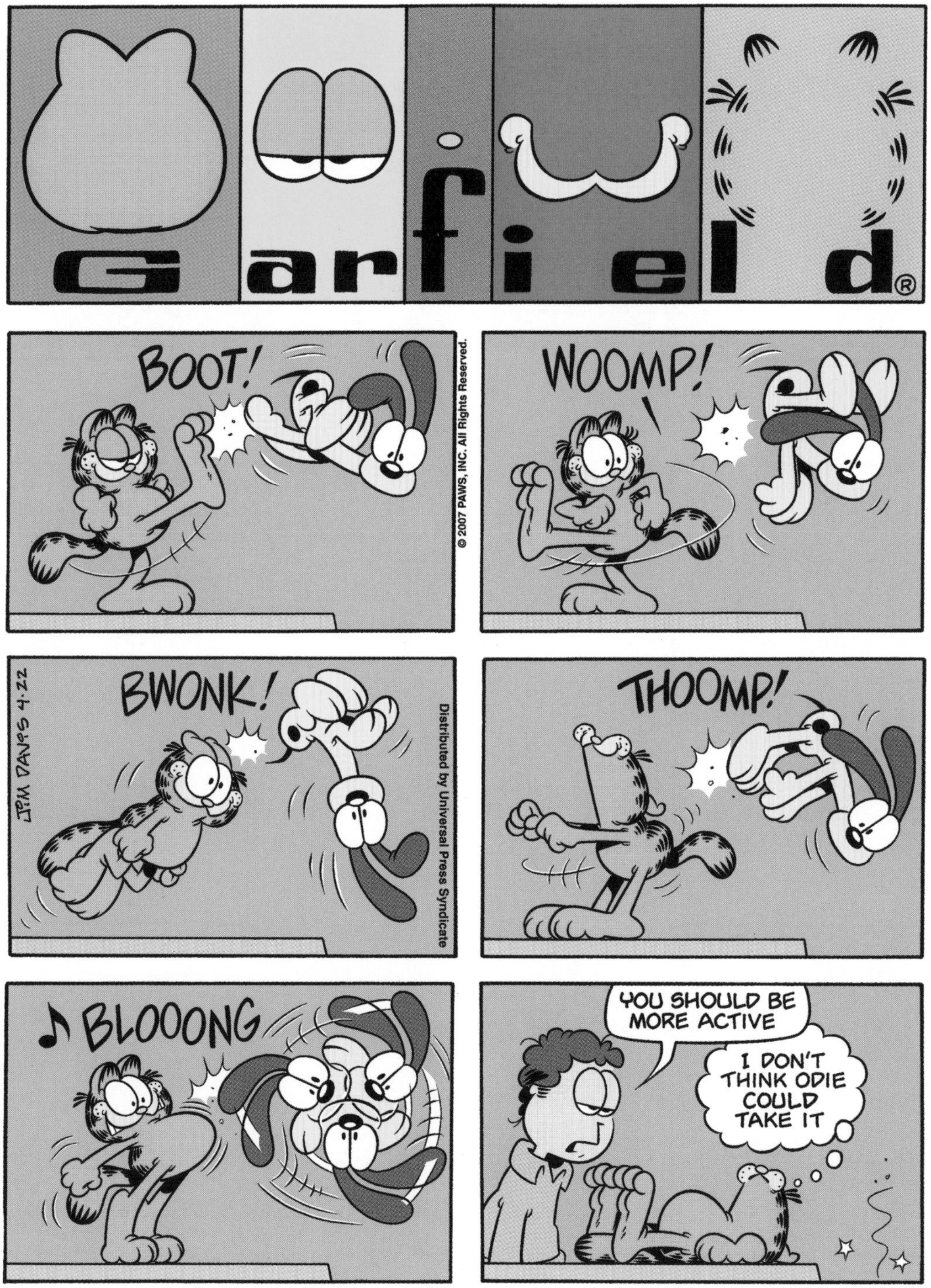
Garfield®
© 2007 PAWS, INC. All Rights Reserved.
BOOT!
WOOMP!
JPM DAVIS 4-22
BWONK!
Distributed by Universal Press Syndicate
THOOMP!
♪ BLOOONG
YOU SHOULD BE MORE ACTIVE
I DON'T THINK ODIE COULD TAKE IT

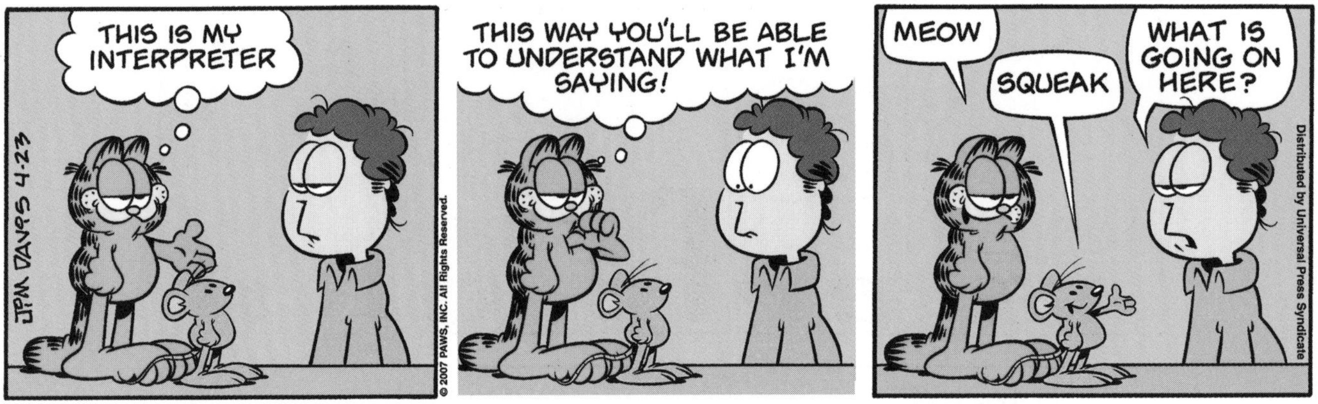
THIS IS MY INTERPRETER
JPM DAVPS 4-23
© 2007 PAWS, INC. All Rights Reserved.
THIS WAY YOU'LL BE ABLE TO UNDERSTAND WHAT I'M SAYING!
MEOW
SQUEAK
WHAT IS GOING ON HERE?
Distributed by Universal Press Syndicate

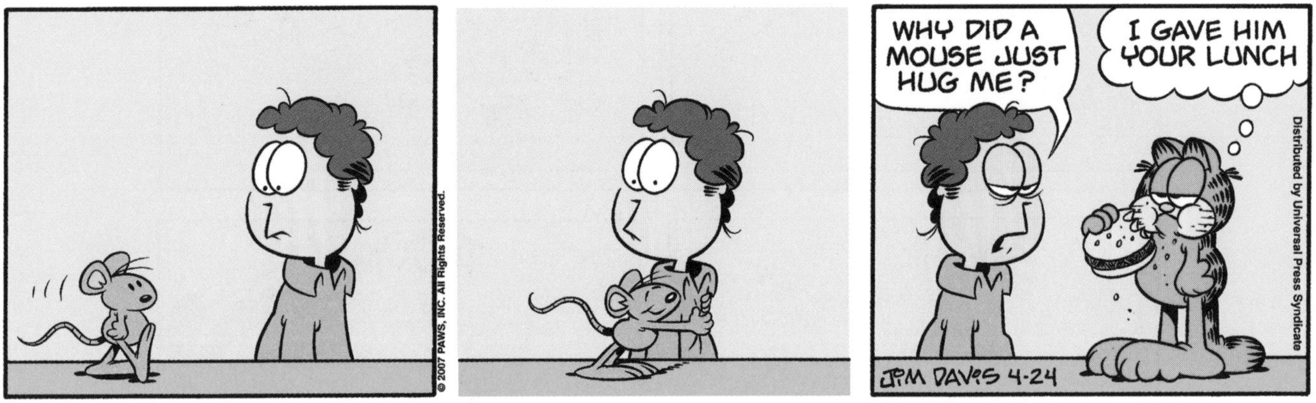
© 2007 PAWS, INC. All Rights Reserved.
WHY DID A MOUSE JUST HUG ME?
I GAVE HIM YOUR LUNCH
Distributed by Universal Press Syndicate
JPM DAVPS 4-24

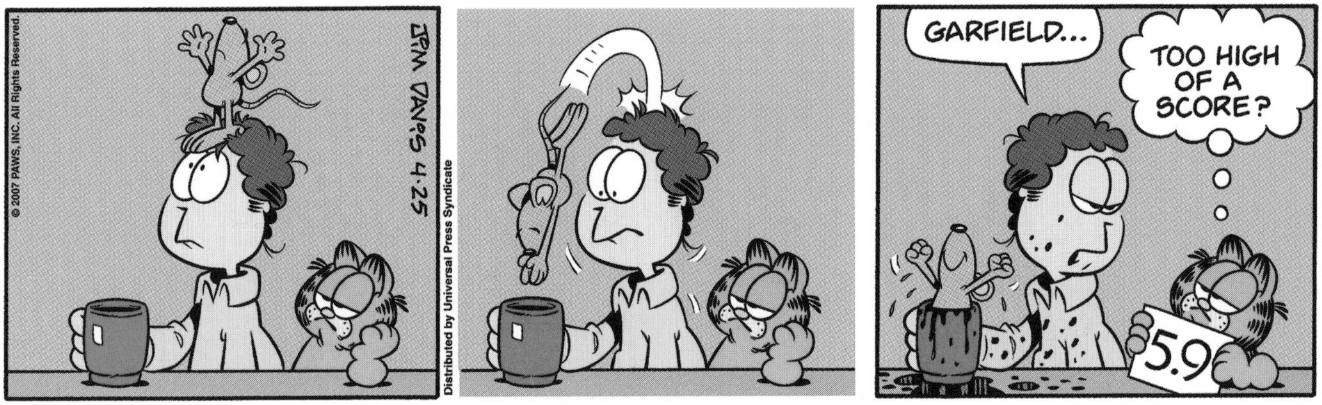
© 2007 PAWS, INC. All Rights Reserved.
JPM DAVPS 4-25
Distributed by Universal Press Syndicate
GARFIELD...
TOO HIGH OF A SCORE?
5.9

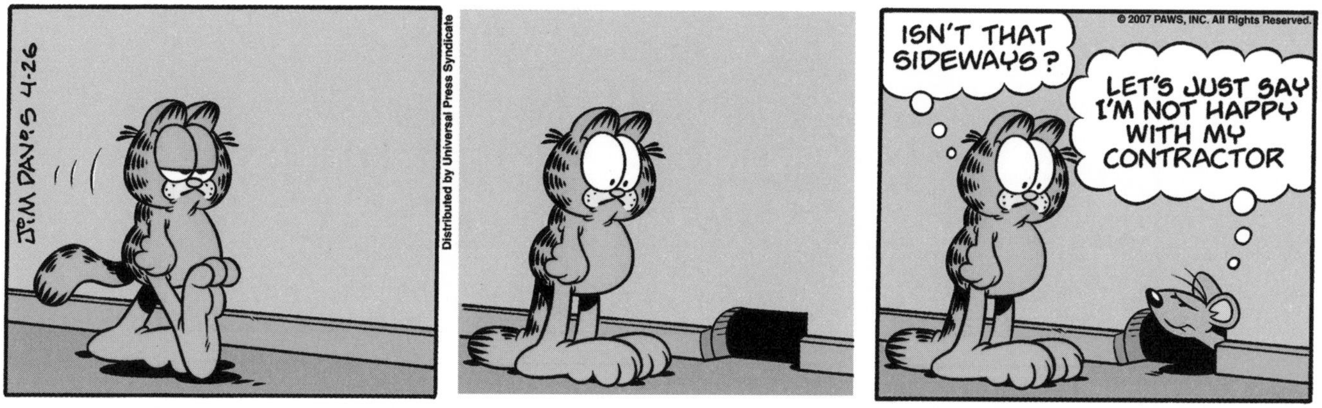
JIM DAVIS 4-26
Distributed by Universal Press Syndicate
© 2007 PAWS, INC. All Rights Reserved.
ISN'T THAT SIDEWAYS?
LET'S JUST SAY I'M NOT HAPPY WITH MY CONTRACTOR

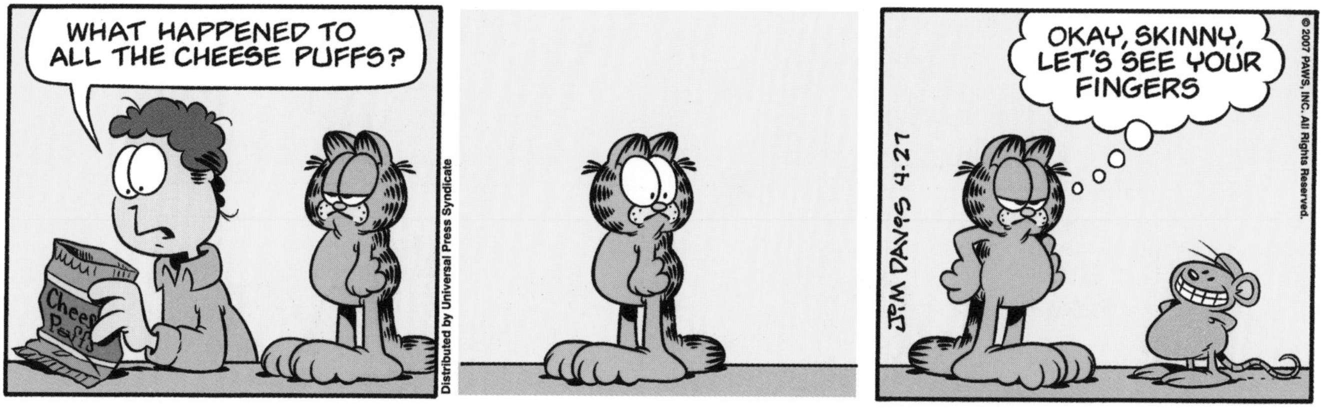
WHAT HAPPENED TO ALL THE CHEESE PUFFS?
Distributed by Universal Press Syndicate
OKAY, SKINNY, LET'S SEE YOUR FINGERS
JIM DAVIS 4-27
© 2007 PAWS, INC. All Rights Reserved.

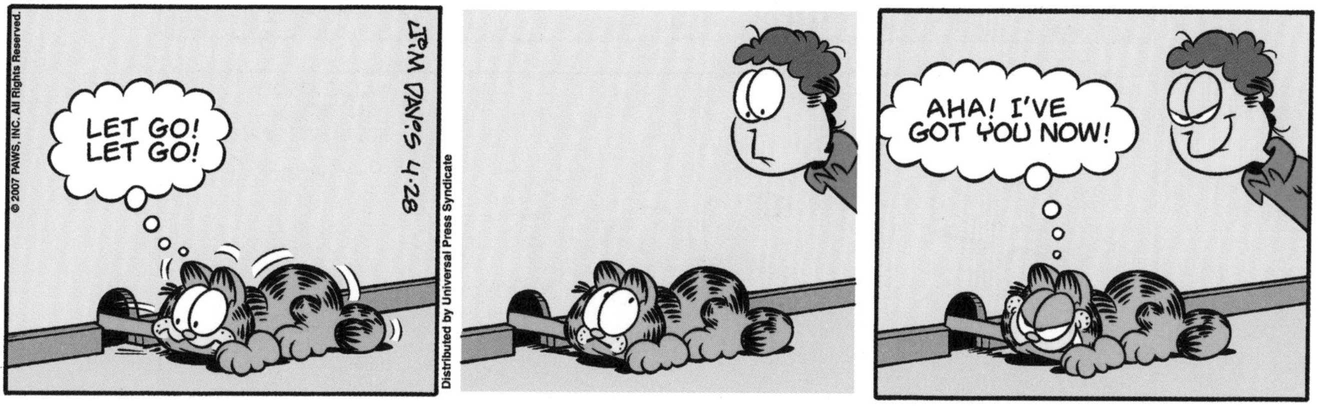
© 2007 PAWS, INC. All Rights Reserved.
LET GO! LET GO!
JIM DAVIS 4-28
Distributed by Universal Press Syndicate
AHA! I'VE GOT YOU NOW!

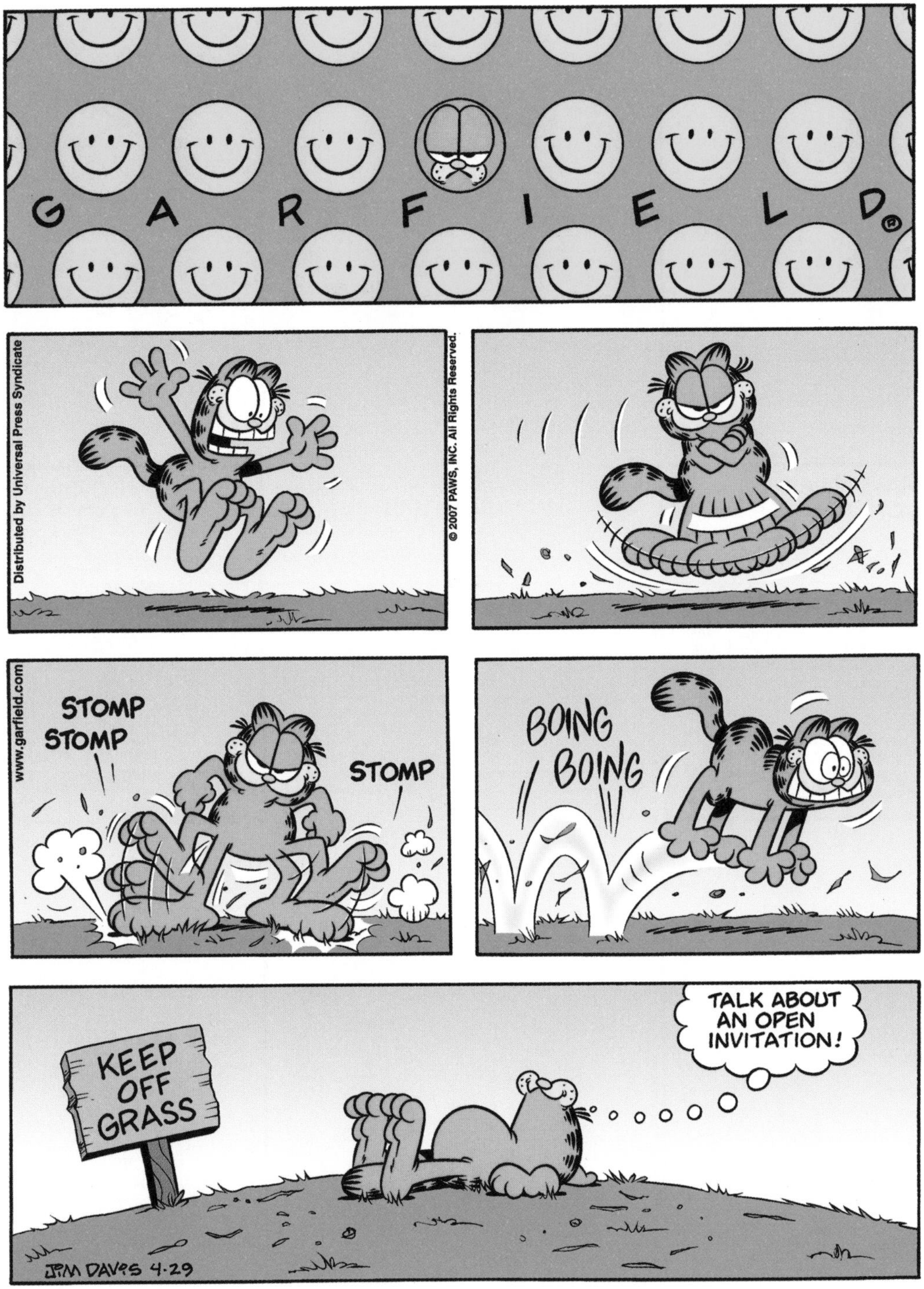
GARFIELD®
Distributed by Universal Press Syndicate
© 2007 PAWS, INC. All Rights Reserved.
www.garfield.com
STOMP
STOMP
STOMP
BOING
BOING
KEEP OFF GRASS
TALK ABOUT AN OPEN INVITATION!
JIM DAVIS 4-29

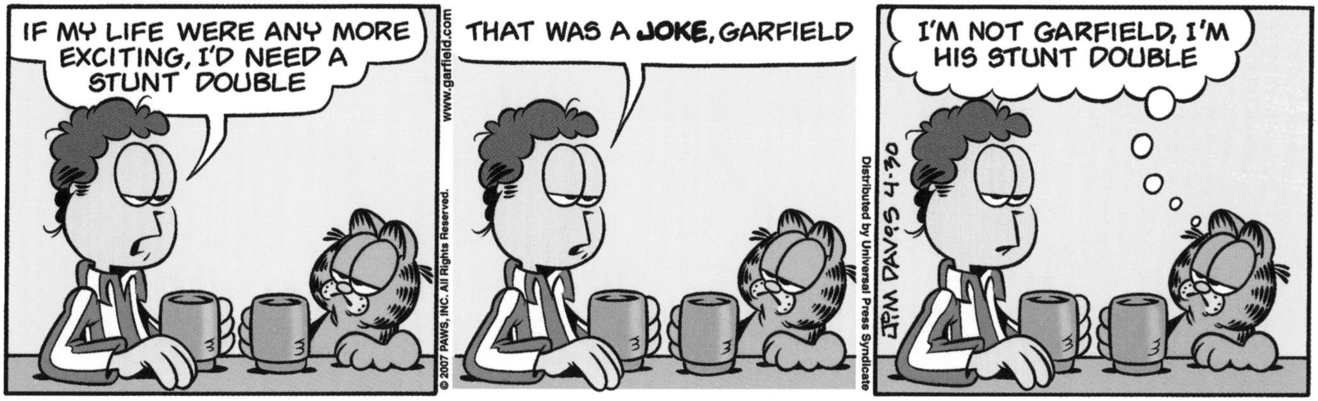
IF MY LIFE WERE ANY MORE EXCITING, I'D NEED A STUNT DOUBLE
THAT WAS A **JOKE**, GARFIELD
I'M NOT GARFIELD, I'M HIS STUNT DOUBLE
JIM DAVIS 4-30
© 2007 PAWS, INC. All Rights Reserved. www.garfield.com
Distributed by Universal Press Syndicate

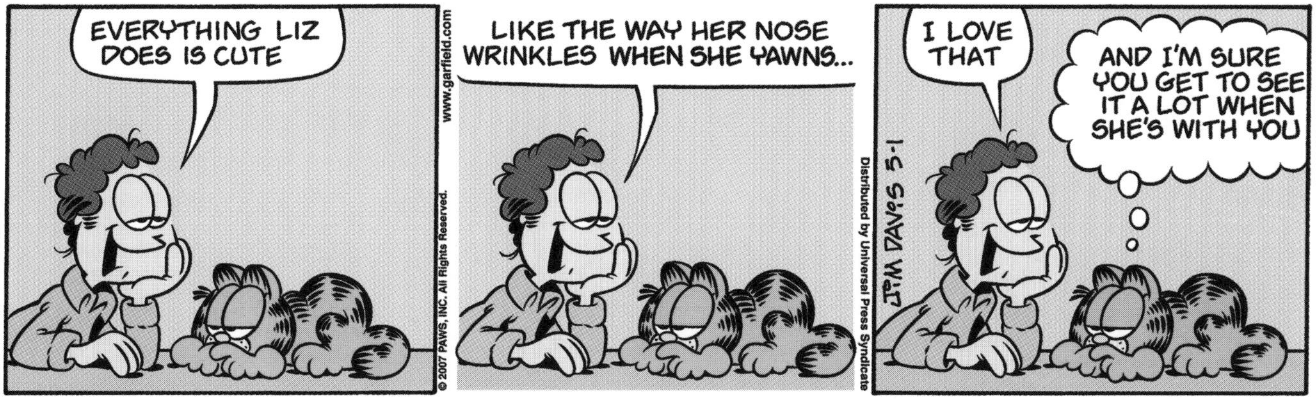
EVERYTHING LIZ DOES IS CUTE
LIKE THE WAY HER NOSE WRINKLES WHEN SHE YAWNS...
I LOVE THAT
AND I'M SURE YOU GET TO SEE IT A LOT WHEN SHE'S WITH YOU
JIM DAVIS 5-1
© 2007 PAWS, INC. All Rights Reserved. www.garfield.com
Distributed by Universal Press Syndicate

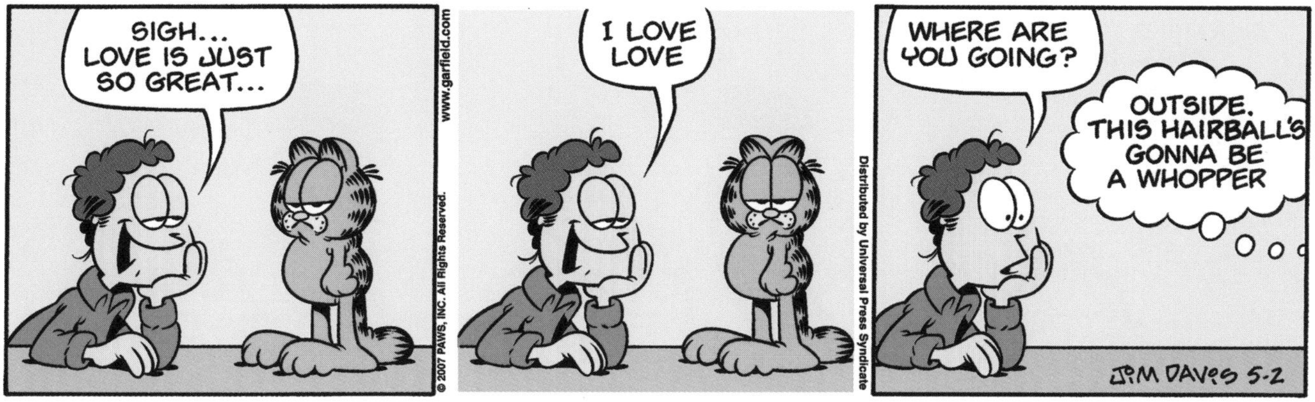
SIGH... LOVE IS JUST SO GREAT...
I LOVE LOVE
WHERE ARE YOU GOING?
OUTSIDE. THIS HAIRBALL'S GONNA BE A WHOPPER
JIM DAVIS 5-2
© 2007 PAWS, INC. All Rights Reserved. www.garfield.com
Distributed by Universal Press Syndicate

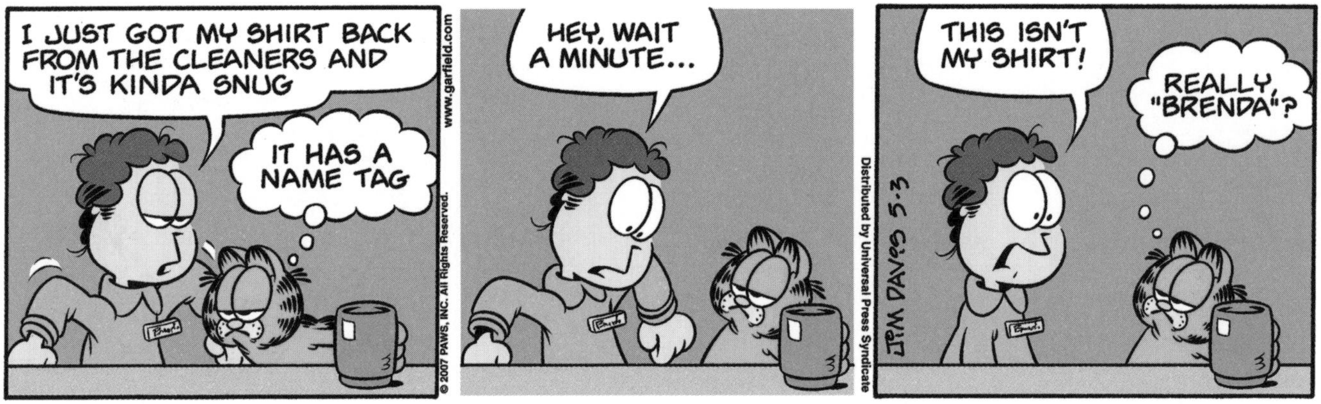
I JUST GOT MY SHIRT BACK FROM THE CLEANERS AND IT'S KINDA SNUG
IT HAS A NAME TAG
© 2007 PAWS, INC. All Rights Reserved. www.garfield.com
HEY, WAIT A MINUTE...
Distributed by Universal Press Syndicate
JIM DAVIS 5-3
THIS ISN'T MY SHIRT!
REALLY, "BRENDA"?

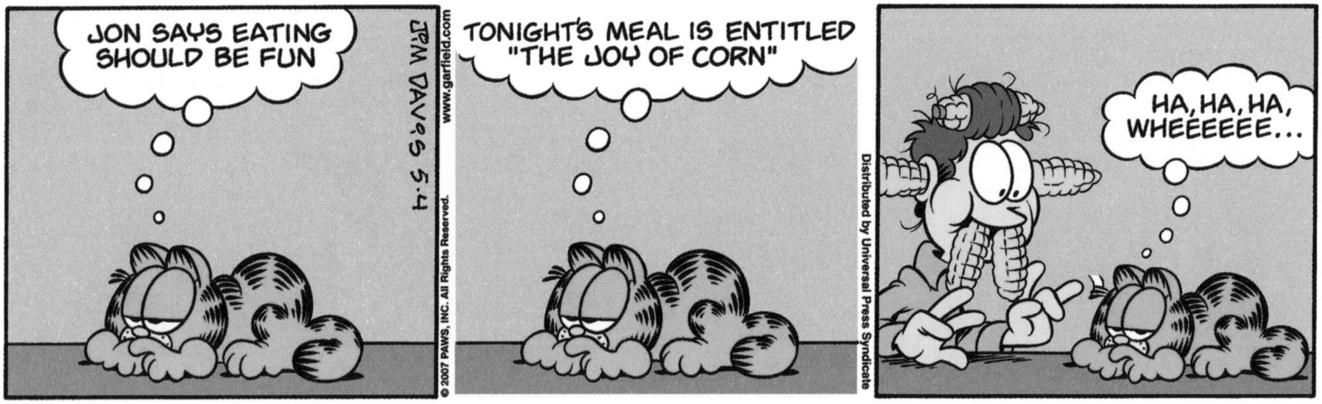
JON SAYS EATING SHOULD BE FUN
JIM DAVIS 5-4
© 2007 PAWS, INC. All Rights Reserved. www.garfield.com
TONIGHT'S MEAL IS ENTITLED "THE JOY OF CORN"
Distributed by Universal Press Syndicate
HA, HA, HA, WHEEEEEE...

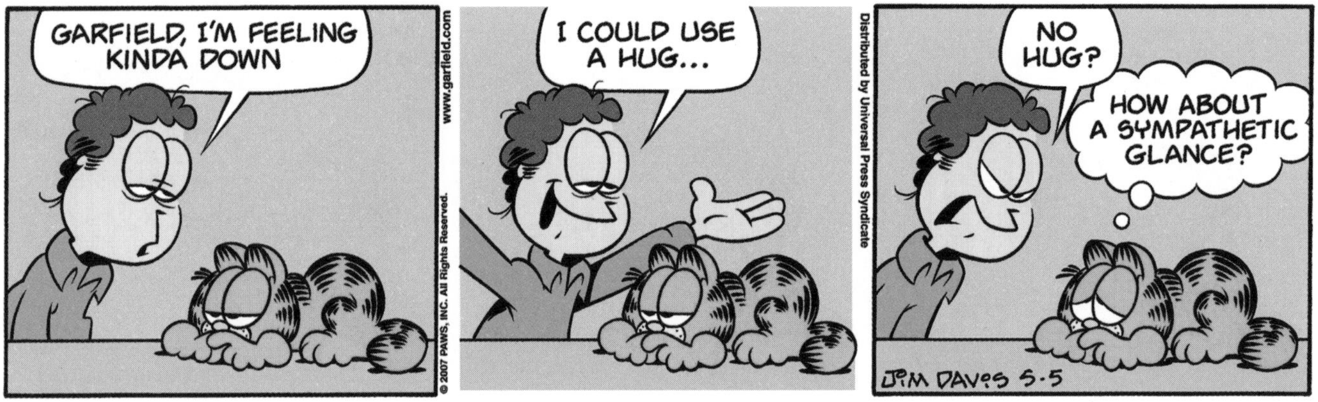
GARFIELD, I'M FEELING KINDA DOWN
© 2007 PAWS, INC. All Rights Reserved. www.garfield.com
I COULD USE A HUG...
Distributed by Universal Press Syndicate
NO HUG?
HOW ABOUT A SYMPATHETIC GLANCE?
JIM DAVIS 5-5

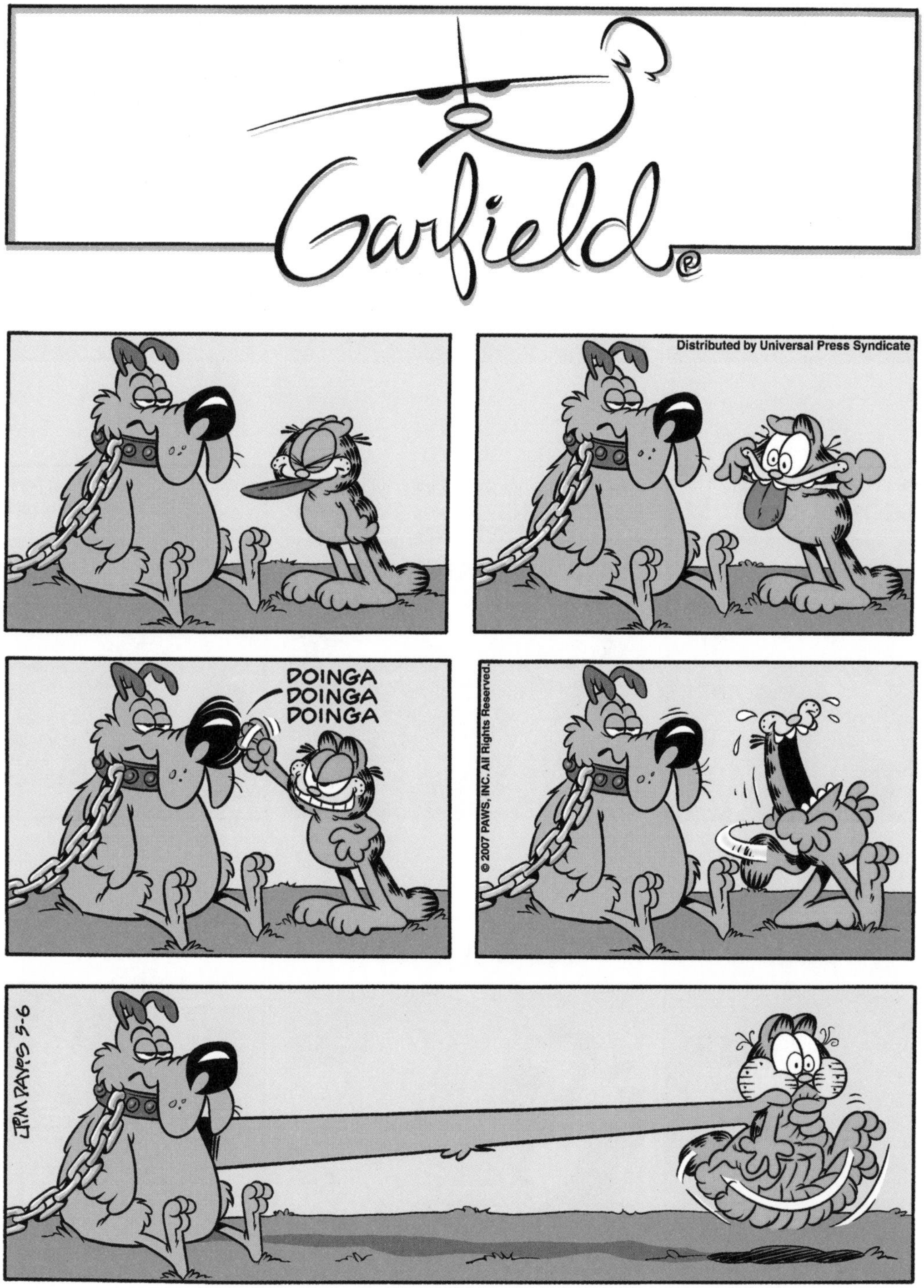
Garfield
Distributed by Universal Press Syndicate
DOINGA
DOINGA
DOINGA
© 2007 PAWS, INC. All Rights Reserved.
JPM DAVIS 5-6

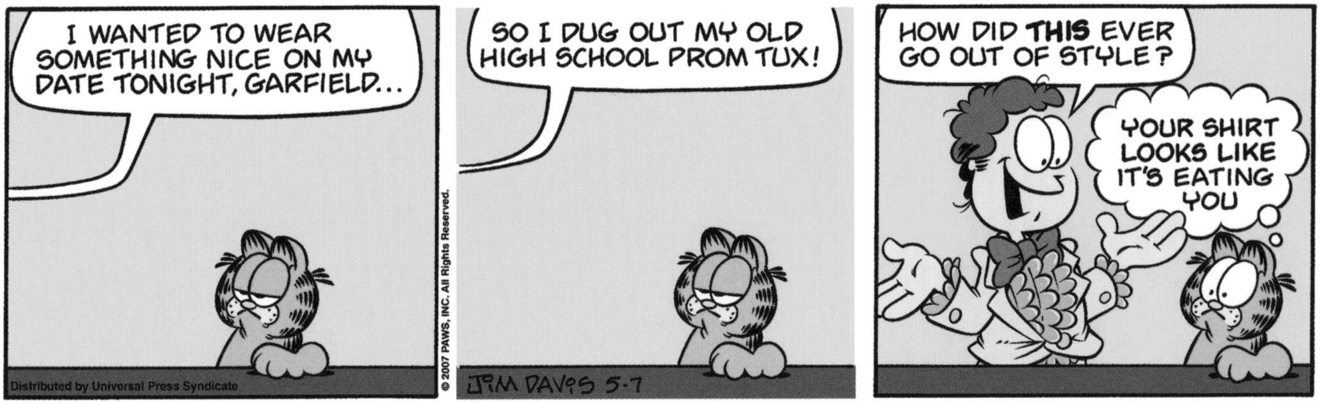
I WANTED TO WEAR SOMETHING NICE ON MY DATE TONIGHT, GARFIELD...
Distributed by Universal Press Syndicate
© 2007 PAWS, INC. All Rights Reserved.
SO I DUG OUT MY OLD HIGH SCHOOL PROM TUX!
JIM DAVIS 5-7
HOW DID **THIS** EVER GO OUT OF STYLE?
YOUR SHIRT LOOKS LIKE IT'S EATING YOU

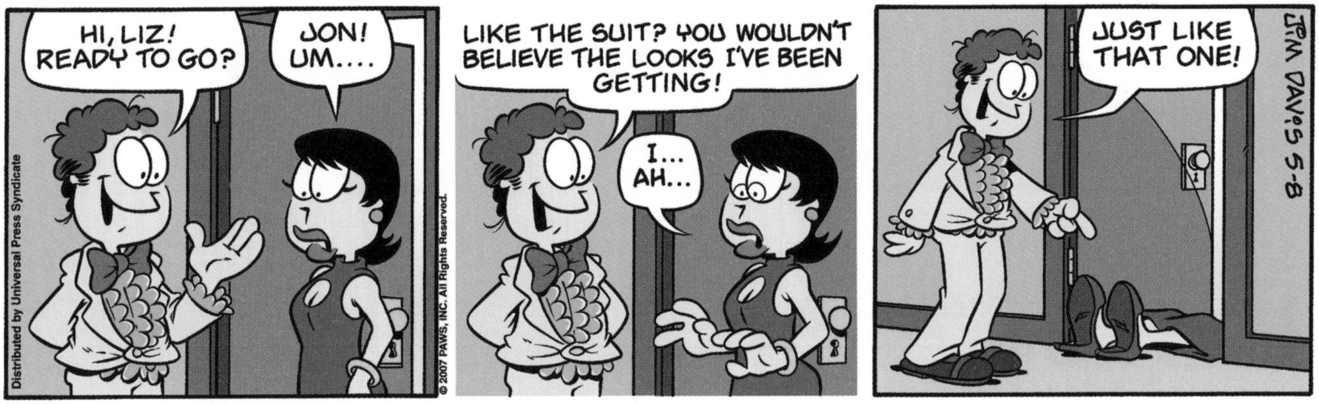
HI, LIZ! READY TO GO?
JON! UM....
Distributed by Universal Press Syndicate
© 2007 PAWS, INC. All Rights Reserved.
LIKE THE SUIT? YOU WOULDN'T BELIEVE THE LOOKS I'VE BEEN GETTING!
I... AH...
JUST LIKE THAT ONE!
JIM DAVIS 5-8

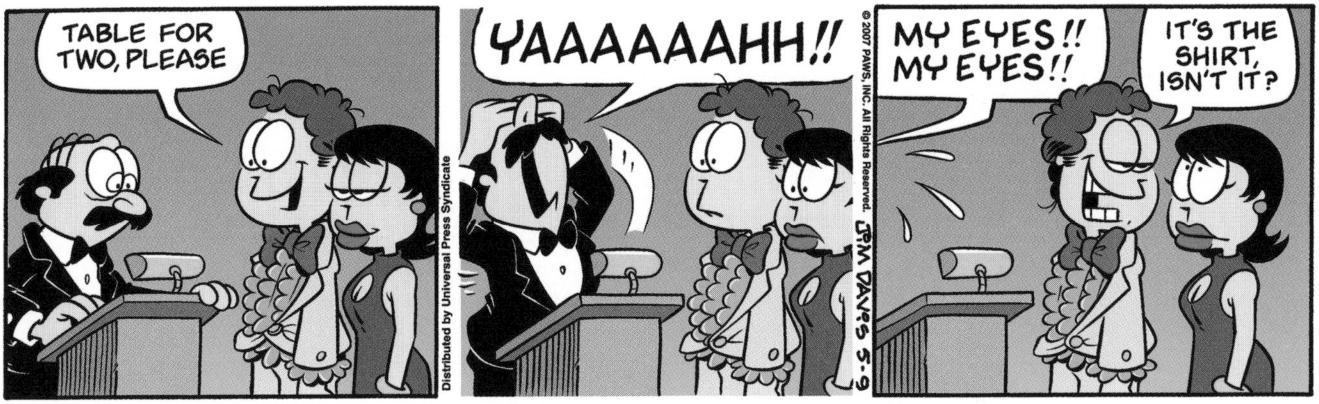
TABLE FOR TWO, PLEASE
Distributed by Universal Press Syndicate
YAAAAAAHH!!
© 2007 PAWS, INC. All Rights Reserved.
JIM DAVIS 5-9
MY EYES!! MY EYES!!
IT'S THE SHIRT, ISN'T IT?

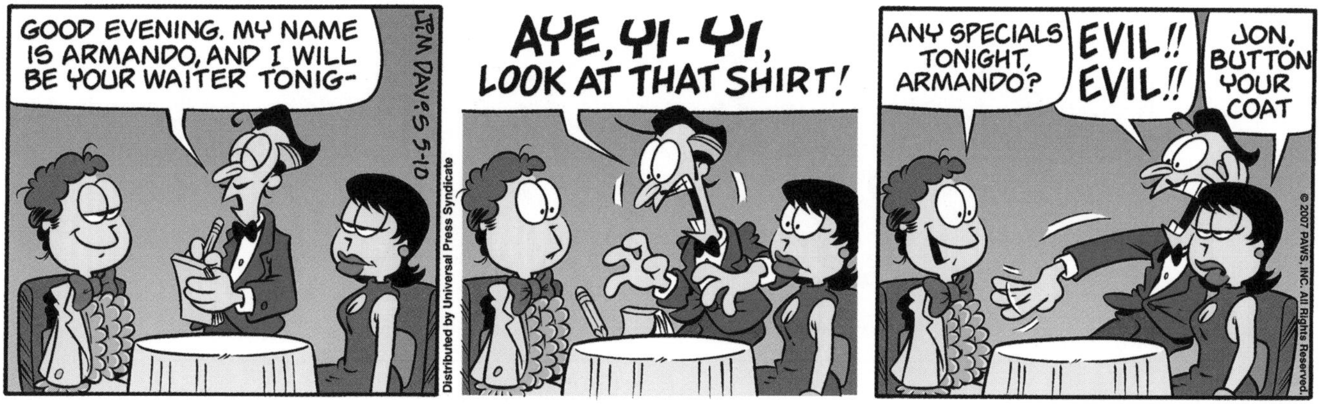
GOOD EVENING. MY NAME IS ARMANDO, AND I WILL BE YOUR WAITER TONIG-
JIM DAVIS 5-10
Distributed by Universal Press Syndicate
AYE, YI-YI, LOOK AT THAT SHIRT!
ANY SPECIALS TONIGHT, ARMANDO?
EVIL!! EVIL!!
JON, BUTTON YOUR COAT
© 2007 PAWS, INC. All Rights Reserved.

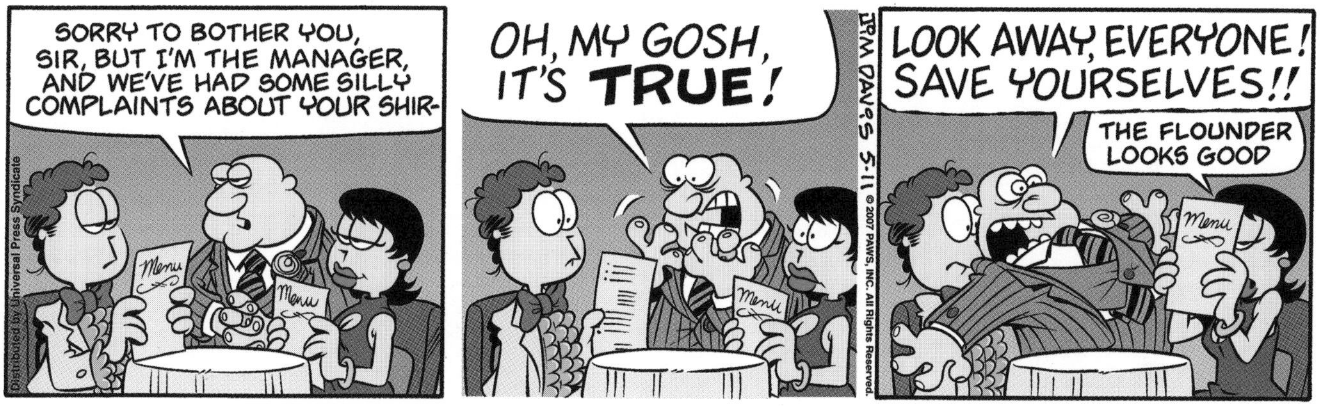
SORRY TO BOTHER YOU, SIR, BUT I'M THE MANAGER, AND WE'VE HAD SOME SILLY COMPLAINTS ABOUT YOUR SHIR-
Distributed by Universal Press Syndicate
Menu
Menu
OH, MY GOSH, IT'S TRUE!
JIM DAVIS 5-11
© 2007 PAWS, INC. All Rights Reserved.
LOOK AWAY, EVERYONE! SAVE YOURSELVES!!
THE FLOUNDER LOOKS GOOD
Menu

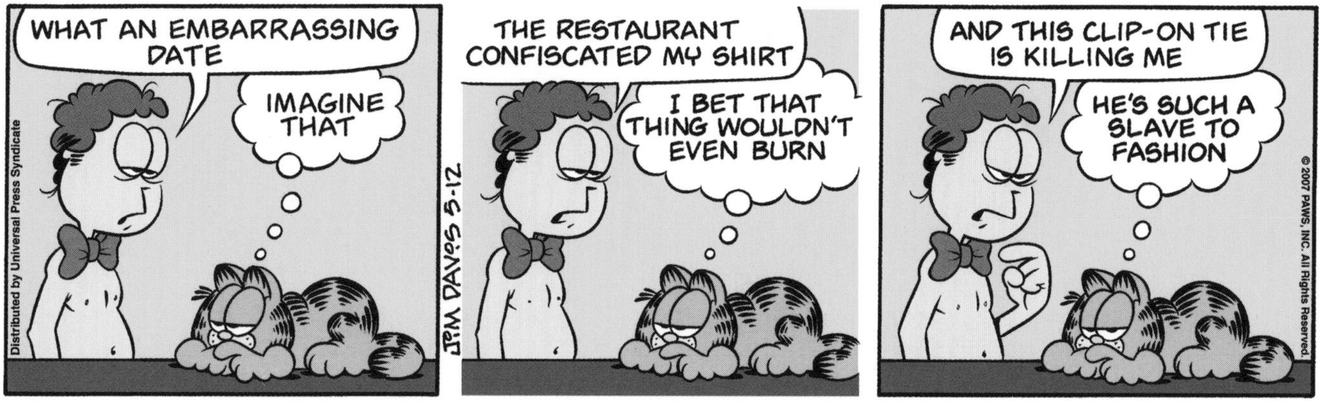
WHAT AN EMBARRASSING DATE
IMAGINE THAT
Distributed by Universal Press Syndicate
JIM DAVIS 5-12
THE RESTAURANT CONFISCATED MY SHIRT
I BET THAT THING WOULDN'T EVEN BURN
AND THIS CLIP-ON TIE IS KILLING ME
HE'S SUCH A SLAVE TO FASHION
© 2007 PAWS, INC. All Rights Reserved.

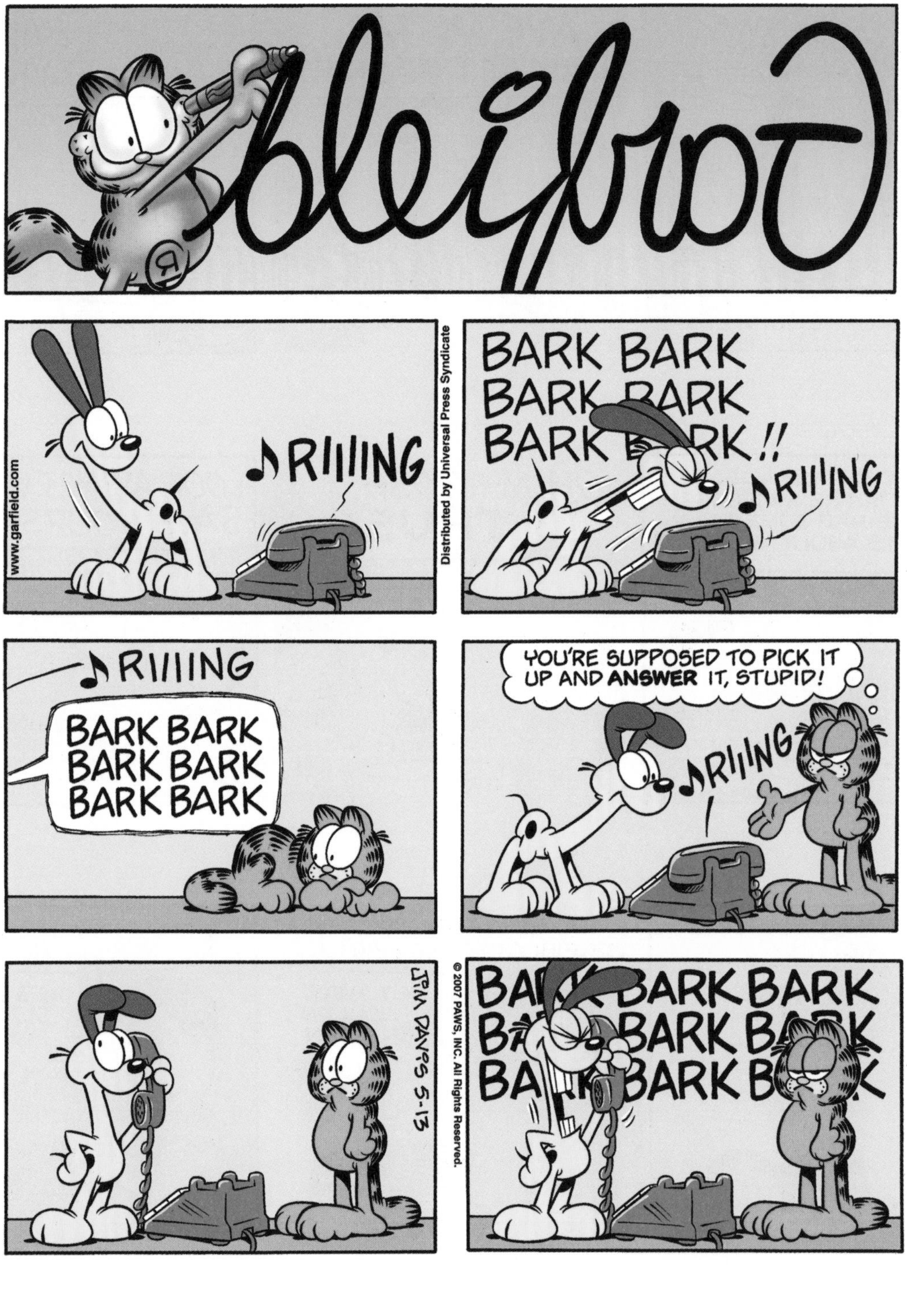
www.garfield.com
RIIIING
Distributed by Universal Press Syndicate
BARK BARK
BARK BARK
BARK BARK !!
RIIIING
RIIIING
BARK BARK
BARK BARK
BARK BARK
YOU'RE SUPPOSED TO PICK IT UP AND **ANSWER** IT, STUPID!
RIIING
JIM DAVIS 5-13
© 2007 PAWS, INC. All Rights Reserved.
BARK BARK BARK
BARK BARK BARK
BARK BARK BARK

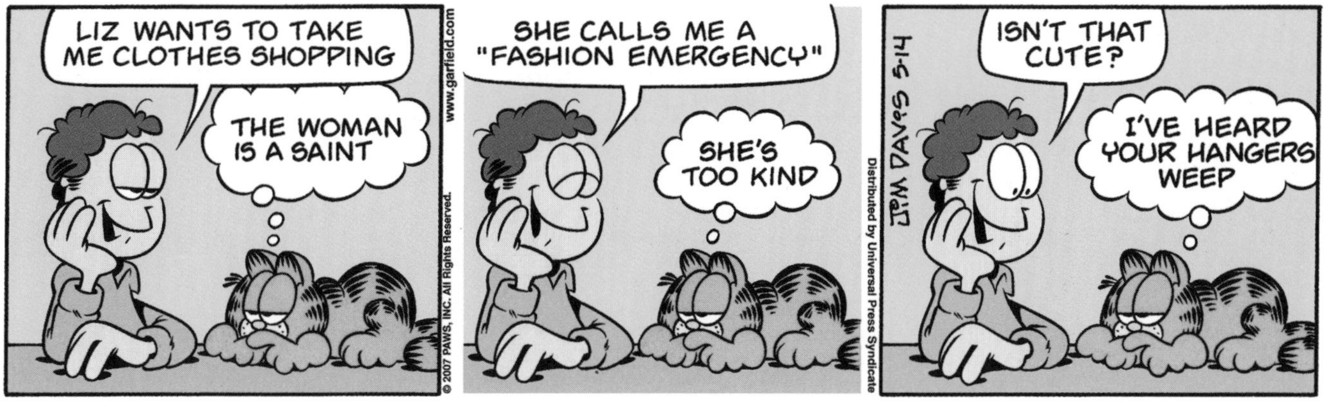
LIZ WANTS TO TAKE ME CLOTHES SHOPPING
THE WOMAN IS A SAINT
© 2007 PAWS, INC. All Rights Reserved. www.garfield.com
SHE CALLS ME A "FASHION EMERGENCY"
SHE'S TOO KIND
Distributed by Universal Press Syndicate
JIM DAVIS 5-14
ISN'T THAT CUTE?
I'VE HEARD YOUR HANGERS WEEP

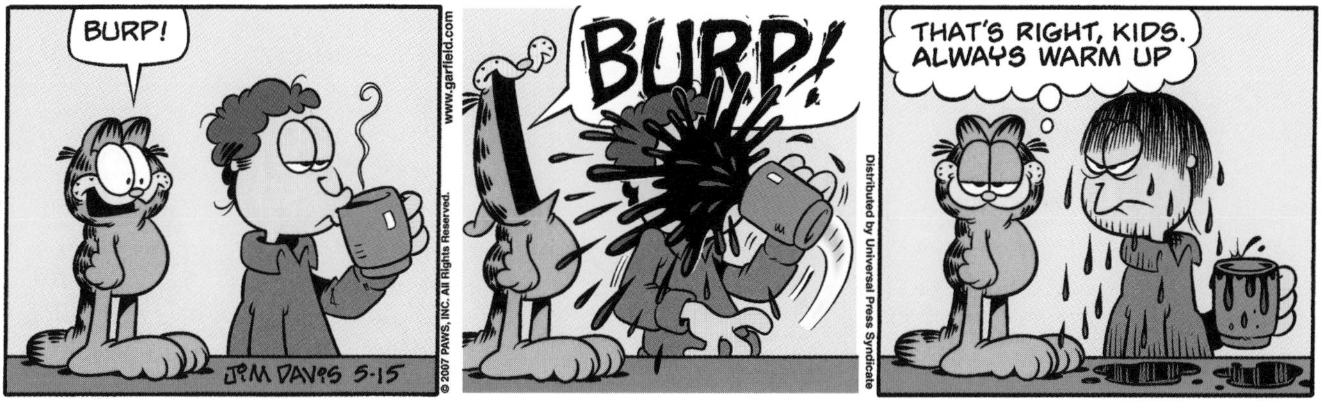
BURP!
JIM DAVIS 5-15
© 2007 PAWS, INC. All Rights Reserved. www.garfield.com
BURP!
Distributed by Universal Press Syndicate
THAT'S RIGHT, KIDS. ALWAYS WARM UP

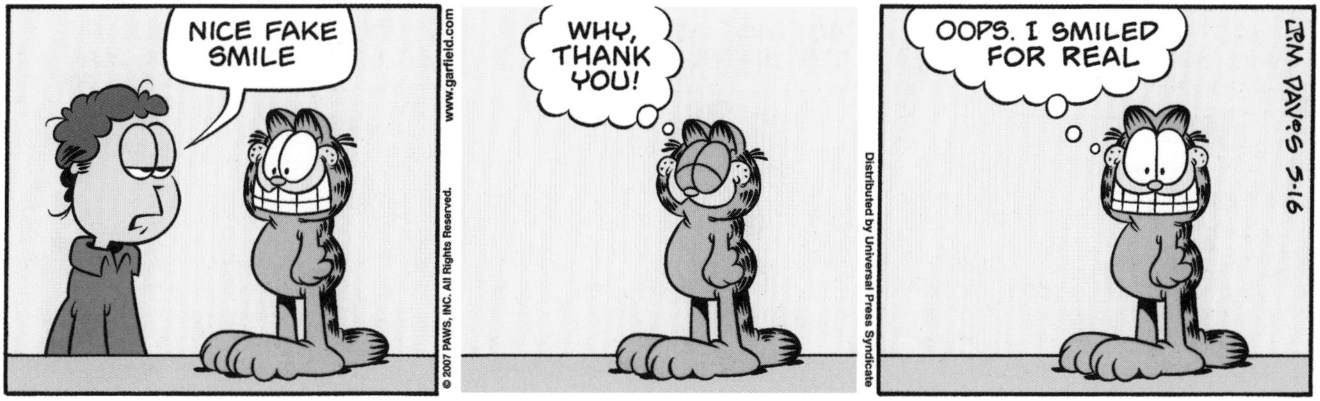
NICE FAKE SMILE
© 2007 PAWS, INC. All Rights Reserved. www.garfield.com
WHY, THANK YOU!
Distributed by Universal Press Syndicate
OOPS. I SMILED FOR REAL
JIM DAVIS 5-16

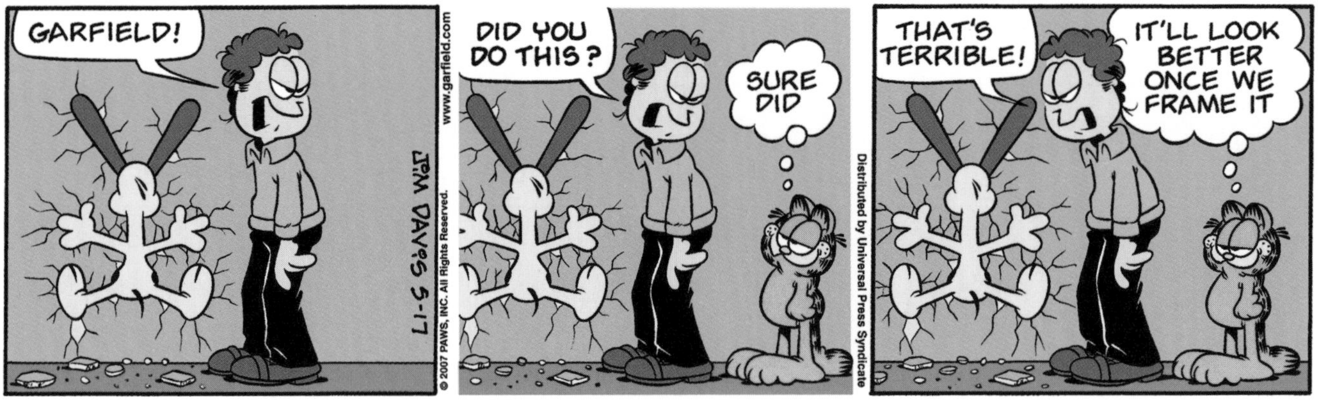
GARFIELD!
JIM DAVIS 5-17
© 2007 PAWS, INC. All Rights Reserved. www.garfield.com
DID YOU DO THIS?
SURE DID
Distributed by Universal Press Syndicate
THAT'S TERRIBLE!
IT'LL LOOK BETTER ONCE WE FRAME IT

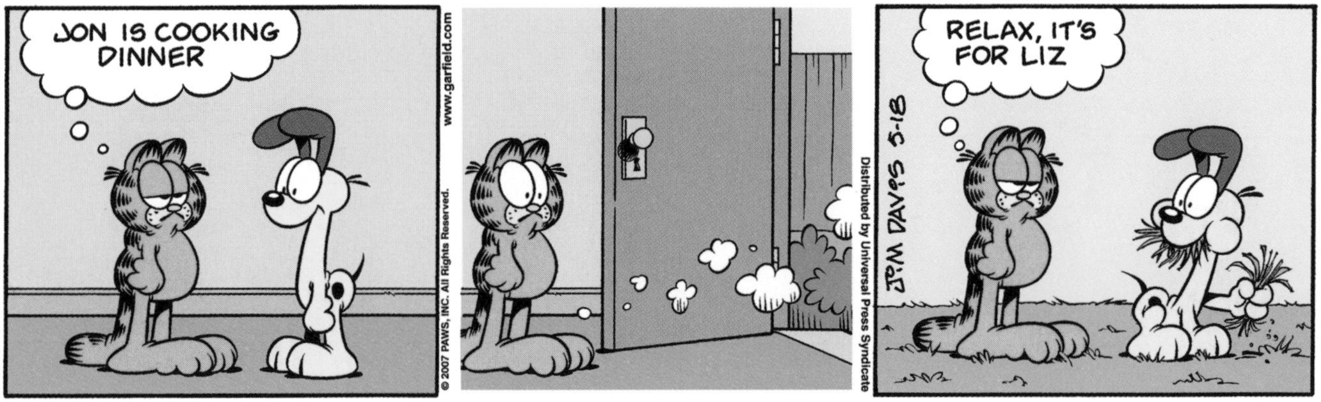
JON IS COOKING DINNER
© 2007 PAWS, INC. All Rights Reserved. www.garfield.com
JIM DAVIS 5-18
Distributed by Universal Press Syndicate
RELAX, IT'S FOR LIZ

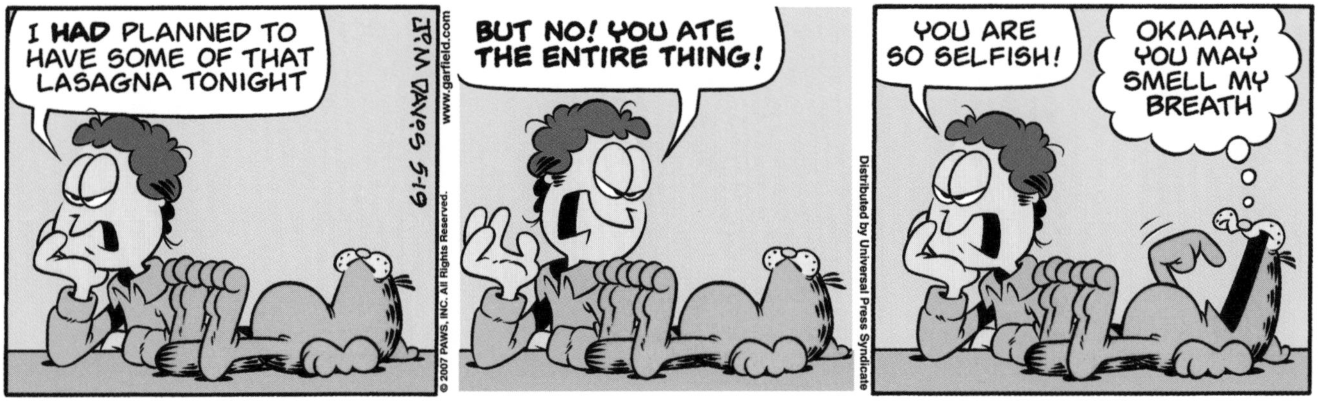
I **HAD** PLANNED TO HAVE SOME OF THAT LASAGNA TONIGHT
JIM DAVIS 5-19
© 2007 PAWS, INC. All Rights Reserved. www.garfield.com
BUT NO! YOU ATE THE ENTIRE THING!
Distributed by Universal Press Syndicate
YOU ARE SO SELFISH!
OKAAAY, YOU MAY SMELL MY BREATH

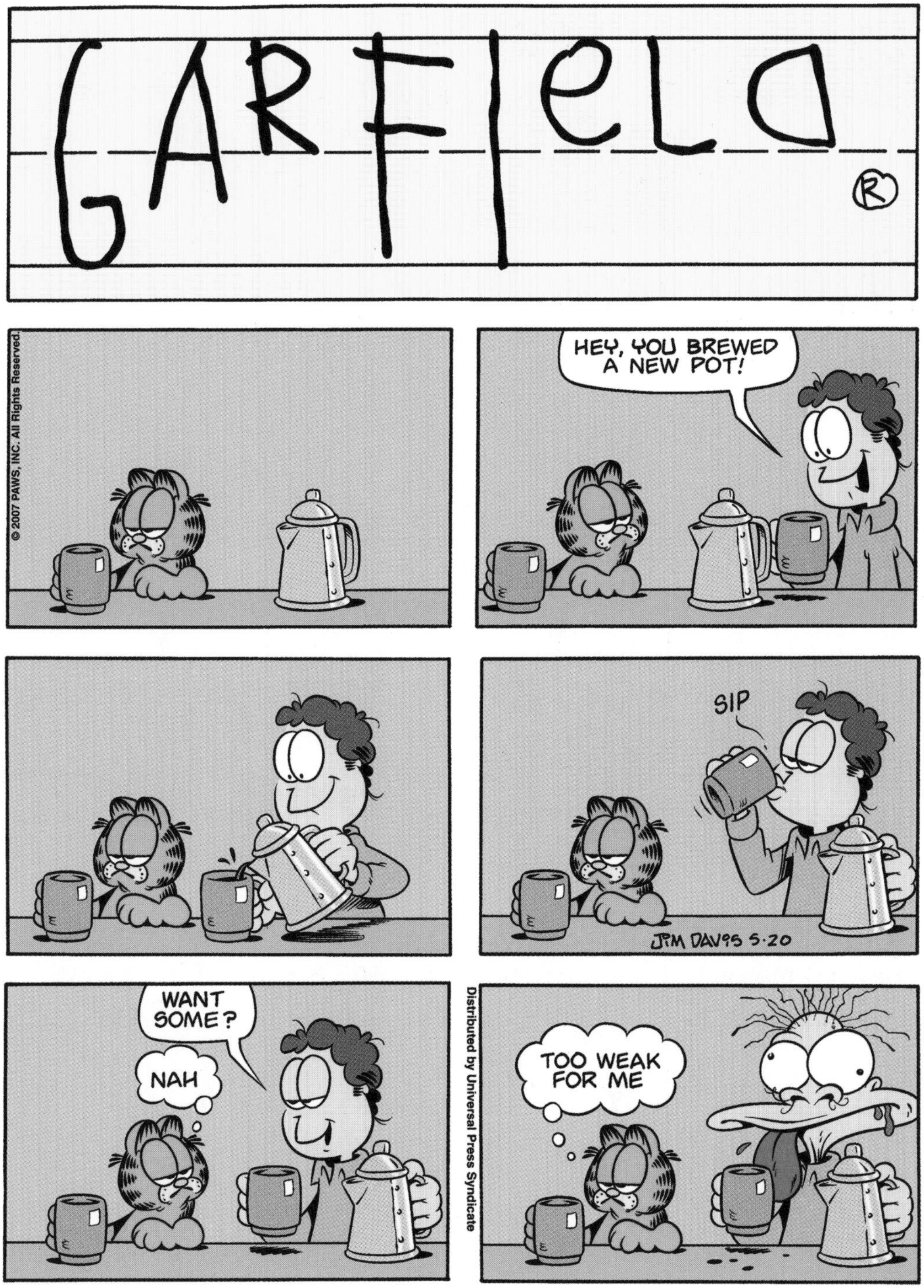
GARFIELD ®
© 2007 PAWS, INC. All Rights Reserved.
HEY, YOU BREWED A NEW POT!
SIP
JIM DAVIS 5·20
WANT SOME?
NAH
Distributed by Universal Press Syndicate
TOO WEAK FOR ME

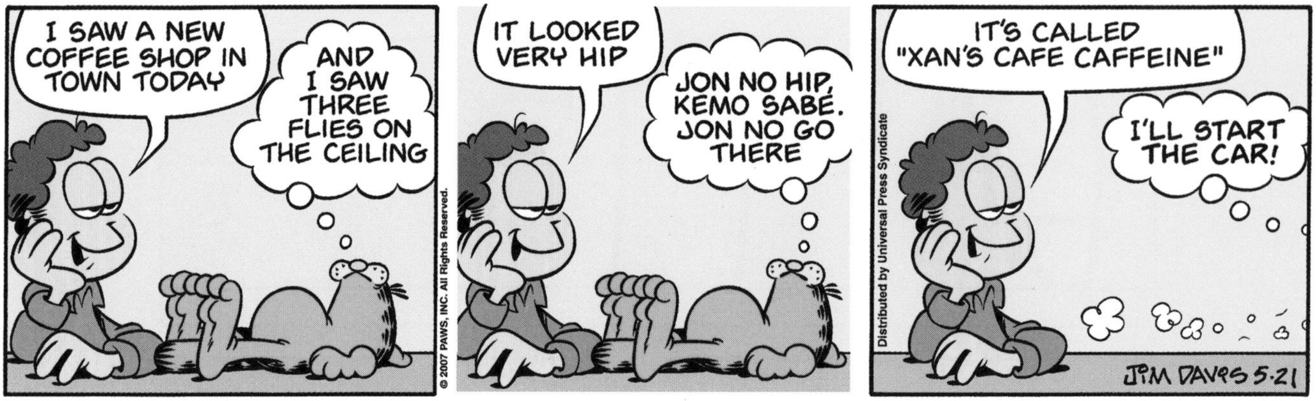
I SAW A NEW COFFEE SHOP IN TOWN TODAY
AND I SAW THREE FLIES ON THE CEILING
© 2007 PAWS, INC. All Rights Reserved.
IT LOOKED VERY HIP
JON NO HIP, KEMO SABÉ. JON NO GO THERE
Distributed by Universal Press Syndicate
IT'S CALLED "XAN'S CAFE CAFFEINE"
I'LL START THE CAR!
JIM DAVIS 5-21

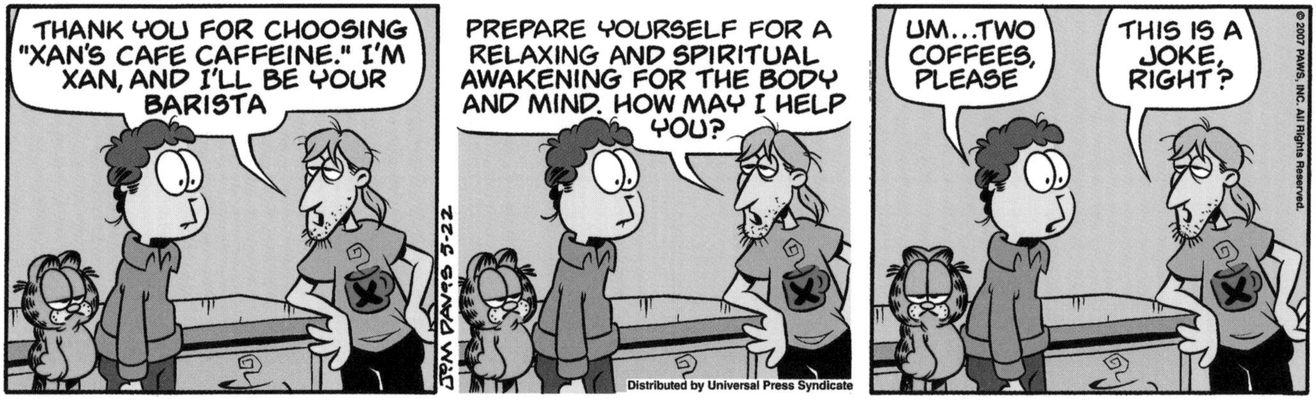
THANK YOU FOR CHOOSING "XAN'S CAFE CAFFEINE." I'M XAN, AND I'LL BE YOUR BARISTA
JIM DAVIS 5-22
PREPARE YOURSELF FOR A RELAXING AND SPIRITUAL AWAKENING FOR THE BODY AND MIND. HOW MAY I HELP YOU?
Distributed by Universal Press Syndicate
UM...TWO COFFEES, PLEASE
THIS IS A JOKE, RIGHT?
© 2007 PAWS, INC. All Rights Reserved.

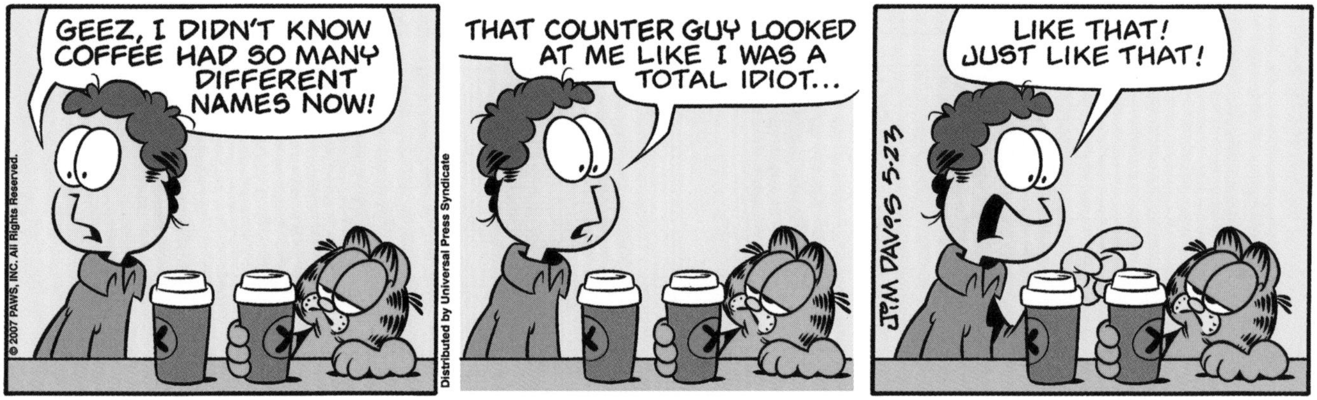
GEEZ, I DIDN'T KNOW COFFEE HAD SO MANY DIFFERENT NAMES NOW!
© 2007 PAWS, INC. All Rights Reserved.
Distributed by Universal Press Syndicate
THAT COUNTER GUY LOOKED AT ME LIKE I WAS A TOTAL IDIOT...
LIKE THAT! JUST LIKE THAT!
JIM DAVIS 5-23

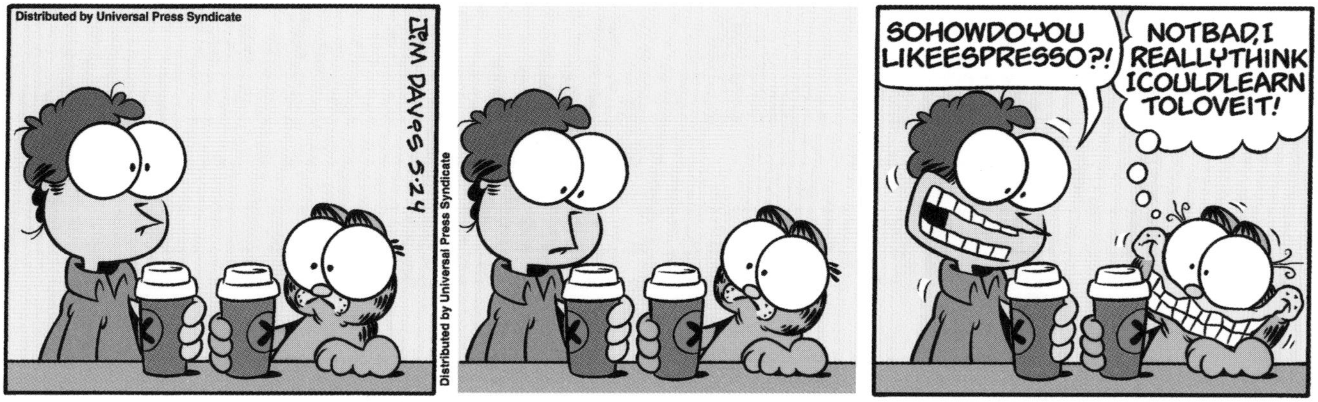
Distributed by Universal Press Syndicate
JIM DAVIS 5-24
Distributed by Universal Press Syndicate
SOHOWDOYOU LIKEESPRESSO?!
NOTBAD,I REALLYTHINK ICOULDLEARN TOLOVEIT!

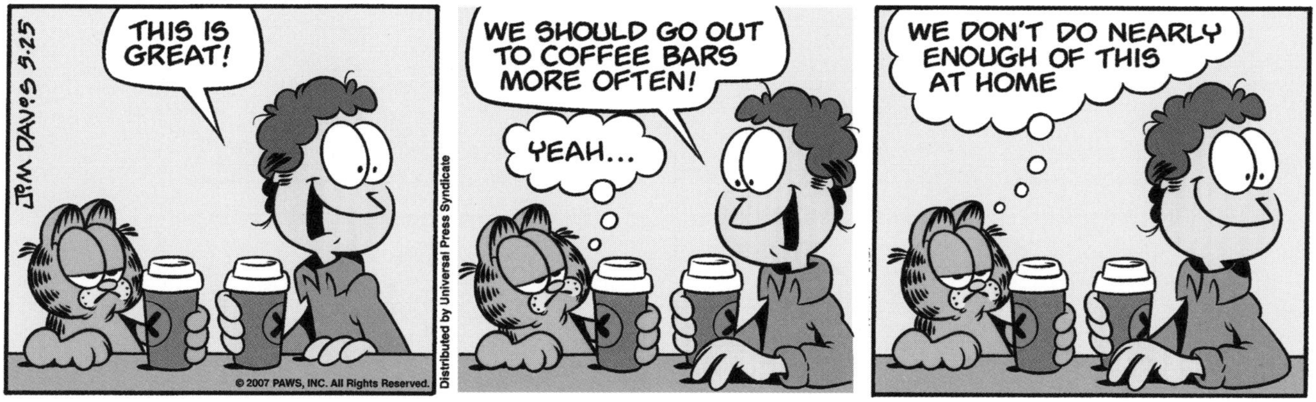
JIM DAVIS 5-25
THIS IS GREAT!
© 2007 PAWS, INC. All Rights Reserved.
Distributed by Universal Press Syndicate
WE SHOULD GO OUT TO COFFEE BARS MORE OFTEN!
YEAH...
WE DON'T DO NEARLY ENOUGH OF THIS AT HOME

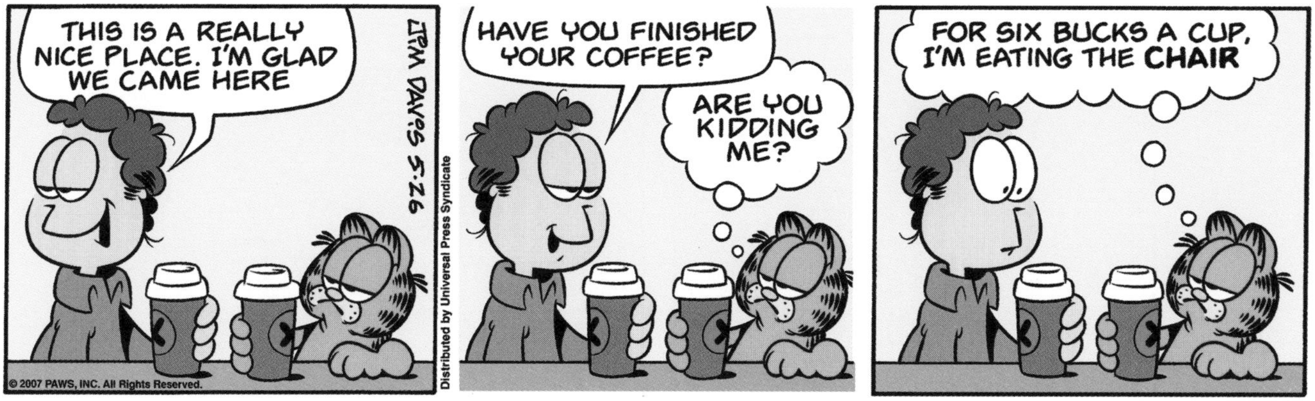
THIS IS A REALLY NICE PLACE. I'M GLAD WE CAME HERE
JIM DAVIS 5-26
© 2007 PAWS, INC. All Rights Reserved.
Distributed by Universal Press Syndicate
HAVE YOU FINISHED YOUR COFFEE?
ARE YOU KIDDING ME?
FOR SIX BUCKS A CUP, I'M EATING THE **CHAIR**

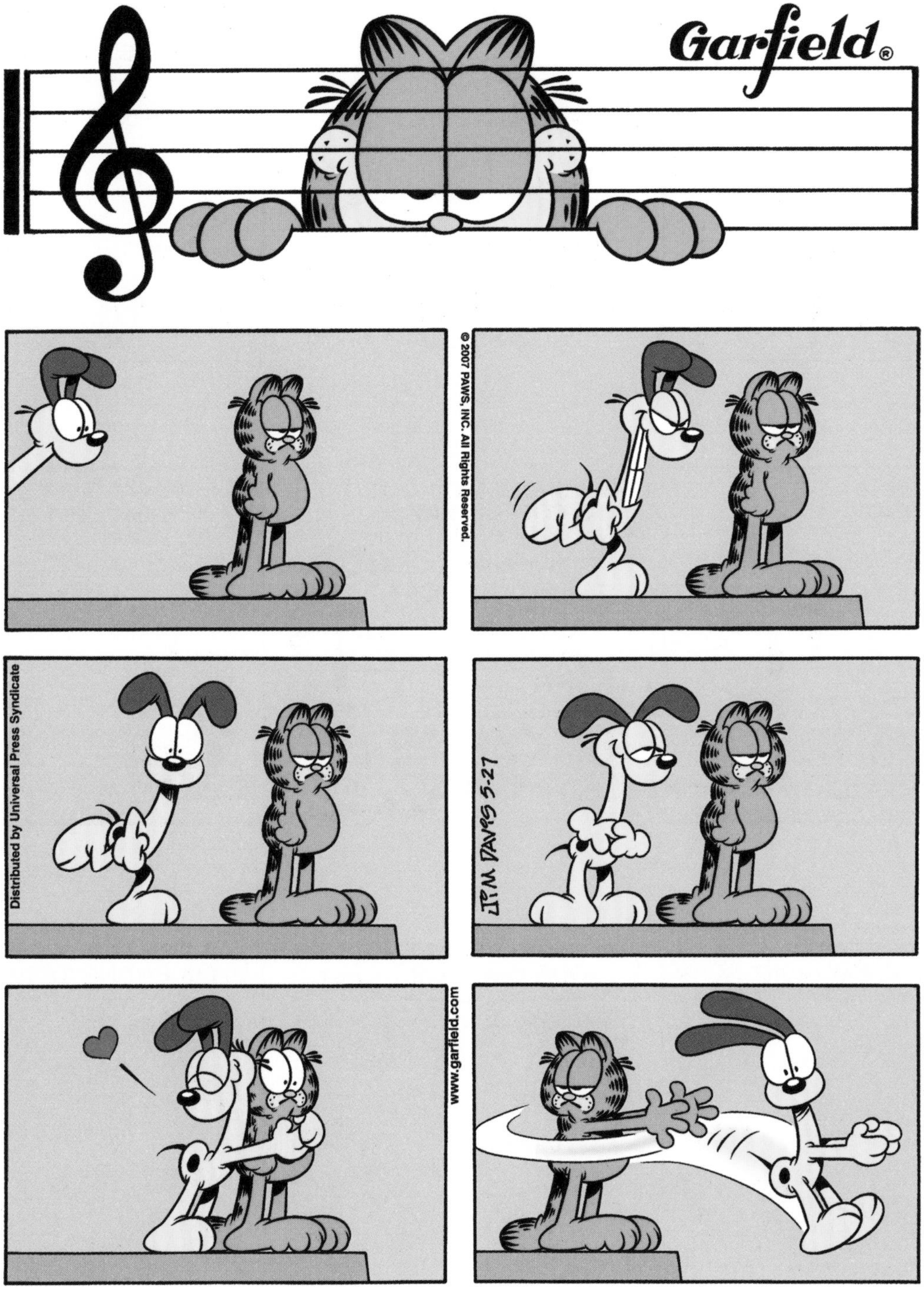
Garfield®
© 2007 PAWS, INC. All Rights Reserved.
Distributed by Universal Press Syndicate
JPM DAVIS 5-27
www.garfield.com

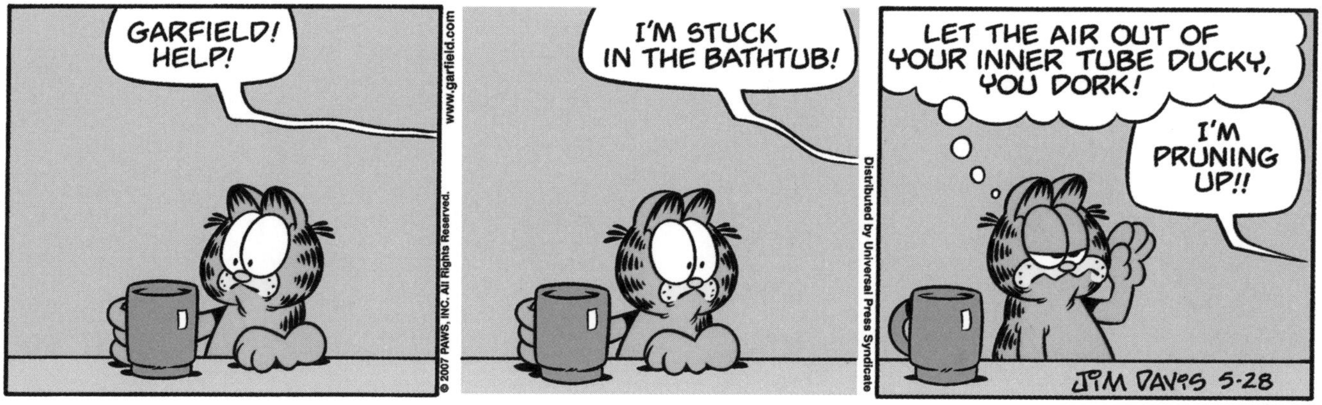
GARFIELD! HELP!
I'M STUCK IN THE BATHTUB!
LET THE AIR OUT OF YOUR INNER TUBE DUCKY, YOU DORK!
I'M PRUNING UP!!
JIM DAVIS 5-28
© 2007 PAWS, INC. All Rights Reserved.
www.garfield.com
Distributed by Universal Press Syndicate

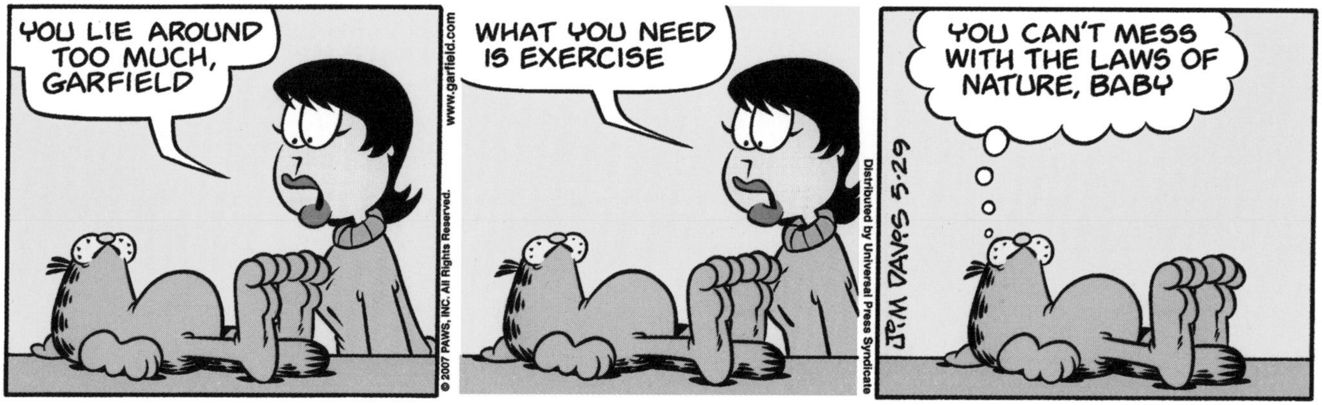
YOU LIE AROUND TOO MUCH, GARFIELD
WHAT YOU NEED IS EXERCISE
YOU CAN'T MESS WITH THE LAWS OF NATURE, BABY
JIM DAVIS 5-29
© 2007 PAWS, INC. All Rights Reserved.
www.garfield.com
Distributed by Universal Press Syndicate

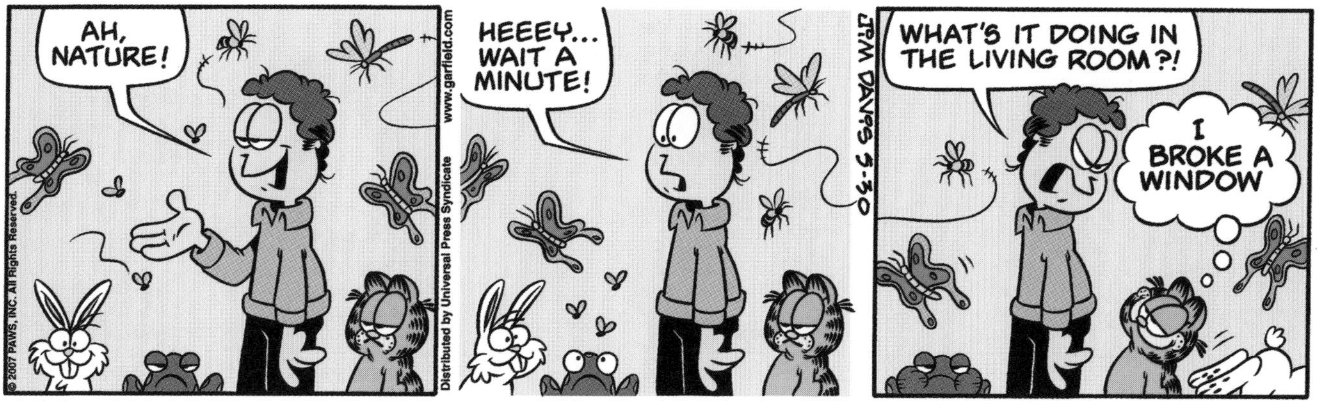
AH, NATURE!
HEEEY... WAIT A MINUTE!
WHAT'S IT DOING IN THE LIVING ROOM?!
I BROKE A WINDOW
JIM DAVIS 5-30
© 2007 PAWS, INC. All Rights Reserved.
www.garfield.com
Distributed by Universal Press Syndicate

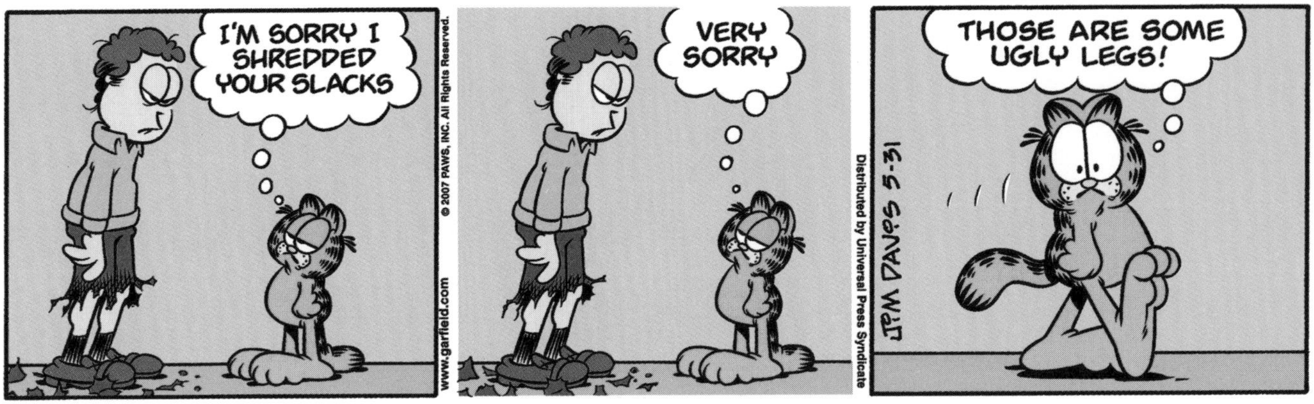
I'M SORRY I SHREDDED YOUR SLACKS
VERY SORRY
THOSE ARE SOME UGLY LEGS!
JIM DAVIS 5-31
© 2007 PAWS, INC. All Rights Reserved.
www.garfield.com
Distributed by Universal Press Syndicate

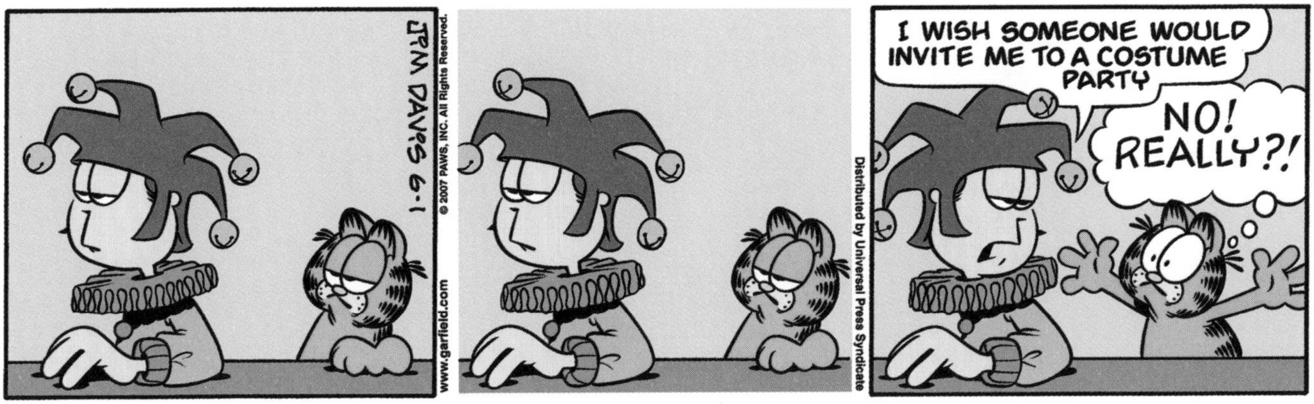
JIM DAVIS 6-1
© 2007 PAWS, INC. All Rights Reserved.
www.garfield.com
Distributed by Universal Press Syndicate
I WISH SOMEONE WOULD INVITE ME TO A COSTUME PARTY
NO! REALLY?!

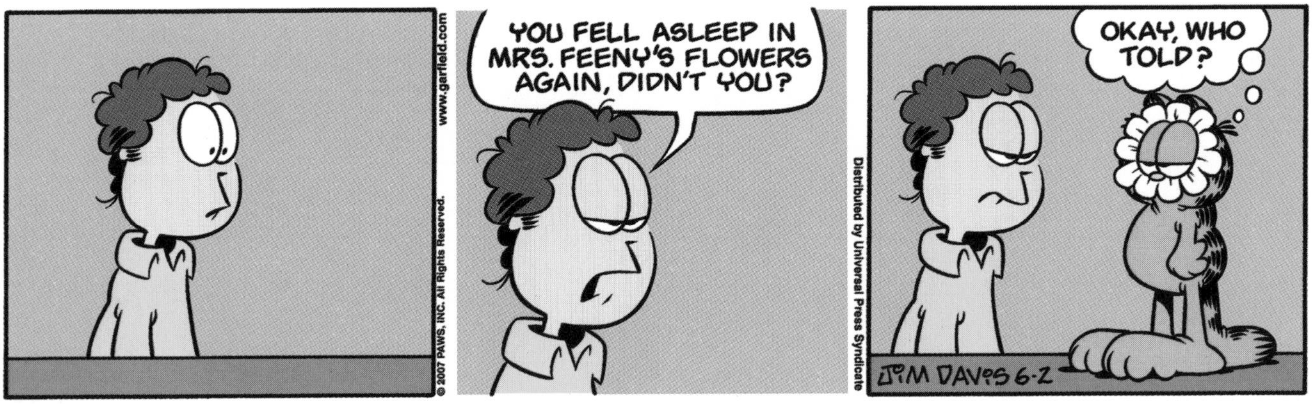
www.garfield.com
© 2007 PAWS, INC. All Rights Reserved.
YOU FELL ASLEEP IN MRS. FEENY'S FLOWERS AGAIN, DIDN'T YOU?
Distributed by Universal Press Syndicate
OKAY, WHO TOLD?
JIM DAVIS 6-2

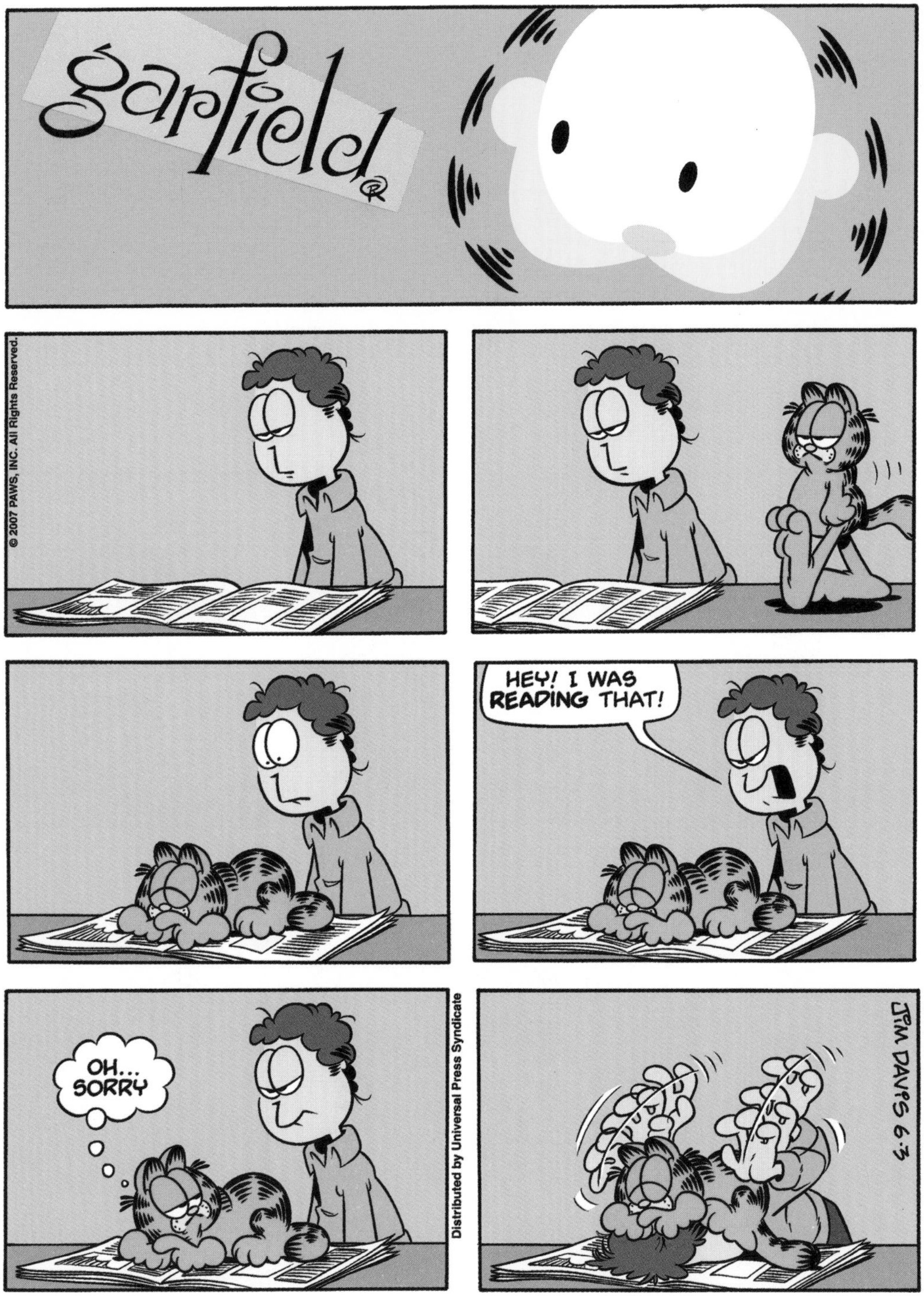
garfield®
© 2007 PAWS, INC. All Rights Reserved.
HEY! I WAS READING THAT!
OH... SORRY
Distributed by Universal Press Syndicate
JIM DAVIS 6-3

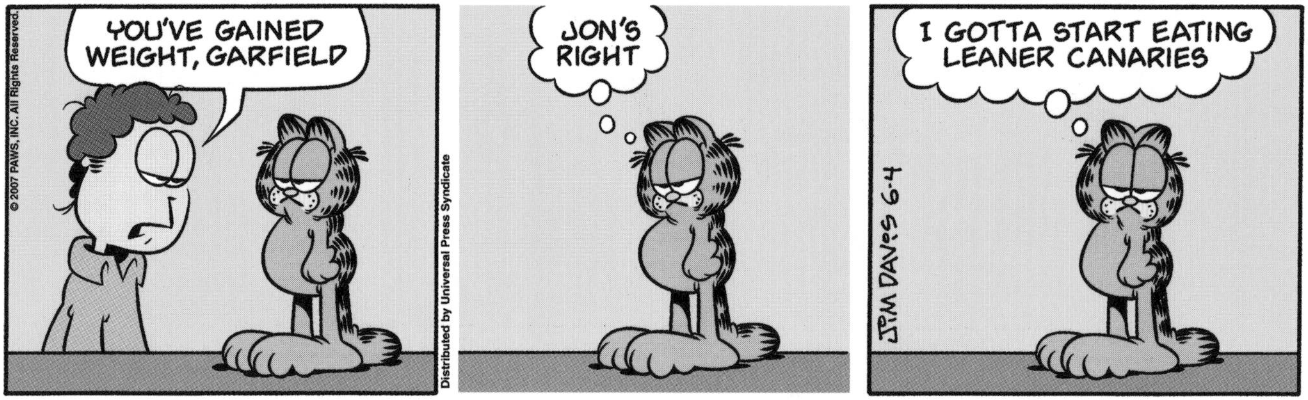
© 2007 PAWS, INC. All Rights Reserved.
YOU'VE GAINED WEIGHT, GARFIELD
Distributed by Universal Press Syndicate
JON'S RIGHT
I GOTTA START EATING LEANER CANARIES
JIM DAVIS 6-4

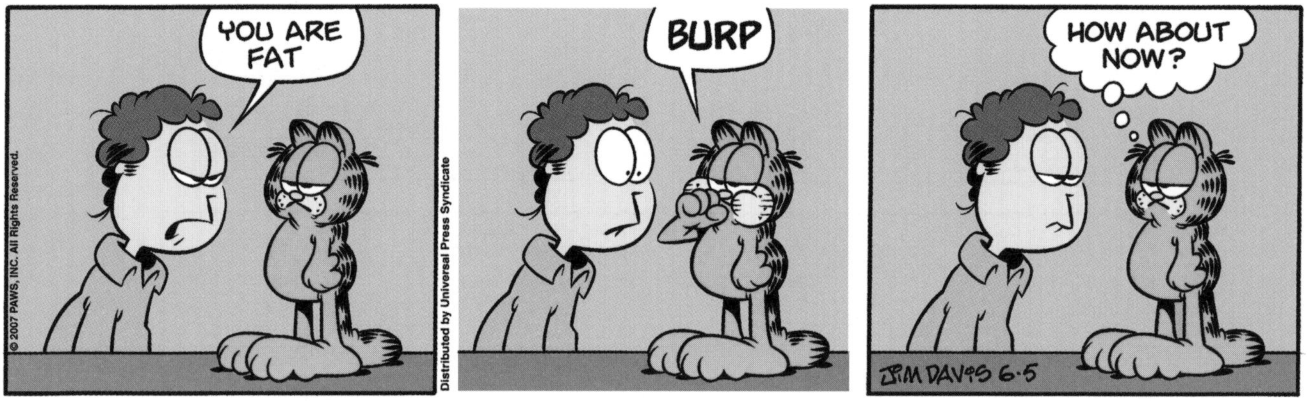
© 2007 PAWS, INC. All Rights Reserved.
YOU ARE FAT
Distributed by Universal Press Syndicate
BURP
HOW ABOUT NOW?
JIM DAVIS 6-5

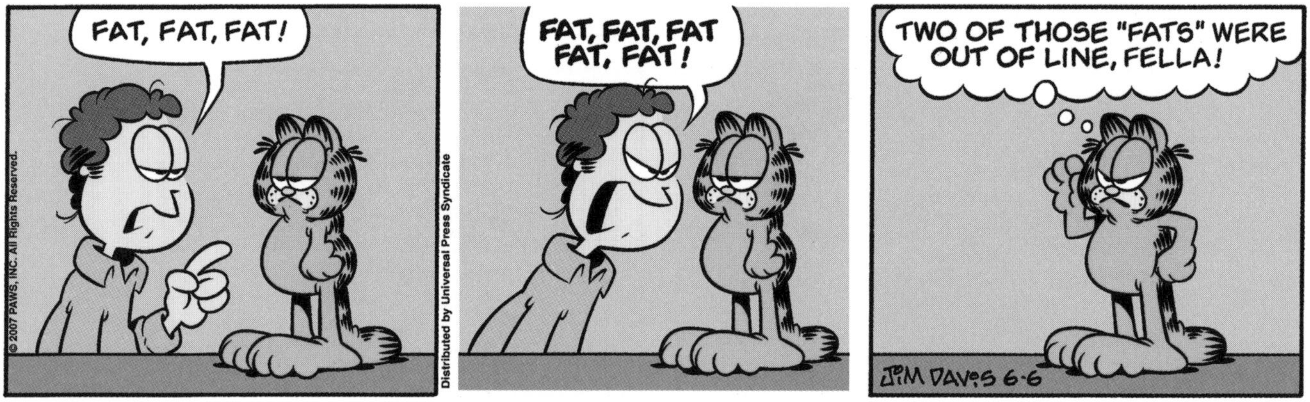
© 2007 PAWS, INC. All Rights Reserved.
FAT, FAT, FAT!
Distributed by Universal Press Syndicate
FAT, FAT, FAT FAT, FAT!
TWO OF THOSE "FATS" WERE OUT OF LINE, FELLA!
JIM DAVIS 6-6

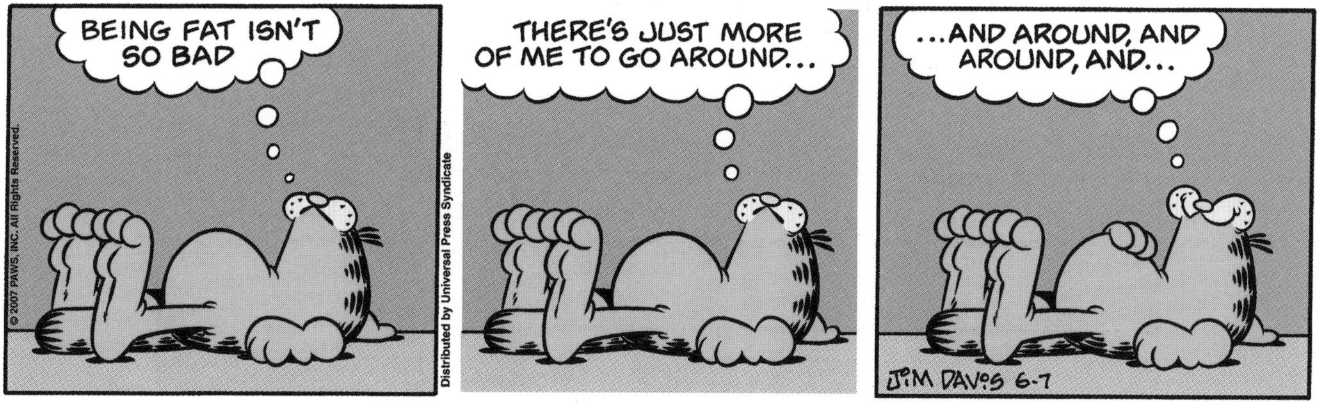
BEING FAT ISN'T SO BAD
THERE'S JUST MORE OF ME TO GO AROUND...
...AND AROUND, AND AROUND, AND...
JIM DAVIS 6-7
© 2007 PAWS, INC. All Rights Reserved.
Distributed by Universal Press Syndicate

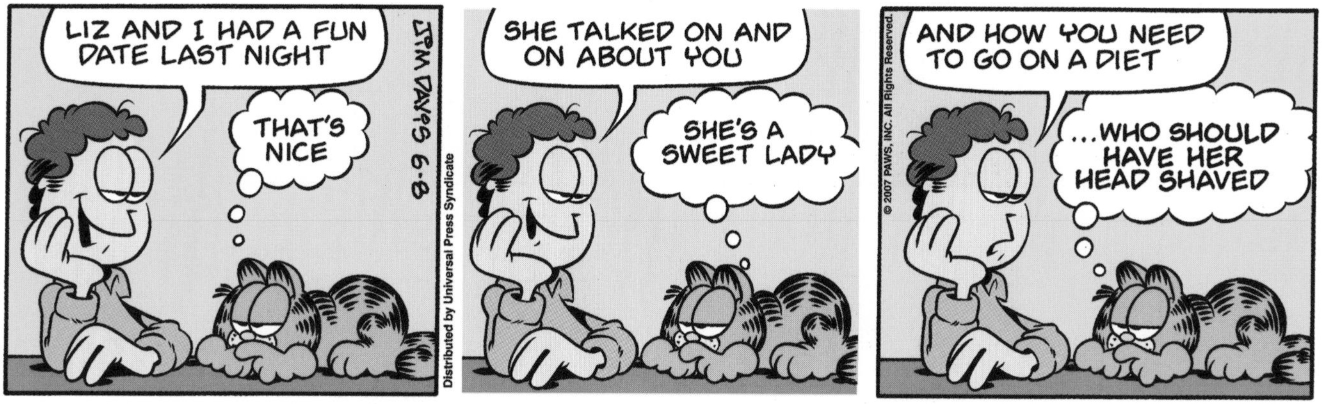
LIZ AND I HAD A FUN DATE LAST NIGHT
THAT'S NICE
JIM DAVIS 6-8
SHE TALKED ON AND ON ABOUT YOU
SHE'S A SWEET LADY
AND HOW YOU NEED TO GO ON A DIET
...WHO SHOULD HAVE HER HEAD SHAVED
Distributed by Universal Press Syndicate
© 2007 PAWS, INC. All Rights Reserved.

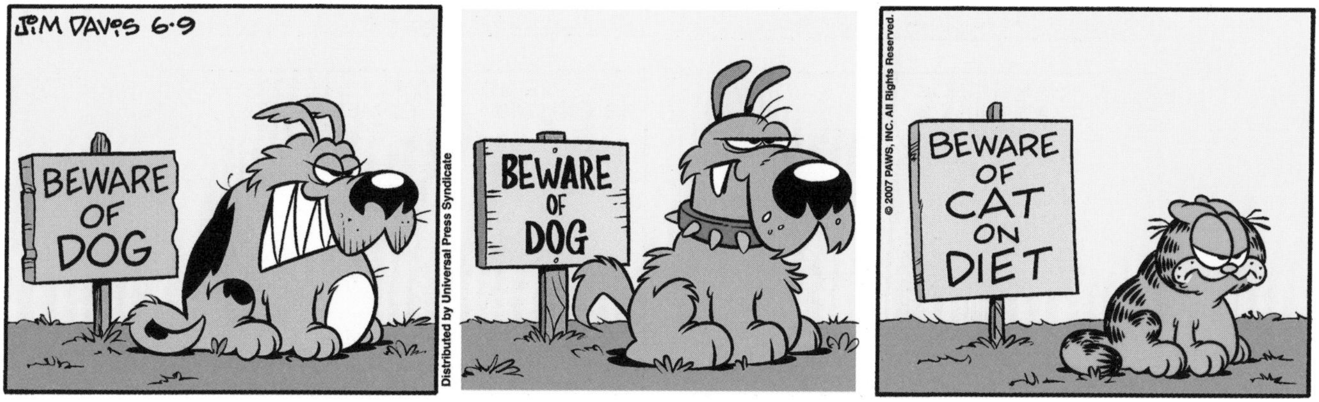
JIM DAVIS 6-9
BEWARE OF DOG
BEWARE OF DOG
BEWARE OF CAT ON DIET
Distributed by Universal Press Syndicate
© 2007 PAWS, INC. All Rights Reserved.

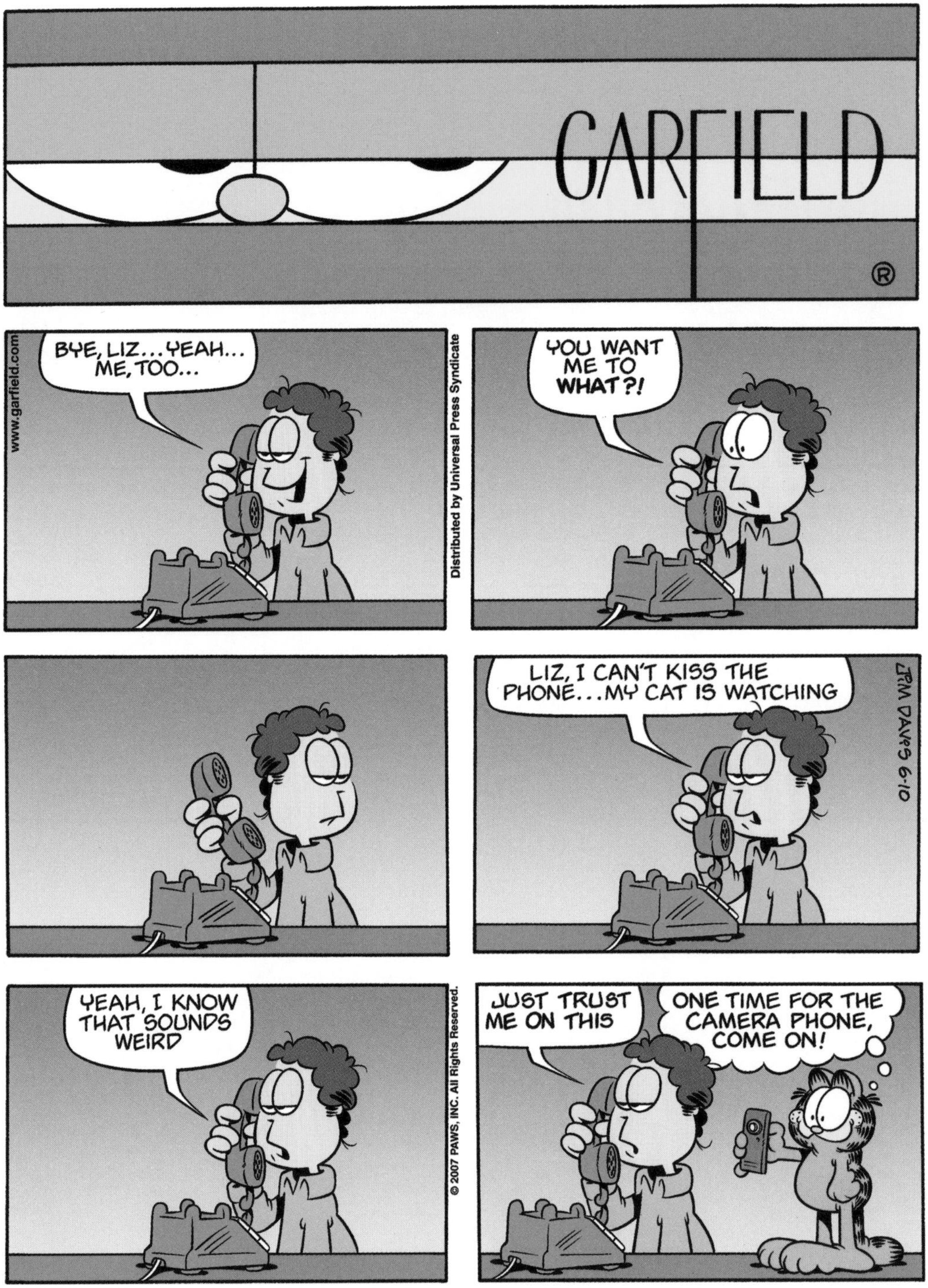
GARFIELD ®
www.garfield.com
BYE, LIZ... YEAH... ME, TOO...
Distributed by Universal Press Syndicate
YOU WANT ME TO WHAT?!
LIZ, I CAN'T KISS THE PHONE... MY CAT IS WATCHING
JIM DAVIS 6-10
YEAH, I KNOW THAT SOUNDS WEIRD
© 2007 PAWS, INC. All Rights Reserved.
JUST TRUST ME ON THIS
ONE TIME FOR THE CAMERA PHONE, COME ON!

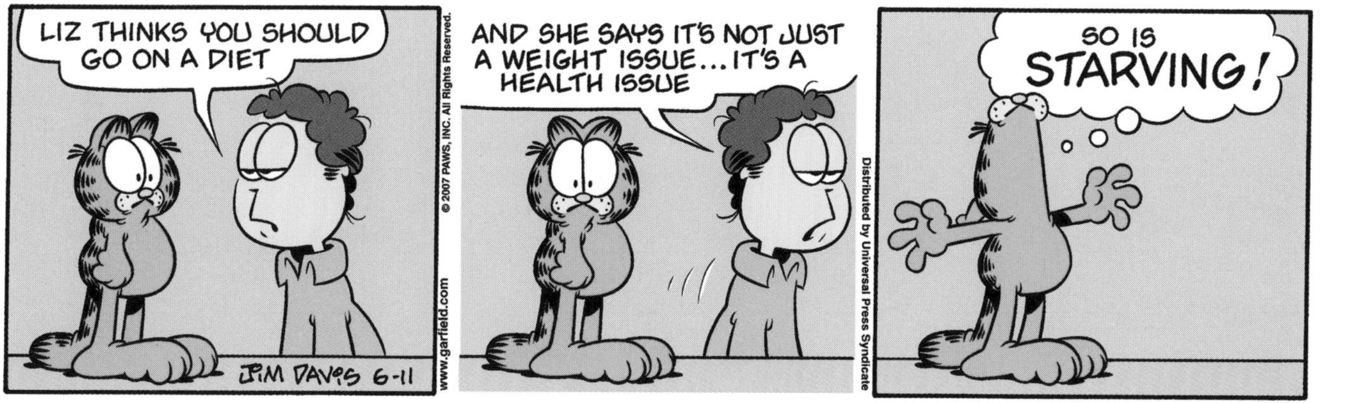
LIZ THINKS YOU SHOULD GO ON A DIET
JIM DAVIS 6-11
© 2007 PAWS, INC. All Rights Reserved.
www.garfield.com
AND SHE SAYS IT'S NOT JUST A WEIGHT ISSUE... IT'S A HEALTH ISSUE
Distributed by Universal Press Syndicate
SO IS STARVING!

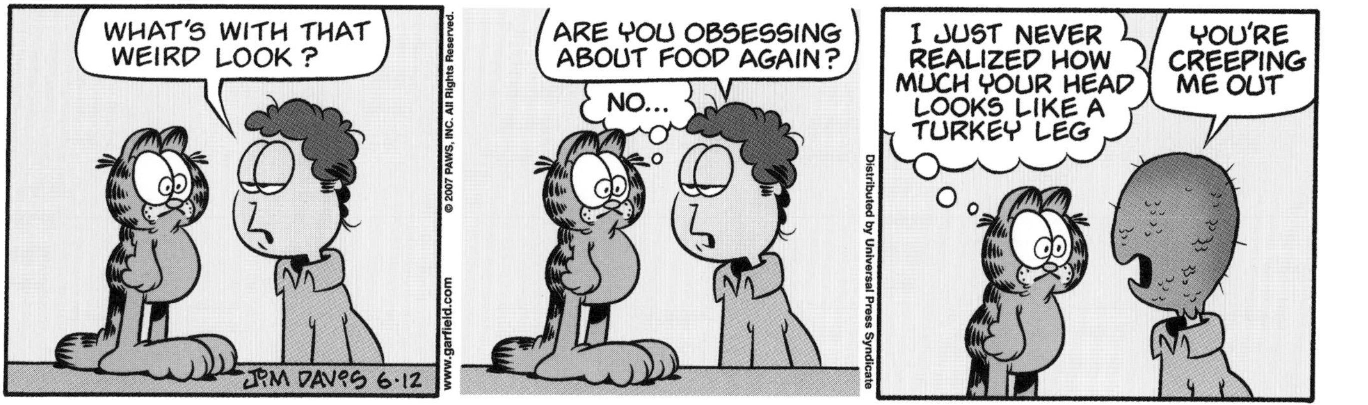
WHAT'S WITH THAT WEIRD LOOK?
JIM DAVIS 6-12
© 2007 PAWS, INC. All Rights Reserved.
www.garfield.com
ARE YOU OBSESSING ABOUT FOOD AGAIN?
NO...
Distributed by Universal Press Syndicate
I JUST NEVER REALIZED HOW MUCH YOUR HEAD LOOKS LIKE A TURKEY LEG
YOU'RE CREEPING ME OUT

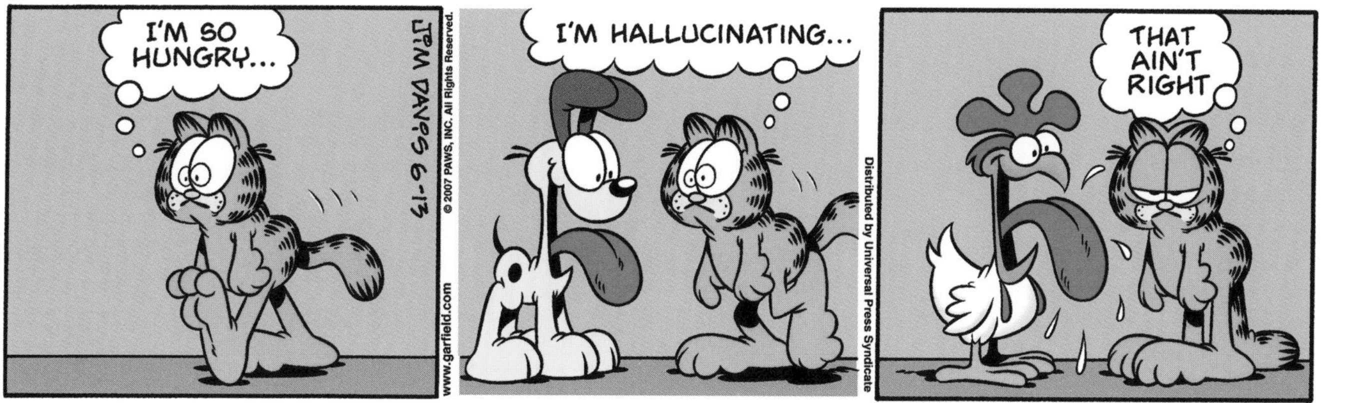
I'M SO HUNGRY...
JIM DAVIS 6-13
© 2007 PAWS, INC. All Rights Reserved.
www.garfield.com
I'M HALLUCINATING...
Distributed by Universal Press Syndicate
THAT AIN'T RIGHT

TOP 50 REASONS TO PARTY!

Somewhere in the world it's Happy Hour

You finally got your sock drawer organized

Nostradamus prophesied it

You want to listen to all 10,000 songs on your MP3 player

You're carrying a party gene

The moon is in a party phase

Because it's daytime

Because it's nighttime

Maturity is overrated

You're dying to wear your new lampshade

You finally potty trained your virtual pet

Your yo-yo stock went up a point

Your place could use a good trashing

You can't think of anything boring to do

You've invested heavily in piñatas

They just passed a law abolishing Mondays

The fun content of your blood is too low

You have a bad reputation to uphold

It's a good way to meet your local law enforcement officials

You don't want to offend the Party Gods

You're tired of playing charades by yourself

It's exactly one week later than this time last week

Fun is a terrible thing to waste

Elvis told you to in a dream

You're not getting any younger

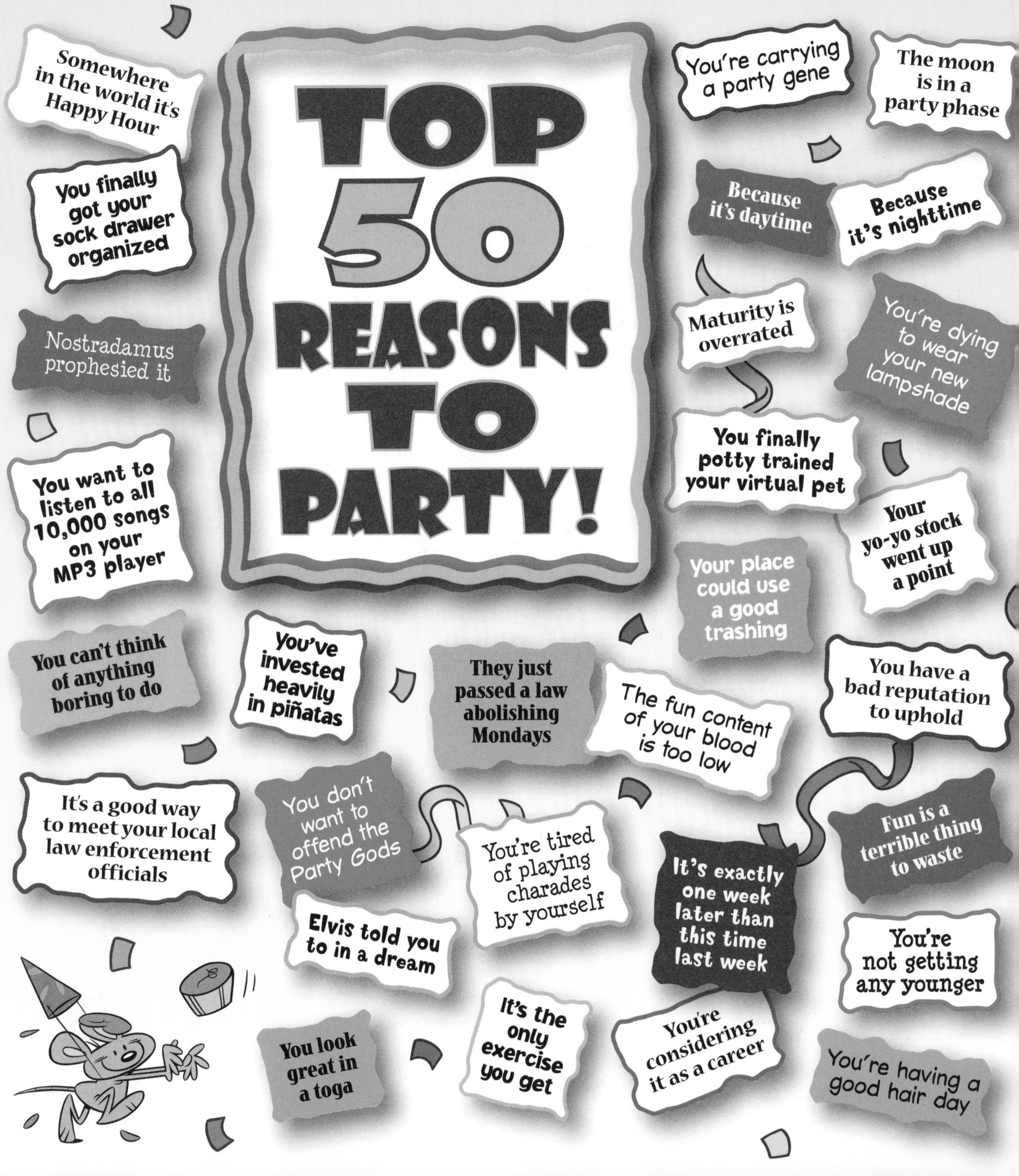

You look great in a toga

It's the only exercise you get

You're considering it as a career

You're having a good hair day

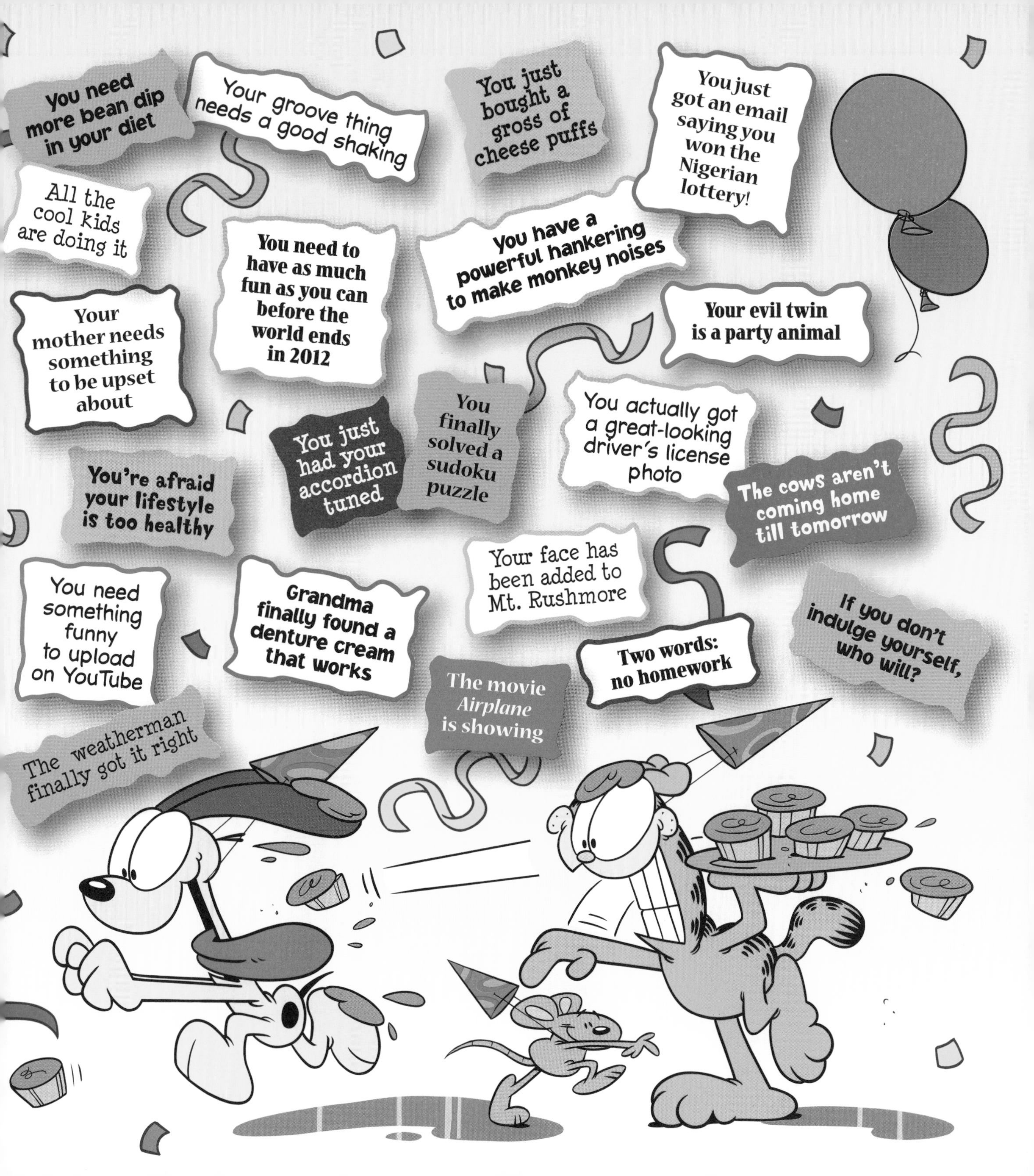

You need more bean dip in your diet
Your groove thing needs a good shaking
You just bought a gross of cheese puffs
You just got an email saying you won the Nigerian lottery!
All the cool kids are doing it
You need to have as much fun as you can before the world ends in 2012
You have a powerful hankering to make monkey noises
Your mother needs something to be upset about
Your evil twin is a party animal
You just had your accordion tuned
You finally solved a sudoku puzzle
You actually got a great-looking driver's license photo
You're afraid your lifestyle is too healthy
The cows aren't coming home till tomorrow
Your face has been added to Mt. Rushmore
You need something funny to upload on YouTube
Grandma finally found a denture cream that works
Two words: no homework
If you don't indulge yourself, who will?
The movie *Airplane* is showing
The weatherman finally got it right

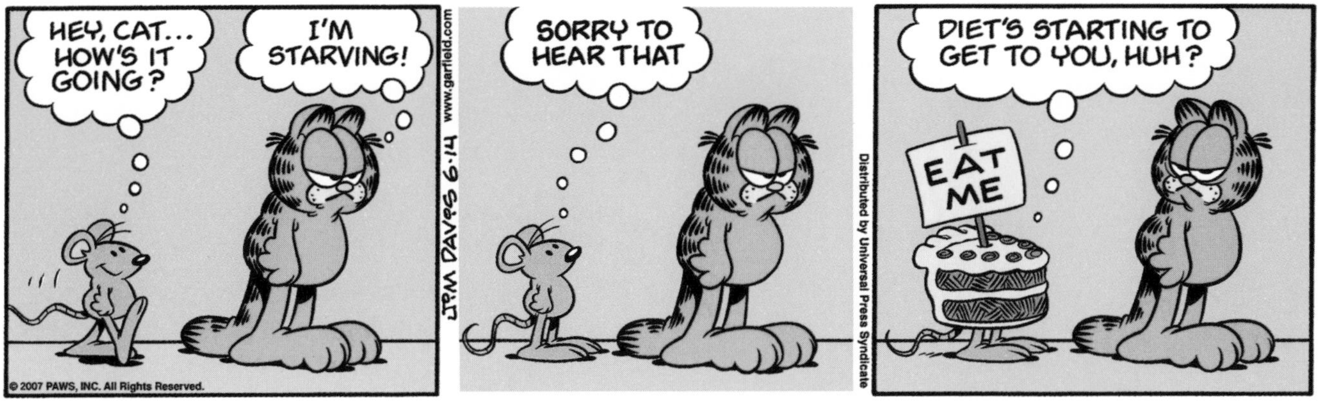
HEY, CAT... HOW'S IT GOING?
I'M STARVING!
SORRY TO HEAR THAT
DIET'S STARTING TO GET TO YOU, HUH?
EAT ME
JIM DAVIS 6-14
www.garfield.com
© 2007 PAWS, INC. All Rights Reserved.
Distributed by Universal Press Syndicate

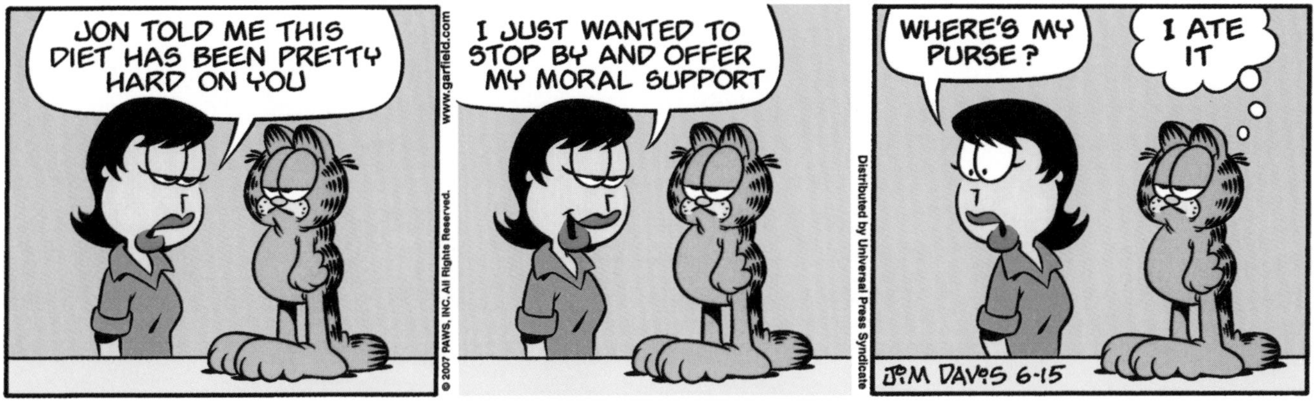
JON TOLD ME THIS DIET HAS BEEN PRETTY HARD ON YOU
I JUST WANTED TO STOP BY AND OFFER MY MORAL SUPPORT
WHERE'S MY PURSE?
I ATE IT
JIM DAVIS 6-15
www.garfield.com
© 2007 PAWS, INC. All Rights Reserved.
Distributed by Universal Press Syndicate

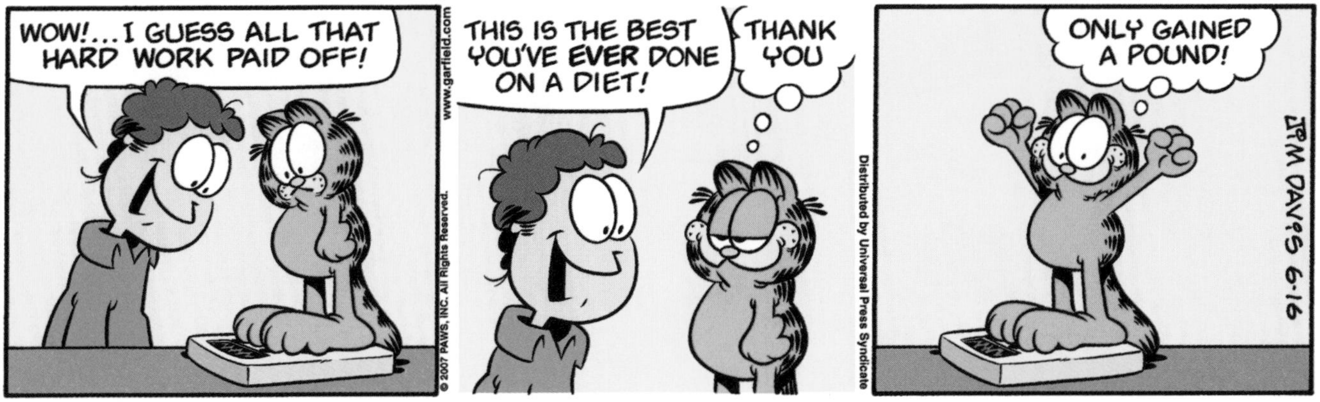
WOW!... I GUESS ALL THAT HARD WORK PAID OFF!
THIS IS THE BEST YOU'VE **EVER** DONE ON A DIET!
THANK YOU
ONLY GAINED A POUND!
JIM DAVIS 6-16
www.garfield.com
© 2007 PAWS, INC. All Rights Reserved.
Distributed by Universal Press Syndicate

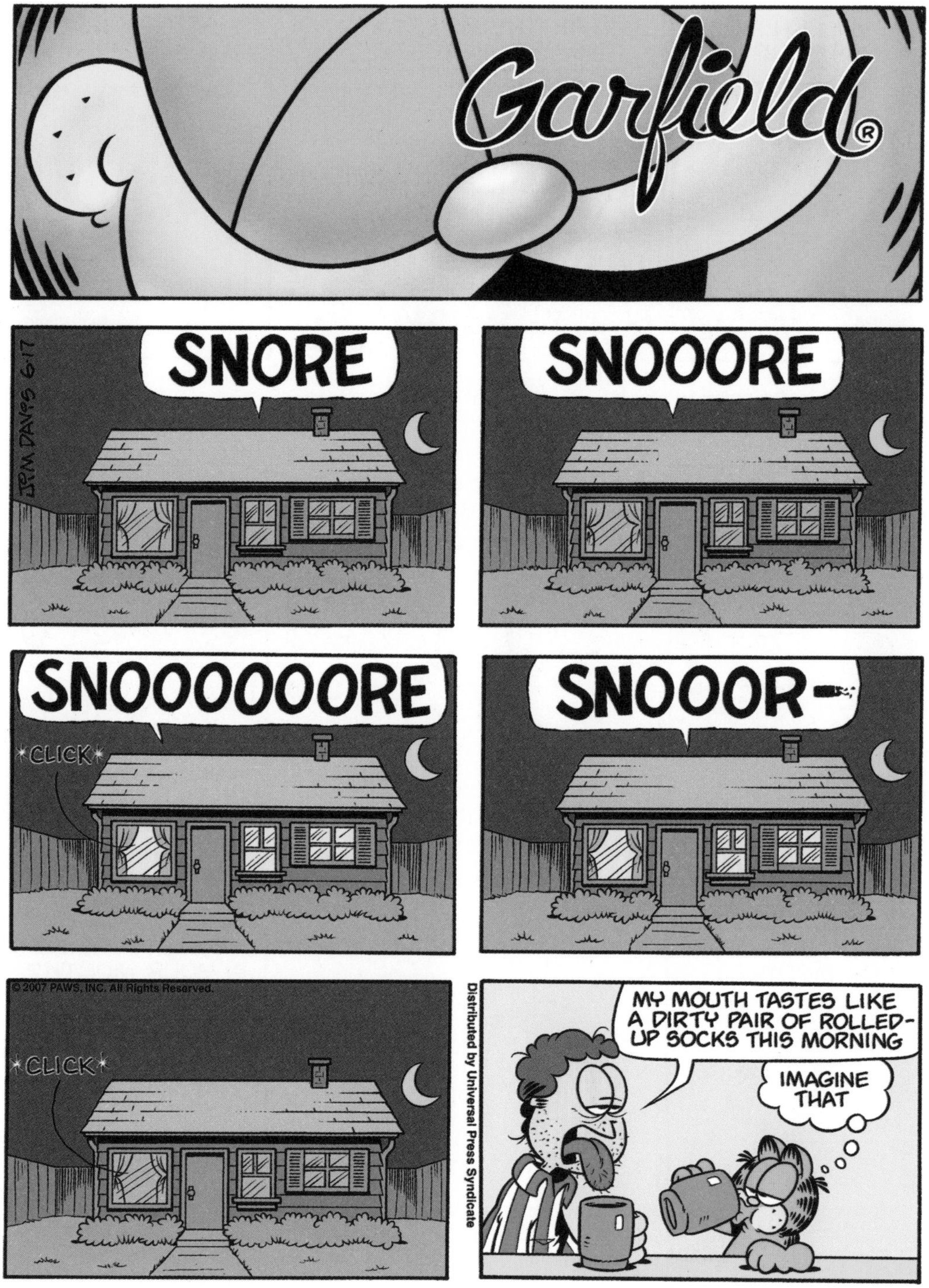
Garfield®
JPM DAVIS 6-17
SNORE
SNOOORE
SNOOOOOORE
CLICK
SNOOOR-
© 2007 PAWS, INC. All Rights Reserved.
CLICK
Distributed by Universal Press Syndicate
MY MOUTH TASTES LIKE A DIRTY PAIR OF ROLLED-UP SOCKS THIS MORNING
IMAGINE THAT

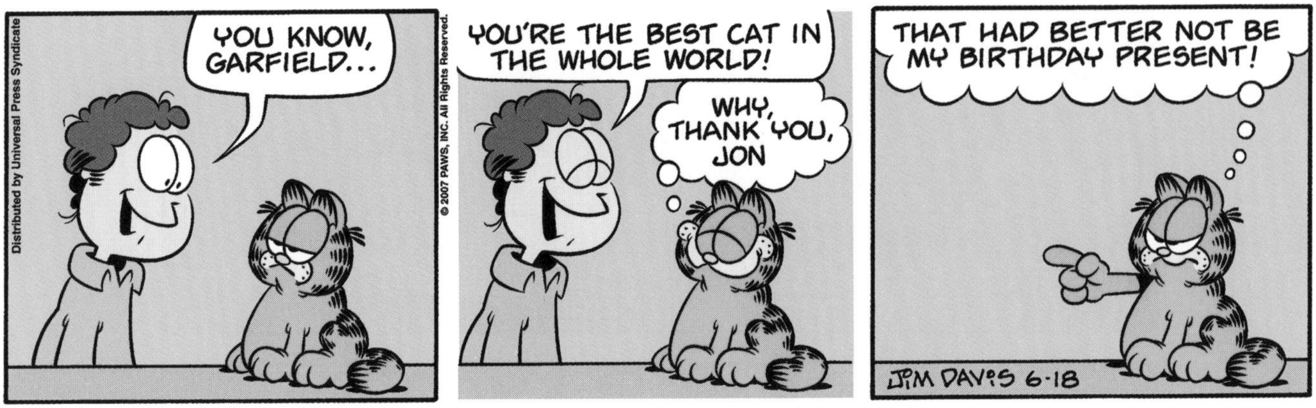
YOU KNOW, GARFIELD...
YOU'RE THE BEST CAT IN THE WHOLE WORLD!
WHY, THANK YOU, JON
THAT HAD BETTER NOT BE MY BIRTHDAY PRESENT!
JIM DAVIS 6-18
Distributed by Universal Press Syndicate
© 2007 PAWS, INC. All Rights Reserved.

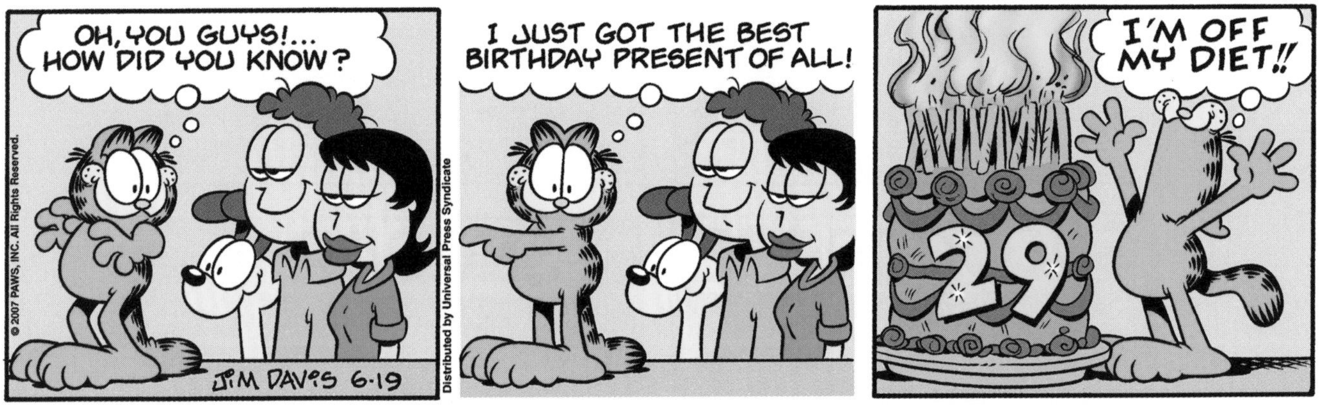
OH, YOU GUYS!... HOW DID YOU KNOW?
JIM DAVIS 6-19
I JUST GOT THE BEST BIRTHDAY PRESENT OF ALL!
29
I'M OFF MY DIET!!
© 2007 PAWS, INC. All Rights Reserved.
Distributed by Universal Press Syndicate

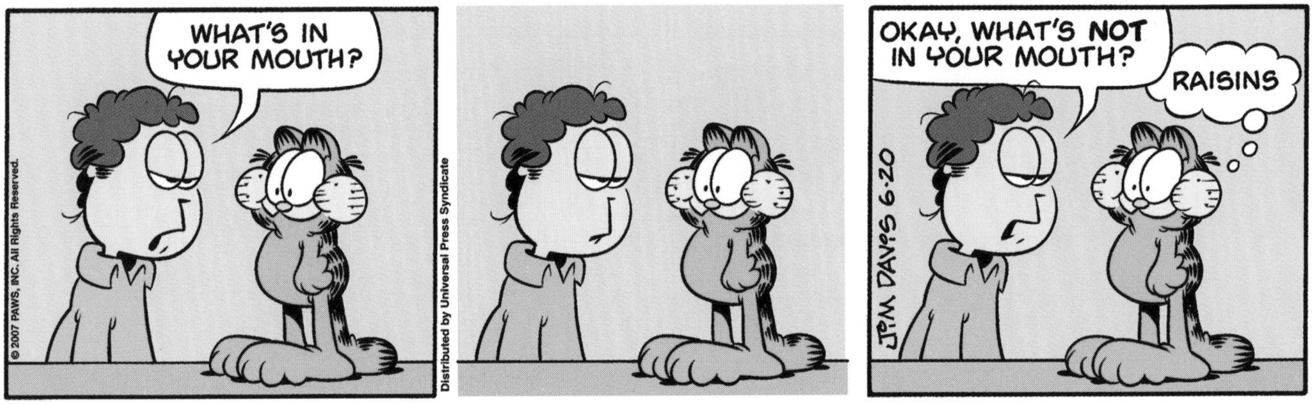
WHAT'S IN YOUR MOUTH?
OKAY, WHAT'S NOT IN YOUR MOUTH?
RAISINS
JIM DAVIS 6-20
© 2007 PAWS, INC. All Rights Reserved.
Distributed by Universal Press Syndicate

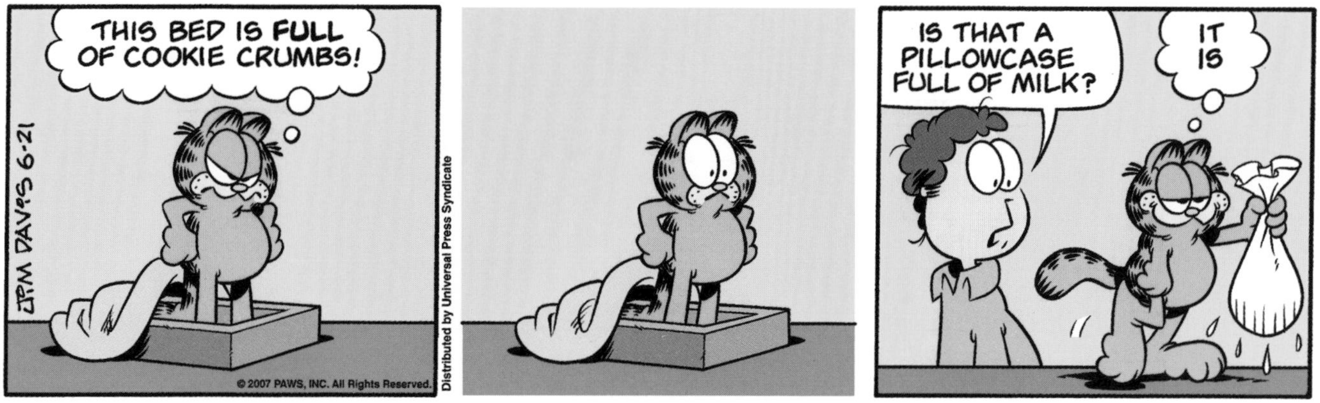
THIS BED IS FULL OF COOKIE CRUMBS!
JIM DAVIS 6-21
© 2007 PAWS, INC. All Rights Reserved.
Distributed by Universal Press Syndicate
IS THAT A PILLOWCASE FULL OF MILK?
IT IS

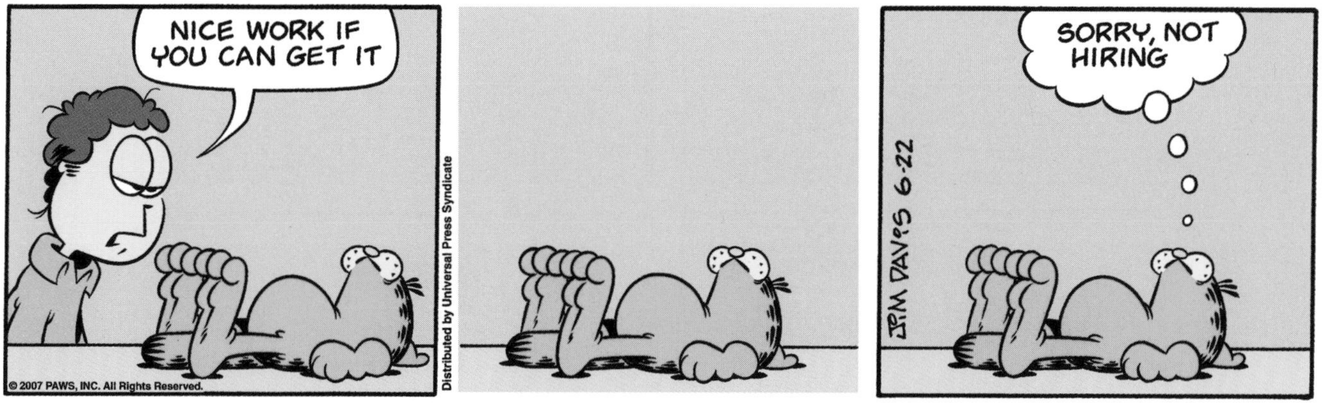
NICE WORK IF YOU CAN GET IT
© 2007 PAWS, INC. All Rights Reserved.
Distributed by Universal Press Syndicate
JIM DAVIS 6-22
SORRY, NOT HIRING

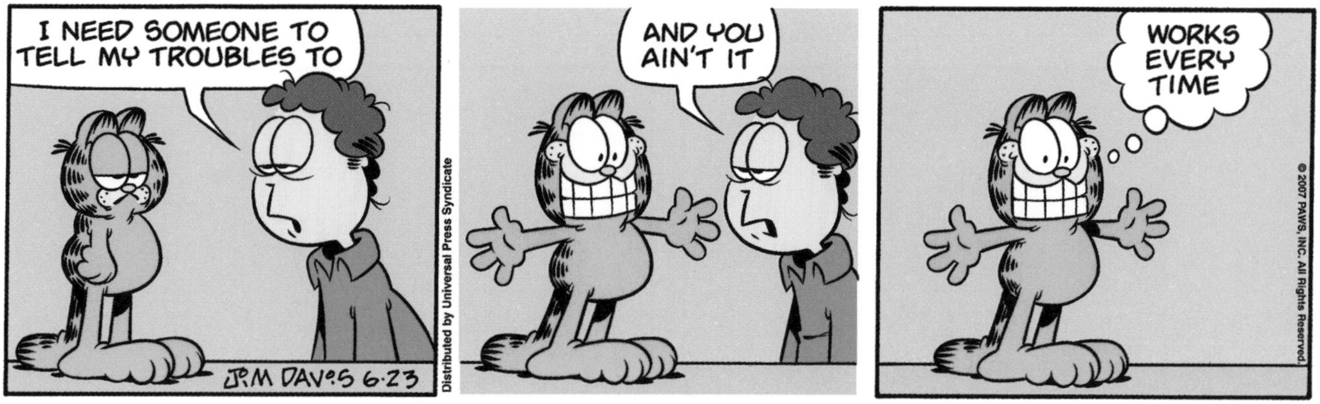
I NEED SOMEONE TO TELL MY TROUBLES TO
JIM DAVIS 6-23
Distributed by Universal Press Syndicate
AND YOU AIN'T IT
WORKS EVERY TIME
© 2007 PAWS, INC. All Rights Reserved.

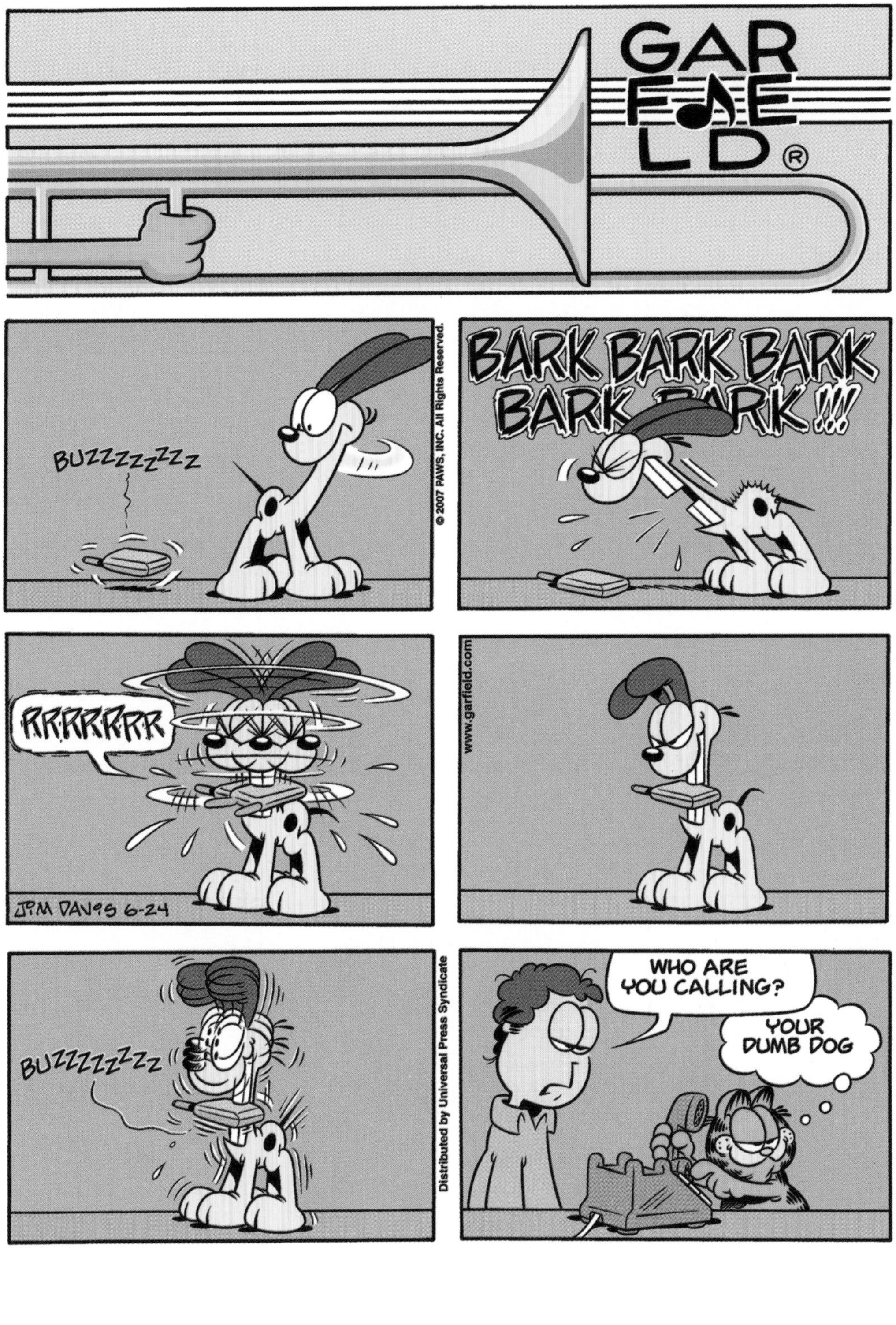
GARFIELD®
BUZZZZZZZZZ
© 2007 PAWS, INC. All Rights Reserved.
BARK BARK BARK BARK BARK !!!
RRRRRRRR
JIM DAVIS 6-24
www.garfield.com
BUZZZZZZZZZ
Distributed by Universal Press Syndicate
WHO ARE YOU CALLING?
YOUR DUMB DOG

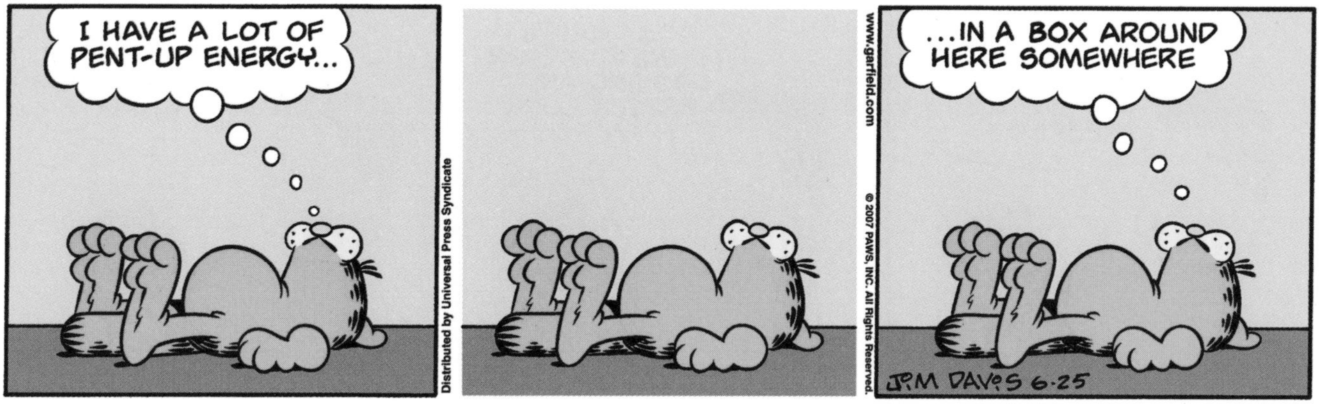
I HAVE A LOT OF PENT-UP ENERGY...
Distributed by Universal Press Syndicate
...IN A BOX AROUND HERE SOMEWHERE
www.garfield.com
© 2007 PAWS, INC. All Rights Reserved.
JIM DAVIS 6-25

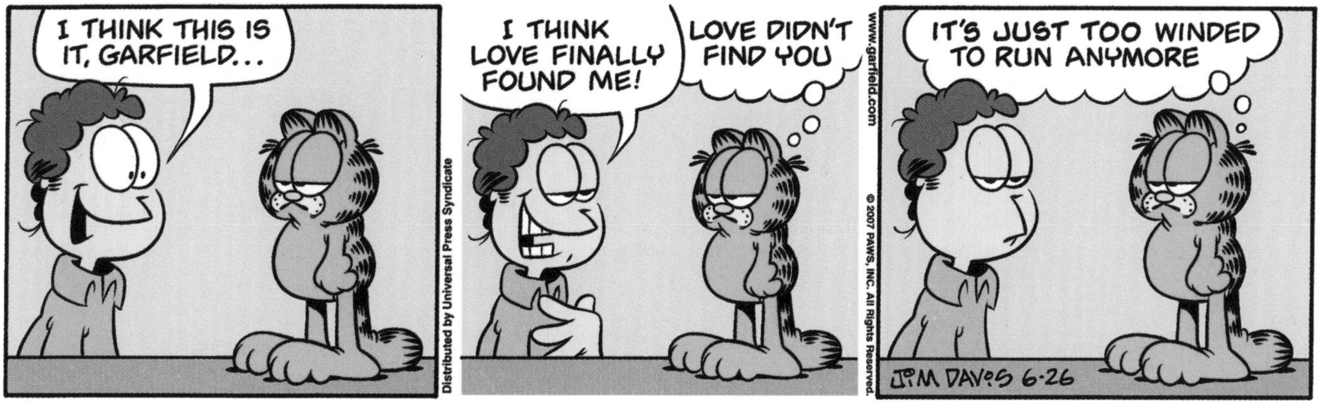
I THINK THIS IS IT, GARFIELD...
Distributed by Universal Press Syndicate
I THINK LOVE FINALLY FOUND ME!
LOVE DIDN'T FIND YOU
www.garfield.com
© 2007 PAWS, INC. All Rights Reserved.
IT'S JUST TOO WINDED TO RUN ANYMORE
JIM DAVIS 6-26

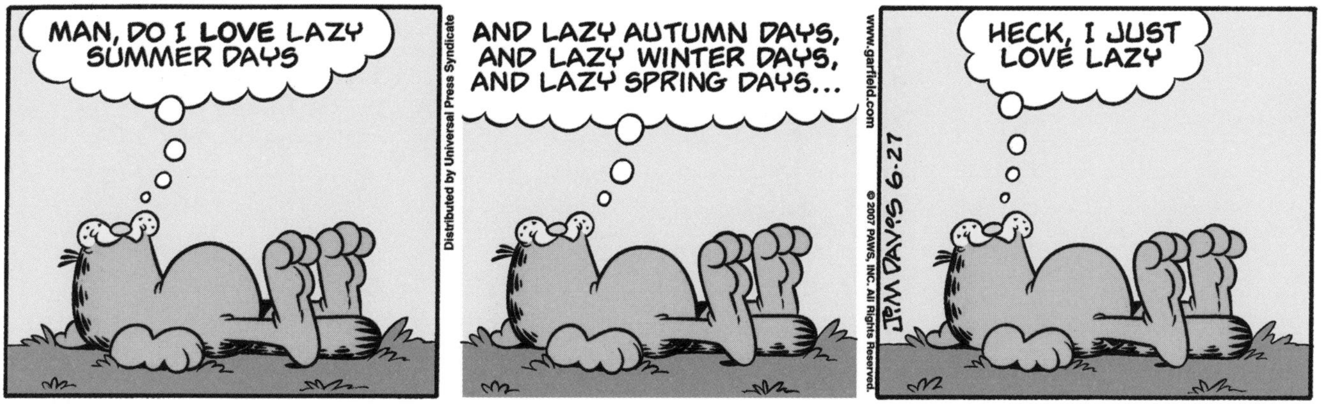
MAN, DO I LOVE LAZY SUMMER DAYS
Distributed by Universal Press Syndicate
AND LAZY AUTUMN DAYS, AND LAZY WINTER DAYS, AND LAZY SPRING DAYS...
www.garfield.com
© 2007 PAWS, INC. All Rights Reserved.
JIM DAVIS 6-27
HECK, I JUST LOVE LAZY

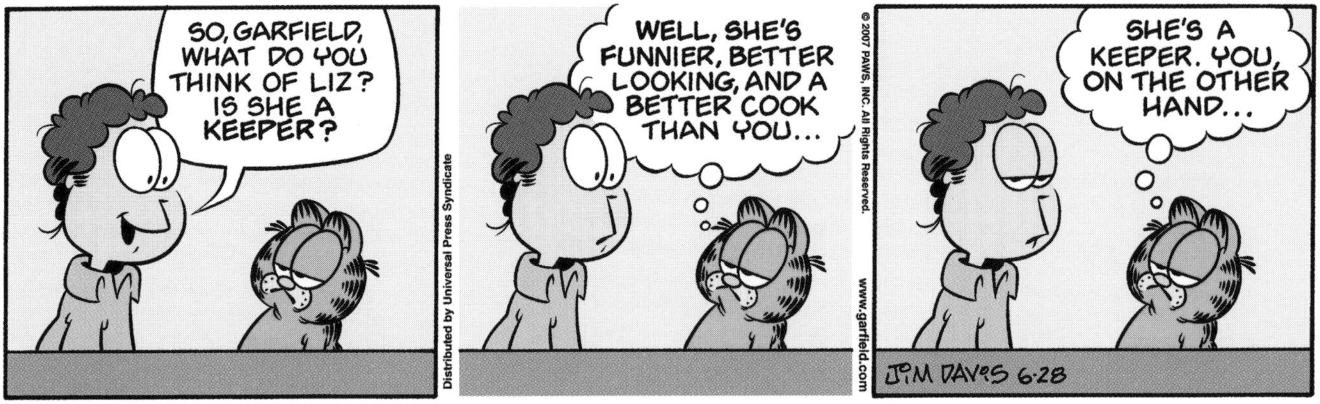
SO, GARFIELD, WHAT DO YOU THINK OF LIZ? IS SHE A KEEPER?
Distributed by Universal Press Syndicate
WELL, SHE'S FUNNIER, BETTER LOOKING, AND A BETTER COOK THAN YOU...
© 2007 PAWS, INC. All Rights Reserved.
www.garfield.com
SHE'S A KEEPER. YOU, ON THE OTHER HAND...
JIM DAVIS 6-28

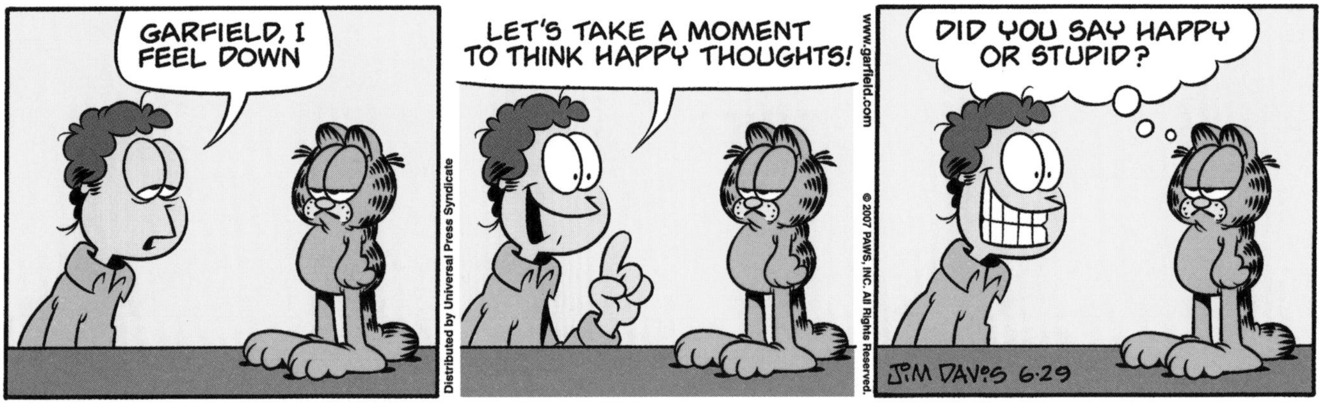
GARFIELD, I FEEL DOWN
Distributed by Universal Press Syndicate
LET'S TAKE A MOMENT TO THINK HAPPY THOUGHTS!
www.garfield.com
© 2007 PAWS, INC. All Rights Reserved.
DID YOU SAY HAPPY OR STUPID?
JIM DAVIS 6-29

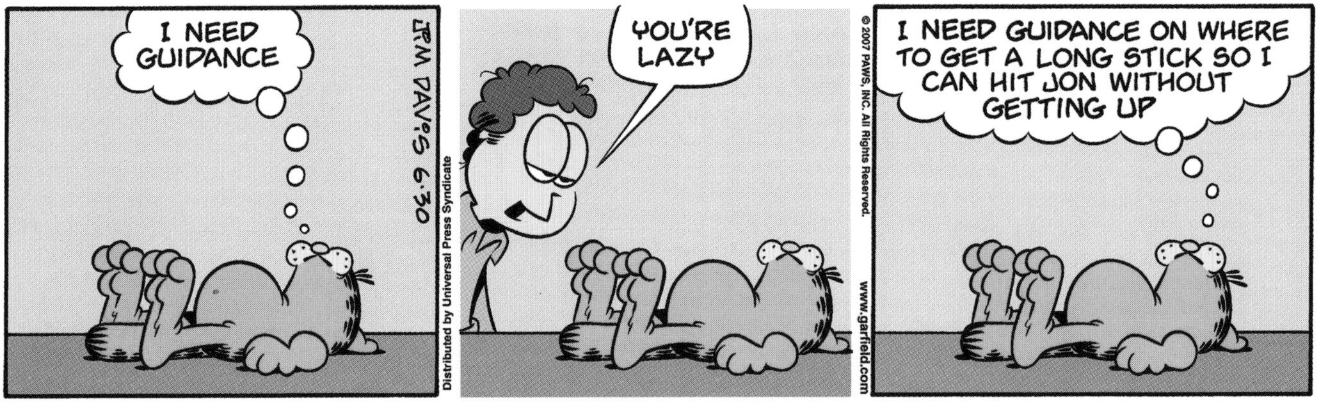
I NEED GUIDANCE
JIM DAVIS 6-30
Distributed by Universal Press Syndicate
YOU'RE LAZY
© 2007 PAWS, INC. All Rights Reserved.
www.garfield.com
I NEED GUIDANCE ON WHERE TO GET A LONG STICK SO I CAN HIT JON WITHOUT GETTING UP

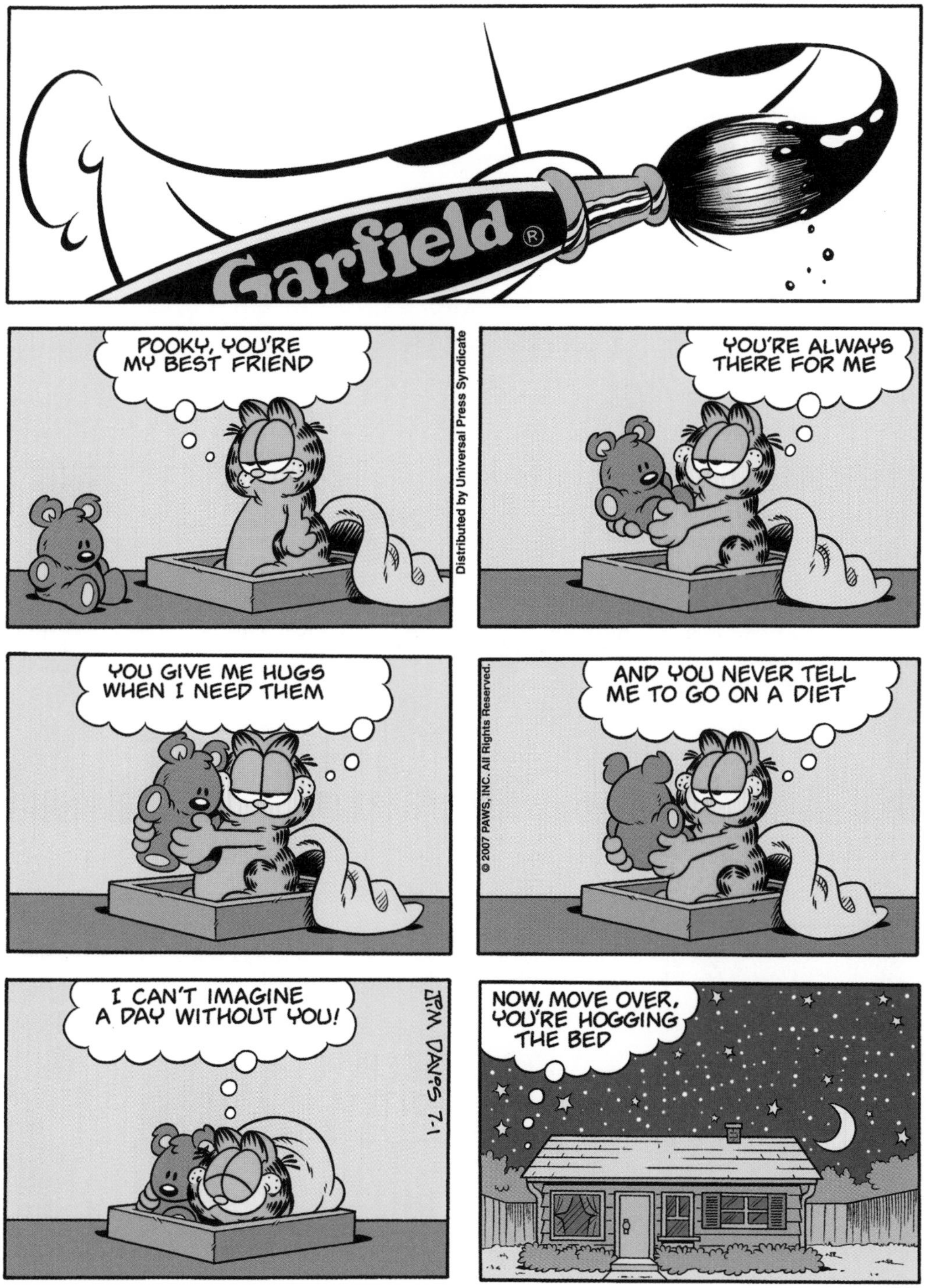
Garfield®
POOKY, YOU'RE MY BEST FRIEND
Distributed by Universal Press Syndicate
YOU'RE ALWAYS THERE FOR ME
YOU GIVE ME HUGS WHEN I NEED THEM
© 2007 PAWS, INC. All Rights Reserved.
AND YOU NEVER TELL ME TO GO ON A DIET
I CAN'T IMAGINE A DAY WITHOUT YOU!
JIM DAVIS 7-1
NOW, MOVE OVER, YOU'RE HOGGING THE BED

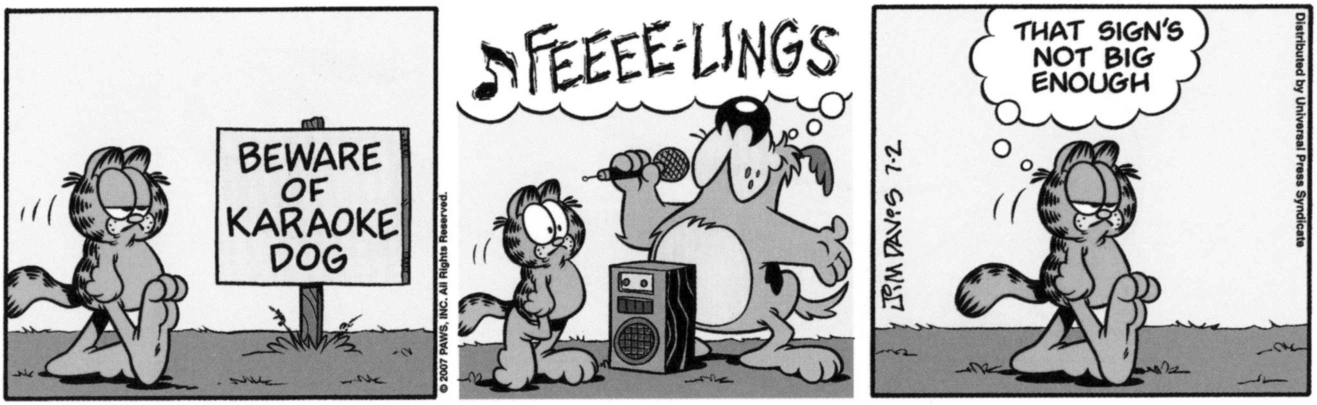
BEWARE OF KARAOKE DOG
FEEEE-LINGS
THAT SIGN'S NOT BIG ENOUGH
© 2007 PAWS, INC. All Rights Reserved.
JIM DAVIS 7·2
Distributed by Universal Press Syndicate

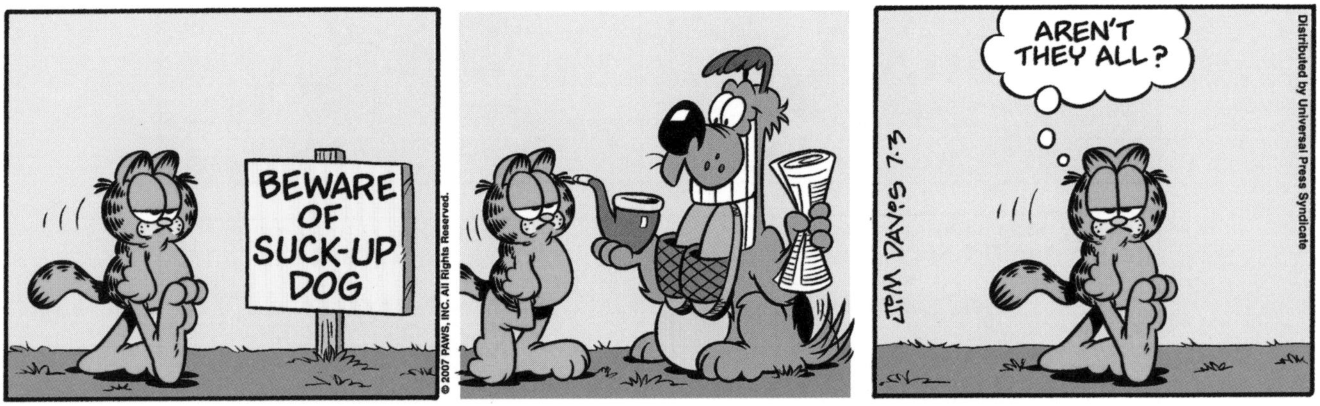
BEWARE OF SUCK-UP DOG
AREN'T THEY ALL?
© 2007 PAWS, INC. All Rights Reserved.
JIM DAVIS 7·3
Distributed by Universal Press Syndicate

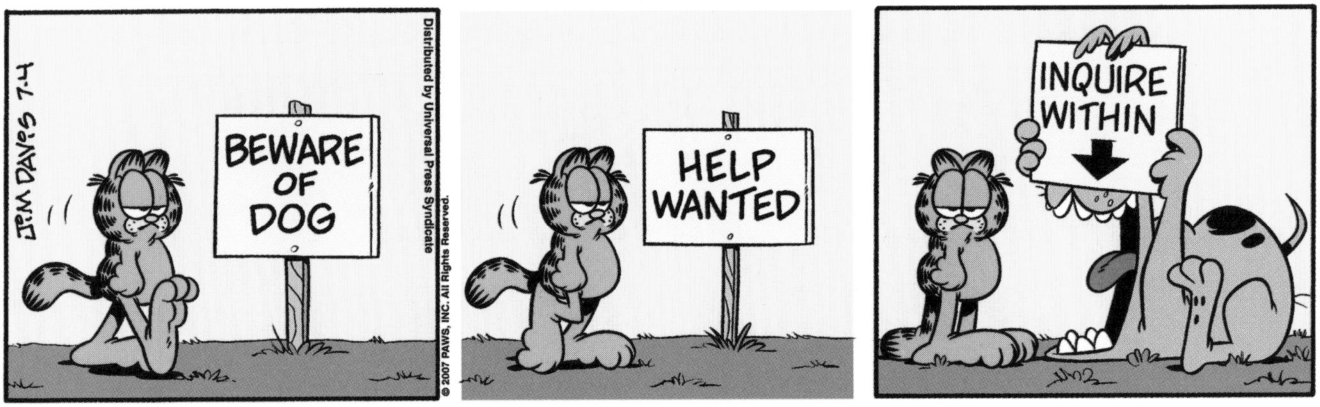
JIM DAVIS 7·4
BEWARE OF DOG
Distributed by Universal Press Syndicate
© 2007 PAWS, INC. All Rights Reserved.
HELP WANTED
INQUIRE WITHIN

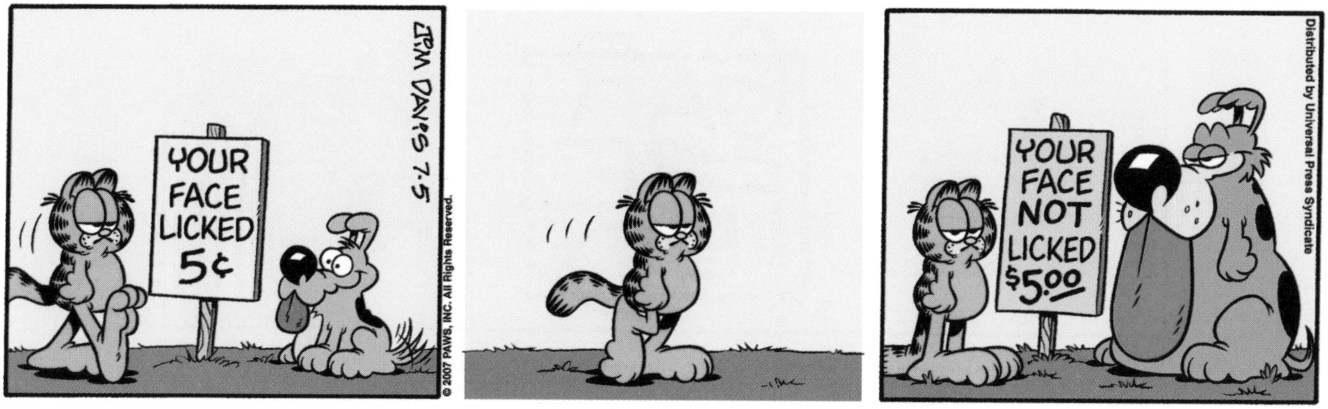
YOUR FACE LICKED 5¢
JIM DAVIS 7-5
© 2007 PAWS, INC. All Rights Reserved.
YOUR FACE NOT LICKED $5.00
Distributed by Universal Press Syndicate

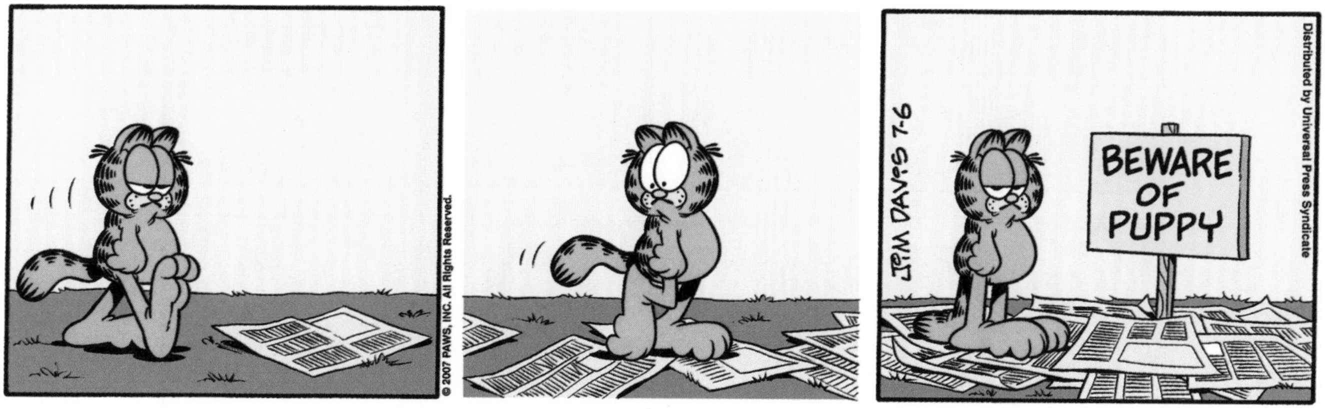
© 2007 PAWS, INC. All Rights Reserved.
JIM DAVIS 7-6
BEWARE OF PUPPY
Distributed by Universal Press Syndicate

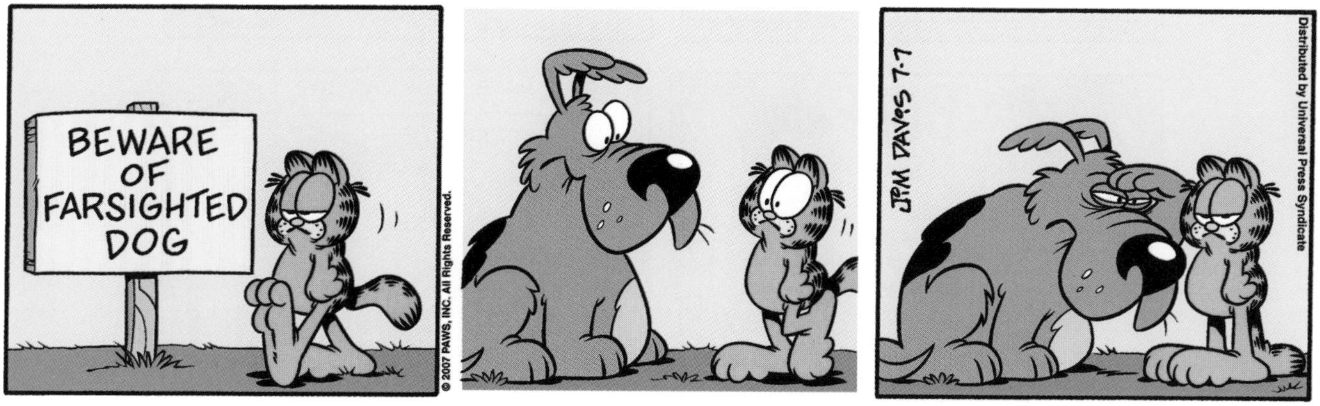
BEWARE OF FARSIGHTED DOG
© 2007 PAWS, INC. All Rights Reserved.
JIM DAVIS 7-7
Distributed by Universal Press Syndicate

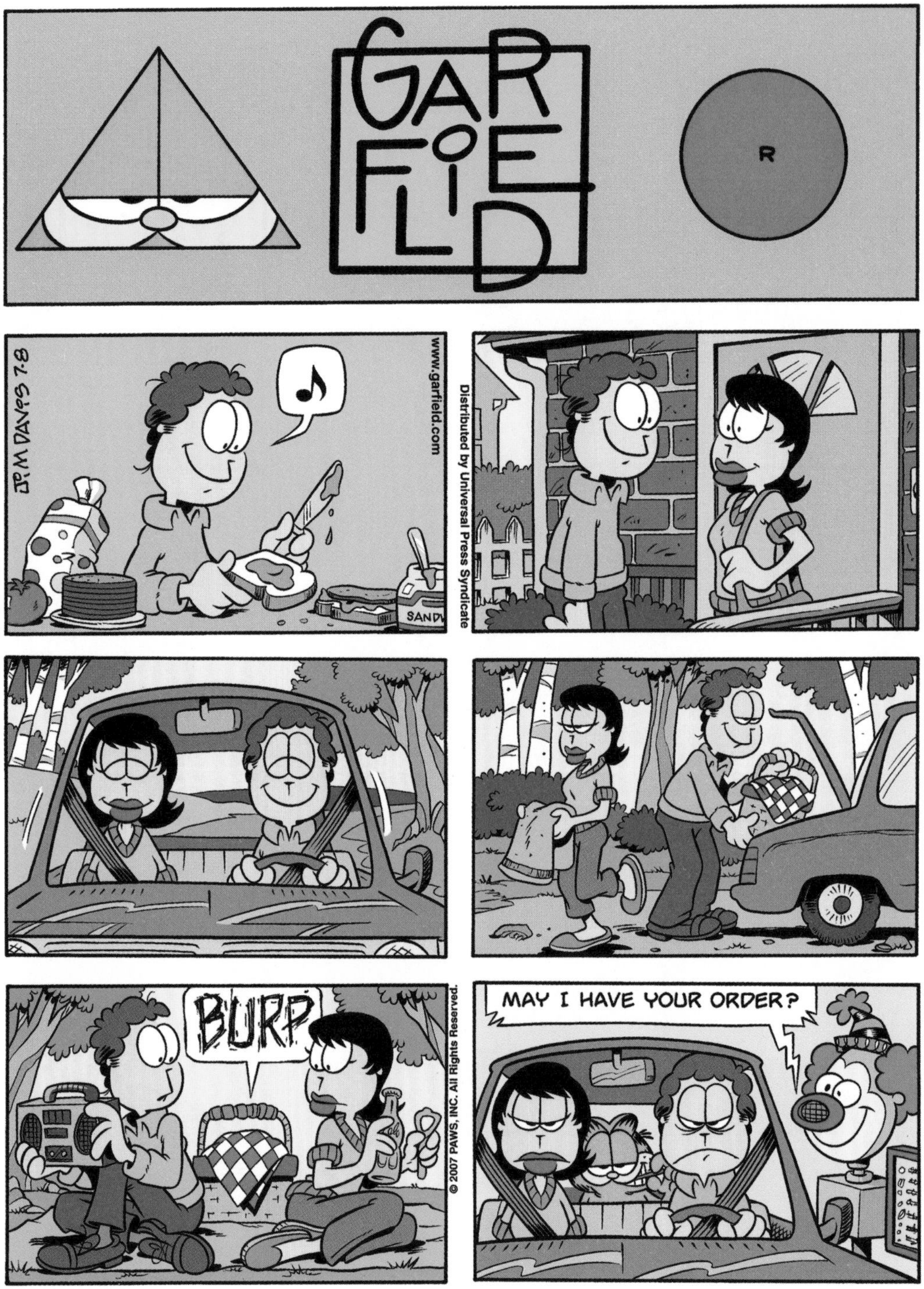
GARFIELD
R
JIM DAVIS 7-8
www.garfield.com
Distributed by Universal Press Syndicate
BURP
© 2007 PAWS, INC. All Rights Reserved.
MAY I HAVE YOUR ORDER?

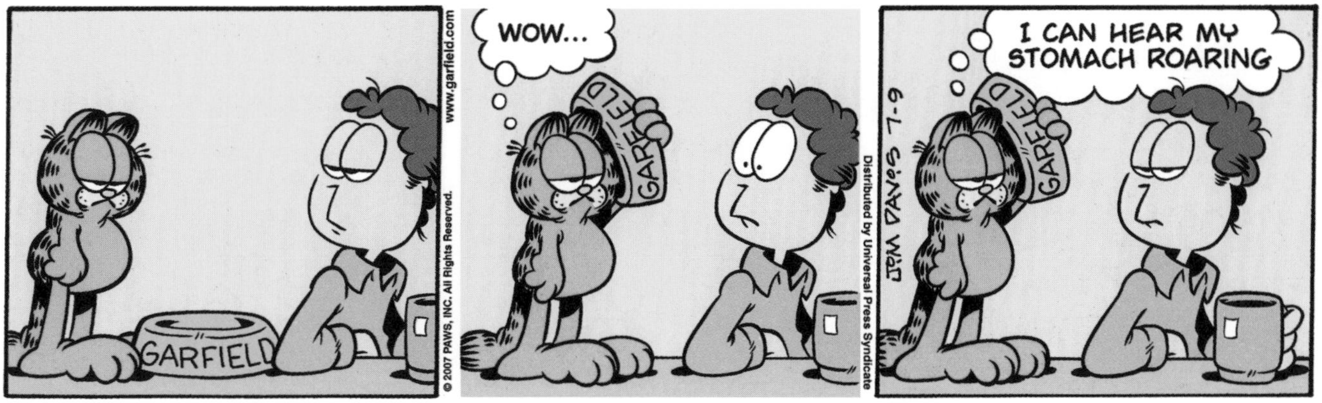
GARFIELD
© 2007 PAWS, INC. All Rights Reserved.
www.garfield.com
WOW...
GARFIELD
Distributed by Universal Press Syndicate
I CAN HEAR MY STOMACH ROARING
JPM DAVIS 7-9
GARFIELD

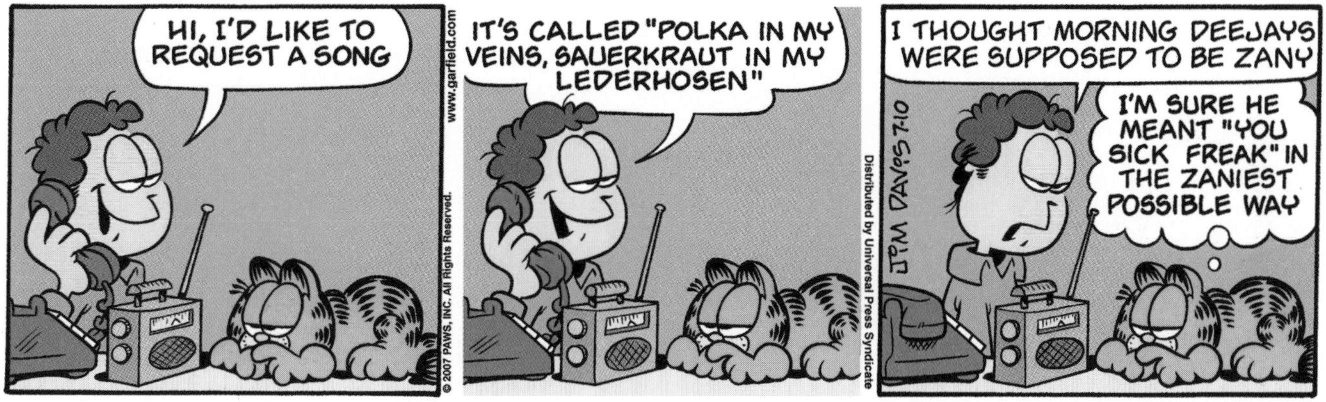
HI, I'D LIKE TO REQUEST A SONG
© 2007 PAWS, INC. All Rights Reserved.
www.garfield.com
IT'S CALLED "POLKA IN MY VEINS, SAUERKRAUT IN MY LEDERHOSEN"
Distributed by Universal Press Syndicate
I THOUGHT MORNING DEEJAYS WERE SUPPOSED TO BE ZANY
I'M SURE HE MEANT "YOU SICK FREAK" IN THE ZANIEST POSSIBLE WAY
JPM DAVIS 7-10

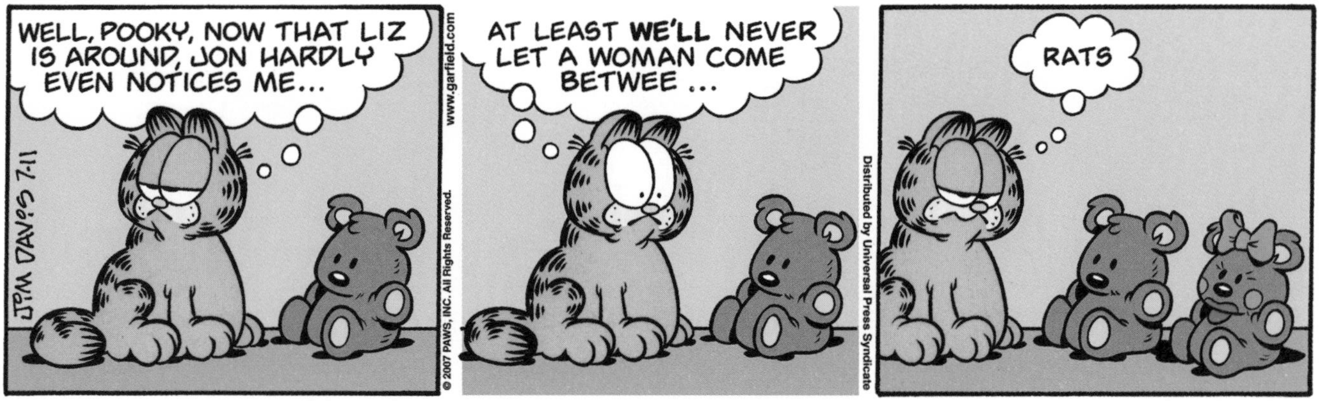
WELL, POOKY, NOW THAT LIZ IS AROUND, JON HARDLY EVEN NOTICES ME...
JPM DAVIS 7-11
© 2007 PAWS, INC. All Rights Reserved.
www.garfield.com
AT LEAST **WE'LL** NEVER LET A WOMAN COME BETWEE ...
Distributed by Universal Press Syndicate
RATS

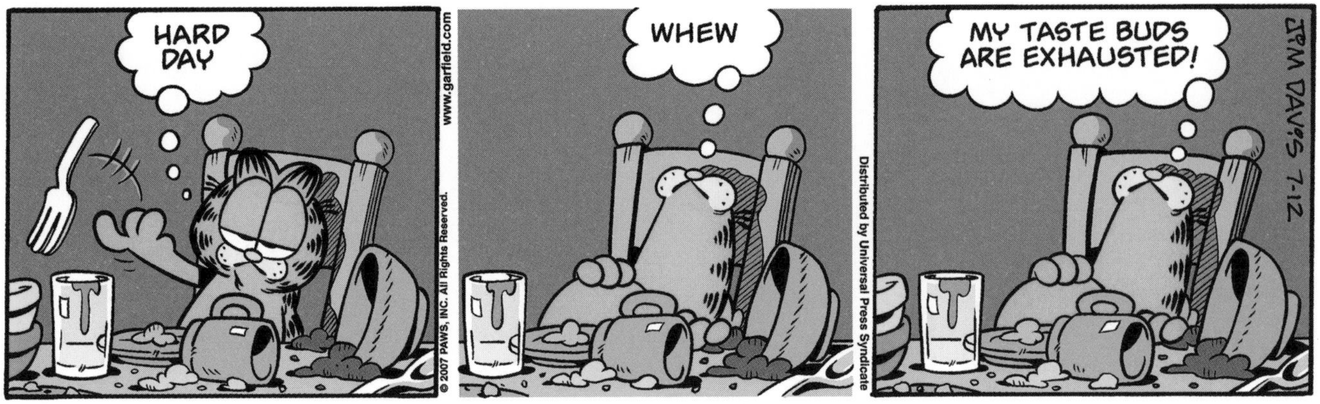
HARD DAY
WHEW
MY TASTE BUDS ARE EXHAUSTED!
JIM DAVIS 7-12
© 2007 PAWS, INC. All Rights Reserved.
www.garfield.com
Distributed by Universal Press Syndicate

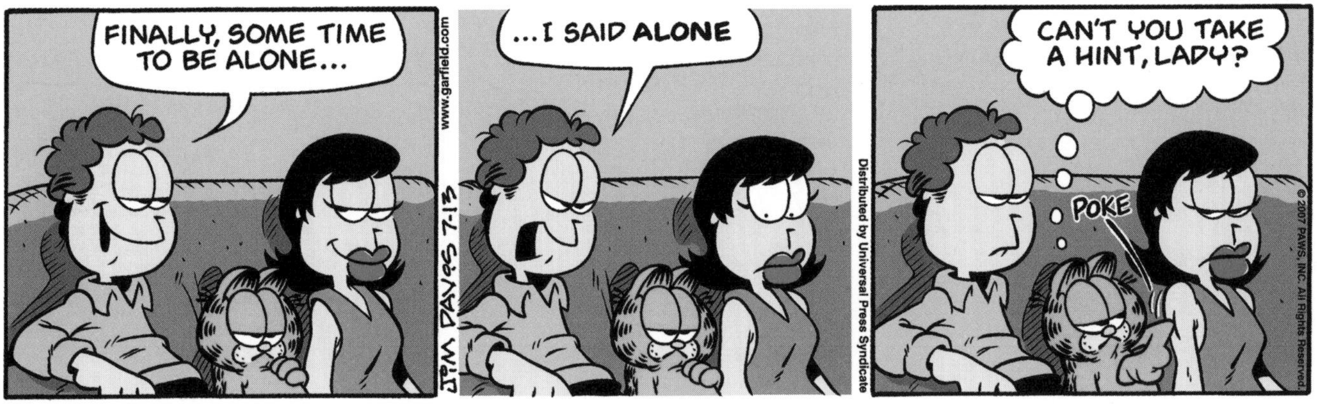
FINALLY, SOME TIME TO BE ALONE...
...I SAID ALONE
CAN'T YOU TAKE A HINT, LADY?
POKE
JIM DAVIS 7-13
www.garfield.com
Distributed by Universal Press Syndicate
© 2007 PAWS, INC. All Rights Reserved.

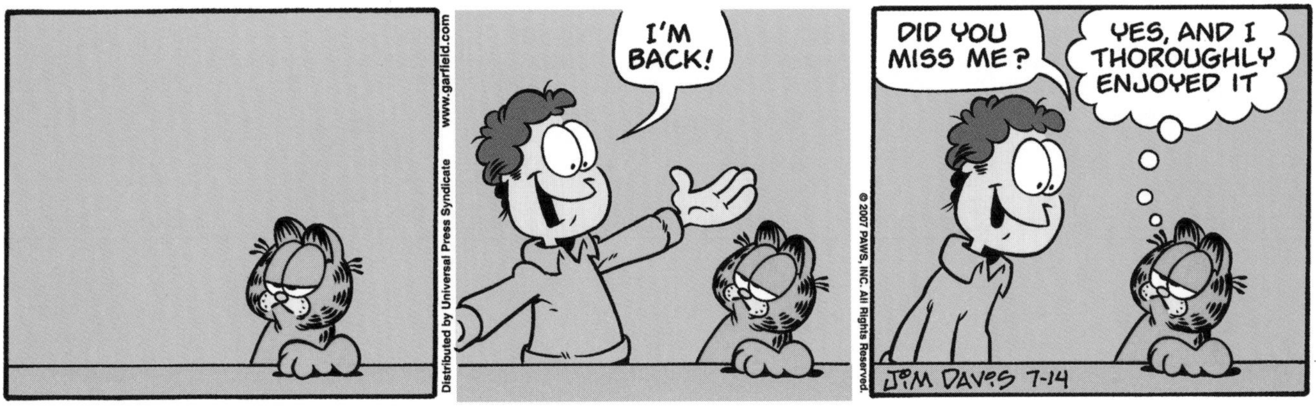
I'M BACK!
DID YOU MISS ME?
YES, AND I THOROUGHLY ENJOYED IT
JIM DAVIS 7-14
www.garfield.com
Distributed by Universal Press Syndicate
© 2007 PAWS, INC. All Rights Reserved.

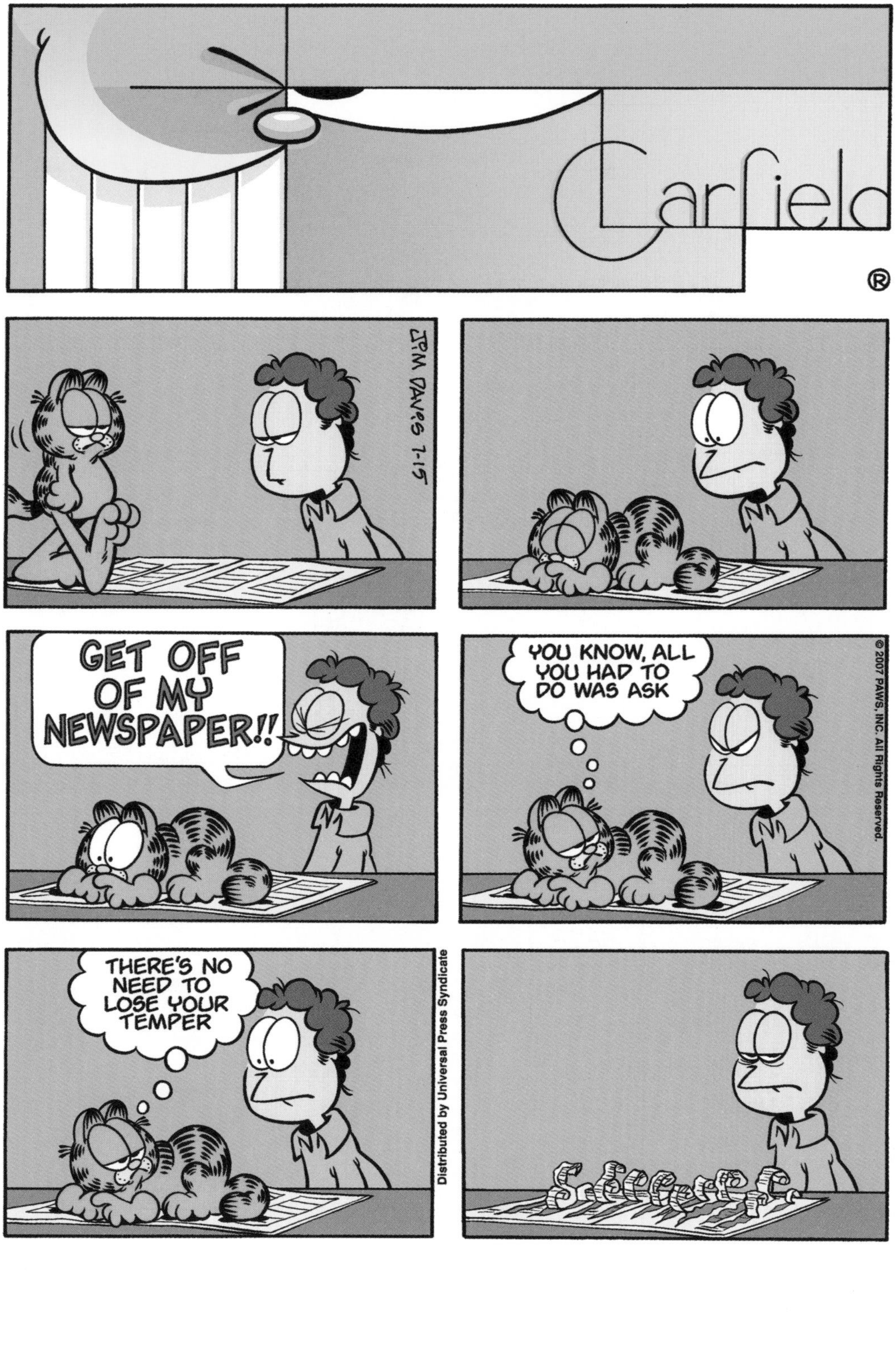
Garfield®
JIM DAVIS 7-15
GET OFF OF MY NEWSPAPER!!
YOU KNOW, ALL YOU HAD TO DO WAS ASK
© 2007 PAWS, INC. All Rights Reserved.
THERE'S NO NEED TO LOSE YOUR TEMPER
Distributed by Universal Press Syndicate

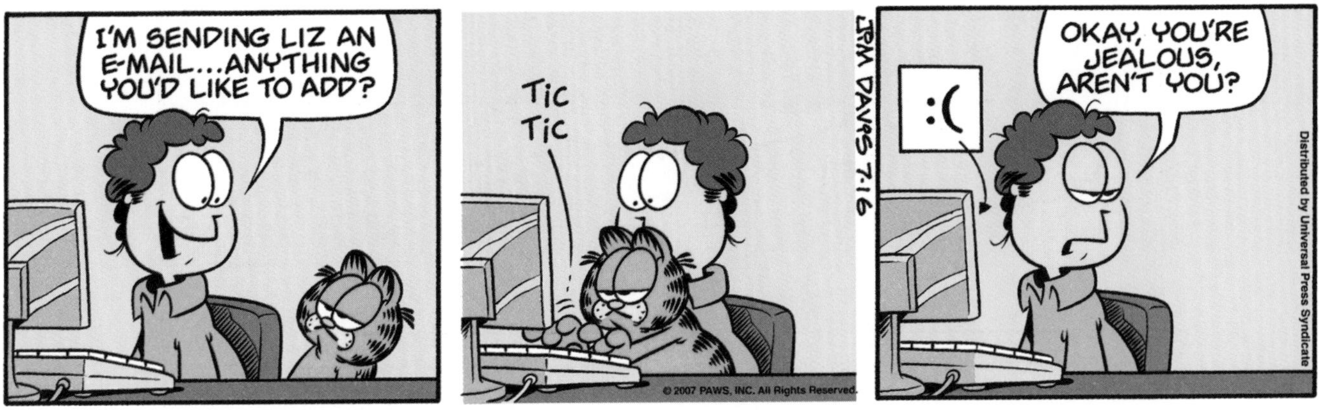
I'M SENDING LIZ AN E-MAIL...ANYTHING YOU'D LIKE TO ADD?
TIC TIC
© 2007 PAWS, INC. All Rights Reserved.
:(
OKAY, YOU'RE JEALOUS, AREN'T YOU?
Distributed by Universal Press Syndicate

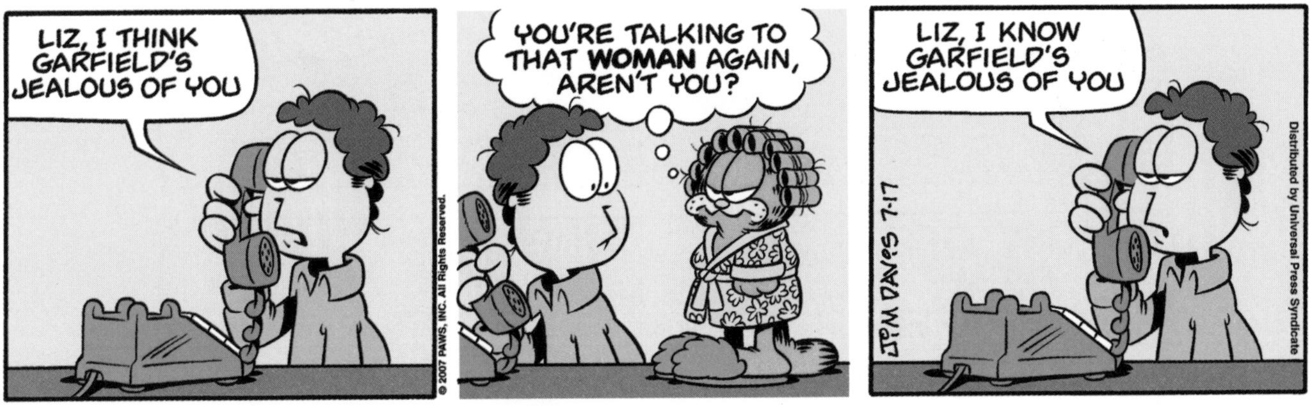
LIZ, I THINK GARFIELD'S JEALOUS OF YOU
© 2007 PAWS, INC. All Rights Reserved.
YOU'RE TALKING TO THAT **WOMAN** AGAIN, AREN'T YOU?
LIZ, I KNOW GARFIELD'S JEALOUS OF YOU
Distributed by Universal Press Syndicate

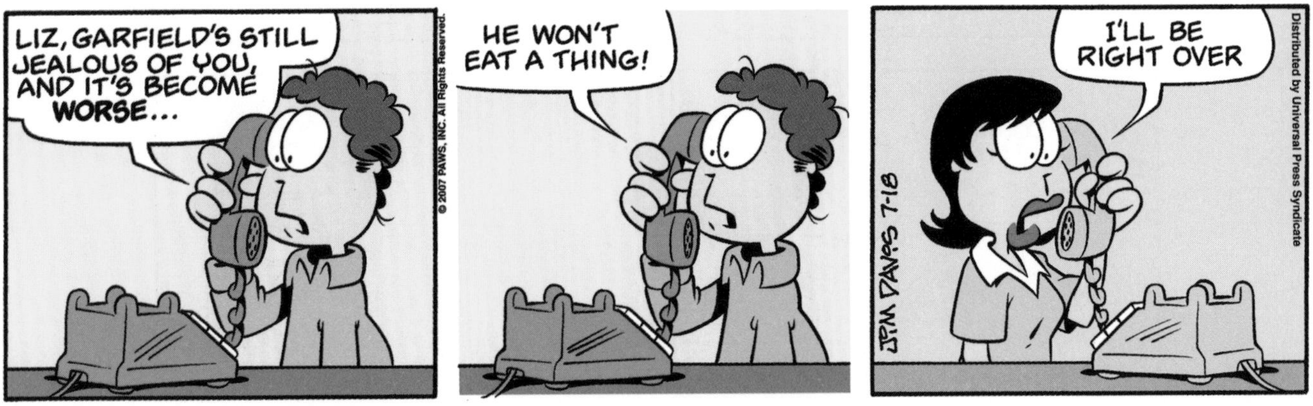
LIZ, GARFIELD'S STILL JEALOUS OF YOU, AND IT'S BECOME **WORSE**...
© 2007 PAWS, INC. All Rights Reserved.
HE WON'T EAT A THING!
I'LL BE RIGHT OVER
Distributed by Universal Press Syndicate

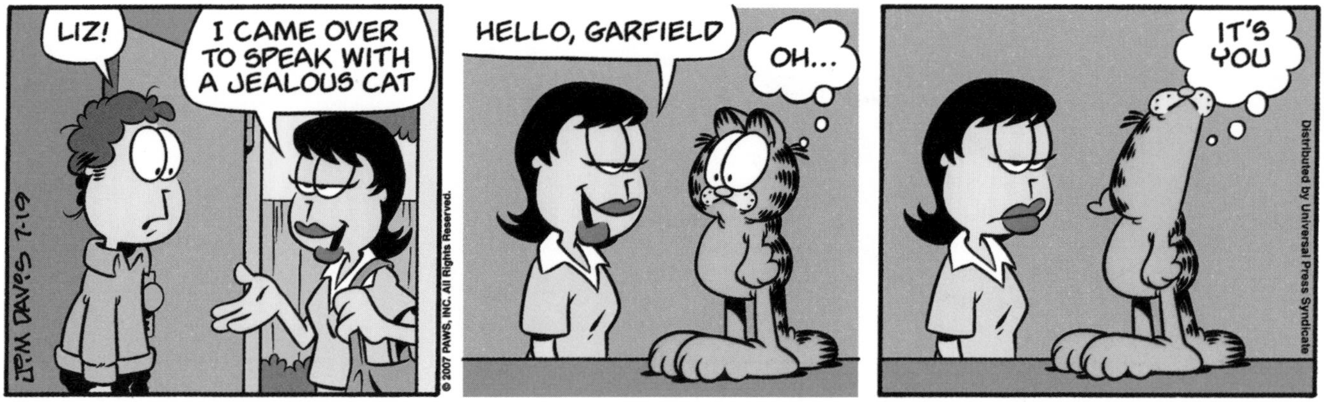
LIZ!
I CAME OVER TO SPEAK WITH A JEALOUS CAT
HELLO, GARFIELD
OH...
IT'S YOU
JPM DAVIS 7-19
© 2007 PAWS, INC. All Rights Reserved.
Distributed by Universal Press Syndicate

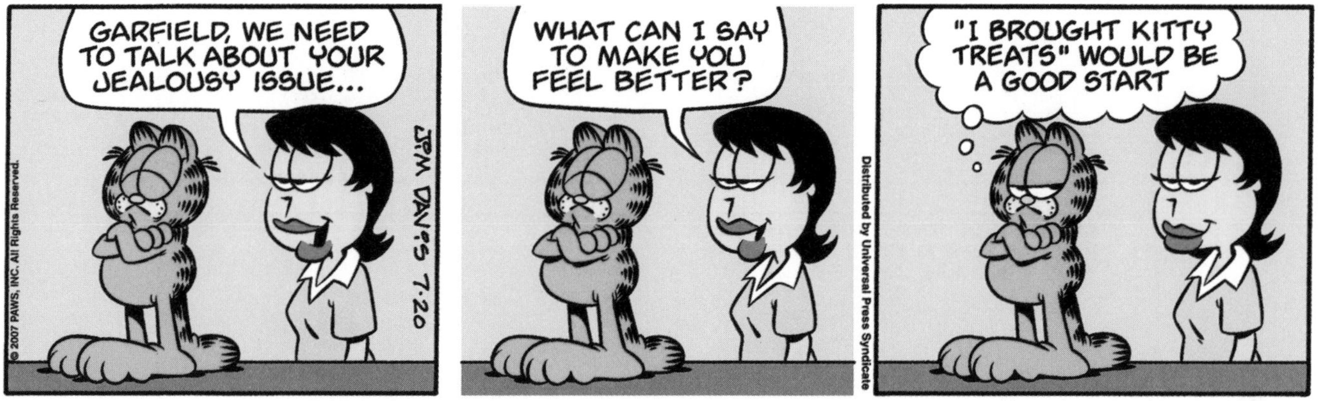
GARFIELD, WE NEED TO TALK ABOUT YOUR JEALOUSY ISSUE...
WHAT CAN I SAY TO MAKE YOU FEEL BETTER?
"I BROUGHT KITTY TREATS" WOULD BE A GOOD START
JPM DAVIS 7-20
© 2007 PAWS, INC. All Rights Reserved.
Distributed by Universal Press Syndicate

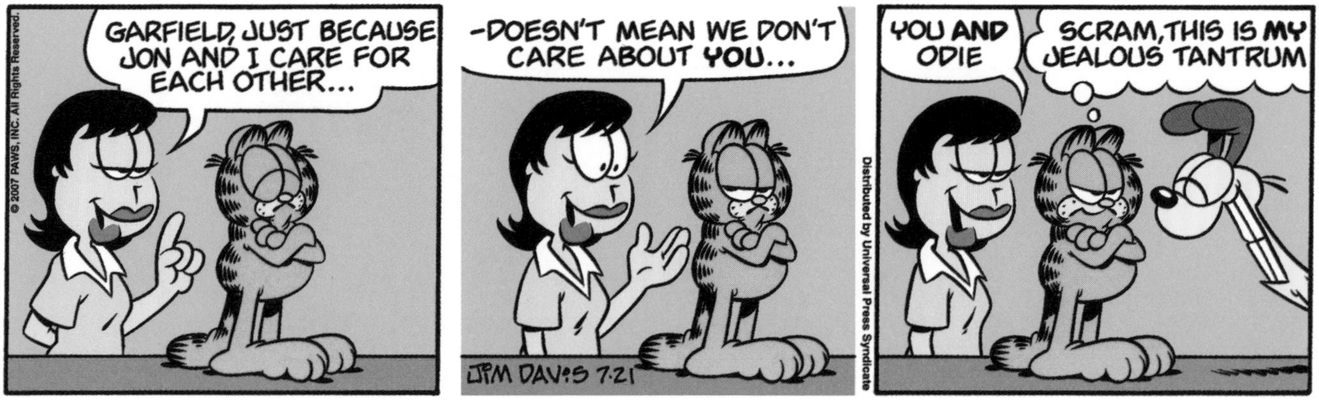
GARFIELD, JUST BECAUSE JON AND I CARE FOR EACH OTHER...
-DOESN'T MEAN WE DON'T CARE ABOUT **YOU**...
YOU **AND** ODIE
SCRAM, THIS IS **MY** JEALOUS TANTRUM
JPM DAVIS 7-21
© 2007 PAWS, INC. All Rights Reserved.
Distributed by Universal Press Syndicate

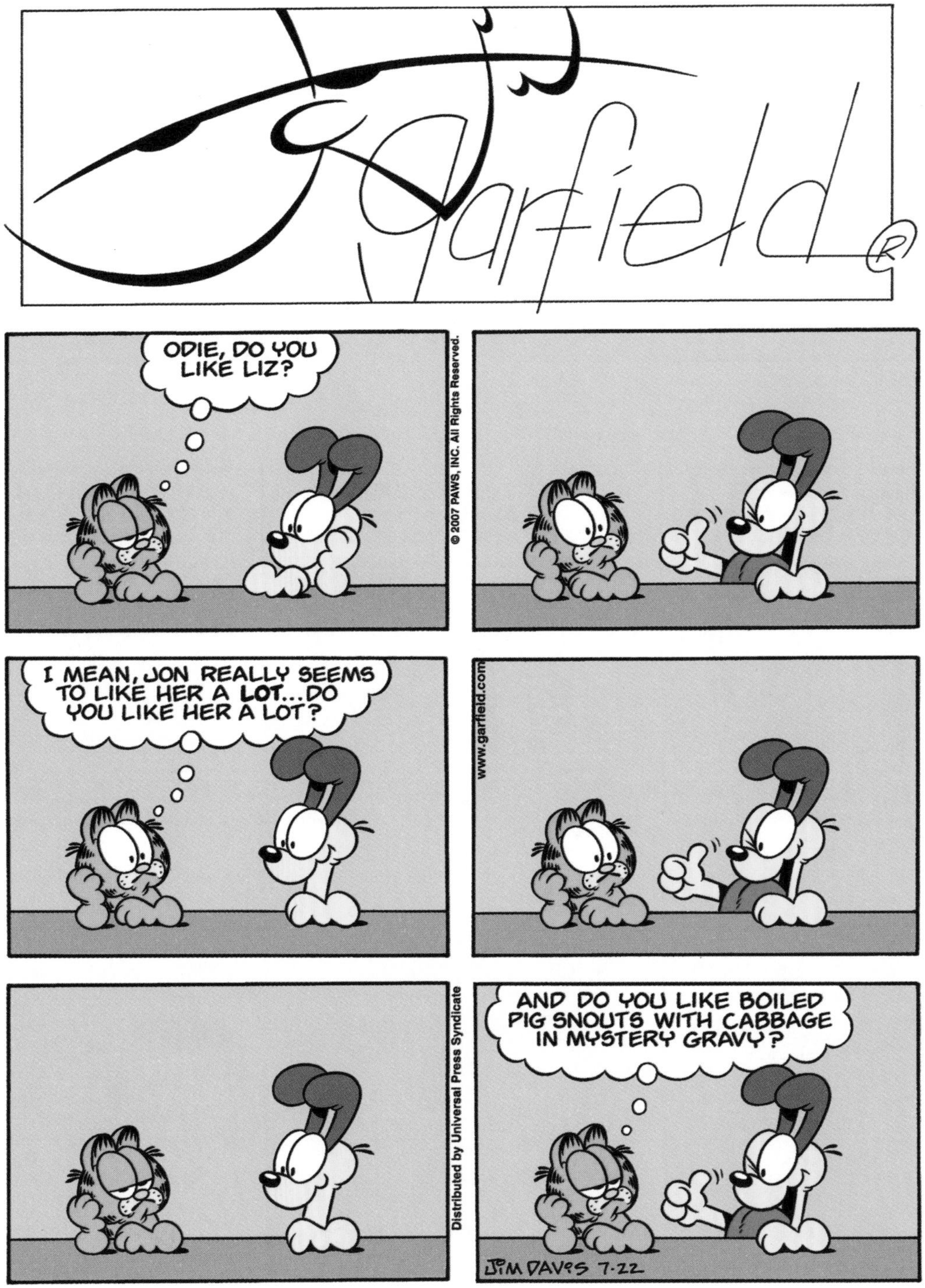
Garfield®
ODIE, DO YOU LIKE LIZ?
© 2007 PAWS, INC. All Rights Reserved.
I MEAN, JON REALLY SEEMS TO LIKE HER A **LOT**...DO YOU LIKE HER A LOT?
www.garfield.com
Distributed by Universal Press Syndicate
AND DO YOU LIKE BOILED PIG SNOUTS WITH CABBAGE IN MYSTERY GRAVY?
JIM DAVIS 7-22

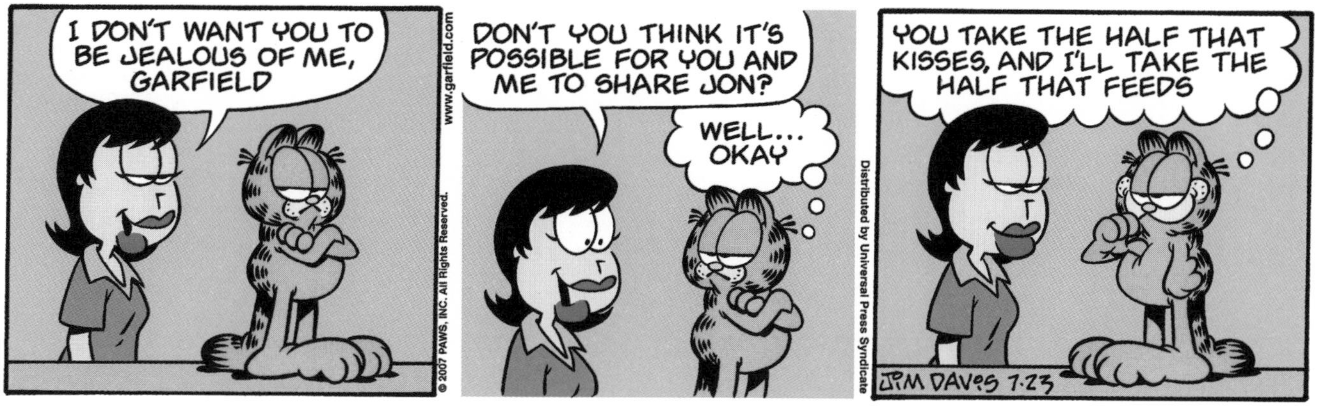
I DON'T WANT YOU TO BE JEALOUS OF ME, GARFIELD
DON'T YOU THINK IT'S POSSIBLE FOR YOU AND ME TO SHARE JON?
WELL... OKAY
YOU TAKE THE HALF THAT KISSES, AND I'LL TAKE THE HALF THAT FEEDS
JIM DAVIS 7-23
www.garfield.com
© 2007 PAWS, INC. All Rights Reserved.
Distributed by Universal Press Syndicate

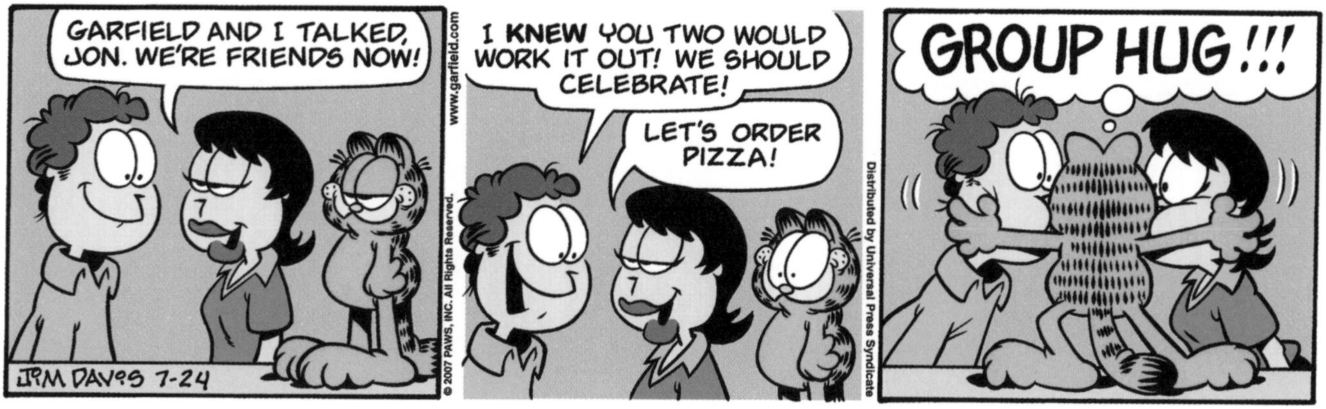
GARFIELD AND I TALKED, JON. WE'RE FRIENDS NOW!
JIM DAVIS 7-24
I **KNEW** YOU TWO WOULD WORK IT OUT! WE SHOULD CELEBRATE!
LET'S ORDER PIZZA!
GROUP HUG!!!
www.garfield.com
© 2007 PAWS, INC. All Rights Reserved.
Distributed by Universal Press Syndicate

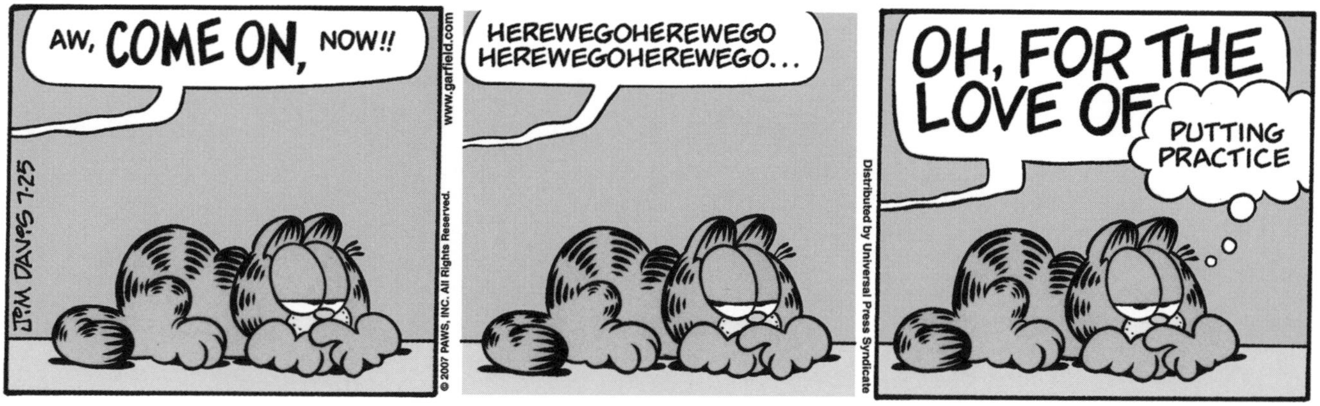
AW, COME ON, NOW!!
JIM DAVIS 7-25
HEREWEGOHEREWEGO HEREWEGOHEREWEGO...
OH, FOR THE LOVE OF
PUTTING PRACTICE
www.garfield.com
© 2007 PAWS, INC. All Rights Reserved.
Distributed by Universal Press Syndicate

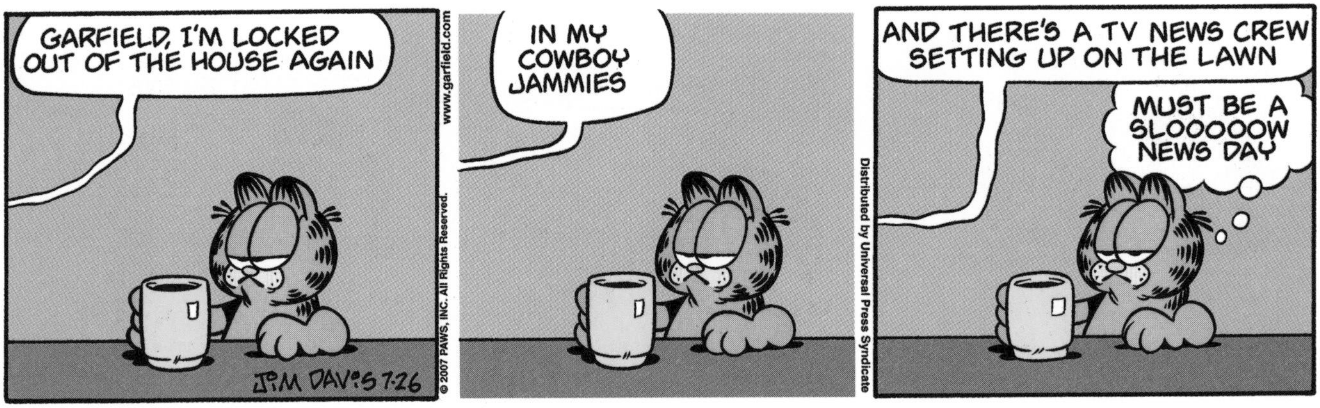
GARFIELD, I'M LOCKED OUT OF THE HOUSE AGAIN
IN MY COWBOY JAMMIES
AND THERE'S A TV NEWS CREW SETTING UP ON THE LAWN
MUST BE A SLOOOOOW NEWS DAY
JIM DAVIS 7-26
© 2007 PAWS, INC. All Rights Reserved.
www.garfield.com
Distributed by Universal Press Syndicate

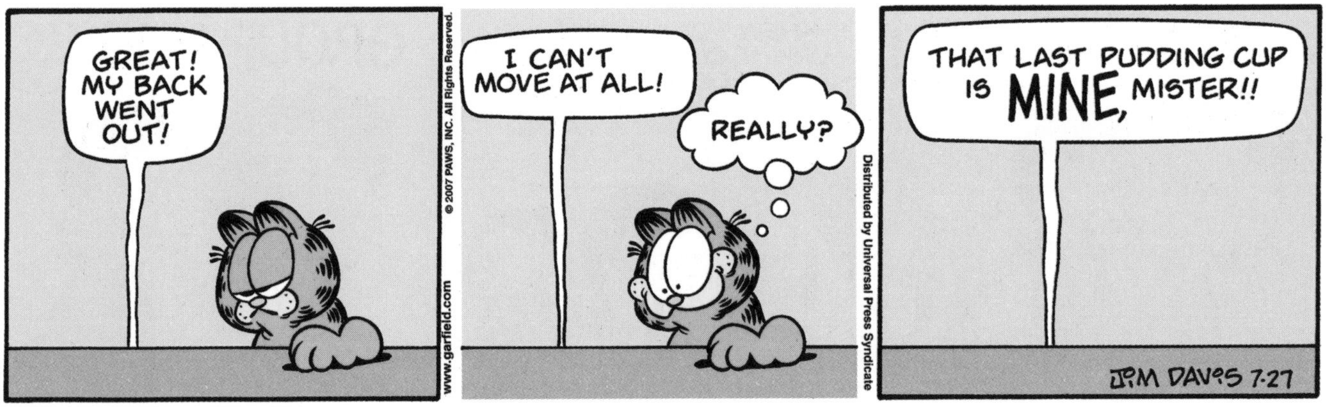
GREAT! MY BACK WENT OUT!
I CAN'T MOVE AT ALL!
REALLY?
THAT LAST PUDDING CUP IS MINE, MISTER!!
JIM DAVIS 7-27
© 2007 PAWS, INC. All Rights Reserved.
www.garfield.com
Distributed by Universal Press Syndicate

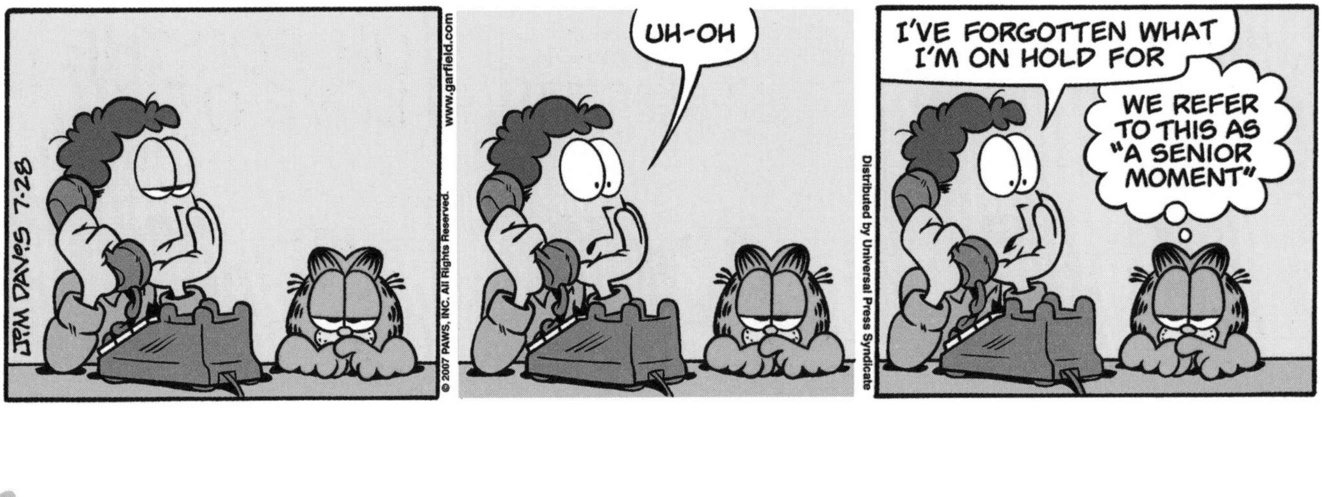
UH-OH
I'VE FORGOTTEN WHAT I'M ON HOLD FOR
WE REFER TO THIS AS "A SENIOR MOMENT"
JIM DAVIS 7-28
© 2007 PAWS, INC. All Rights Reserved.
www.garfield.com
Distributed by Universal Press Syndicate

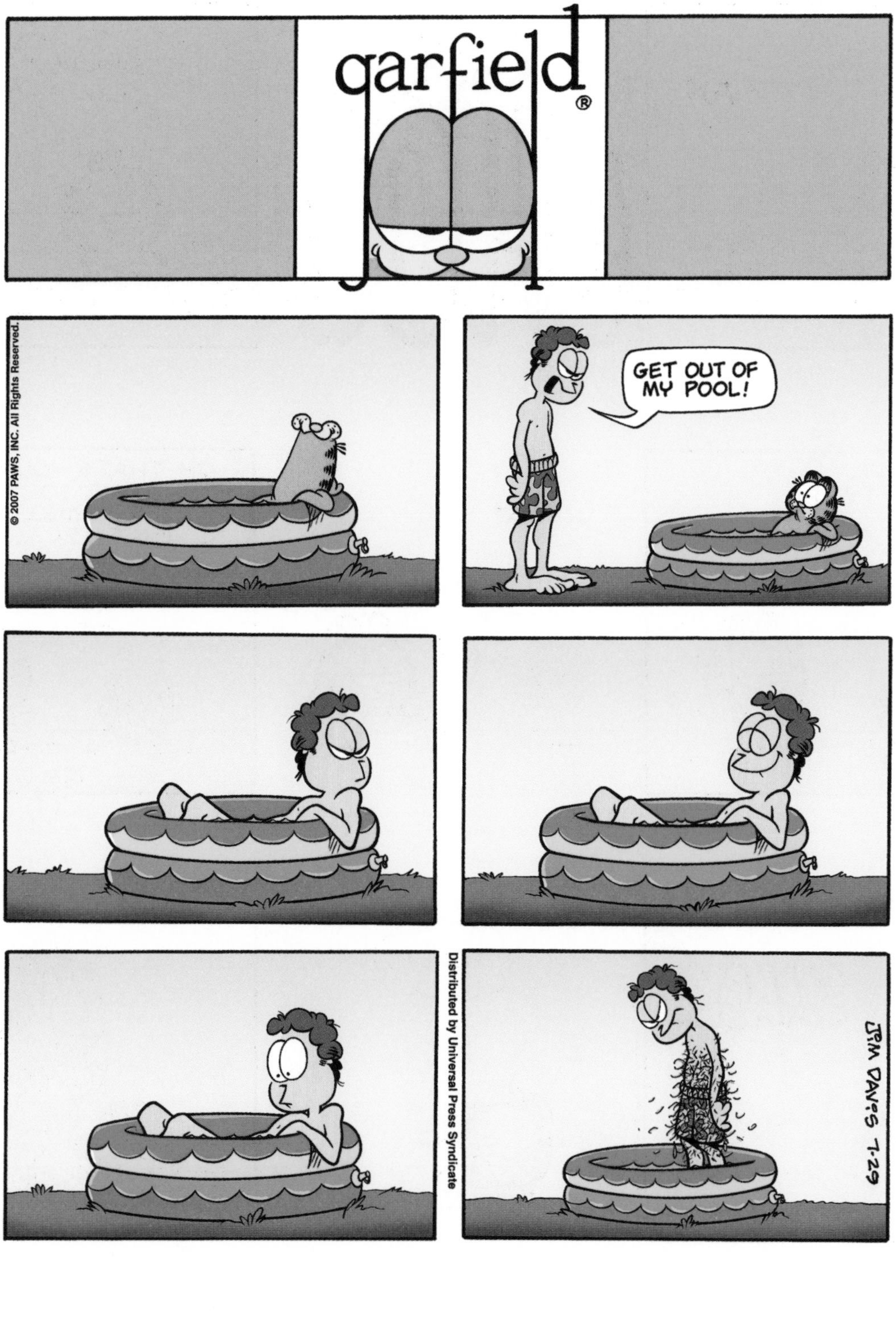
garfield®
GET OUT OF MY POOL!
JIM DAVIS 7-29

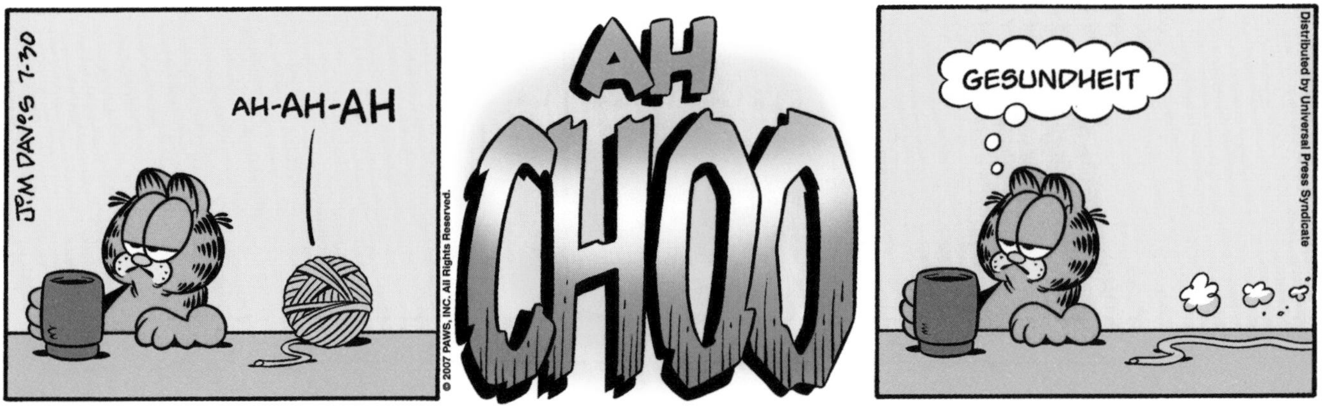
JIM DAVIS 7-30
AH-AH-AH
© 2007 PAWS, INC. All Rights Reserved.
AH CHOO
GESUNDHEIT
Distributed by Universal Press Syndicate

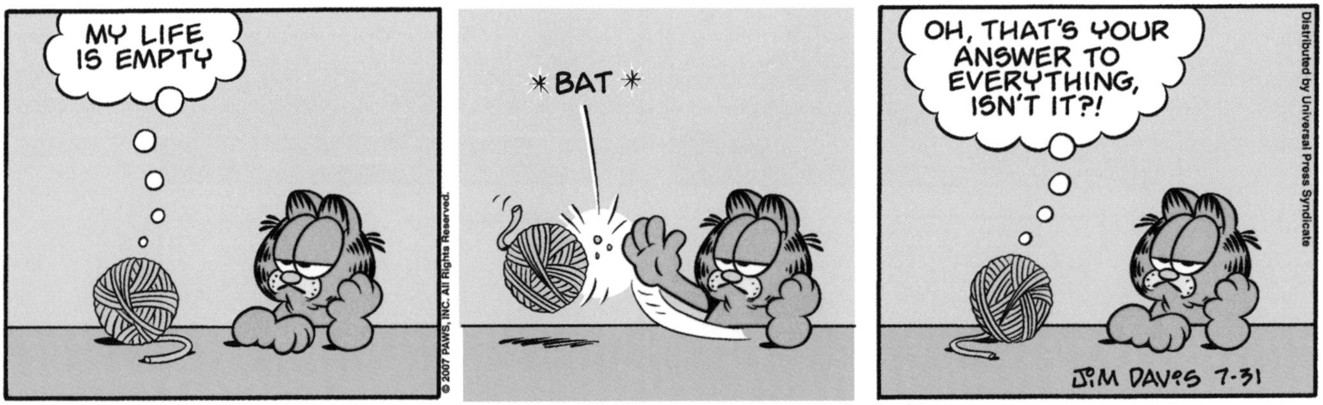
MY LIFE IS EMPTY
© 2007 PAWS, INC. All Rights Reserved.
BAT
OH, THAT'S YOUR ANSWER TO EVERYTHING, ISN'T IT?!
Distributed by Universal Press Syndicate
JIM DAVIS 7-31

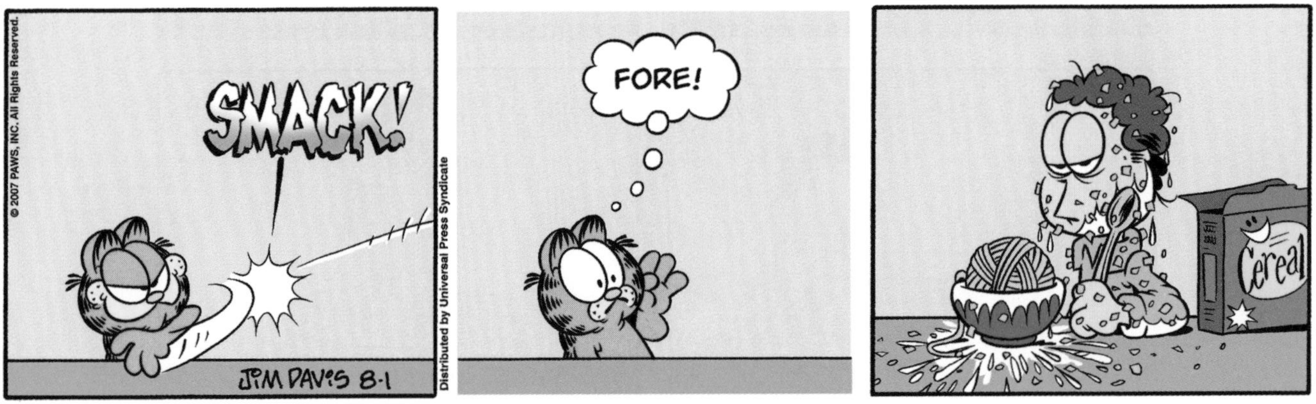
© 2007 PAWS, INC. All Rights Reserved.
SMACK!
JIM DAVIS 8-1
Distributed by Universal Press Syndicate
FORE!
Cereal

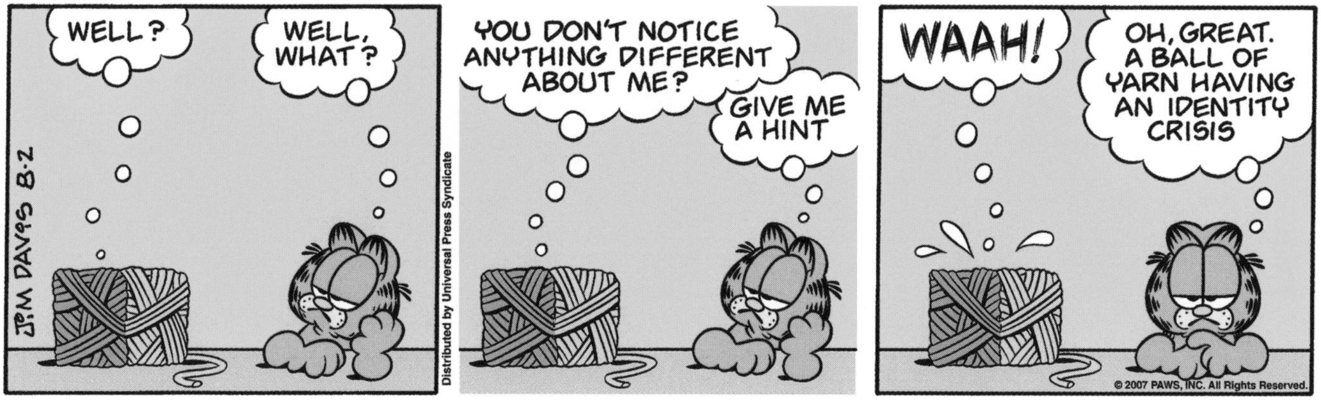
WELL?
WELL, WHAT?
JIM DAVIS 8·2
YOU DON'T NOTICE ANYTHING DIFFERENT ABOUT ME?
GIVE ME A HINT
Distributed by Universal Press Syndicate
WAAH!
OH, GREAT. A BALL OF YARN HAVING AN IDENTITY CRISIS
© 2007 PAWS, INC. All Rights Reserved.

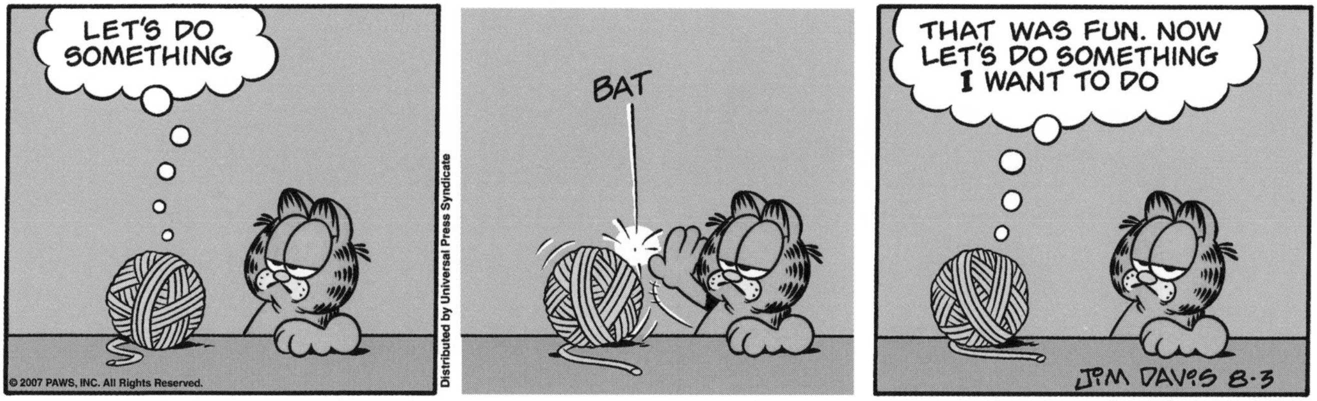
LET'S DO SOMETHING
© 2007 PAWS, INC. All Rights Reserved.
Distributed by Universal Press Syndicate
BAT
THAT WAS FUN. NOW LET'S DO SOMETHING I WANT TO DO
JIM DAVIS 8·3

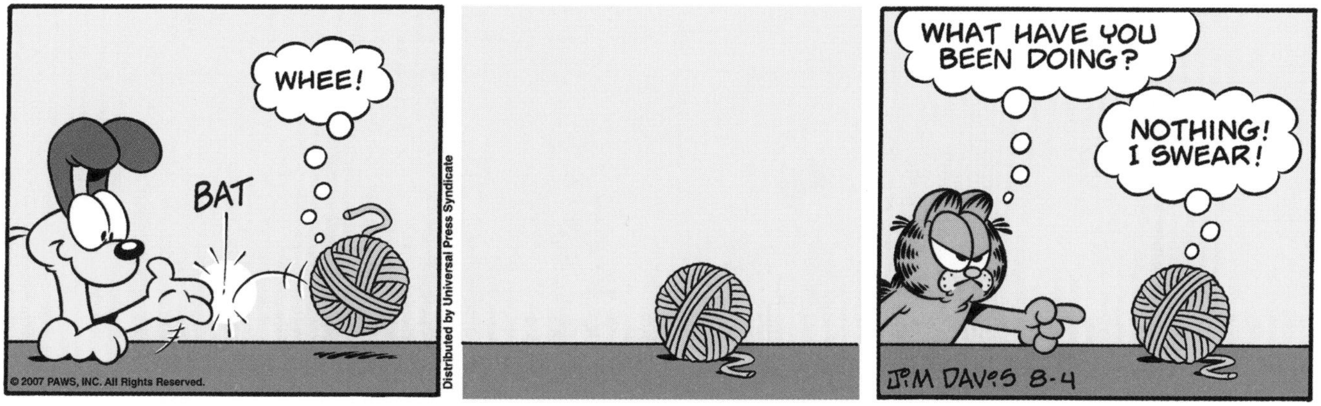
WHEE!
BAT
© 2007 PAWS, INC. All Rights Reserved.
Distributed by Universal Press Syndicate
WHAT HAVE YOU BEEN DOING?
NOTHING! I SWEAR!
JIM DAVIS 8·4

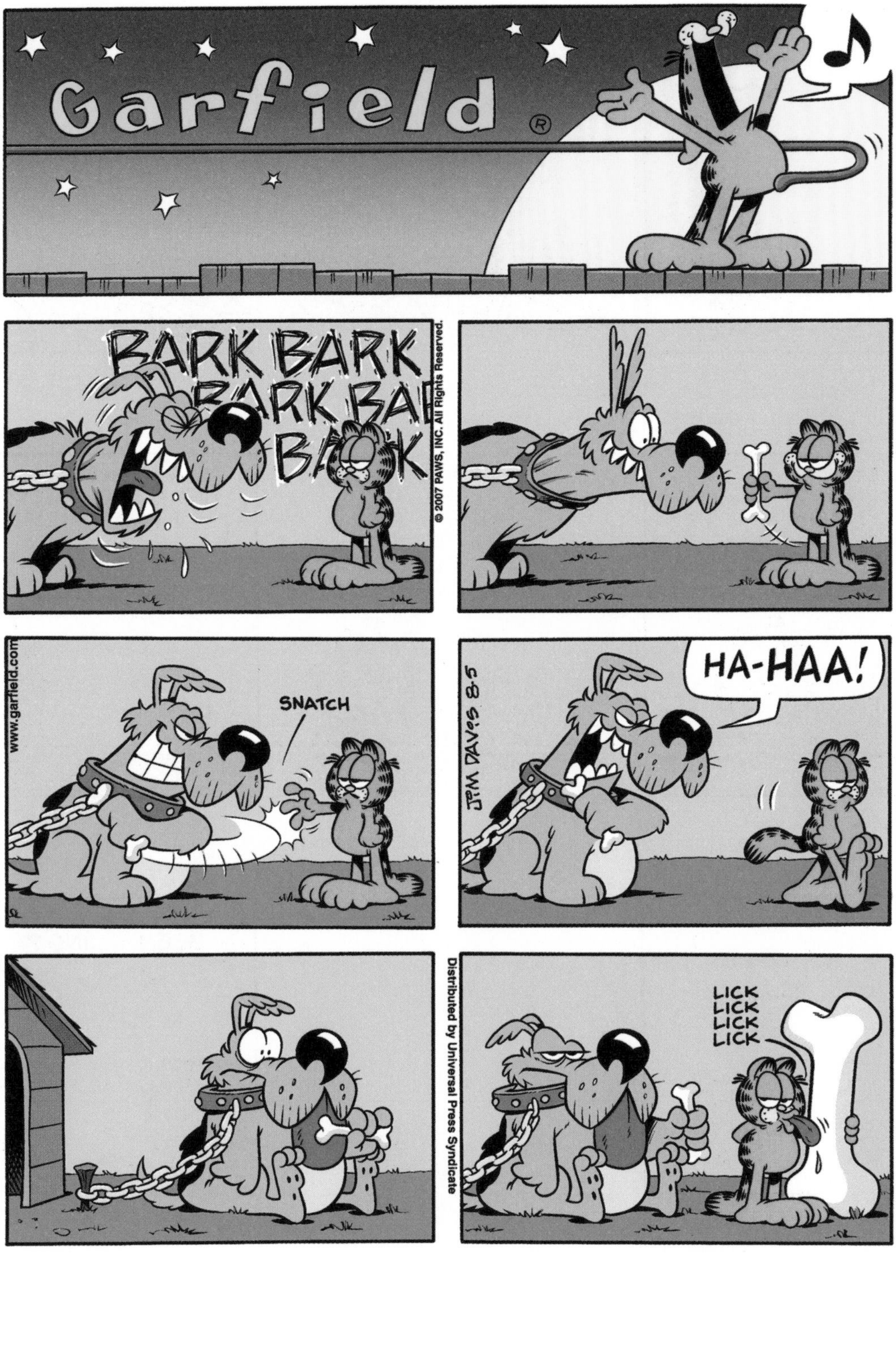
Garfield®
BARK BARK
BARK BA
© 2007 PAWS, INC. All Rights Reserved.
www.garfield.com
SNATCH
JIM DAVIS 8-5
HA-HAA!
Distributed by Universal Press Syndicate
LICK
LICK
LICK
LICK

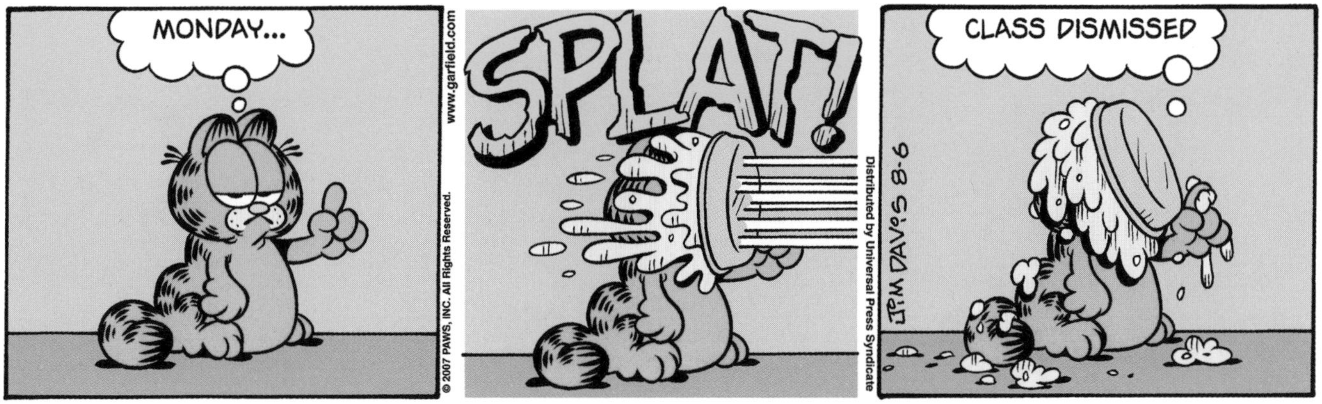
MONDAY...
SPLAT!
CLASS DISMISSED
www.garfield.com
© 2007 PAWS, INC. All Rights Reserved.
Distributed by Universal Press Syndicate
JIM DAVIS 8-6

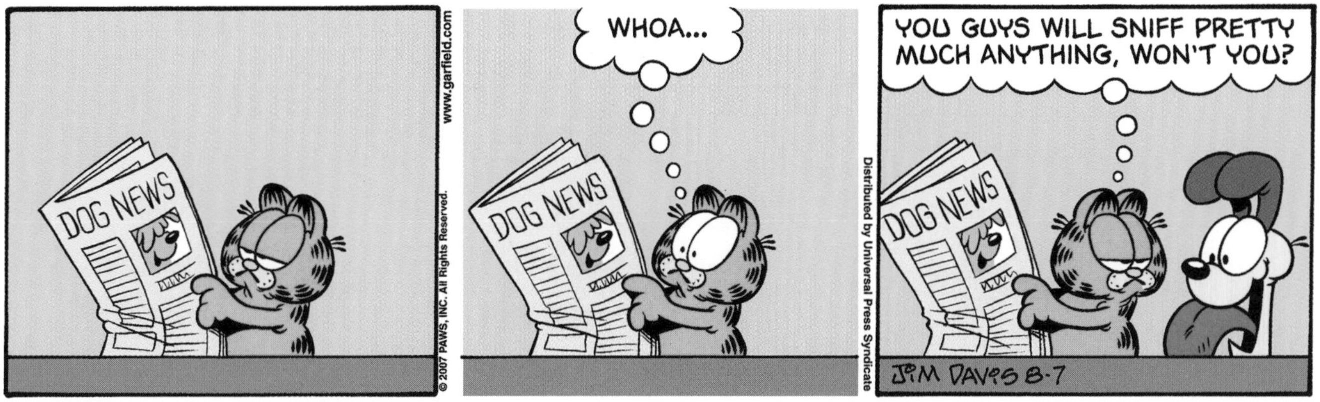
DOG NEWS
WHOA...
YOU GUYS WILL SNIFF PRETTY MUCH ANYTHING, WON'T YOU?
www.garfield.com
© 2007 PAWS, INC. All Rights Reserved.
Distributed by Universal Press Syndicate
JIM DAVIS 8-7

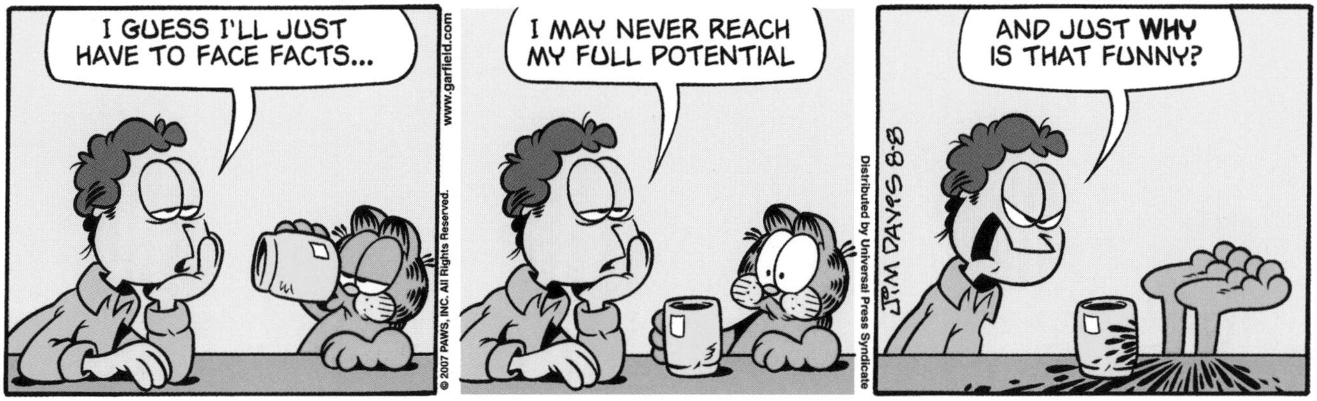
I GUESS I'LL JUST HAVE TO FACE FACTS...
I MAY NEVER REACH MY FULL POTENTIAL
AND JUST WHY IS THAT FUNNY?
www.garfield.com
© 2007 PAWS, INC. All Rights Reserved.
Distributed by Universal Press Syndicate
JIM DAVIS 8-8

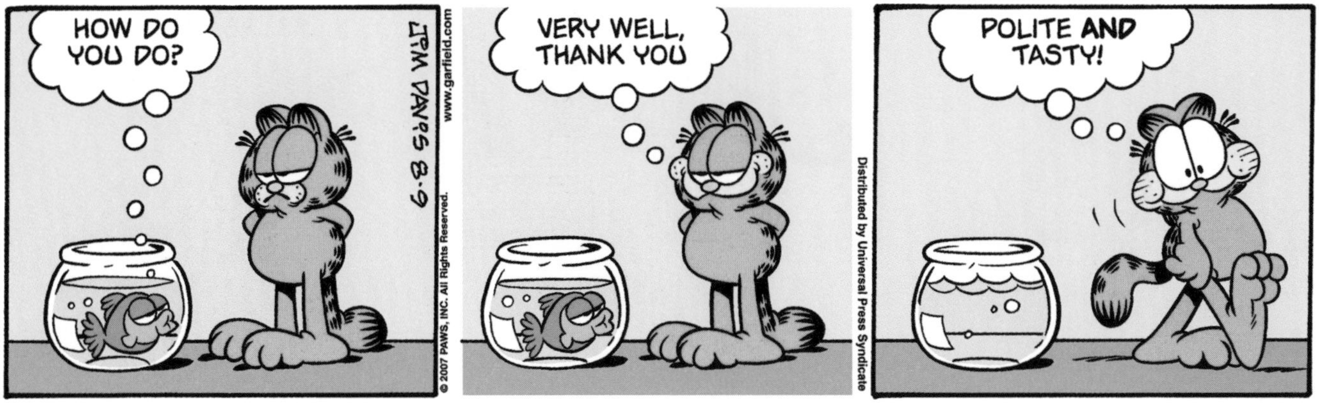
HOW DO YOU DO?
JPM DAVIS 8-9
www.garfield.com
© 2007 PAWS, INC. All Rights Reserved.
VERY WELL, THANK YOU
Distributed by Universal Press Syndicate
POLITE **AND** TASTY!

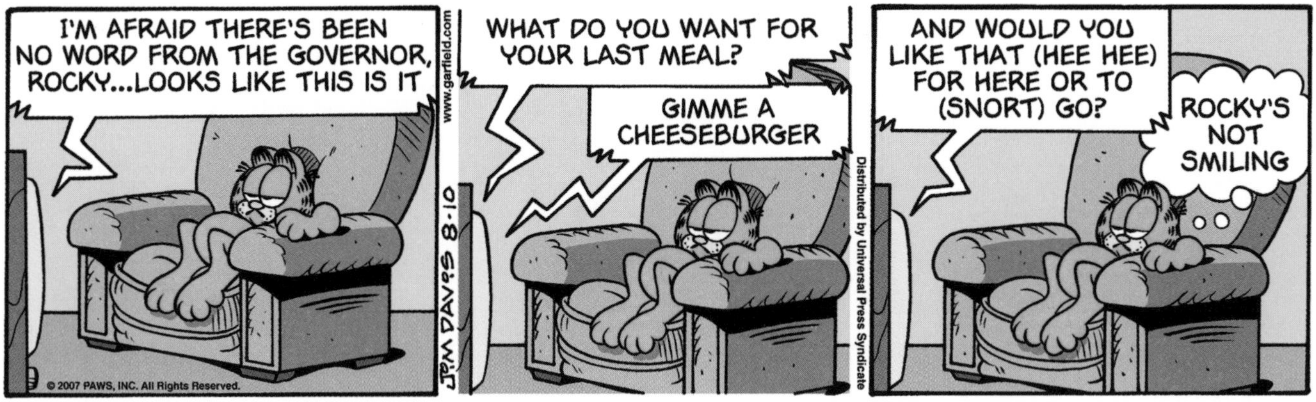
I'M AFRAID THERE'S BEEN NO WORD FROM THE GOVERNOR, ROCKY...LOOKS LIKE THIS IS IT
© 2007 PAWS, INC. All Rights Reserved.
www.garfield.com
JPM DAVIS 8-10
WHAT DO YOU WANT FOR YOUR LAST MEAL?
GIMME A CHEESEBURGER
Distributed by Universal Press Syndicate
AND WOULD YOU LIKE THAT (HEE HEE) FOR HERE OR TO (SNORT) GO?
ROCKY'S NOT SMILING

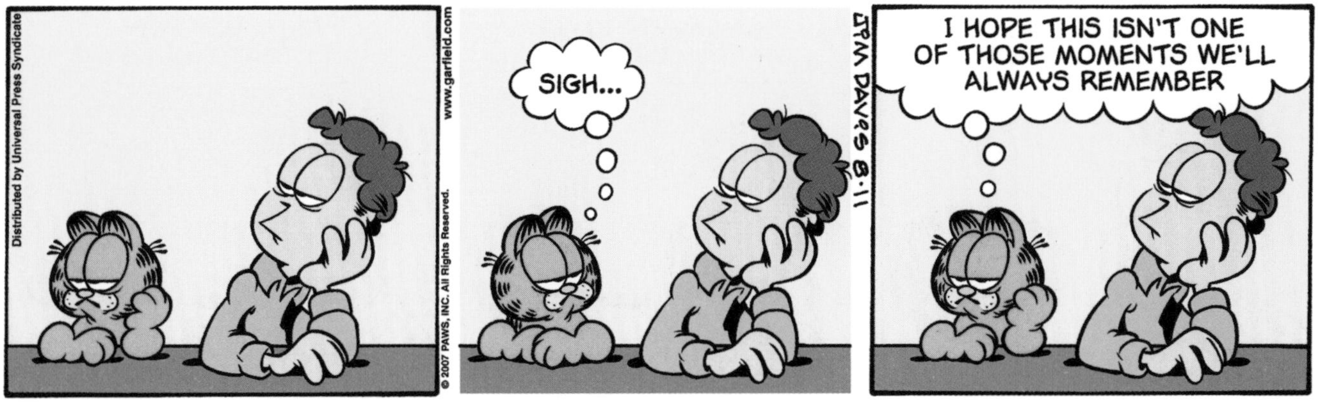
Distributed by Universal Press Syndicate
www.garfield.com
© 2007 PAWS, INC. All Rights Reserved.
SIGH...
JPM DAVIS 8-11
I HOPE THIS ISN'T ONE OF THOSE MOMENTS WE'LL ALWAYS REMEMBER

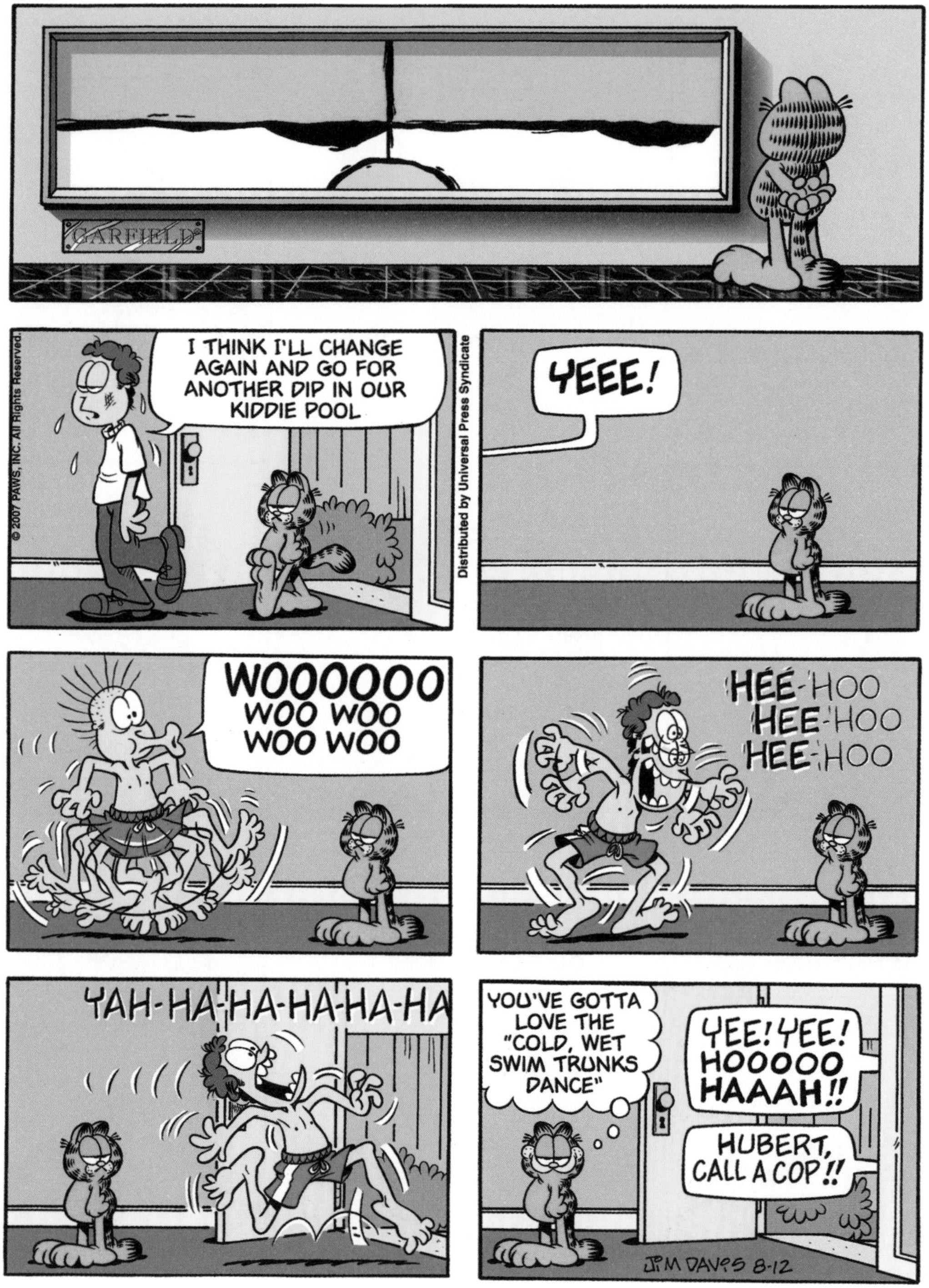

GARFIELD®
© 2007 PAWS, INC. All Rights Reserved.
I THINK I'LL CHANGE AGAIN AND GO FOR ANOTHER DIP IN OUR KIDDIE POOL
Distributed by Universal Press Syndicate
YEEE!
WOOOOOO WOO WOO WOO WOO
HEE-HOO HEE-HOO HEE-HOO
YAH-HA-HA-HA-HA-HA
YOU'VE GOTTA LOVE THE "COLD, WET SWIM TRUNKS DANCE"
YEE! YEE! HOOOOO HAAAH!!
HUBERT, CALL A COP!!
JIM DAVIS 8-12

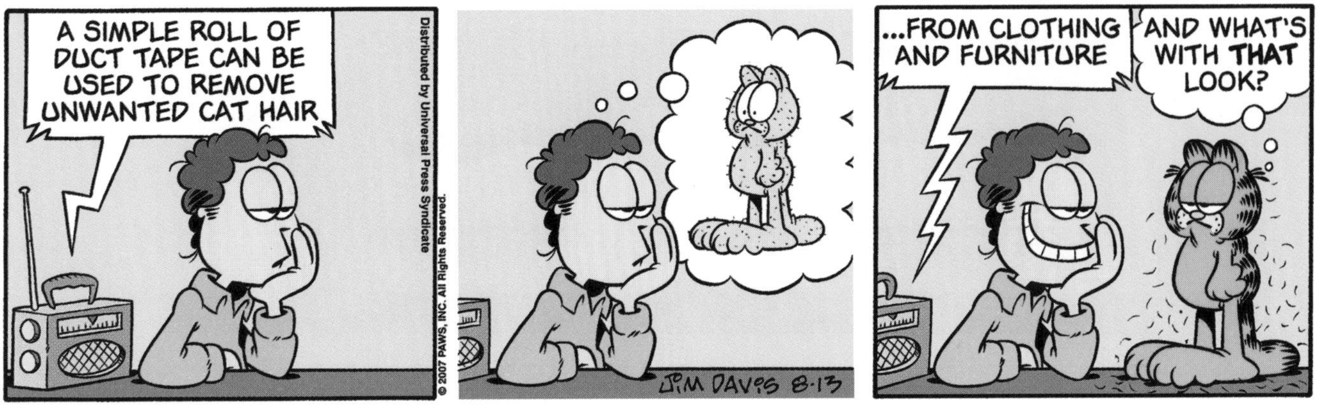
A SIMPLE ROLL OF DUCT TAPE CAN BE USED TO REMOVE UNWANTED CAT HAIR
Distributed by Universal Press Syndicate
© 2007 PAWS, INC. All Rights Reserved.
JIM DAVIS 8-13
...FROM CLOTHING AND FURNITURE
AND WHAT'S WITH **THAT** LOOK?

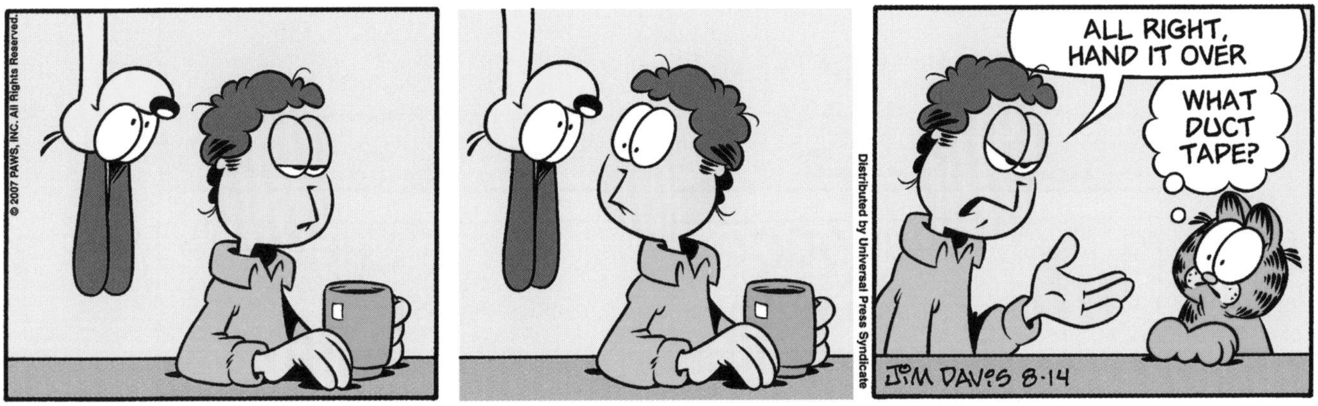
© 2007 PAWS, INC. All Rights Reserved.
Distributed by Universal Press Syndicate
ALL RIGHT, HAND IT OVER
WHAT DUCT TAPE?
JIM DAVIS 8-14

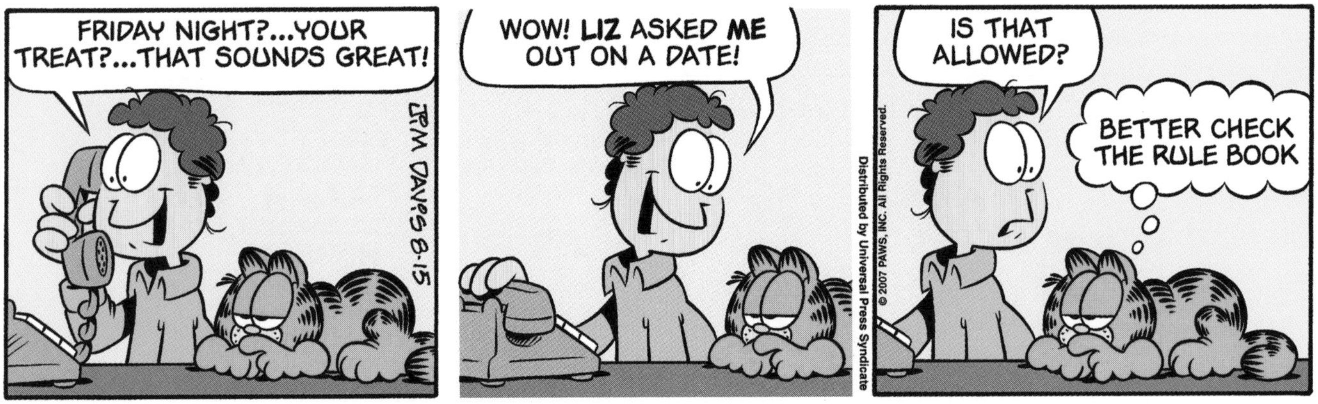
FRIDAY NIGHT?...YOUR TREAT?...THAT SOUNDS GREAT!
JIM DAVIS 8-15
WOW! **LIZ** ASKED **ME** OUT ON A DATE!
© 2007 PAWS, INC. All Rights Reserved.
Distributed by Universal Press Syndicate
IS THAT ALLOWED?
BETTER CHECK THE RULE BOOK

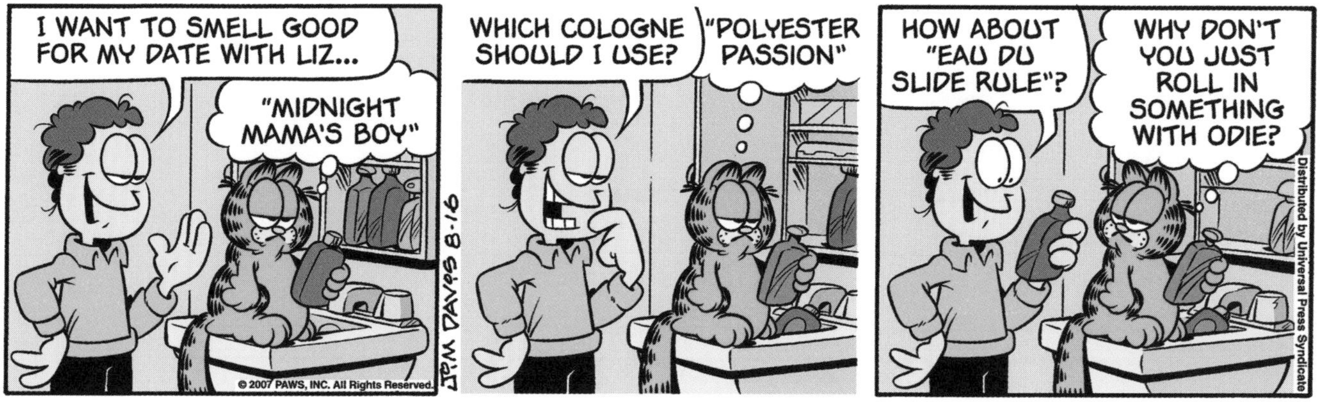
I WANT TO SMELL GOOD FOR MY DATE WITH LIZ...
"MIDNIGHT MAMA'S BOY"
© 2007 PAWS, INC. All Rights Reserved.
JIM DAVIS 8-16
WHICH COLOGNE SHOULD I USE?
"POLYESTER PASSION"
HOW ABOUT "EAU DU SLIDE RULE"?
WHY DON'T YOU JUST ROLL IN SOMETHING WITH ODIE?
Distributed by Universal Press Syndicate

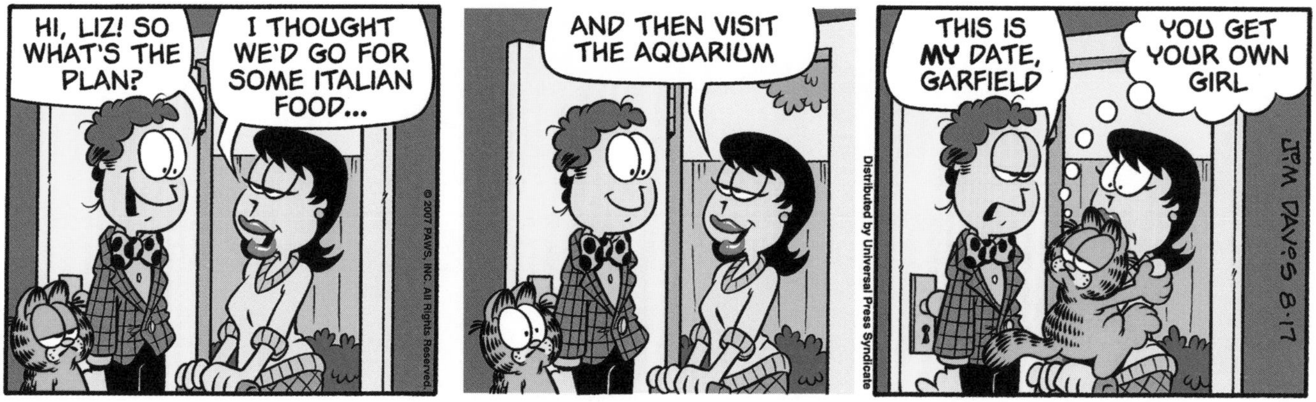
HI, LIZ! SO WHAT'S THE PLAN?
I THOUGHT WE'D GO FOR SOME ITALIAN FOOD...
© 2007 PAWS, INC. All Rights Reserved.
AND THEN VISIT THE AQUARIUM
Distributed by Universal Press Syndicate
THIS IS MY DATE, GARFIELD
YOU GET YOUR OWN GIRL
JIM DAVIS 8-17

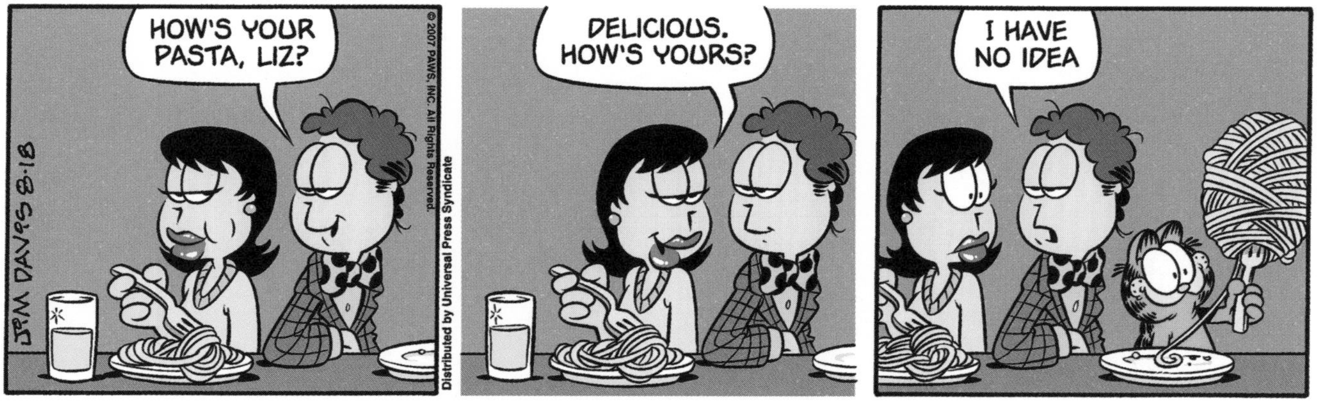
JIM DAVIS 8-18
HOW'S YOUR PASTA, LIZ?
© 2007 PAWS, INC. All Rights Reserved.
Distributed by Universal Press Syndicate
DELICIOUS. HOW'S YOURS?
I HAVE NO IDEA

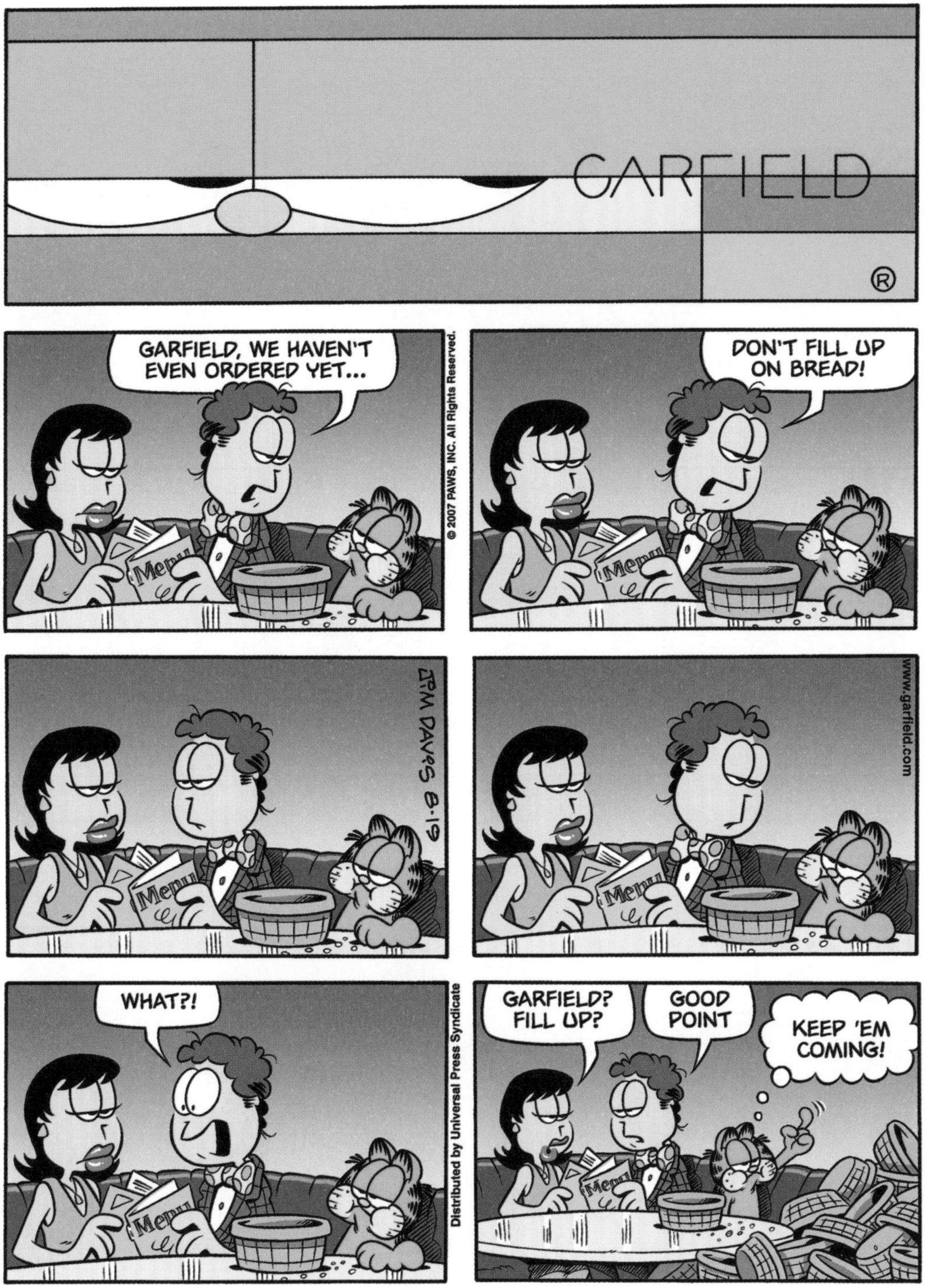
GARFIELD
GARFIELD, WE HAVEN'T EVEN ORDERED YET...
© 2007 PAWS, INC. All Rights Reserved.
DON'T FILL UP ON BREAD!
JIM DAVIS 8-19
www.garfield.com
WHAT?!
Distributed by Universal Press Syndicate
GARFIELD? FILL UP?
GOOD POINT
KEEP 'EM COMING!

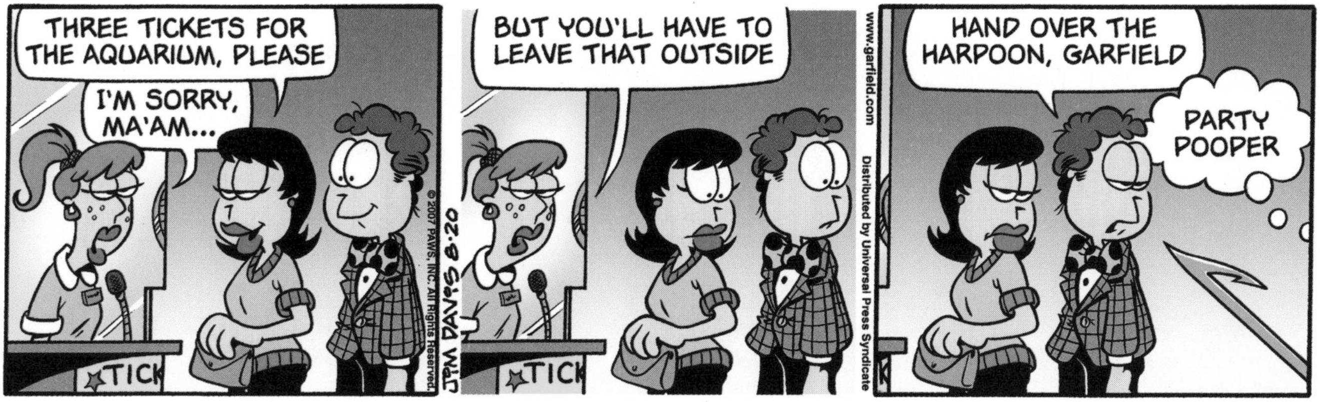
THREE TICKETS FOR THE AQUARIUM, PLEASE
I'M SORRY, MA'AM...
TICK
© 2007 PAWS, INC. All Rights Reserved.
JIM DAVIS 8·20
BUT YOU'LL HAVE TO LEAVE THAT OUTSIDE
TICK
www.garfield.com
Distributed by Universal Press Syndicate
HAND OVER THE HARPOON, GARFIELD
PARTY POOPER

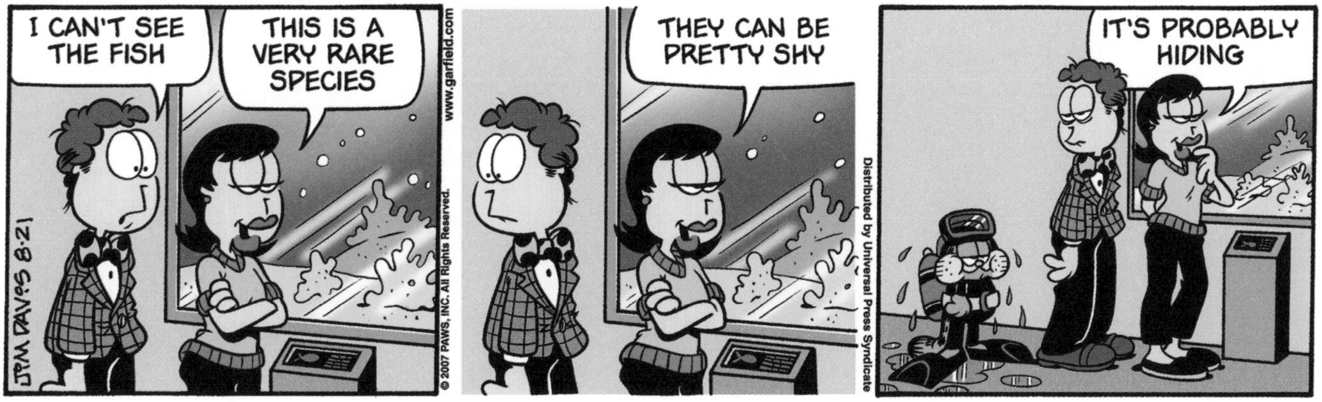
I CAN'T SEE THE FISH
THIS IS A VERY RARE SPECIES
JIM DAVIS 8·21
www.garfield.com
© 2007 PAWS, INC. All Rights Reserved.
THEY CAN BE PRETTY SHY
Distributed by Universal Press Syndicate
IT'S PROBABLY HIDING

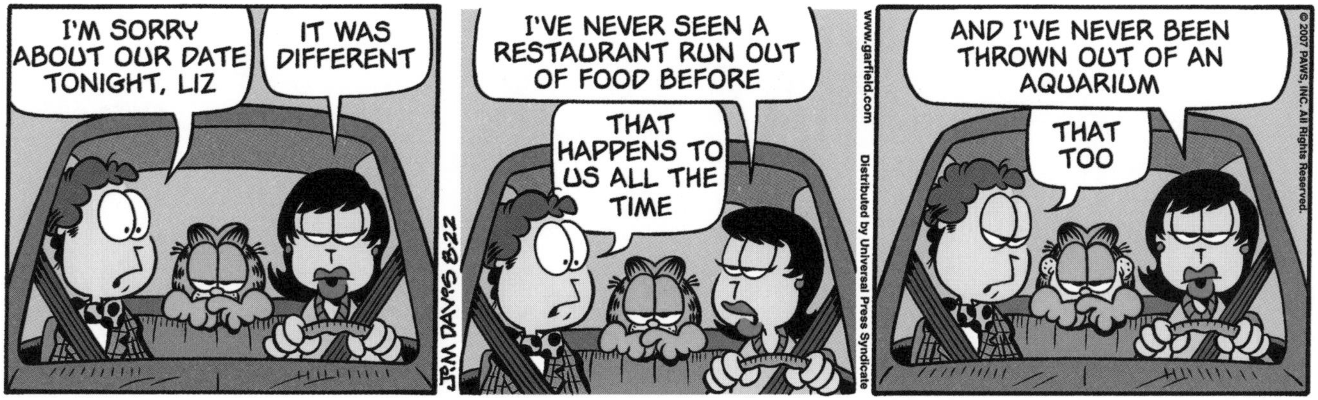
I'M SORRY ABOUT OUR DATE TONIGHT, LIZ
IT WAS DIFFERENT
JIM DAVIS 8·22
I'VE NEVER SEEN A RESTAURANT RUN OUT OF FOOD BEFORE
THAT HAPPENS TO US ALL THE TIME
www.garfield.com
Distributed by Universal Press Syndicate
AND I'VE NEVER BEEN THROWN OUT OF AN AQUARIUM
THAT TOO
© 2007 PAWS, INC. All Rights Reserved.

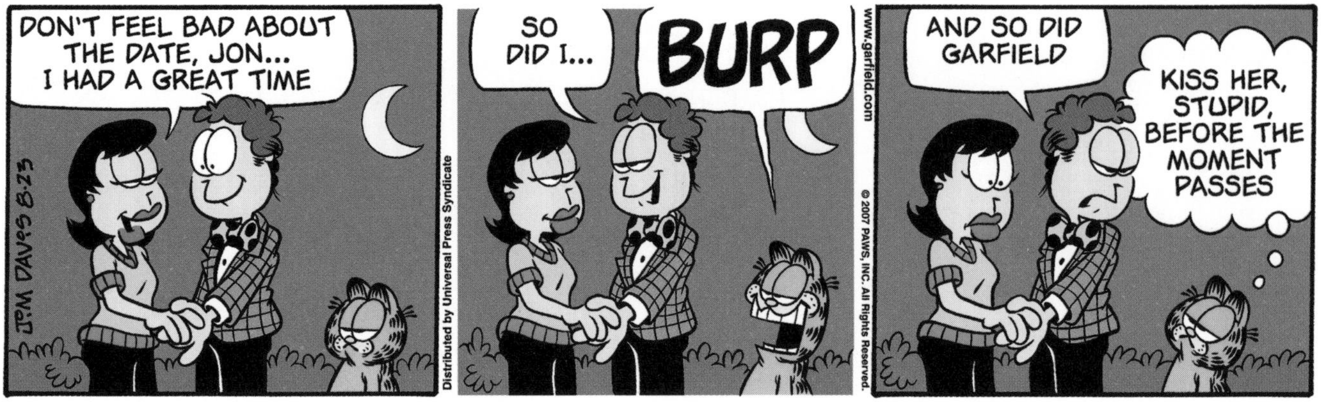
DON'T FEEL BAD ABOUT THE DATE, JON... I HAD A GREAT TIME
JIM DAVIS 8-23
Distributed by Universal Press Syndicate
SO DID I...
BURP
© 2007 PAWS, INC. All Rights Reserved.
www.garfield.com
AND SO DID GARFIELD
KISS HER, STUPID, BEFORE THE MOMENT PASSES

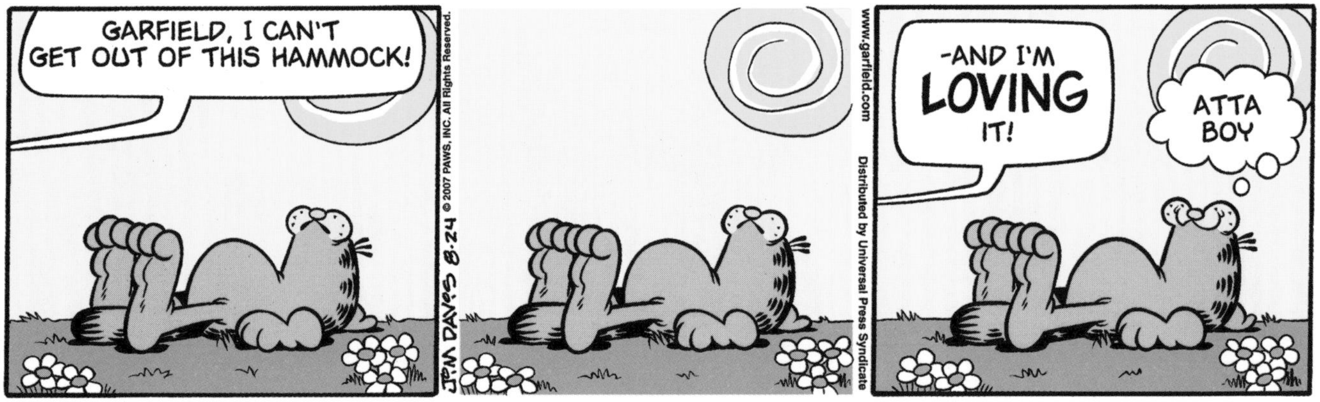
GARFIELD, I CAN'T GET OUT OF THIS HAMMOCK!
JIM DAVIS 8-24 © 2007 PAWS, INC. All Rights Reserved.
www.garfield.com
Distributed by Universal Press Syndicate
-AND I'M LOVING IT!
ATTA BOY

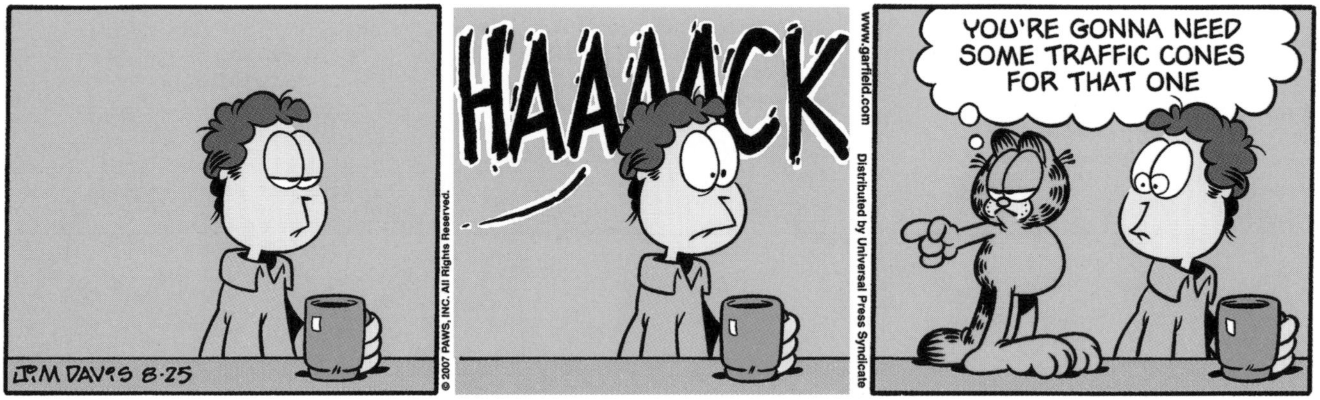
JIM DAVIS 8-25
© 2007 PAWS, INC. All Rights Reserved.
HAAAACK
www.garfield.com
Distributed by Universal Press Syndicate
YOU'RE GONNA NEED SOME TRAFFIC CONES FOR THAT ONE

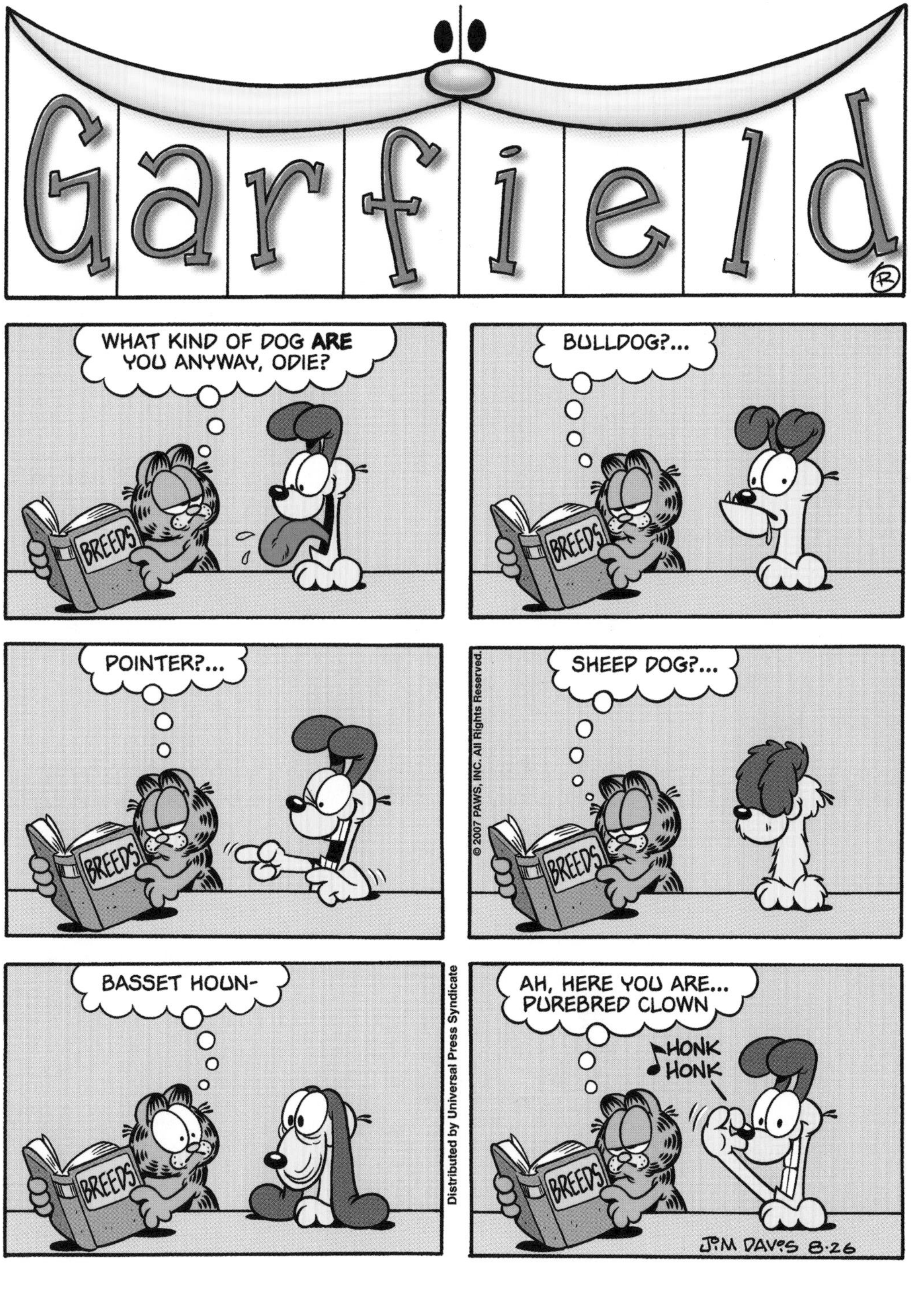

Garfield®
WHAT KIND OF DOG ARE YOU ANYWAY, ODIE?
BREEDS
BULLDOG?...
POINTER?...
SHEEP DOG?...
BASSET HOUN-
AH, HERE YOU ARE... PUREBRED CLOWN
HONK HONK
JIM DAVIS 8-26
© 2007 PAWS, INC. All Rights Reserved.
Distributed by Universal Press Syndicate

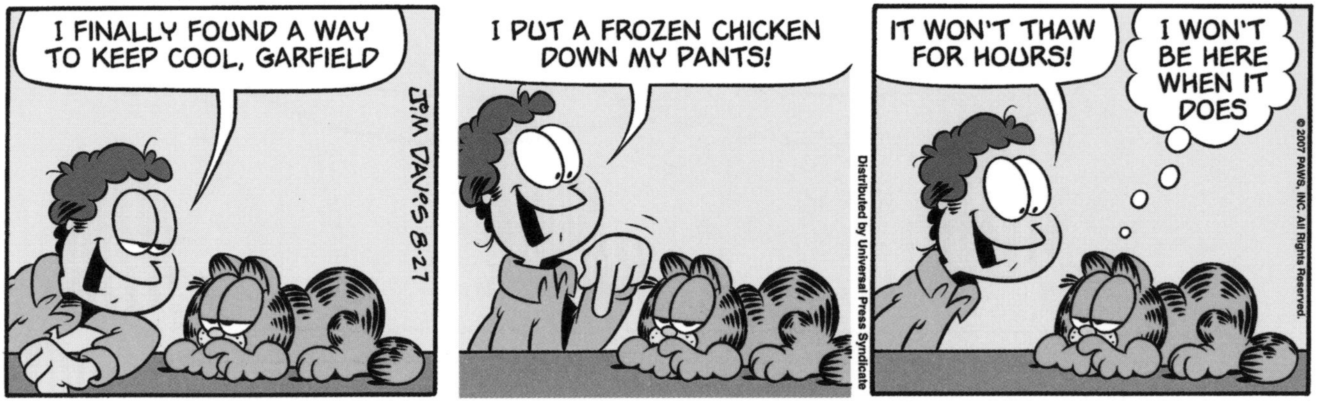
I FINALLY FOUND A WAY TO KEEP COOL, GARFIELD
JIM DAVIS 8·27
I PUT A FROZEN CHICKEN DOWN MY PANTS!
Distributed by Universal Press Syndicate
IT WON'T THAW FOR HOURS!
I WON'T BE HERE WHEN IT DOES
© 2007 PAWS, INC. All Rights Reserved.

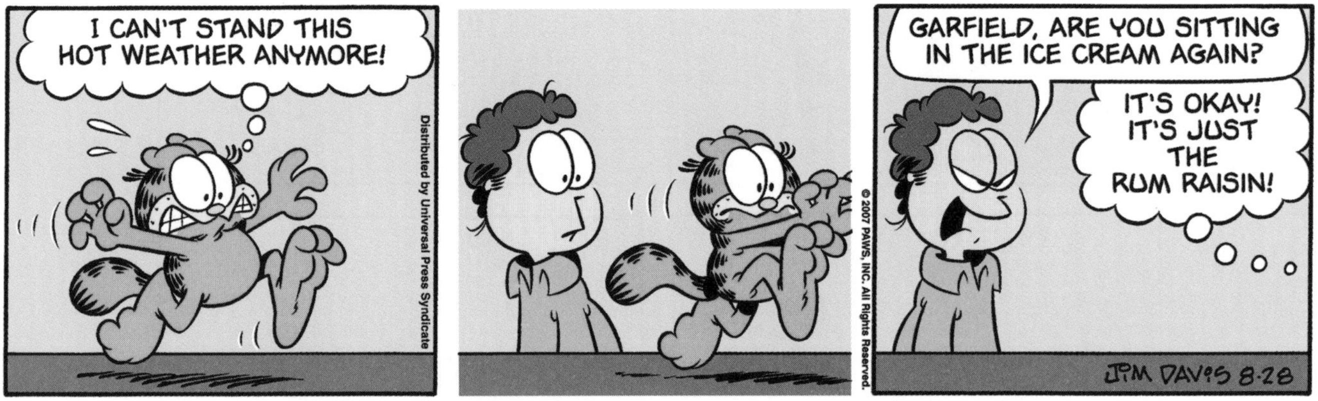
I CAN'T STAND THIS HOT WEATHER ANYMORE!
Distributed by Universal Press Syndicate
© 2007 PAWS, INC. All Rights Reserved.
GARFIELD, ARE YOU SITTING IN THE ICE CREAM AGAIN?
IT'S OKAY! IT'S JUST THE RUM RAISIN!
JIM DAVIS 8·28

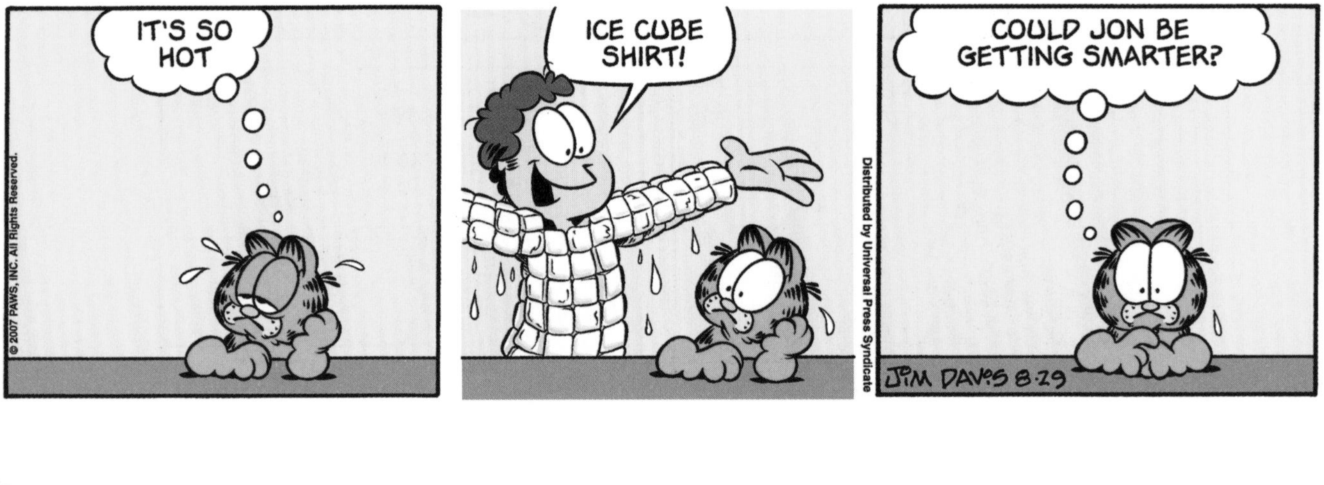
IT'S SO HOT
© 2007 PAWS, INC. All Rights Reserved.
ICE CUBE SHIRT!
Distributed by Universal Press Syndicate
COULD JON BE GETTING SMARTER?
JIM DAVIS 8·29

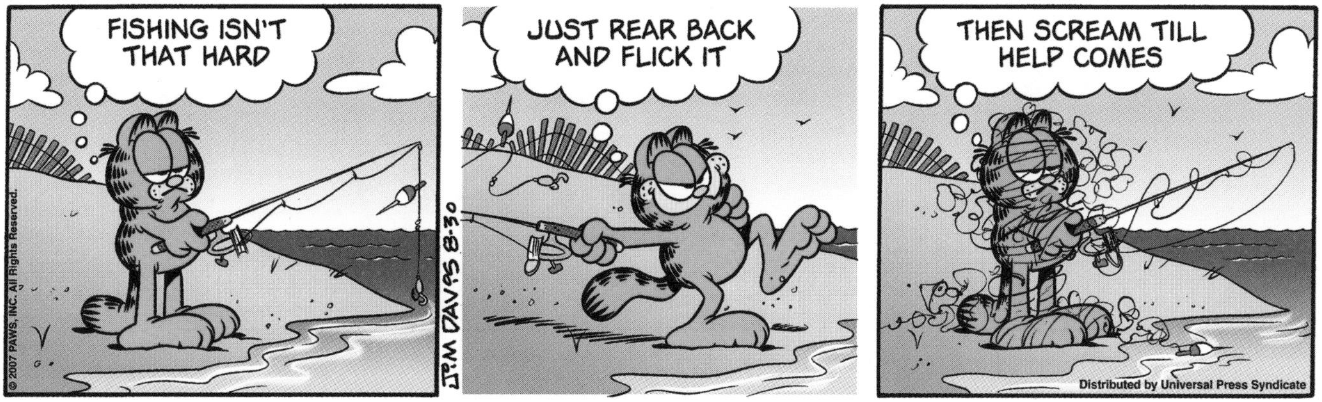
FISHING ISN'T THAT HARD
JUST REAR BACK AND FLICK IT
THEN SCREAM TILL HELP COMES
JIM DAVIS 8-30
© 2007 PAWS, INC. All Rights Reserved.
Distributed by Universal Press Syndicate

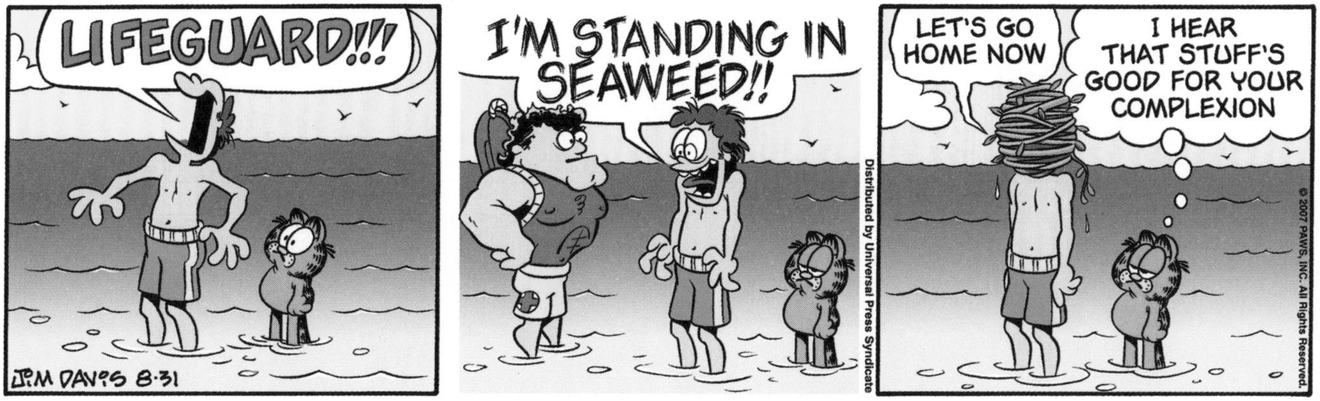
LIFEGUARD!!!
I'M STANDING IN SEAWEED!!
LET'S GO HOME NOW
I HEAR THAT STUFF'S GOOD FOR YOUR COMPLEXION
JIM DAVIS 8-31
Distributed by Universal Press Syndicate
© 2007 PAWS, INC. All Rights Reserved.

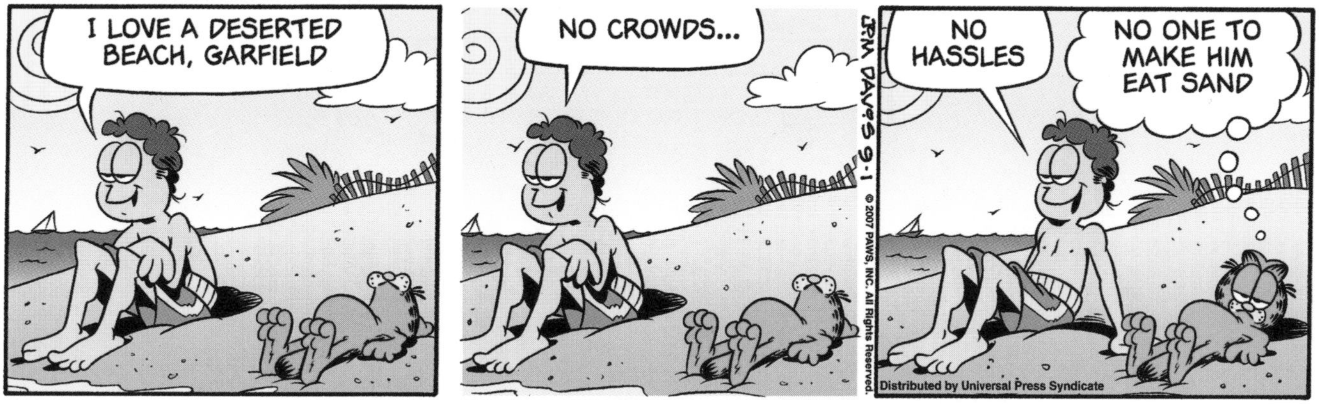
I LOVE A DESERTED BEACH, GARFIELD
NO CROWDS...
NO HASSLES
NO ONE TO MAKE HIM EAT SAND
JIM DAVIS 9-1
© 2007 PAWS, INC. All Rights Reserved.
Distributed by Universal Press Syndicate

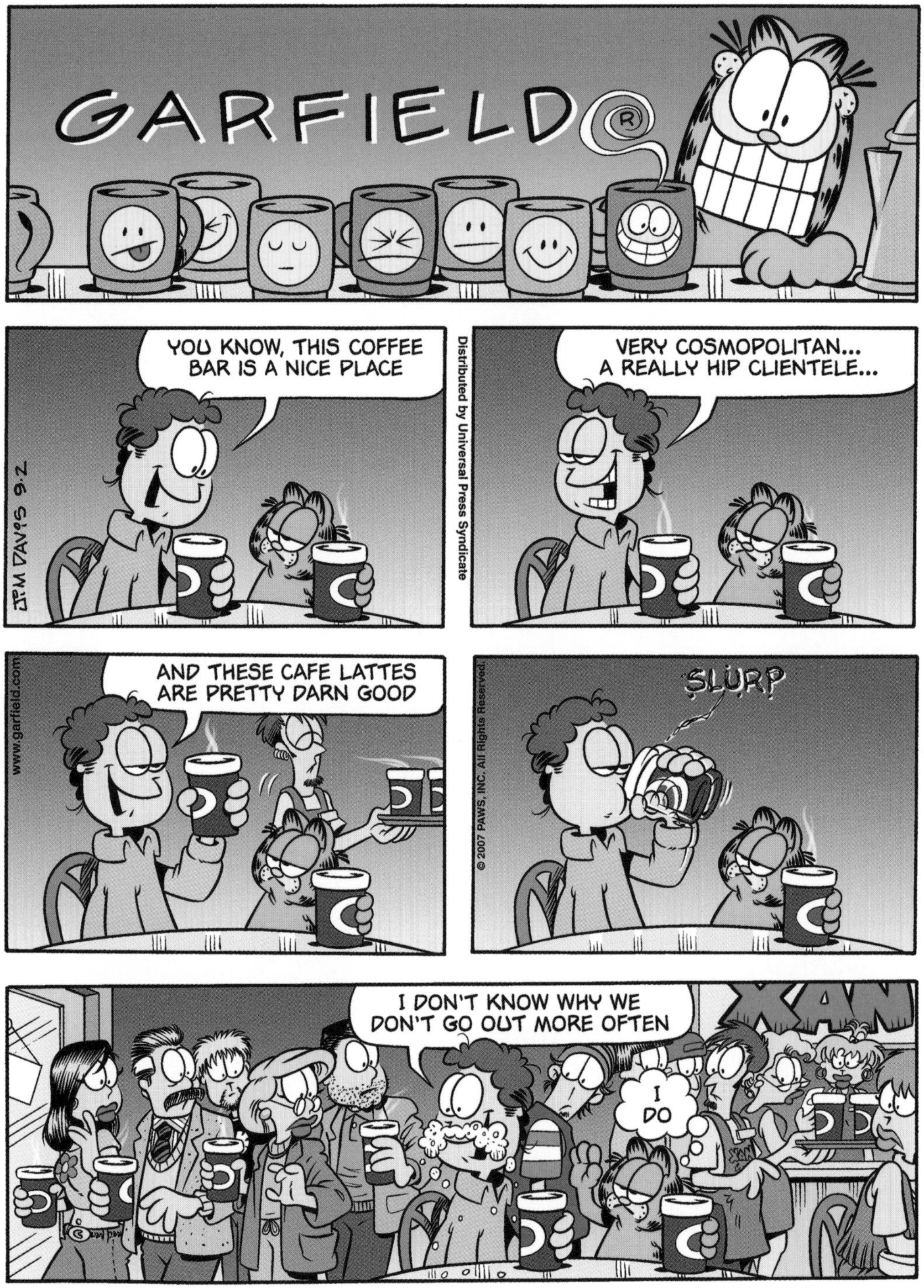
GARFIELD
YOU KNOW, THIS COFFEE BAR IS A NICE PLACE
JIM DAVIS 9.2
Distributed by Universal Press Syndicate
VERY COSMOPOLITAN... A REALLY HIP CLIENTELE...
www.garfield.com
AND THESE CAFE LATTES ARE PRETTY DARN GOOD
© 2007 PAWS, INC. All Rights Reserved.
SLURP
I DON'T KNOW WHY WE DON'T GO OUT MORE OFTEN
I DO

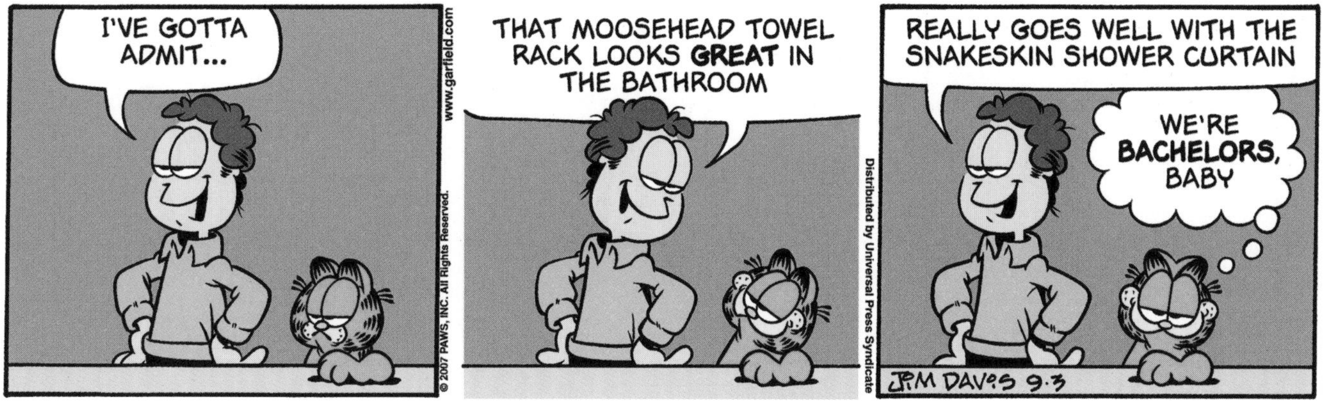
I'VE GOTTA ADMIT...
© 2007 PAWS, INC. All Rights Reserved. www.garfield.com
THAT MOOSEHEAD TOWEL RACK LOOKS GREAT IN THE BATHROOM
Distributed by Universal Press Syndicate
REALLY GOES WELL WITH THE SNAKESKIN SHOWER CURTAIN
WE'RE BACHELORS, BABY
JIM DAVIS 9-3

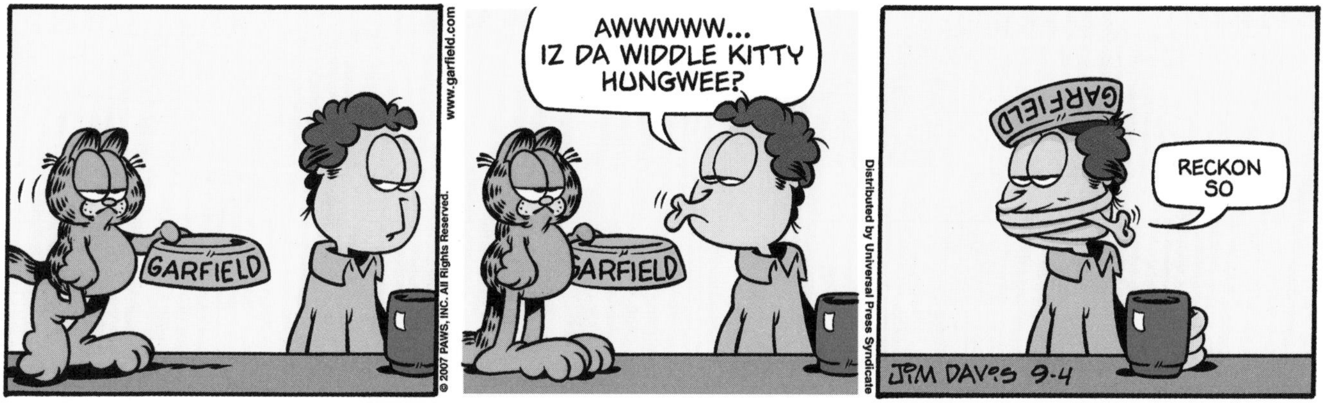
GARFIELD
© 2007 PAWS, INC. All Rights Reserved. www.garfield.com
AWWWWW... IZ DA WIDDLE KITTY HUNGWEE?
GARFIELD
Distributed by Universal Press Syndicate
GARFIELD
RECKON SO
JIM DAVIS 9-4

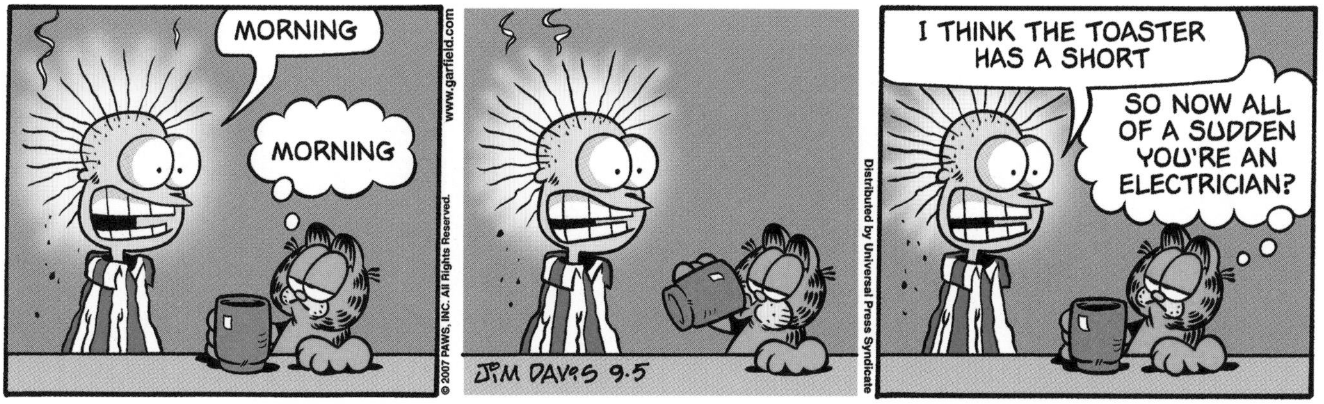
MORNING
MORNING
© 2007 PAWS, INC. All Rights Reserved. www.garfield.com
JIM DAVIS 9-5
Distributed by Universal Press Syndicate
I THINK THE TOASTER HAS A SHORT
SO NOW ALL OF A SUDDEN YOU'RE AN ELECTRICIAN?

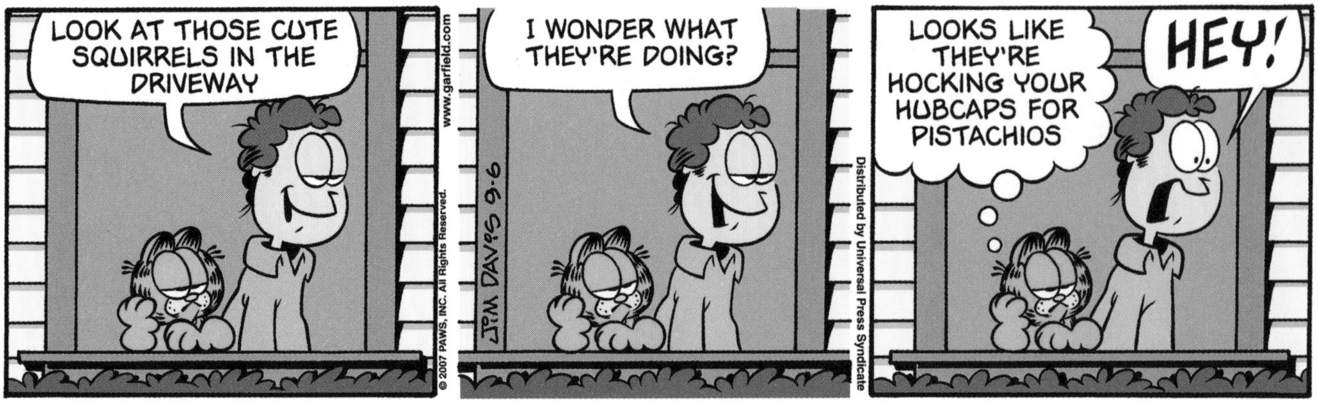
LOOK AT THOSE CUTE SQUIRRELS IN THE DRIVEWAY
© 2007 PAWS, INC. All Rights Reserved.
www.garfield.com
JIM DAVIS 9-6
I WONDER WHAT THEY'RE DOING?
Distributed by Universal Press Syndicate
LOOKS LIKE THEY'RE HOCKING YOUR HUBCAPS FOR PISTACHIOS
HEY!

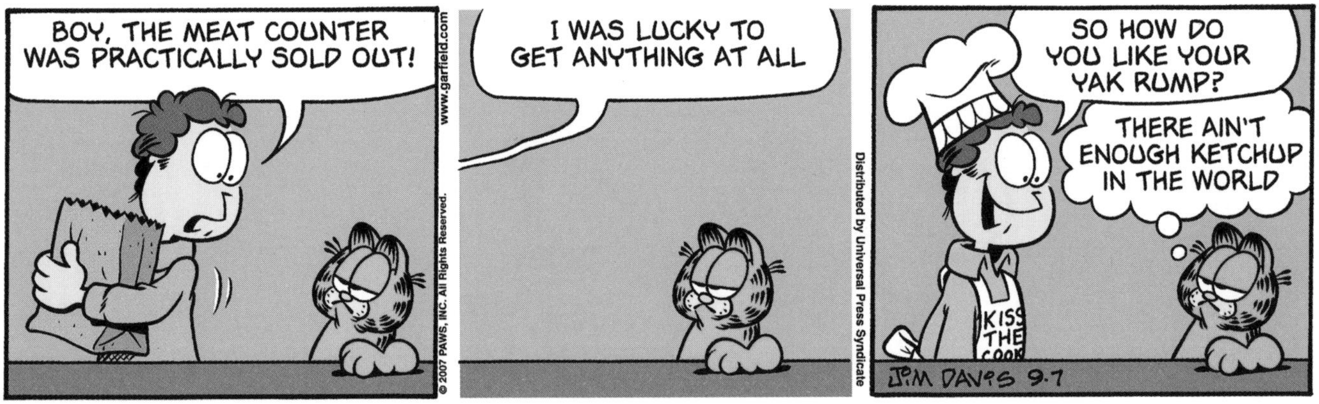
BOY, THE MEAT COUNTER WAS PRACTICALLY SOLD OUT!
© 2007 PAWS, INC. All Rights Reserved.
www.garfield.com
I WAS LUCKY TO GET ANYTHING AT ALL
Distributed by Universal Press Syndicate
SO HOW DO YOU LIKE YOUR YAK RUMP?
THERE AIN'T ENOUGH KETCHUP IN THE WORLD
KISS THE
JIM DAVIS 9-7

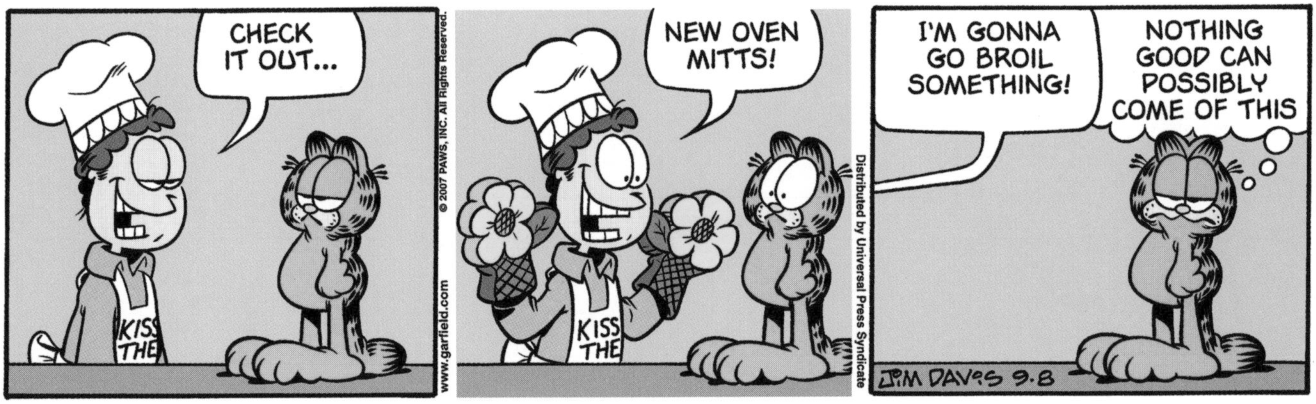
CHECK IT OUT...
KISS THE
© 2007 PAWS, INC. All Rights Reserved.
www.garfield.com
NEW OVEN MITTS!
KISS THE
Distributed by Universal Press Syndicate
I'M GONNA GO BROIL SOMETHING!
NOTHING GOOD CAN POSSIBLY COME OF THIS
JIM DAVIS 9-8

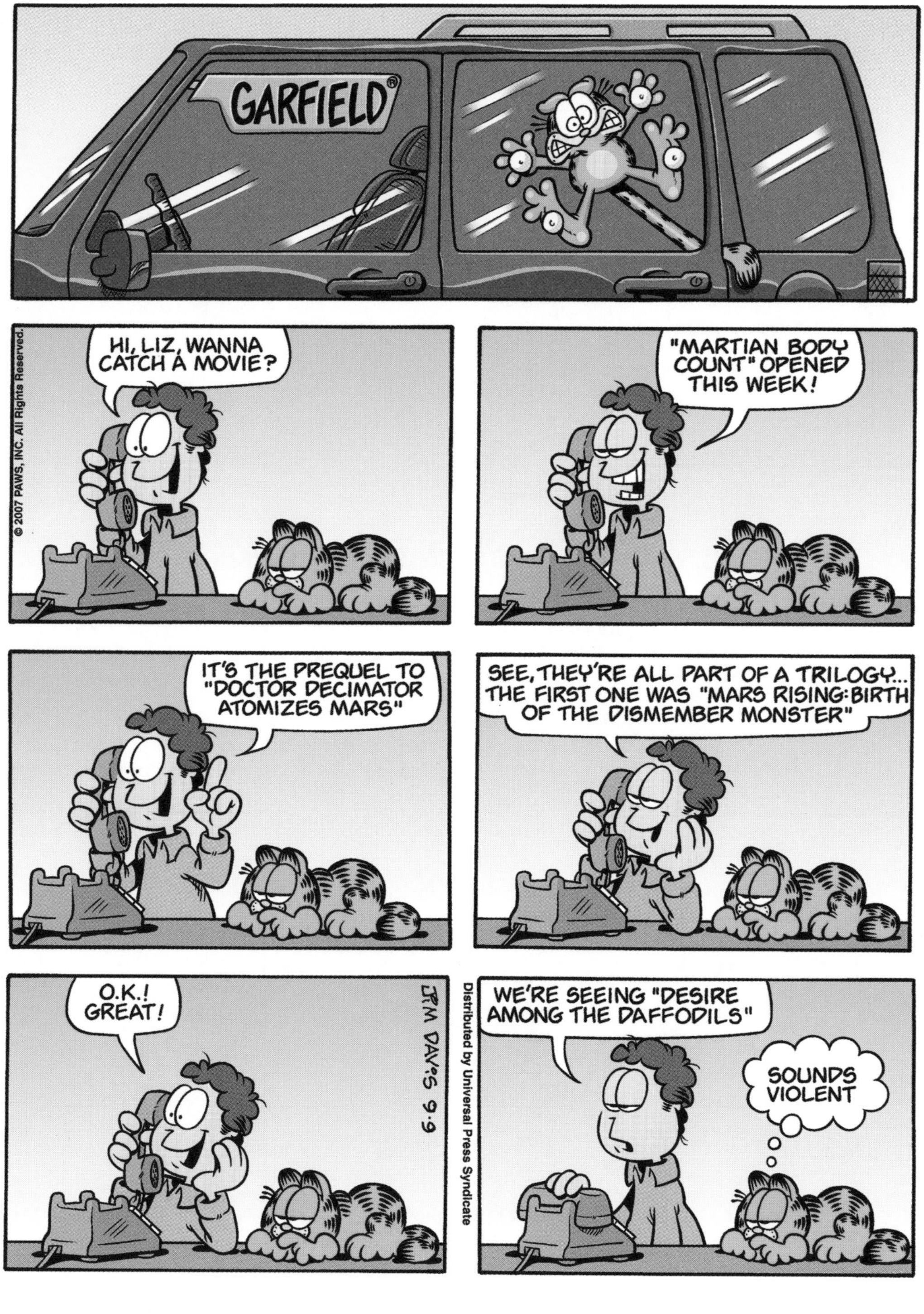

GARFIELD®
HI, LIZ, WANNA CATCH A MOVIE?
"MARTIAN BODY COUNT" OPENED THIS WEEK!
IT'S THE PREQUEL TO "DOCTOR DECIMATOR ATOMIZES MARS"
SEE, THEY'RE ALL PART OF A TRILOGY... THE FIRST ONE WAS "MARS RISING: BIRTH OF THE DISMEMBER MONSTER"
O.K.! GREAT!
JIM DAVIS 9-9
WE'RE SEEING "DESIRE AMONG THE DAFFODILS"
SOUNDS VIOLENT

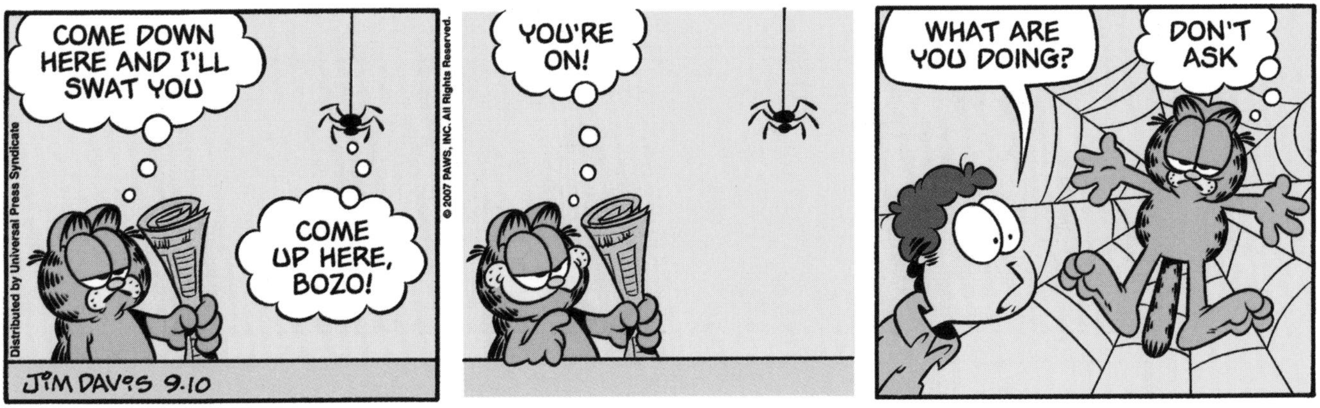
COME DOWN HERE AND I'LL SWAT YOU
COME UP HERE, BOZO!
JIM DAVIS 9.10
Distributed by Universal Press Syndicate
© 2007 PAWS, INC. All Rights Reserved.
YOU'RE ON!
WHAT ARE YOU DOING?
DON'T ASK

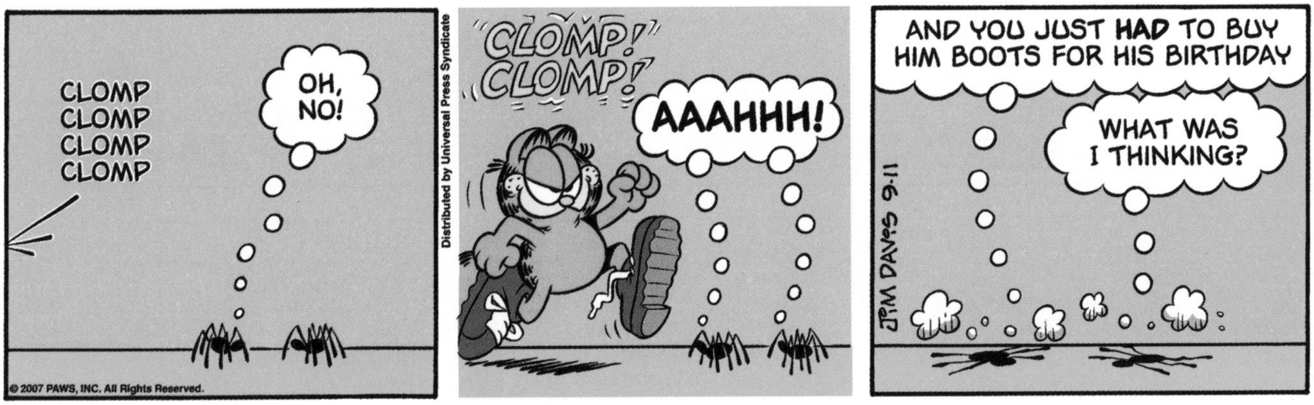
CLOMP CLOMP CLOMP CLOMP
OH, NO!
© 2007 PAWS, INC. All Rights Reserved.
Distributed by Universal Press Syndicate
CLOMP! CLOMP!
AAAHHH!
AND YOU JUST HAD TO BUY HIM BOOTS FOR HIS BIRTHDAY
WHAT WAS I THINKING?
JIM DAVIS 9.11

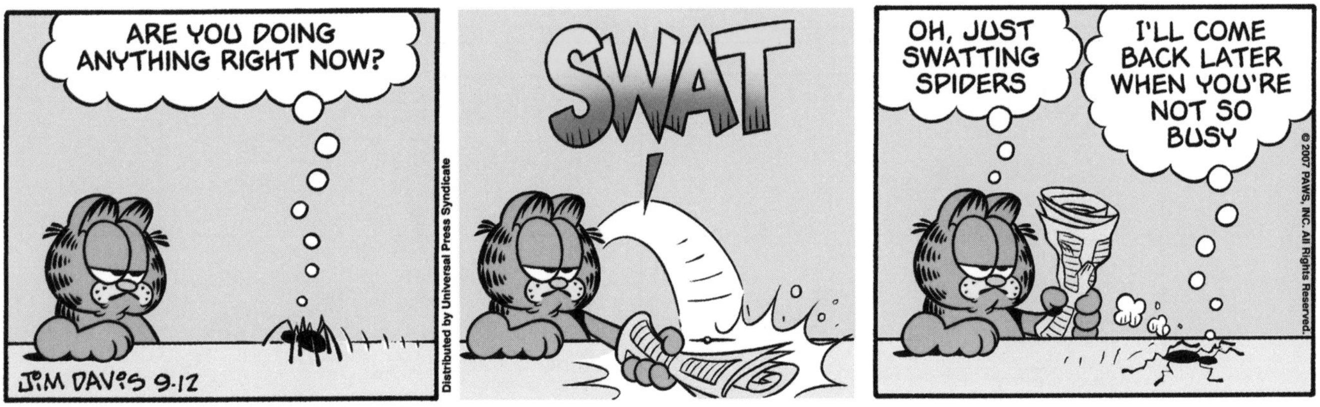
ARE YOU DOING ANYTHING RIGHT NOW?
JIM DAVIS 9.12
Distributed by Universal Press Syndicate
SWAT
OH, JUST SWATTING SPIDERS
I'LL COME BACK LATER WHEN YOU'RE NOT SO BUSY
© 2007 PAWS, INC. All Rights Reserved.

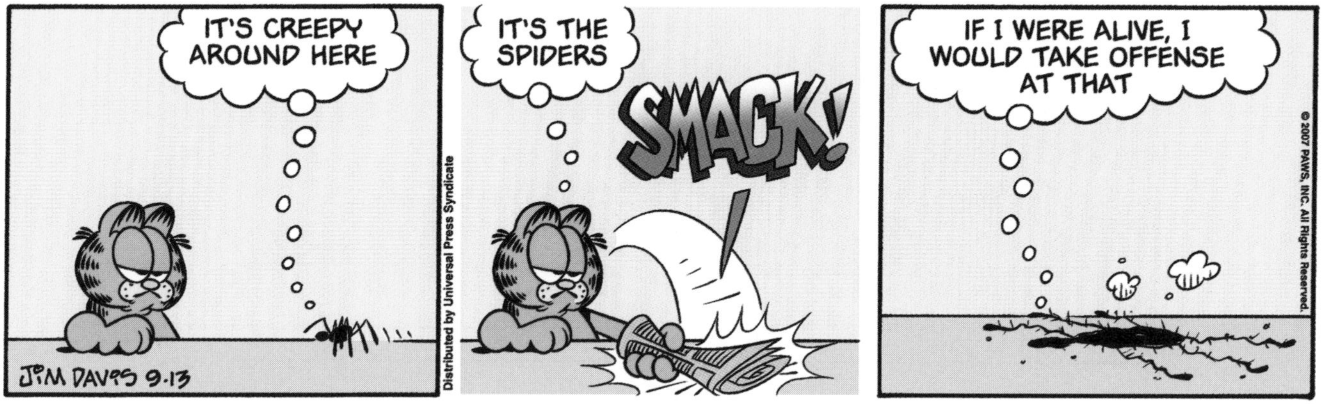
IT'S CREEPY AROUND HERE
JIM DAVIS 9.13
Distributed by Universal Press Syndicate
IT'S THE SPIDERS
SMACK!
IF I WERE ALIVE, I WOULD TAKE OFFENSE AT THAT
© 2007 PAWS, INC. All Rights Reserved.

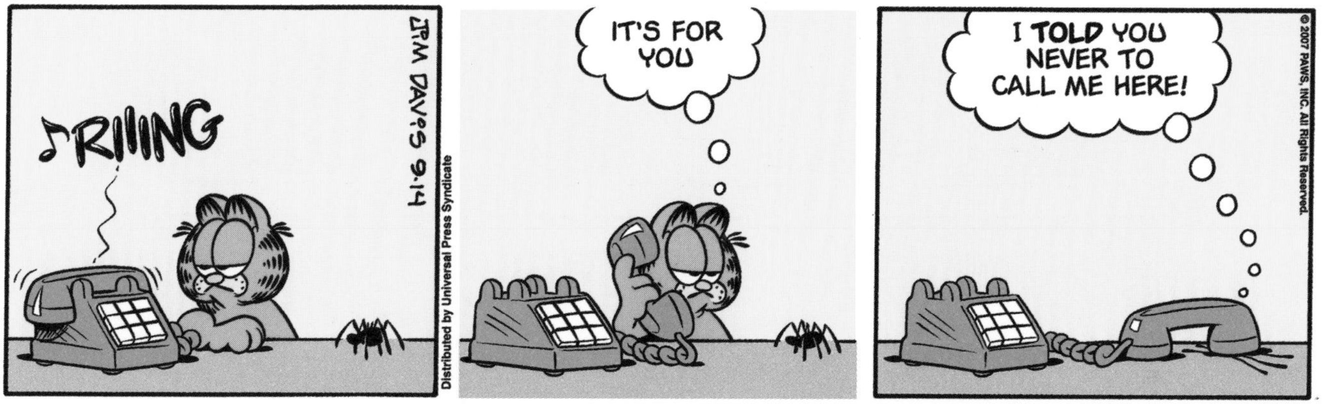
♪RIIING
JIM DAVIS 9.14
Distributed by Universal Press Syndicate
IT'S FOR YOU
I **TOLD** YOU NEVER TO CALL ME HERE!
© 2007 PAWS, INC. All Rights Reserved.

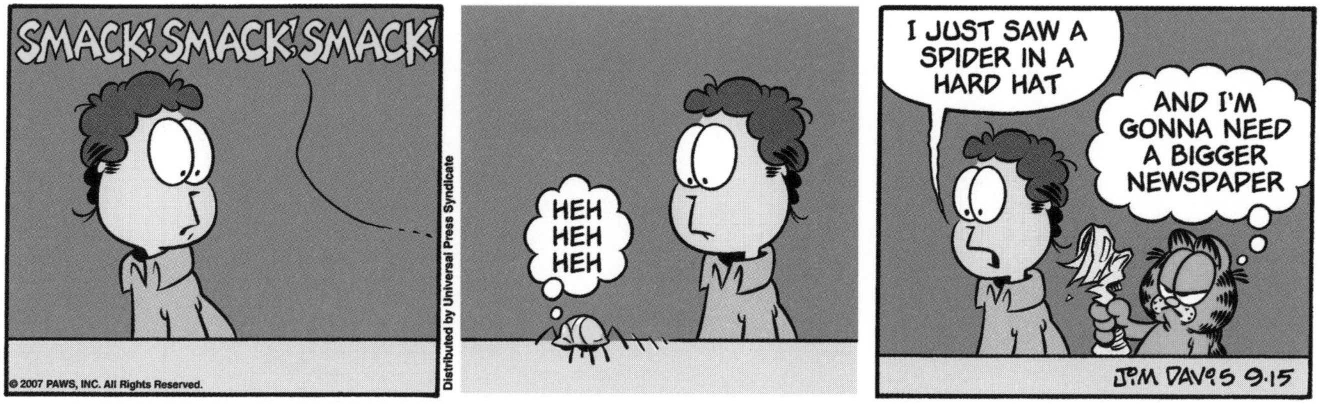
SMACK! SMACK! SMACK!
© 2007 PAWS, INC. All Rights Reserved.
Distributed by Universal Press Syndicate
HEH HEH HEH
I JUST SAW A SPIDER IN A HARD HAT
AND I'M GONNA NEED A BIGGER NEWSPAPER
JIM DAVIS 9.15

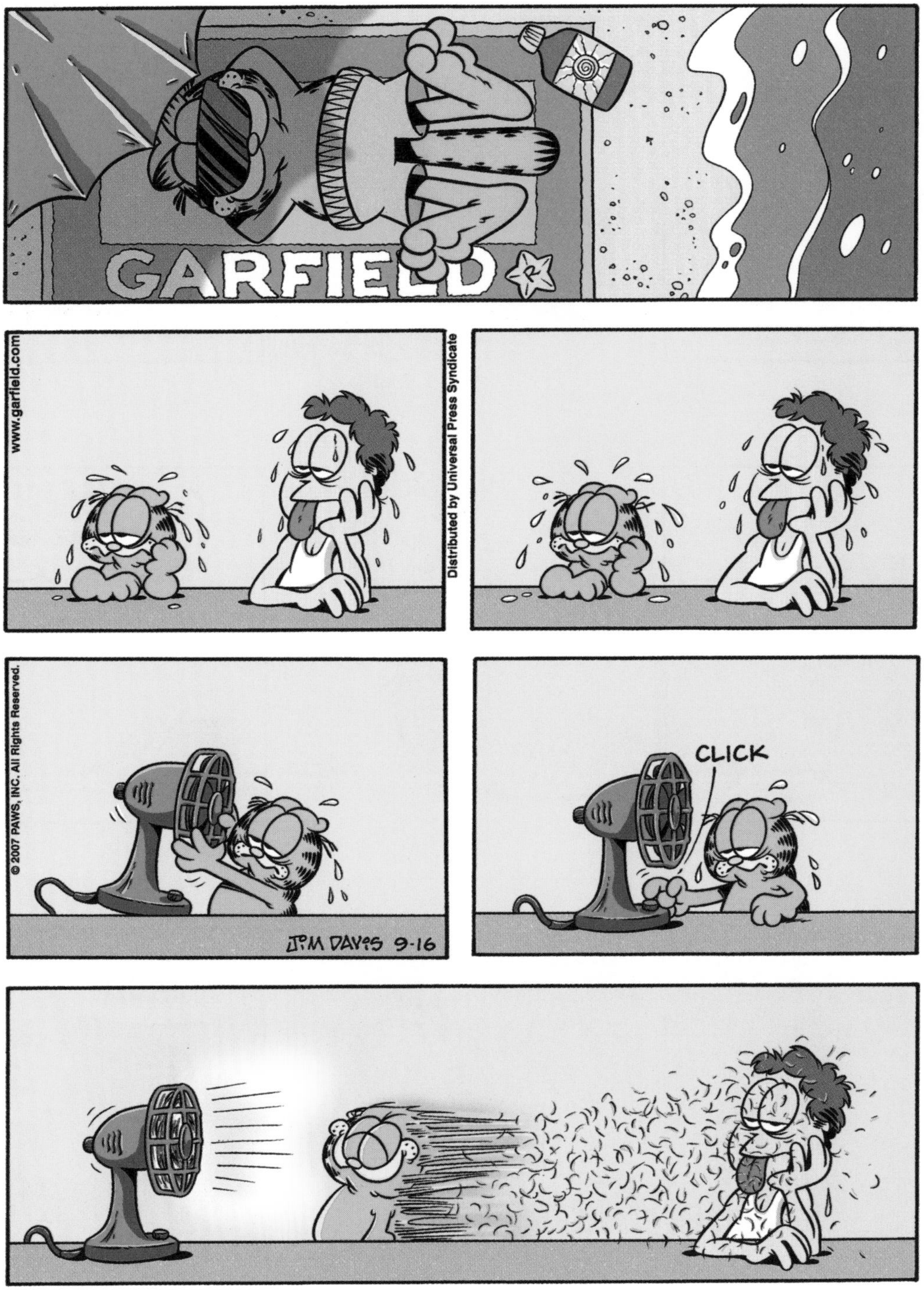
GARFIELD
www.garfield.com
Distributed by Universal Press Syndicate
© 2007 PAWS, INC. All Rights Reserved.
JIM DAVIS 9-16
CLICK

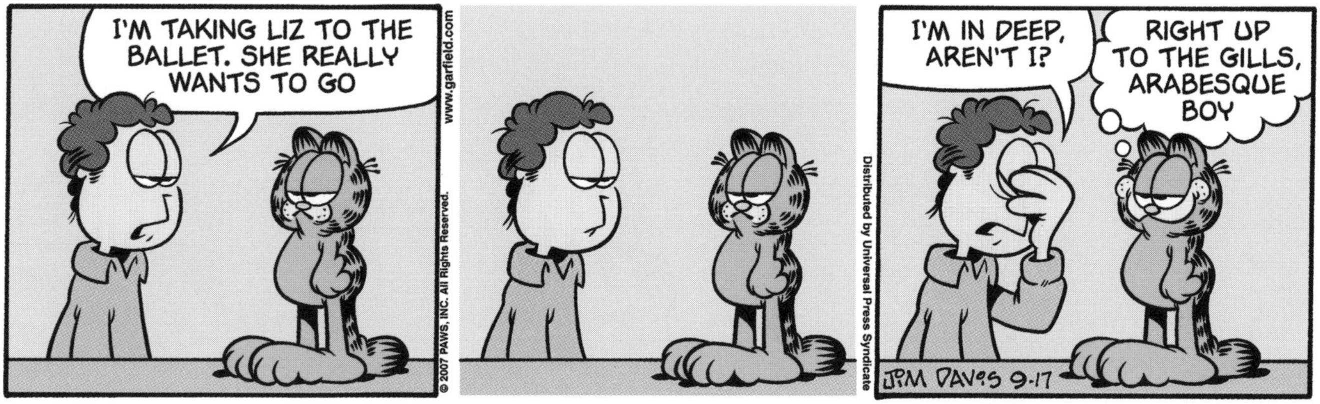
I'M TAKING LIZ TO THE BALLET. SHE REALLY WANTS TO GO
www.garfield.com
© 2007 PAWS, INC. All Rights Reserved.
I'M IN DEEP, AREN'T I?
RIGHT UP TO THE GILLS, ARABESQUE BOY
Distributed by Universal Press Syndicate
JPM DAVPS 9-17

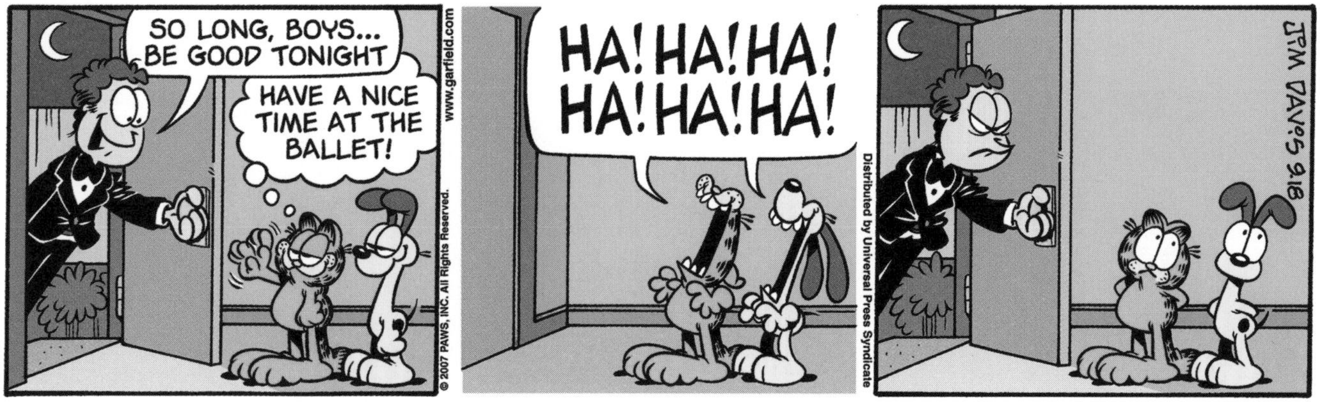
SO LONG, BOYS... BE GOOD TONIGHT
HAVE A NICE TIME AT THE BALLET!
www.garfield.com
© 2007 PAWS, INC. All Rights Reserved.
HA! HA! HA! HA! HA! HA!
Distributed by Universal Press Syndicate
JPM DAVPS 9-18

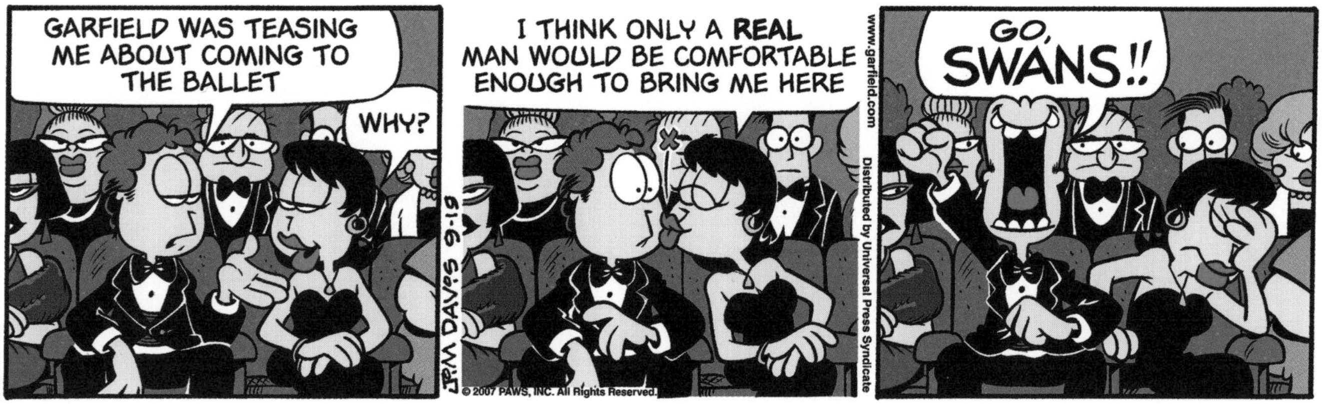
GARFIELD WAS TEASING ME ABOUT COMING TO THE BALLET
WHY?
JPM DAVPS 9-19
I THINK ONLY A **REAL** MAN WOULD BE COMFORTABLE ENOUGH TO BRING ME HERE
© 2007 PAWS, INC. All Rights Reserved.
www.garfield.com
Distributed by Universal Press Syndicate
GO, SWANS!!

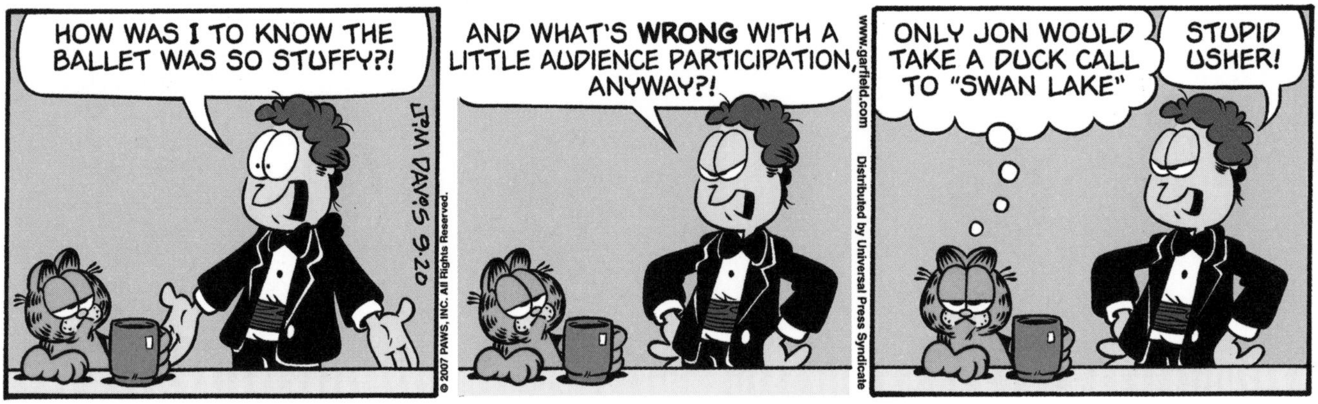
HOW WAS I TO KNOW THE BALLET WAS SO STUFFY?!
JIM DAVIS 9-20
© 2007 PAWS, INC. All Rights Reserved.
AND WHAT'S WRONG WITH A LITTLE AUDIENCE PARTICIPATION, ANYWAY?!
www.garfield.com Distributed by Universal Press Syndicate
ONLY JON WOULD TAKE A DUCK CALL TO "SWAN LAKE"
STUPID USHER!

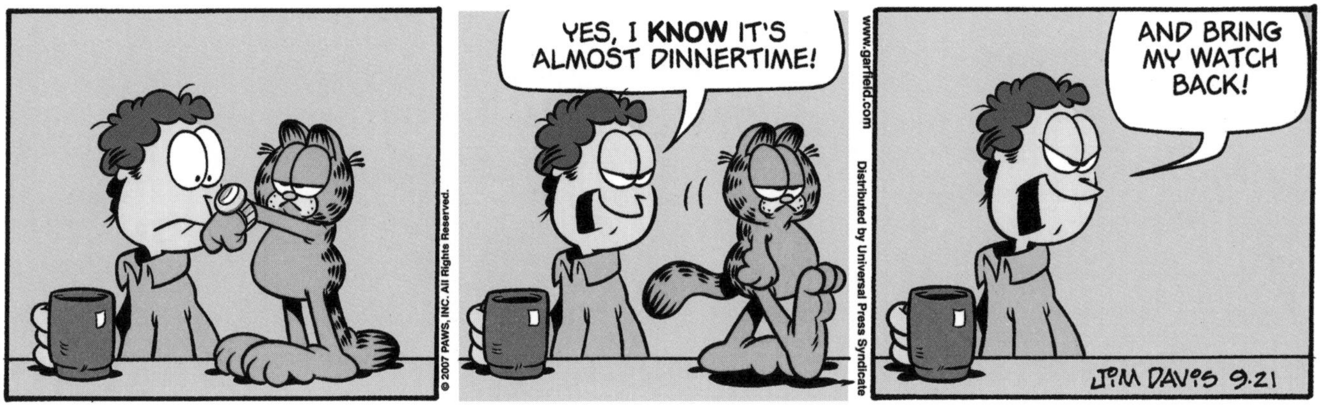
© 2007 PAWS, INC. All Rights Reserved.
YES, I KNOW IT'S ALMOST DINNERTIME!
www.garfield.com Distributed by Universal Press Syndicate
AND BRING MY WATCH BACK!
JIM DAVIS 9-21

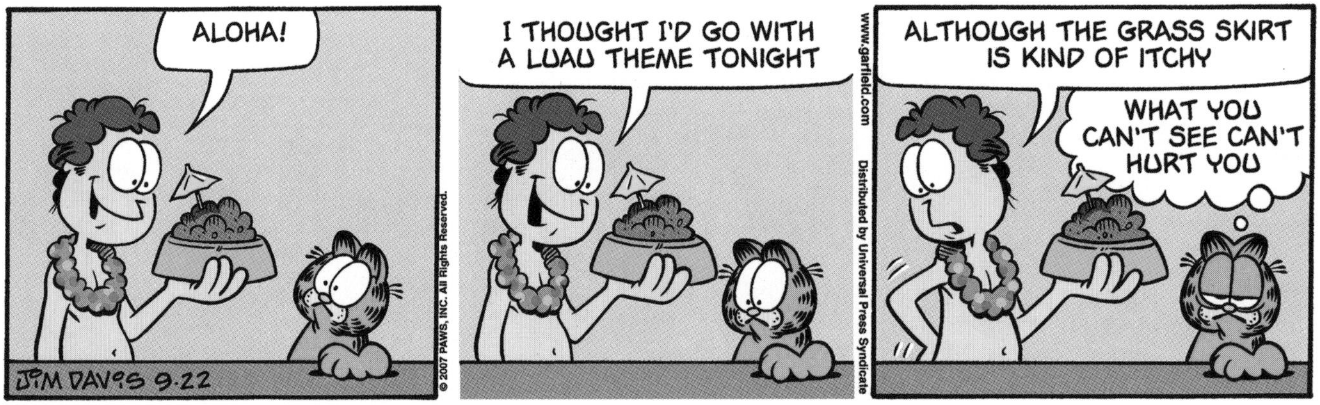
ALOHA!
JIM DAVIS 9-22
© 2007 PAWS, INC. All Rights Reserved.
I THOUGHT I'D GO WITH A LUAU THEME TONIGHT
www.garfield.com Distributed by Universal Press Syndicate
ALTHOUGH THE GRASS SKIRT IS KIND OF ITCHY
WHAT YOU CAN'T SEE CAN'T HURT YOU

PLAY
GARFIELD
R
HEY! THAT SQUIRREL IS STEALING SEEDS FROM OUR BIRD FEEDER AGAIN!
SLAM!
SHOO! SHOO, YOU STUPID SQUIRREL!
SLAM!
JIM DAVIS 9.23
© 2007 PAWS, INC. All Rights Reserved.
Distributed by Universal Press Syndicate
HEY! WHERE'S MY HAMBURGER?

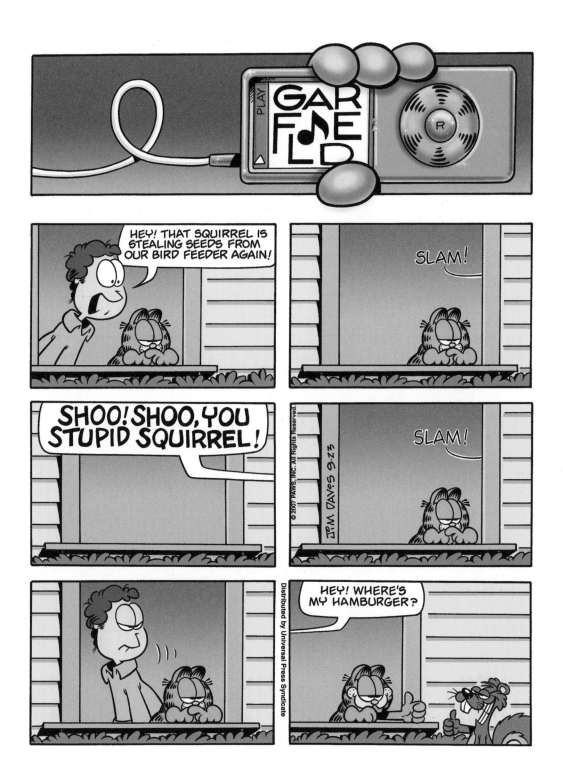

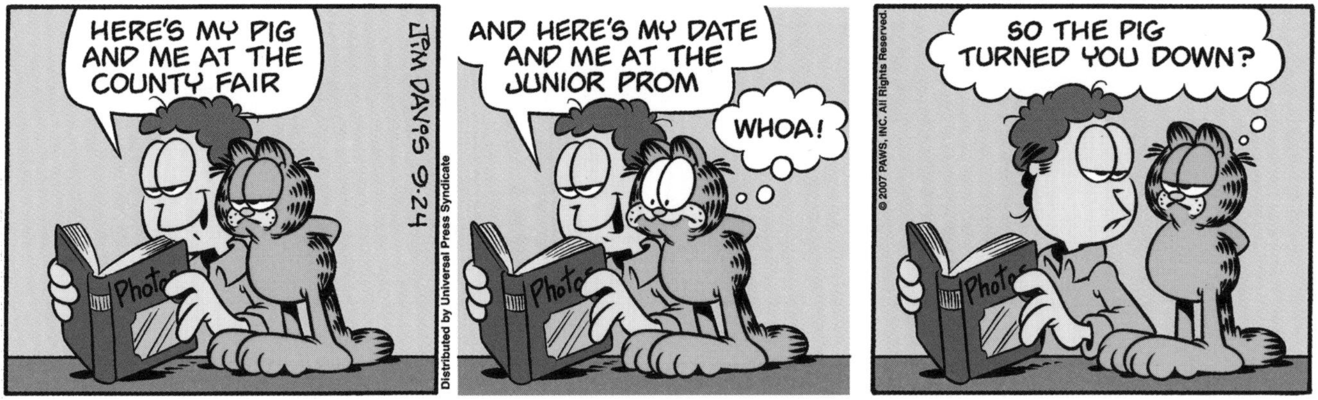
HERE'S MY PIG AND ME AT THE COUNTY FAIR
JIM DAVIS 9-24
AND HERE'S MY DATE AND ME AT THE JUNIOR PROM
WHOA!
Distributed by Universal Press Syndicate
SO THE PIG TURNED YOU DOWN?
© 2007 PAWS, INC. All Rights Reserved.

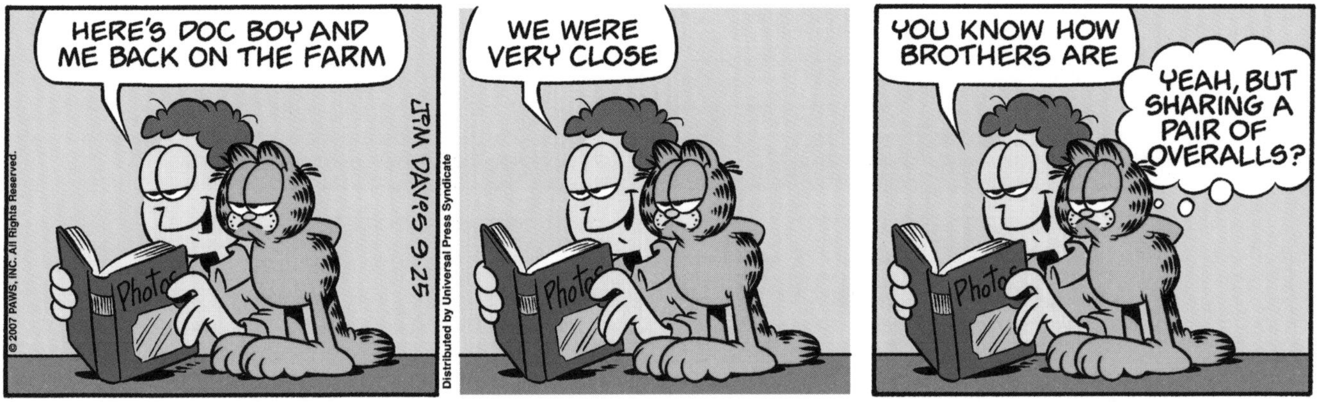
HERE'S DOC BOY AND ME BACK ON THE FARM
© 2007 PAWS, INC. All Rights Reserved.
JIM DAVIS 9-25
Distributed by Universal Press Syndicate
WE WERE VERY CLOSE
YOU KNOW HOW BROTHERS ARE
YEAH, BUT SHARING A PAIR OF OVERALLS?

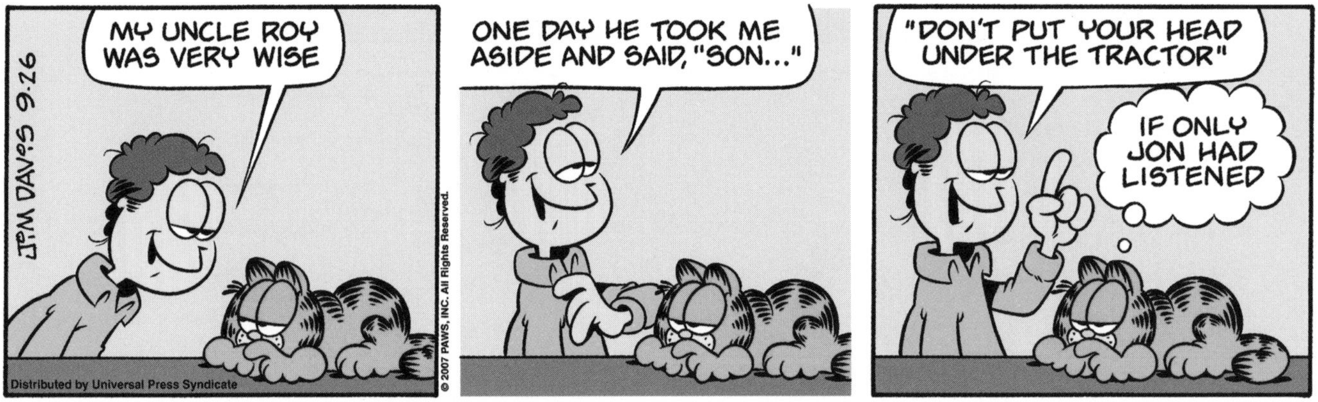
JIM DAVIS 9-26
MY UNCLE ROY WAS VERY WISE
Distributed by Universal Press Syndicate
© 2007 PAWS, INC. All Rights Reserved.
ONE DAY HE TOOK ME ASIDE AND SAID, "SON..."
"DON'T PUT YOUR HEAD UNDER THE TRACTOR"
IF ONLY JON HAD LISTENED

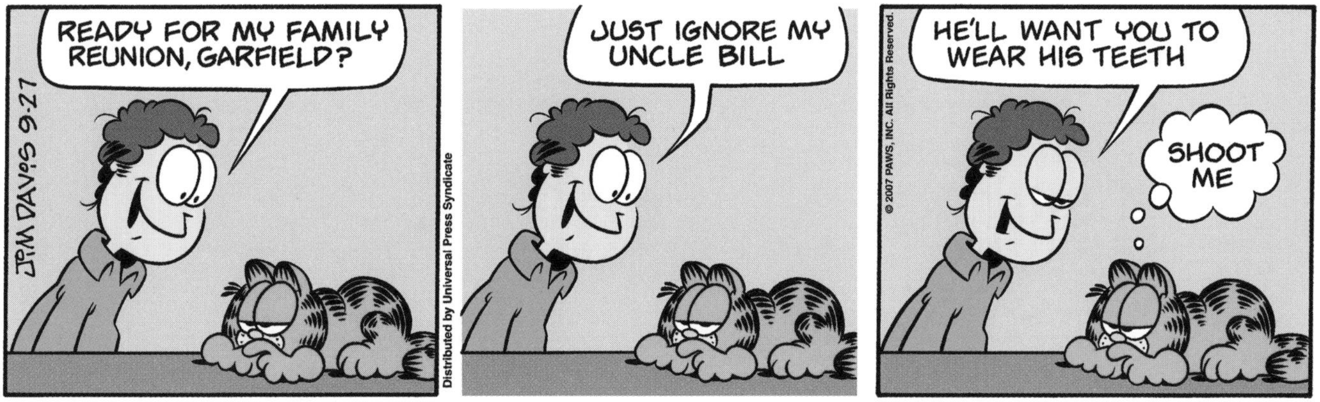
READY FOR MY FAMILY REUNION, GARFIELD?
JUST IGNORE MY UNCLE BILL
HE'LL WANT YOU TO WEAR HIS TEETH
SHOOT ME
JIM DAVIS 9·27
Distributed by Universal Press Syndicate
© 2007 PAWS, INC. All Rights Reserved.

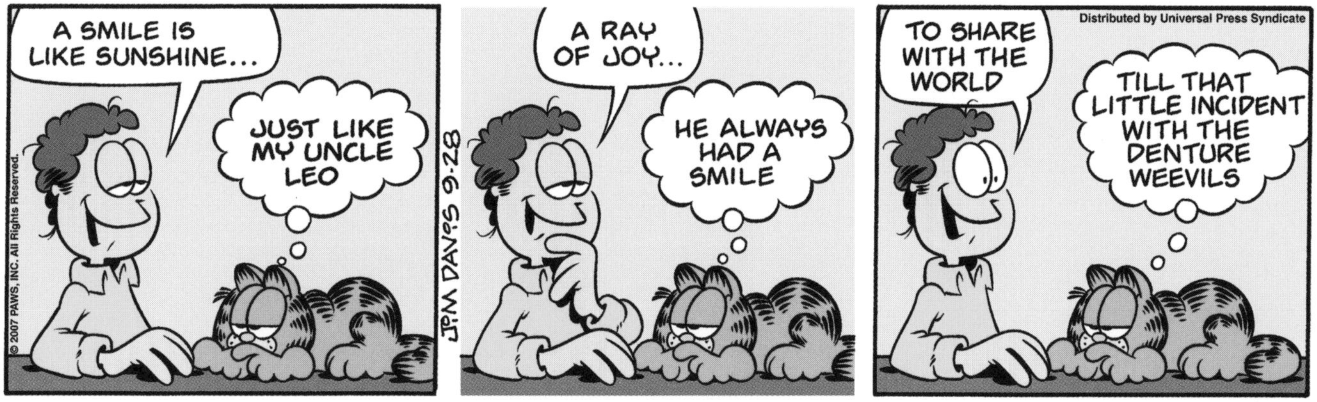
A SMILE IS LIKE SUNSHINE...
JUST LIKE MY UNCLE LEO
A RAY OF JOY...
HE ALWAYS HAD A SMILE
TO SHARE WITH THE WORLD
TILL THAT LITTLE INCIDENT WITH THE DENTURE WEEVILS
JIM DAVIS 9·28
© 2007 PAWS, INC. All Rights Reserved.
Distributed by Universal Press Syndicate

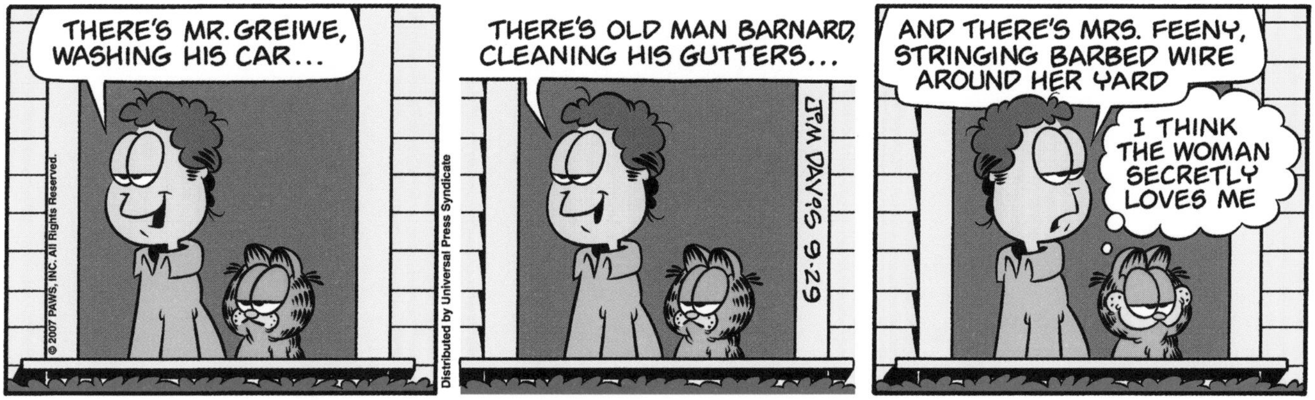
THERE'S MR. GREIWE, WASHING HIS CAR...
THERE'S OLD MAN BARNARD, CLEANING HIS GUTTERS...
AND THERE'S MRS. FEENY, STRINGING BARBED WIRE AROUND HER YARD
I THINK THE WOMAN SECRETLY LOVES ME
JIM DAVIS 9·29
© 2007 PAWS, INC. All Rights Reserved.
Distributed by Universal Press Syndicate

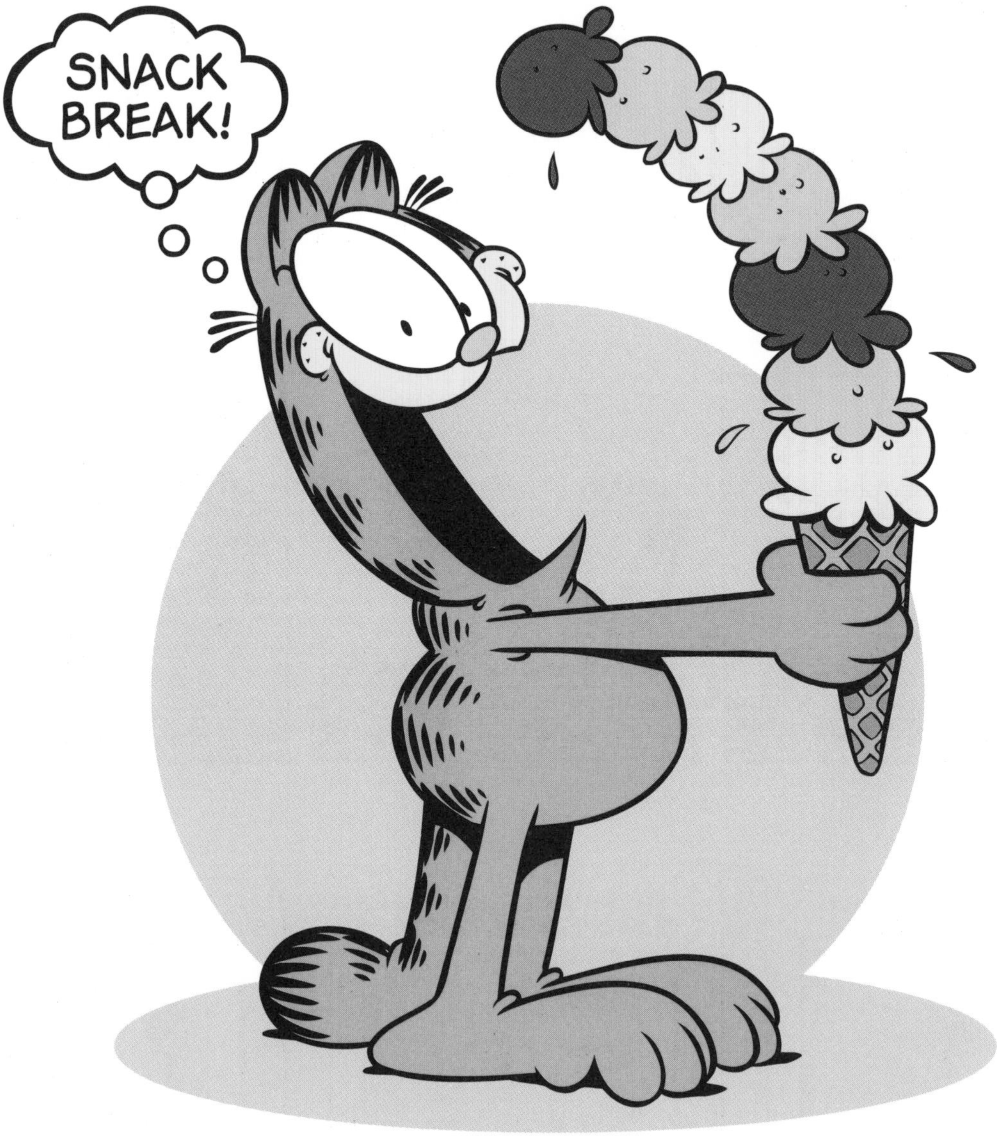
SNACK BREAK!

Garfield SHOVELS IT IN

BY JIM DAVIS

Ballantine Books Trade Paperbacks • **New York**

Garfield's FURRY TALES

Hansel and Gobbler

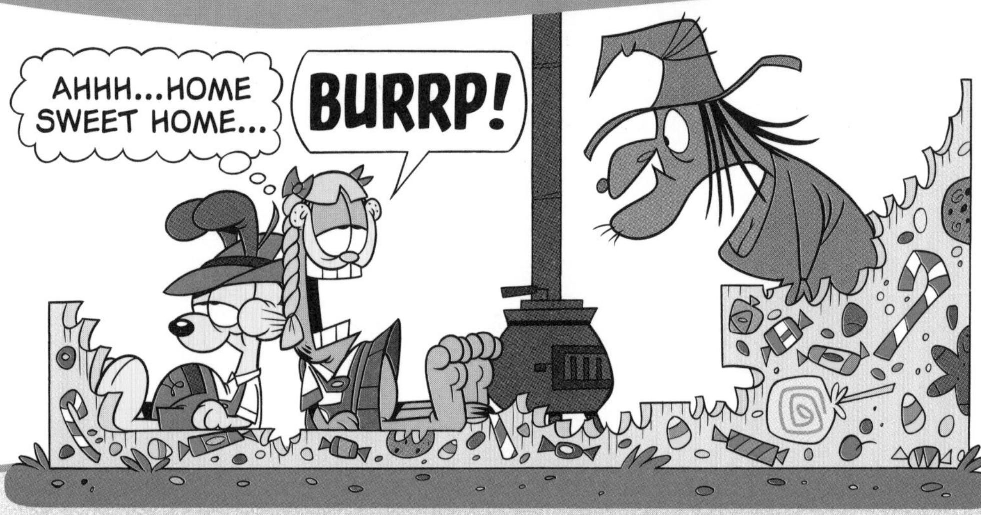
AHHH...HOME SWEET HOME...
BURRP!

Little Red Riding Dog

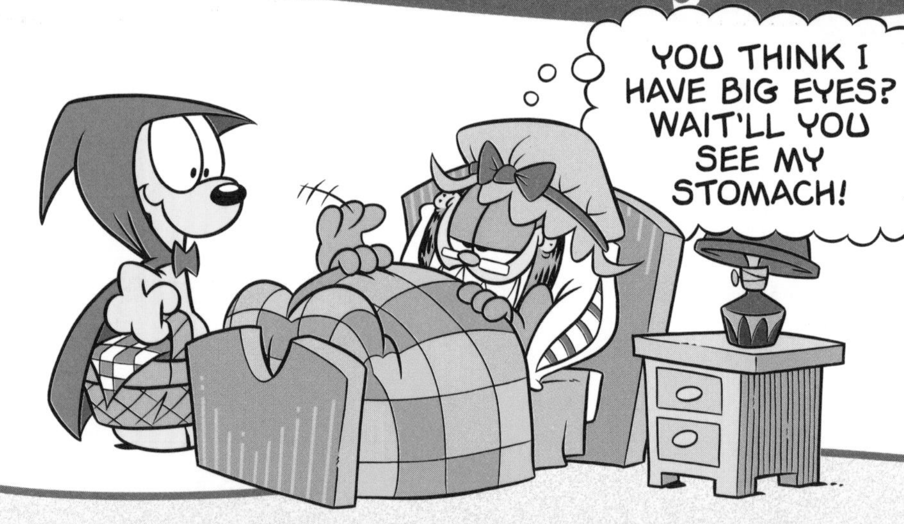
YOU THINK I HAVE BIG EYES? WAIT'LL YOU SEE MY STOMACH!

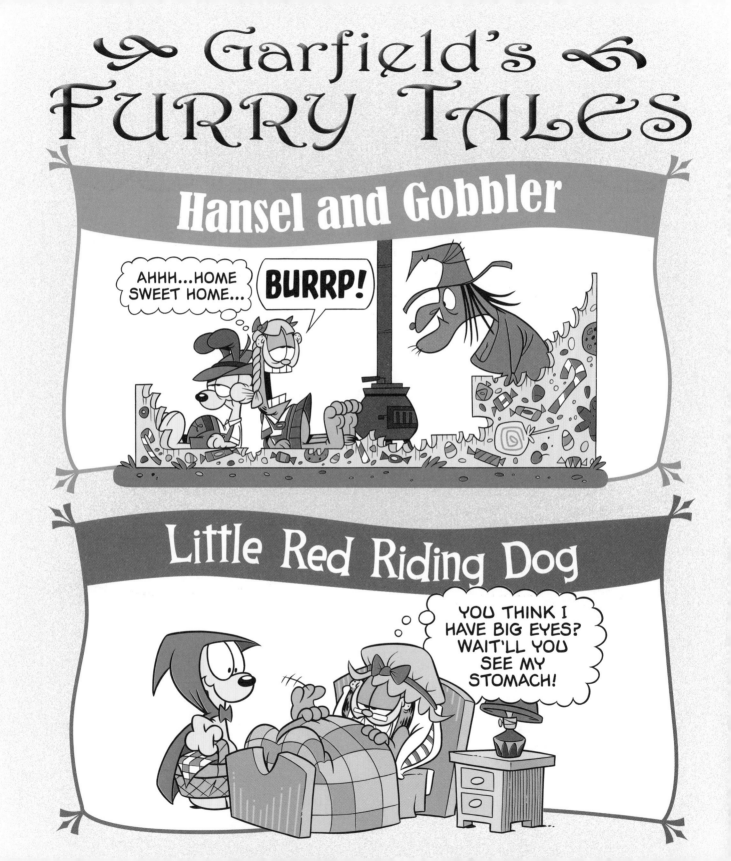

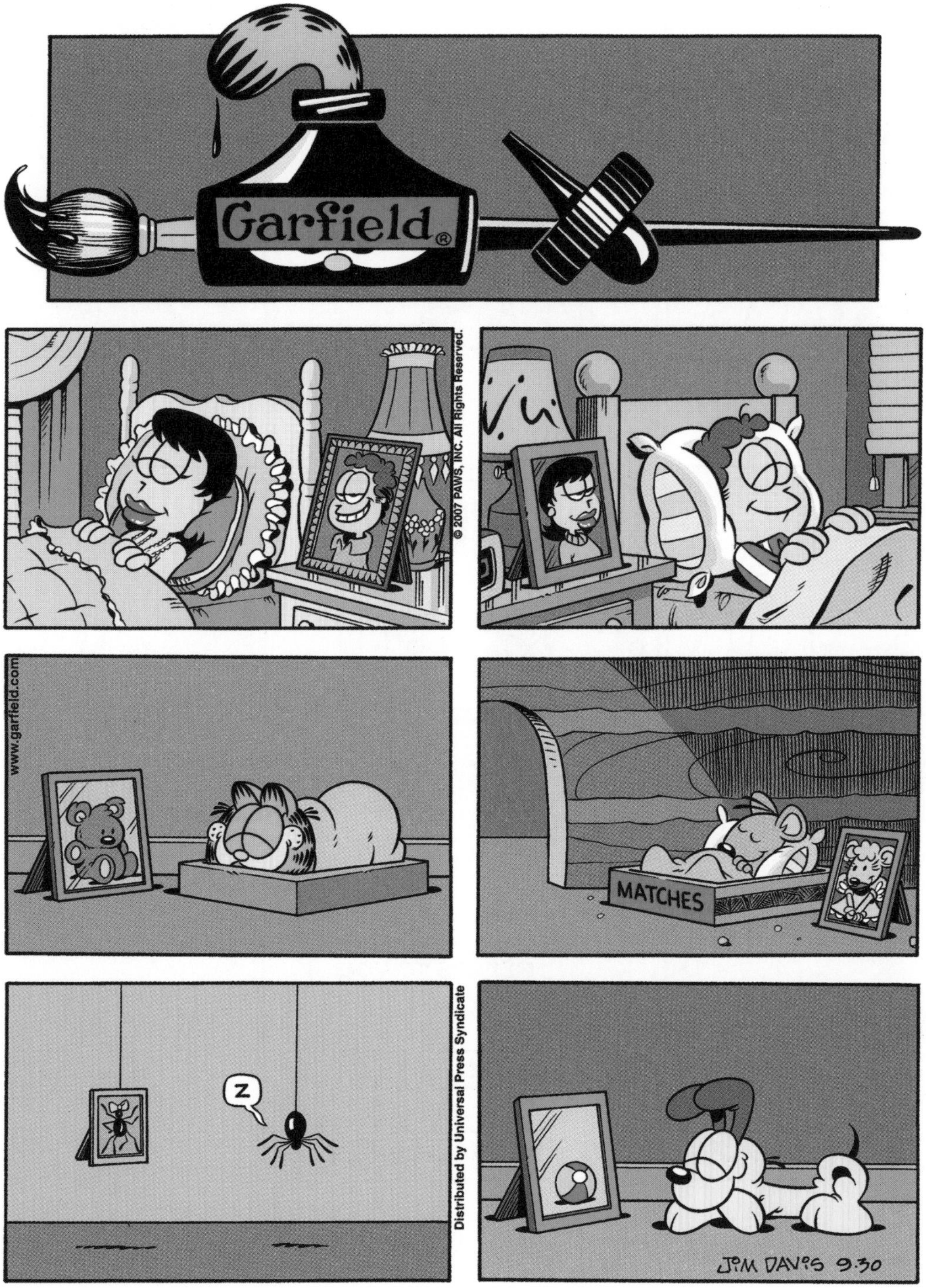
Garfield®
© 2007 PAWS, INC. All Rights Reserved.
www.garfield.com
MATCHES
Z
Distributed by Universal Press Syndicate
JIM DAVIS 9-30

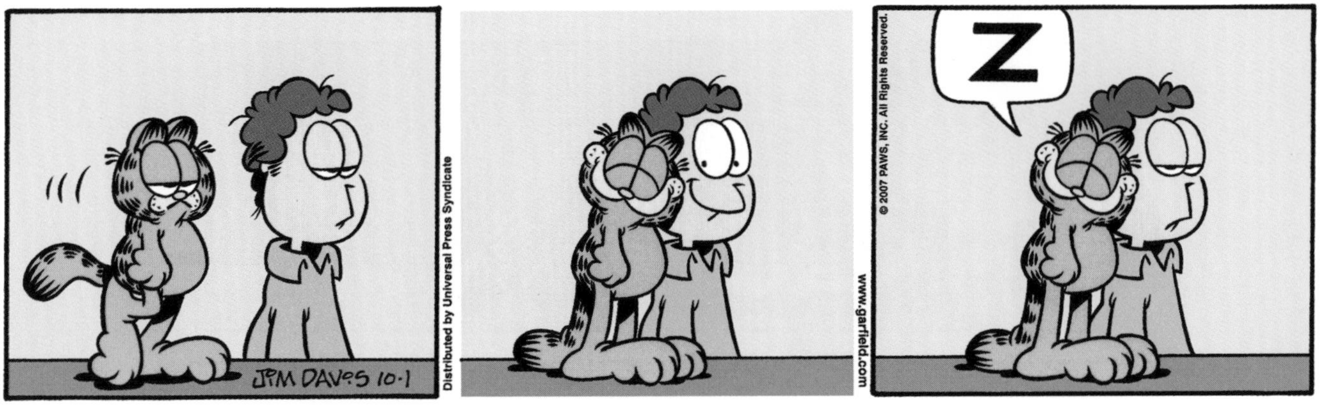
JIM DAVIS 10-1
Distributed by Universal Press Syndicate
www.garfield.com
© 2007 PAWS, INC. All Rights Reserved.
Z

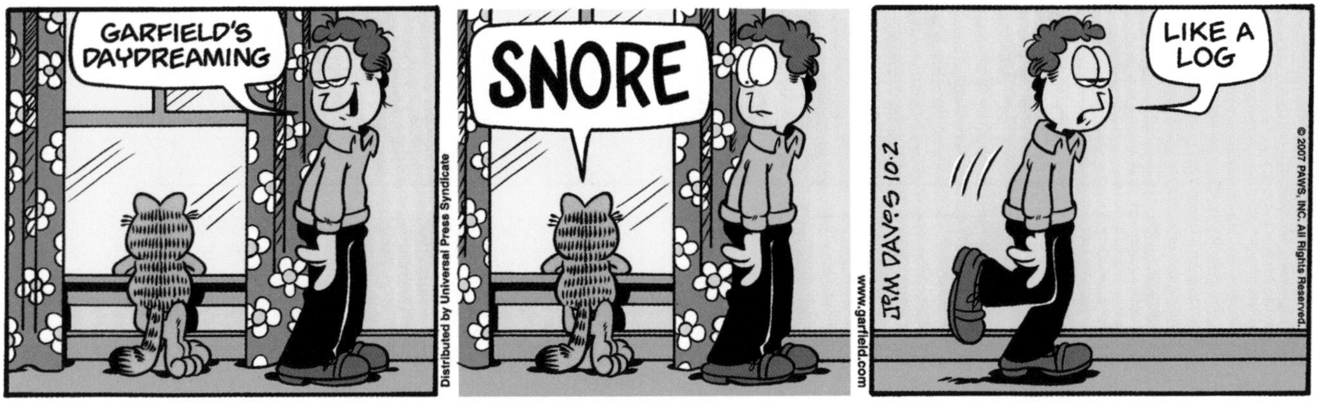
GARFIELD'S DAYDREAMING
Distributed by Universal Press Syndicate
SNORE
www.garfield.com
JIM DAVIS 10-2
LIKE A LOG
© 2007 PAWS, INC. All Rights Reserved.

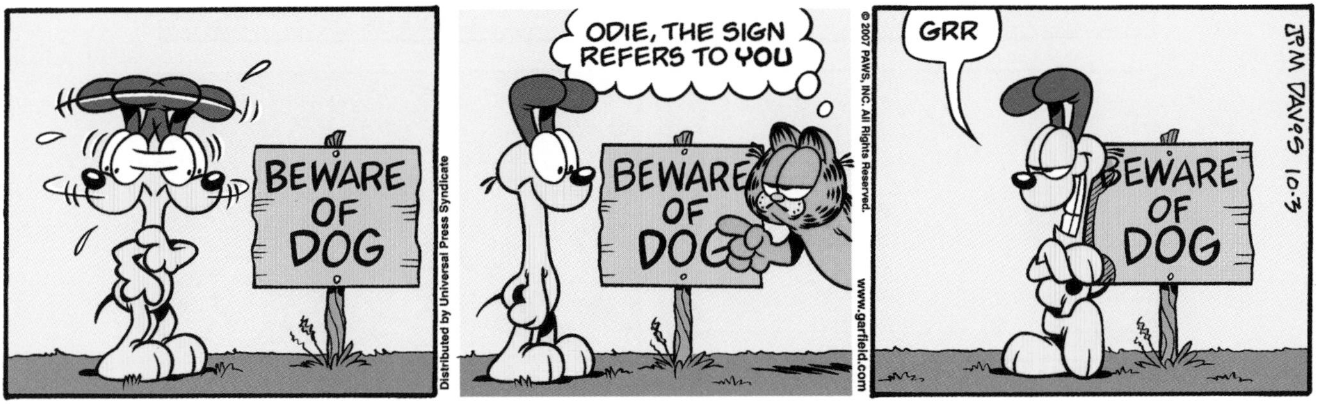
BEWARE OF DOG
Distributed by Universal Press Syndicate
ODIE, THE SIGN REFERS TO **YOU**
BEWARE OF DOG
© 2007 PAWS, INC. All Rights Reserved.
www.garfield.com
GRR
BEWARE OF DOG
JIM DAVIS 10-3

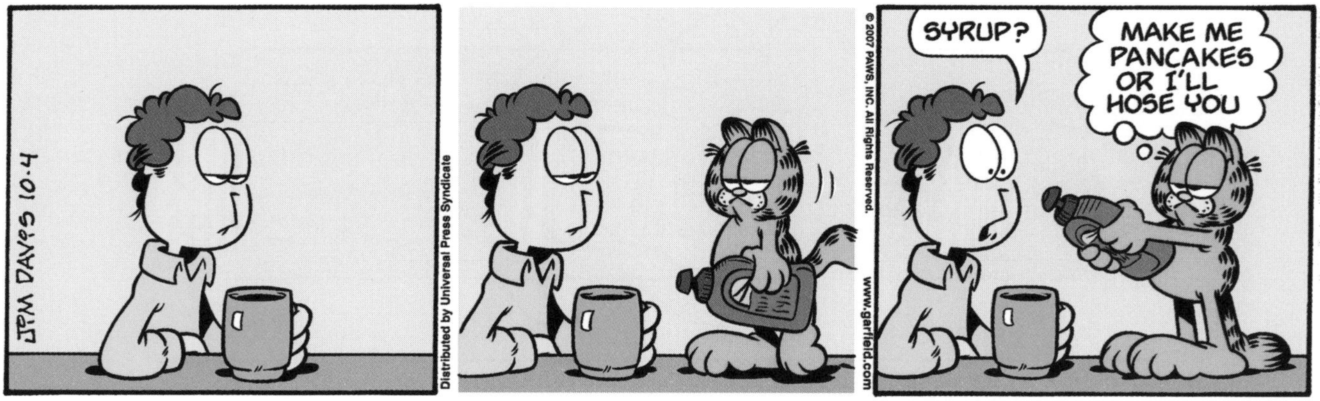
SYRUP?
MAKE ME PANCAKES OR I'LL HOSE YOU

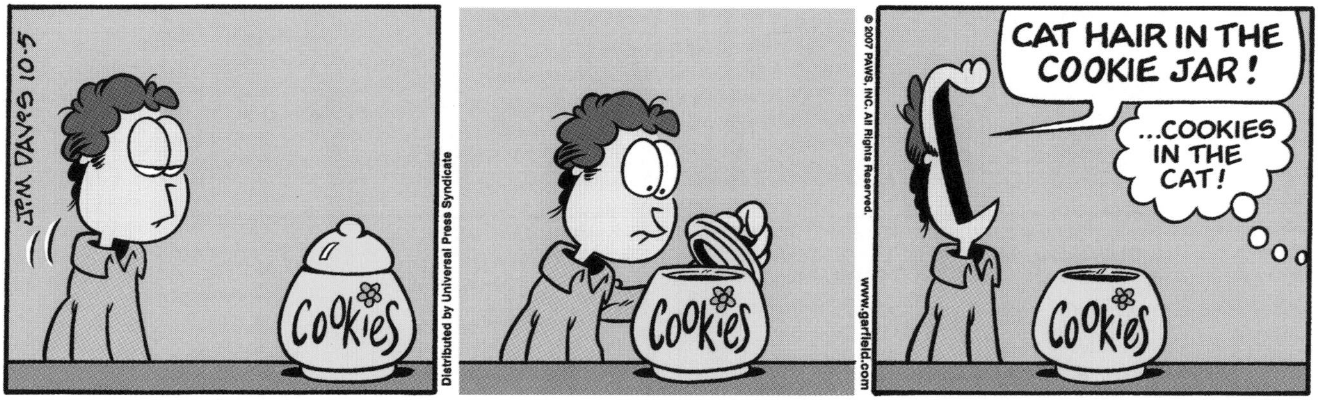
CAT HAIR IN THE COOKIE JAR!
...COOKIES IN THE CAT!

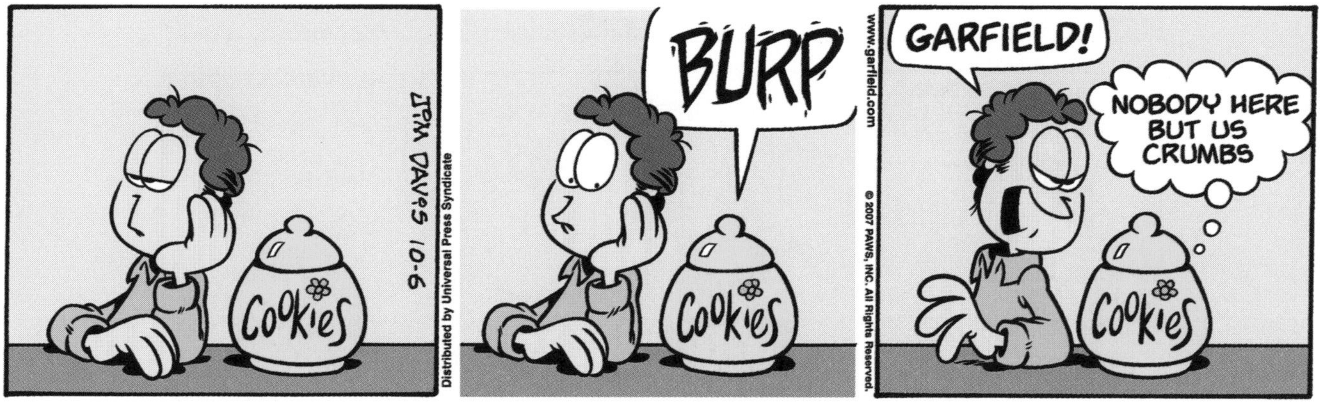
BURP
GARFIELD!
NOBODY HERE BUT US CRUMBS

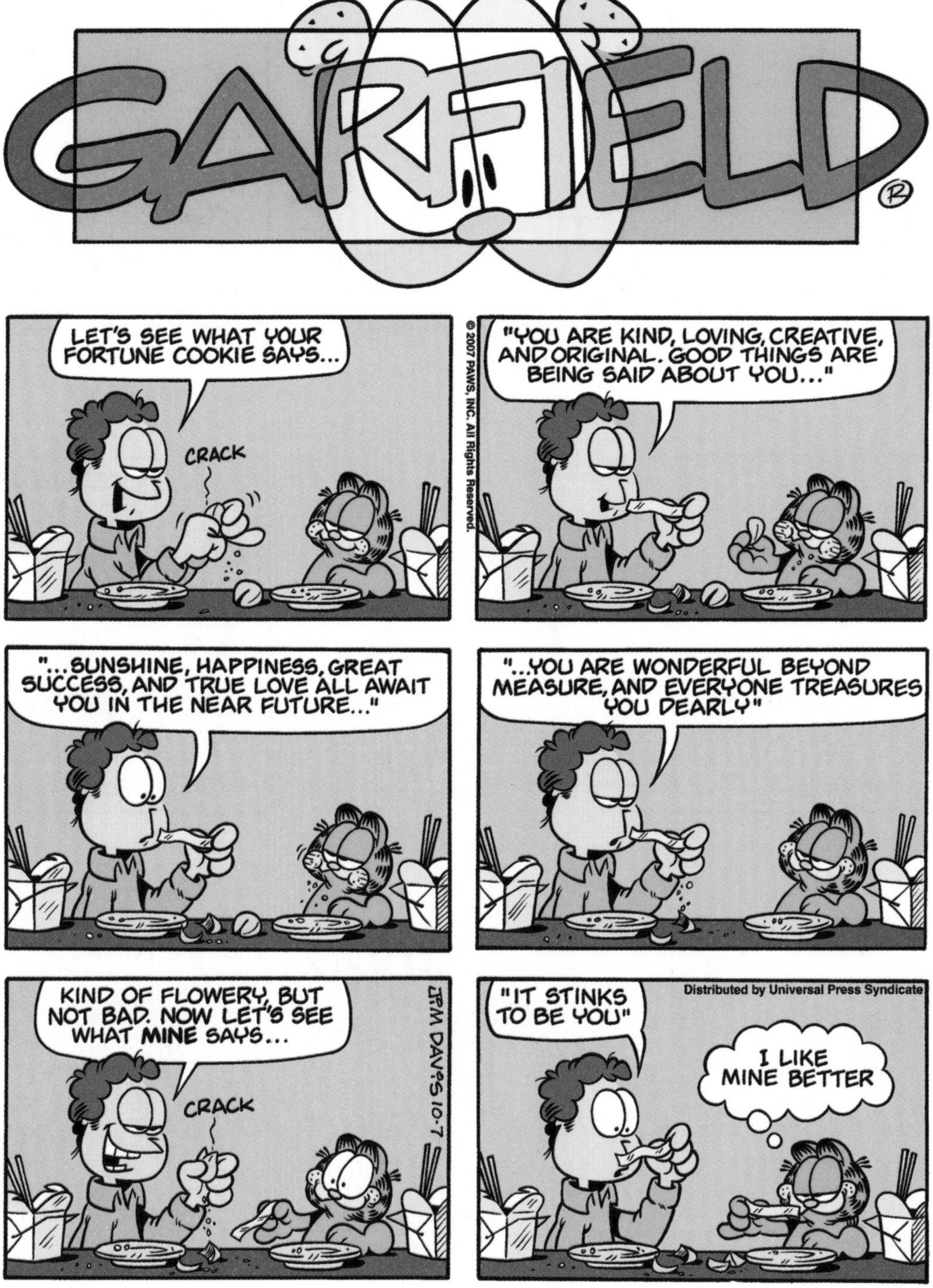
GARFIELD®
LET'S SEE WHAT YOUR FORTUNE COOKIE SAYS...
CRACK
© 2007 PAWS, INC. All Rights Reserved.
"YOU ARE KIND, LOVING, CREATIVE, AND ORIGINAL. GOOD THINGS ARE BEING SAID ABOUT YOU..."
"...SUNSHINE, HAPPINESS, GREAT SUCCESS, AND TRUE LOVE ALL AWAIT YOU IN THE NEAR FUTURE..."
"...YOU ARE WONDERFUL BEYOND MEASURE, AND EVERYONE TREASURES YOU DEARLY"
KIND OF FLOWERY, BUT NOT BAD. NOW LET'S SEE WHAT MINE SAYS...
CRACK
JIM DAVIS 10-7
Distributed by Universal Press Syndicate
"IT STINKS TO BE YOU"
I LIKE MINE BETTER

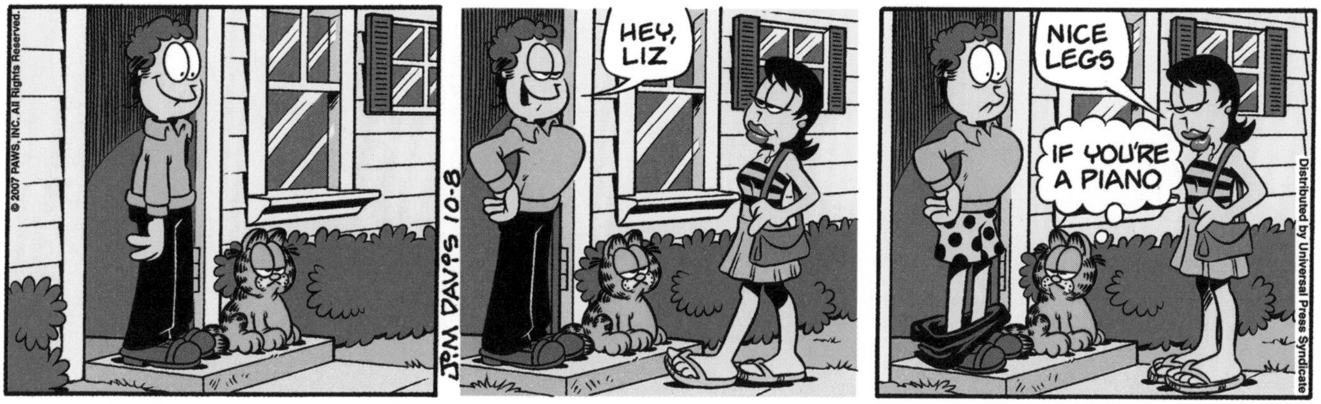
HEY, LIZ
NICE LEGS
IF YOU'RE A PIANO
JIM DAVIS 10-8

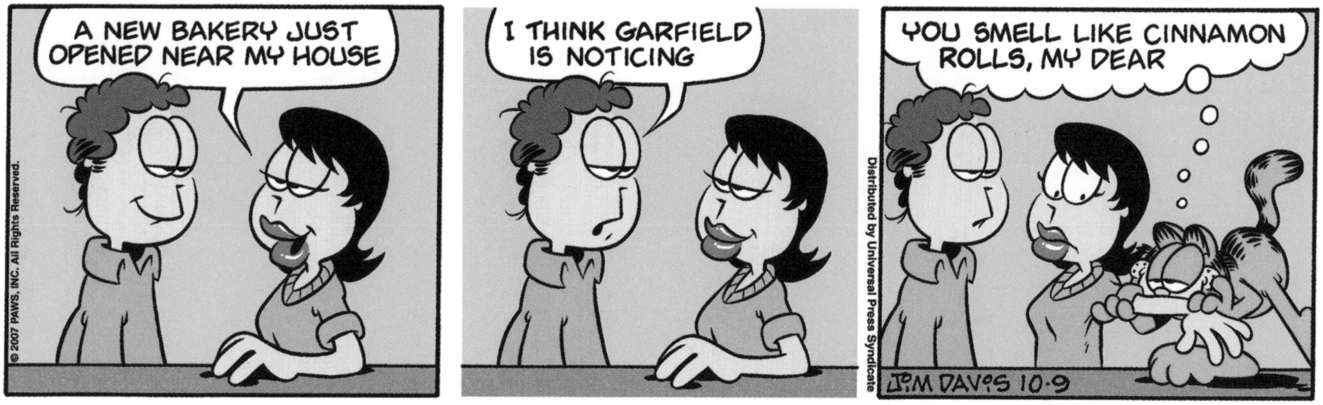
A NEW BAKERY JUST OPENED NEAR MY HOUSE
I THINK GARFIELD IS NOTICING
YOU SMELL LIKE CINNAMON ROLLS, MY DEAR
JIM DAVIS 10-9

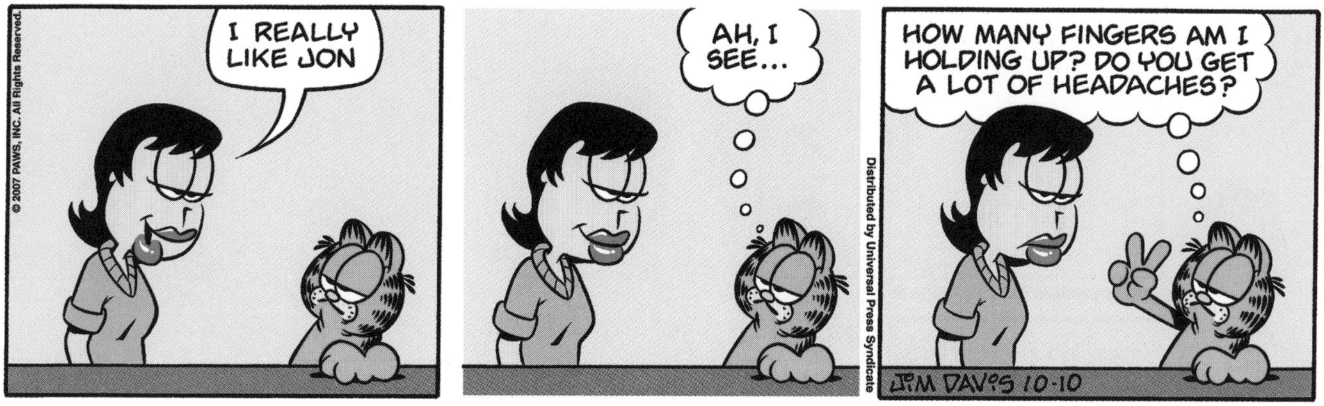
I REALLY LIKE JON
AH, I SEE...
HOW MANY FINGERS AM I HOLDING UP? DO YOU GET A LOT OF HEADACHES?
JIM DAVIS 10-10

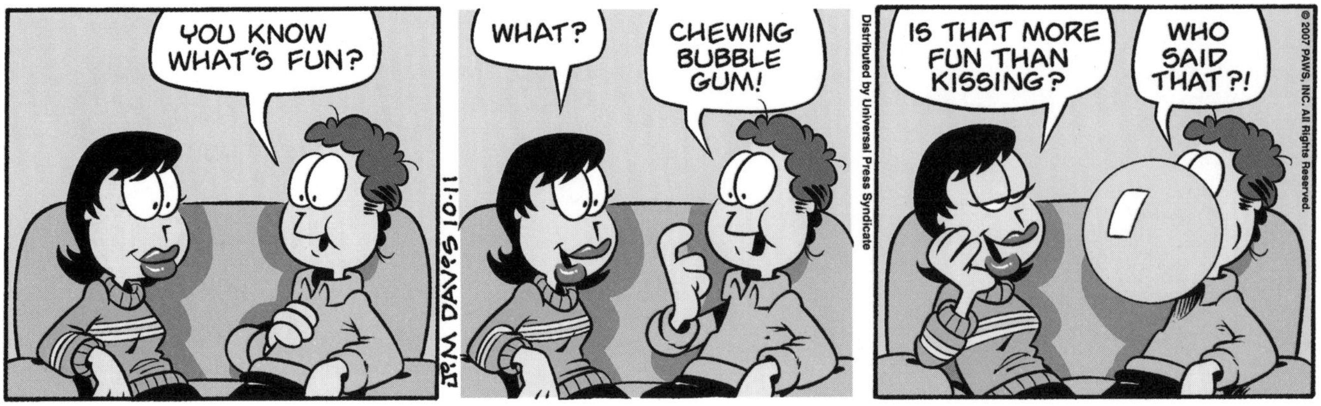
YOU KNOW WHAT'S FUN?
JIM DAVIS 10-11
WHAT?
CHEWING BUBBLE GUM!
Distributed by Universal Press Syndicate
IS THAT MORE FUN THAN KISSING?
WHO SAID THAT?!
© 2007 PAWS, INC. All Rights Reserved.

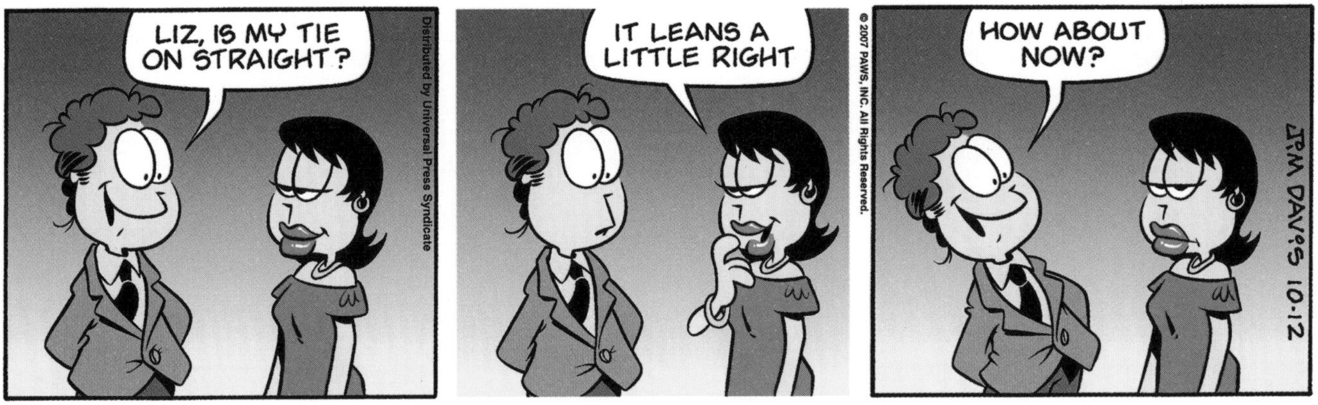
LIZ, IS MY TIE ON STRAIGHT?
Distributed by Universal Press Syndicate
IT LEANS A LITTLE RIGHT
© 2007 PAWS, INC. All Rights Reserved.
HOW ABOUT NOW?
JIM DAVIS 10-12

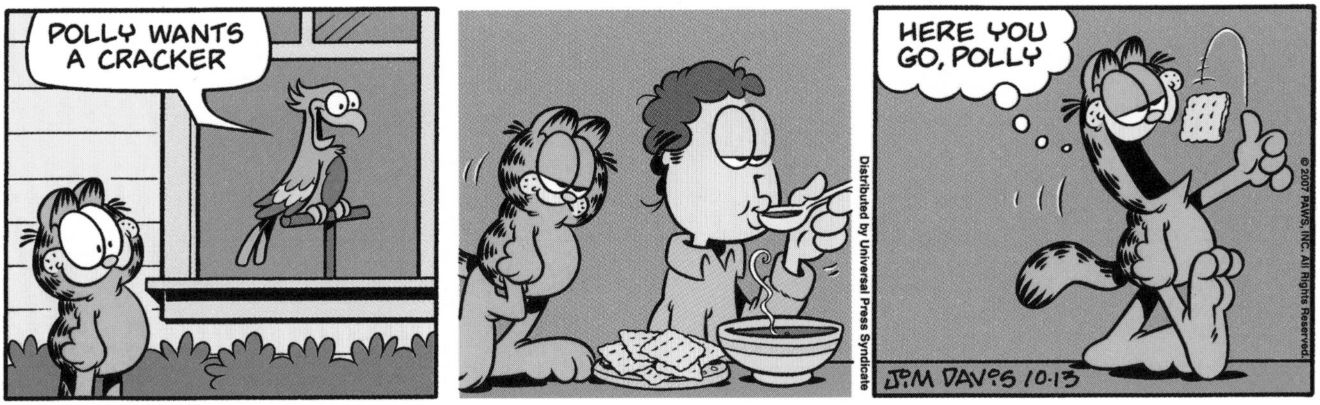
POLLY WANTS A CRACKER
Distributed by Universal Press Syndicate
HERE YOU GO, POLLY
© 2007 PAWS, INC. All Rights Reserved.
JIM DAVIS 10-13

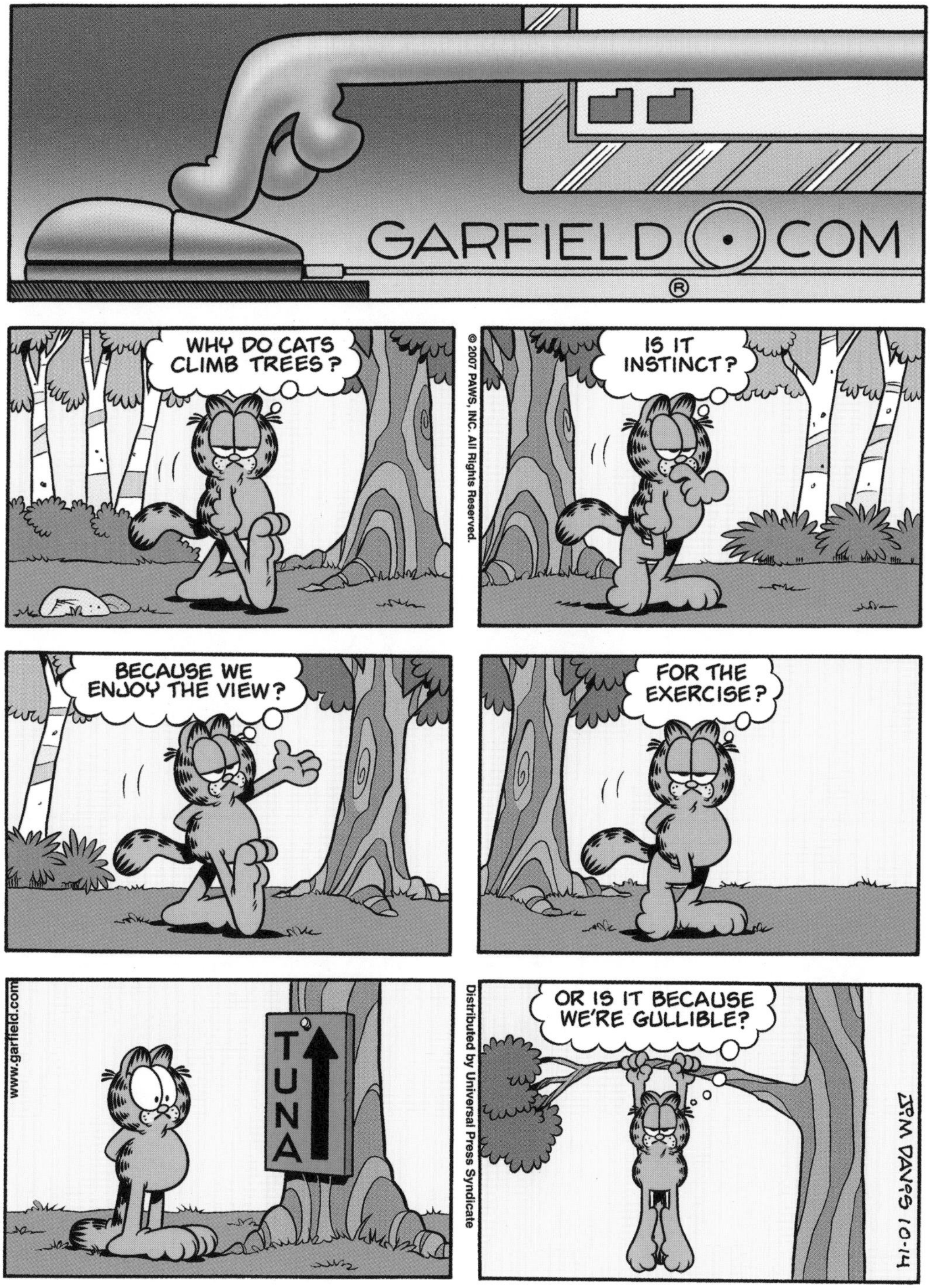
GARFIELD.COM
WHY DO CATS CLIMB TREES?
© 2007 PAWS, INC. All Rights Reserved.
IS IT INSTINCT?
BECAUSE WE ENJOY THE VIEW?
FOR THE EXERCISE?
www.garfield.com
TUNA
Distributed by Universal Press Syndicate
OR IS IT BECAUSE WE'RE GULLIBLE?
JIM DAVIS 10-14

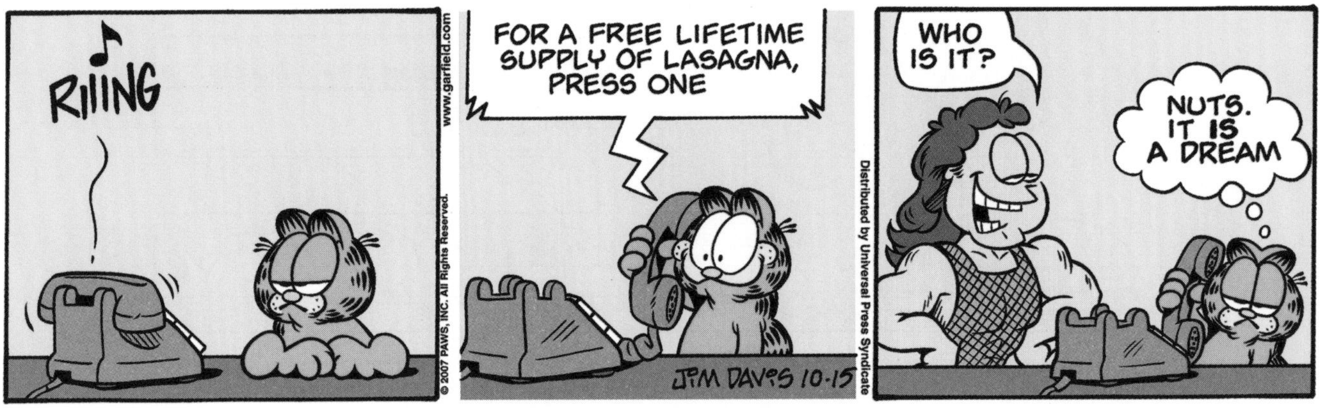
RIIING
FOR A FREE LIFETIME SUPPLY OF LASAGNA, PRESS ONE
WHO IS IT?
NUTS. IT IS A DREAM
JIM DAVIS 10-15
© 2007 PAWS, INC. All Rights Reserved. www.garfield.com
Distributed by Universal Press Syndicate

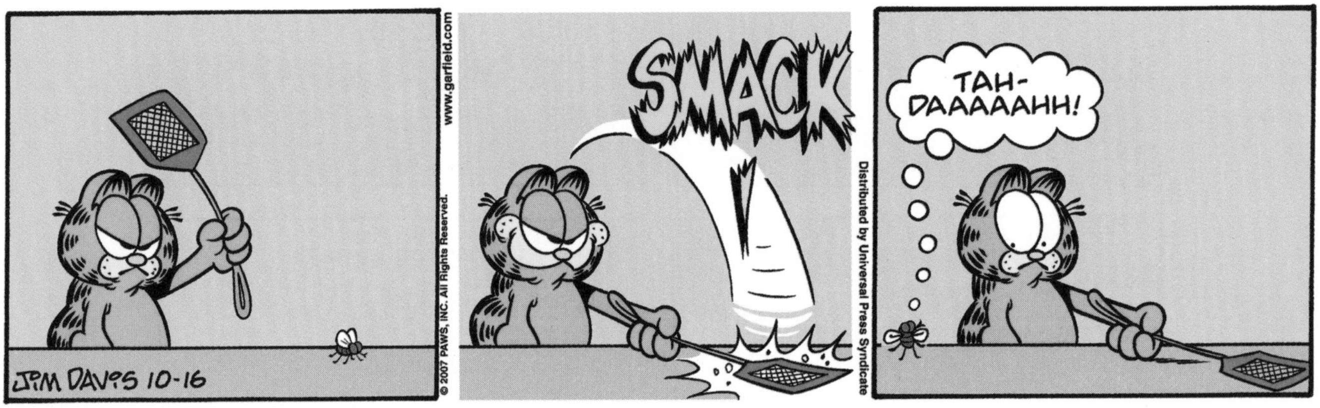
JIM DAVIS 10-16
SMACK
TAH-DAAAAAHH!
© 2007 PAWS, INC. All Rights Reserved. www.garfield.com
Distributed by Universal Press Syndicate

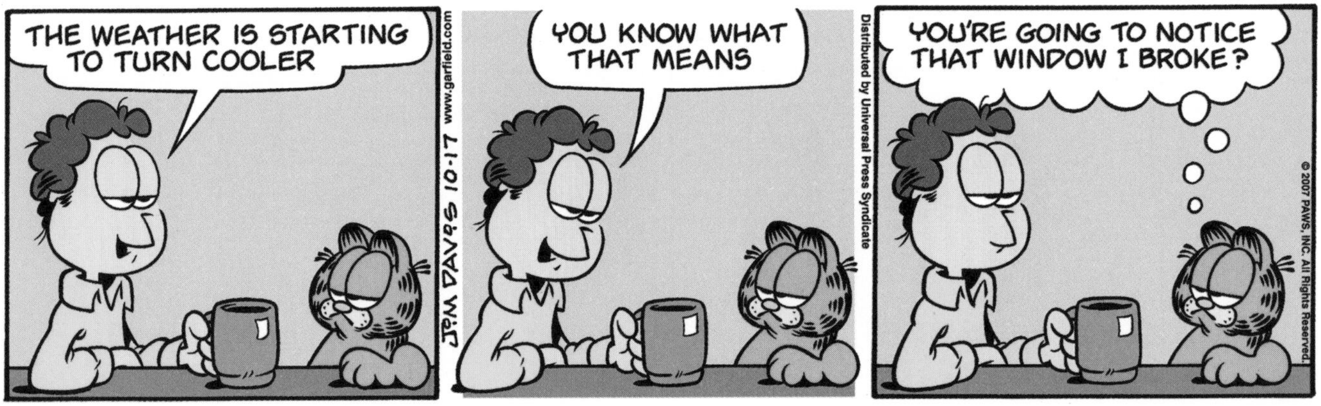
THE WEATHER IS STARTING TO TURN COOLER
YOU KNOW WHAT THAT MEANS
YOU'RE GOING TO NOTICE THAT WINDOW I BROKE?
JIM DAVIS 10-17
www.garfield.com
Distributed by Universal Press Syndicate
© 2007 PAWS, INC. All Rights Reserved.

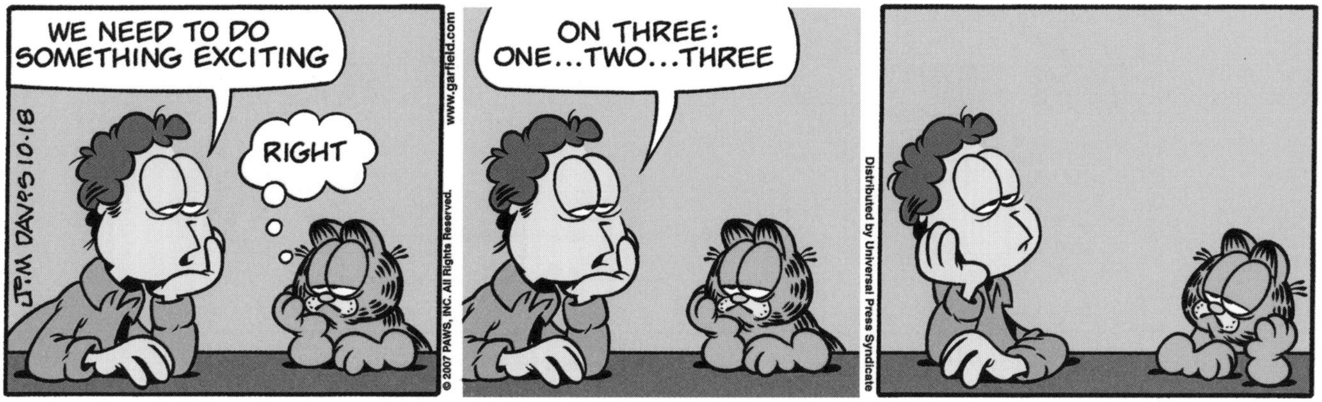
WE NEED TO DO SOMETHING EXCITING
RIGHT
ON THREE: ONE...TWO...THREE
JIM DAVIS 10-18
© 2007 PAWS, INC. All Rights Reserved.
www.garfield.com
Distributed by Universal Press Syndicate

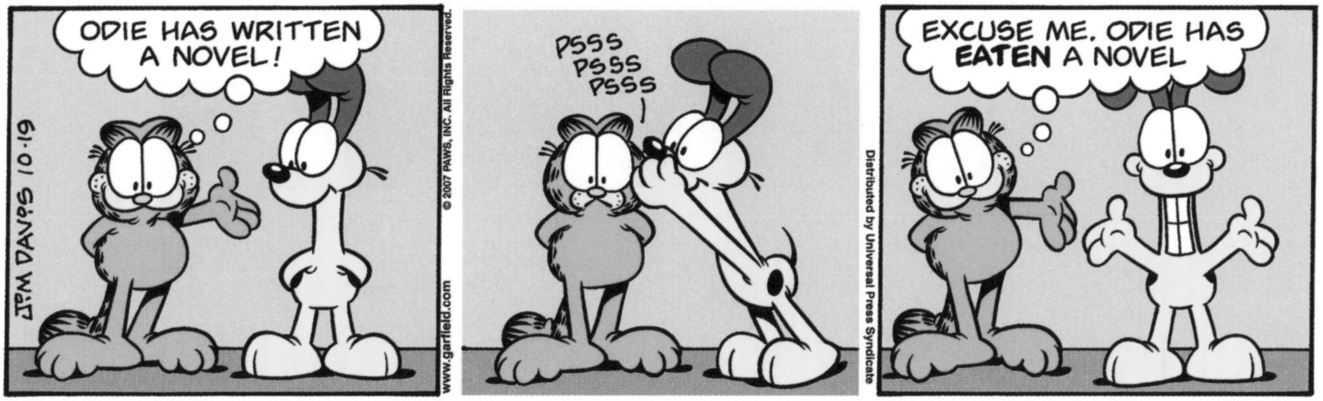
ODIE HAS WRITTEN A NOVEL!
PSSS PSSS PSSS
EXCUSE ME. ODIE HAS **EATEN** A NOVEL
JIM DAVIS 10-19
© 2007 PAWS, INC. All Rights Reserved.
www.garfield.com
Distributed by Universal Press Syndicate

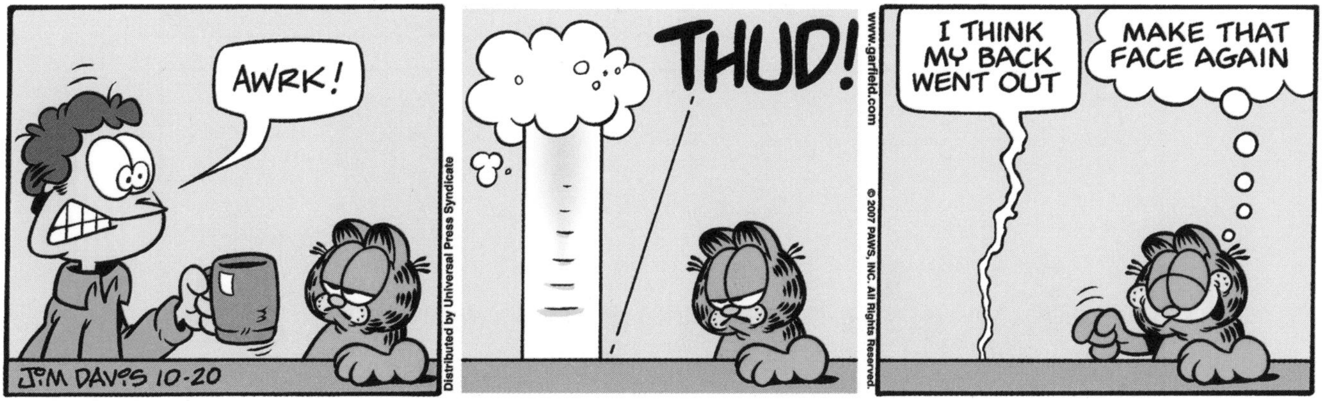
AWRK!
THUD!
I THINK MY BACK WENT OUT
MAKE THAT FACE AGAIN
JIM DAVIS 10-20
Distributed by Universal Press Syndicate
www.garfield.com
© 2007 PAWS, INC. All Rights Reserved.

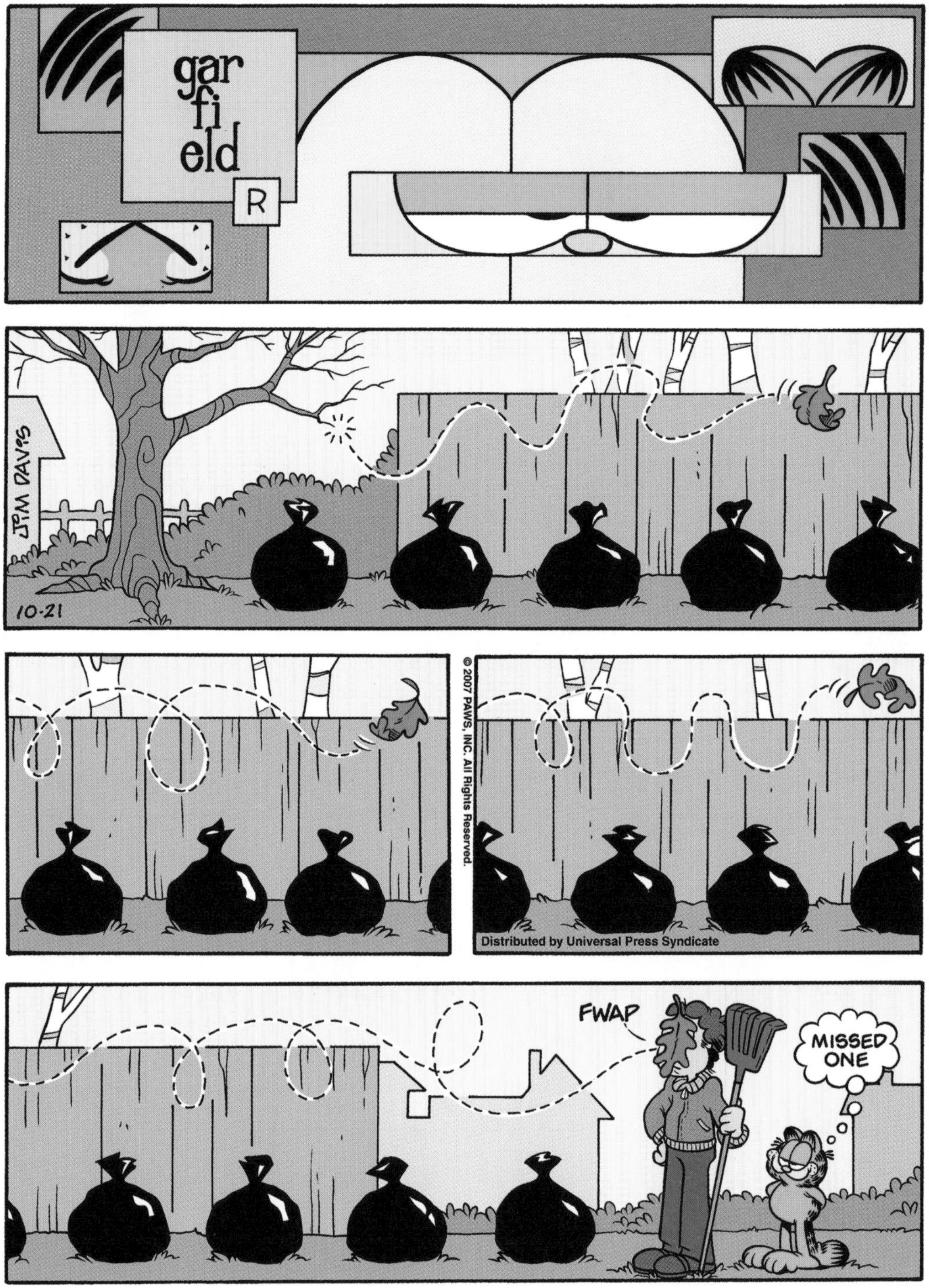
garfield
R
JIM DAVIS
10-21
© 2007 PAWS, INC. All Rights Reserved.
Distributed by Universal Press Syndicate
FWAP
MISSED ONE

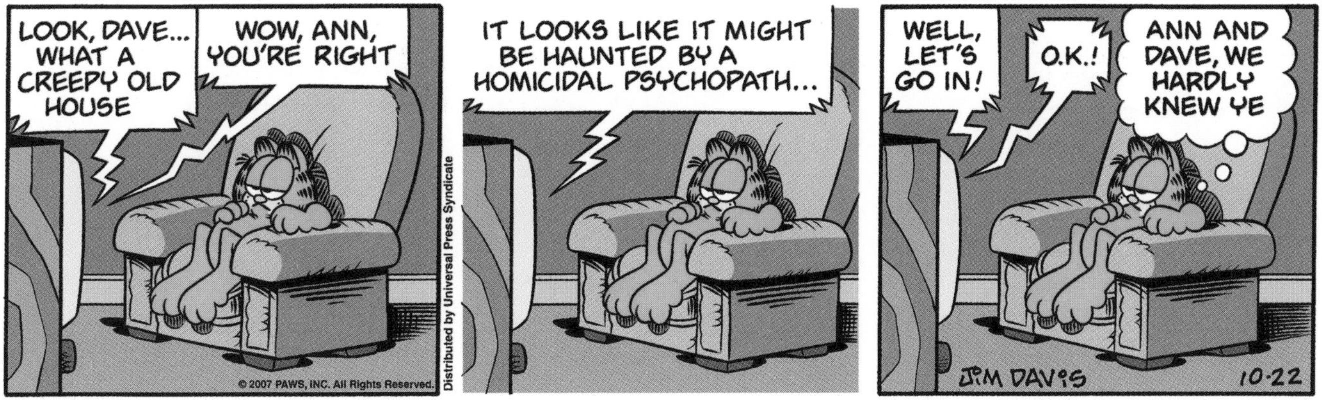
LOOK, DAVE... WHAT A CREEPY OLD HOUSE
WOW, ANN, YOU'RE RIGHT
© 2007 PAWS, INC. All Rights Reserved.
Distributed by Universal Press Syndicate
IT LOOKS LIKE IT MIGHT BE HAUNTED BY A HOMICIDAL PSYCHOPATH...
WELL, LET'S GO IN!
O.K.!
ANN AND DAVE, WE HARDLY KNEW YE
JIM DAVIS
10-22

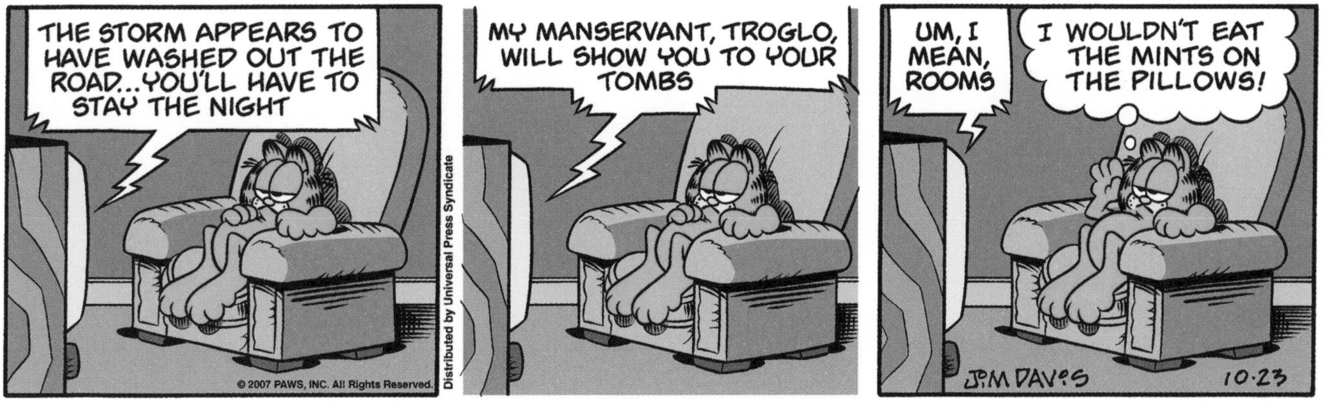
THE STORM APPEARS TO HAVE WASHED OUT THE ROAD...YOU'LL HAVE TO STAY THE NIGHT
© 2007 PAWS, INC. All Rights Reserved.
Distributed by Universal Press Syndicate
MY MANSERVANT, TROGLO, WILL SHOW YOU TO YOUR TOMBS
UM, I MEAN, ROOMS
I WOULDN'T EAT THE MINTS ON THE PILLOWS!
JIM DAVIS
10-23

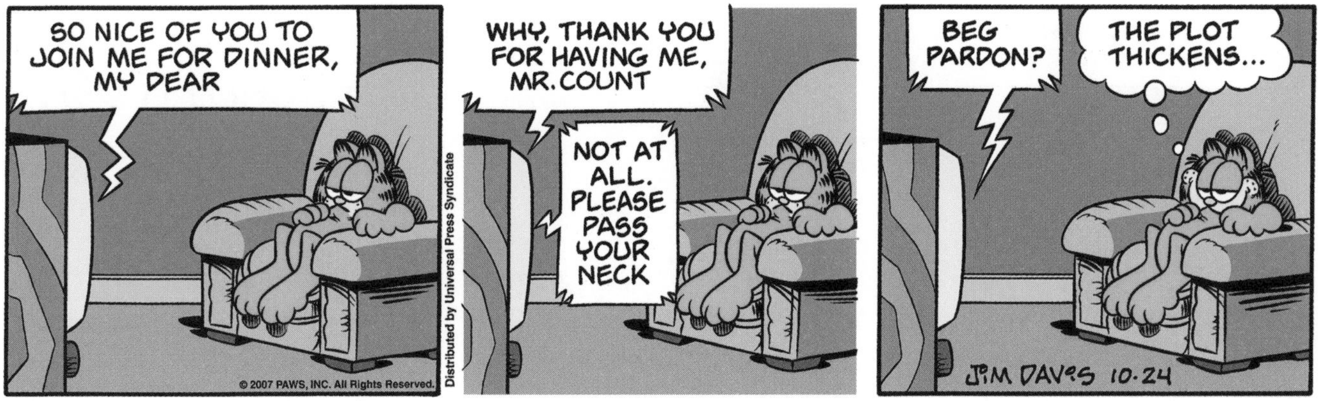
SO NICE OF YOU TO JOIN ME FOR DINNER, MY DEAR
© 2007 PAWS, INC. All Rights Reserved.
Distributed by Universal Press Syndicate
WHY, THANK YOU FOR HAVING ME, MR. COUNT
NOT AT ALL. PLEASE PASS YOUR NECK
BEG PARDON?
THE PLOT THICKENS...
JIM DAVIS 10-24

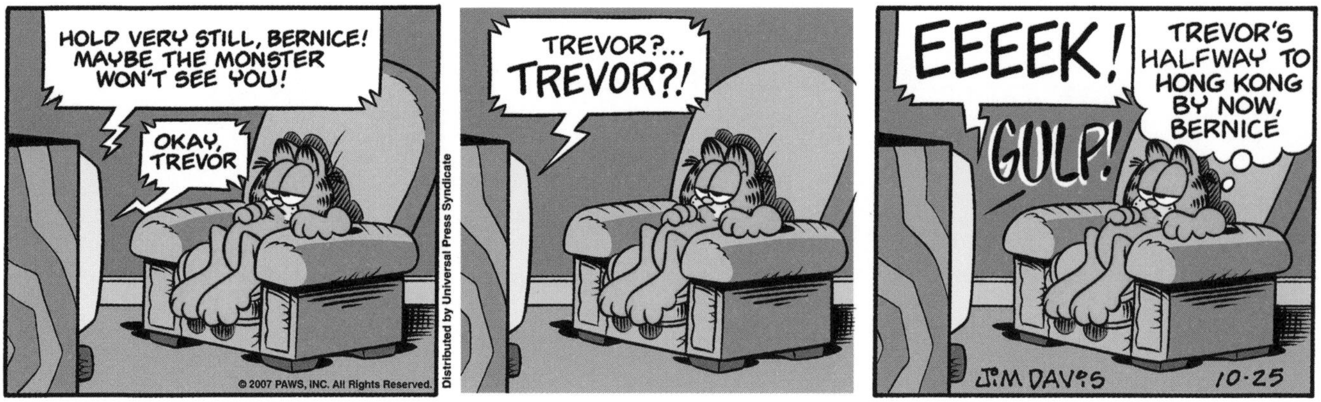

HOLD VERY STILL, BERNICE! MAYBE THE MONSTER WON'T SEE YOU!
OKAY, TREVOR
© 2007 PAWS, INC. All Rights Reserved.
Distributed by Universal Press Syndicate
TREVOR?... TREVOR?!
EEEEK!
GULP!
TREVOR'S HALFWAY TO HONG KONG BY NOW, BERNICE
JIM DAVIS
10-25

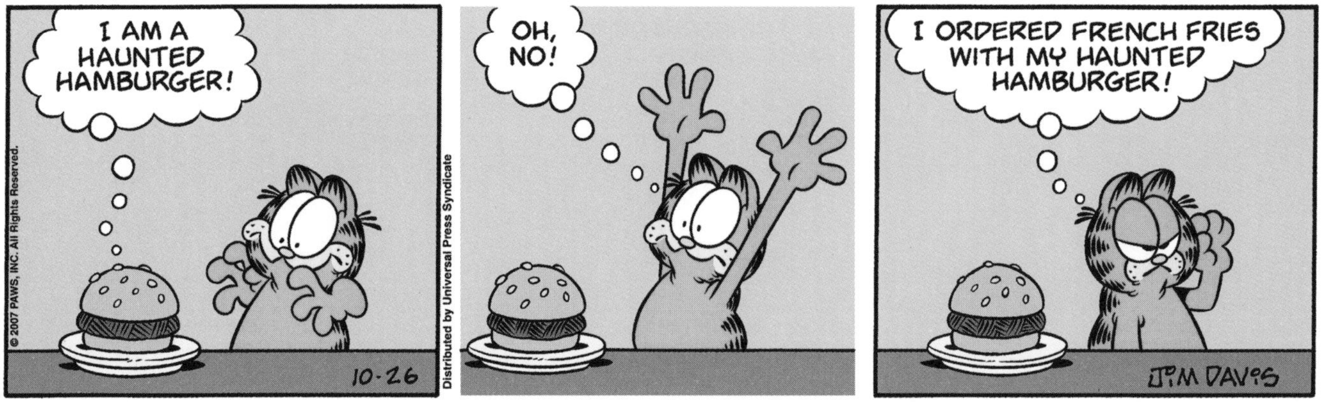

I AM A HAUNTED HAMBURGER!
© 2007 PAWS, INC. All Rights Reserved.
10-26
Distributed by Universal Press Syndicate
OH, NO!
I ORDERED FRENCH FRIES WITH MY HAUNTED HAMBURGER!
JIM DAVIS

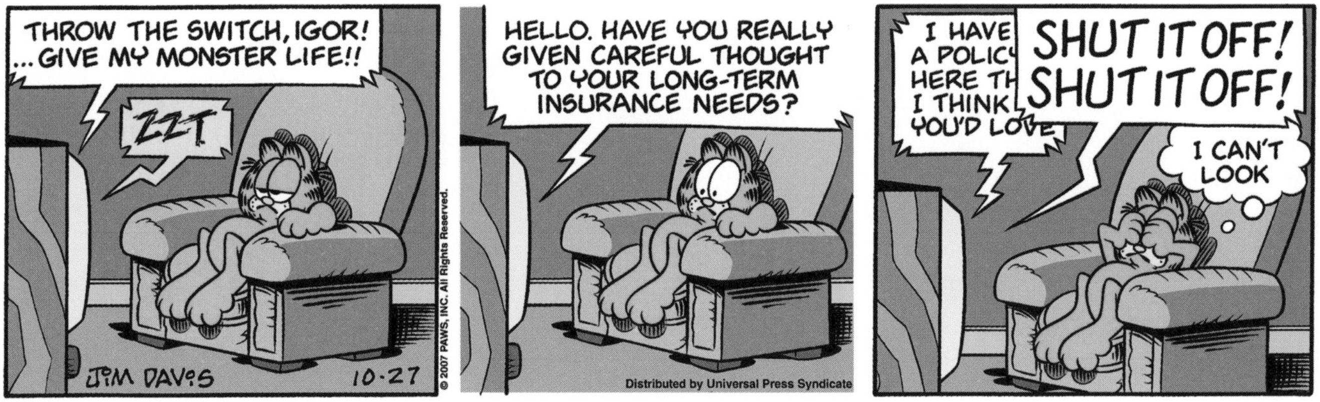

THROW THE SWITCH, IGOR! ...GIVE MY MONSTER LIFE!!
ZZT
JIM DAVIS
10-27
© 2007 PAWS, INC. All Rights Reserved.
HELLO. HAVE YOU REALLY GIVEN CAREFUL THOUGHT TO YOUR LONG-TERM INSURANCE NEEDS?
Distributed by Universal Press Syndicate
I HAVE A POLICY HERE TH I THINK YOU'D LOVE
SHUT IT OFF! SHUT IT OFF!
I CAN'T LOOK

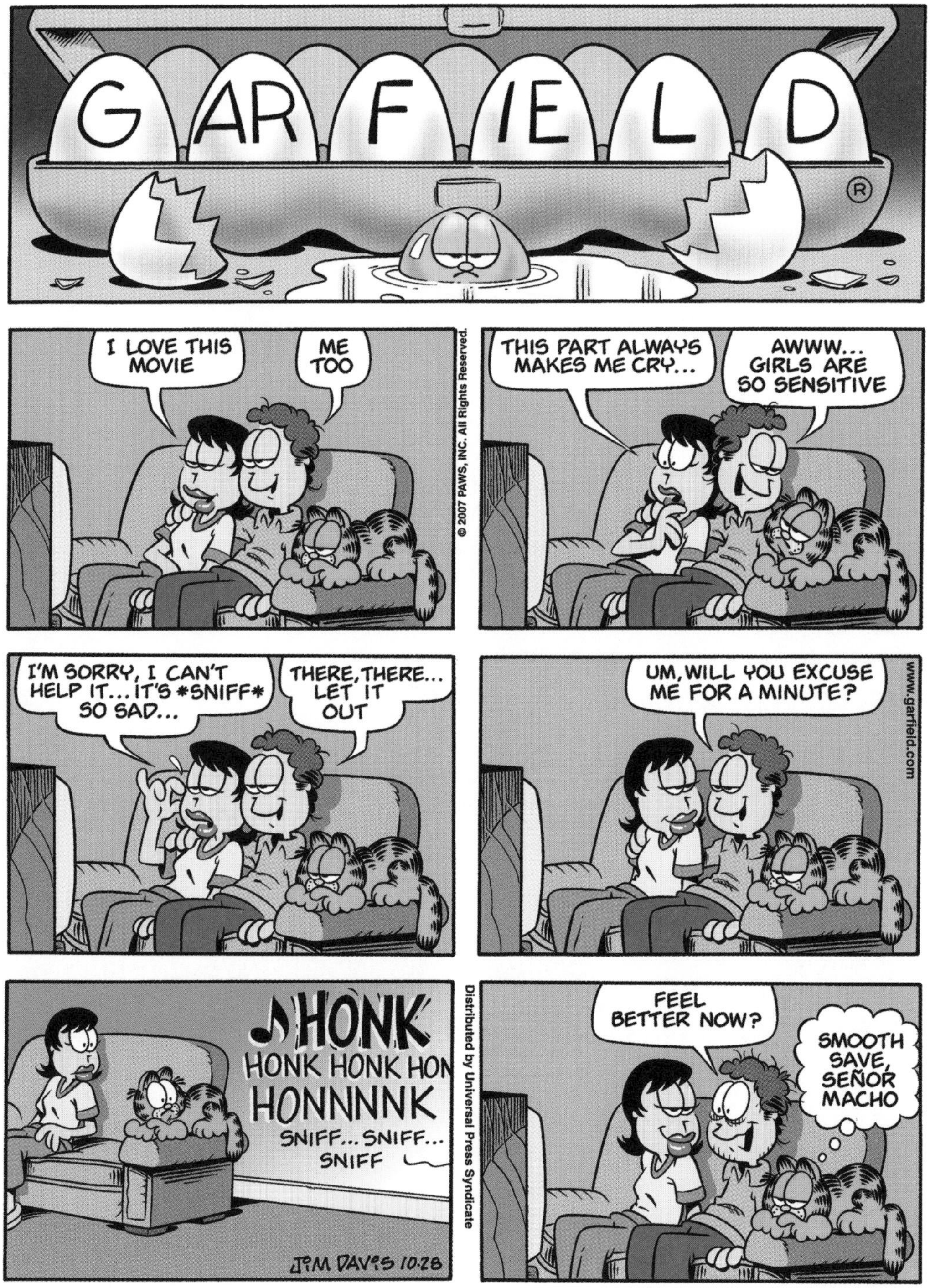
GARFIELD ®
I LOVE THIS MOVIE
ME TOO
© 2007 PAWS, INC. All Rights Reserved.
THIS PART ALWAYS MAKES ME CRY...
AWWW... GIRLS ARE SO SENSITIVE
I'M SORRY, I CAN'T HELP IT... IT'S *SNIFF* SO SAD...
THERE, THERE... LET IT OUT
UM, WILL YOU EXCUSE ME FOR A MINUTE?
www.garfield.com
♪HONK
HONK HONK HON
HONNNNK
SNIFF... SNIFF... SNIFF
Distributed by Universal Press Syndicate
JIM DAVIS 10-28
FEEL BETTER NOW?
SMOOTH SAVE, SEÑOR MACHO

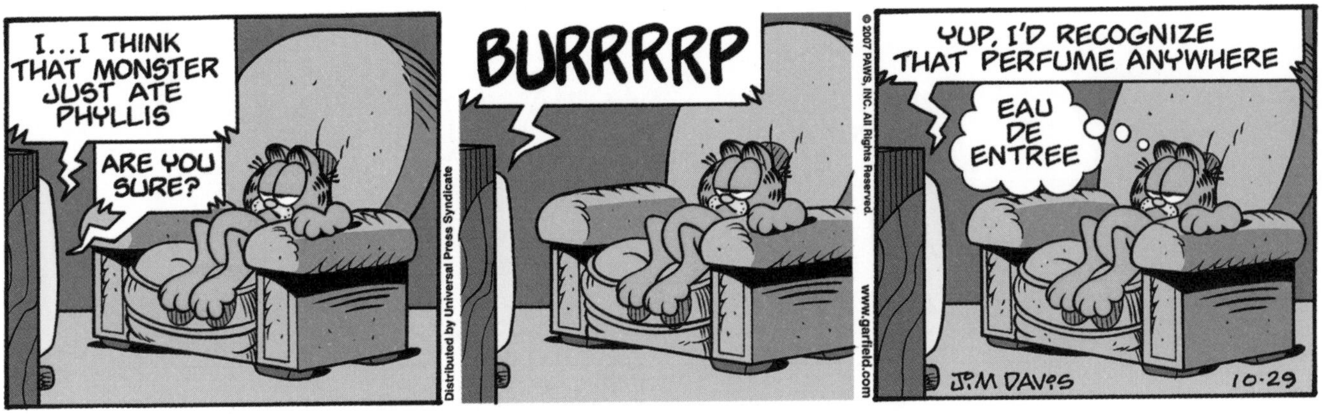
I...I THINK THAT MONSTER JUST ATE PHYLLIS
ARE YOU SURE?
BURRRRP
YUP, I'D RECOGNIZE THAT PERFUME ANYWHERE
EAU DE ENTREE
JIM DAVIS 10-29
Distributed by Universal Press Syndicate
© 2007 PAWS, INC. All Rights Reserved.
www.garfield.com

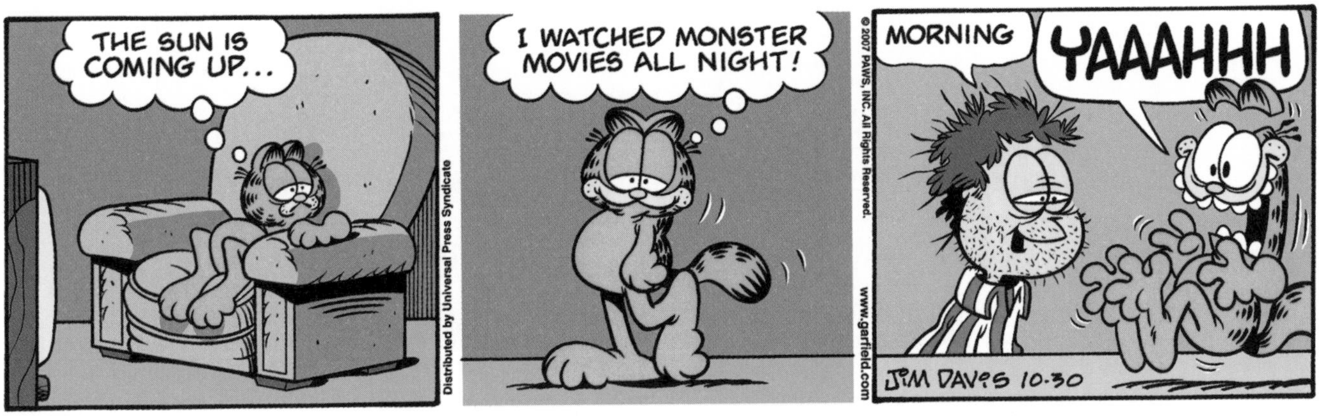
THE SUN IS COMING UP...
I WATCHED MONSTER MOVIES ALL NIGHT!
MORNING
YAAAHHH
JIM DAVIS 10-30
Distributed by Universal Press Syndicate
© 2007 PAWS, INC. All Rights Reserved.
www.garfield.com

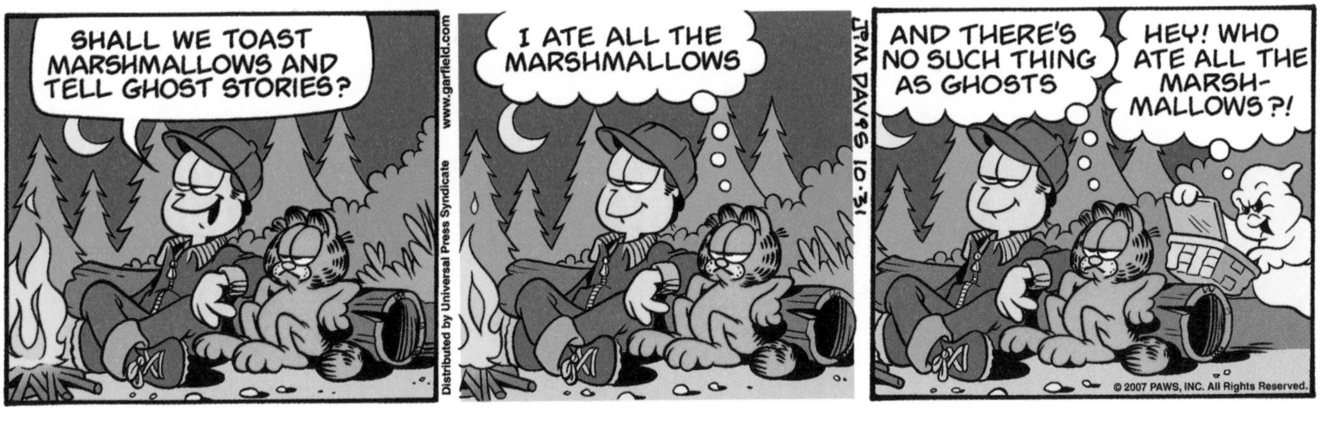
SHALL WE TOAST MARSHMALLOWS AND TELL GHOST STORIES?
I ATE ALL THE MARSHMALLOWS
AND THERE'S NO SUCH THING AS GHOSTS
HEY! WHO ATE ALL THE MARSH-MALLOWS?!
JIM DAVIS 10-31
www.garfield.com
Distributed by Universal Press Syndicate
© 2007 PAWS, INC. All Rights Reserved.

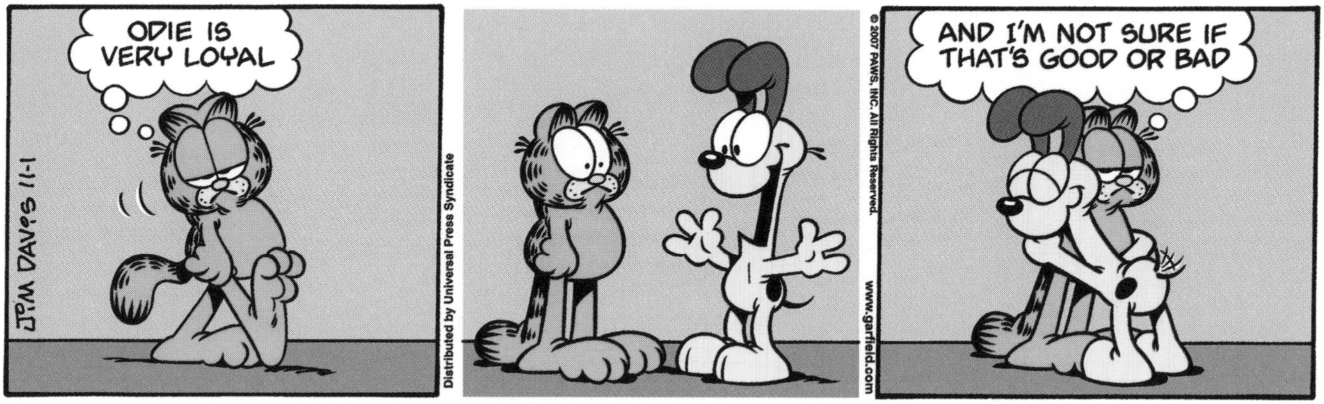
ODIE IS VERY LOYAL
JPM DAVIS 11-1
Distributed by Universal Press Syndicate
© 2007 PAWS, INC. All Rights Reserved.
www.garfield.com
AND I'M NOT SURE IF THAT'S GOOD OR BAD

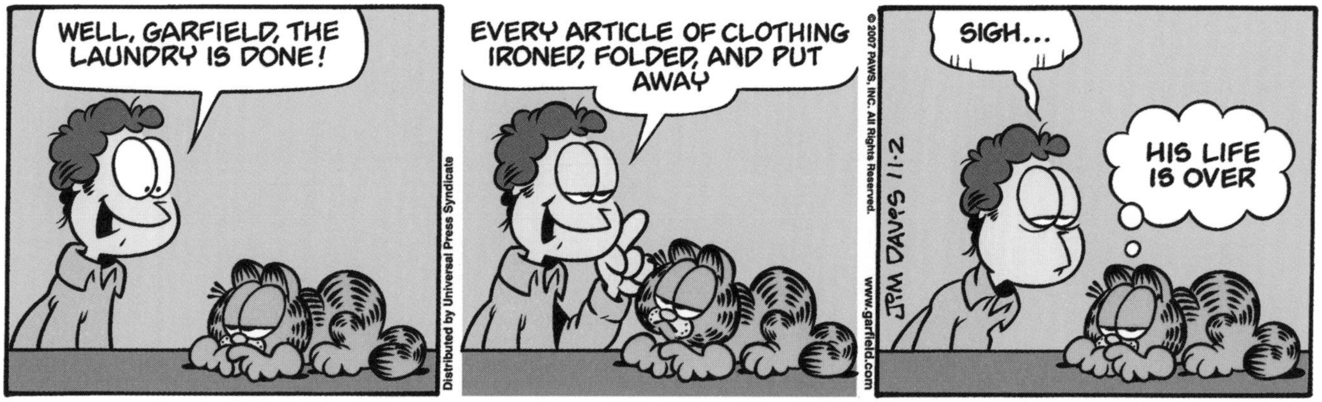
WELL, GARFIELD, THE LAUNDRY IS DONE!
Distributed by Universal Press Syndicate
EVERY ARTICLE OF CLOTHING IRONED, FOLDED, AND PUT AWAY
© 2007 PAWS, INC. All Rights Reserved.
www.garfield.com
SIGH...
HIS LIFE IS OVER
JPM DAVIS 11-2

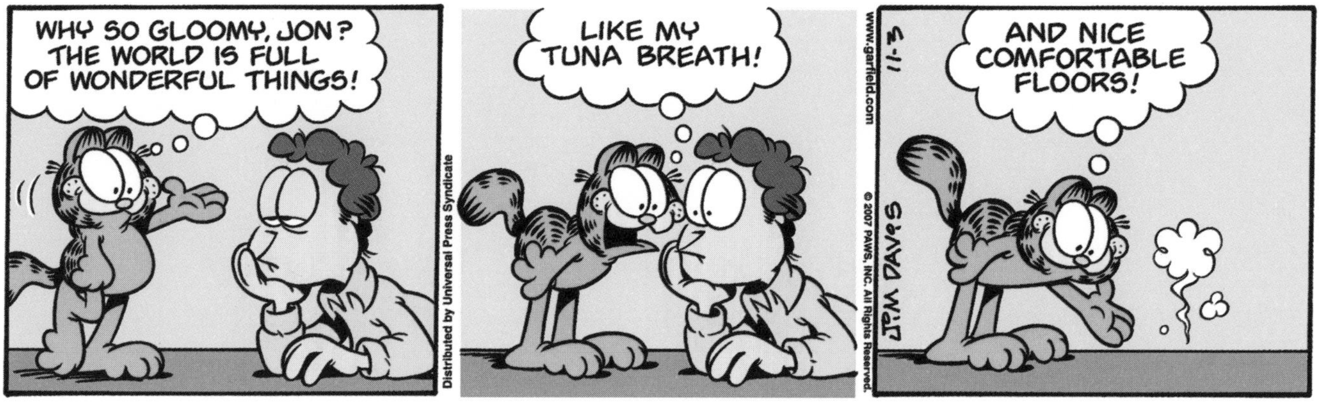
WHY SO GLOOMY, JON? THE WORLD IS FULL OF WONDERFUL THINGS!
Distributed by Universal Press Syndicate
LIKE MY TUNA BREATH!
www.garfield.com
© 2007 PAWS, INC. All Rights Reserved.
AND NICE COMFORTABLE FLOORS!
JPM DAVIS 11-3

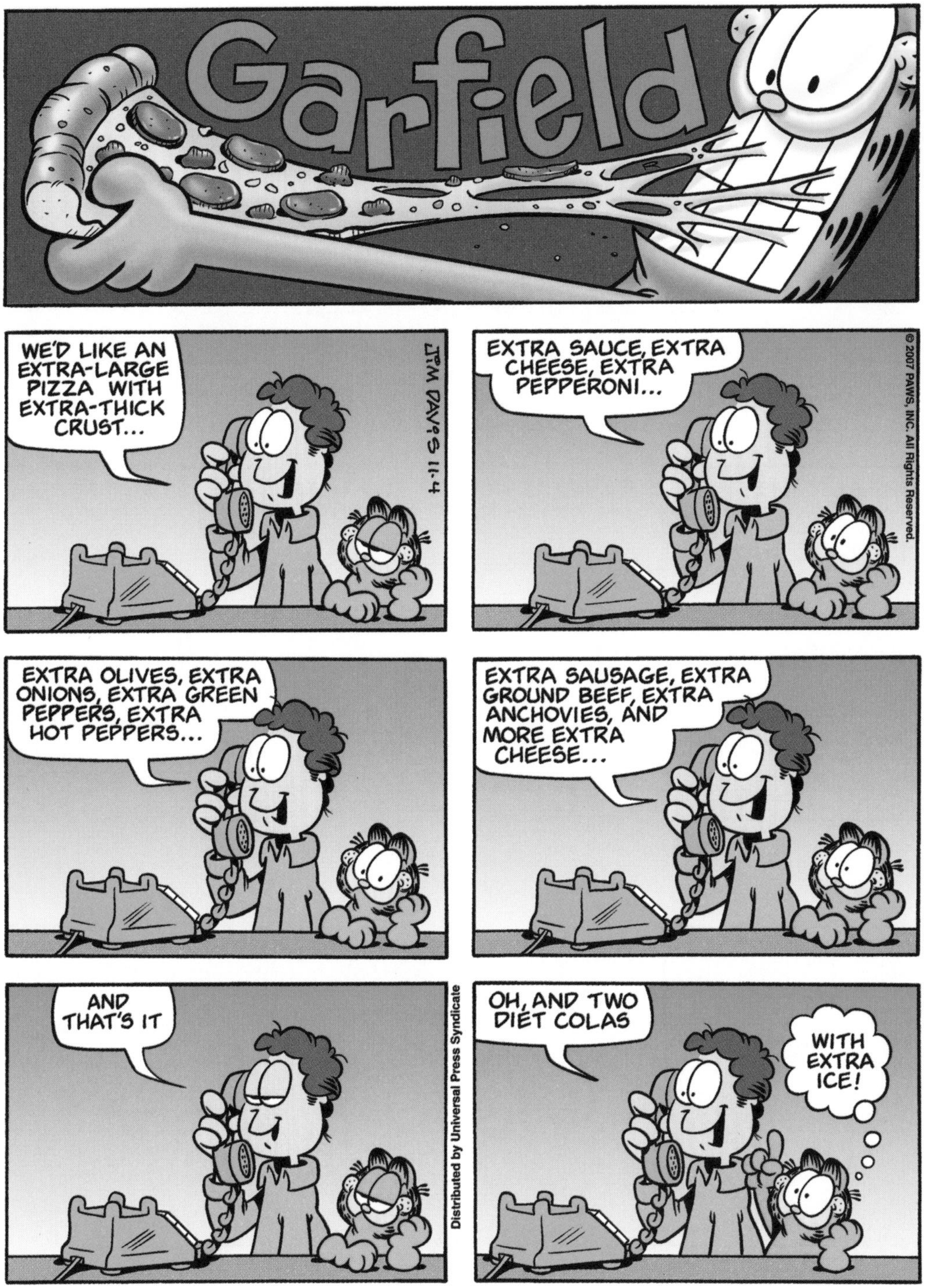
Garfield
JPM DAVPS 11-4
WE'D LIKE AN EXTRA-LARGE PIZZA WITH EXTRA-THICK CRUST...
EXTRA SAUCE, EXTRA CHEESE, EXTRA PEPPERONI...
© 2007 PAWS, INC. All Rights Reserved.
EXTRA OLIVES, EXTRA ONIONS, EXTRA GREEN PEPPERS, EXTRA HOT PEPPERS...
EXTRA SAUSAGE, EXTRA GROUND BEEF, EXTRA ANCHOVIES, AND MORE EXTRA CHEESE...
AND THAT'S IT
Distributed by Universal Press Syndicate
OH, AND TWO DIET COLAS
WITH EXTRA ICE!

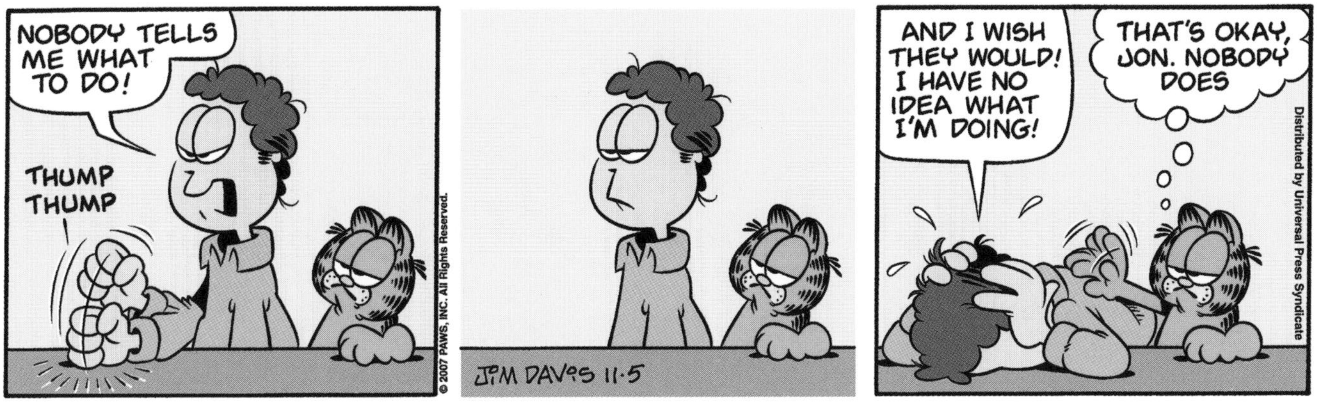
NOBODY TELLS ME WHAT TO DO!
THUMP THUMP
© 2007 PAWS, INC. All Rights Reserved.
JIM DAVIS 11-5
AND I WISH THEY WOULD! I HAVE NO IDEA WHAT I'M DOING!
THAT'S OKAY, JON. NOBODY DOES
Distributed by Universal Press Syndicate

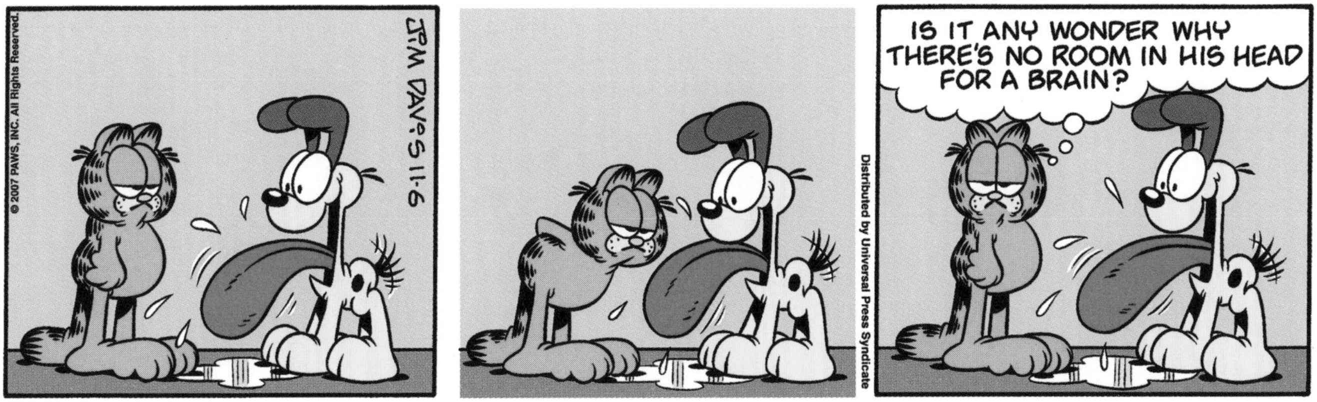
© 2007 PAWS, INC. All Rights Reserved.
JIM DAVIS 11-6
Distributed by Universal Press Syndicate
IS IT ANY WONDER WHY THERE'S NO ROOM IN HIS HEAD FOR A BRAIN?

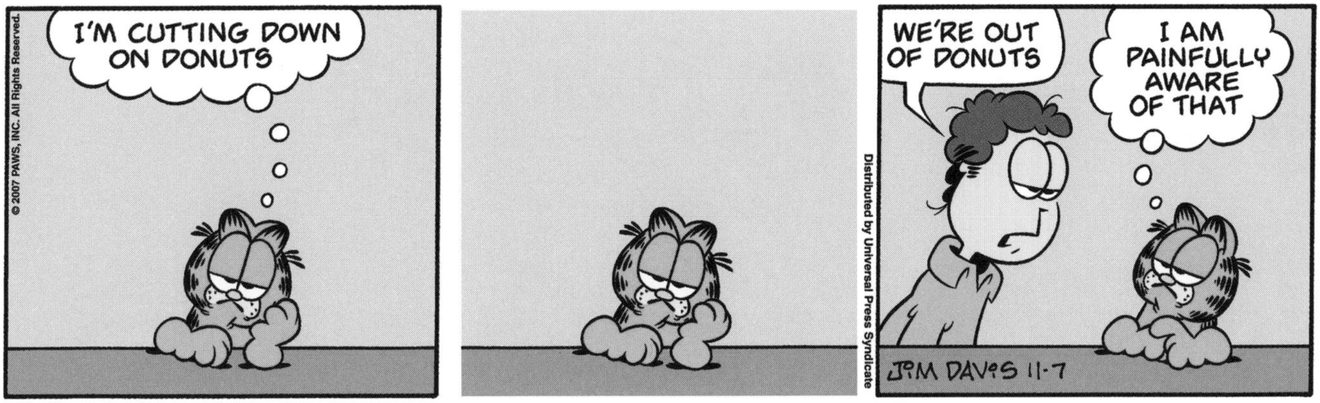
© 2007 PAWS, INC. All Rights Reserved.
I'M CUTTING DOWN ON DONUTS
Distributed by Universal Press Syndicate
WE'RE OUT OF DONUTS
I AM PAINFULLY AWARE OF THAT
JIM DAVIS 11-7

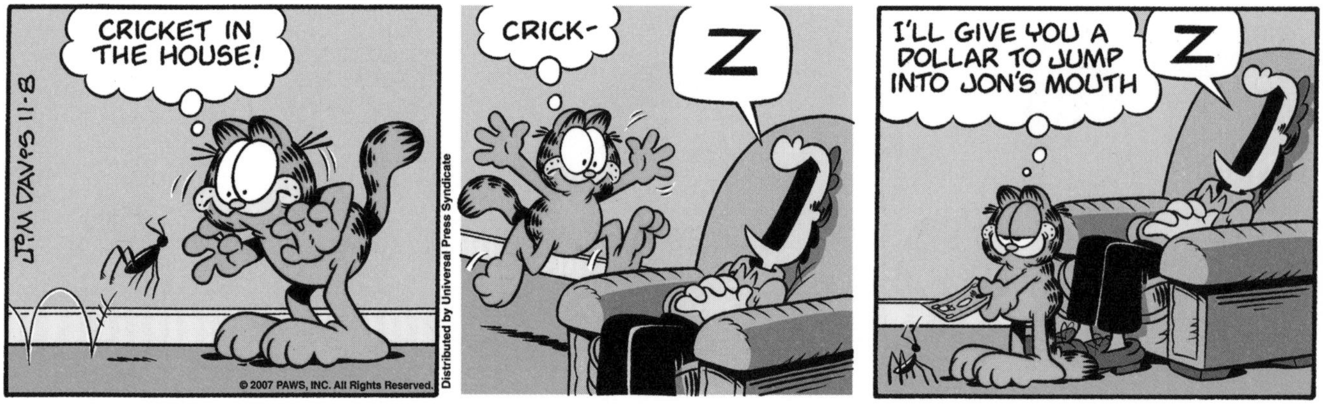
CRICKET IN THE HOUSE!
JPM DAVPS 11-8
© 2007 PAWS, INC. All Rights Reserved.
Distributed by Universal Press Syndicate
CRICK-
Z
I'LL GIVE YOU A DOLLAR TO JUMP INTO JON'S MOUTH
Z

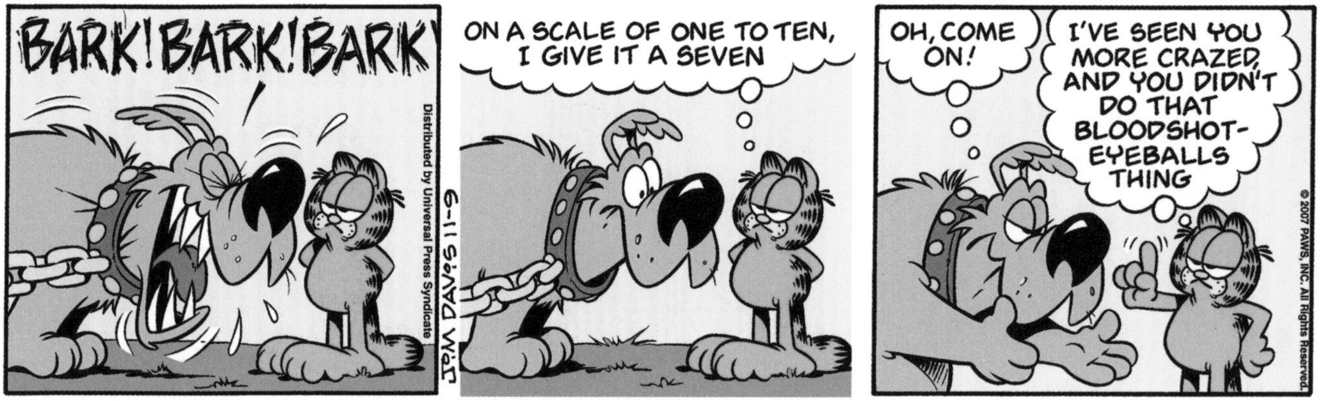
BARK! BARK! BARK!
Distributed by Universal Press Syndicate
JPM DAVPS 11-9
ON A SCALE OF ONE TO TEN, I GIVE IT A SEVEN
OH, COME ON!
I'VE SEEN YOU MORE CRAZED, AND YOU DIDN'T DO THAT BLOODSHOT-EYEBALLS THING
© 2007 PAWS, INC. All Rights Reserved.

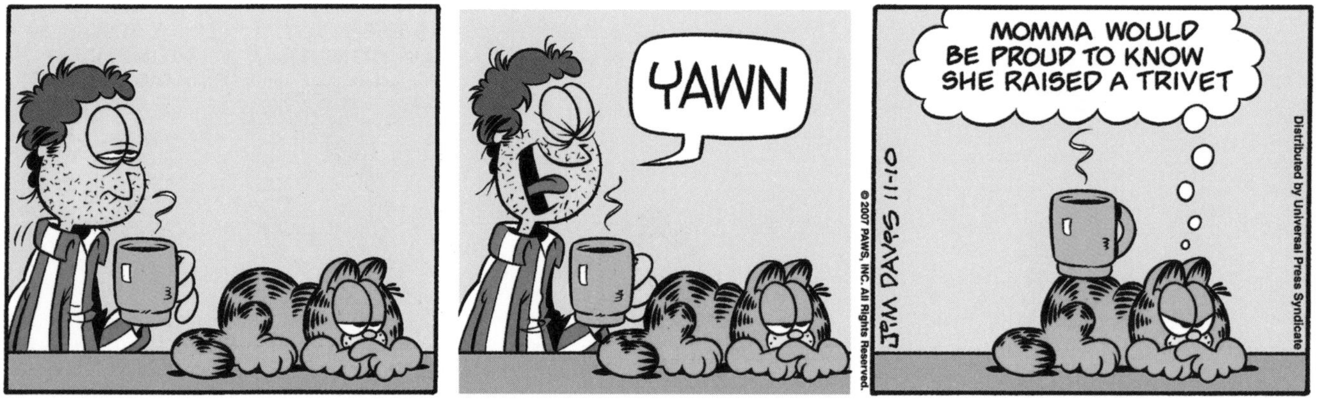
YAWN
© 2007 PAWS, INC. All Rights Reserved.
JPM DAVPS 11-10
MOMMA WOULD BE PROUD TO KNOW SHE RAISED A TRIVET
Distributed by Universal Press Syndicate

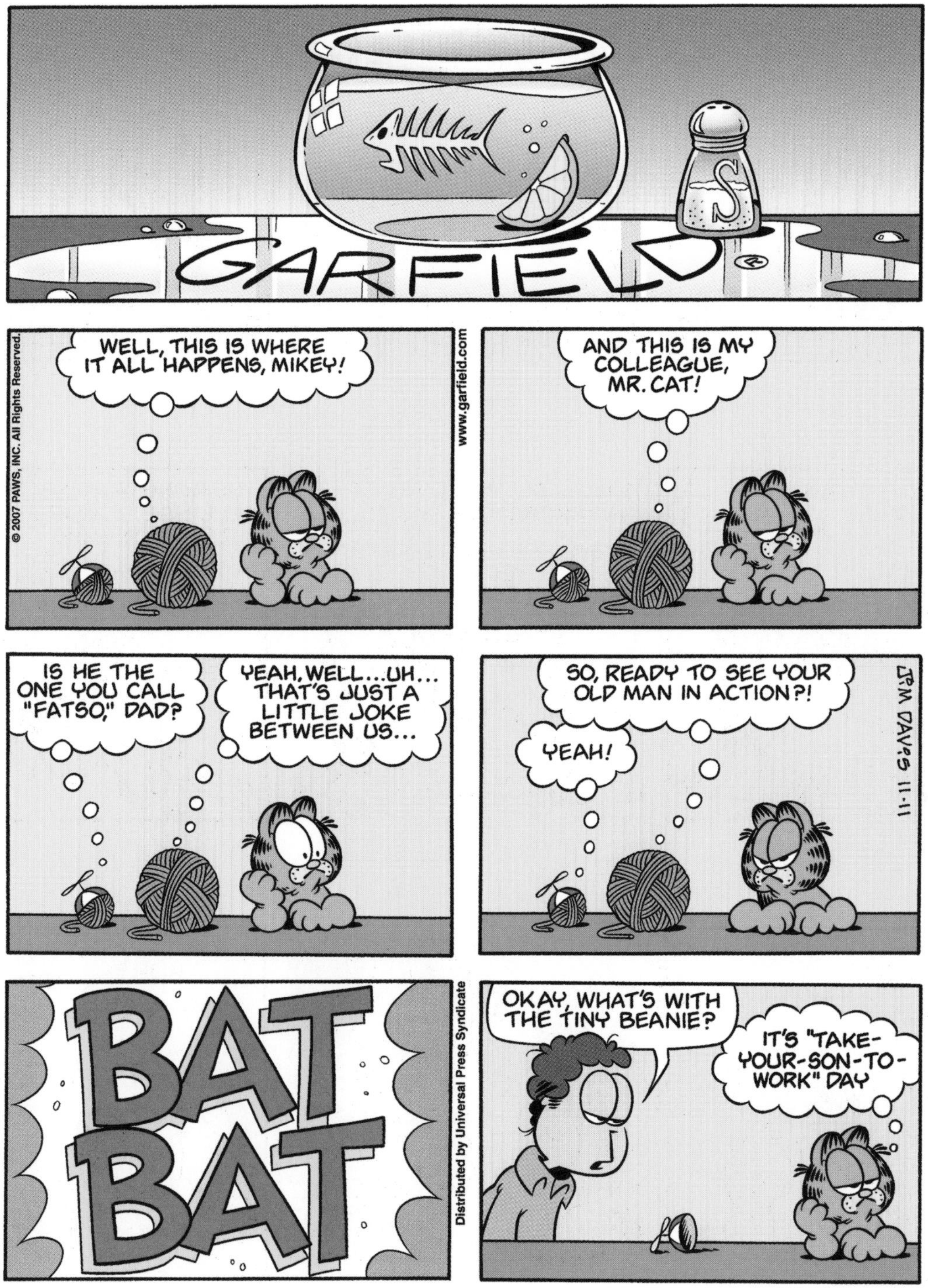
GARFIELD
© 2007 PAWS, INC. All Rights Reserved.
www.garfield.com
WELL, THIS IS WHERE IT ALL HAPPENS, MIKEY!
AND THIS IS MY COLLEAGUE, MR. CAT!
IS HE THE ONE YOU CALL "FATSO," DAD?
YEAH, WELL...UH... THAT'S JUST A LITTLE JOKE BETWEEN US...
SO, READY TO SEE YOUR OLD MAN IN ACTION?!
YEAH!
JIM DAVIS 11-11
BAT BAT
Distributed by Universal Press Syndicate
OKAY, WHAT'S WITH THE TINY BEANIE?
IT'S "TAKE-YOUR-SON-TO-WORK" DAY

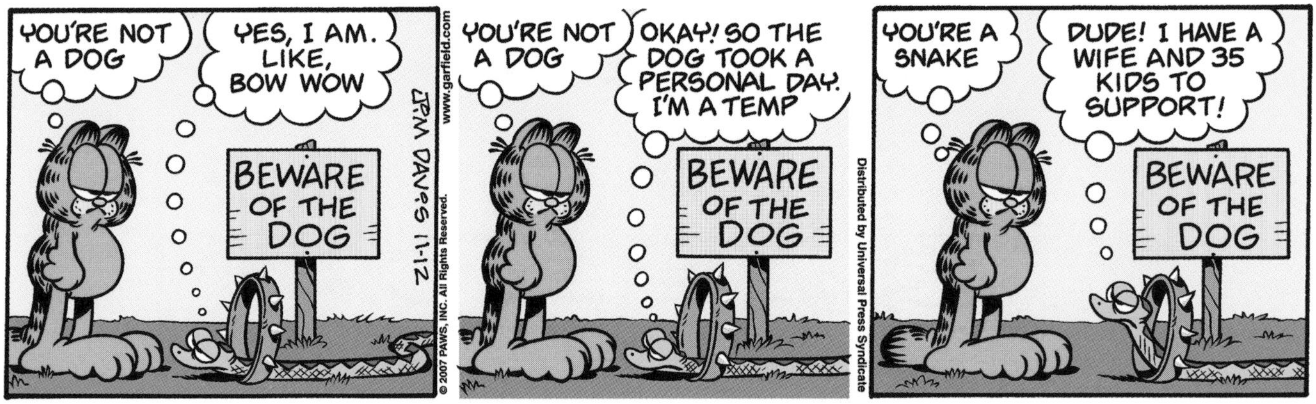
YOU'RE NOT A DOG
YES, I AM. LIKE, BOW WOW
BEWARE OF THE DOG
JPM DAVIS 11-12
© 2007 PAWS, INC. All Rights Reserved.
www.garfield.com
YOU'RE NOT A DOG
OKAY! SO THE DOG TOOK A PERSONAL DAY. I'M A TEMP
BEWARE OF THE DOG
Distributed by Universal Press Syndicate
YOU'RE A SNAKE
DUDE! I HAVE A WIFE AND 35 KIDS TO SUPPORT!
BEWARE OF THE DOG

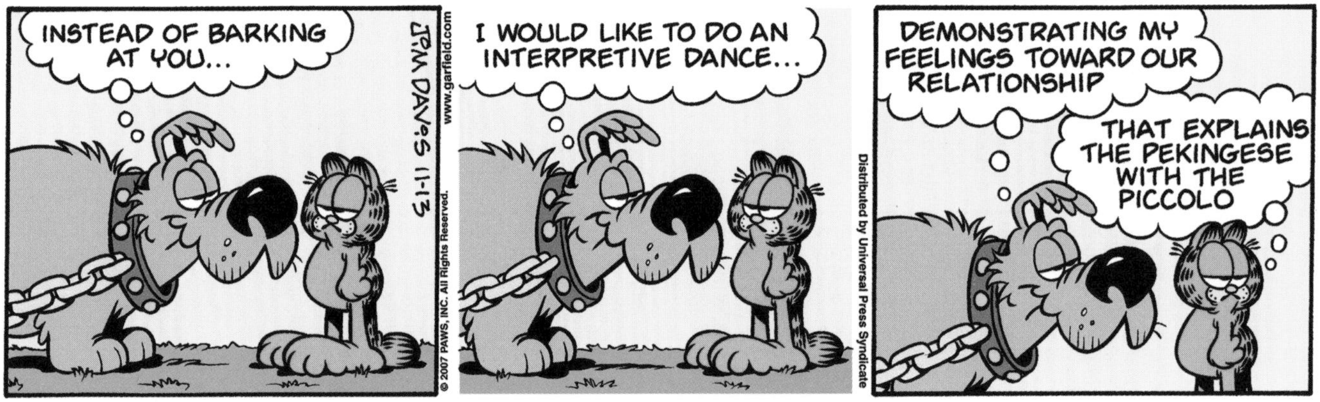
INSTEAD OF BARKING AT YOU...
JPM DAVIS 11-13
© 2007 PAWS, INC. All Rights Reserved.
www.garfield.com
I WOULD LIKE TO DO AN INTERPRETIVE DANCE...
Distributed by Universal Press Syndicate
DEMONSTRATING MY FEELINGS TOWARD OUR RELATIONSHIP
THAT EXPLAINS THE PEKINGESE WITH THE PICCOLO

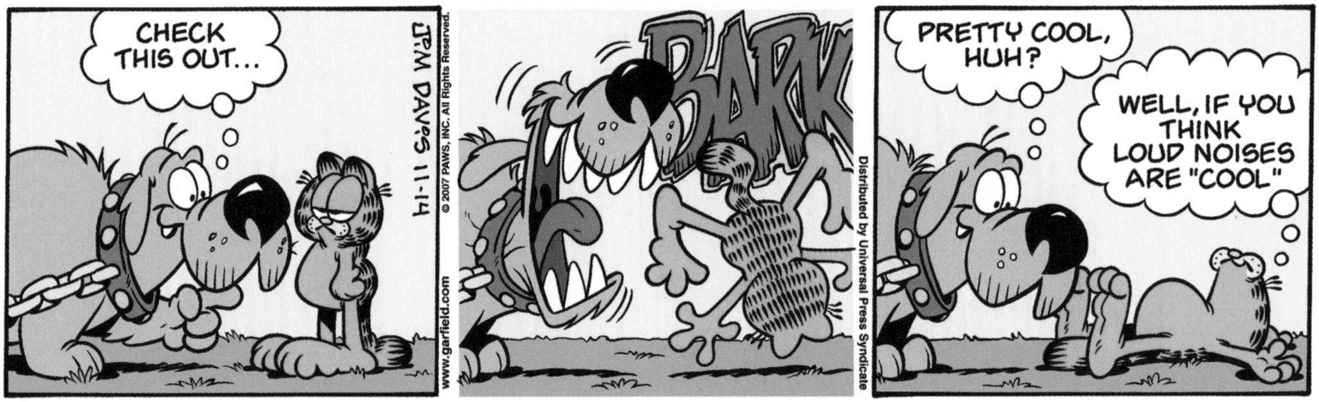
CHECK THIS OUT...
JPM DAVIS 11-14
© 2007 PAWS, INC. All Rights Reserved.
www.garfield.com
BARK
Distributed by Universal Press Syndicate
PRETTY COOL, HUH?
WELL, IF YOU THINK LOUD NOISES ARE "COOL"

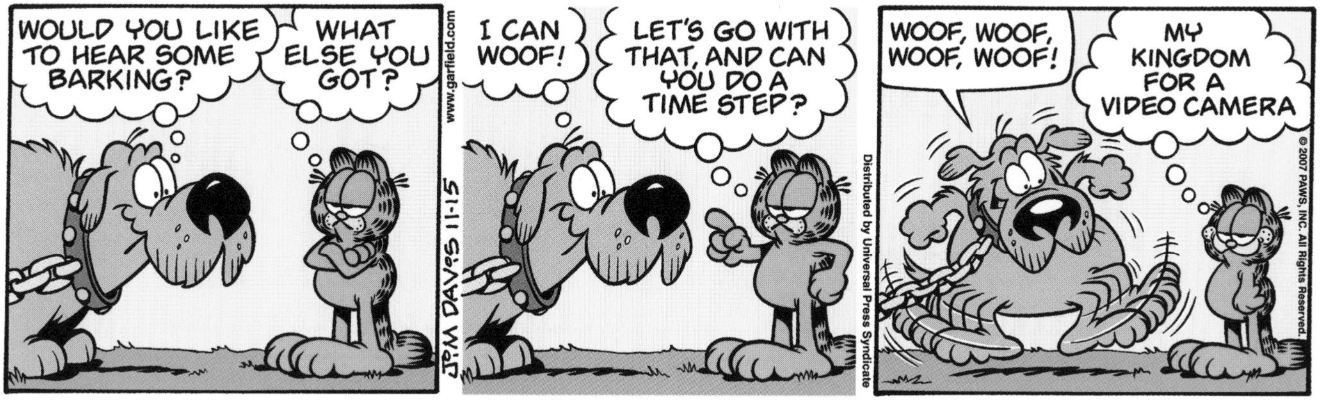
WOULD YOU LIKE TO HEAR SOME BARKING?
WHAT ELSE YOU GOT?
www.garfield.com
JIM DAVIS 11-15
I CAN WOOF!
LET'S GO WITH THAT, AND CAN YOU DO A TIME STEP?
Distributed by Universal Press Syndicate
WOOF, WOOF, WOOF, WOOF!
MY KINGDOM FOR A VIDEO CAMERA
© 2007 PAWS, INC. All Rights Reserved.

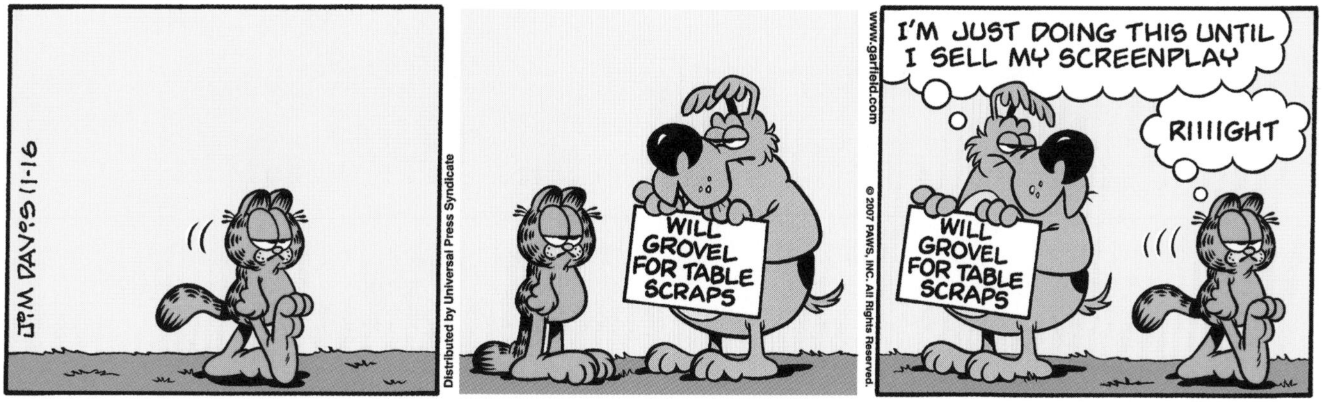
JIM DAVIS 11-16
Distributed by Universal Press Syndicate
WILL GROVEL FOR TABLE SCRAPS
www.garfield.com
© 2007 PAWS, INC. All Rights Reserved.
I'M JUST DOING THIS UNTIL I SELL MY SCREENPLAY
RIIIIGHT
WILL GROVEL FOR TABLE SCRAPS

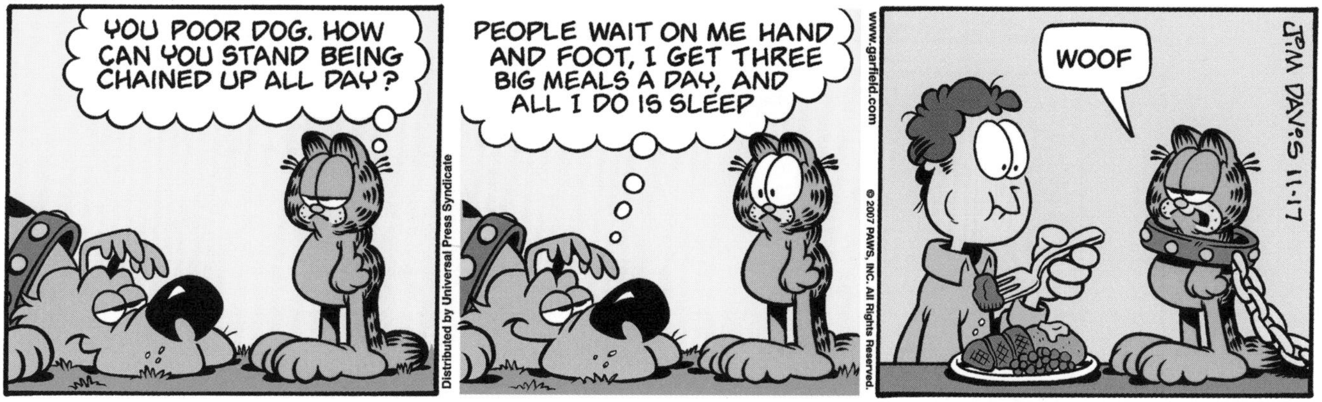
YOU POOR DOG. HOW CAN YOU STAND BEING CHAINED UP ALL DAY?
Distributed by Universal Press Syndicate
PEOPLE WAIT ON ME HAND AND FOOT, I GET THREE BIG MEALS A DAY, AND ALL I DO IS SLEEP
www.garfield.com
© 2007 PAWS, INC. All Rights Reserved.
WOOF
JIM DAVIS 11-17

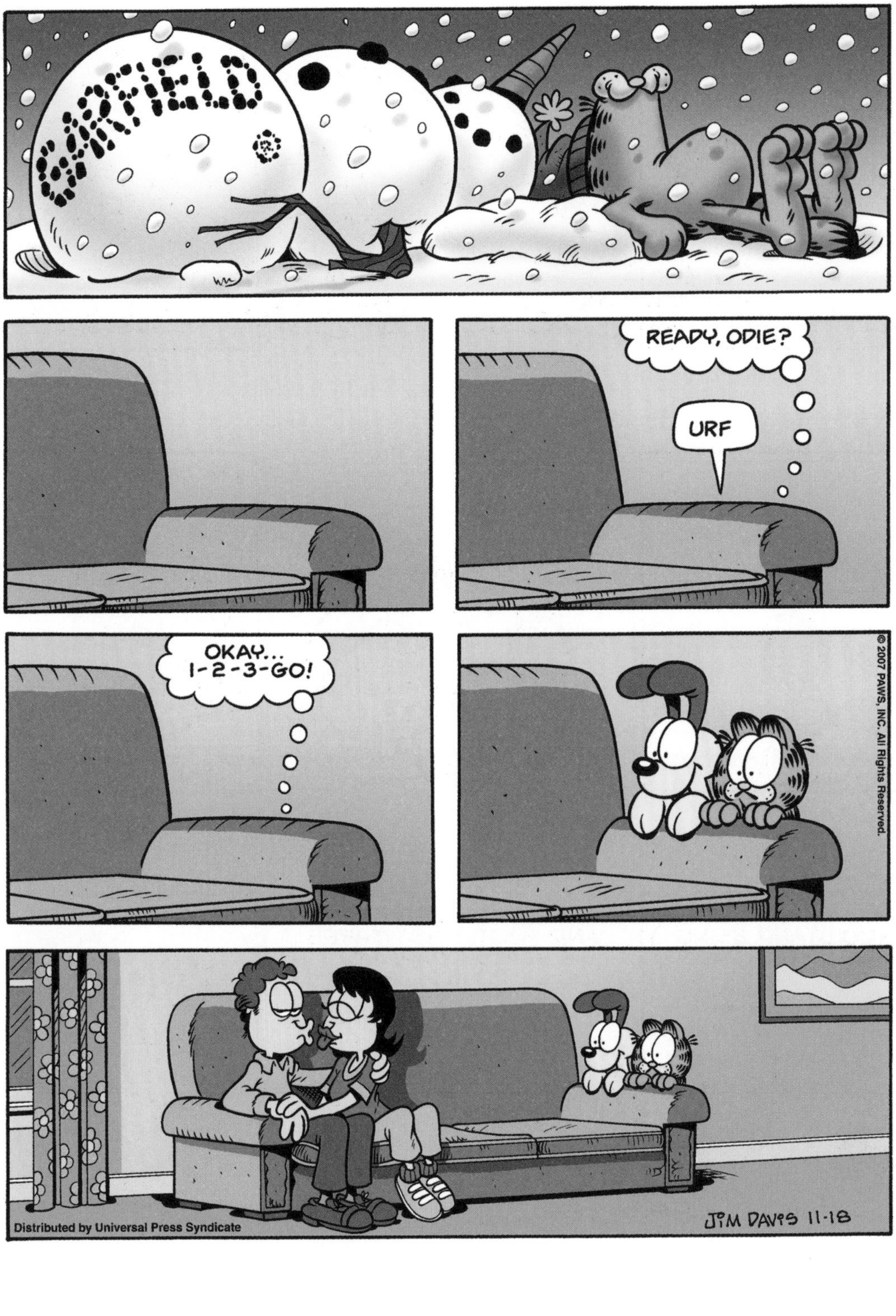
GARFIELD
READY, ODIE?
URF
OKAY... 1-2-3-GO!
© 2007 PAWS, INC. All Rights Reserved.
Distributed by Universal Press Syndicate
JIM DAVIS 11-18

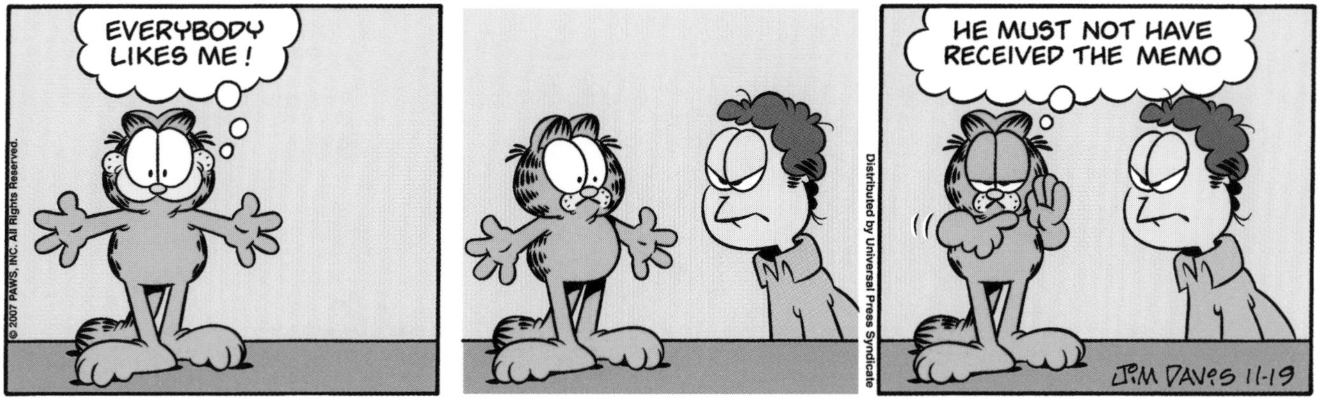
EVERYBODY LIKES ME!
HE MUST NOT HAVE RECEIVED THE MEMO
JIM DAVIS 11-19
© 2007 PAWS, INC. All Rights Reserved.
Distributed by Universal Press Syndicate

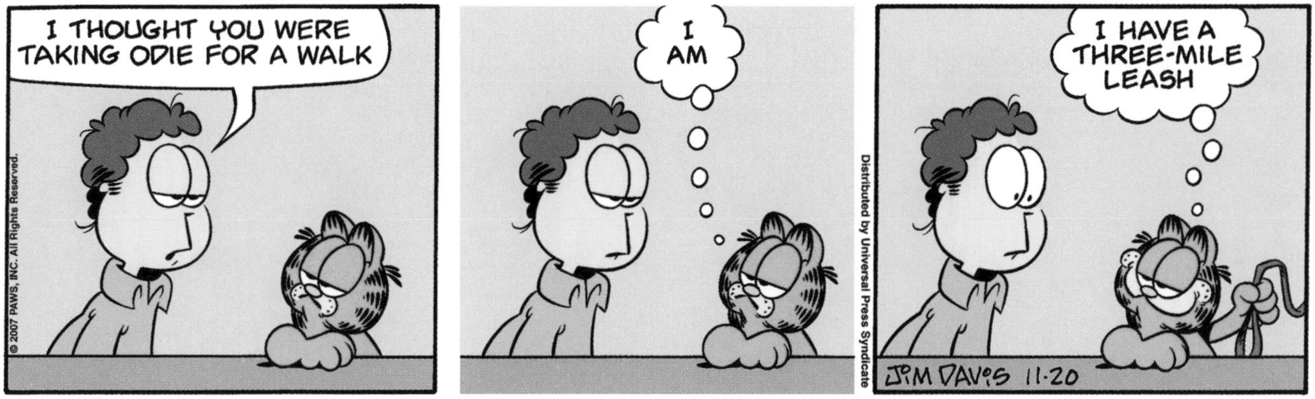
I THOUGHT YOU WERE TAKING ODIE FOR A WALK
I AM
I HAVE A THREE-MILE LEASH
JIM DAVIS 11-20
© 2007 PAWS, INC. All Rights Reserved.
Distributed by Universal Press Syndicate

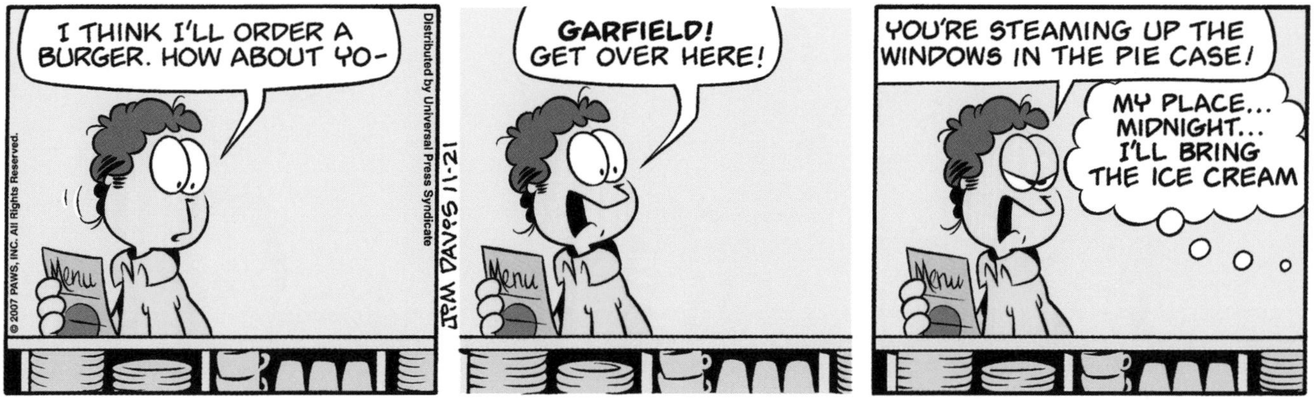
I THINK I'LL ORDER A BURGER. HOW ABOUT YO-
GARFIELD! GET OVER HERE!
YOU'RE STEAMING UP THE WINDOWS IN THE PIE CASE!
MY PLACE... MIDNIGHT... I'LL BRING THE ICE CREAM
Menu
JIM DAVIS 11-21
© 2007 PAWS, INC. All Rights Reserved.
Distributed by Universal Press Syndicate

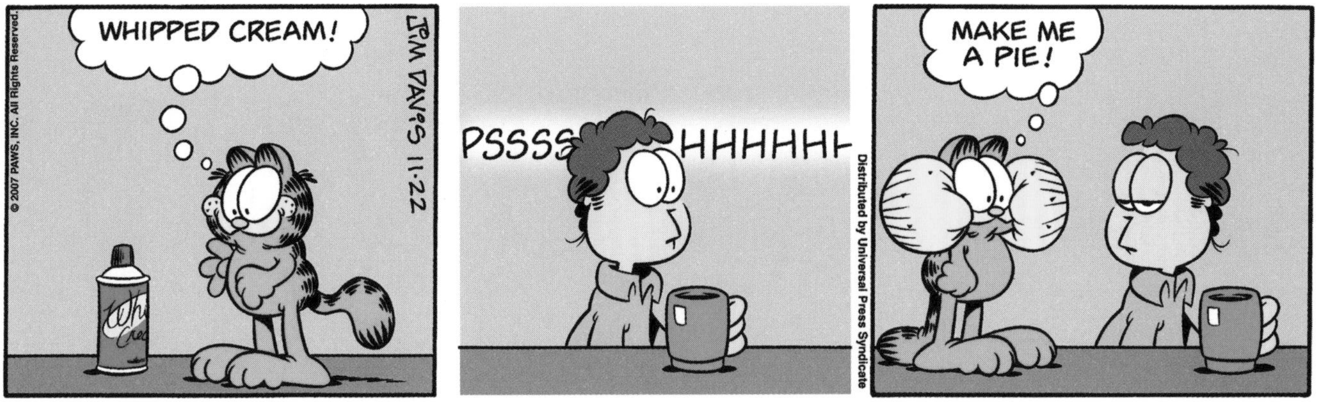

WHIPPED CREAM!
PSSSSHHHHHH
MAKE ME A PIE!
JIM DAVIS 11·22
© 2007 PAWS, INC. All Rights Reserved.
Distributed by Universal Press Syndicate

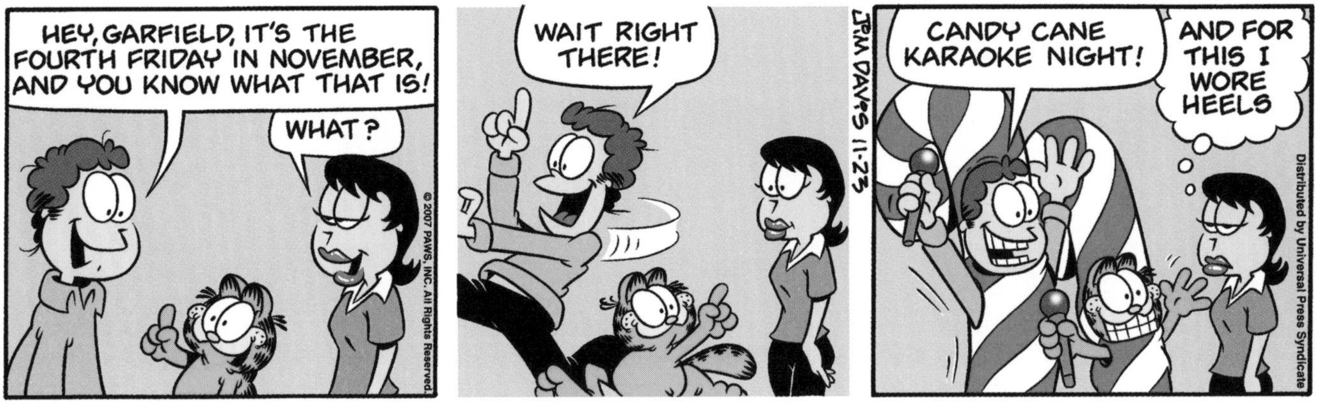

HEY, GARFIELD, IT'S THE FOURTH FRIDAY IN NOVEMBER, AND YOU KNOW WHAT THAT IS!
WHAT?
WAIT RIGHT THERE!
CANDY CANE KARAOKE NIGHT!
AND FOR THIS I WORE HEELS
JIM DAVIS 11·23
© 2007 PAWS, INC. All Rights Reserved.
Distributed by Universal Press Syndicate

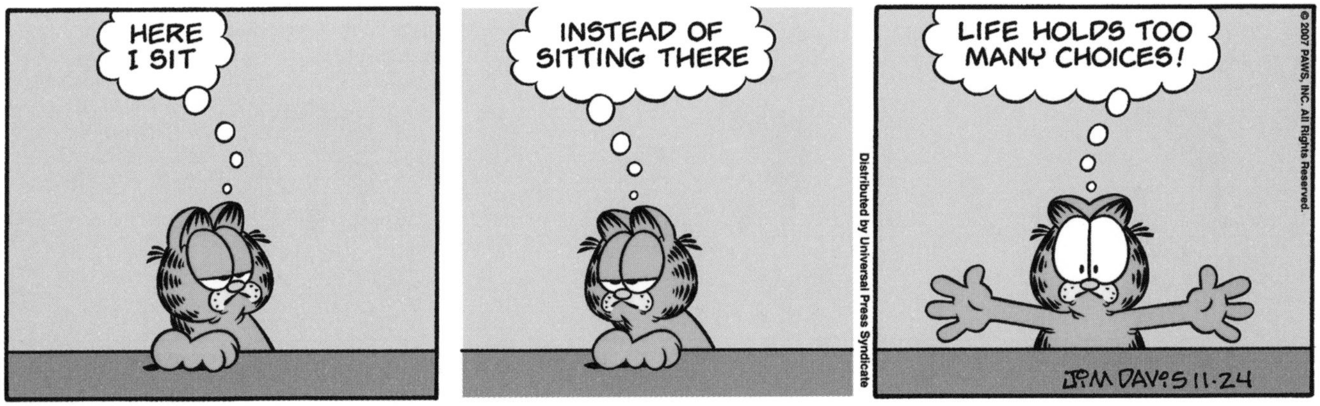

HERE I SIT
INSTEAD OF SITTING THERE
LIFE HOLDS TOO MANY CHOICES!
JIM DAVIS 11·24
© 2007 PAWS, INC. All Rights Reserved.
Distributed by Universal Press Syndicate

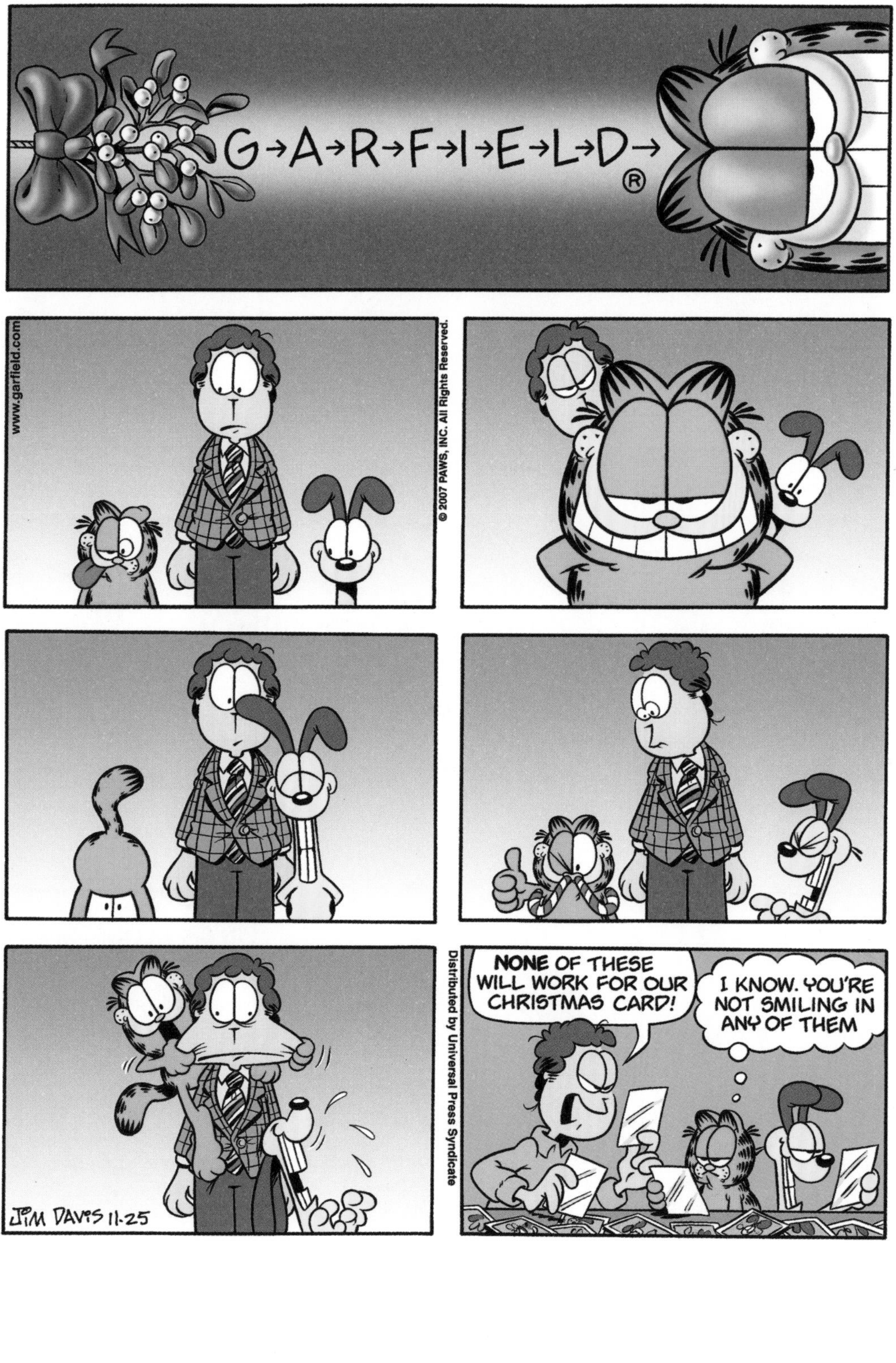
G→A→R→F→I→E→L→D→ ®
www.garfield.com
© 2007 PAWS, INC. All Rights Reserved.
JIM DAVIS 11-25
Distributed by Universal Press Syndicate
NONE OF THESE WILL WORK FOR OUR CHRISTMAS CARD!
I KNOW. YOU'RE NOT SMILING IN ANY OF THEM

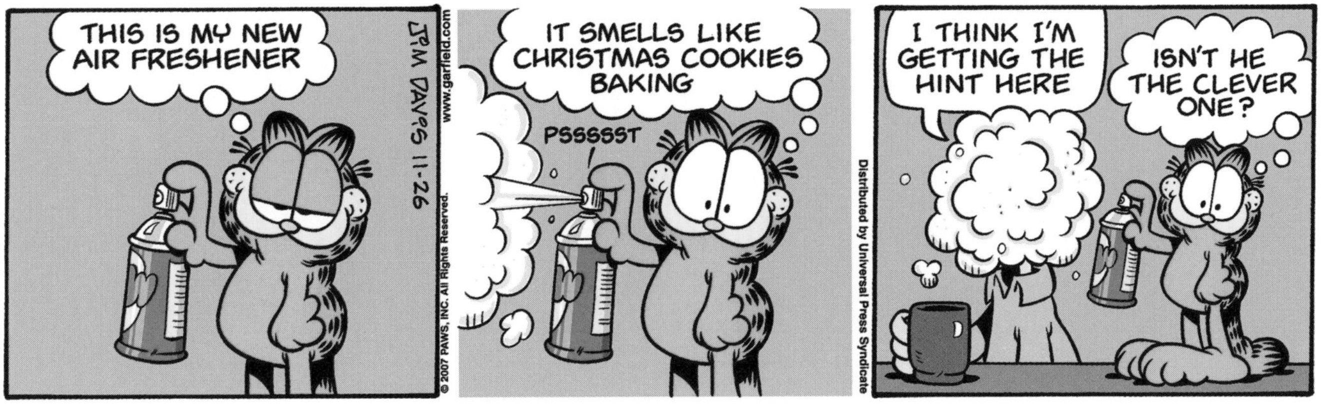
THIS IS MY NEW AIR FRESHENER
JPM DAVIS 11-26
www.garfield.com
© 2007 PAWS, INC. All Rights Reserved.
IT SMELLS LIKE CHRISTMAS COOKIES BAKING
PSSSSST
Distributed by Universal Press Syndicate
I THINK I'M GETTING THE HINT HERE
ISN'T HE THE CLEVER ONE?

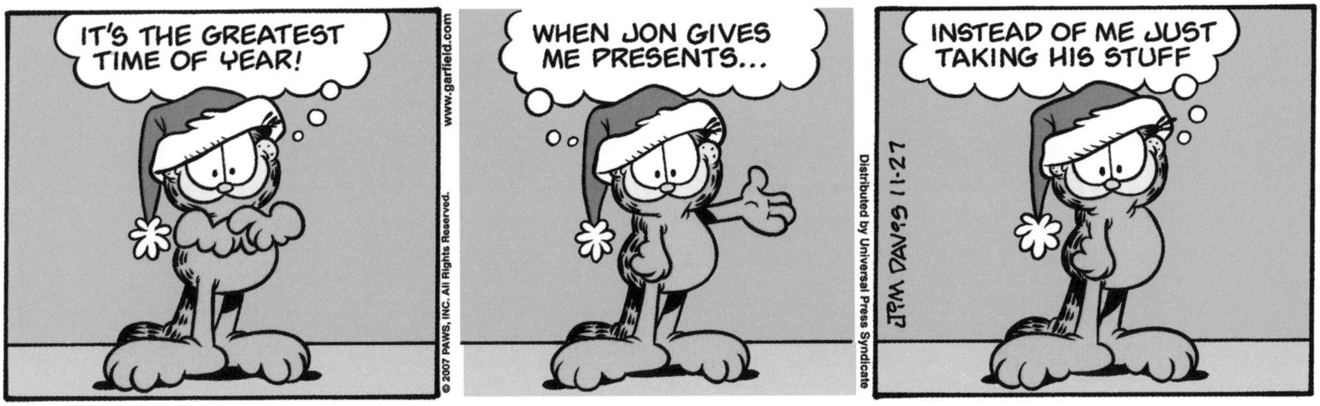
IT'S THE GREATEST TIME OF YEAR!
www.garfield.com
© 2007 PAWS, INC. All Rights Reserved.
WHEN JON GIVES ME PRESENTS...
Distributed by Universal Press Syndicate
JPM DAVIS 11-27
INSTEAD OF ME JUST TAKING HIS STUFF

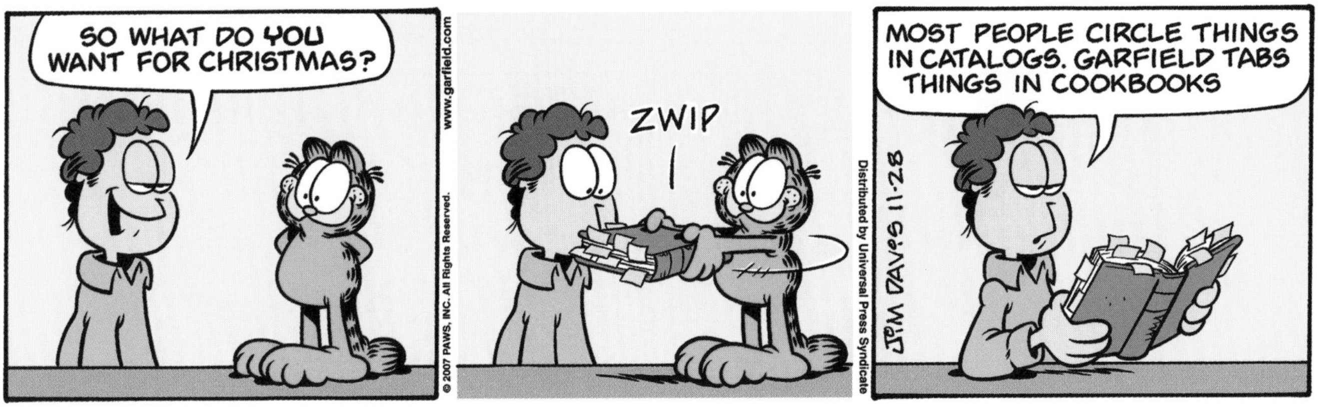
SO WHAT DO YOU WANT FOR CHRISTMAS?
www.garfield.com
© 2007 PAWS, INC. All Rights Reserved.
ZWIP
Distributed by Universal Press Syndicate
JPM DAVIS 11-28
MOST PEOPLE CIRCLE THINGS IN CATALOGS. GARFIELD TABS THINGS IN COOKBOOKS

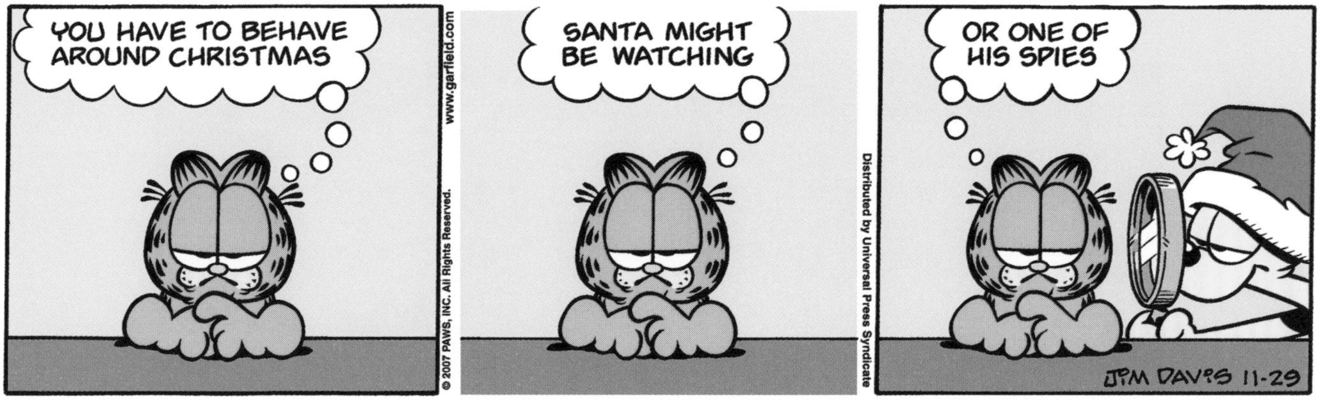
YOU HAVE TO BEHAVE AROUND CHRISTMAS
SANTA MIGHT BE WATCHING
OR ONE OF HIS SPIES
JIM DAVIS 11-29
© 2007 PAWS, INC. All Rights Reserved. www.garfield.com
Distributed by Universal Press Syndicate

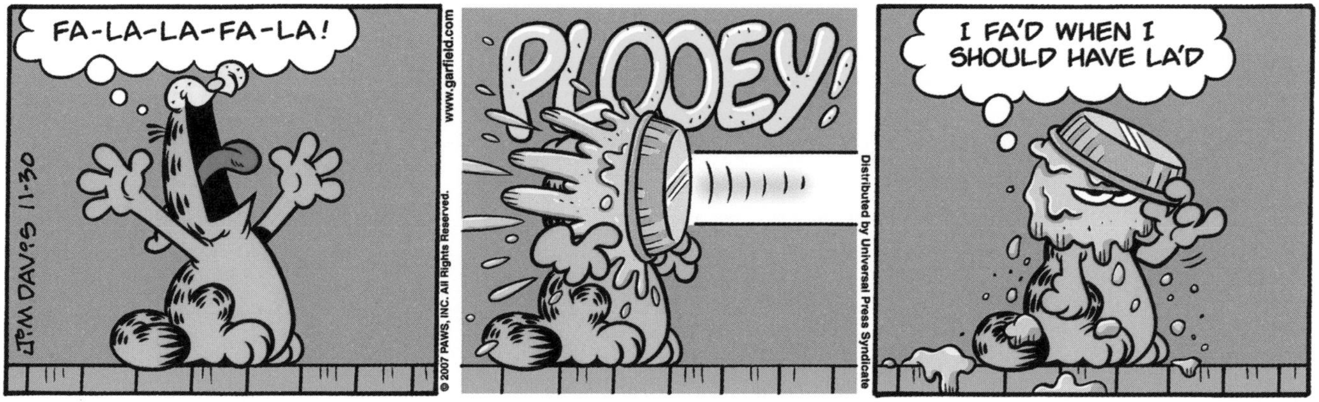
FA-LA-LA-FA-LA!
JIM DAVIS 11-30
PLOOEY!
I FA'D WHEN I SHOULD HAVE LA'D
© 2007 PAWS, INC. All Rights Reserved. www.garfield.com
Distributed by Universal Press Syndicate

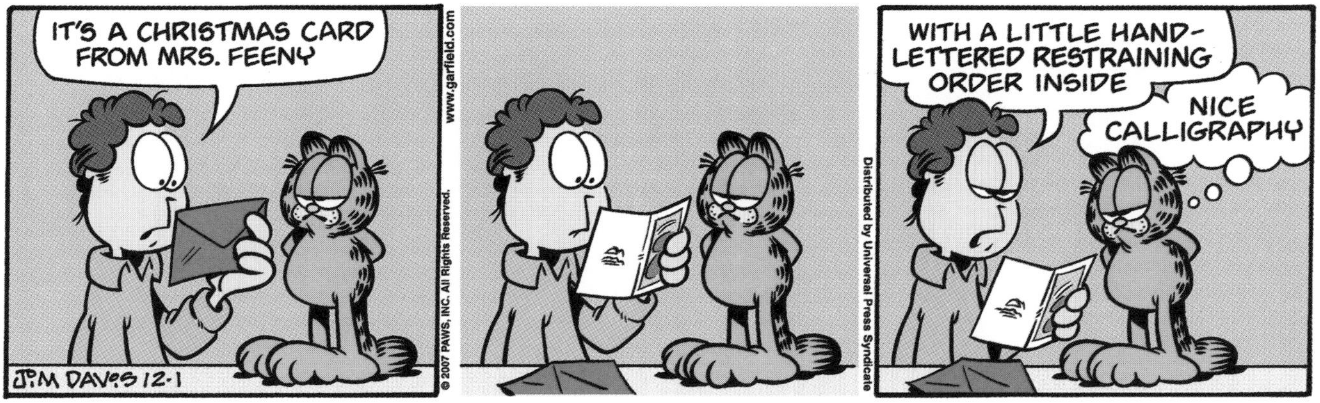
IT'S A CHRISTMAS CARD FROM MRS. FEENY
JIM DAVIS 12-1
WITH A LITTLE HAND-LETTERED RESTRAINING ORDER INSIDE
NICE CALLIGRAPHY
© 2007 PAWS, INC. All Rights Reserved. www.garfield.com
Distributed by Universal Press Syndicate

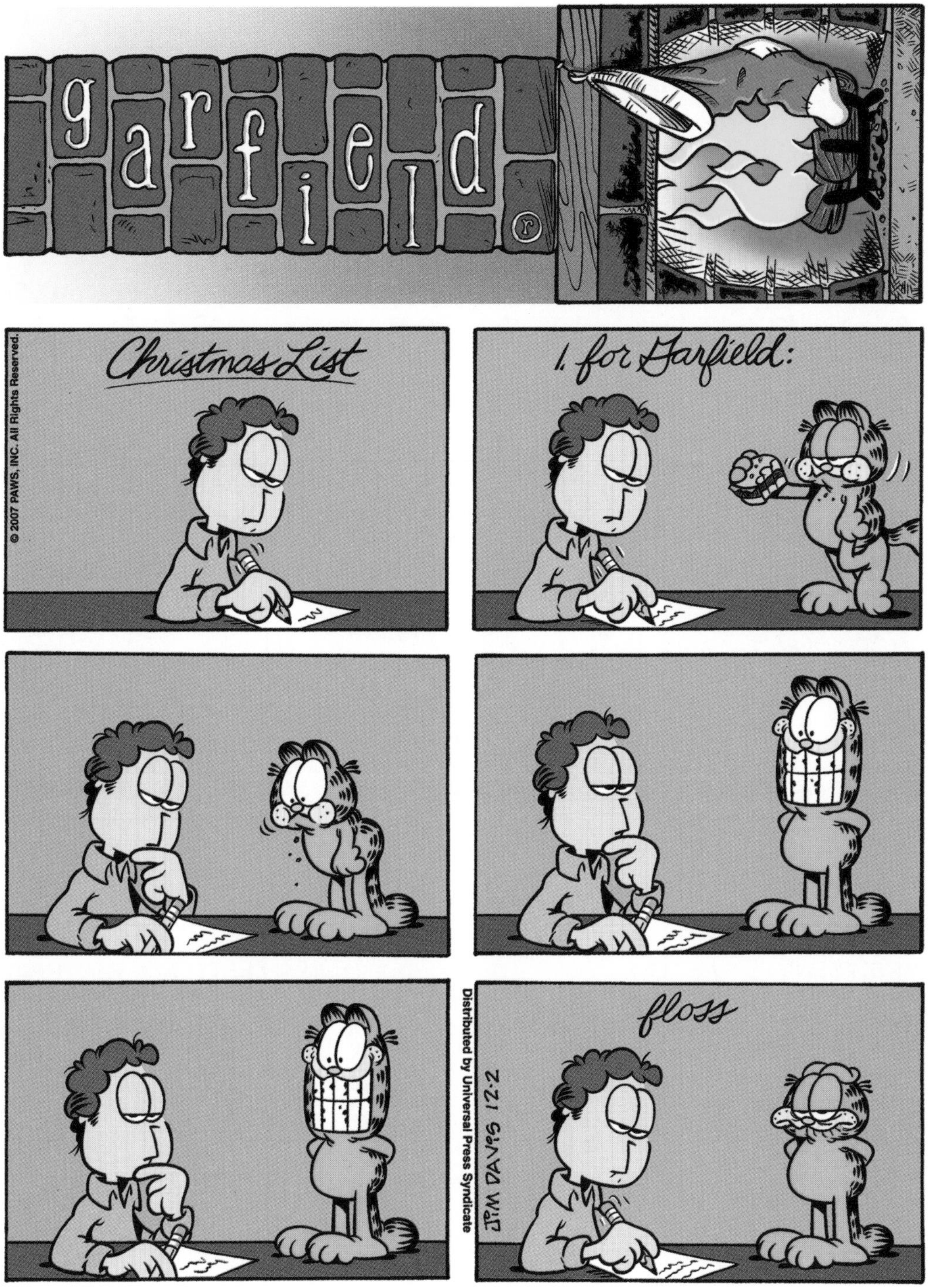
garfield®
Christmas List
© 2007 PAWS, INC. All Rights Reserved.
1. for Garfield:
Distributed by Universal Press Syndicate
JPM DAVPS 12·2
floss

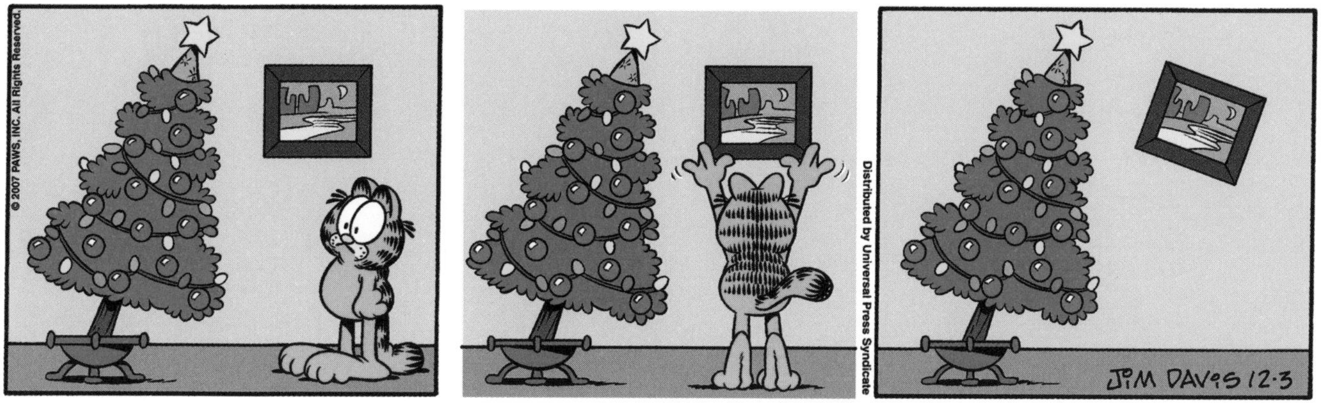
© 2007 PAWS, INC. All Rights Reserved.
Distributed by Universal Press Syndicate
JIM DAVIS 12-3

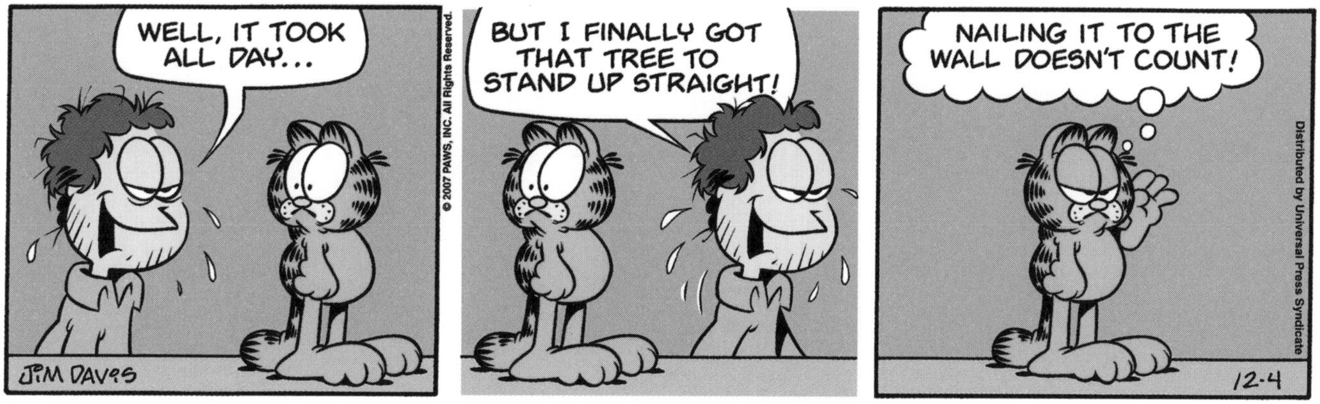
WELL, IT TOOK ALL DAY...
JIM DAVIS
© 2007 PAWS, INC. All Rights Reserved.
BUT I FINALLY GOT THAT TREE TO STAND UP STRAIGHT!
NAILING IT TO THE WALL DOESN'T COUNT!
Distributed by Universal Press Syndicate
12-4

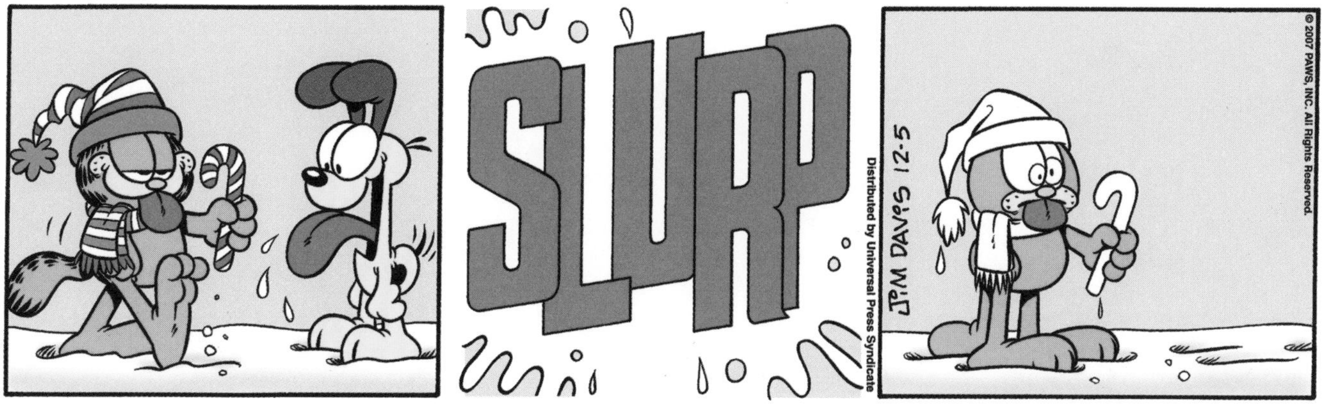
SLURP
Distributed by Universal Press Syndicate
JIM DAVIS 12-5
© 2007 PAWS, INC. All Rights Reserved.

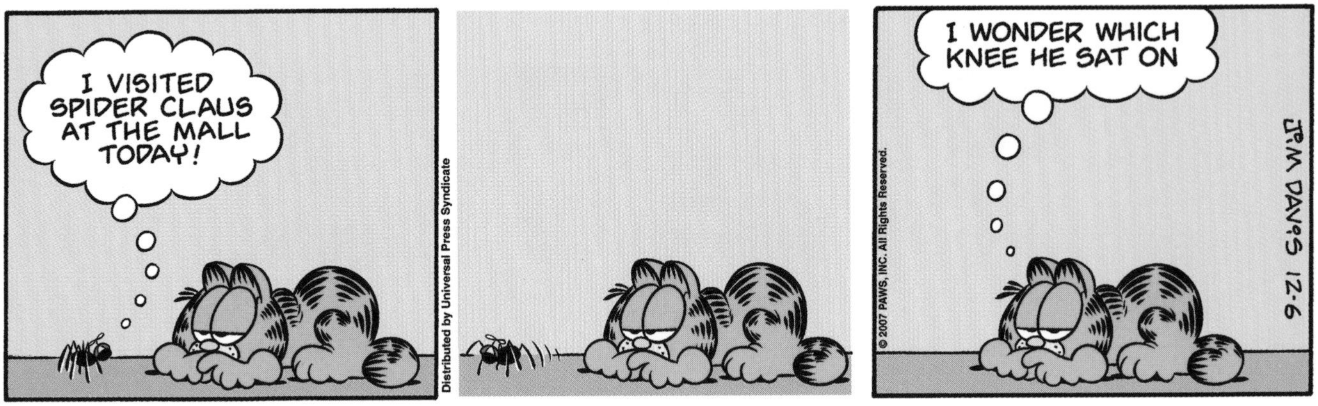
I VISITED SPIDER CLAUS AT THE MALL TODAY!
I WONDER WHICH KNEE HE SAT ON
JIM DAVIS 12-6
Distributed by Universal Press Syndicate
© 2007 PAWS, INC. All Rights Reserved.

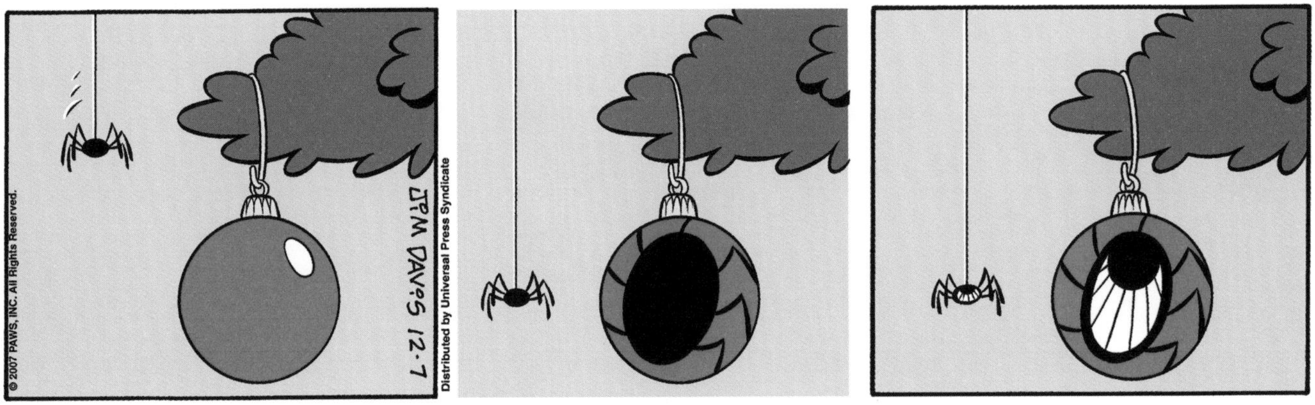
JIM DAVIS 12-7
© 2007 PAWS, INC. All Rights Reserved.
Distributed by Universal Press Syndicate

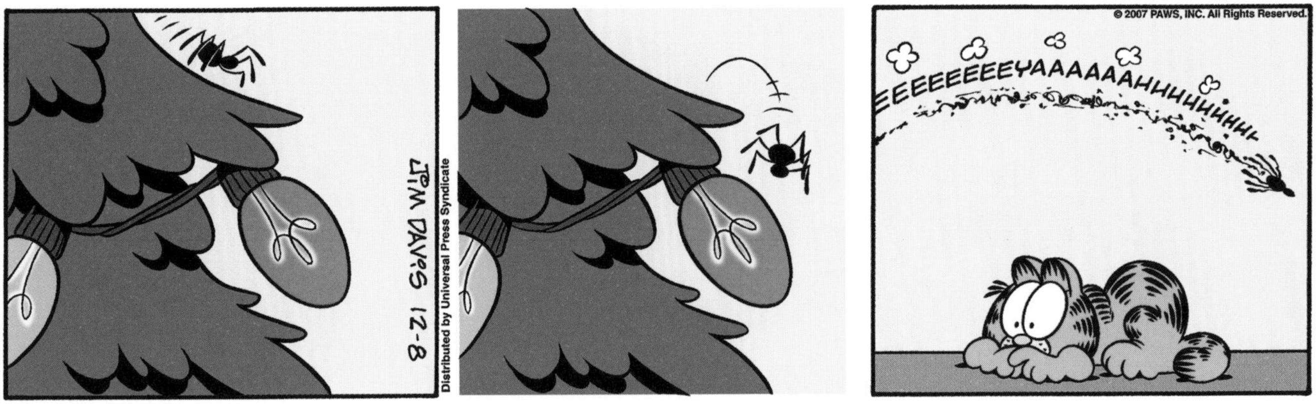
JIM DAVIS 12-8
Distributed by Universal Press Syndicate
© 2007 PAWS, INC. All Rights Reserved.
EEEEEEEEYAAAAAAHHHHHHHH!

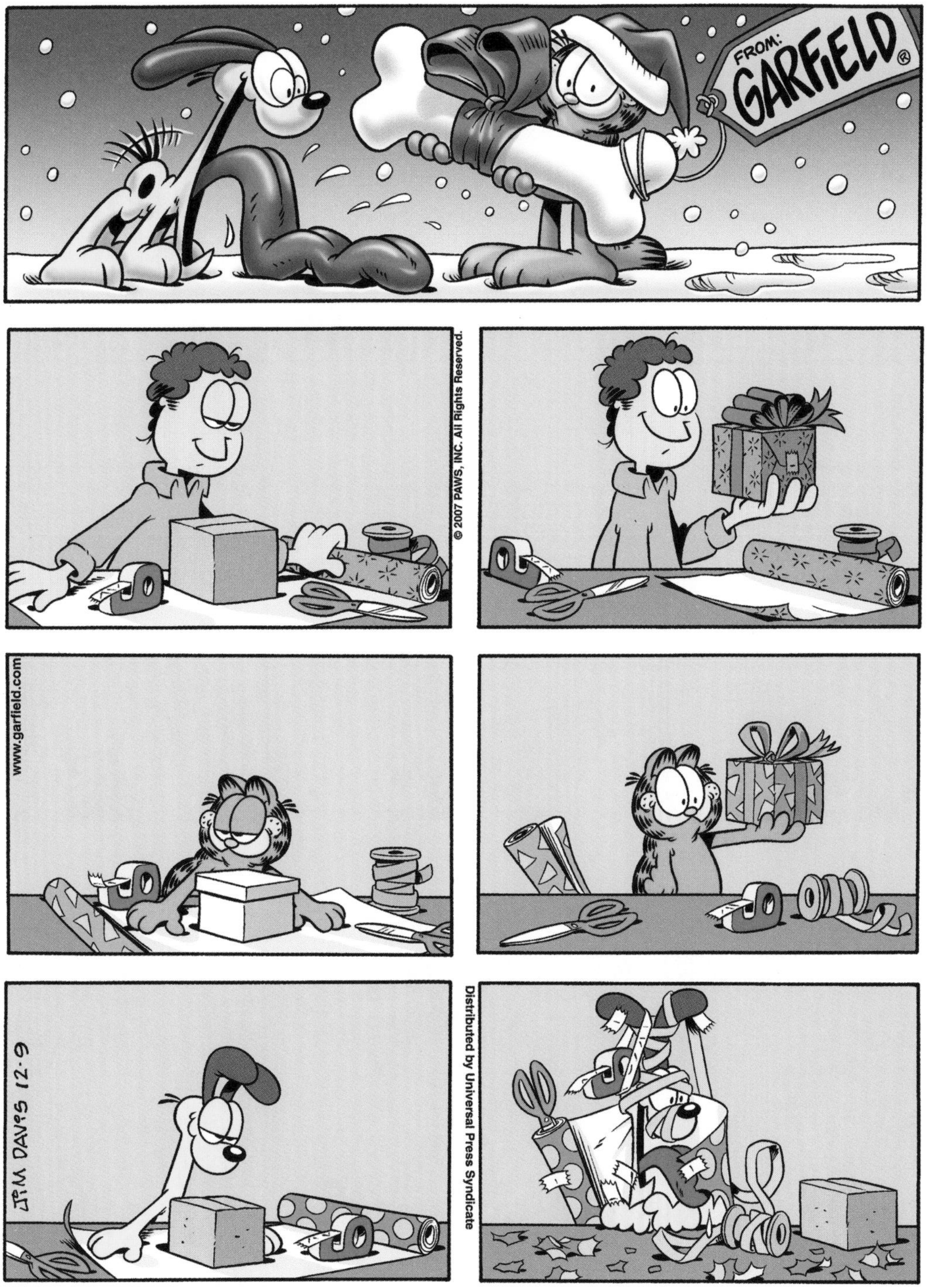
FROM:
GARFIELD®
© 2007 PAWS, INC. All Rights Reserved.
www.garfield.com
JIM DAVIS 12-9
Distributed by Universal Press Syndicate

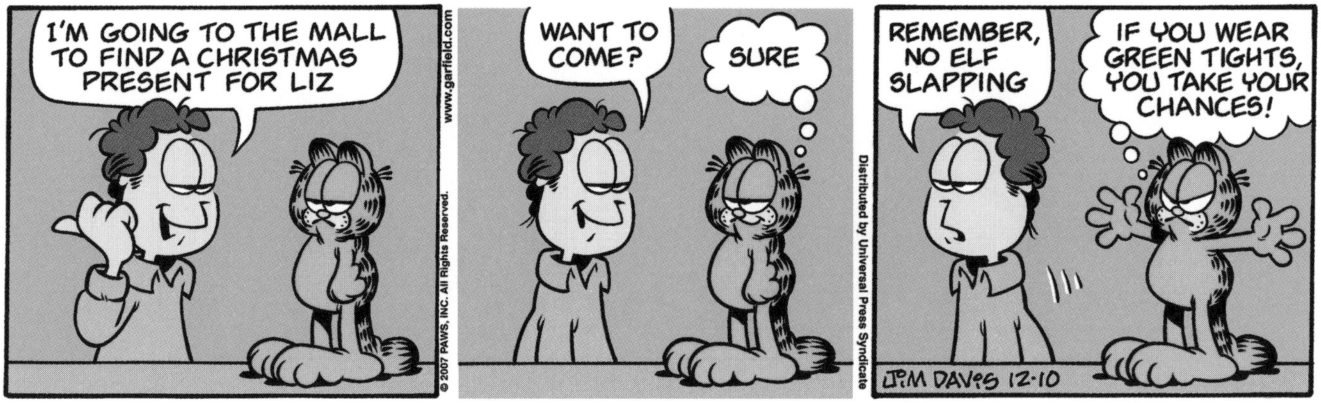
I'M GOING TO THE MALL TO FIND A CHRISTMAS PRESENT FOR LIZ
WANT TO COME?
SURE
REMEMBER, NO ELF SLAPPING
IF YOU WEAR GREEN TIGHTS, YOU TAKE YOUR CHANCES!
JIM DAVIS 12-10
www.garfield.com
© 2007 PAWS, INC. All Rights Reserved.
Distributed by Universal Press Syndicate

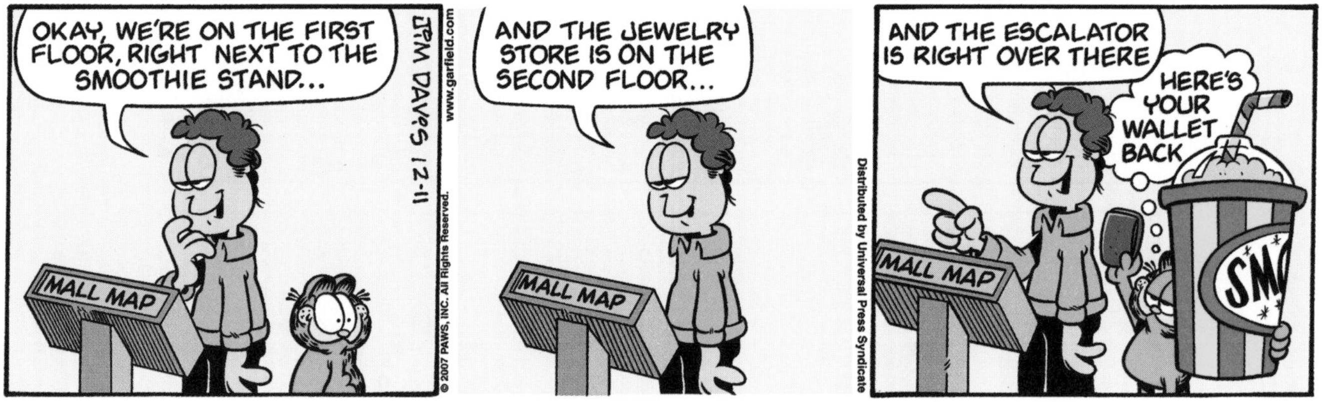
OKAY, WE'RE ON THE FIRST FLOOR, RIGHT NEXT TO THE SMOOTHIE STAND...
MALL MAP
AND THE JEWELRY STORE IS ON THE SECOND FLOOR...
MALL MAP
AND THE ESCALATOR IS RIGHT OVER THERE
HERE'S YOUR WALLET BACK
MALL MAP
JIM DAVIS 12-11
www.garfield.com
© 2007 PAWS, INC. All Rights Reserved.
Distributed by Universal Press Syndicate

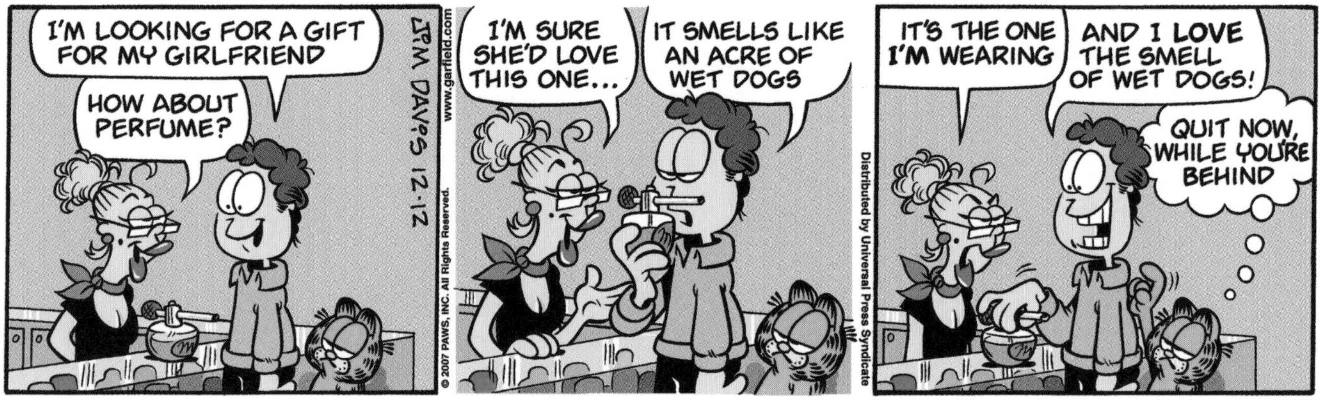
I'M LOOKING FOR A GIFT FOR MY GIRLFRIEND
HOW ABOUT PERFUME?
I'M SURE SHE'D LOVE THIS ONE...
IT SMELLS LIKE AN ACRE OF WET DOGS
IT'S THE ONE I'M WEARING
AND I LOVE THE SMELL OF WET DOGS!
QUIT NOW, WHILE YOU'RE BEHIND
JIM DAVIS 12-12
www.garfield.com
© 2007 PAWS, INC. All Rights Reserved.
Distributed by Universal Press Syndicate

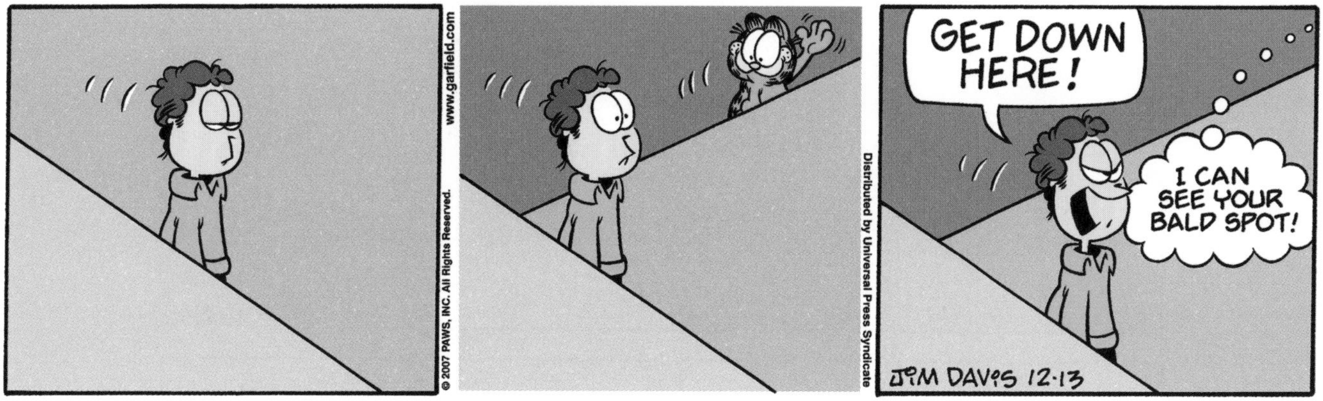
GET DOWN HERE!
I CAN SEE YOUR BALD SPOT!
JIM DAVIS 12-13
© 2007 PAWS, INC. All Rights Reserved.
www.garfield.com
Distributed by Universal Press Syndicate

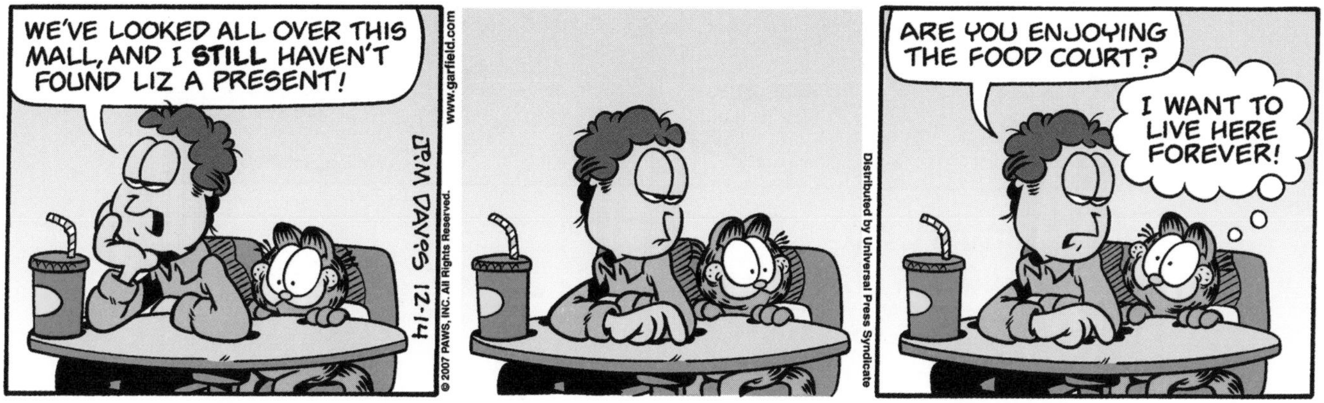
WE'VE LOOKED ALL OVER THIS MALL, AND I STILL HAVEN'T FOUND LIZ A PRESENT!
ARE YOU ENJOYING THE FOOD COURT?
I WANT TO LIVE HERE FOREVER!
JIM DAVIS 12-14
© 2007 PAWS, INC. All Rights Reserved.
www.garfield.com
Distributed by Universal Press Syndicate

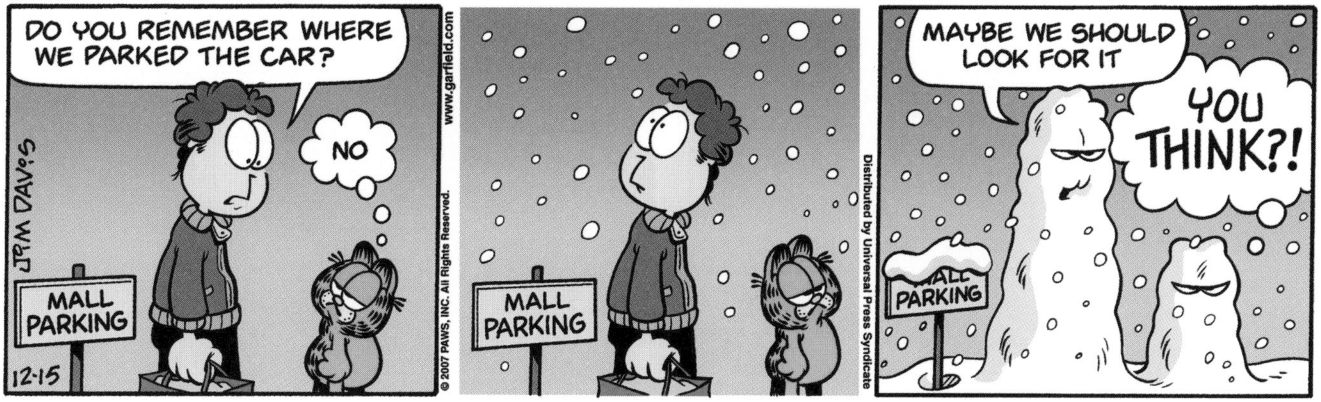
DO YOU REMEMBER WHERE WE PARKED THE CAR?
NO
MALL PARKING
MALL PARKING
MAYBE WE SHOULD LOOK FOR IT
YOU THINK?!
PARKING
JIM DAVIS 12-15
© 2007 PAWS, INC. All Rights Reserved.
www.garfield.com
Distributed by Universal Press Syndicate

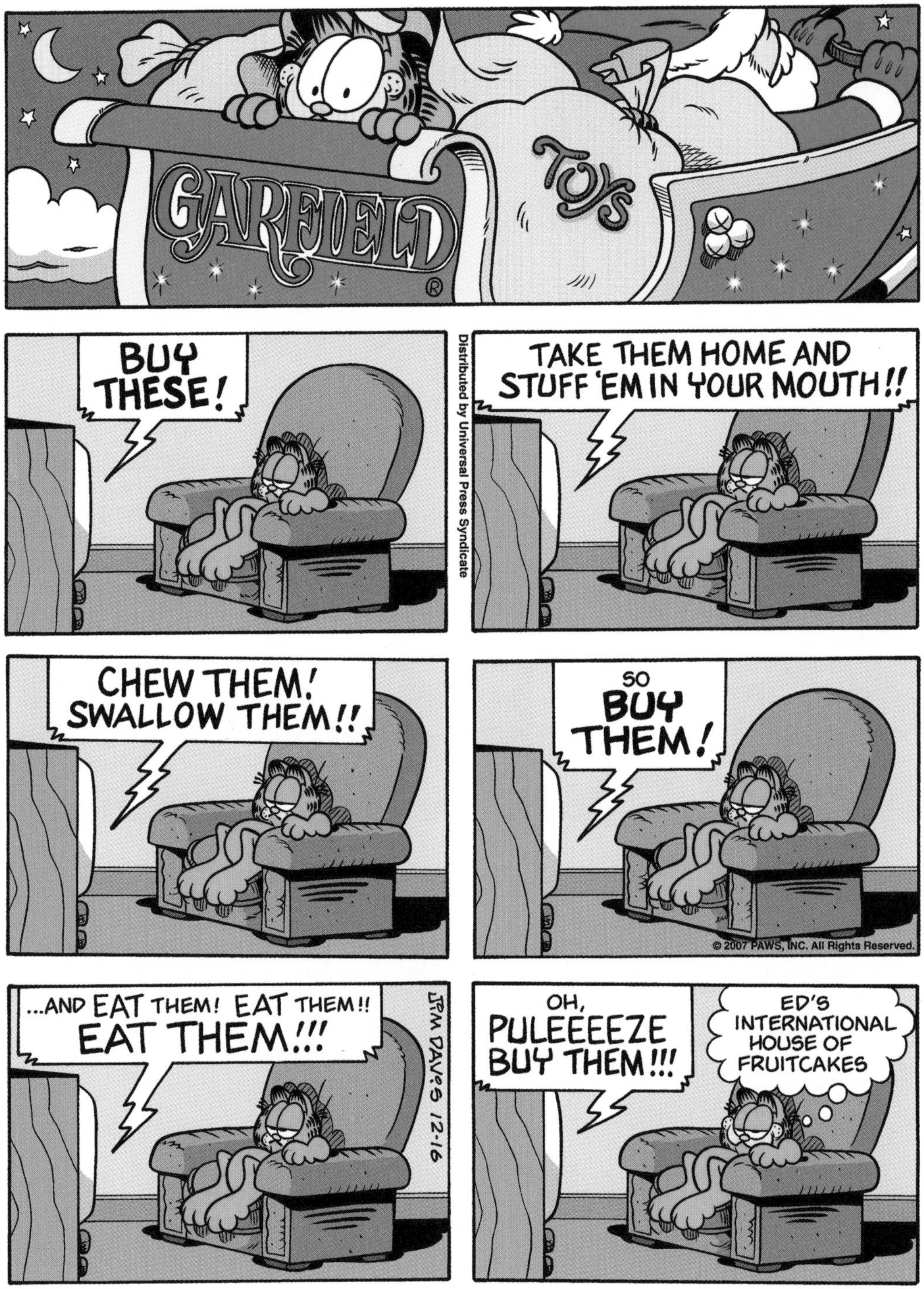
GARFIELD
TOYS
Distributed by Universal Press Syndicate
BUY THESE!
TAKE THEM HOME AND STUFF 'EM IN YOUR MOUTH!!
CHEW THEM! SWALLOW THEM!!
SO BUY THEM!
© 2007 PAWS, INC. All Rights Reserved.
...AND EAT THEM! EAT THEM!! EAT THEM!!!
JIM DAVIS 12-16
OH, PULEEEEZE BUY THEM!!!
ED'S INTERNATIONAL HOUSE OF FRUITCAKES

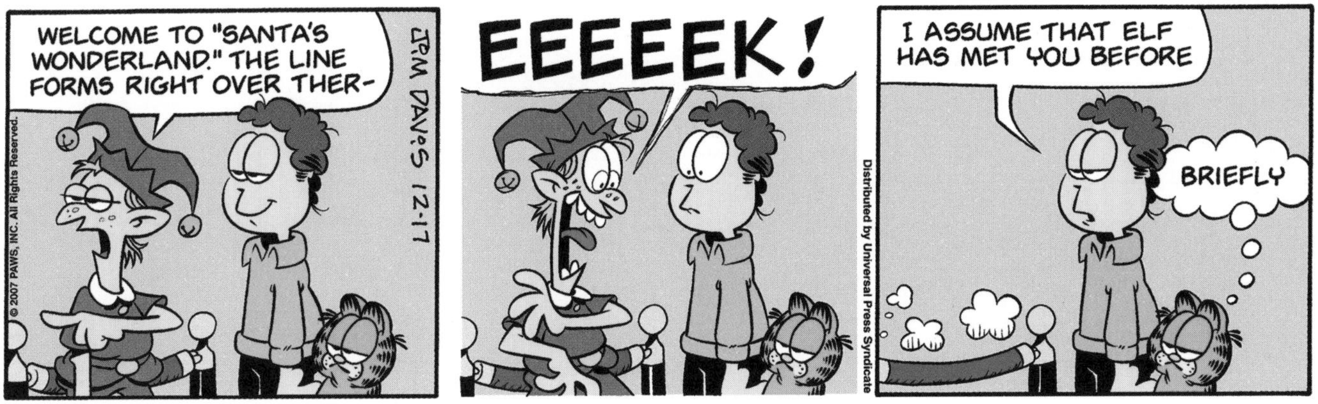
WELCOME TO "SANTA'S WONDERLAND." THE LINE FORMS RIGHT OVER THER-
JIM DAVIS 12-17
© 2007 PAWS, INC. All Rights Reserved.
EEEEEK!
I ASSUME THAT ELF HAS MET YOU BEFORE
BRIEFLY
Distributed by Universal Press Syndicate

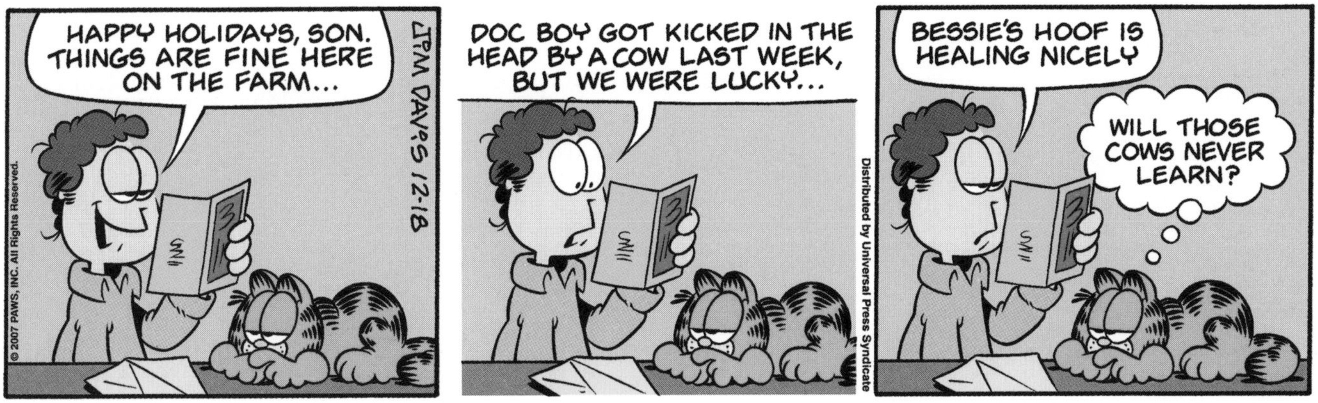
HAPPY HOLIDAYS, SON. THINGS ARE FINE HERE ON THE FARM...
JIM DAVIS 12-18
© 2007 PAWS, INC. All Rights Reserved.
DOC BOY GOT KICKED IN THE HEAD BY A COW LAST WEEK, BUT WE WERE LUCKY...
BESSIE'S HOOF IS HEALING NICELY
WILL THOSE COWS NEVER LEARN?
Distributed by Universal Press Syndicate

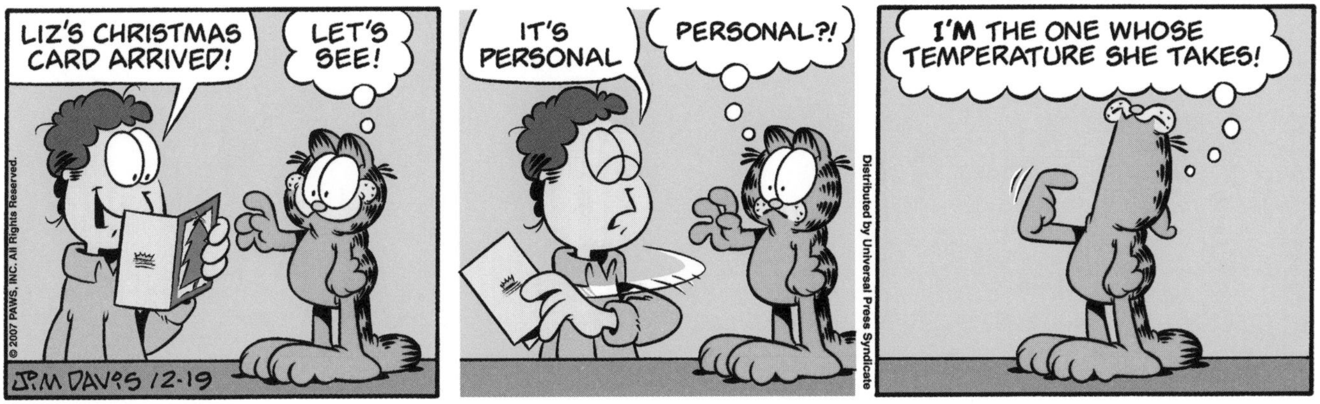
LIZ'S CHRISTMAS CARD ARRIVED!
LET'S SEE!
© 2007 PAWS, INC. All Rights Reserved.
JIM DAVIS 12-19
IT'S PERSONAL
PERSONAL?!
I'M THE ONE WHOSE TEMPERATURE SHE TAKES!
Distributed by Universal Press Syndicate

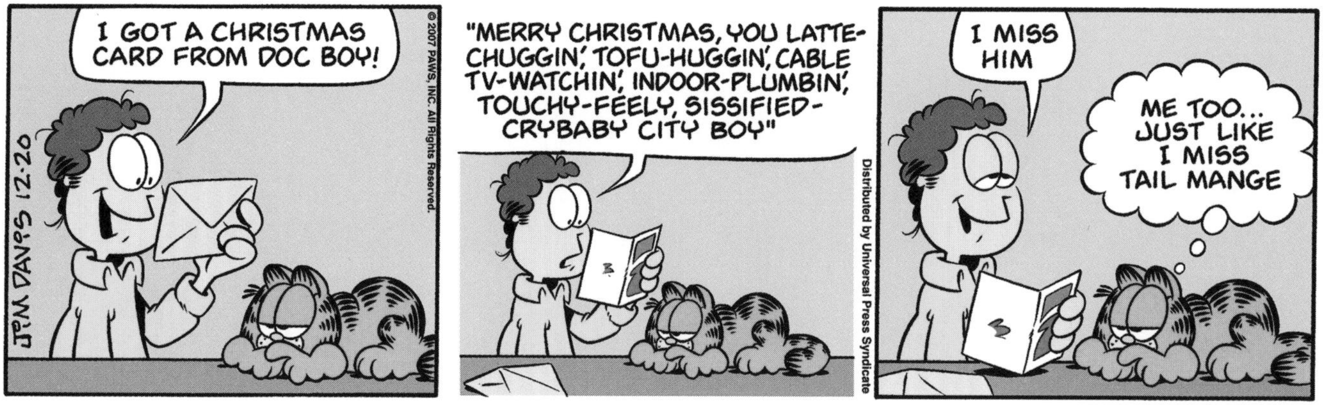
JIM DAVIS 12-20
© 2007 PAWS, INC. All Rights Reserved.
I GOT A CHRISTMAS CARD FROM DOC BOY!
"MERRY CHRISTMAS, YOU LATTE-CHUGGIN', TOFU-HUGGIN', CABLE TV-WATCHIN', INDOOR-PLUMBIN', TOUCHY-FEELY, SISSIFIED-CRYBABY CITY BOY"
Distributed by Universal Press Syndicate
I MISS HIM
ME TOO... JUST LIKE I MISS TAIL MANGE

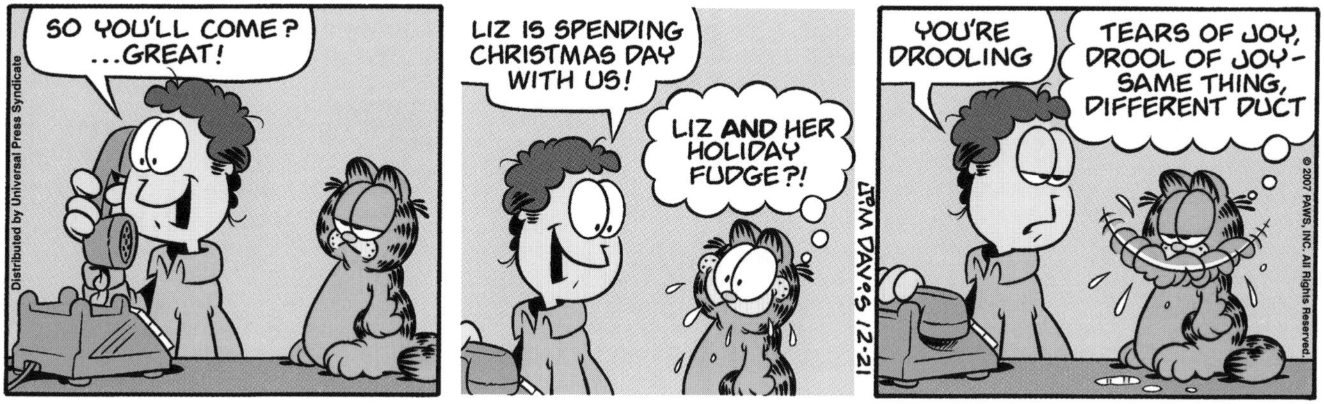
Distributed by Universal Press Syndicate
SO YOU'LL COME? ...GREAT!
LIZ IS SPENDING CHRISTMAS DAY WITH US!
LIZ AND HER HOLIDAY FUDGE?!
JIM DAVIS 12-21
YOU'RE DROOLING
TEARS OF JOY, DROOL OF JOY-SAME THING, DIFFERENT DUCT
© 2007 PAWS, INC. All Rights Reserved.

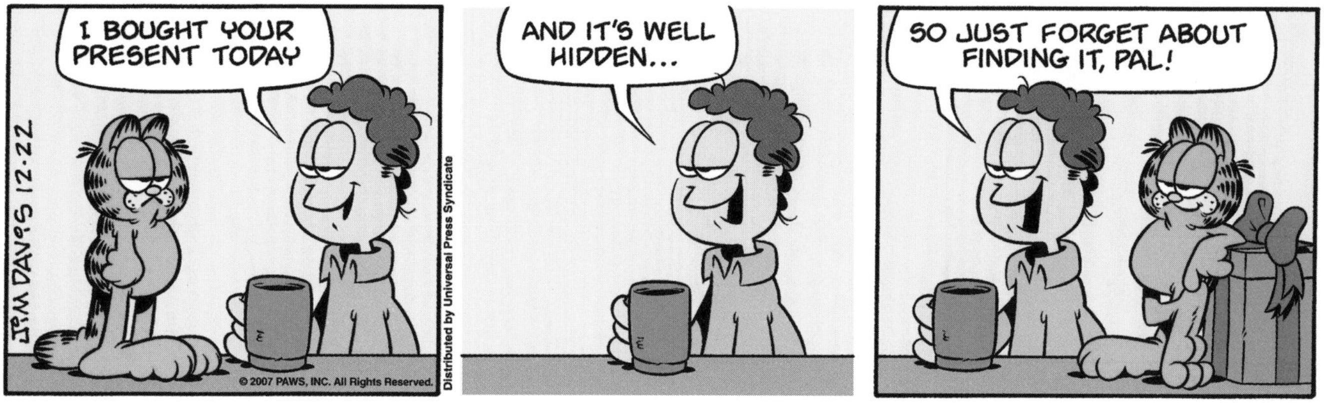
JIM DAVIS 12-22
I BOUGHT YOUR PRESENT TODAY
© 2007 PAWS, INC. All Rights Reserved.
Distributed by Universal Press Syndicate
AND IT'S WELL HIDDEN...
SO JUST FORGET ABOUT FINDING IT, PAL!

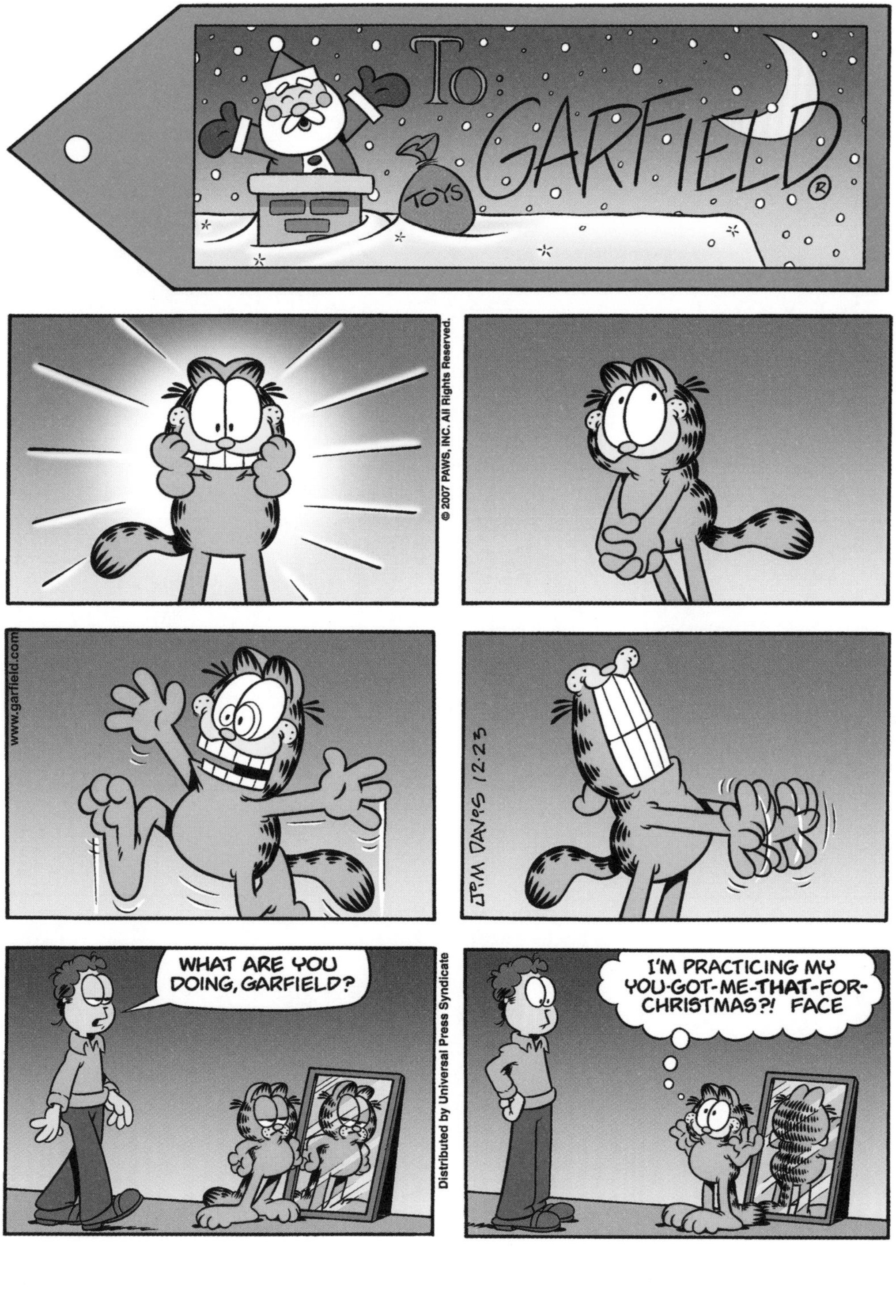
TO GARFIELD
TOYS
© 2007 PAWS, INC. All Rights Reserved.
www.garfield.com
JPM DAVIS 12-23
Distributed by Universal Press Syndicate
WHAT ARE YOU DOING, GARFIELD?
I'M PRACTICING MY YOU-GOT-ME-THAT-FOR-CHRISTMAS?! FACE

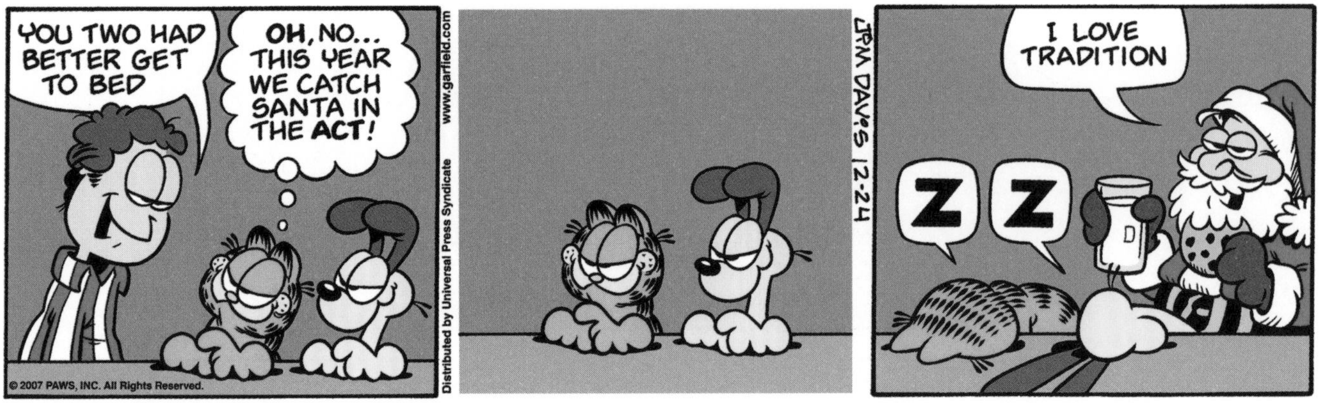
YOU TWO HAD BETTER GET TO BED
OH, NO... THIS YEAR WE CATCH SANTA IN THE ACT!
I LOVE TRADITION
Z
Z
© 2007 PAWS, INC. All Rights Reserved.
Distributed by Universal Press Syndicate
www.garfield.com
JIM DAVIS 12-24

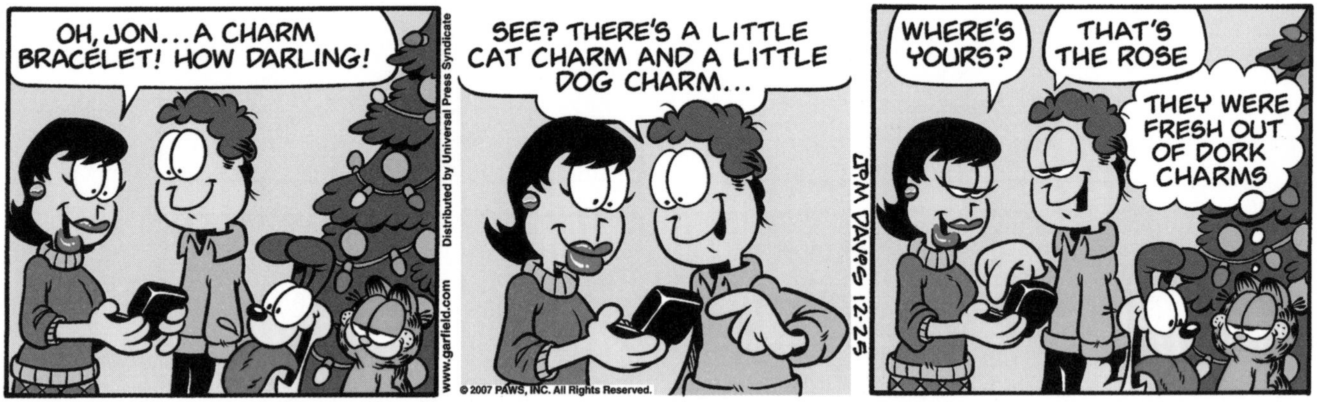
OH, JON... A CHARM BRACELET! HOW DARLING!
SEE? THERE'S A LITTLE CAT CHARM AND A LITTLE DOG CHARM...
WHERE'S YOURS?
THAT'S THE ROSE
THEY WERE FRESH OUT OF DORK CHARMS
www.garfield.com
Distributed by Universal Press Syndicate
© 2007 PAWS, INC. All Rights Reserved.
JIM DAVIS 12-25

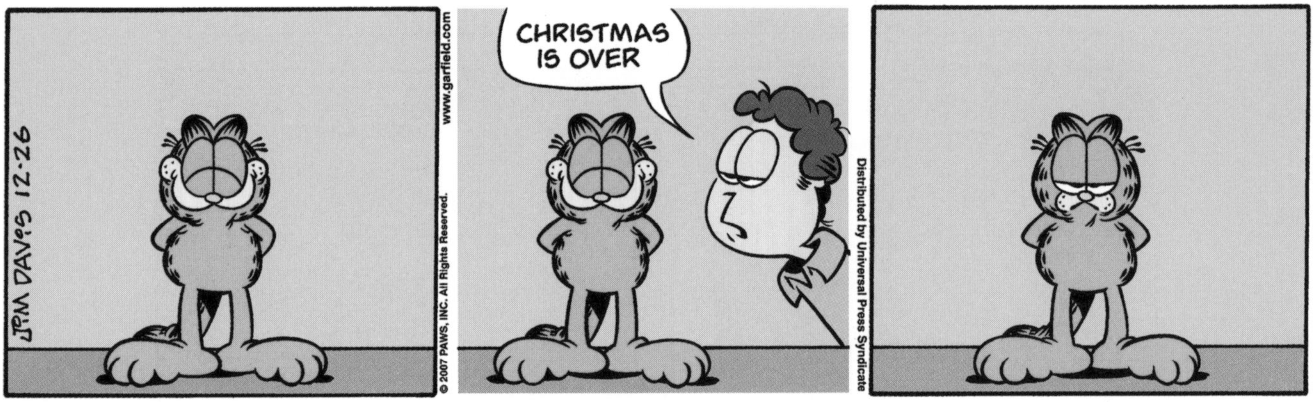
JIM DAVIS 12-26
© 2007 PAWS, INC. All Rights Reserved.
www.garfield.com
CHRISTMAS IS OVER
Distributed by Universal Press Syndicate

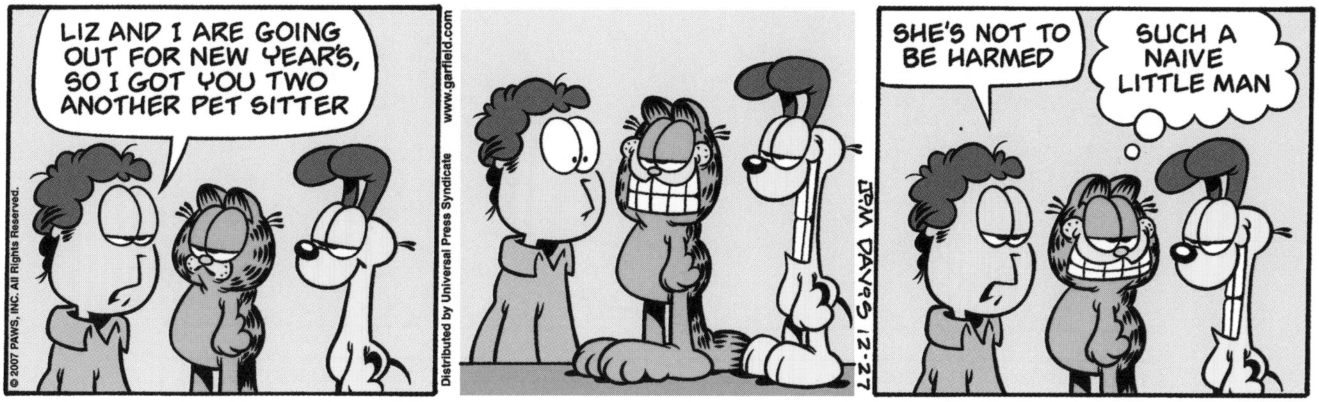
LIZ AND I ARE GOING OUT FOR NEW YEAR'S, SO I GOT YOU TWO ANOTHER PET SITTER
© 2007 PAWS, INC. All Rights Reserved.
Distributed by Universal Press Syndicate www.garfield.com
JIM DAVIS 12-27
SHE'S NOT TO BE HARMED
SUCH A NAIVE LITTLE MAN

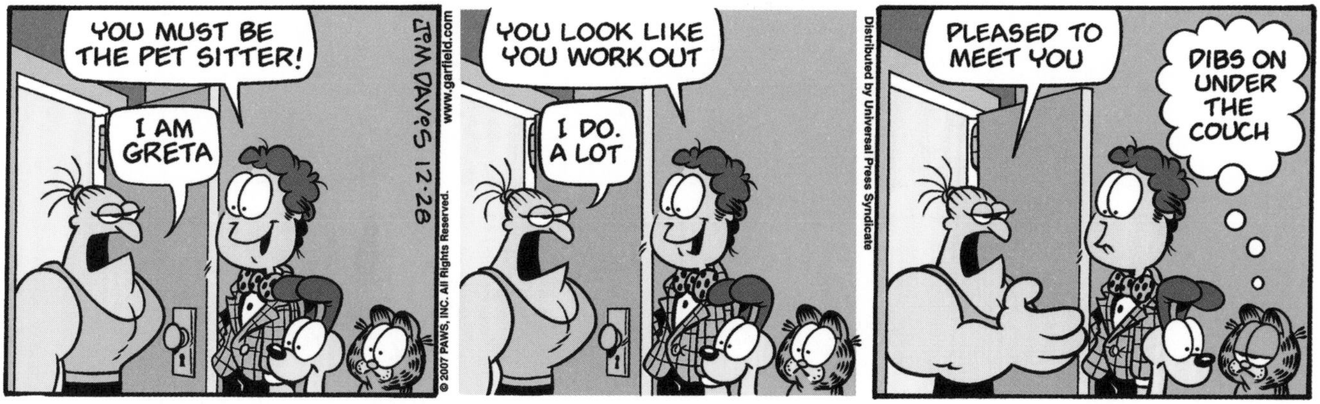
YOU MUST BE THE PET SITTER!
I AM GRETA
JIM DAVIS 12-28
www.garfield.com
© 2007 PAWS, INC. All Rights Reserved.
YOU LOOK LIKE YOU WORK OUT
I DO. A LOT
Distributed by Universal Press Syndicate
PLEASED TO MEET YOU
DIBS ON UNDER THE COUCH

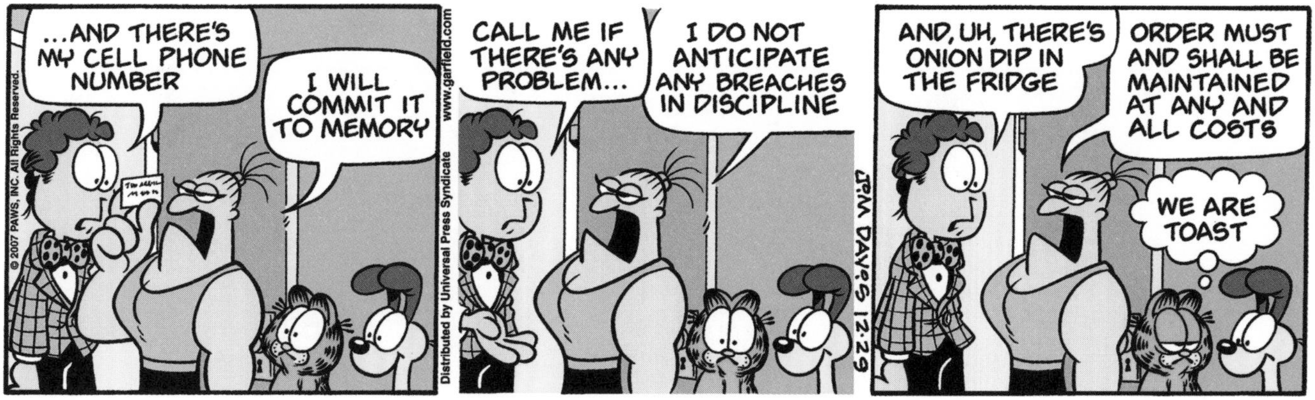
...AND THERE'S MY CELL PHONE NUMBER
I WILL COMMIT IT TO MEMORY
© 2007 PAWS, INC. All Rights Reserved.
Distributed by Universal Press Syndicate www.garfield.com
CALL ME IF THERE'S ANY PROBLEM...
I DO NOT ANTICIPATE ANY BREACHES IN DISCIPLINE
JIM DAVIS 12-29
AND, UH, THERE'S ONION DIP IN THE FRIDGE
ORDER MUST AND SHALL BE MAINTAINED AT ANY AND ALL COSTS
WE ARE TOAST

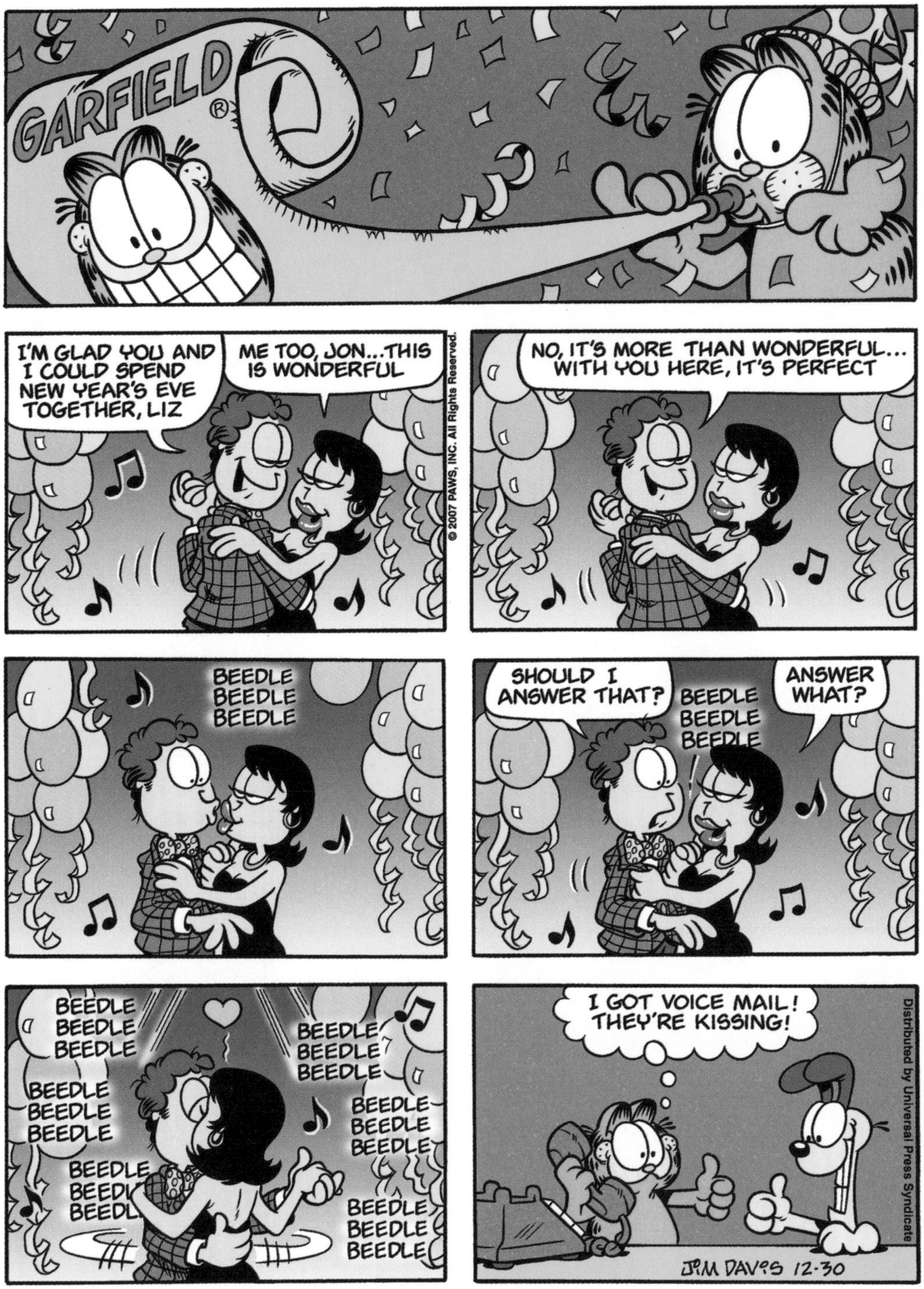
GARFIELD®
I'M GLAD YOU AND I COULD SPEND NEW YEAR'S EVE TOGETHER, LIZ
ME TOO, JON...THIS IS WONDERFUL
© 2007 PAWS, INC. All Rights Reserved.
NO, IT'S MORE THAN WONDERFUL... WITH YOU HERE, IT'S PERFECT
BEEDLE BEEDLE BEEDLE
SHOULD I ANSWER THAT?
BEEDLE BEEDLE BEEDLE
ANSWER WHAT?
BEEDLE BEEDLE BEEDLE
BEEDLE BEEDLE BEEDLE
BEEDLE BEEDLE BEEDLE
BEEDLE BEEDLE BEEDLE
BEEDLE BEEDLE BEEDLE
I GOT VOICE MAIL! THEY'RE KISSING!
Distributed by Universal Press Syndicate
JIM DAVIS 12-30

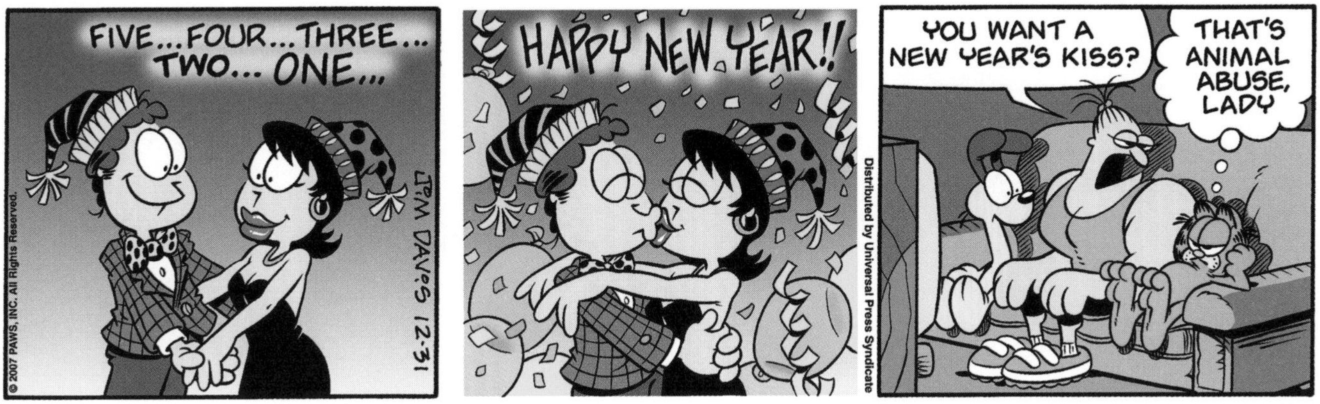
FIVE... FOUR... THREE... TWO... ONE...
JIM DAVIS 12-31
© 2007 PAWS, INC. All Rights Reserved.
HAPPY NEW YEAR!!
Distributed by Universal Press Syndicate
YOU WANT A NEW YEAR'S KISS?
THAT'S ANIMAL ABUSE, LADY

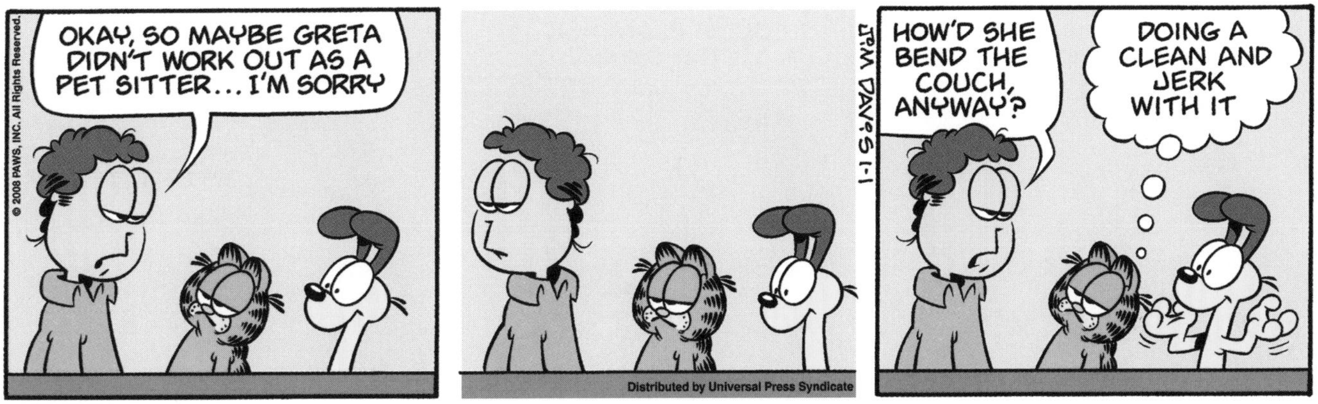
© 2008 PAWS, INC. All Rights Reserved.
OKAY, SO MAYBE GRETA DIDN'T WORK OUT AS A PET SITTER... I'M SORRY
Distributed by Universal Press Syndicate
JIM DAVIS 1-1
HOW'D SHE BEND THE COUCH, ANYWAY?
DOING A CLEAN AND JERK WITH IT

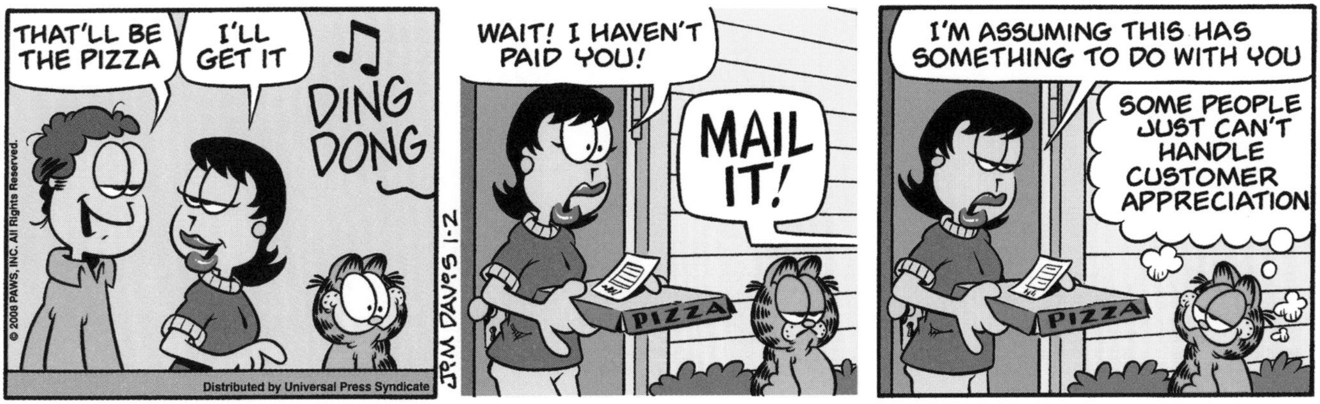
© 2008 PAWS, INC. All Rights Reserved.
THAT'LL BE THE PIZZA
I'LL GET IT
DING DONG
Distributed by Universal Press Syndicate
JIM DAVIS 1-2
WAIT! I HAVEN'T PAID YOU!
MAIL IT!
PIZZA
I'M ASSUMING THIS HAS SOMETHING TO DO WITH YOU
SOME PEOPLE JUST CAN'T HANDLE CUSTOMER APPRECIATION
PIZZA

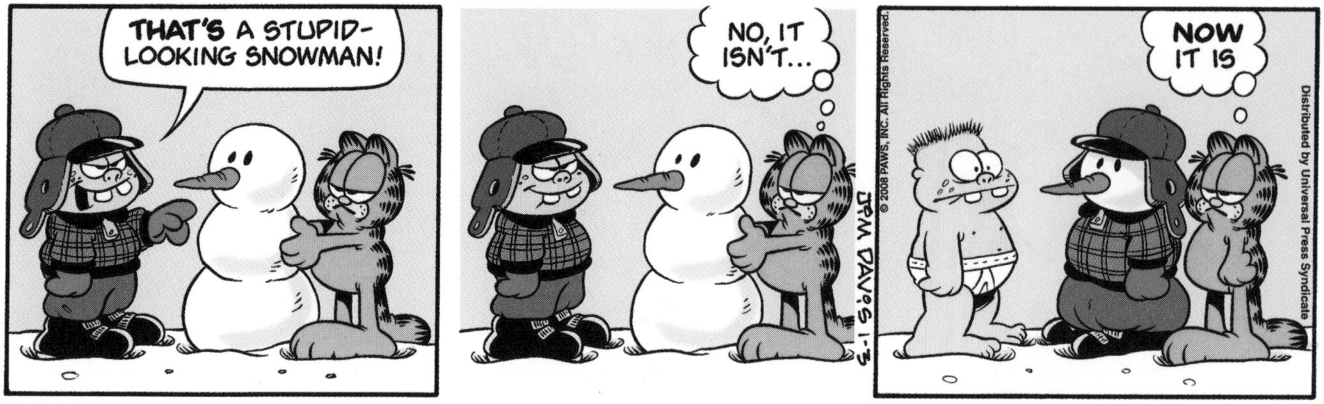
THAT'S A STUPID-LOOKING SNOWMAN!
NO, IT ISN'T...
NOW IT IS
JPM DAVPS 1-3
© 2008 PAWS, INC. All Rights Reserved.
Distributed by Universal Press Syndicate

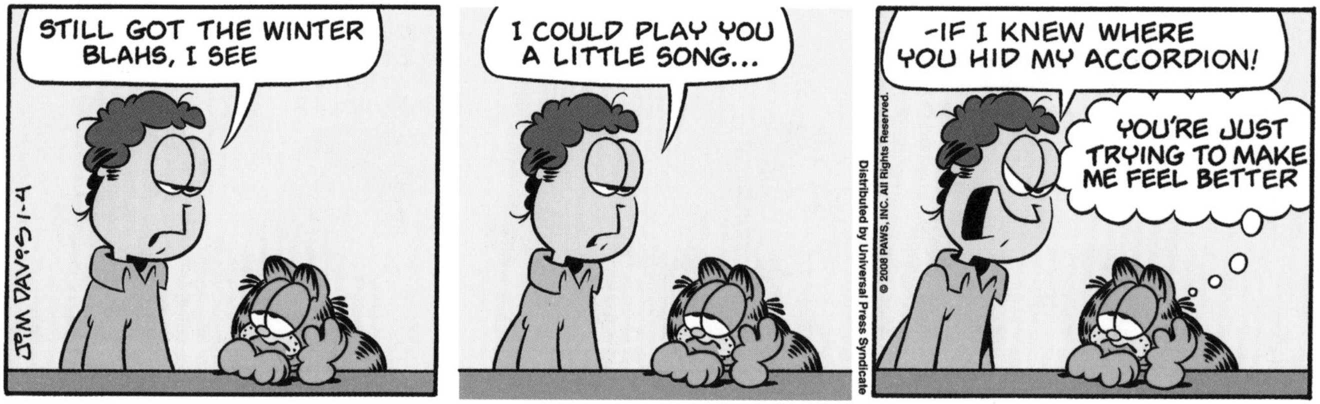
STILL GOT THE WINTER BLAHS, I SEE
I COULD PLAY YOU A LITTLE SONG...
-IF I KNEW WHERE YOU HID MY ACCORDION!
YOU'RE JUST TRYING TO MAKE ME FEEL BETTER
JPM DAVPS 1-4
© 2008 PAWS, INC. All Rights Reserved.
Distributed by Universal Press Syndicate

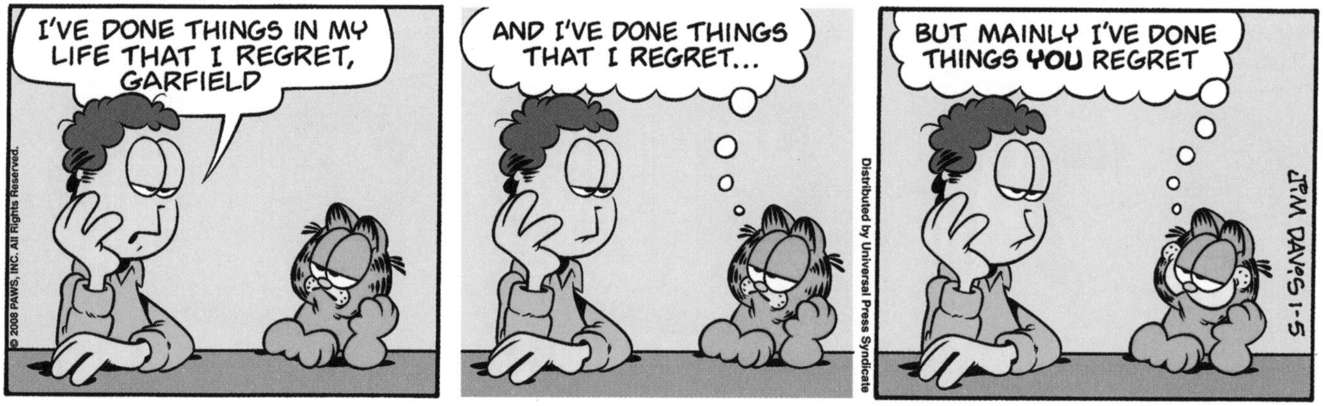
I'VE DONE THINGS IN MY LIFE THAT I REGRET, GARFIELD
AND I'VE DONE THINGS THAT I REGRET...
BUT MAINLY I'VE DONE THINGS YOU REGRET
JPM DAVPS 1-5
© 2008 PAWS, INC. All Rights Reserved.
Distributed by Universal Press Syndicate

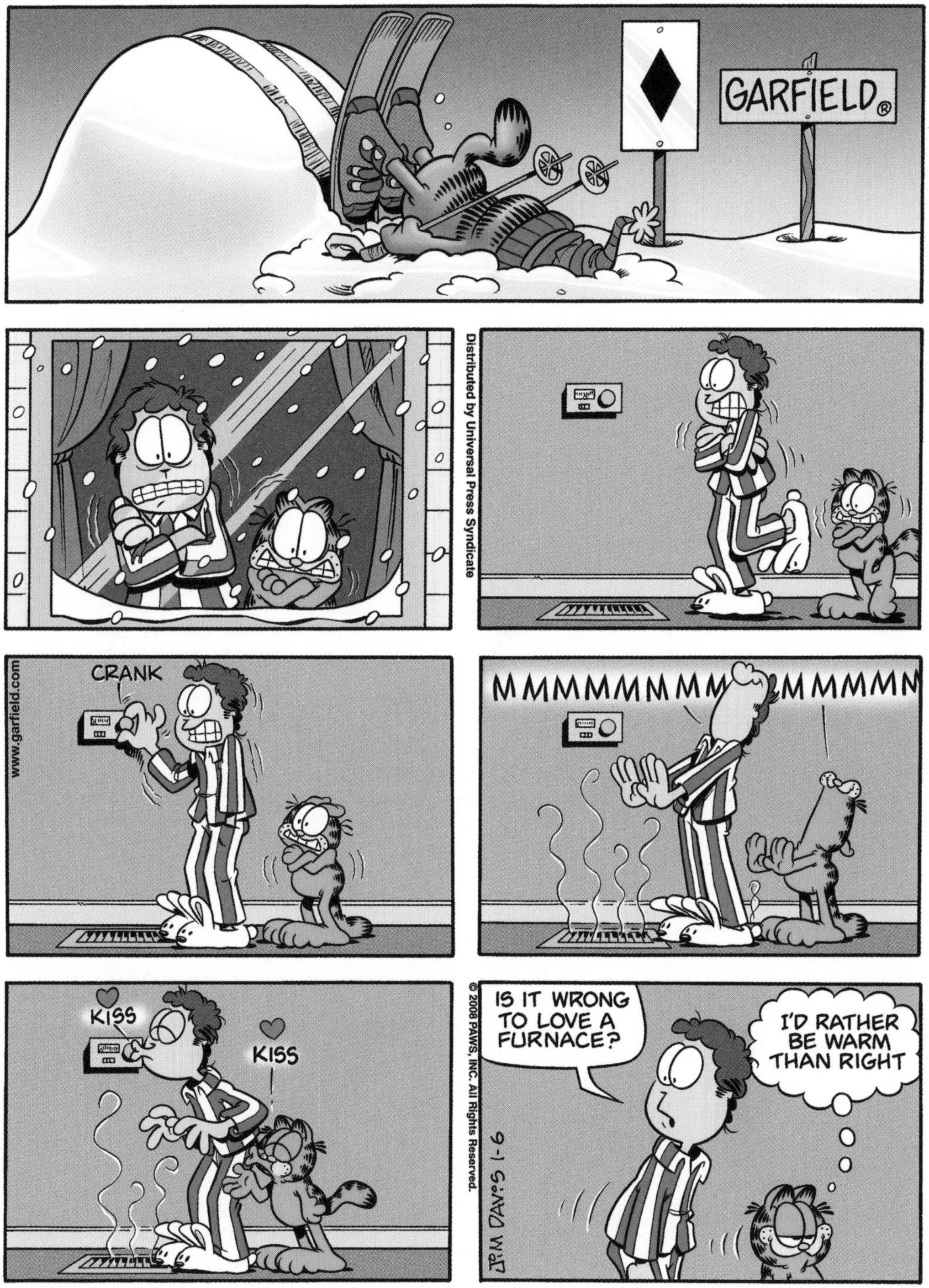
GARFIELD®
Distributed by Universal Press Syndicate
www.garfield.com
CRANK
MMMMMMMMMMMMMMMMN
KISS
KISS
© 2008 PAWS, INC. All Rights Reserved.
JPM DAVIS 1-6
IS IT WRONG TO LOVE A FURNACE?
I'D RATHER BE WARM THAN RIGHT

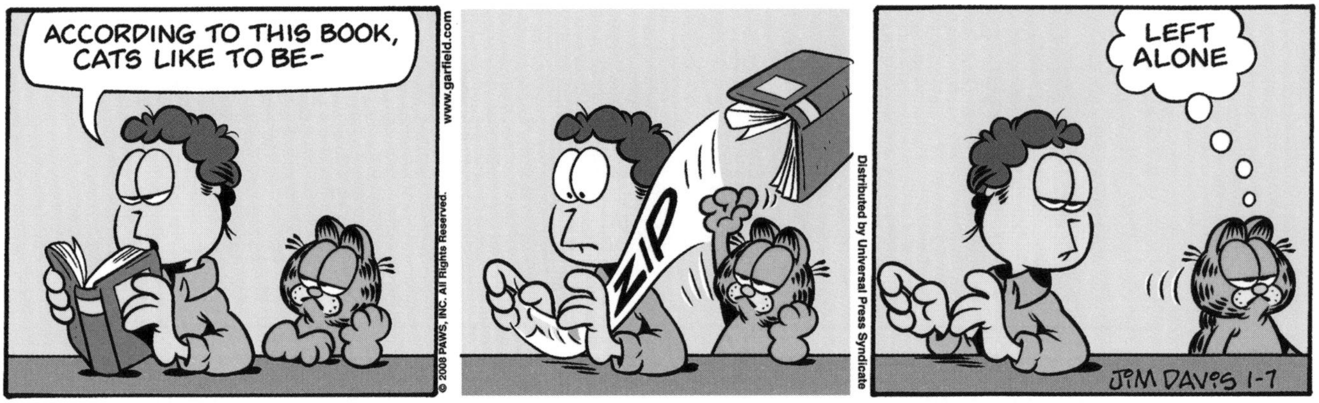
ACCORDING TO THIS BOOK, CATS LIKE TO BE-
© 2008 PAWS, INC. All Rights Reserved. www.garfield.com
ZIP
Distributed by Universal Press Syndicate
LEFT ALONE
JIM DAVIS 1-7

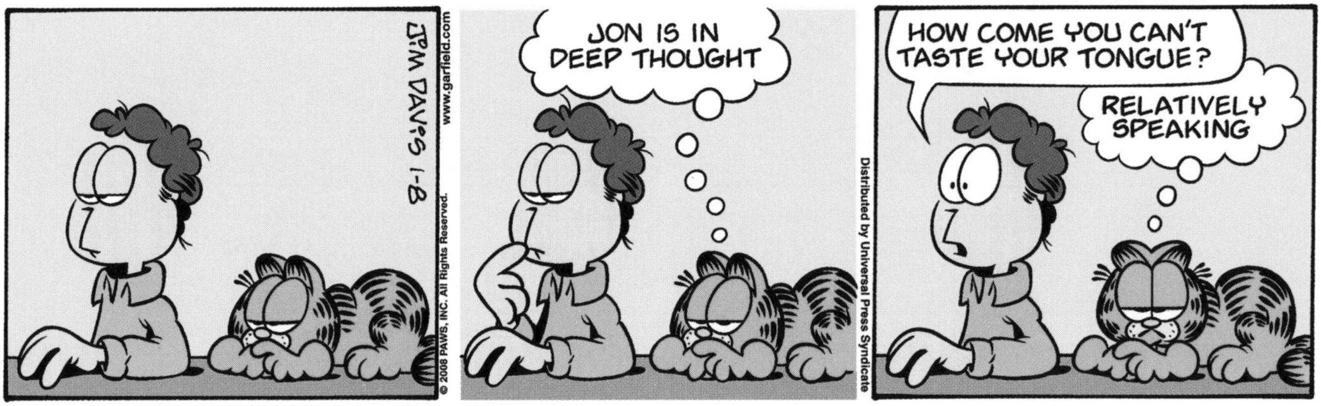
JIM DAVIS 1-8
© 2008 PAWS, INC. All Rights Reserved. www.garfield.com
JON IS IN DEEP THOUGHT
Distributed by Universal Press Syndicate
HOW COME YOU CAN'T TASTE YOUR TONGUE?
RELATIVELY SPEAKING

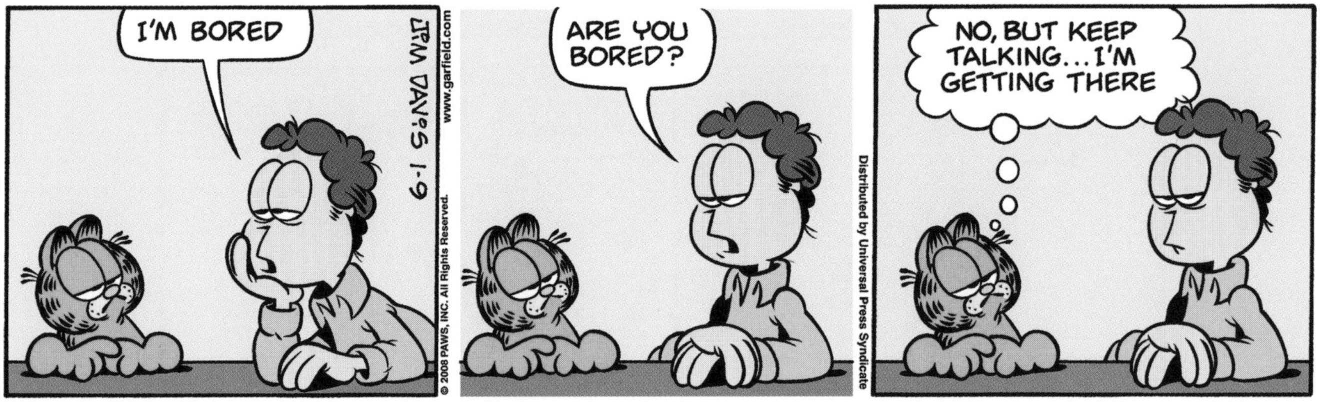
I'M BORED
JIM DAVIS 1-9
© 2008 PAWS, INC. All Rights Reserved. www.garfield.com
ARE YOU BORED?
Distributed by Universal Press Syndicate
NO, BUT KEEP TALKING... I'M GETTING THERE

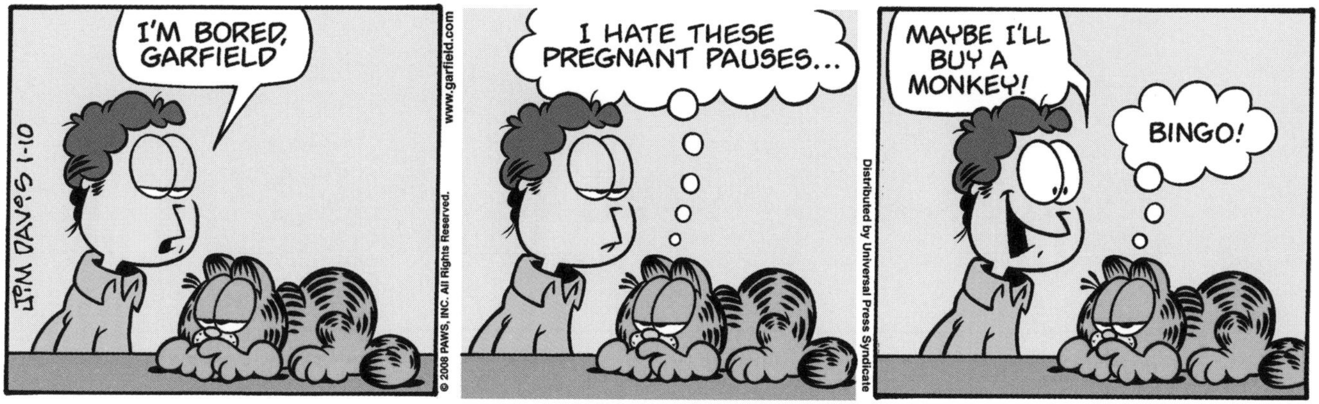
JIM DAVIS 1-10
I'M BORED, GARFIELD
© 2008 PAWS, INC. All Rights Reserved. www.garfield.com
I HATE THESE PREGNANT PAUSES...
Distributed by Universal Press Syndicate
MAYBE I'LL BUY A MONKEY!
BINGO!

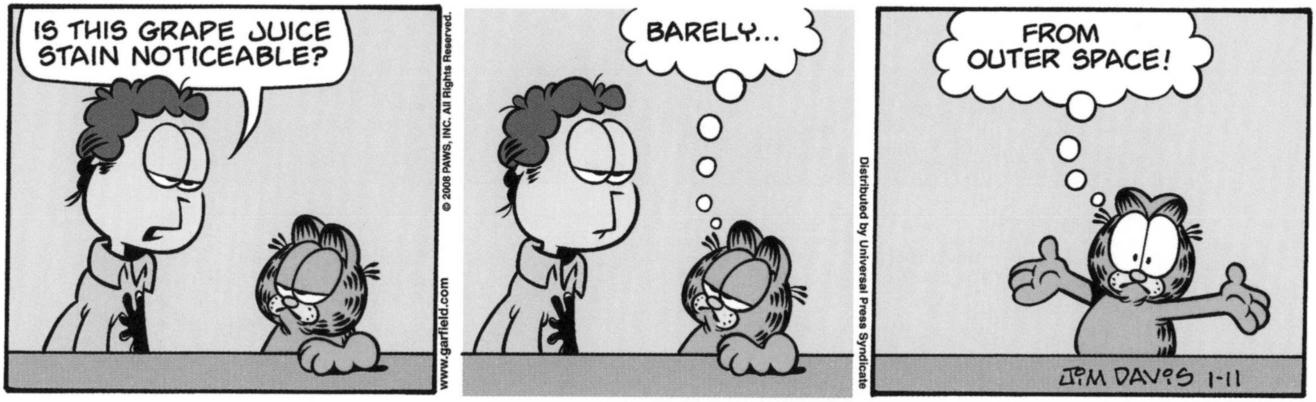
IS THIS GRAPE JUICE STAIN NOTICEABLE?
© 2008 PAWS, INC. All Rights Reserved. www.garfield.com
BARELY...
Distributed by Universal Press Syndicate
FROM OUTER SPACE!
JIM DAVIS 1-11

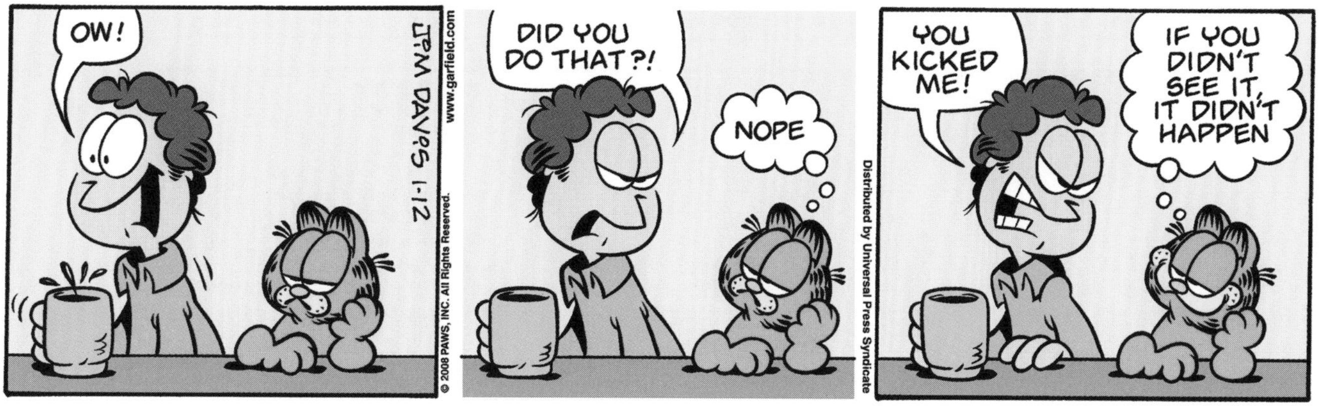
OW!
JIM DAVIS 1-12
© 2008 PAWS, INC. All Rights Reserved. www.garfield.com
DID YOU DO THAT?!
NOPE
Distributed by Universal Press Syndicate
YOU KICKED ME!
IF YOU DIDN'T SEE IT, IT DIDN'T HAPPEN

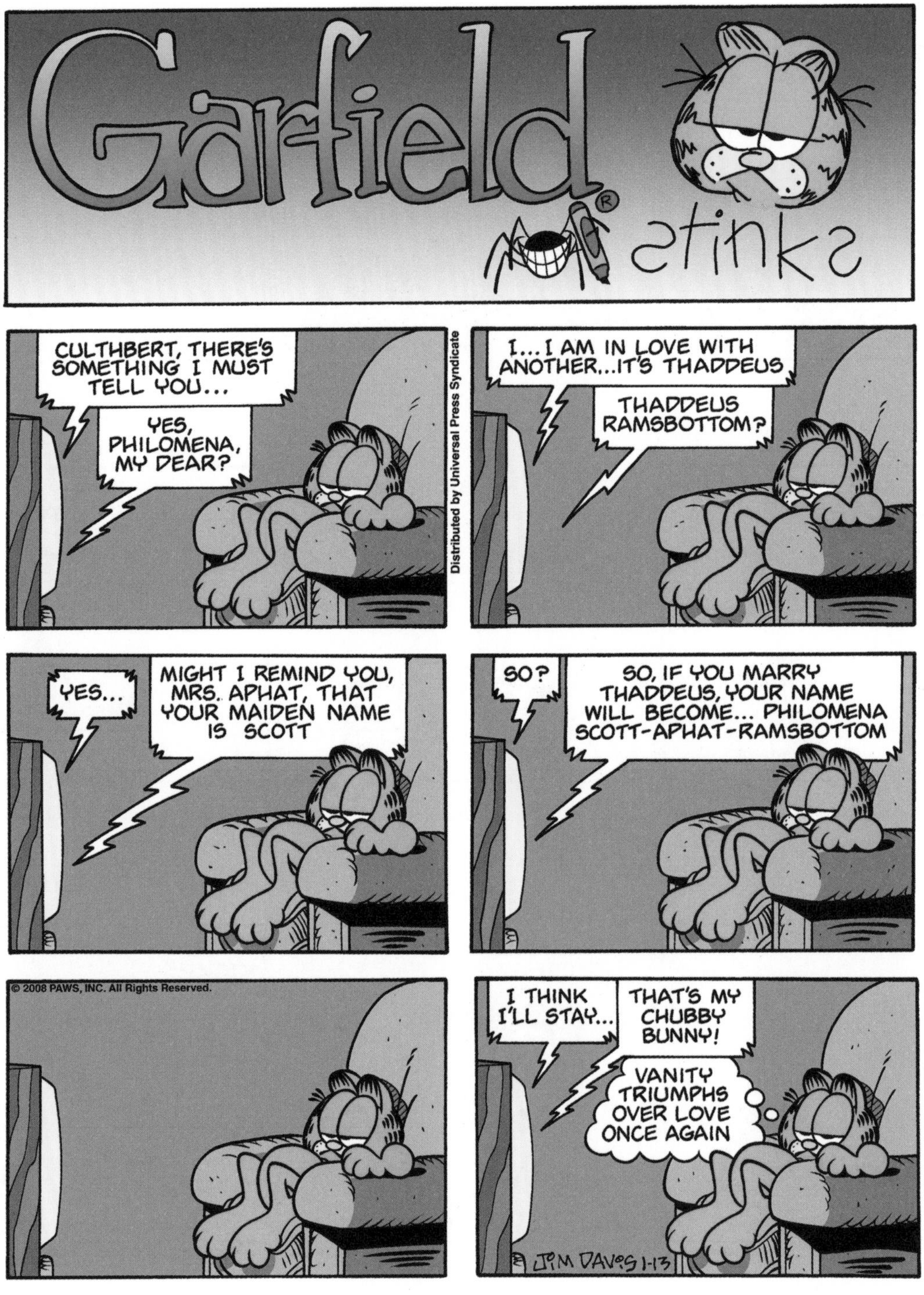
Garfield
stinks
CULTHBERT, THERE'S SOMETHING I MUST TELL YOU...
YES, PHILOMENA, MY DEAR?
Distributed by Universal Press Syndicate
I... I AM IN LOVE WITH ANOTHER...IT'S THADDEUS
THADDEUS RAMSBOTTOM?
YES...
MIGHT I REMIND YOU, MRS. APHAT, THAT YOUR MAIDEN NAME IS SCOTT
SO?
SO, IF YOU MARRY THADDEUS, YOUR NAME WILL BECOME... PHILOMENA SCOTT-APHAT-RAMSBOTTOM
© 2008 PAWS, INC. All Rights Reserved.
I THINK I'LL STAY...
THAT'S MY CHUBBY BUNNY!
VANITY TRIUMPHS OVER LOVE ONCE AGAIN
JIM DAVIS 1-13

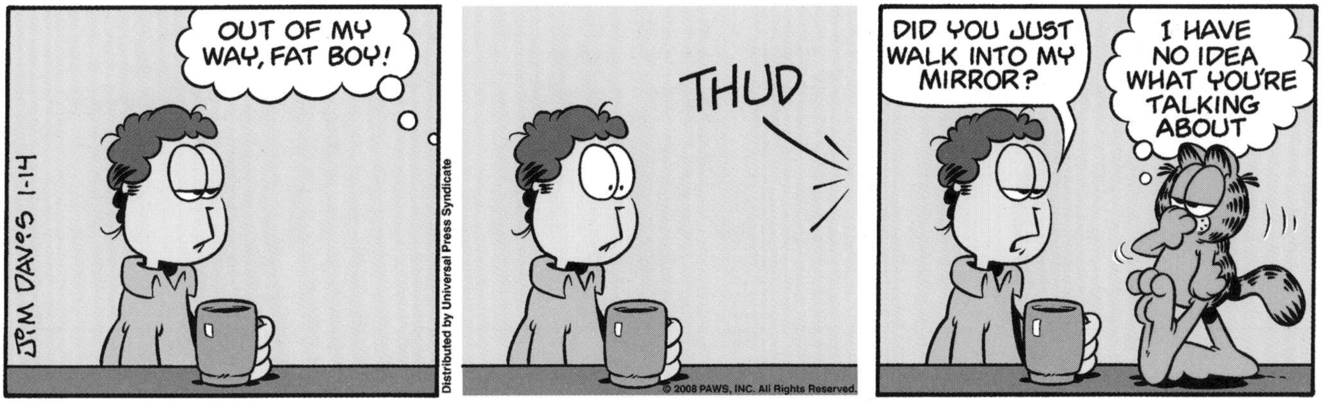
JIM DAVIS 1-14
OUT OF MY WAY, FAT BOY!
THUD
DID YOU JUST WALK INTO MY MIRROR?
I HAVE NO IDEA WHAT YOU'RE TALKING ABOUT
Distributed by Universal Press Syndicate
© 2008 PAWS, INC. All Rights Reserved.

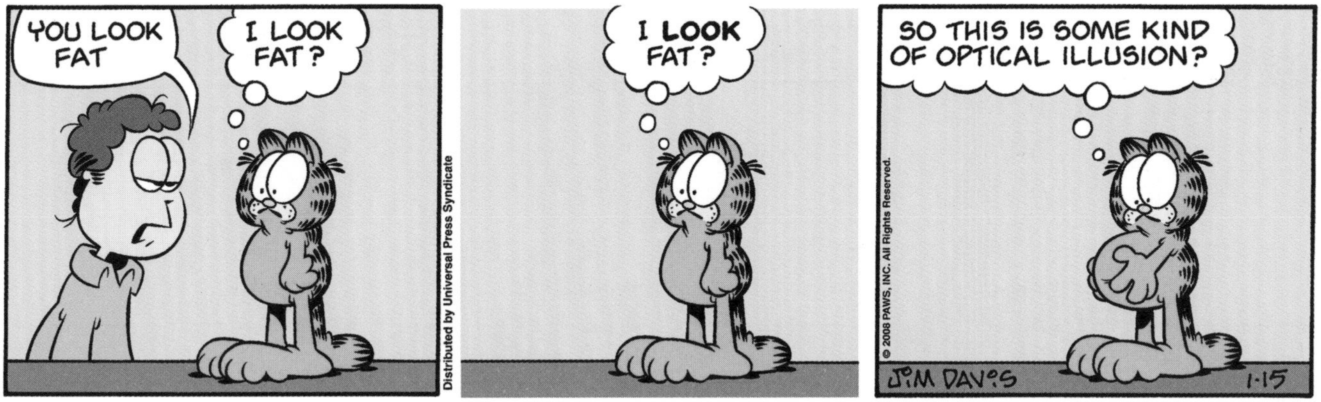
YOU LOOK FAT
I LOOK FAT?
I **LOOK** FAT?
SO THIS IS SOME KIND OF OPTICAL ILLUSION?
Distributed by Universal Press Syndicate
© 2008 PAWS, INC. All Rights Reserved.
JIM DAVIS 1-15

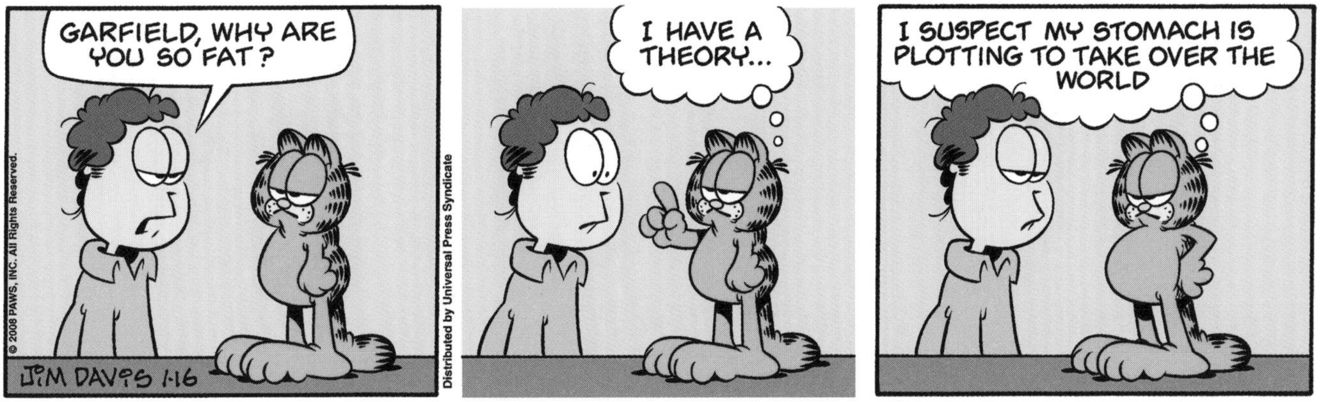
GARFIELD, WHY ARE YOU SO FAT?
I HAVE A THEORY...
I SUSPECT MY STOMACH IS PLOTTING TO TAKE OVER THE WORLD
© 2008 PAWS, INC. All Rights Reserved.
JIM DAVIS 1-16
Distributed by Universal Press Syndicate

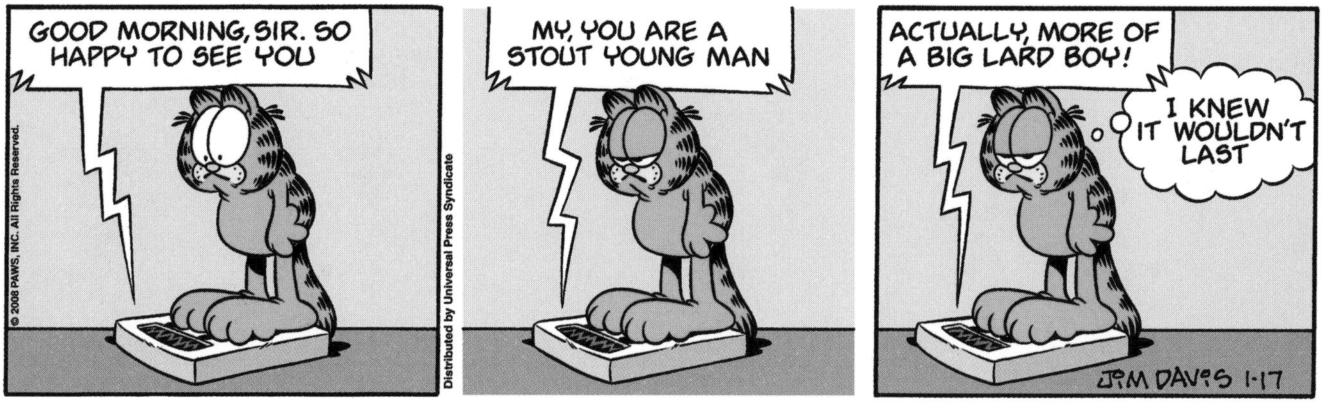
GOOD MORNING, SIR. SO HAPPY TO SEE YOU
© 2008 PAWS, INC. All Rights Reserved.
Distributed by Universal Press Syndicate
MY, YOU ARE A STOUT YOUNG MAN
ACTUALLY, MORE OF A BIG LARD BOY!
I KNEW IT WOULDN'T LAST
JIM DAVIS 1-17

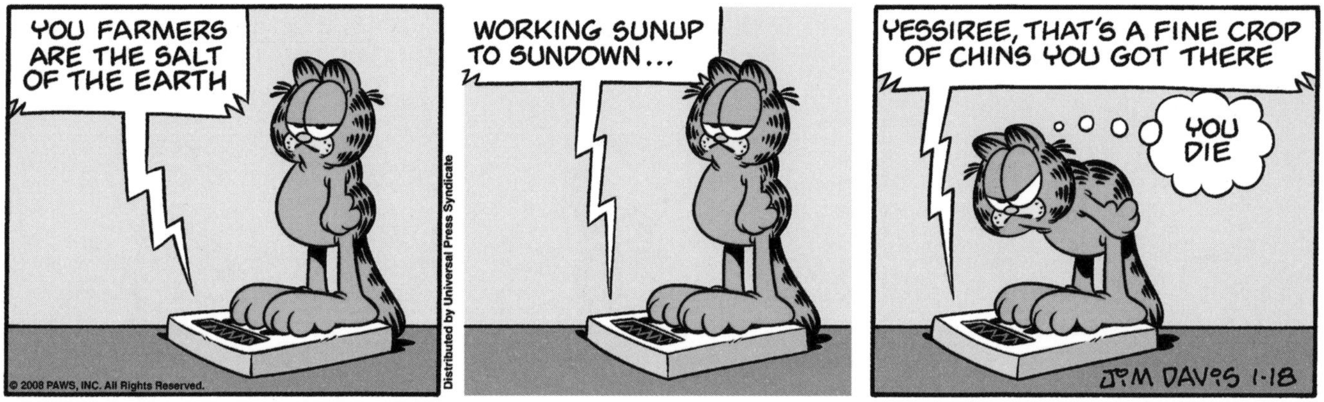
YOU FARMERS ARE THE SALT OF THE EARTH
© 2008 PAWS, INC. All Rights Reserved.
Distributed by Universal Press Syndicate
WORKING SUNUP TO SUNDOWN...
YESSIREE, THAT'S A FINE CROP OF CHINS YOU GOT THERE
YOU DIE
JIM DAVIS 1-18

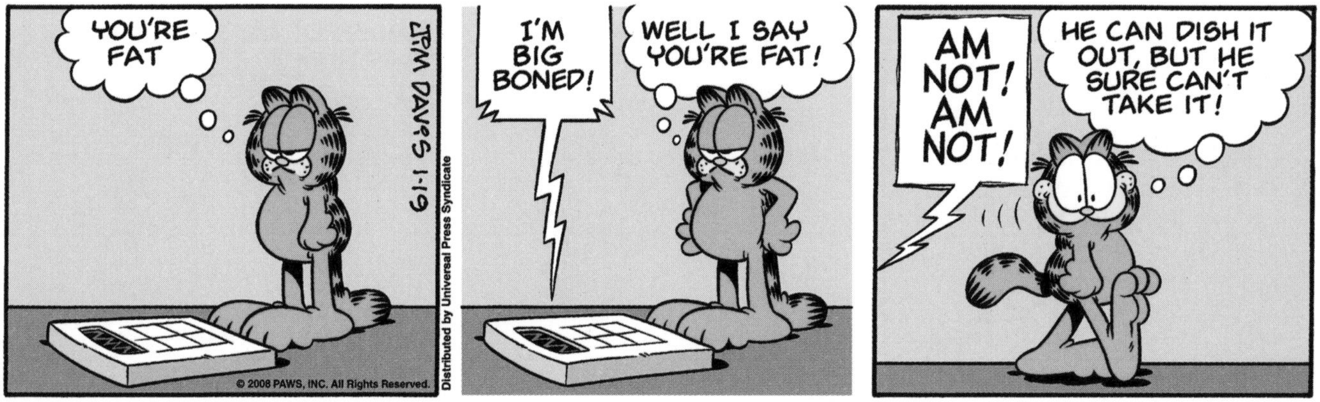
YOU'RE FAT
JIM DAVIS 1-19
© 2008 PAWS, INC. All Rights Reserved.
Distributed by Universal Press Syndicate
I'M BIG BONED!
WELL I SAY YOU'RE FAT!
AM NOT! AM NOT!
HE CAN DISH IT OUT, BUT HE SURE CAN'T TAKE IT!

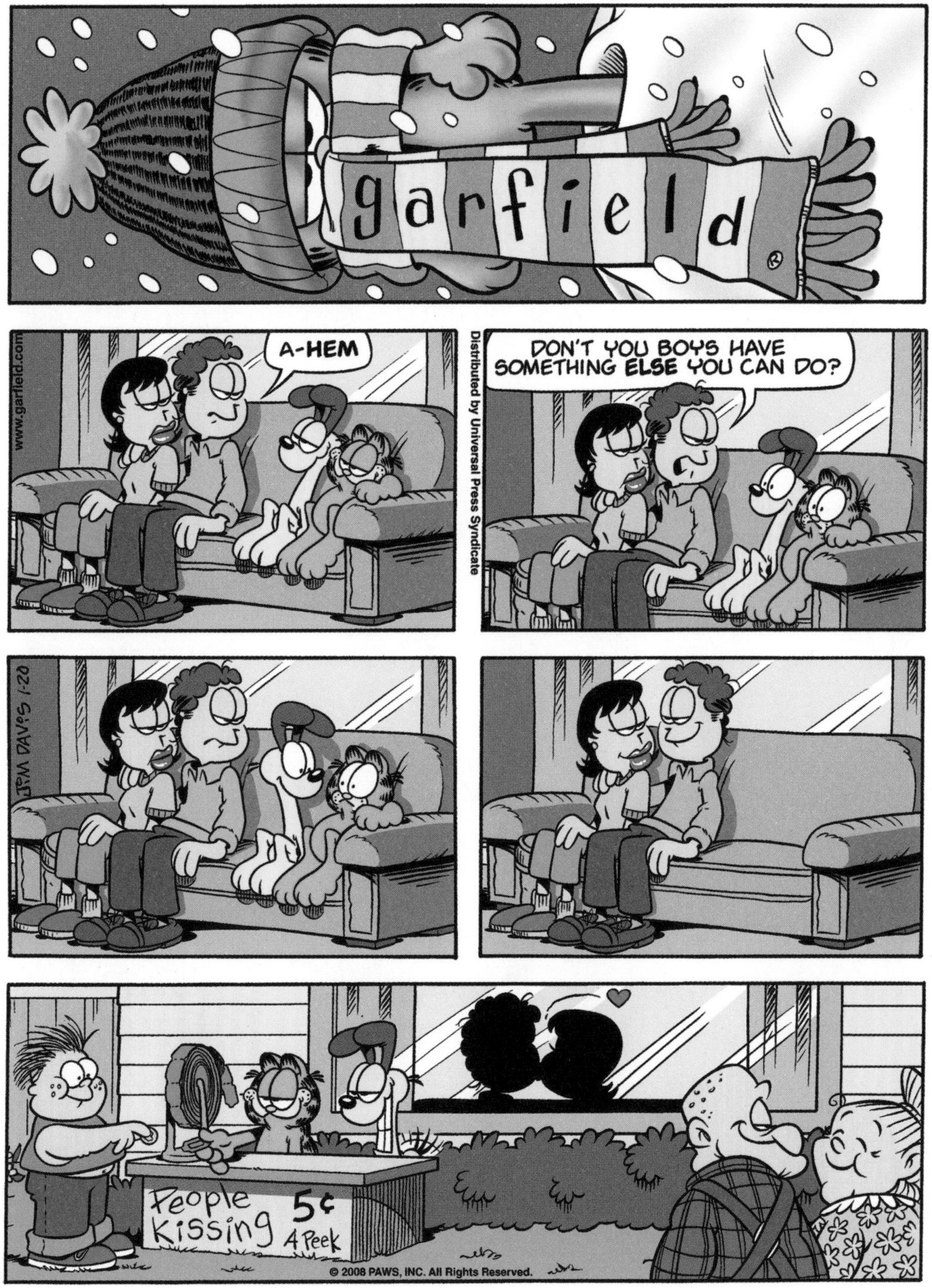
garfield
www.garfield.com
A-HEM
Distributed by Universal Press Syndicate
DON'T YOU BOYS HAVE SOMETHING ELSE YOU CAN DO?
JPM DAVPS 1-20
People Kissing 5¢ 4 Peek
© 2008 PAWS, INC. All Rights Reserved.

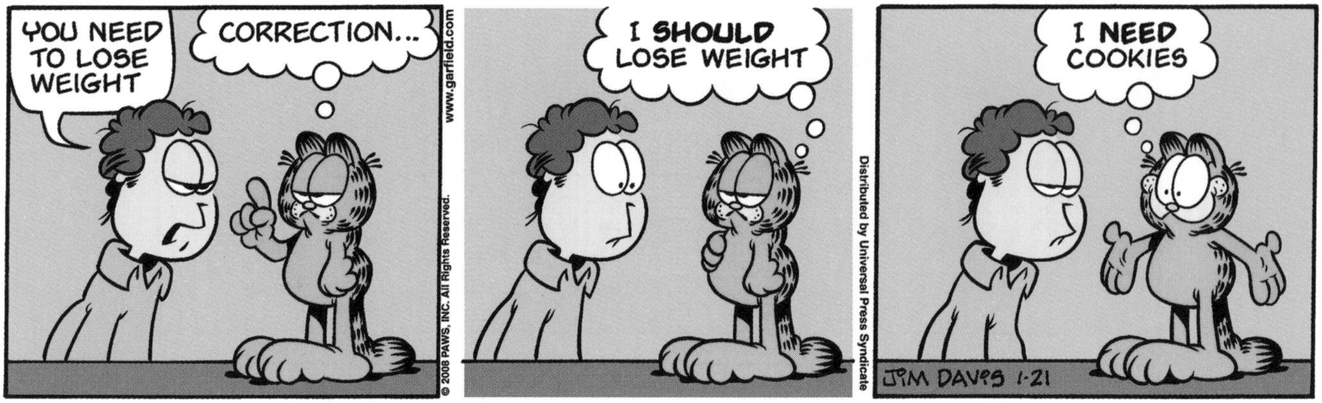
YOU NEED TO LOSE WEIGHT
CORRECTION...
I SHOULD LOSE WEIGHT
I NEED COOKIES
JIM DAVIS 1-21
© 2008 PAWS, INC. All Rights Reserved.
www.garfield.com
Distributed by Universal Press Syndicate

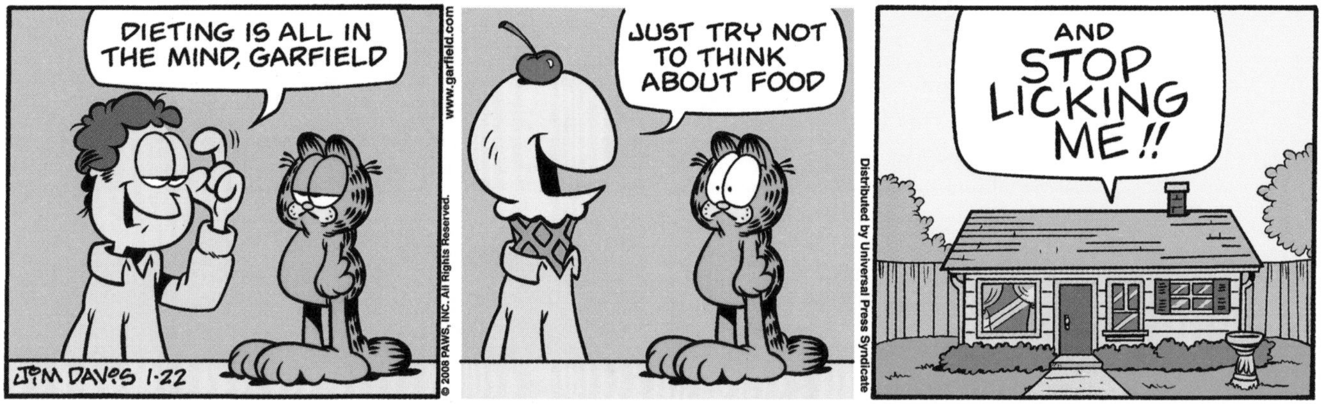
DIETING IS ALL IN THE MIND, GARFIELD
JIM DAVIS 1-22
JUST TRY NOT TO THINK ABOUT FOOD
AND STOP LICKING ME!!
© 2008 PAWS, INC. All Rights Reserved.
www.garfield.com
Distributed by Universal Press Syndicate

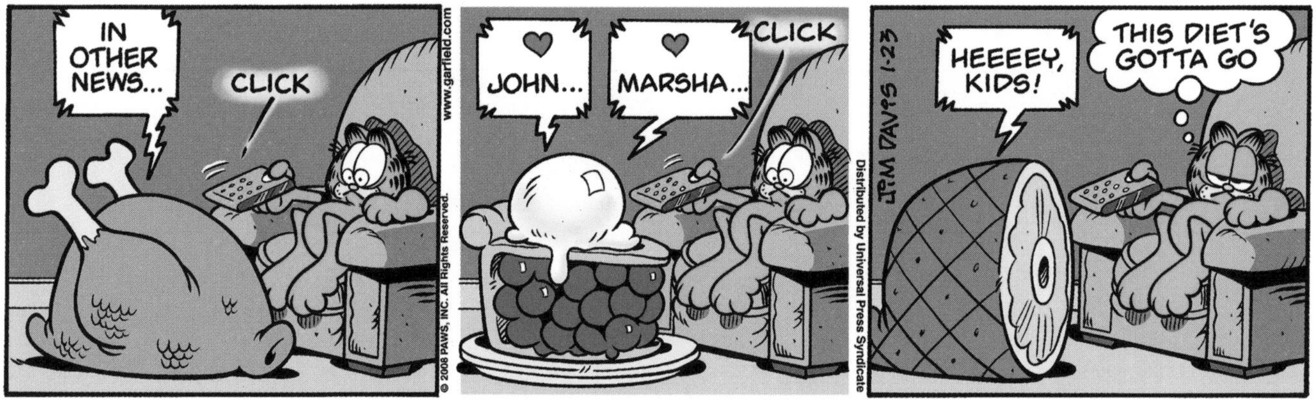
IN OTHER NEWS...
CLICK
JOHN...
MARSHA...
CLICK
HEEEEY, KIDS!
THIS DIET'S GOTTA GO
JIM DAVIS 1-23
© 2008 PAWS, INC. All Rights Reserved.
www.garfield.com
Distributed by Universal Press Syndicate

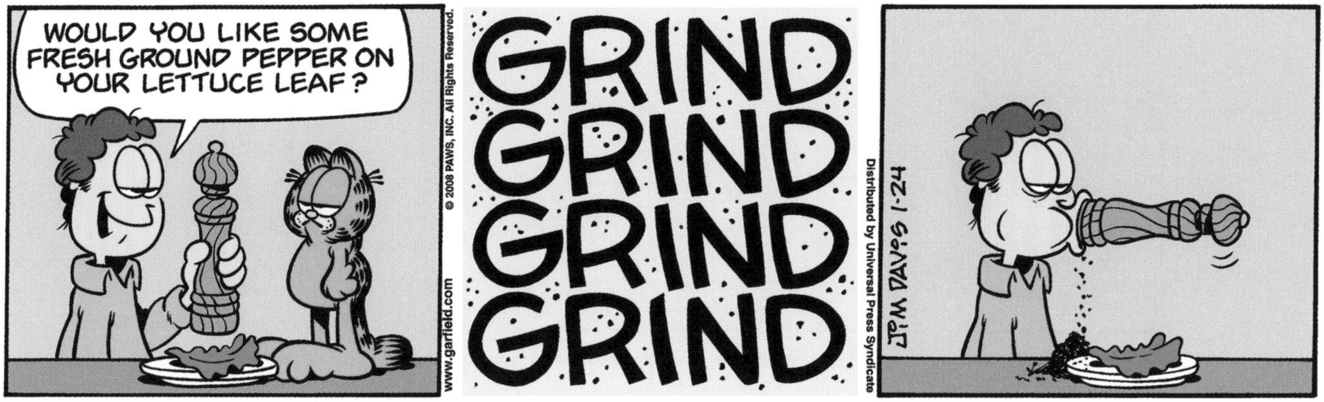
WOULD YOU LIKE SOME FRESH GROUND PEPPER ON YOUR LETTUCE LEAF?
GRIND GRIND GRIND GRIND
JIM DAVIS 1-24
© 2008 PAWS, INC. All Rights Reserved.
www.garfield.com
Distributed by Universal Press Syndicate

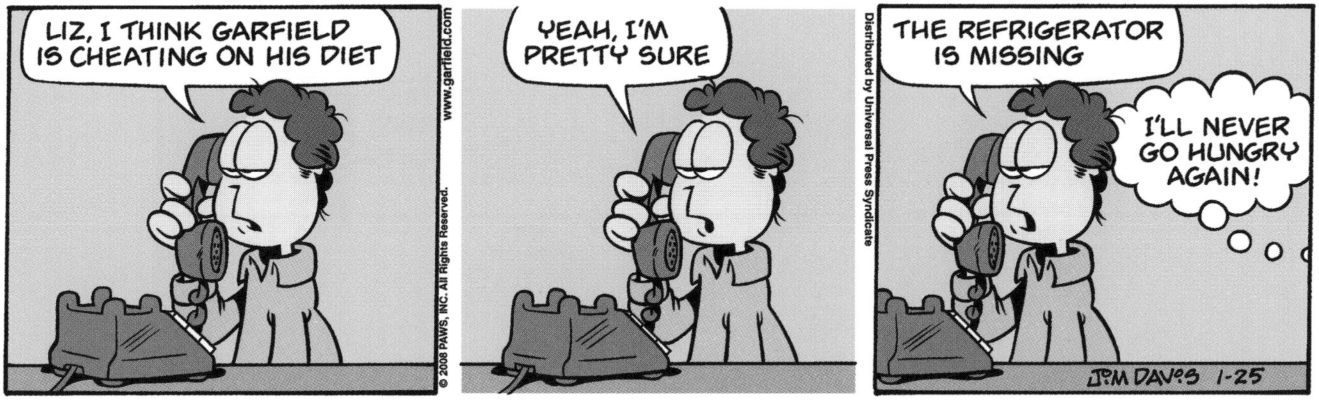
LIZ, I THINK GARFIELD IS CHEATING ON HIS DIET
YEAH, I'M PRETTY SURE
THE REFRIGERATOR IS MISSING
I'LL NEVER GO HUNGRY AGAIN!
JIM DAVIS 1-25
© 2008 PAWS, INC. All Rights Reserved.
www.garfield.com
Distributed by Universal Press Syndicate

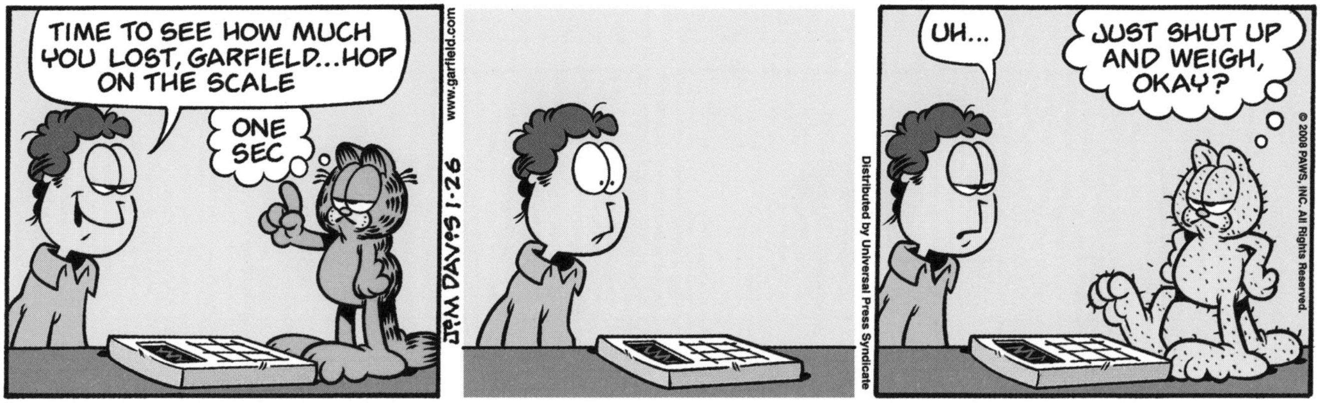
TIME TO SEE HOW MUCH YOU LOST, GARFIELD...HOP ON THE SCALE
ONE SEC
UH...
JUST SHUT UP AND WEIGH, OKAY?
JIM DAVIS 1-26
© 2008 PAWS, INC. All Rights Reserved.
www.garfield.com
Distributed by Universal Press Syndicate

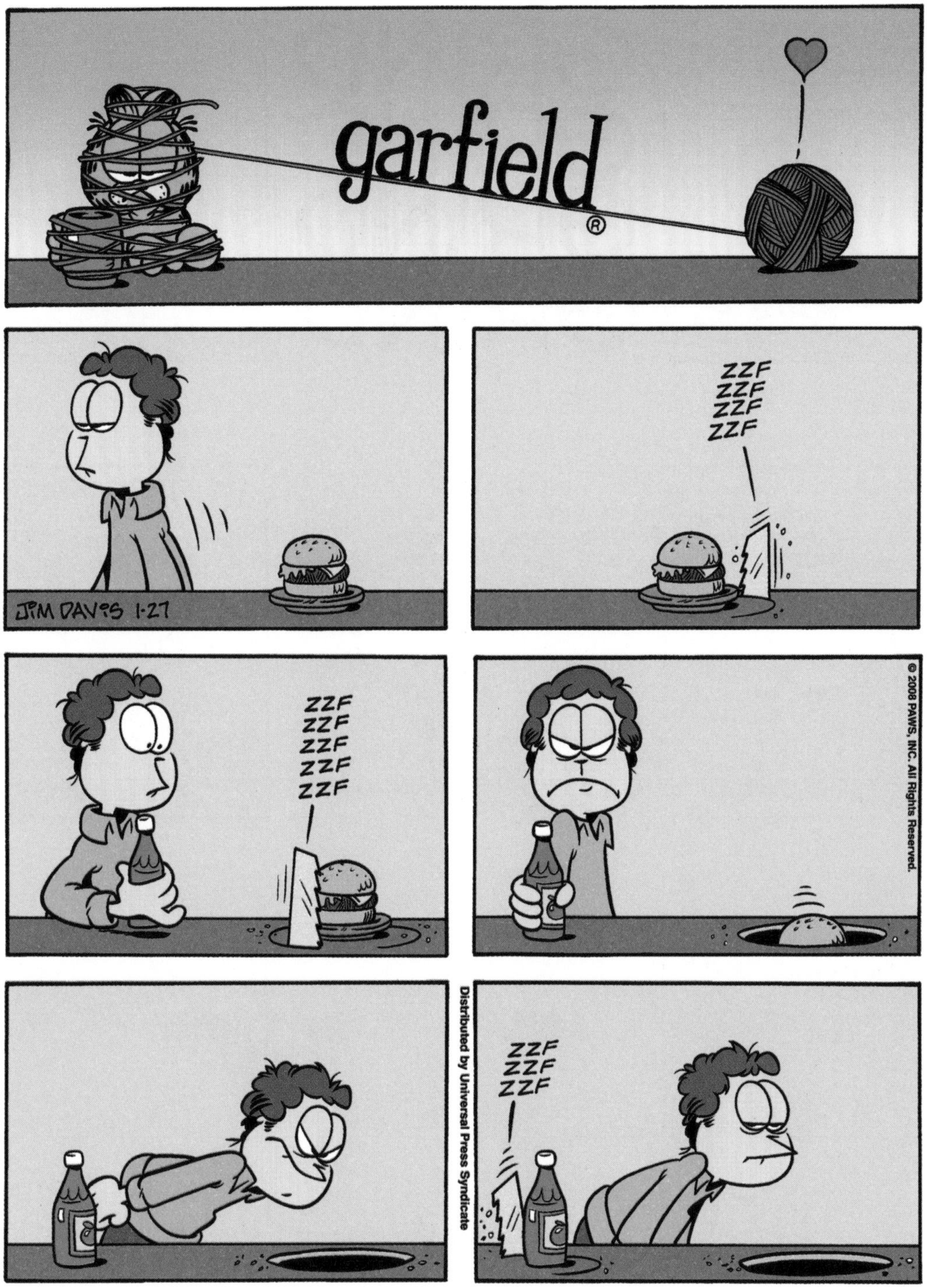
garfield
JIM DAVIS 1-27
ZZF ZZF ZZF ZZF
ZZF ZZF ZZF ZZF ZZF
ZZF ZZF ZZF

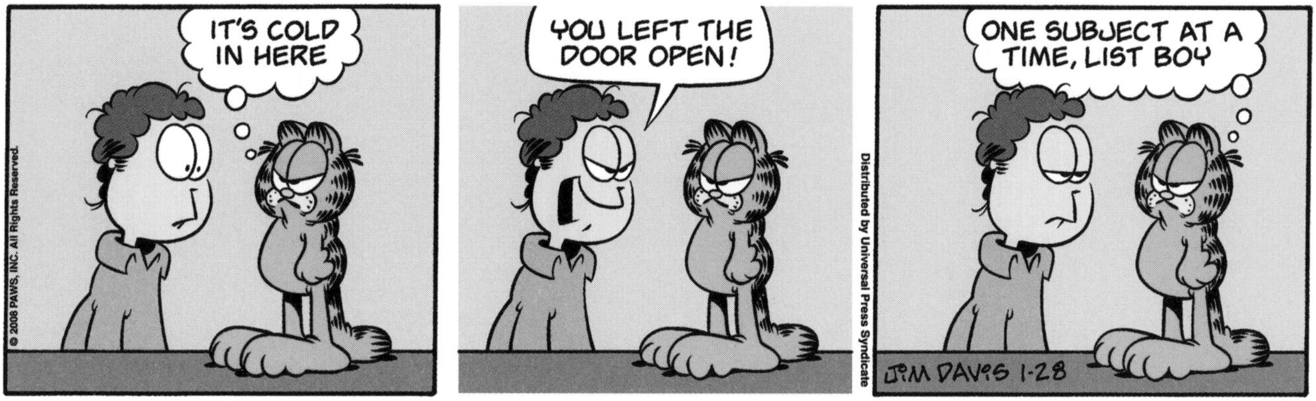
IT'S COLD IN HERE
YOU LEFT THE DOOR OPEN!
ONE SUBJECT AT A TIME, LIST BOY
JIM DAVIS 1-28
© 2008 PAWS, INC. All Rights Reserved.
Distributed by Universal Press Syndicate

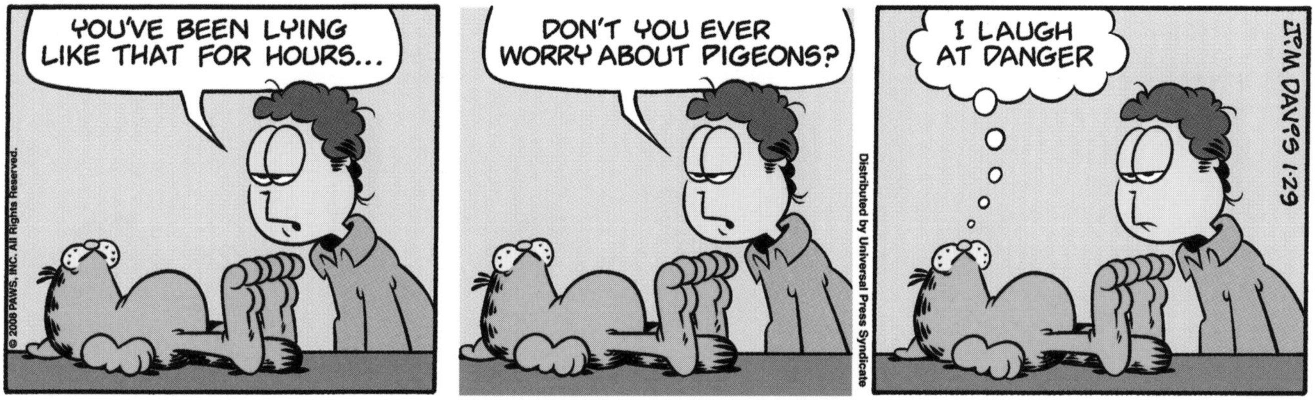
YOU'VE BEEN LYING LIKE THAT FOR HOURS...
DON'T YOU EVER WORRY ABOUT PIGEONS?
I LAUGH AT DANGER
JIM DAVIS 1-29
© 2008 PAWS, INC. All Rights Reserved.
Distributed by Universal Press Syndicate

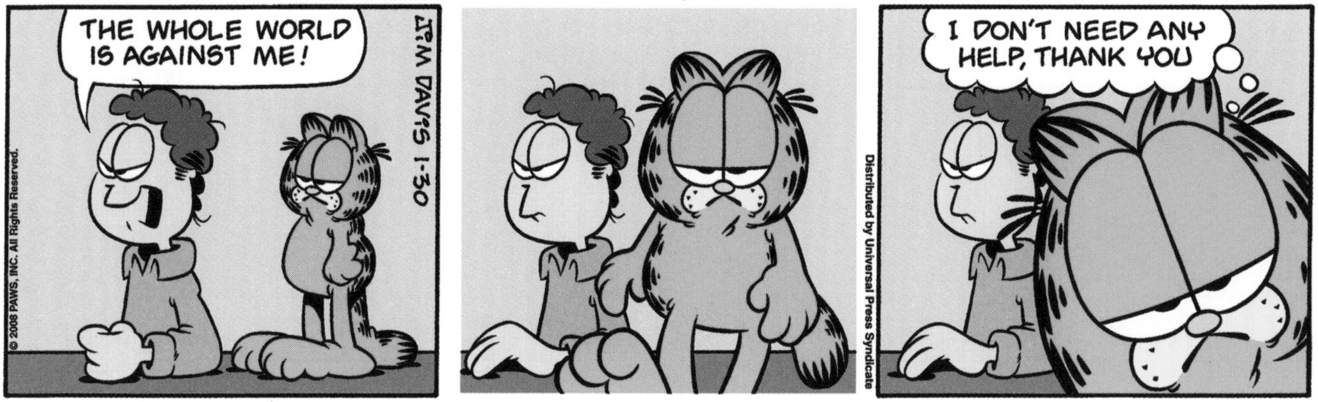
THE WHOLE WORLD IS AGAINST ME!
JIM DAVIS 1-30
I DON'T NEED ANY HELP, THANK YOU
© 2008 PAWS, INC. All Rights Reserved.
Distributed by Universal Press Syndicate

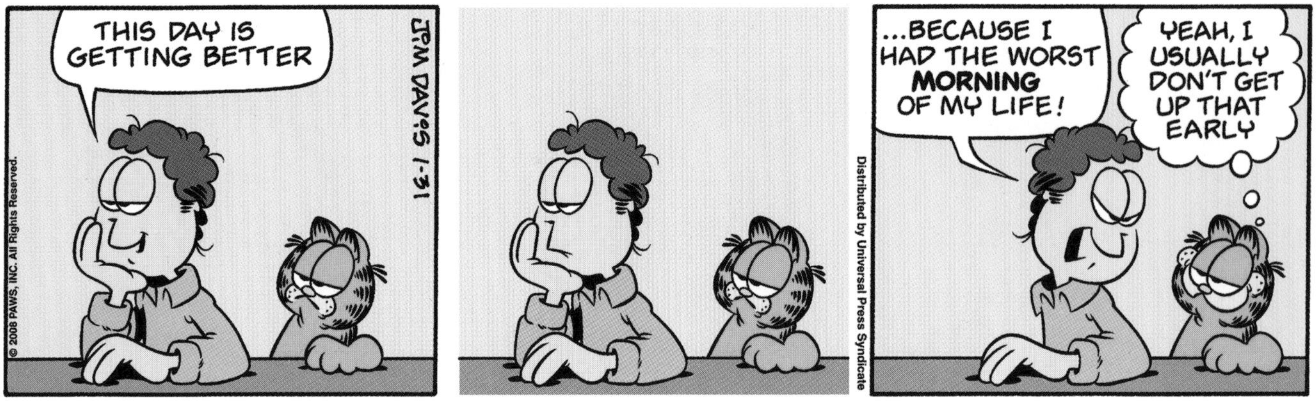
THIS DAY IS GETTING BETTER
JIM DAVIS 1-31
© 2008 PAWS, INC. All Rights Reserved.
...BECAUSE I HAD THE WORST **MORNING** OF MY LIFE!
YEAH, I USUALLY DON'T GET UP THAT EARLY
Distributed by Universal Press Syndicate

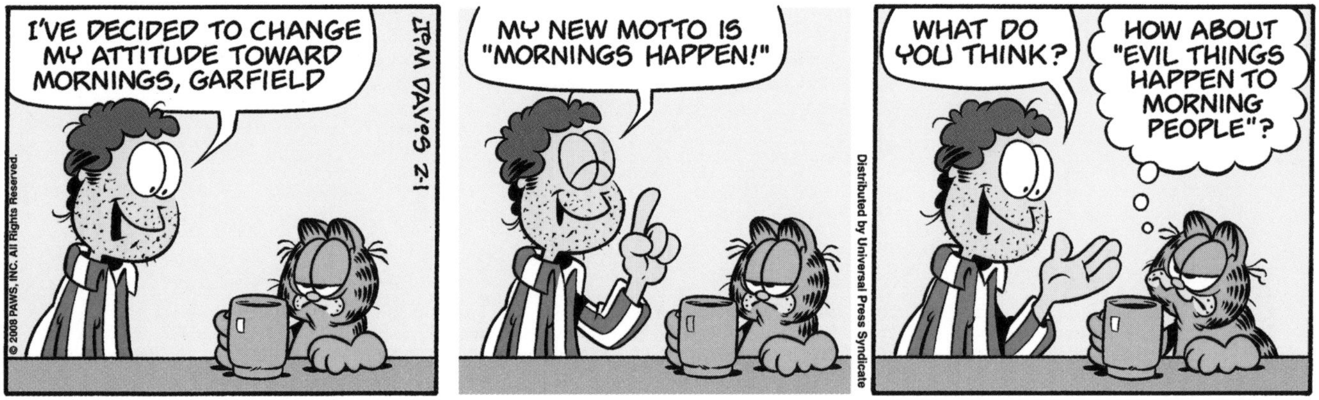
I'VE DECIDED TO CHANGE MY ATTITUDE TOWARD MORNINGS, GARFIELD
JIM DAVIS 2-1
© 2008 PAWS, INC. All Rights Reserved.
MY NEW MOTTO IS "MORNINGS HAPPEN!"
WHAT DO YOU THINK?
HOW ABOUT "EVIL THINGS HAPPEN TO MORNING PEOPLE"?
Distributed by Universal Press Syndicate

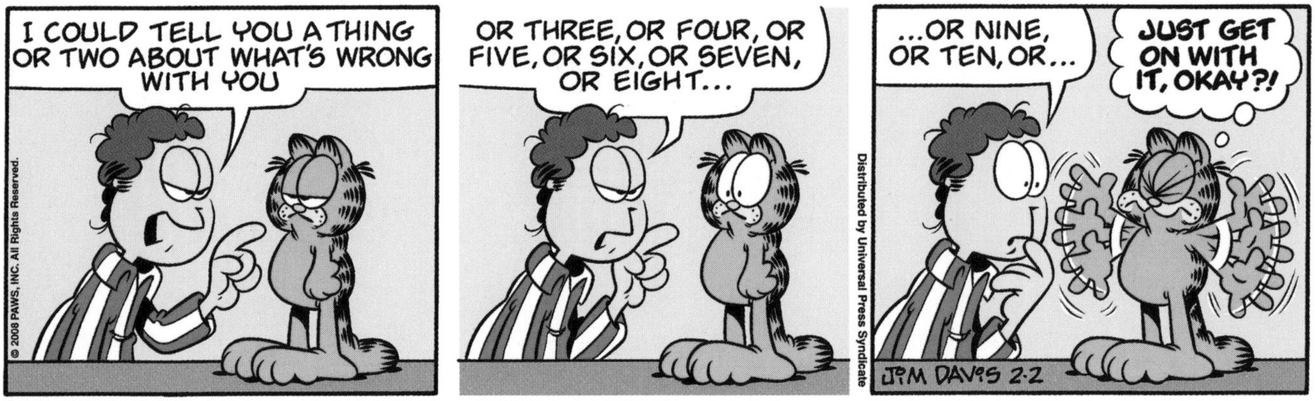
I COULD TELL YOU A THING OR TWO ABOUT WHAT'S WRONG WITH YOU
© 2008 PAWS, INC. All Rights Reserved.
OR THREE, OR FOUR, OR FIVE, OR SIX, OR SEVEN, OR EIGHT...
...OR NINE, OR TEN, OR...
JUST GET ON WITH IT, OKAY?!
JIM DAVIS 2-2
Distributed by Universal Press Syndicate

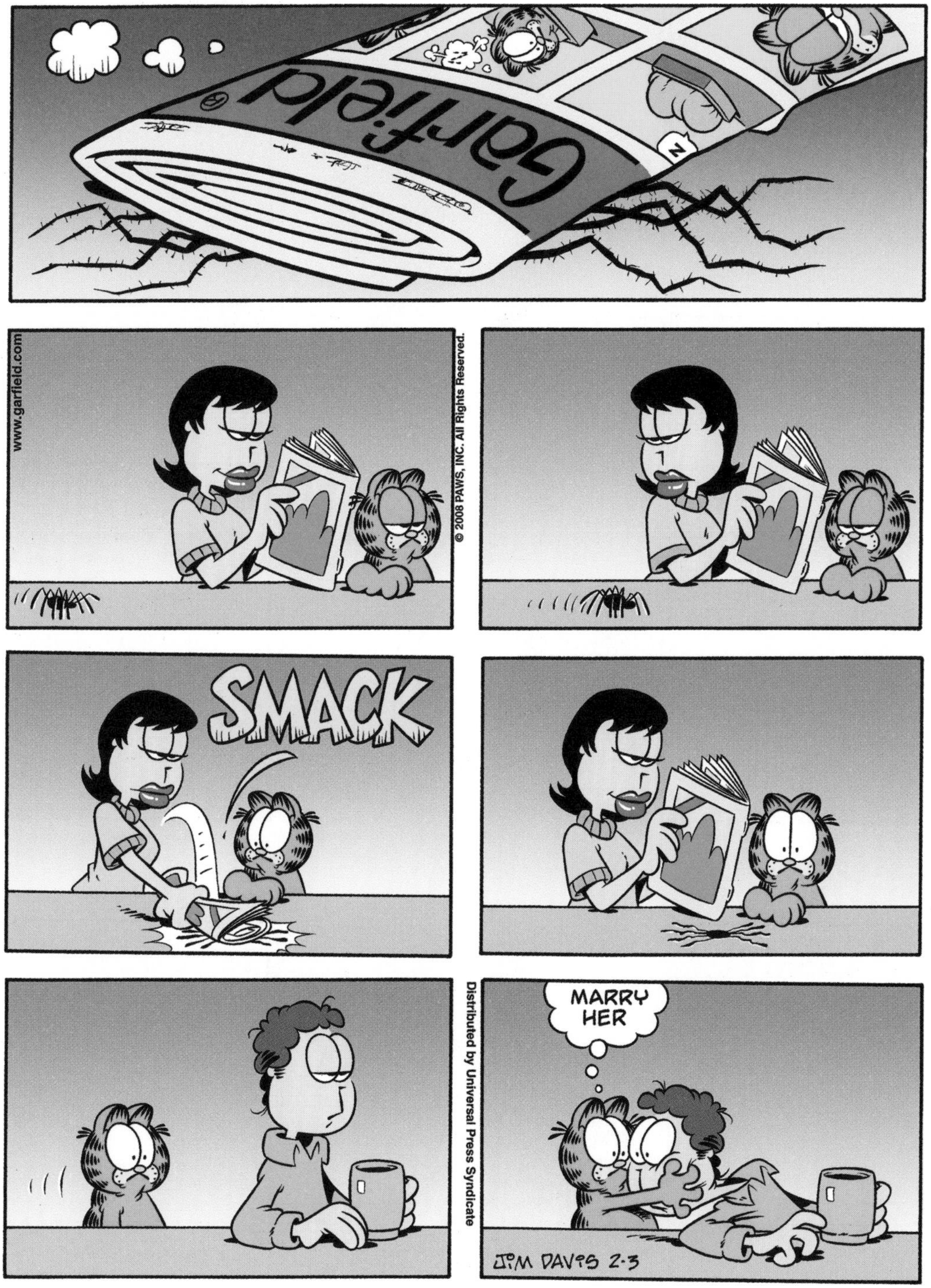

Garfield
www.garfield.com
© 2008 PAWS, INC. All Rights Reserved.
SMACK
Distributed by Universal Press Syndicate
MARRY HER
JIM DAVIS 2-3

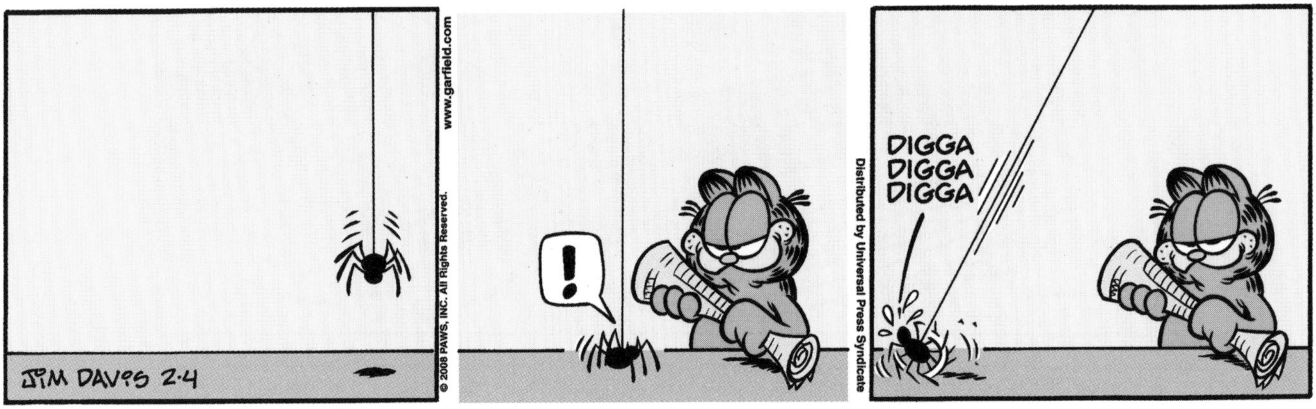
JIM DAVIS 2·4
© 2008 PAWS, INC. All Rights Reserved. www.garfield.com
!
Distributed by Universal Press Syndicate
DIGGA
DIGGA
DIGGA

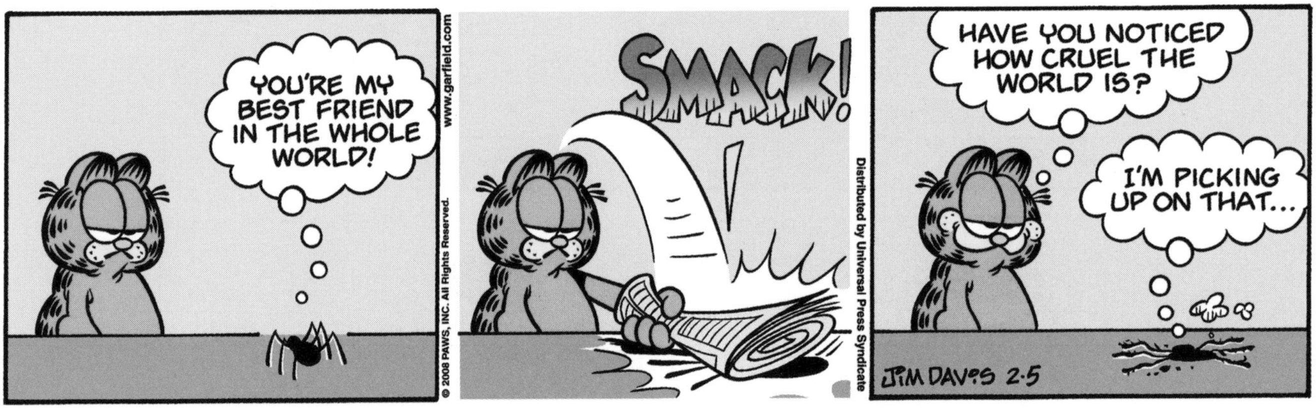
YOU'RE MY BEST FRIEND IN THE WHOLE WORLD!
© 2008 PAWS, INC. All Rights Reserved. www.garfield.com
SMACK!
Distributed by Universal Press Syndicate
HAVE YOU NOTICED HOW CRUEL THE WORLD IS?
I'M PICKING UP ON THAT...
JIM DAVIS 2·5

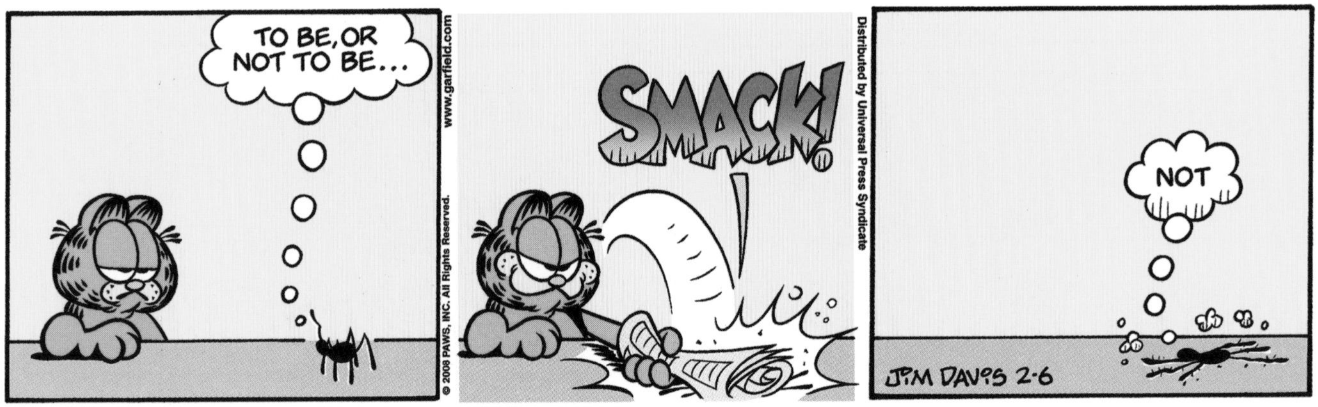
TO BE, OR NOT TO BE...
© 2008 PAWS, INC. All Rights Reserved. www.garfield.com
SMACK!
Distributed by Universal Press Syndicate
NOT
JIM DAVIS 2·6

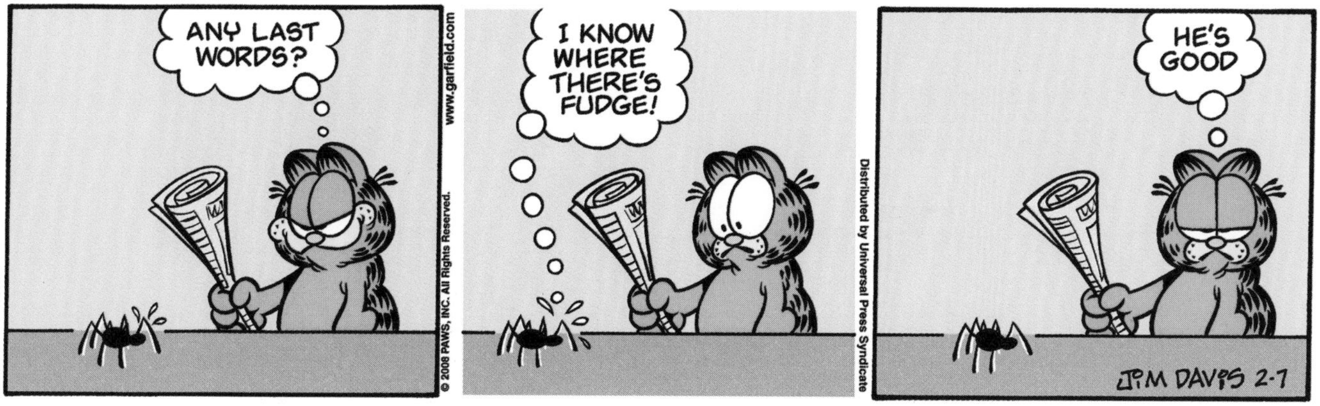
ANY LAST WORDS?
I KNOW WHERE THERE'S FUDGE!
HE'S GOOD
© 2008 PAWS, INC. All Rights Reserved. www.garfield.com
Distributed by Universal Press Syndicate
JIM DAVIS 2-7

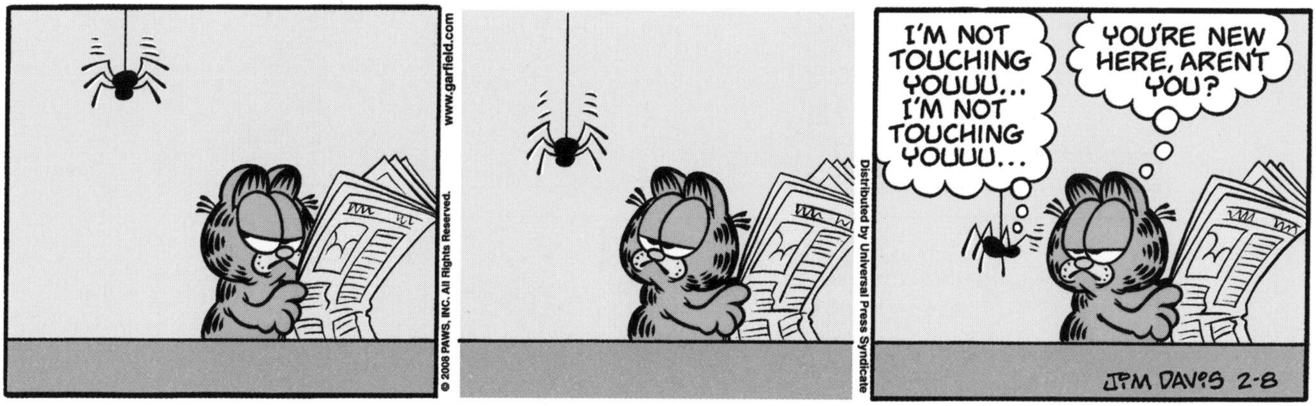
I'M NOT TOUCHING YOUUU... I'M NOT TOUCHING YOUUU...
YOU'RE NEW HERE, AREN'T YOU?
© 2008 PAWS, INC. All Rights Reserved. www.garfield.com
Distributed by Universal Press Syndicate
JIM DAVIS 2-8

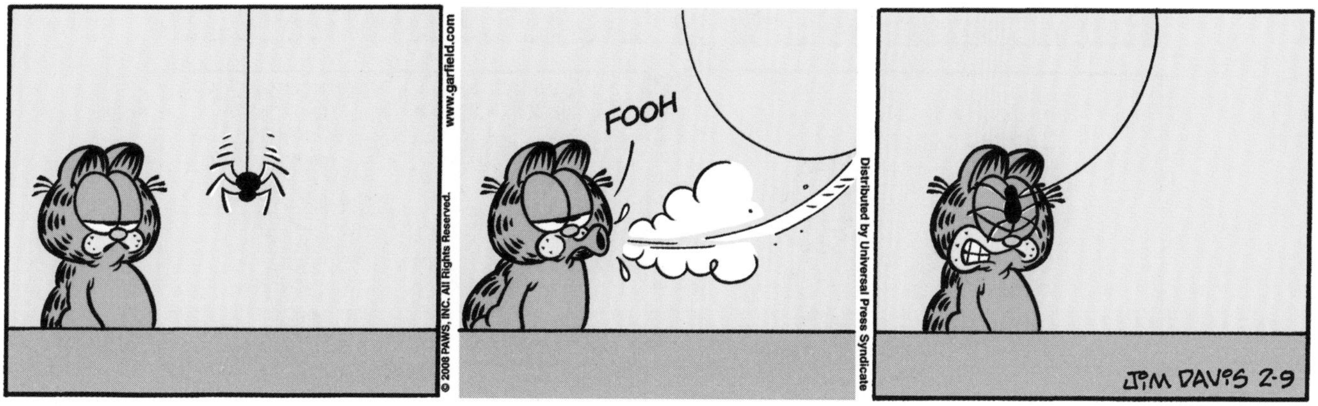
FOOH
© 2008 PAWS, INC. All Rights Reserved. www.garfield.com
Distributed by Universal Press Syndicate
JIM DAVIS 2-9

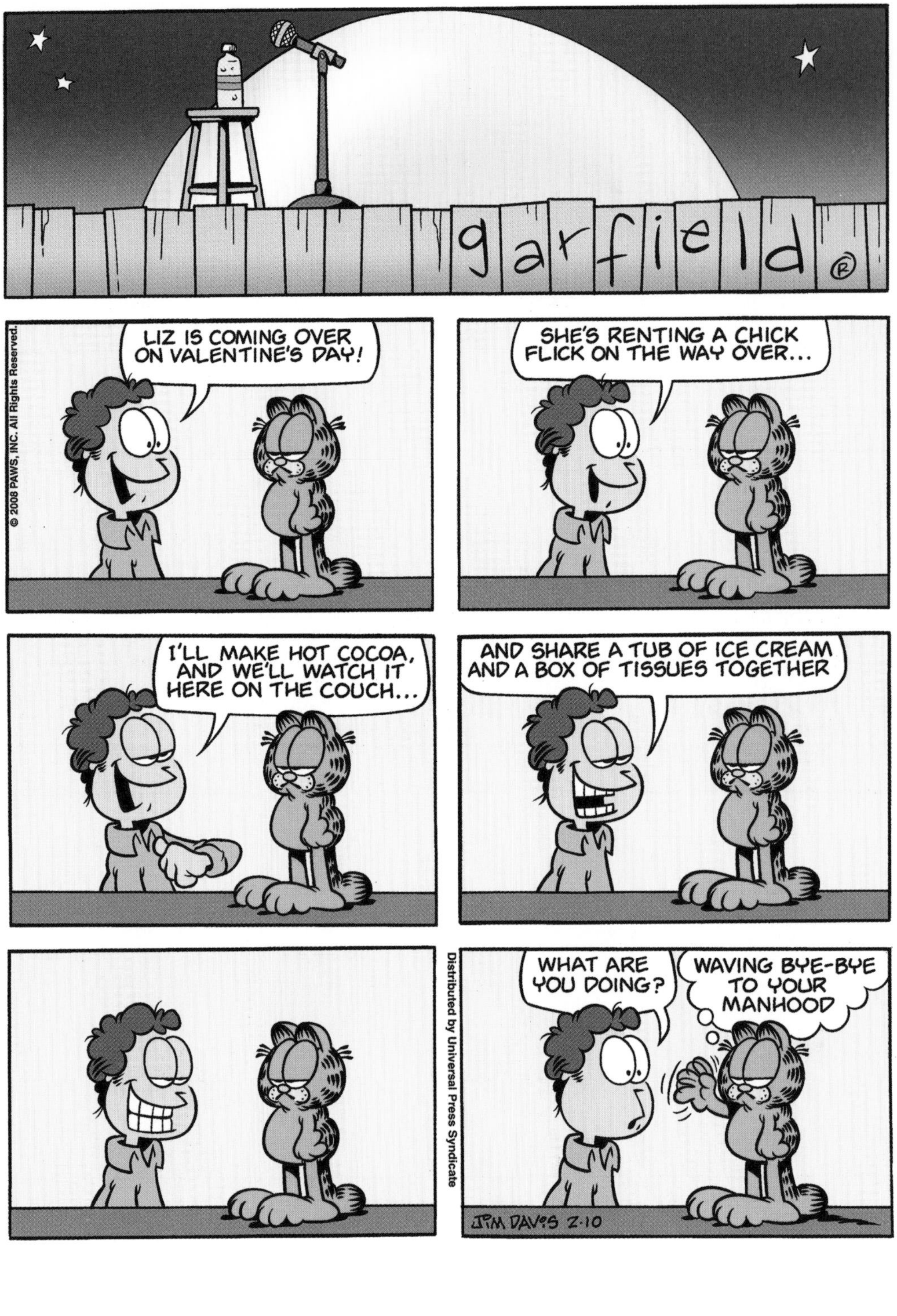
garfield
LIZ IS COMING OVER ON VALENTINE'S DAY!
SHE'S RENTING A CHICK FLICK ON THE WAY OVER...
I'LL MAKE HOT COCOA, AND WE'LL WATCH IT HERE ON THE COUCH...
AND SHARE A TUB OF ICE CREAM AND A BOX OF TISSUES TOGETHER
WHAT ARE YOU DOING?
WAVING BYE-BYE TO YOUR MANHOOD
© 2008 PAWS, INC. All Rights Reserved.
Distributed by Universal Press Syndicate
JIM DAVIS 2-10

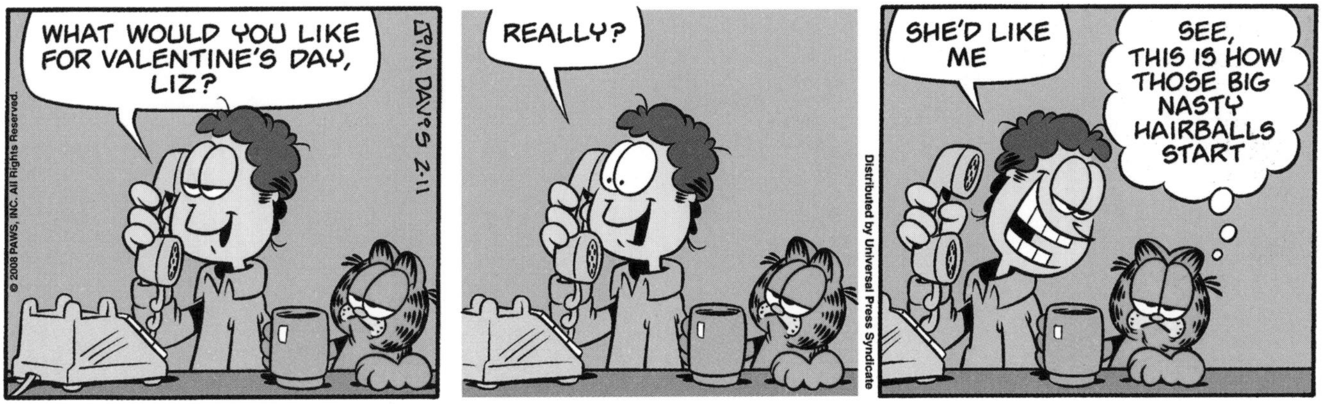
WHAT WOULD YOU LIKE FOR VALENTINE'S DAY, LIZ?
JPM DAVIS 2-11
© 2008 PAWS, INC. All Rights Reserved.
REALLY?
SHE'D LIKE ME
SEE, THIS IS HOW THOSE BIG NASTY HAIRBALLS START
Distributed by Universal Press Syndicate

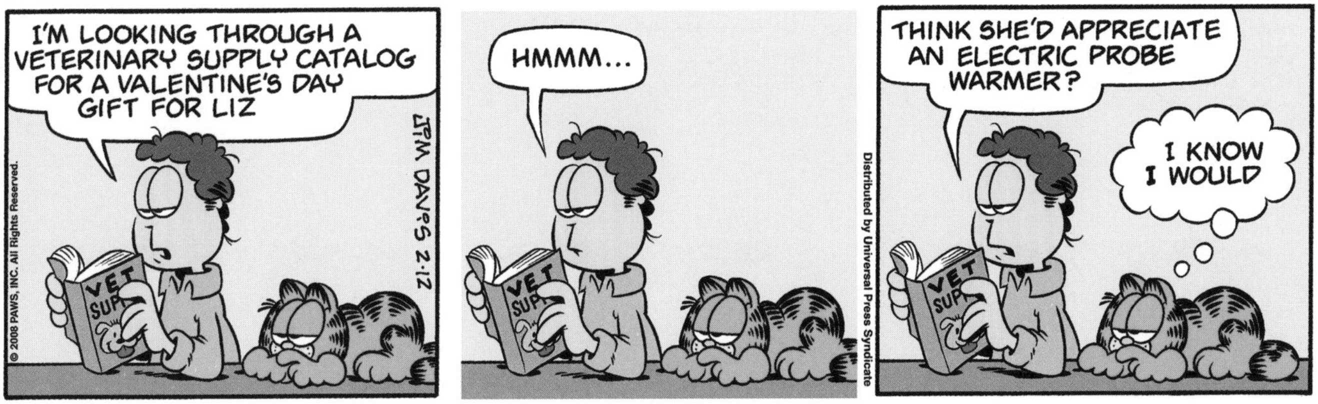
I'M LOOKING THROUGH A VETERINARY SUPPLY CATALOG FOR A VALENTINE'S DAY GIFT FOR LIZ
JPM DAVIS 2-12
© 2008 PAWS, INC. All Rights Reserved.
HMMM...
THINK SHE'D APPRECIATE AN ELECTRIC PROBE WARMER?
I KNOW I WOULD
Distributed by Universal Press Syndicate

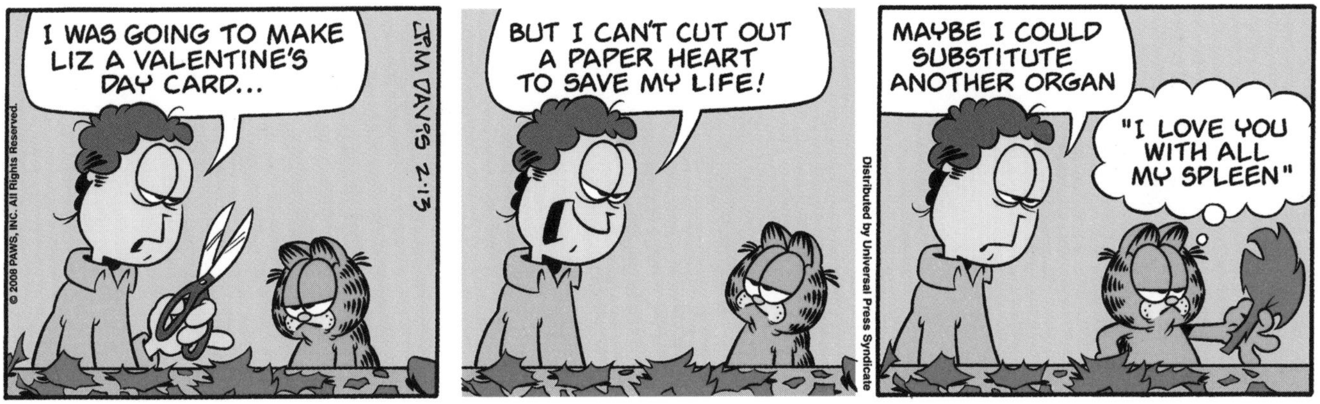
I WAS GOING TO MAKE LIZ A VALENTINE'S DAY CARD...
JPM DAVIS 2-13
© 2008 PAWS, INC. All Rights Reserved.
BUT I CAN'T CUT OUT A PAPER HEART TO SAVE MY LIFE!
MAYBE I COULD SUBSTITUTE ANOTHER ORGAN
"I LOVE YOU WITH ALL MY SPLEEN"
Distributed by Universal Press Syndicate

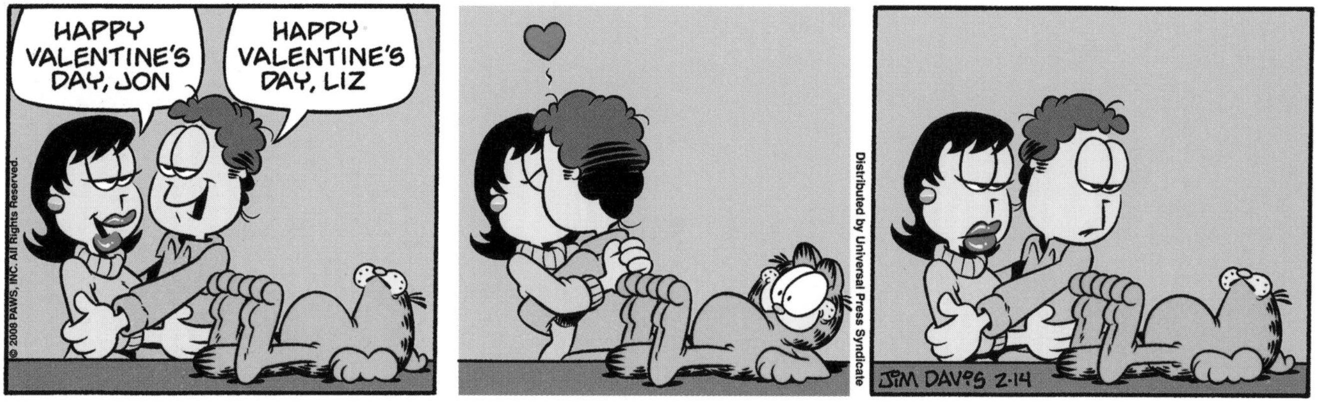
HAPPY VALENTINE'S DAY, JON
HAPPY VALENTINE'S DAY, LIZ
© 2008 PAWS, INC. All Rights Reserved.
Distributed by Universal Press Syndicate
JIM DAVIS 2-14

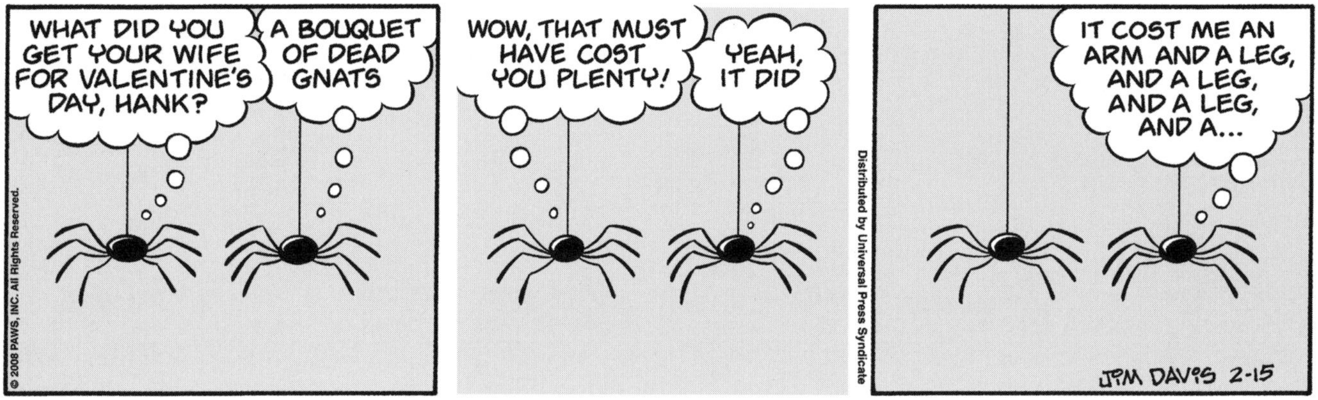
WHAT DID YOU GET YOUR WIFE FOR VALENTINE'S DAY, HANK?
A BOUQUET OF DEAD GNATS
WOW, THAT MUST HAVE COST YOU PLENTY!
YEAH, IT DID
IT COST ME AN ARM AND A LEG, AND A LEG, AND A LEG, AND A...
© 2008 PAWS, INC. All Rights Reserved.
Distributed by Universal Press Syndicate
JIM DAVIS 2-15

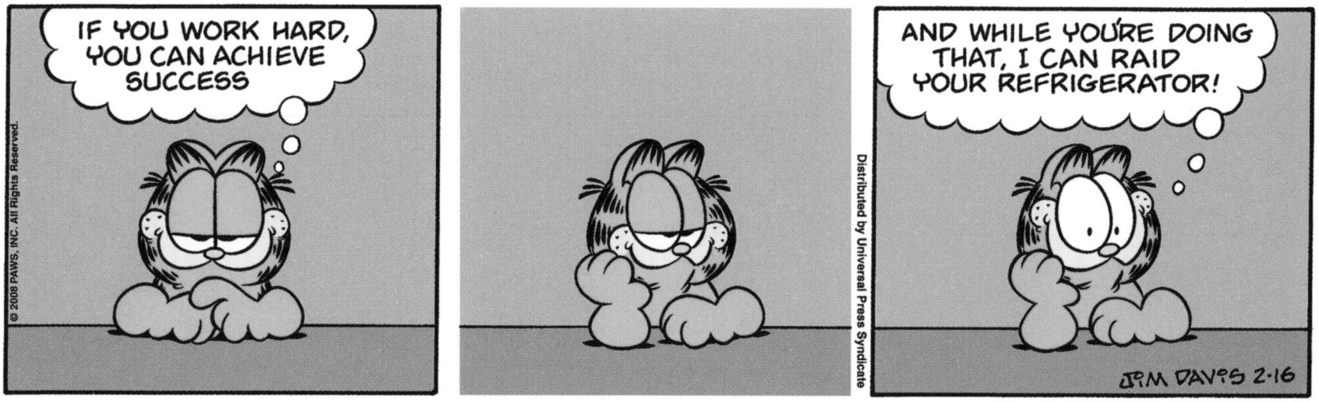
IF YOU WORK HARD, YOU CAN ACHIEVE SUCCESS
AND WHILE YOU'RE DOING THAT, I CAN RAID YOUR REFRIGERATOR!
© 2008 PAWS, INC. All Rights Reserved.
Distributed by Universal Press Syndicate
JIM DAVIS 2-16

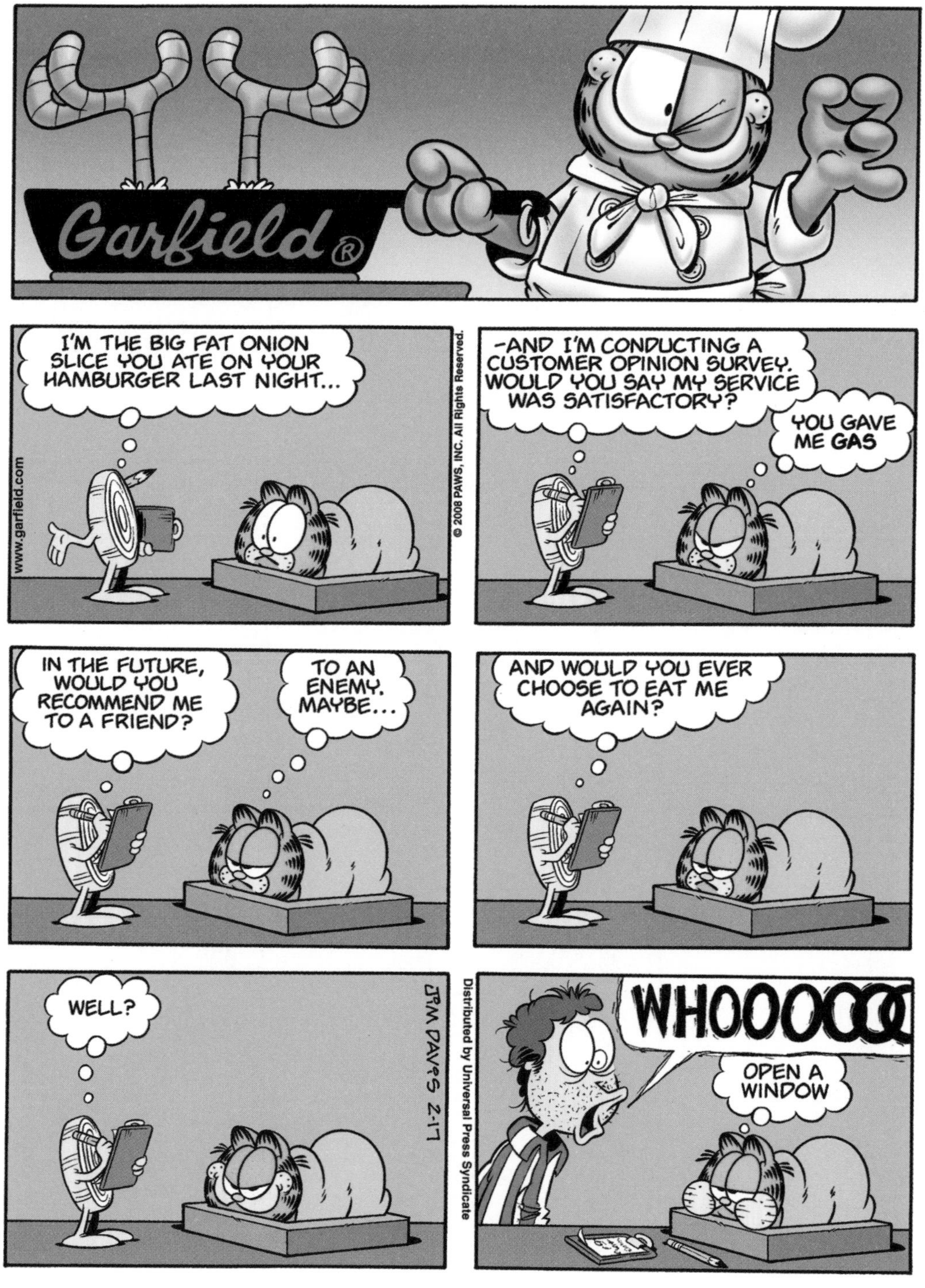
Garfield®
www.garfield.com
I'M THE BIG FAT ONION SLICE YOU ATE ON YOUR HAMBURGER LAST NIGHT...
© 2008 PAWS, INC. All Rights Reserved.
-AND I'M CONDUCTING A CUSTOMER OPINION SURVEY. WOULD YOU SAY MY SERVICE WAS SATISFACTORY?
YOU GAVE ME **GAS**
IN THE FUTURE, WOULD YOU RECOMMEND ME TO A FRIEND?
TO AN ENEMY. MAYBE...
AND WOULD YOU EVER CHOOSE TO EAT ME AGAIN?
WELL?
JIM DAVIS 2-17
Distributed by Universal Press Syndicate
WHOOOOOO
OPEN A WINDOW

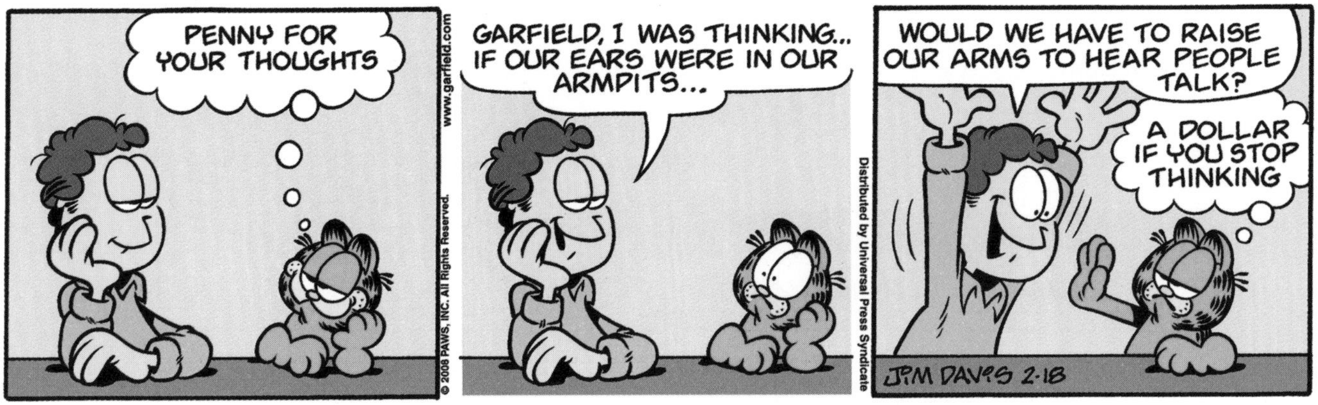
PENNY FOR YOUR THOUGHTS
© 2008 PAWS, INC. All Rights Reserved. www.garfield.com
GARFIELD, I WAS THINKING... IF OUR EARS WERE IN OUR ARMPITS...
Distributed by Universal Press Syndicate
WOULD WE HAVE TO RAISE OUR ARMS TO HEAR PEOPLE TALK?
A DOLLAR IF YOU STOP THINKING
JIM DAVIS 2·18

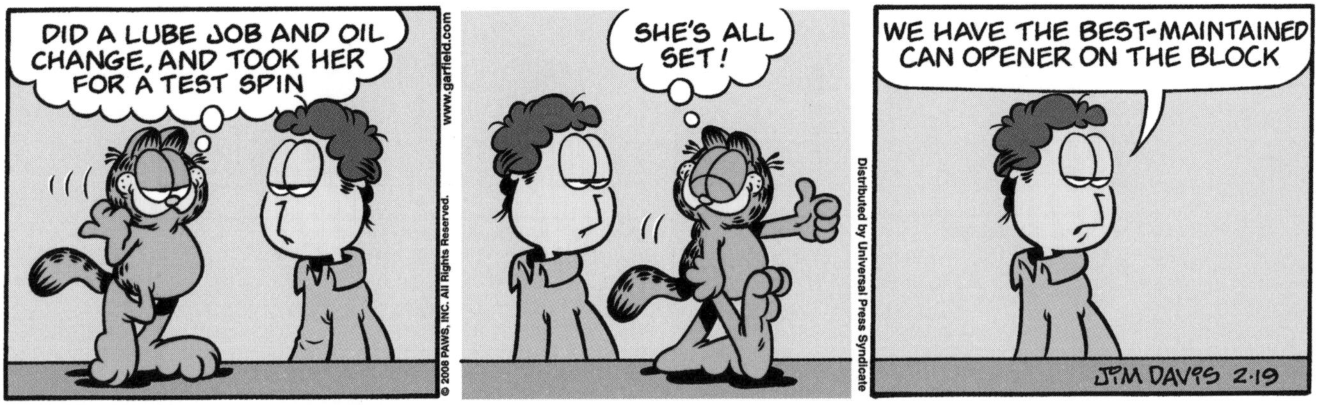
DID A LUBE JOB AND OIL CHANGE, AND TOOK HER FOR A TEST SPIN
© 2008 PAWS, INC. All Rights Reserved. www.garfield.com
SHE'S ALL SET!
Distributed by Universal Press Syndicate
WE HAVE THE BEST-MAINTAINED CAN OPENER ON THE BLOCK
JIM DAVIS 2·19

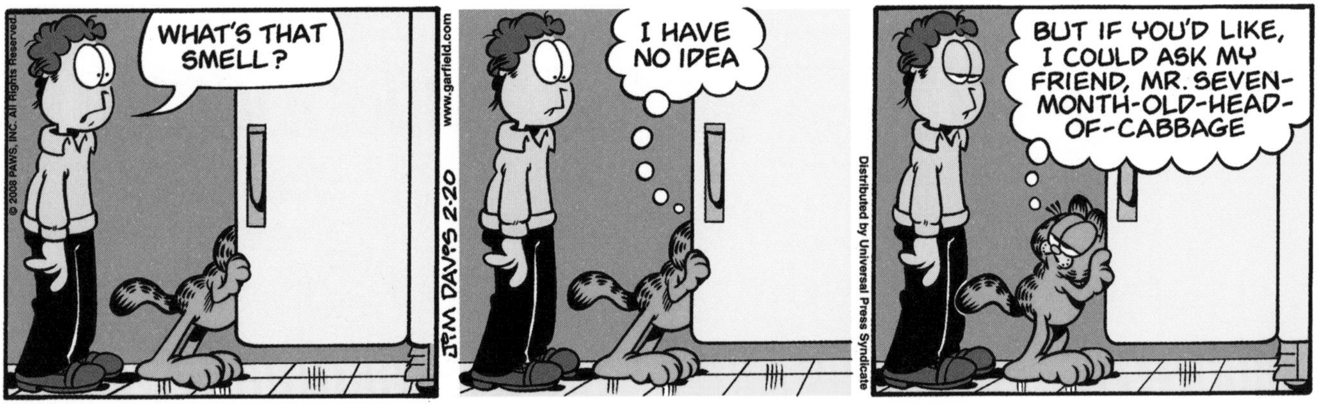
© 2008 PAWS, INC. All Rights Reserved.
WHAT'S THAT SMELL?
www.garfield.com
JIM DAVIS 2·20
I HAVE NO IDEA
Distributed by Universal Press Syndicate
BUT IF YOU'D LIKE, I COULD ASK MY FRIEND, MR. SEVEN-MONTH-OLD-HEAD-OF-CABBAGE

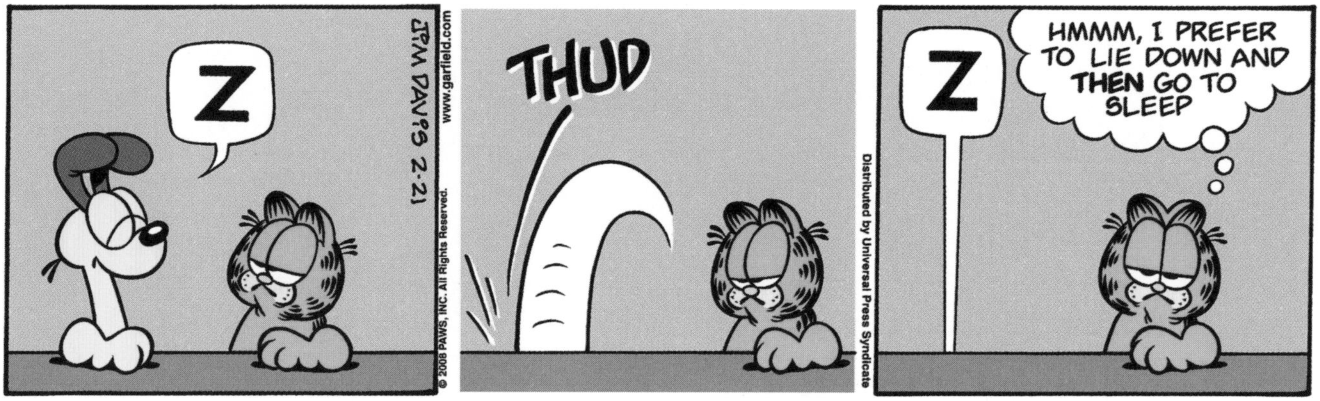
JIM DAVIS 2-21
www.garfield.com
© 2008 PAWS, INC. All Rights Reserved.
Z
THUD
Distributed by Universal Press Syndicate
Z
HMMM, I PREFER TO LIE DOWN AND THEN GO TO SLEEP

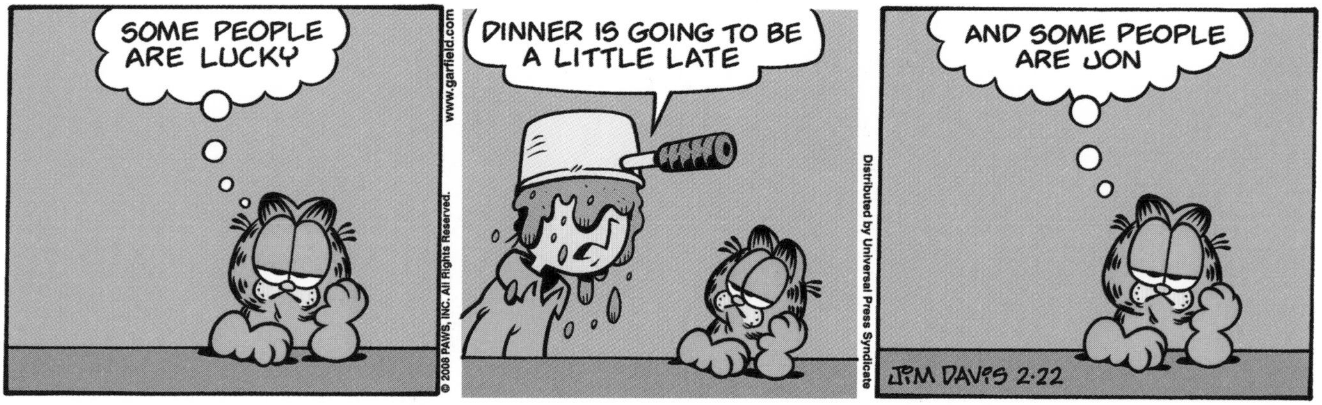
SOME PEOPLE ARE LUCKY
www.garfield.com
© 2008 PAWS, INC. All Rights Reserved.
DINNER IS GOING TO BE A LITTLE LATE
Distributed by Universal Press Syndicate
AND SOME PEOPLE ARE JON
JIM DAVIS 2-22

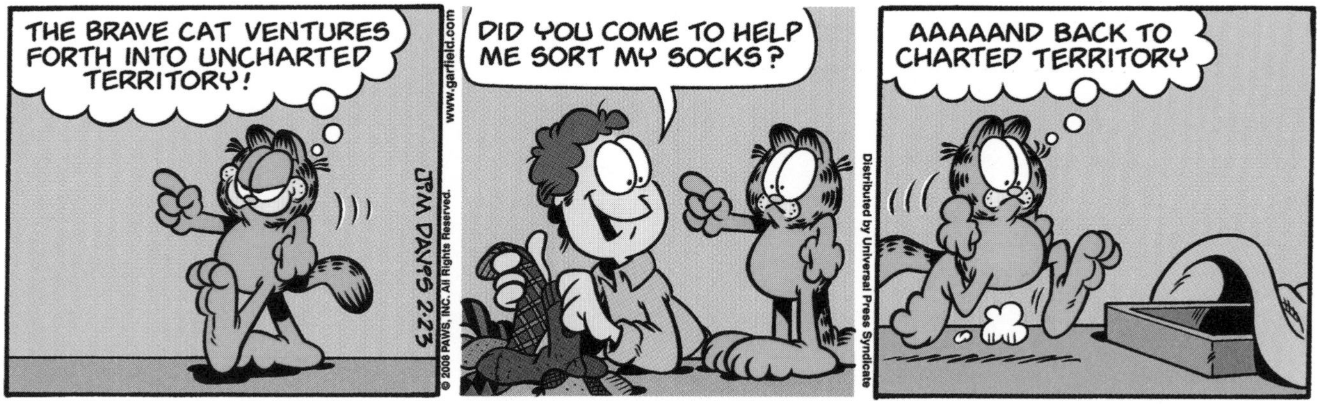
THE BRAVE CAT VENTURES FORTH INTO UNCHARTED TERRITORY!
JIM DAVIS 2-23
www.garfield.com
© 2008 PAWS, INC. All Rights Reserved.
DID YOU COME TO HELP ME SORT MY SOCKS?
Distributed by Universal Press Syndicate
AAAAAND BACK TO CHARTED TERRITORY

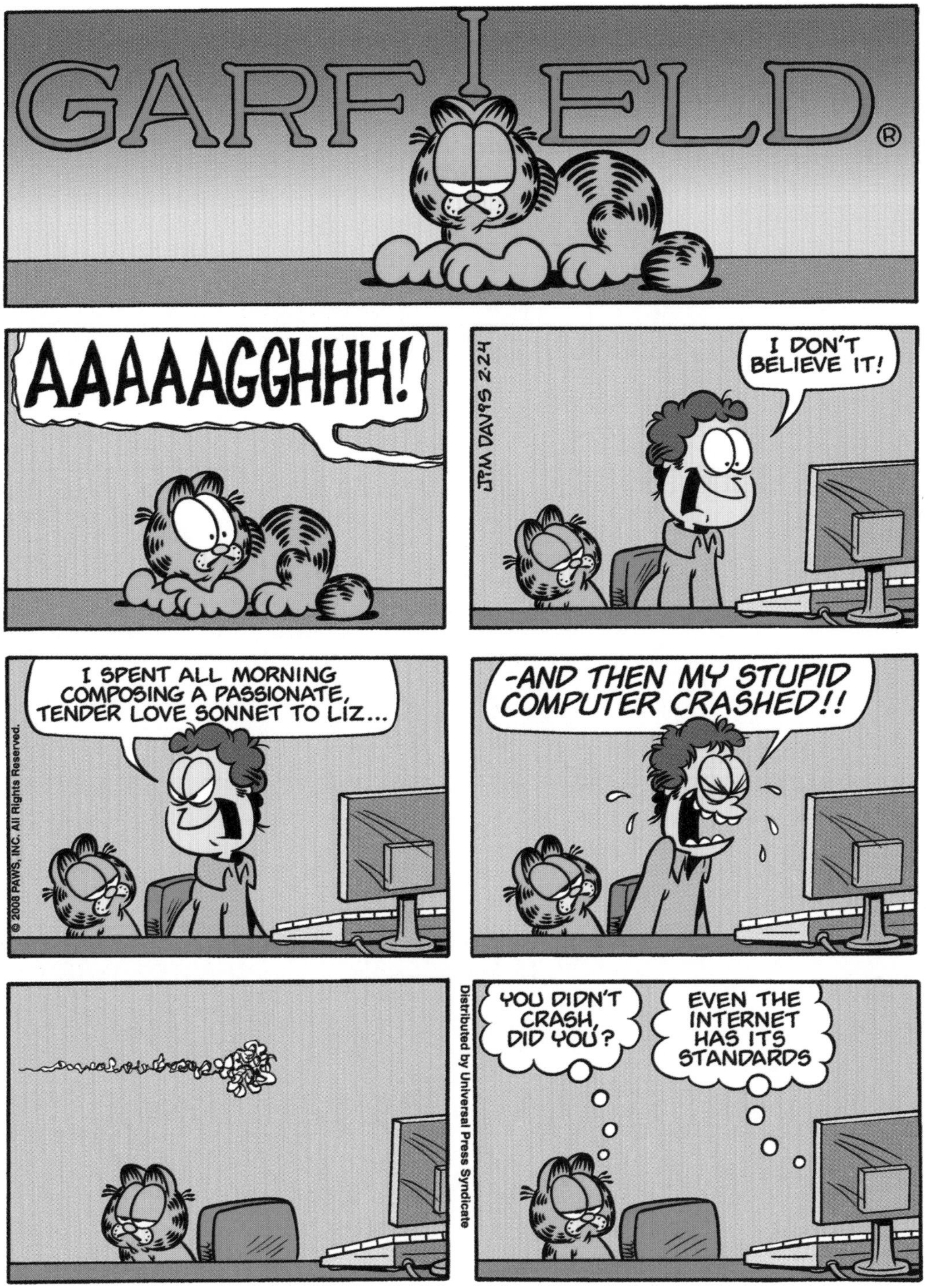
GARFIELD®
AAAAAGGHHH!
JPM DAVPS 2-24
I DON'T BELIEVE IT!
© 2008 PAWS, INC. All Rights Reserved.
I SPENT ALL MORNING COMPOSING A PASSIONATE, TENDER LOVE SONNET TO LIZ...
-AND THEN MY STUPID COMPUTER CRASHED!!
Distributed by Universal Press Syndicate
YOU DIDN'T CRASH, DID YOU?
EVEN THE INTERNET HAS ITS STANDARDS

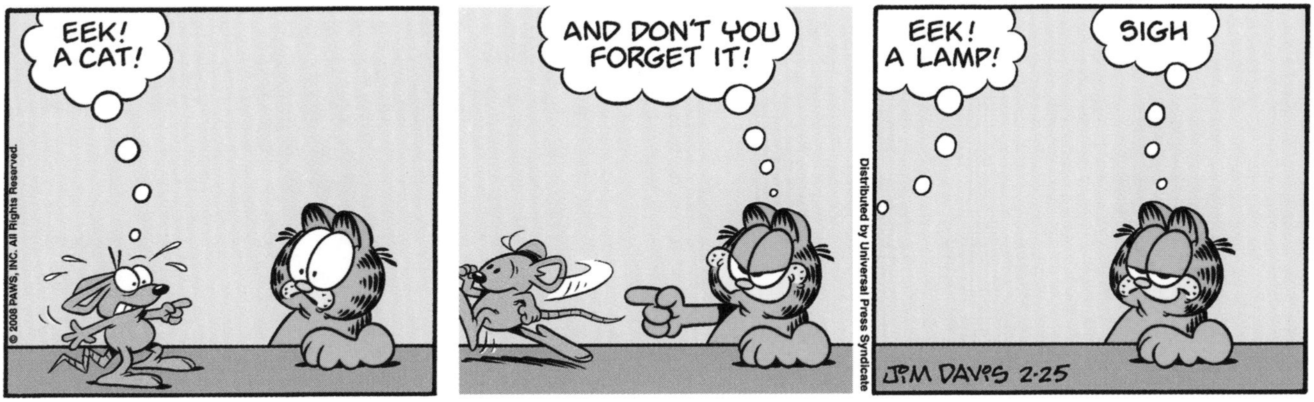
EEK! A CAT!
AND DON'T YOU FORGET IT!
EEK! A LAMP!
SIGH
© 2008 PAWS, INC. All Rights Reserved.
Distributed by Universal Press Syndicate
JIM DAVIS 2·25

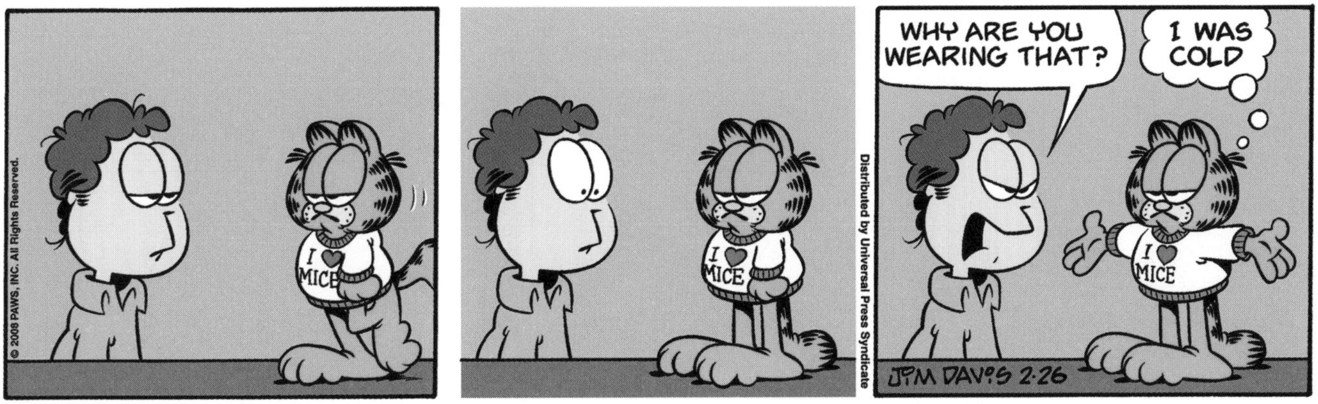
I ♥ MICE
WHY ARE YOU WEARING THAT?
I WAS COLD
© 2008 PAWS, INC. All Rights Reserved.
Distributed by Universal Press Syndicate
JIM DAVIS 2·26

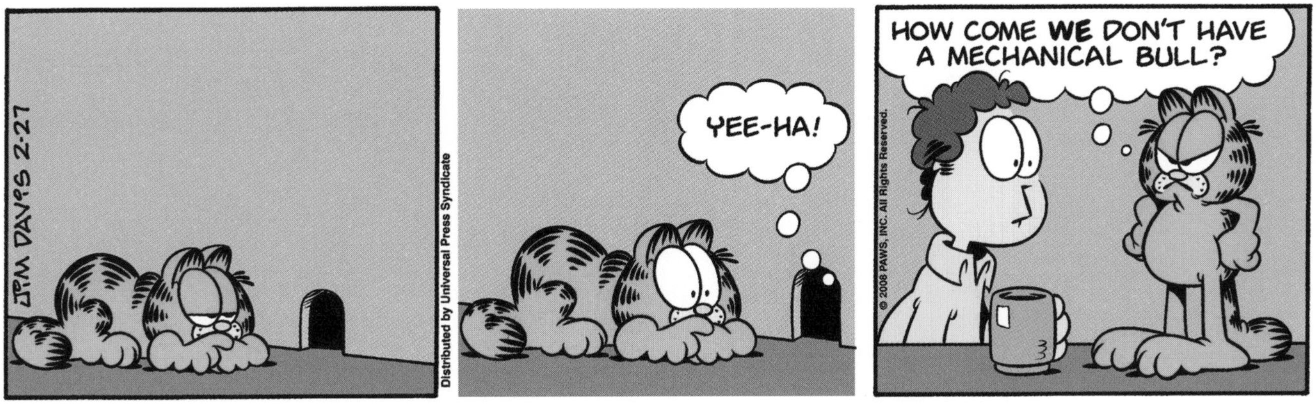
JIM DAVIS 2·27
YEE-HA!
HOW COME **WE** DON'T HAVE A MECHANICAL BULL?
Distributed by Universal Press Syndicate
© 2008 PAWS, INC. All Rights Reserved.

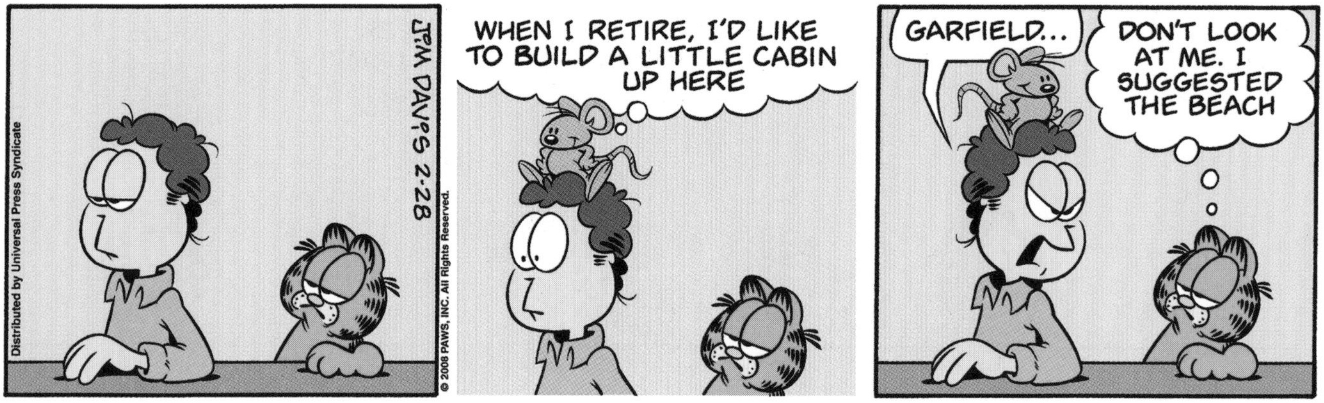
JIM DAVIS 2-28
Distributed by Universal Press Syndicate
© 2008 PAWS, INC. All Rights Reserved.
WHEN I RETIRE, I'D LIKE TO BUILD A LITTLE CABIN UP HERE
GARFIELD...
DON'T LOOK AT ME. I SUGGESTED THE BEACH

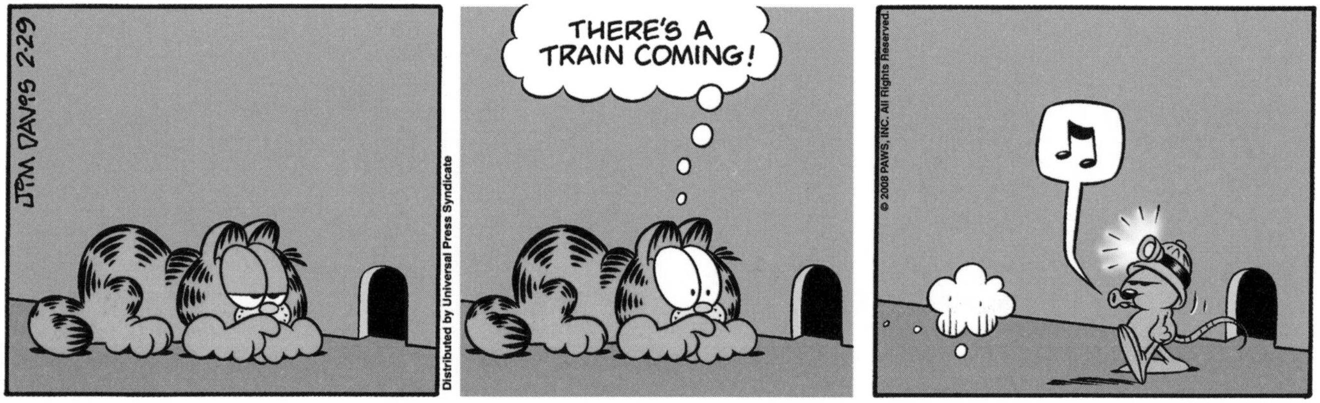
JIM DAVIS 2-29
Distributed by Universal Press Syndicate
THERE'S A TRAIN COMING!
© 2008 PAWS, INC. All Rights Reserved.

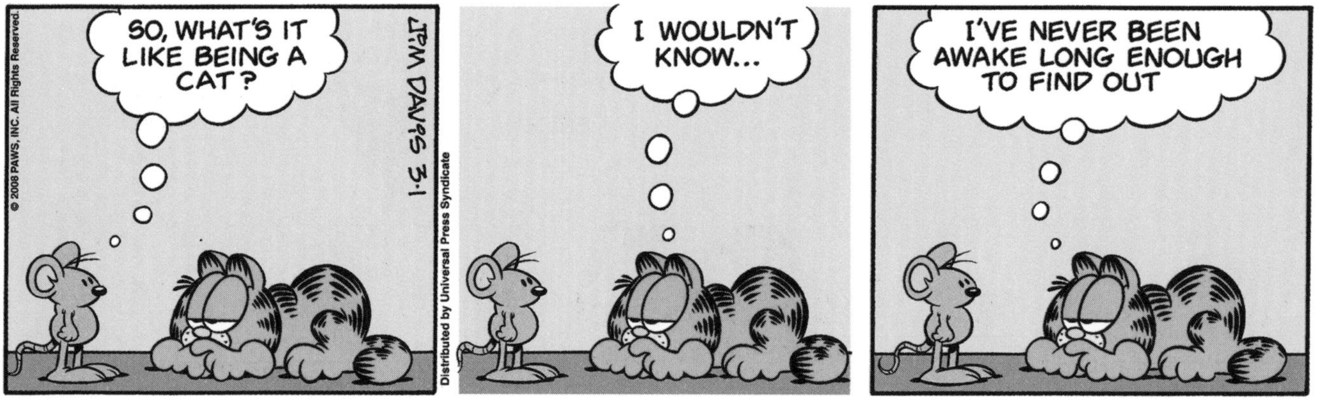
© 2008 PAWS, INC. All Rights Reserved.
SO, WHAT'S IT LIKE BEING A CAT?
JIM DAVIS 3-1
Distributed by Universal Press Syndicate
I WOULDN'T KNOW...
I'VE NEVER BEEN AWAKE LONG ENOUGH TO FIND OUT

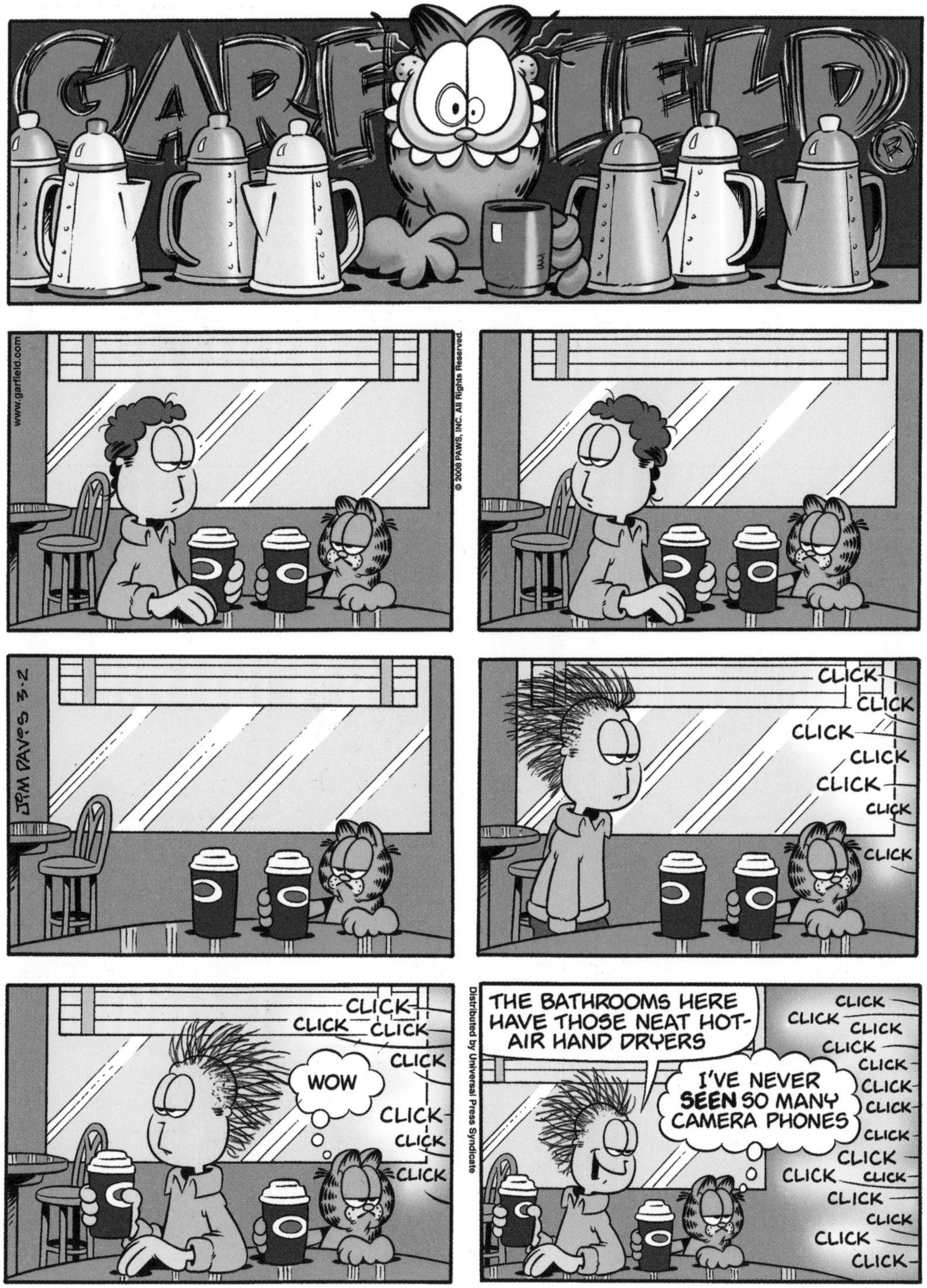
GARFIELD®
www.garfield.com
© 2008 PAWS, INC. All Rights Reserved.
JPM DAVPS 3-2
Distributed by Universal Press Syndicate
CLICK CLICK CLICK CLICK CLICK CLICK CLICK
CLICK CLICK CLICK CLICK CLICK CLICK CLICK
WOW
THE BATHROOMS HERE HAVE THOSE NEAT HOT-AIR HAND DRYERS
I'VE NEVER **SEEN** SO MANY CAMERA PHONES
CLICK CLICK CLICK CLICK CLICK CLICK CLICK CLICK CLICK CLICK CLICK CLICK CLICK CLICK CLICK CLICK

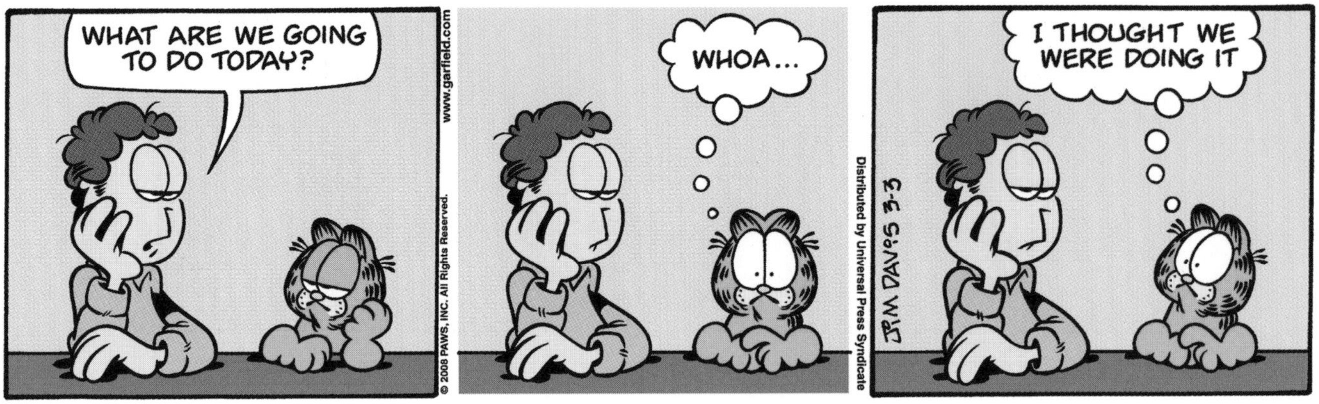
WHAT ARE WE GOING TO DO TODAY?
© 2008 PAWS, INC. All Rights Reserved. www.garfield.com
WHOA...
I THOUGHT WE WERE DOING IT
JPM DAV!S 3-3
Distributed by Universal Press Syndicate

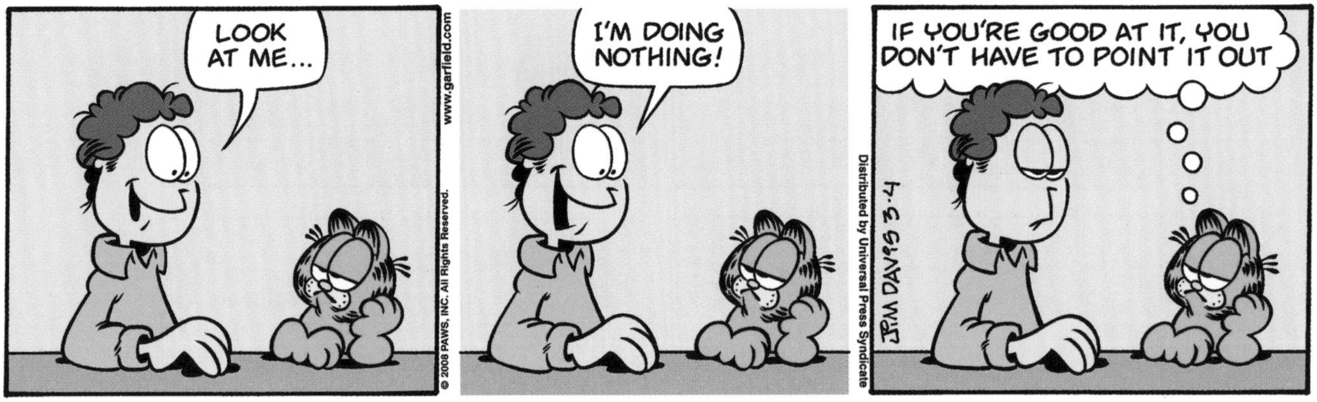
LOOK AT ME...
© 2008 PAWS, INC. All Rights Reserved. www.garfield.com
I'M DOING NOTHING!
IF YOU'RE GOOD AT IT, YOU DON'T HAVE TO POINT IT OUT
JPM DAV!S 3-4
Distributed by Universal Press Syndicate

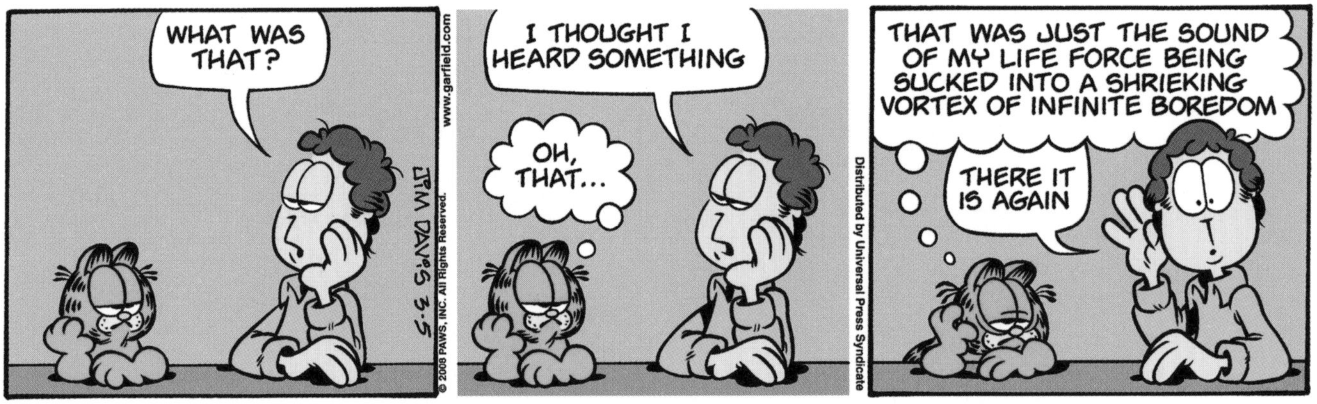
WHAT WAS THAT?
JPM DAV!S 3-5
© 2008 PAWS, INC. All Rights Reserved. www.garfield.com
I THOUGHT I HEARD SOMETHING
OH, THAT...
THAT WAS JUST THE SOUND OF MY LIFE FORCE BEING SUCKED INTO A SHRIEKING VORTEX OF INFINITE BOREDOM
THERE IT IS AGAIN
Distributed by Universal Press Syndicate

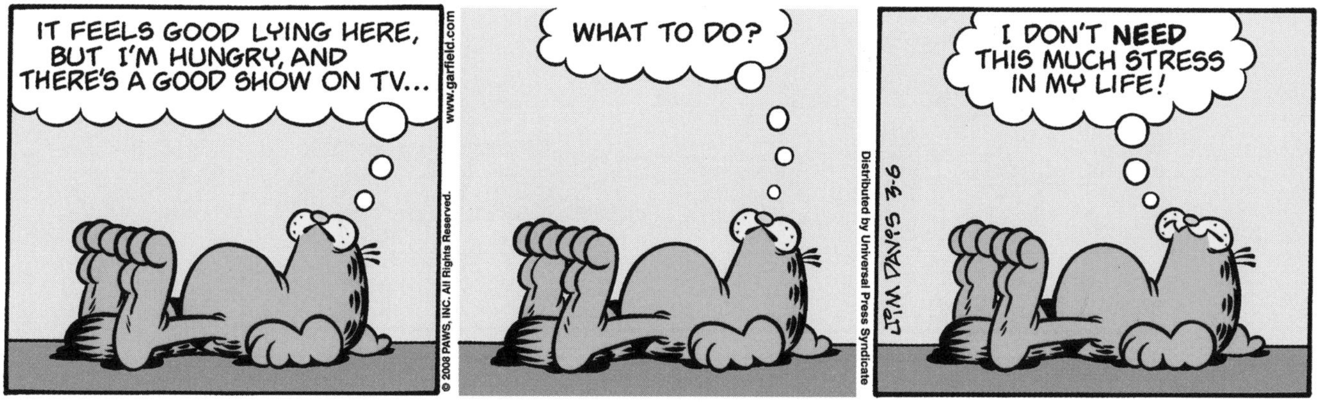
IT FEELS GOOD LYING HERE, BUT I'M HUNGRY, AND THERE'S A GOOD SHOW ON TV...
WHAT TO DO?
I DON'T NEED THIS MUCH STRESS IN MY LIFE!
www.garfield.com
© 2008 PAWS, INC. All Rights Reserved.
Distributed by Universal Press Syndicate
JIM DAVIS 3-6

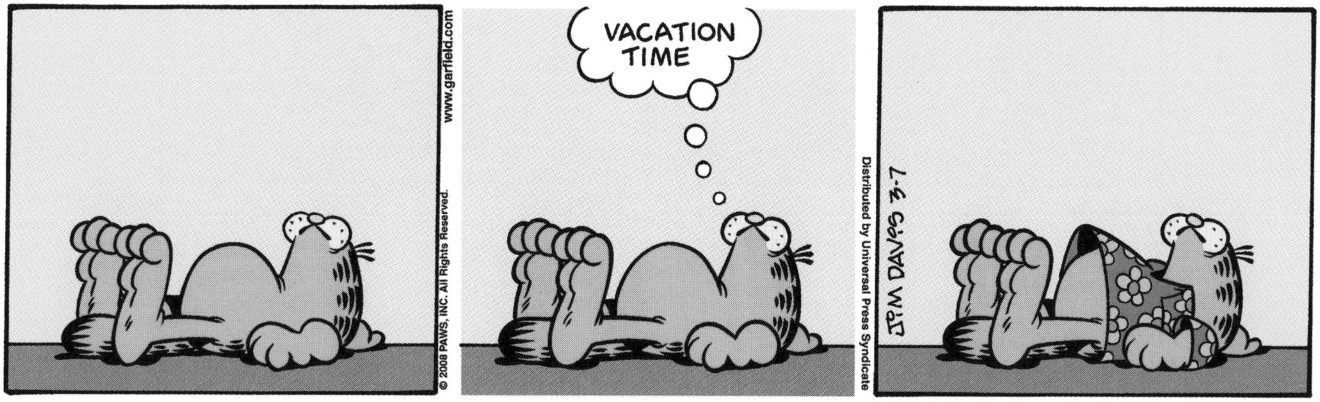
VACATION TIME
www.garfield.com
© 2008 PAWS, INC. All Rights Reserved.
Distributed by Universal Press Syndicate
JIM DAVIS 3-7

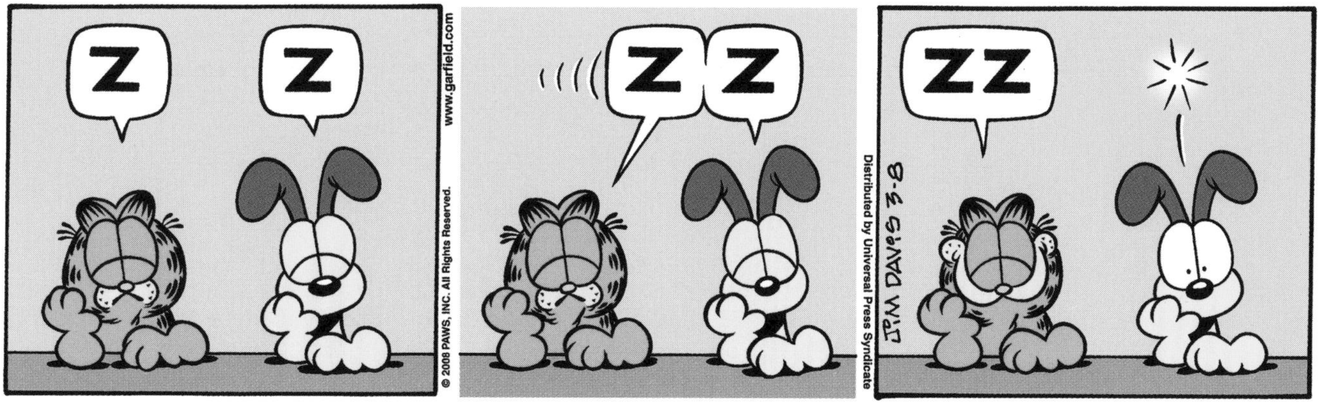
Z
Z
Z
Z
ZZ
www.garfield.com
© 2008 PAWS, INC. All Rights Reserved.
Distributed by Universal Press Syndicate
JIM DAVIS 3-8

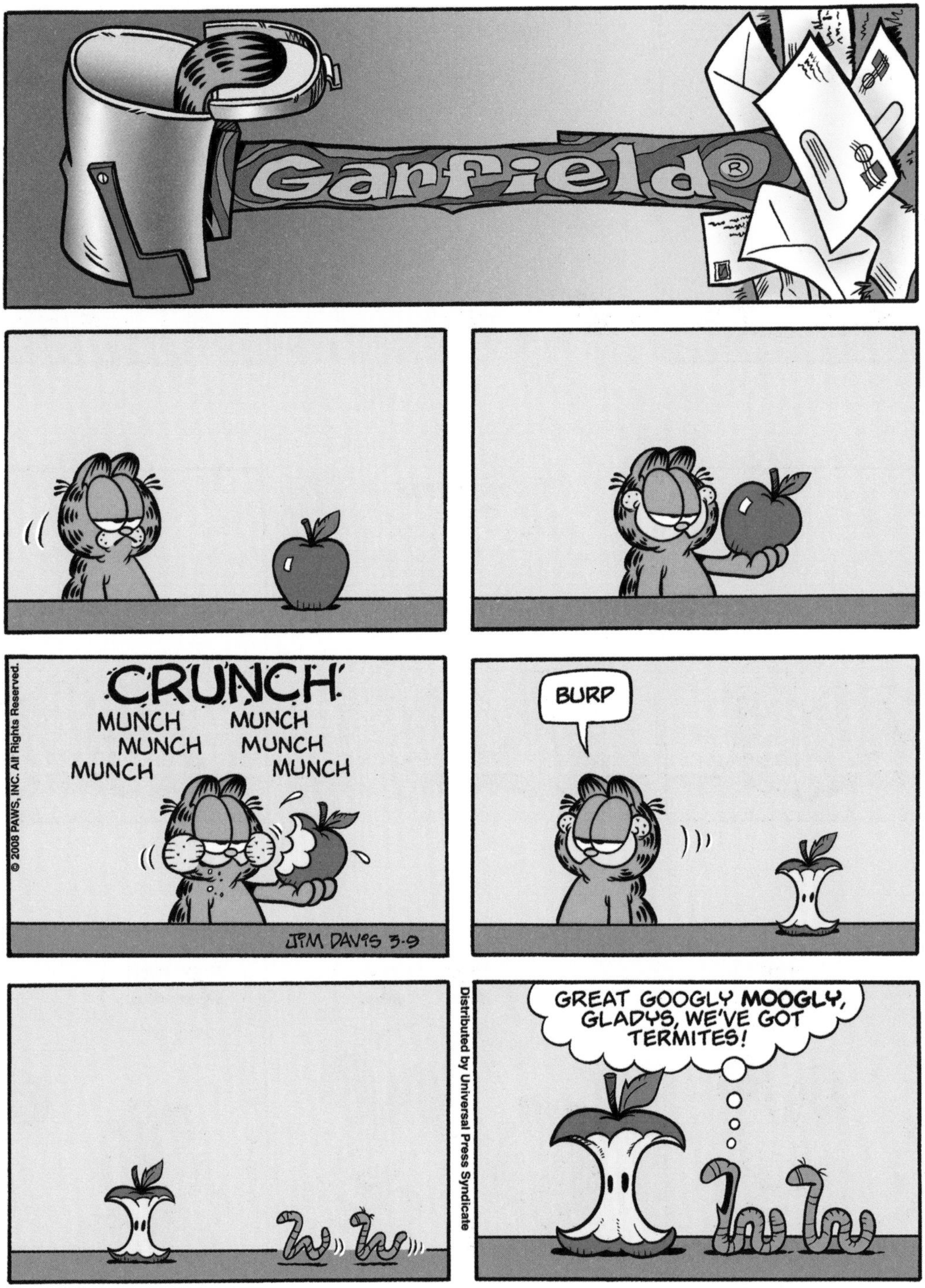
Garfield®
CRUNCH
MUNCH MUNCH MUNCH MUNCH MUNCH MUNCH
© 2008 PAWS, INC. All Rights Reserved.
JIM DAVIS 3-9
BURP
Distributed by Universal Press Syndicate
GREAT GOOGLY MOOGLY, GLADYS, WE'VE GOT TERMITES!

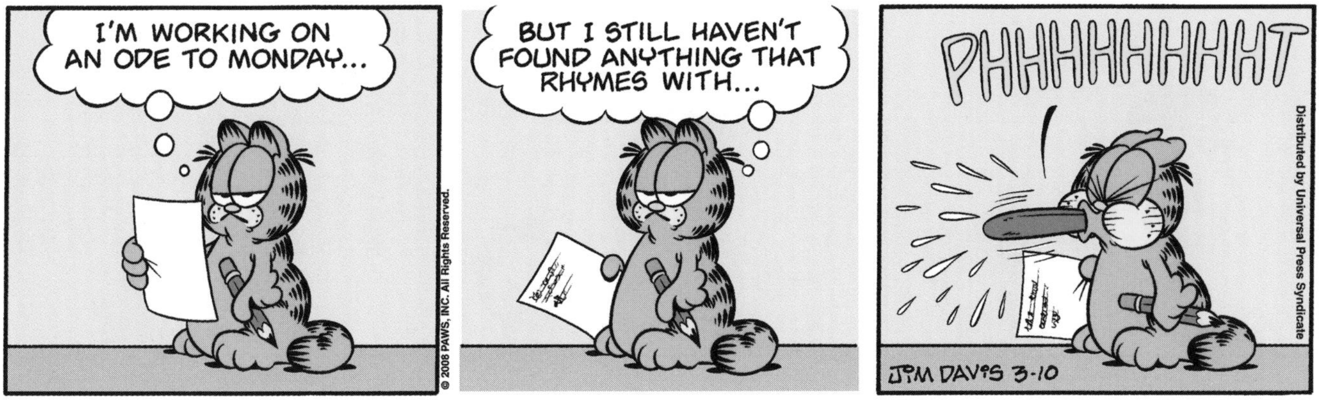
I'M WORKING ON AN ODE TO MONDAY...
BUT I STILL HAVEN'T FOUND ANYTHING THAT RHYMES WITH...
PHHHHHHHHT
JIM DAVIS 3-10
© 2008 PAWS, INC. All Rights Reserved.
Distributed by Universal Press Syndicate

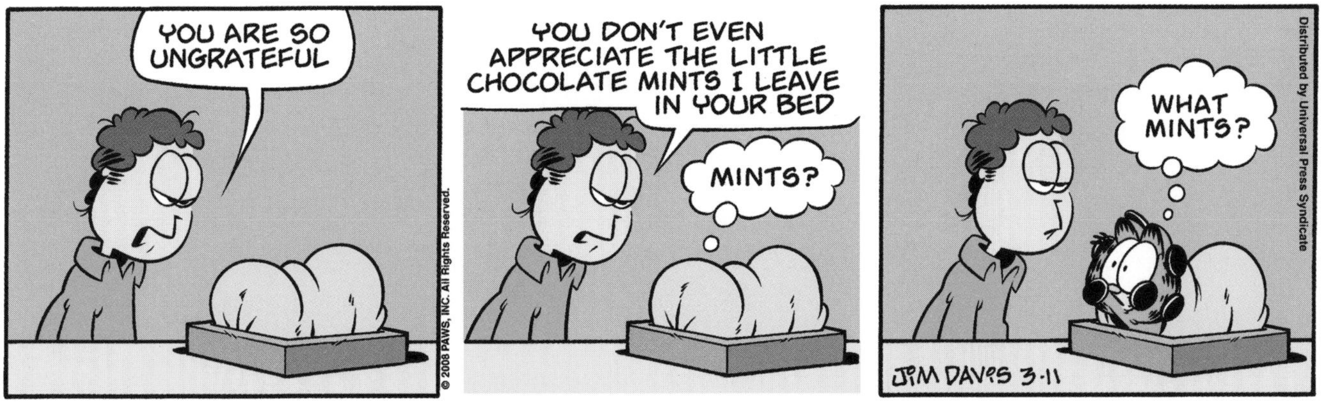
YOU ARE SO UNGRATEFUL
YOU DON'T EVEN APPRECIATE THE LITTLE CHOCOLATE MINTS I LEAVE IN YOUR BED
MINTS?
WHAT MINTS?
JIM DAVIS 3-11
© 2008 PAWS, INC. All Rights Reserved.
Distributed by Universal Press Syndicate

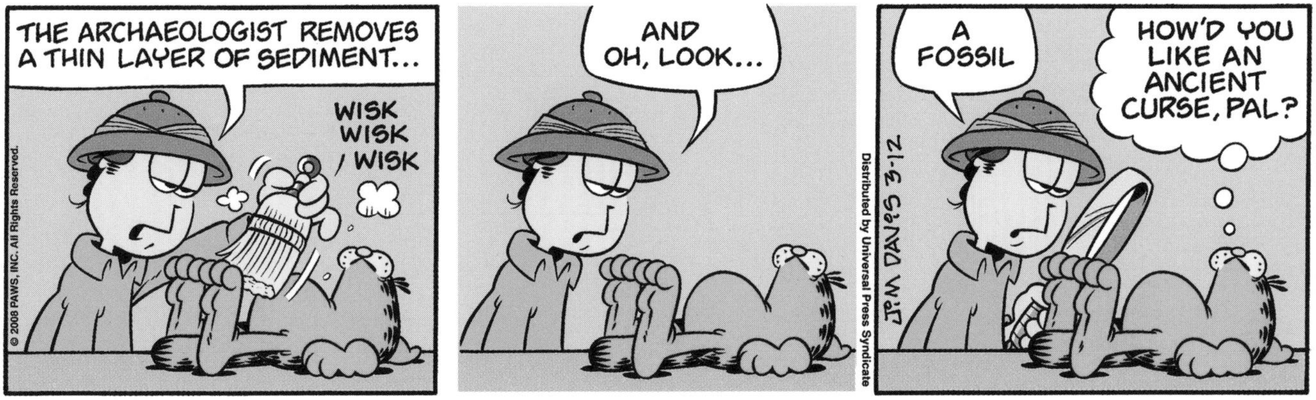
THE ARCHAEOLOGIST REMOVES A THIN LAYER OF SEDIMENT...
WISK WISK WISK
AND OH, LOOK...
A FOSSIL
HOW'D YOU LIKE AN ANCIENT CURSE, PAL?
JIM DAVIS 3-12
© 2008 PAWS, INC. All Rights Reserved.
Distributed by Universal Press Syndicate

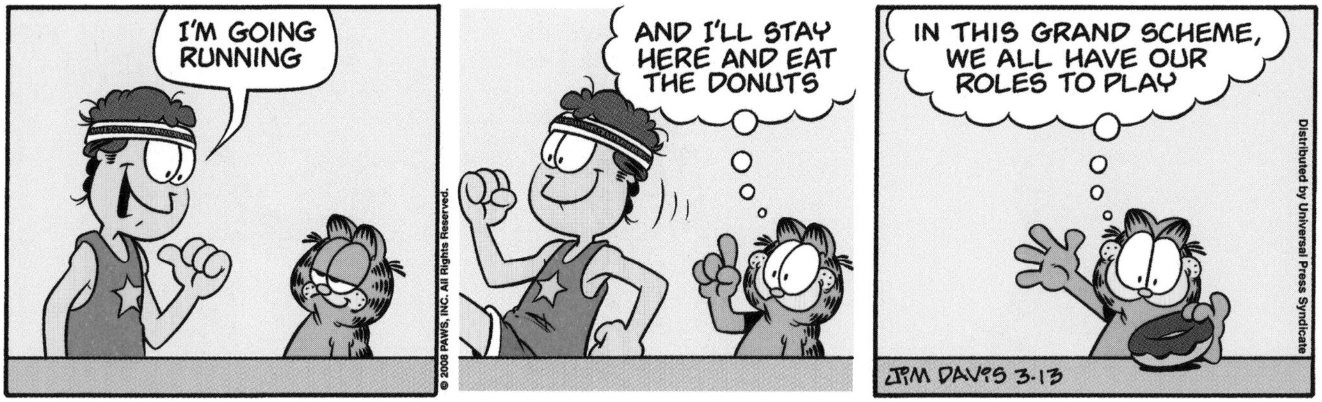
I'M GOING RUNNING
AND I'LL STAY HERE AND EAT THE DONUTS
IN THIS GRAND SCHEME, WE ALL HAVE OUR ROLES TO PLAY
JIM DAVIS 3-13
© 2008 PAWS, INC. All Rights Reserved.
Distributed by Universal Press Syndicate

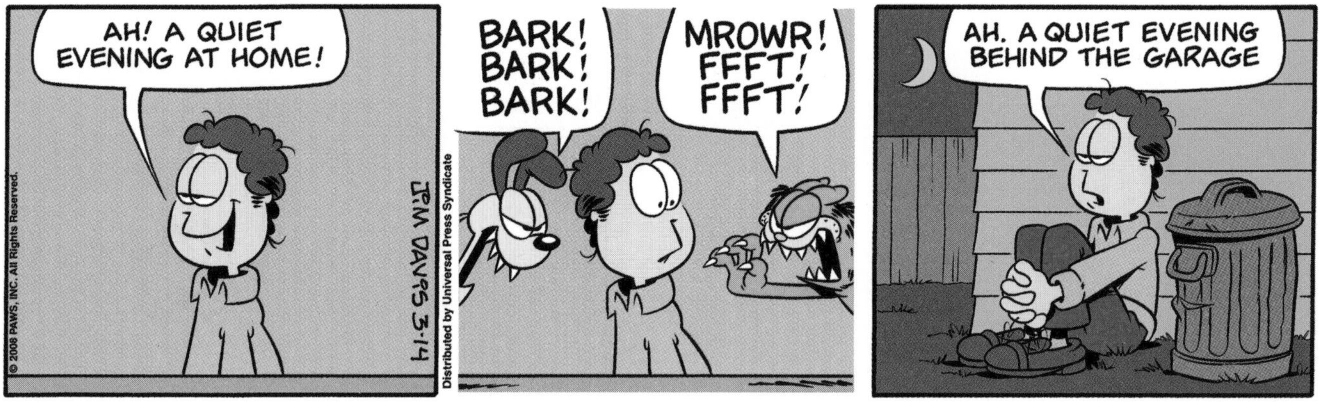
AH! A QUIET EVENING AT HOME!
BARK! BARK! BARK!
MROWR! FFFT! FFFT!
AH. A QUIET EVENING BEHIND THE GARAGE
JIM DAVIS 3-14
© 2008 PAWS, INC. All Rights Reserved.
Distributed by Universal Press Syndicate

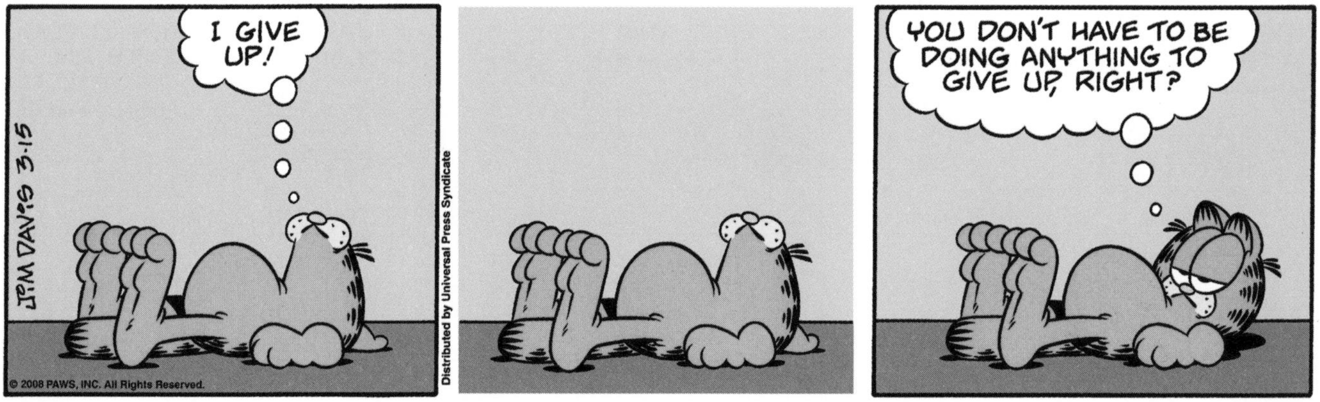
I GIVE UP!
YOU DON'T HAVE TO BE DOING ANYTHING TO GIVE UP, RIGHT?
JIM DAVIS 3-15
© 2008 PAWS, INC. All Rights Reserved.
Distributed by Universal Press Syndicate

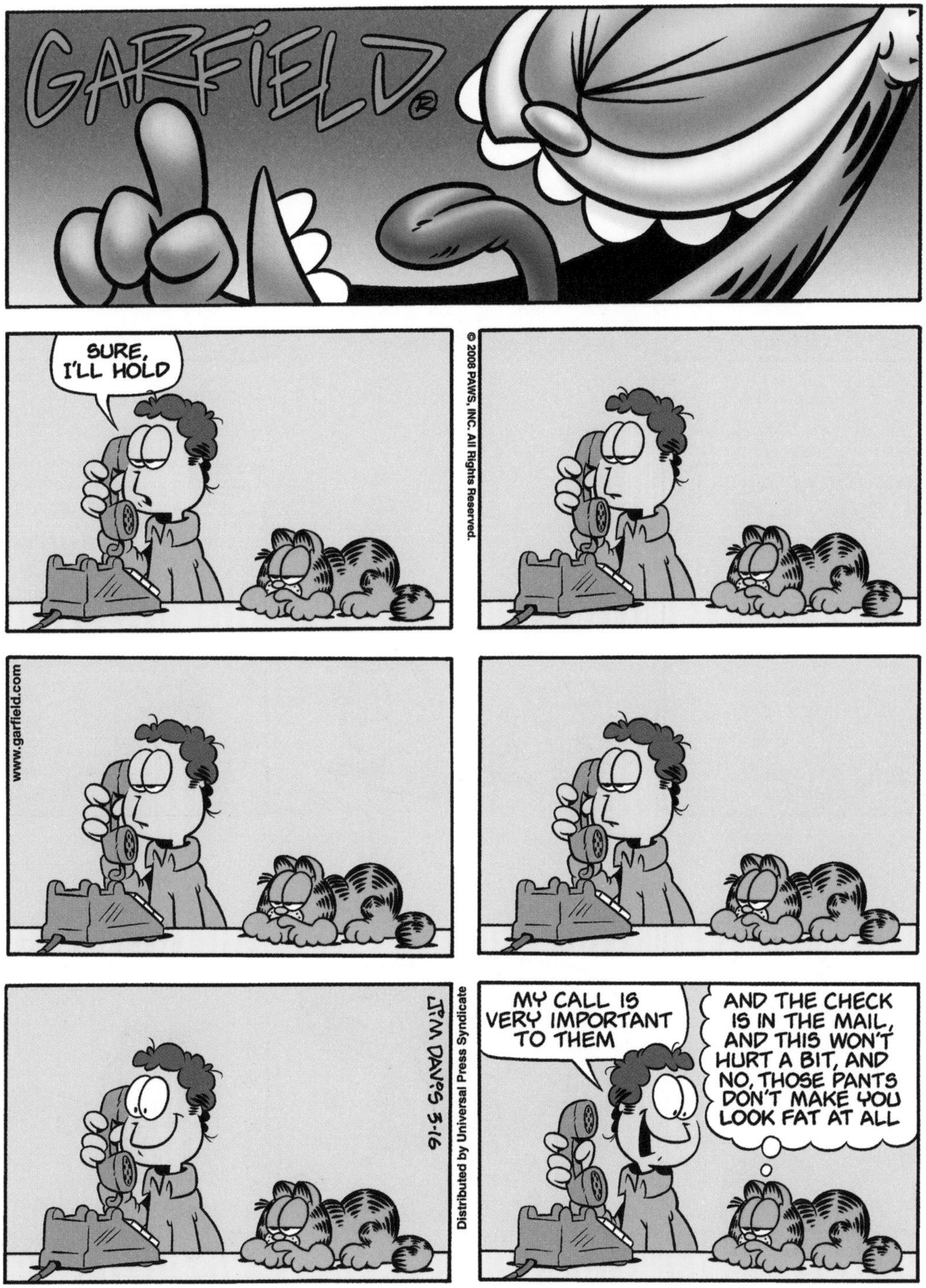
GARFIELD®
SURE, I'LL HOLD
© 2008 PAWS, INC. All Rights Reserved.
www.garfield.com
JPM DAVFS 3-16
Distributed by Universal Press Syndicate
MY CALL IS VERY IMPORTANT TO THEM
AND THE CHECK IS IN THE MAIL, AND THIS WON'T HURT A BIT, AND NO, THOSE PANTS DON'T MAKE YOU LOOK FAT AT ALL

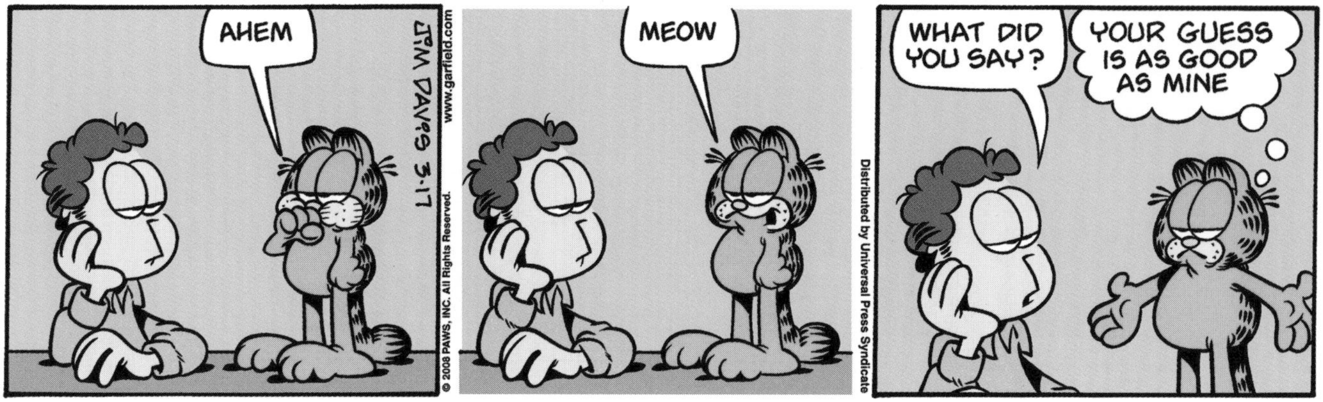
AHEM
JIM DAVIS 3.17
www.garfield.com
© 2008 PAWS, INC. All Rights Reserved.
MEOW
Distributed by Universal Press Syndicate
WHAT DID YOU SAY?
YOUR GUESS IS AS GOOD AS MINE

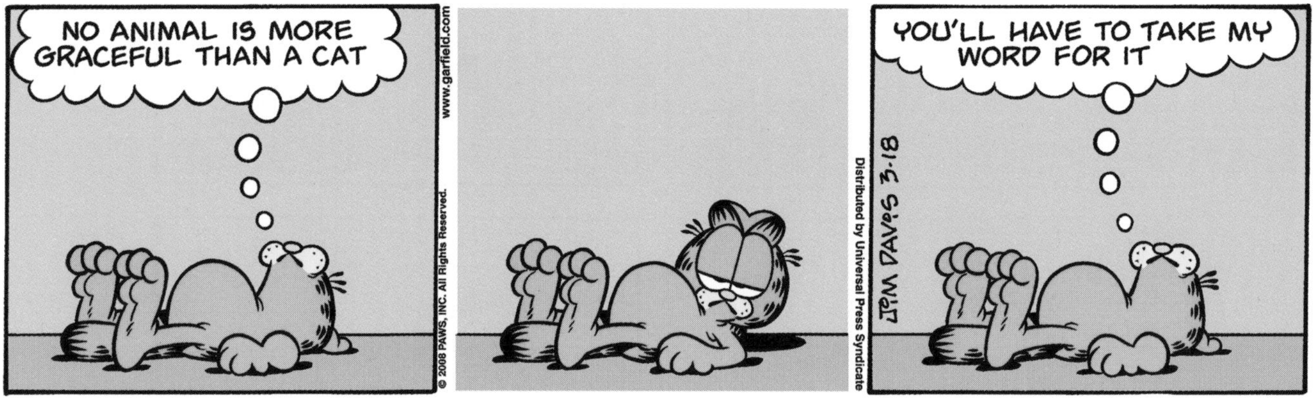
NO ANIMAL IS MORE GRACEFUL THAN A CAT
www.garfield.com
© 2008 PAWS, INC. All Rights Reserved.
Distributed by Universal Press Syndicate
JIM DAVIS 3.18
YOU'LL HAVE TO TAKE MY WORD FOR IT

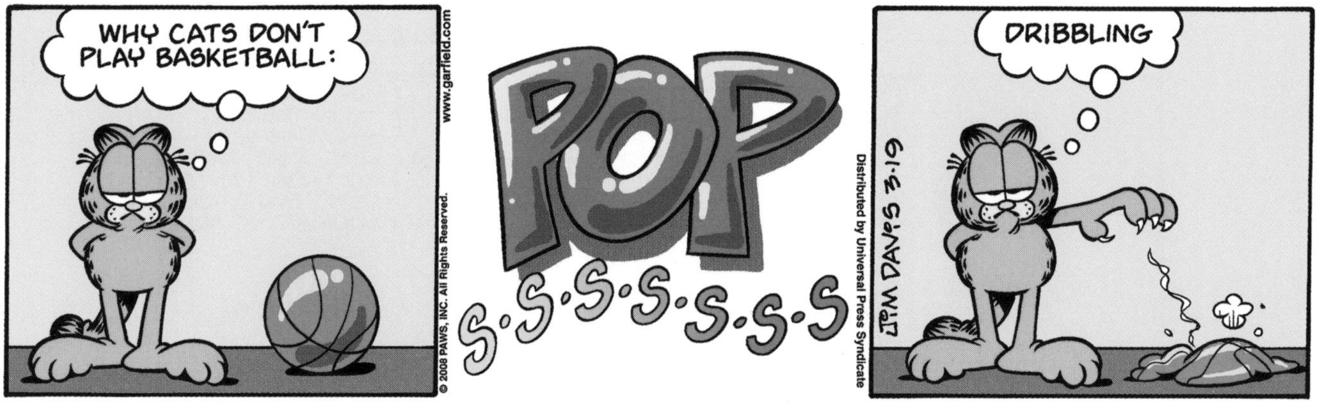
WHY CATS DON'T PLAY BASKETBALL:
www.garfield.com
© 2008 PAWS, INC. All Rights Reserved.
POP
S-S-S-S-S-S-S-S-S
Distributed by Universal Press Syndicate
JIM DAVIS 3.19
DRIBBLING

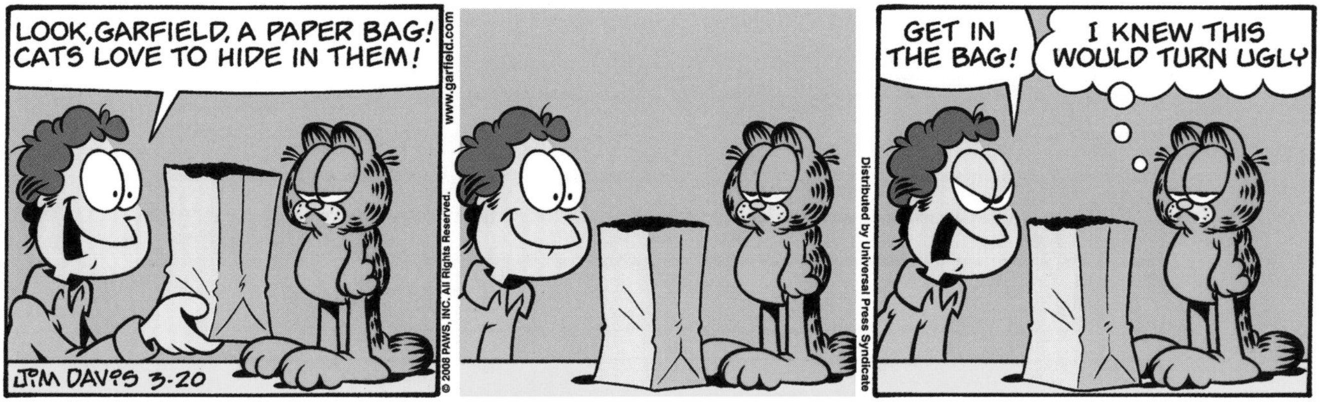
LOOK, GARFIELD, A PAPER BAG! CATS LOVE TO HIDE IN THEM!
JIM DAVIS 3-20
GET IN THE BAG!
I KNEW THIS WOULD TURN UGLY
© 2008 PAWS, INC. All Rights Reserved. www.garfield.com
Distributed by Universal Press Syndicate

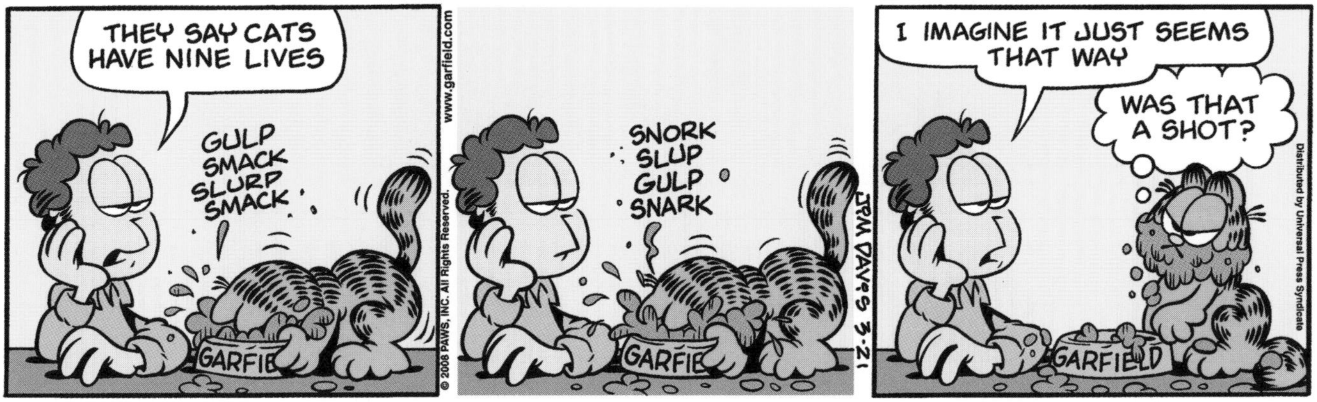
THEY SAY CATS HAVE NINE LIVES
GULP SMACK SLURP SMACK
GARFIE
SNORK SLUP GULP SNARK
GARFIE
JIM DAVIS 3-21
I IMAGINE IT JUST SEEMS THAT WAY
WAS THAT A SHOT?
GARFIELD
© 2008 PAWS, INC. All Rights Reserved. www.garfield.com
Distributed by Universal Press Syndicate

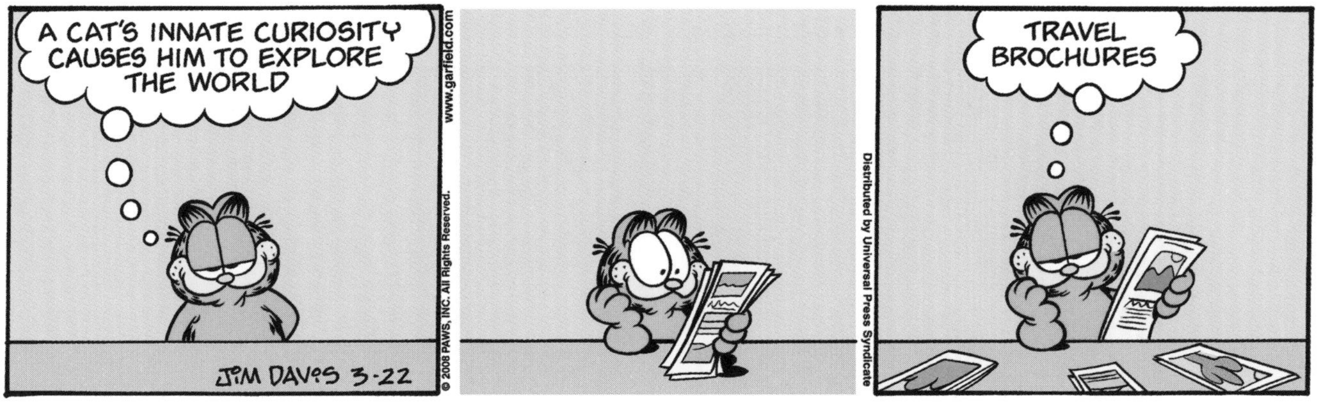
A CAT'S INNATE CURIOSITY CAUSES HIM TO EXPLORE THE WORLD
JIM DAVIS 3-22
TRAVEL BROCHURES
© 2008 PAWS, INC. All Rights Reserved. www.garfield.com
Distributed by Universal Press Syndicate

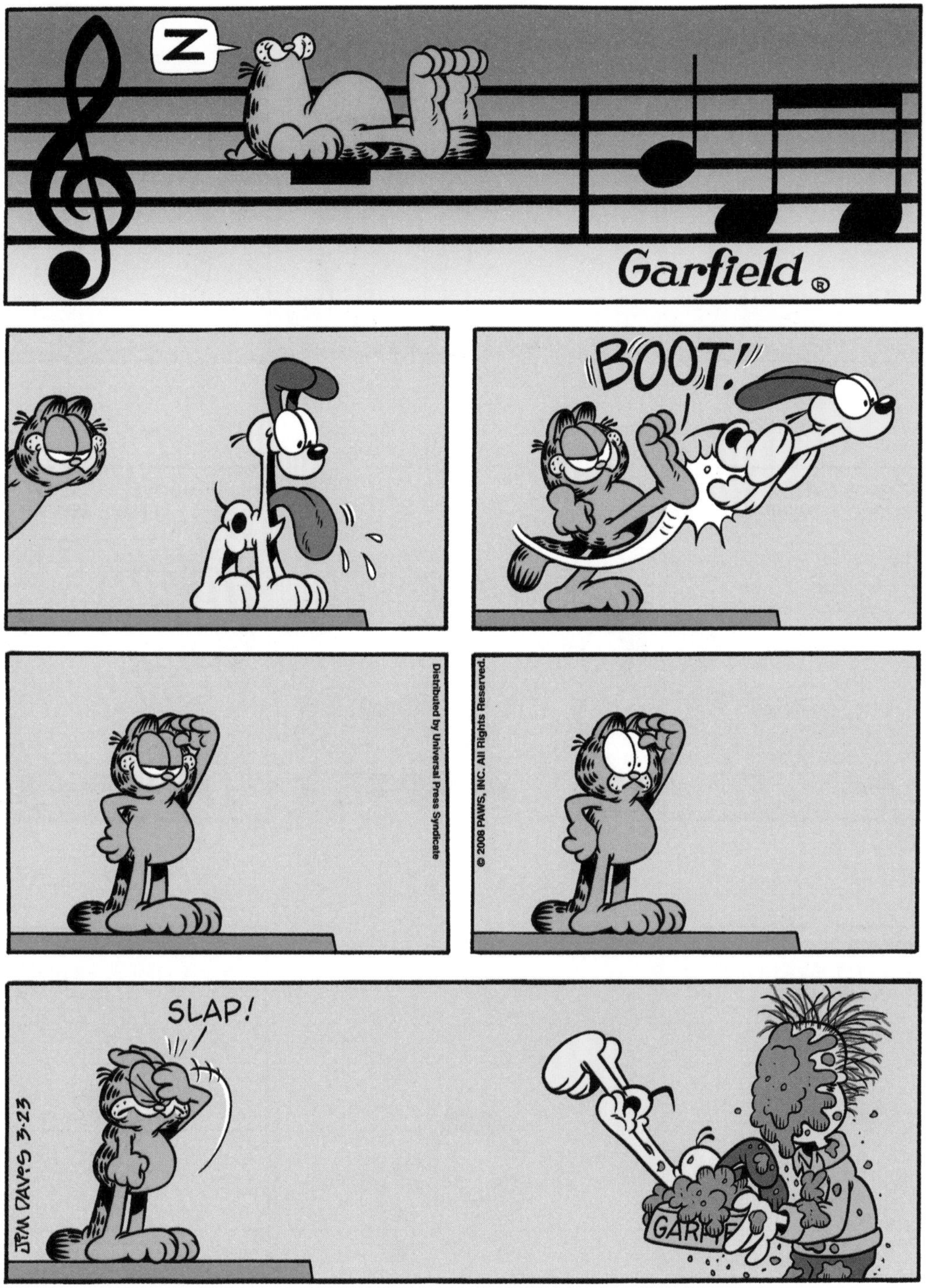
Z
Garfield ®
BOOT!
Distributed by Universal Press Syndicate
© 2008 PAWS, INC. All Rights Reserved.
SLAP!
JPM DAVPS 3·23
GARF

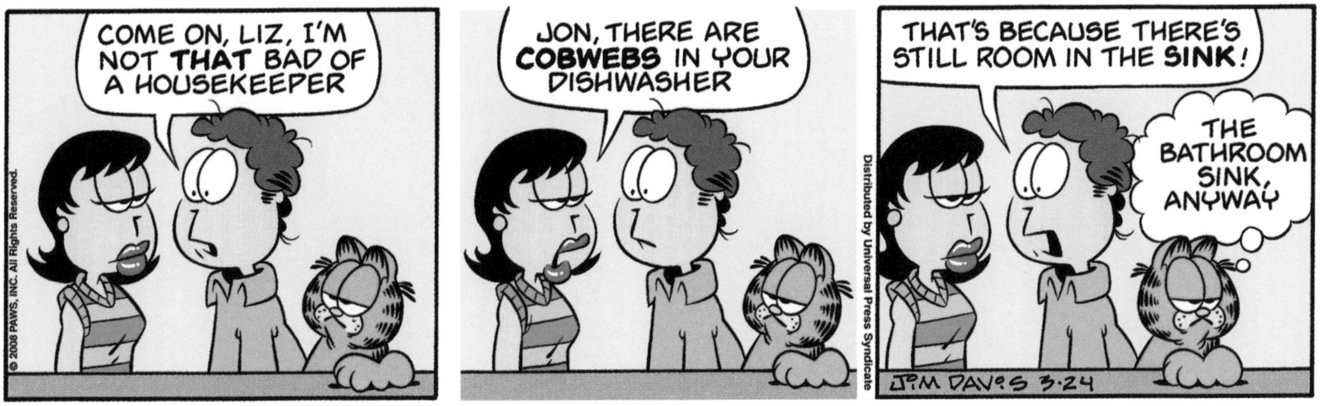
COME ON, LIZ, I'M NOT **THAT** BAD OF A HOUSEKEEPER
© 2008 PAWS, INC. All Rights Reserved.
JON, THERE ARE **COBWEBS** IN YOUR DISHWASHER
Distributed by Universal Press Syndicate
THAT'S BECAUSE THERE'S STILL ROOM IN THE **SINK**!
THE BATHROOM SINK, ANYWAY
JIM DAVIS 3-24

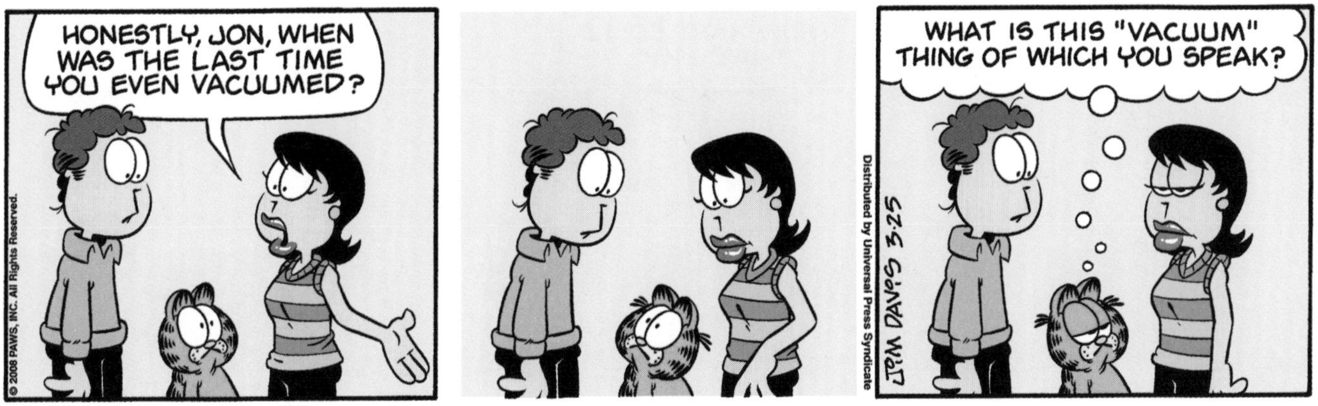
HONESTLY, JON, WHEN WAS THE LAST TIME YOU EVEN VACUUMED?
© 2008 PAWS, INC. All Rights Reserved.
Distributed by Universal Press Syndicate
WHAT IS THIS "VACUUM" THING OF WHICH YOU SPEAK?
JIM DAVIS 3-25

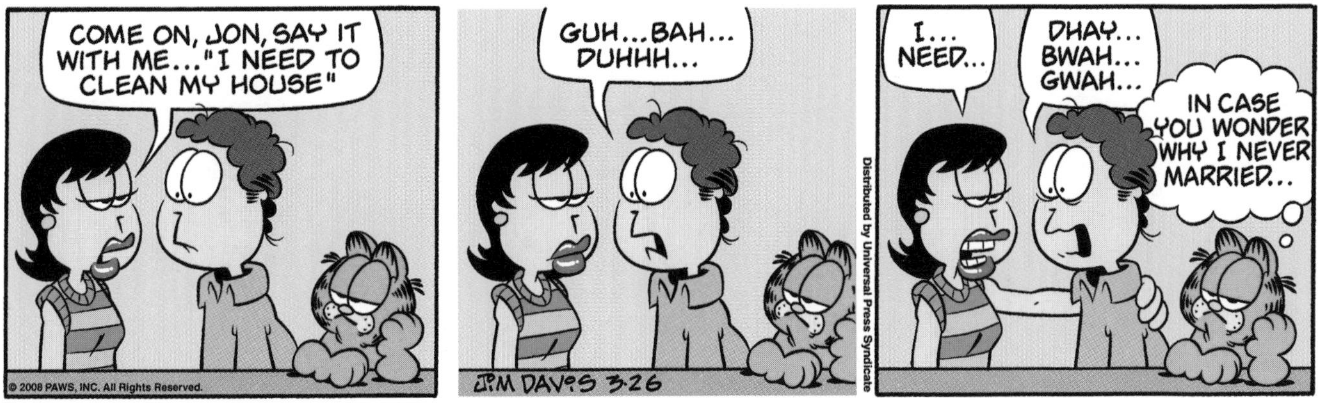
COME ON, JON, SAY IT WITH ME..."I NEED TO CLEAN MY HOUSE"
© 2008 PAWS, INC. All Rights Reserved.
GUH...BAH... DUHHH...
JIM DAVIS 3-26
Distributed by Universal Press Syndicate
I... NEED...
DHAY... BWAH... GWAH...
IN CASE YOU WONDER WHY I NEVER MARRIED...

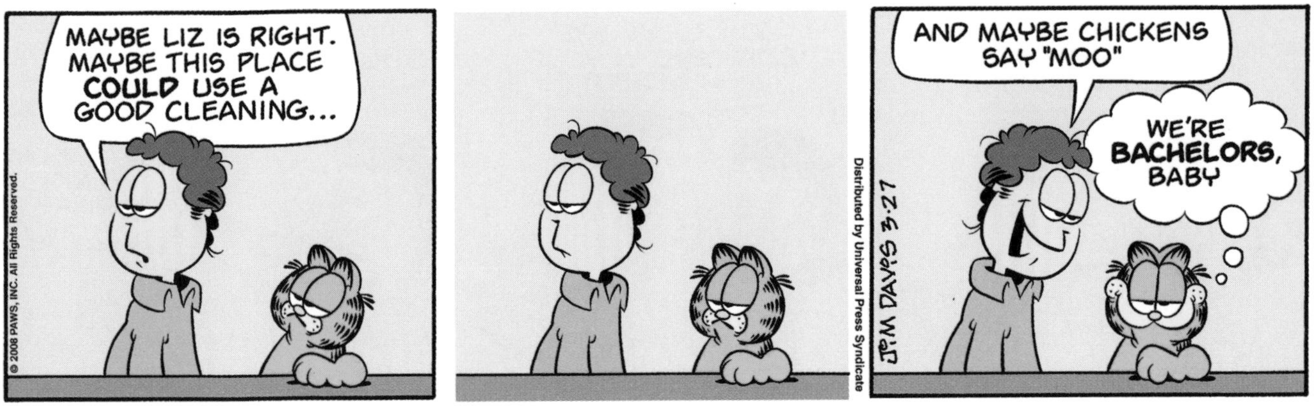
MAYBE LIZ IS RIGHT. MAYBE THIS PLACE **COULD** USE A GOOD CLEANING...
AND MAYBE CHICKENS SAY "MOO"
WE'RE **BACHELORS**, BABY
© 2008 PAWS, INC. All Rights Reserved.
Distributed by Universal Press Syndicate

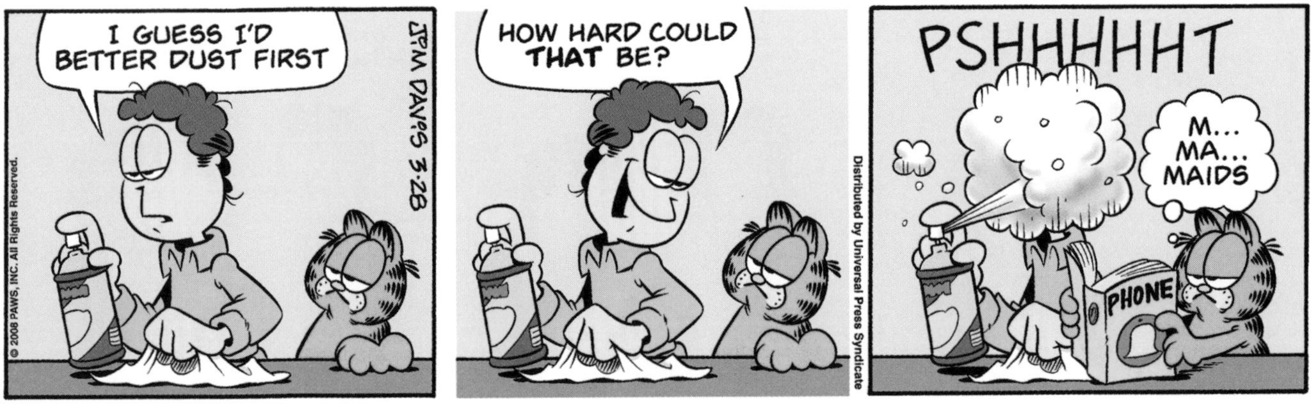
I GUESS I'D BETTER DUST FIRST
HOW HARD COULD **THAT** BE?
PSHHHHHT
M... MA... MAIDS
PHONE
© 2008 PAWS, INC. All Rights Reserved.
Distributed by Universal Press Syndicate

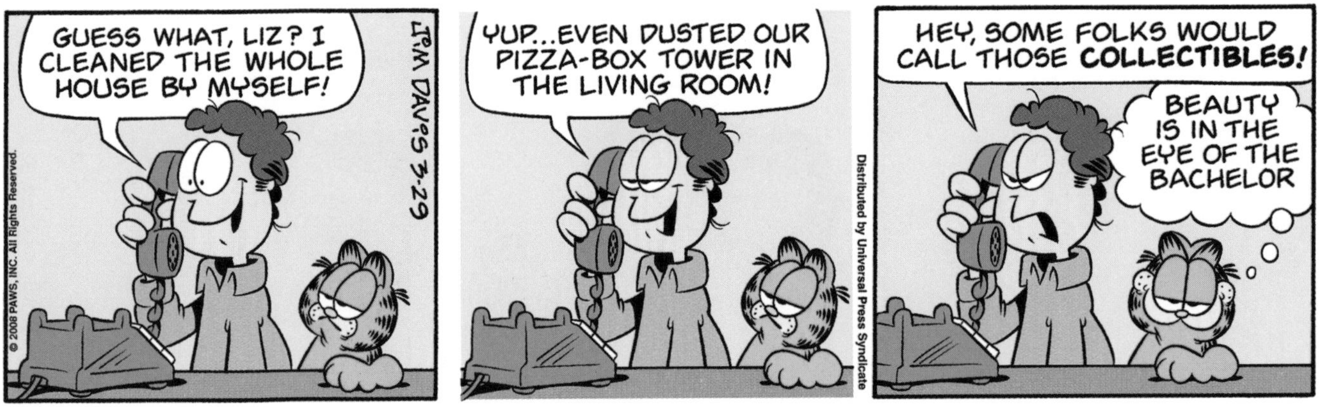
GUESS WHAT, LIZ? I CLEANED THE WHOLE HOUSE BY MYSELF!
YUP...EVEN DUSTED OUR PIZZA-BOX TOWER IN THE LIVING ROOM!
HEY, SOME FOLKS WOULD CALL THOSE **COLLECTIBLES!**
BEAUTY IS IN THE EYE OF THE BACHELOR
© 2008 PAWS, INC. All Rights Reserved.
Distributed by Universal Press Syndicate

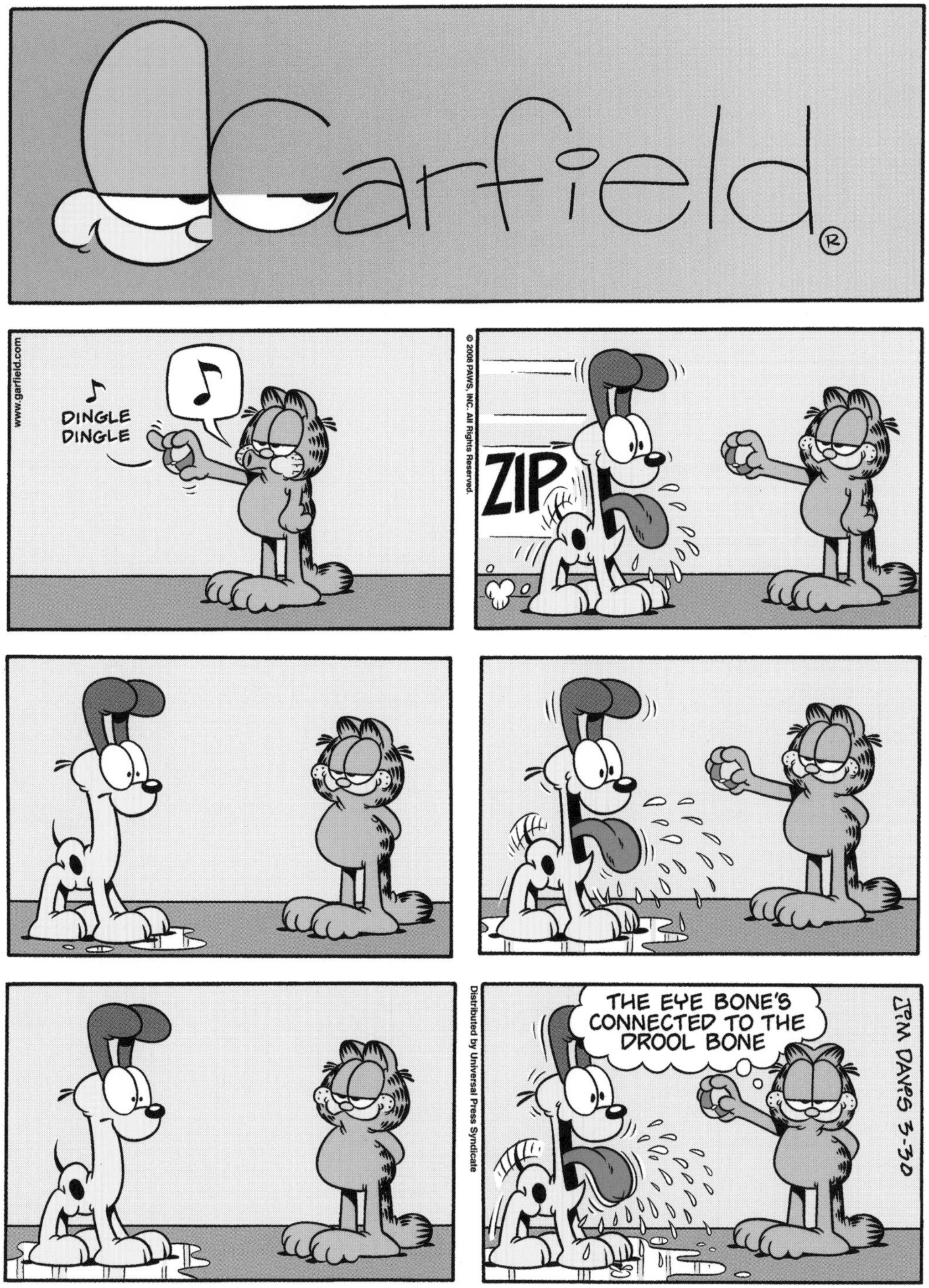
Garfield
www.garfield.com
DINGLE DINGLE
© 2006 PAWS, INC. All Rights Reserved.
ZIP
Distributed by Universal Press Syndicate
THE EYE BONE'S CONNECTED TO THE DROOL BONE
JPM DAVIS 3-30

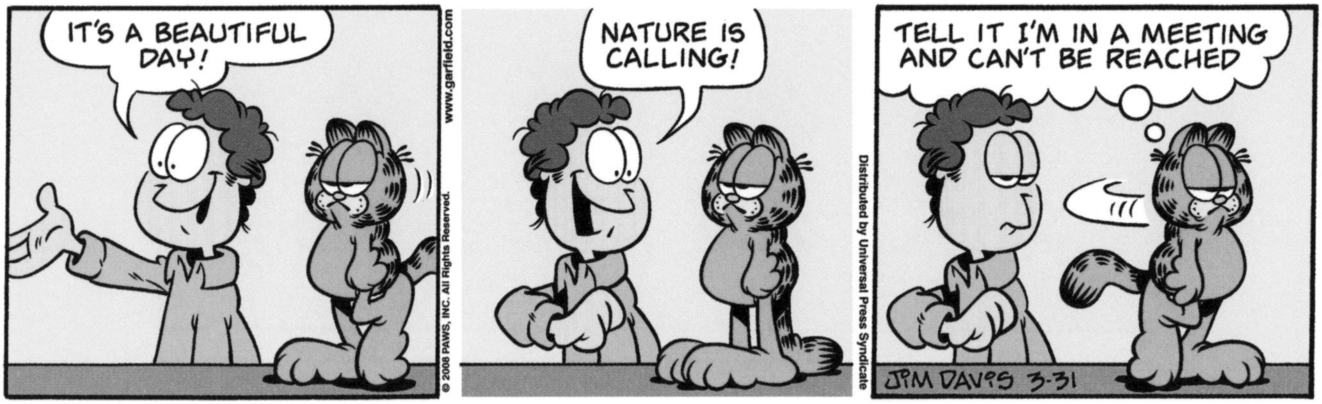
IT'S A BEAUTIFUL DAY!
NATURE IS CALLING!
TELL IT I'M IN A MEETING AND CAN'T BE REACHED
JIM DAVIS 3-31
© 2008 PAWS, INC. All Rights Reserved. www.garfield.com
Distributed by Universal Press Syndicate

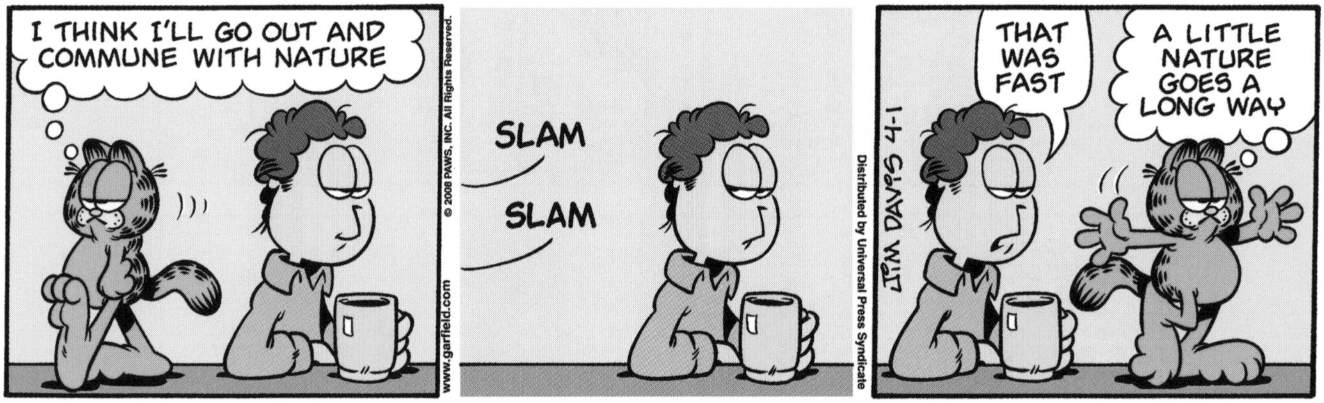
I THINK I'LL GO OUT AND COMMUNE WITH NATURE
SLAM
SLAM
THAT WAS FAST
A LITTLE NATURE GOES A LONG WAY
JIM DAVIS 4-1
© 2008 PAWS, INC. All Rights Reserved. www.garfield.com
Distributed by Universal Press Syndicate

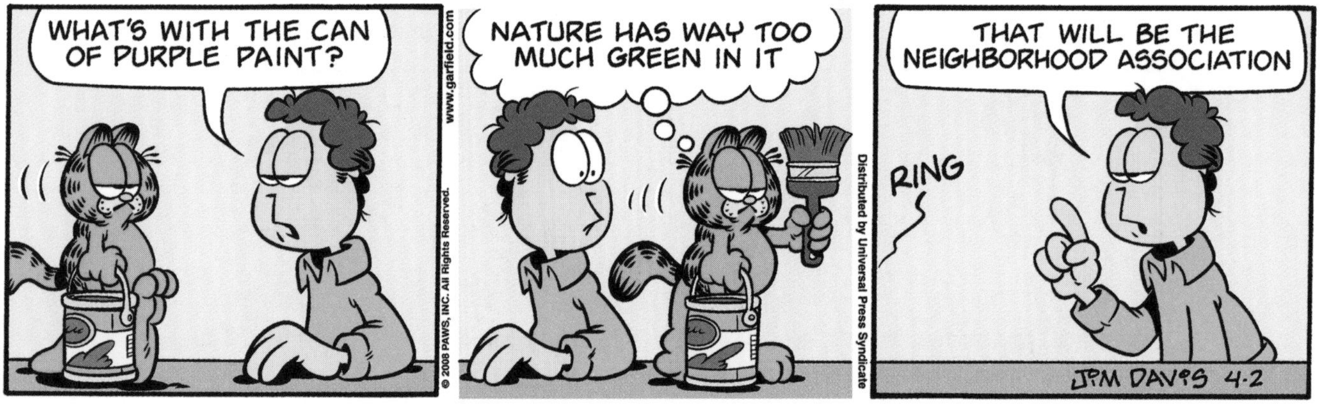
WHAT'S WITH THE CAN OF PURPLE PAINT?
NATURE HAS WAY TOO MUCH GREEN IN IT
RING
THAT WILL BE THE NEIGHBORHOOD ASSOCIATION
JIM DAVIS 4-2
© 2008 PAWS, INC. All Rights Reserved. www.garfield.com
Distributed by Universal Press Syndicate

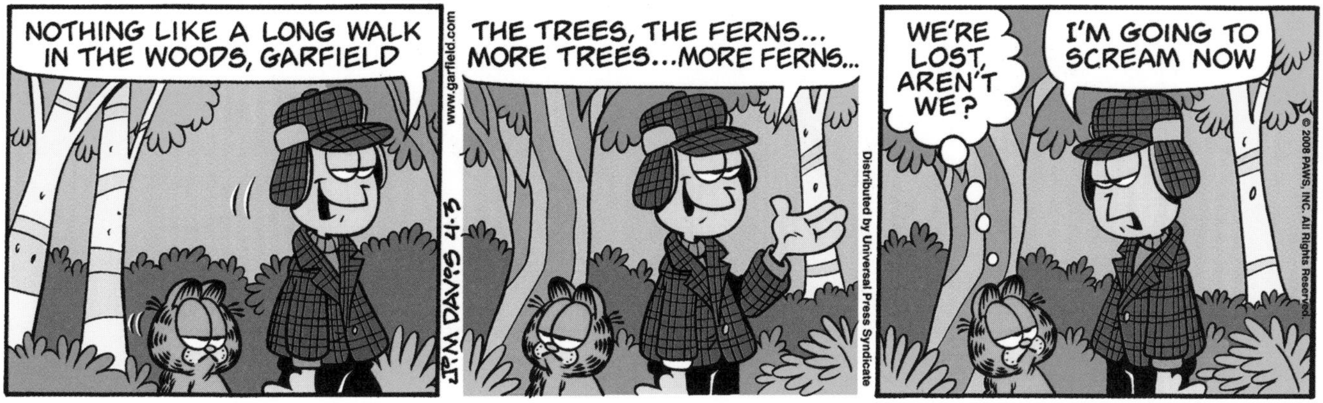
NOTHING LIKE A LONG WALK IN THE WOODS, GARFIELD
www.garfield.com
JIM DAVIS 4-3
THE TREES, THE FERNS... MORE TREES...MORE FERNS...
Distributed by Universal Press Syndicate
WE'RE LOST, AREN'T WE?
I'M GOING TO SCREAM NOW
© 2008 PAWS, INC. All Rights Reserved.

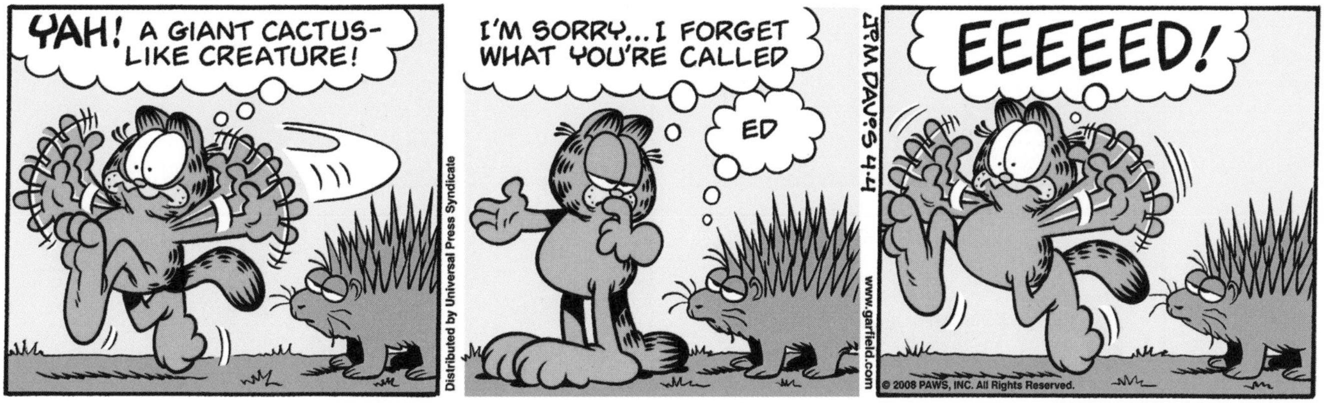
YAH! A GIANT CACTUS-LIKE CREATURE!
Distributed by Universal Press Syndicate
I'M SORRY...I FORGET WHAT YOU'RE CALLED
ED
JIM DAVIS 4-4
www.garfield.com
EEEEED!
© 2008 PAWS, INC. All Rights Reserved.

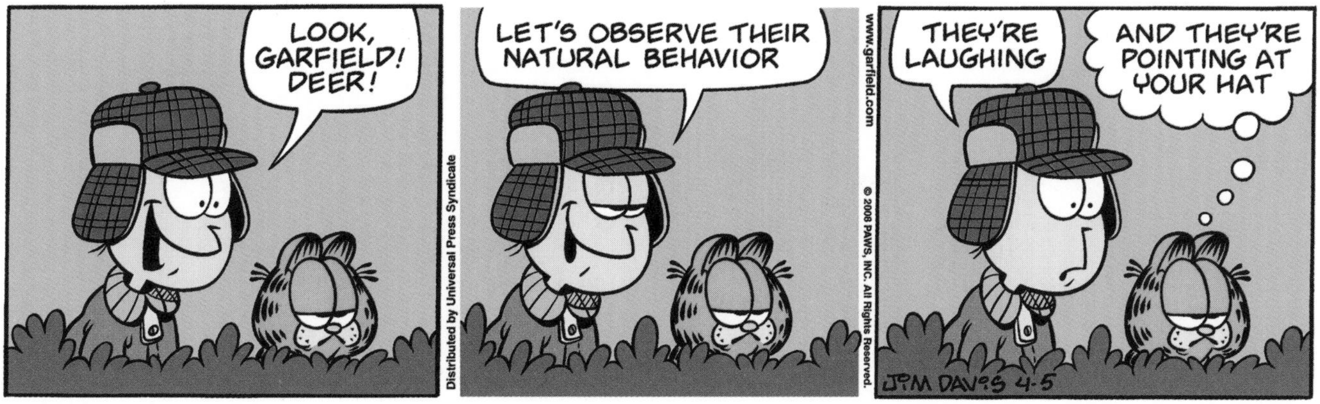
LOOK, GARFIELD! DEER!
Distributed by Universal Press Syndicate
LET'S OBSERVE THEIR NATURAL BEHAVIOR
www.garfield.com
© 2008 PAWS, INC. All Rights Reserved.
THEY'RE LAUGHING
AND THEY'RE POINTING AT YOUR HAT
JIM DAVIS 4-5

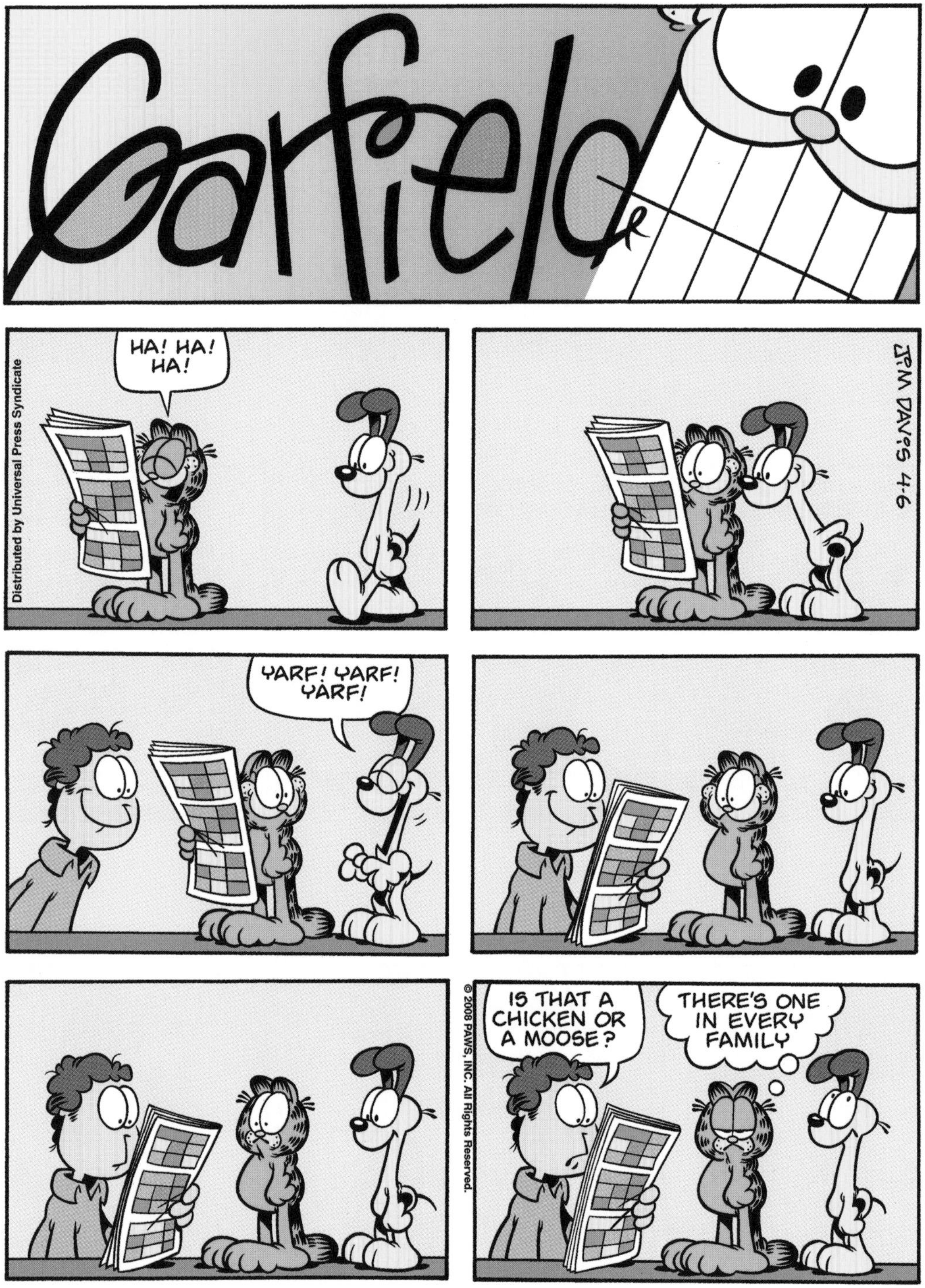
Garfield
HA! HA! HA!
Distributed by Universal Press Syndicate
JPM DAVPS 4-6
YARF! YARF! YARF!
© 2008 PAWS, INC. All Rights Reserved.
IS THAT A CHICKEN OR A MOOSE?
THERE'S ONE IN EVERY FAMILY

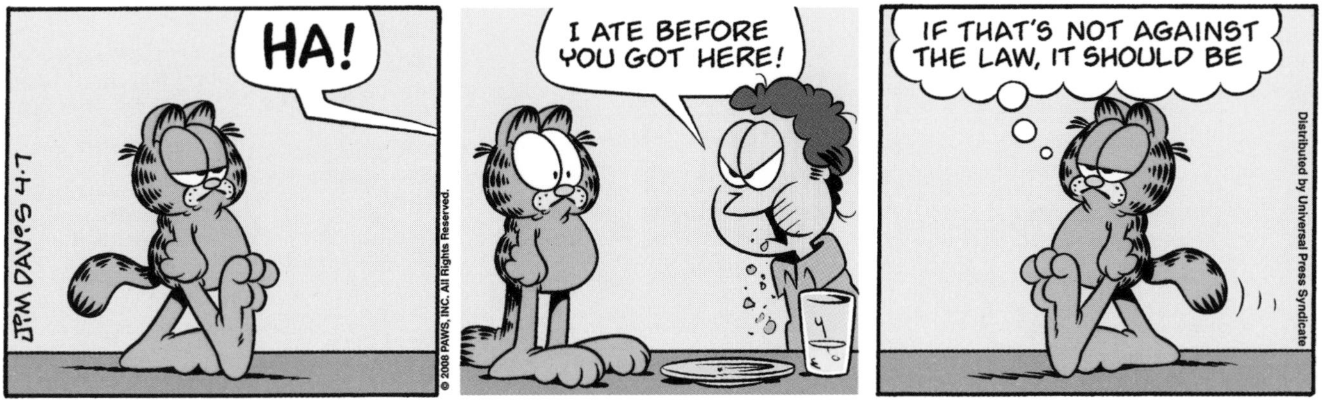
JIM DAVIS 4·7
HA!
© 2008 PAWS, INC. All Rights Reserved.
I ATE BEFORE YOU GOT HERE!
IF THAT'S NOT AGAINST THE LAW, IT SHOULD BE
Distributed by Universal Press Syndicate

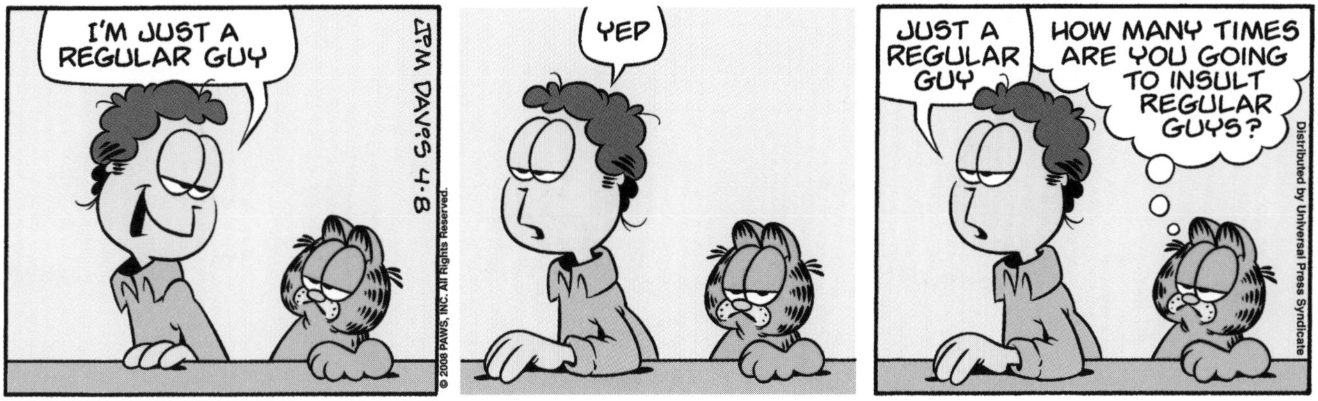
I'M JUST A REGULAR GUY
JIM DAVIS 4·8
© 2008 PAWS, INC. All Rights Reserved.
YEP
JUST A REGULAR GUY
HOW MANY TIMES ARE YOU GOING TO INSULT REGULAR GUYS?
Distributed by Universal Press Syndicate

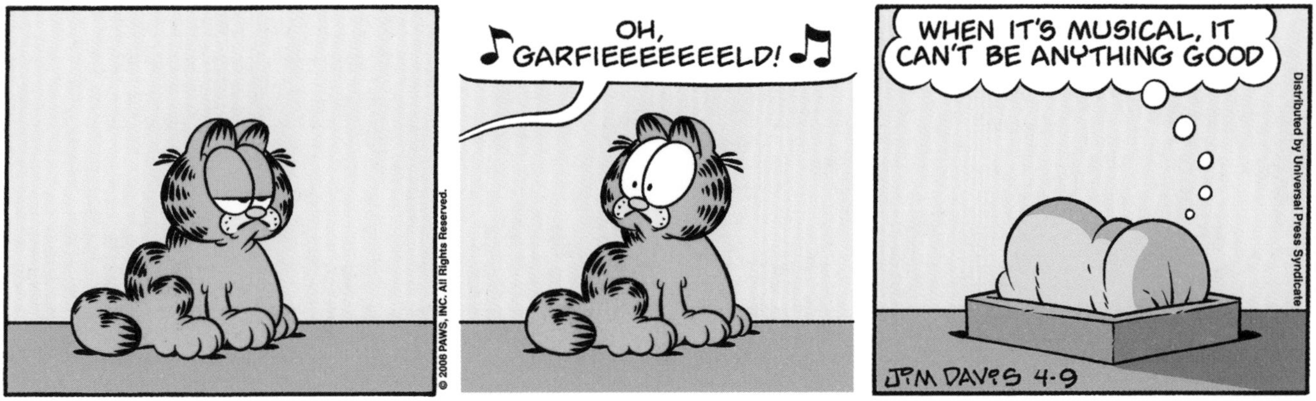
© 2008 PAWS, INC. All Rights Reserved.
OH, GARFIEEEEEEELD!
WHEN IT'S MUSICAL, IT CAN'T BE ANYTHING GOOD
Distributed by Universal Press Syndicate
JIM DAVIS 4·9

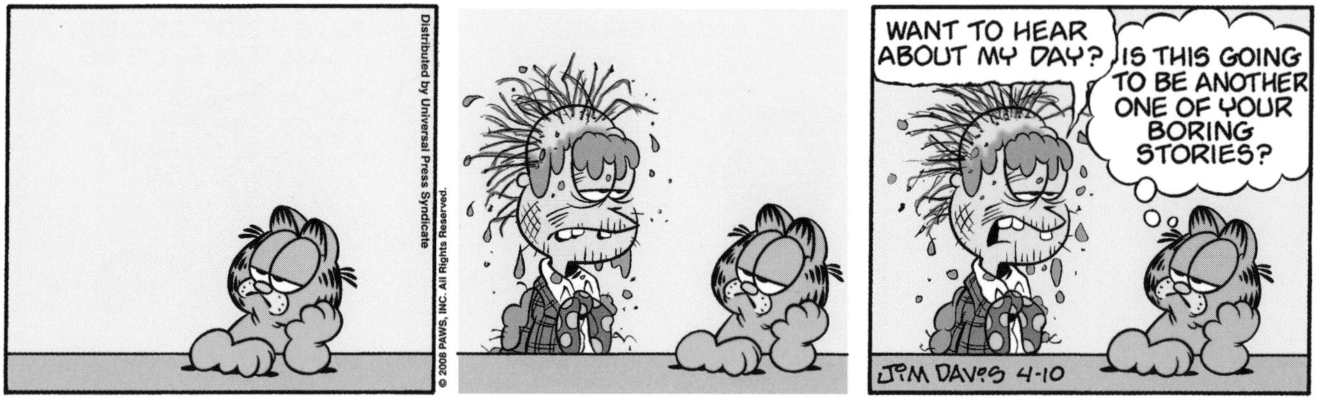
Distributed by Universal Press Syndicate
© 2008 PAWS, INC. All Rights Reserved.
WANT TO HEAR ABOUT MY DAY?
IS THIS GOING TO BE ANOTHER ONE OF YOUR BORING STORIES?
JIM DAVIS 4-10

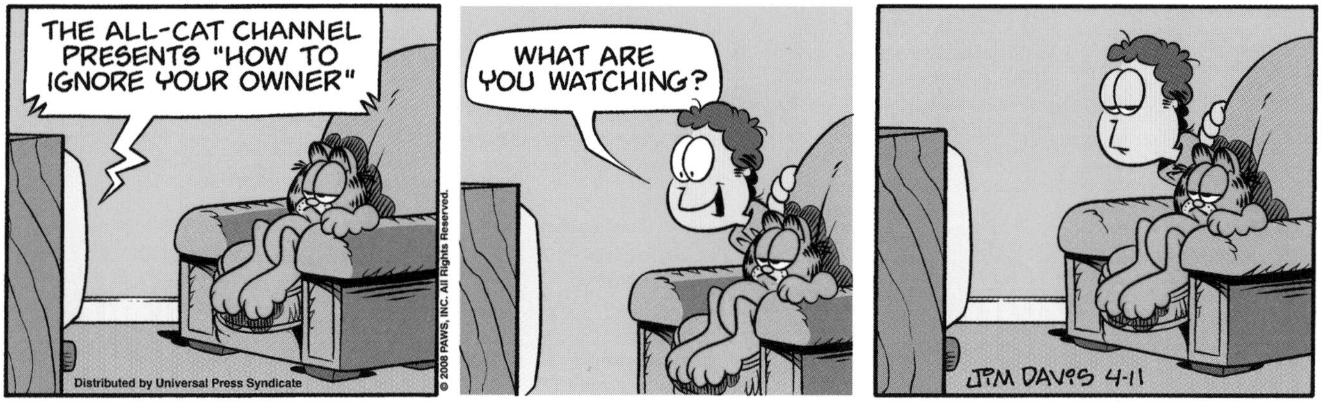
THE ALL-CAT CHANNEL PRESENTS "HOW TO IGNORE YOUR OWNER"
Distributed by Universal Press Syndicate
© 2008 PAWS, INC. All Rights Reserved.
WHAT ARE YOU WATCHING?
JIM DAVIS 4-11

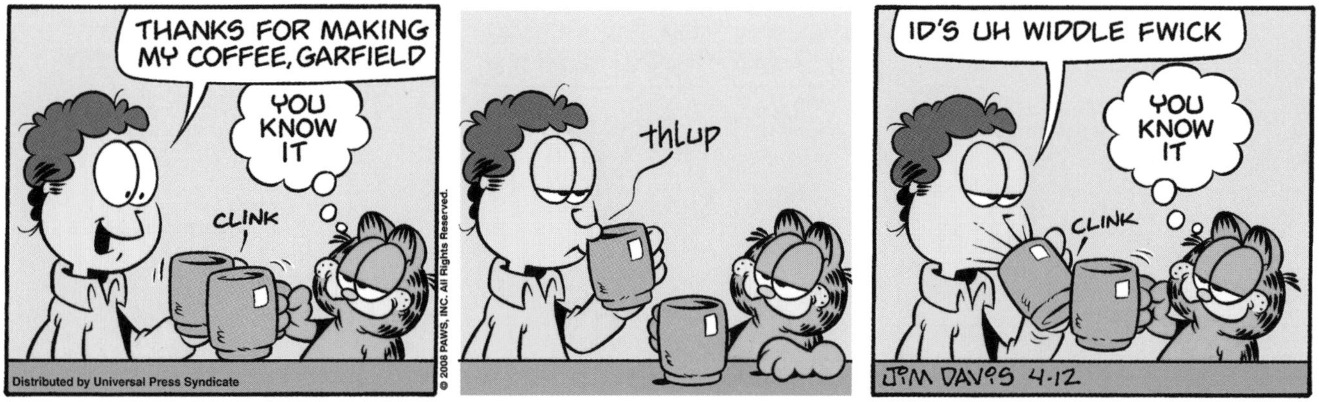
THANKS FOR MAKING MY COFFEE, GARFIELD
YOU KNOW IT
CLINK
Distributed by Universal Press Syndicate
© 2008 PAWS, INC. All Rights Reserved.
thlup
ID'S UH WIDDLE FWICK
YOU KNOW IT
CLINK
JIM DAVIS 4-12

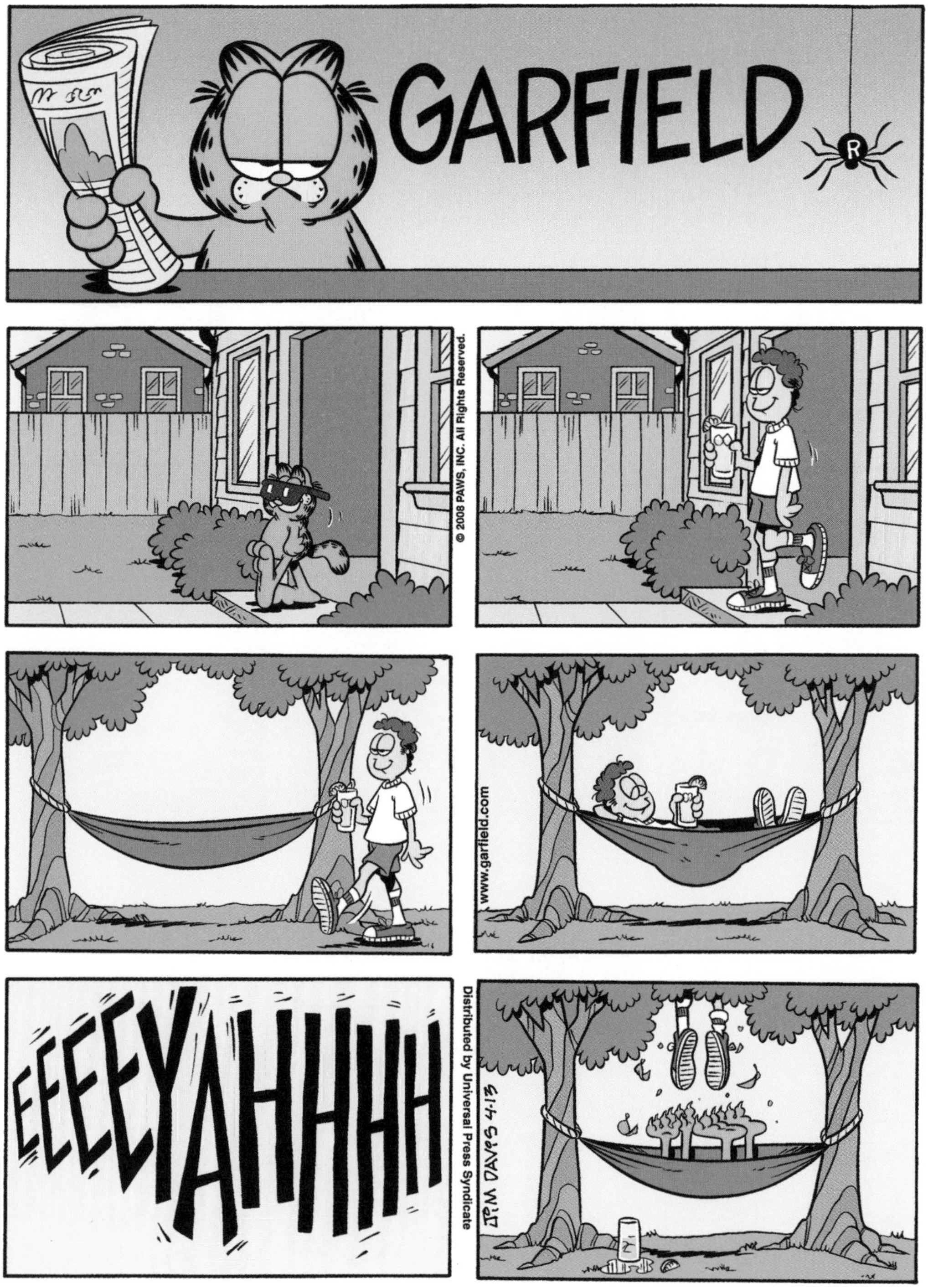
GARFIELD
© 2008 PAWS, INC. All Rights Reserved.
www.garfield.com
EEEEYAHHHH
Distributed by Universal Press Syndicate
JPM DAVIS 4-13

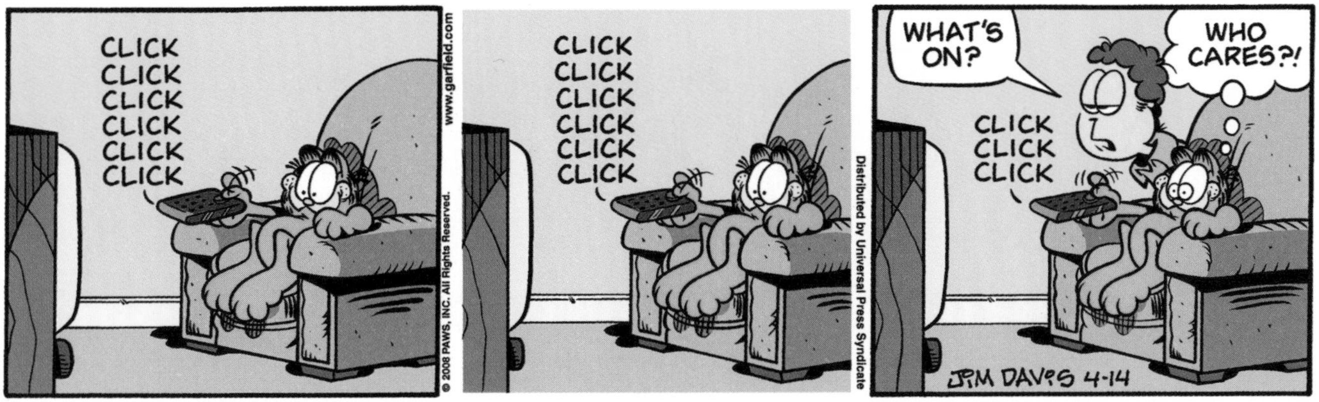
CLICK CLICK CLICK CLICK CLICK CLICK
CLICK CLICK CLICK CLICK CLICK CLICK
WHAT'S ON?
CLICK CLICK CLICK
WHO CARES?!
JIM DAVIS 4-14
© 2008 PAWS, INC. All Rights Reserved. www.garfield.com
Distributed by Universal Press Syndicate

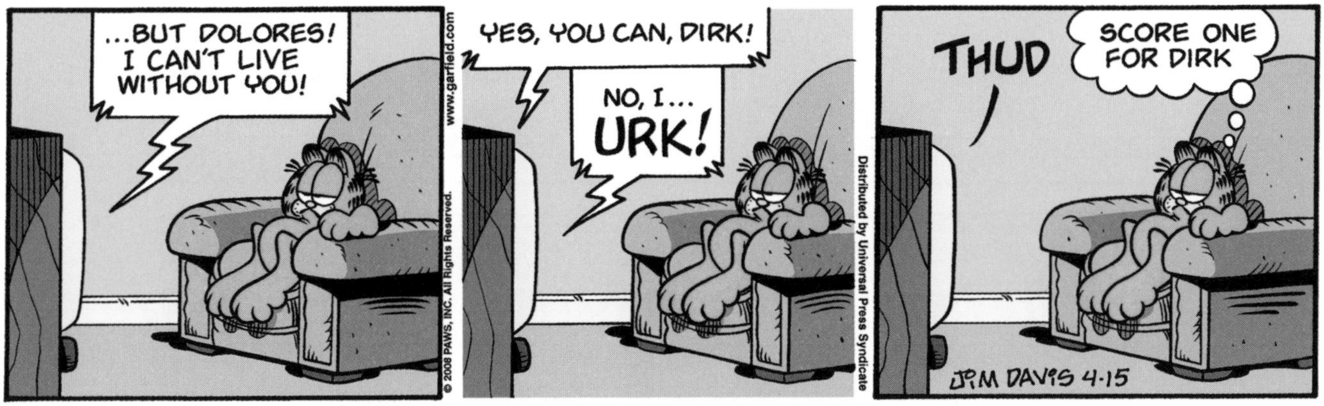
...BUT DOLORES! I CAN'T LIVE WITHOUT YOU!
YES, YOU CAN, DIRK!
NO, I... URK!
THUD
SCORE ONE FOR DIRK
JIM DAVIS 4-15
© 2008 PAWS, INC. All Rights Reserved. www.garfield.com
Distributed by Universal Press Syndicate

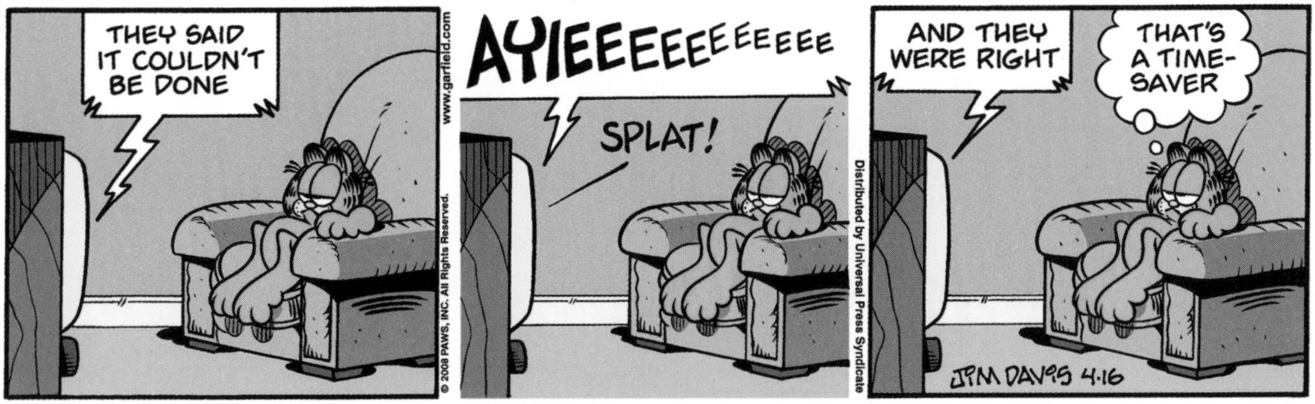
THEY SAID IT COULDN'T BE DONE
AYIEEEEEEEEEEE
SPLAT!
AND THEY WERE RIGHT
THAT'S A TIME-SAVER
JIM DAVIS 4-16
© 2008 PAWS, INC. All Rights Reserved. www.garfield.com
Distributed by Universal Press Syndicate

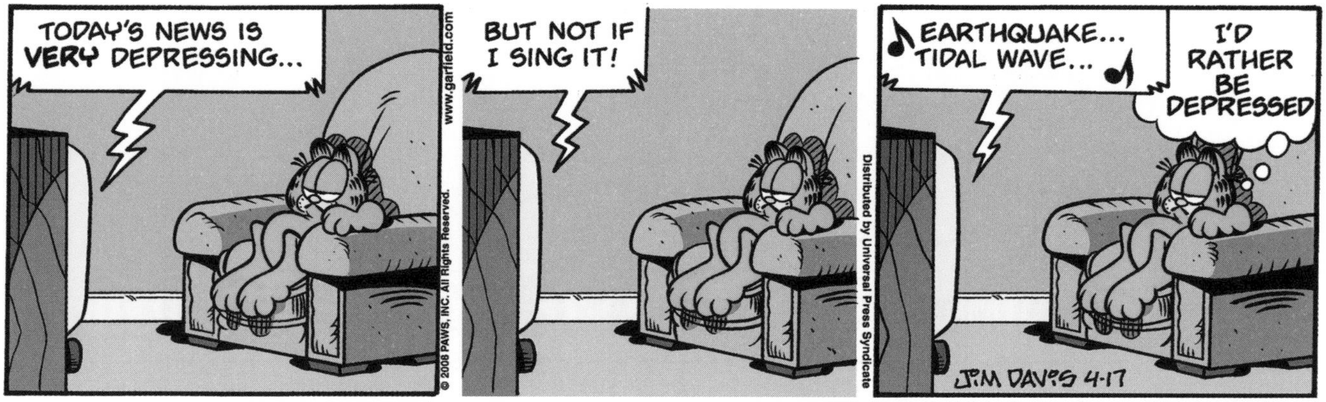
TODAY'S NEWS IS VERY DEPRESSING...
BUT NOT IF I SING IT!
EARTHQUAKE... TIDAL WAVE...
I'D RATHER BE DEPRESSED
JIM DAVIS 4-17
© 2008 PAWS, INC. All Rights Reserved.
www.garfield.com
Distributed by Universal Press Syndicate

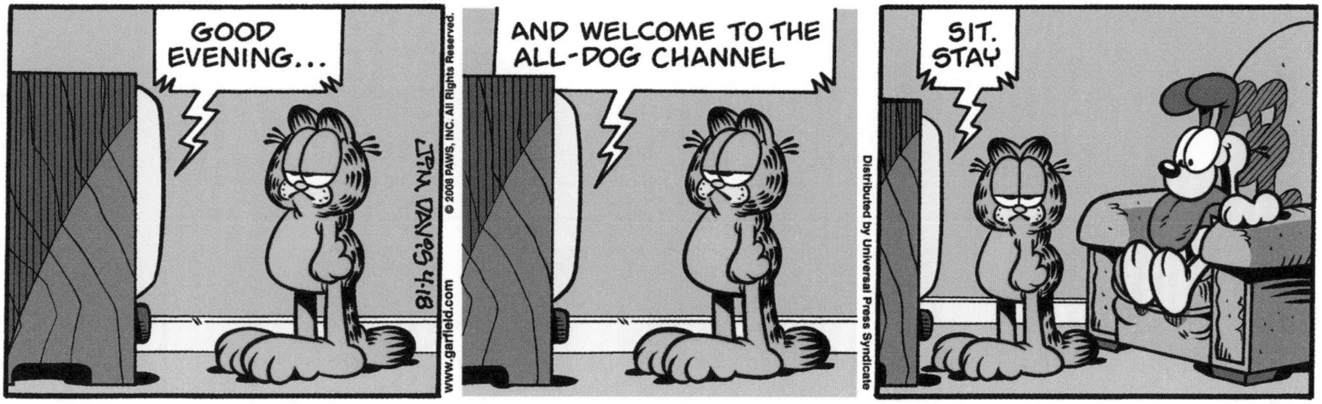
GOOD EVENING...
AND WELCOME TO THE ALL-DOG CHANNEL
SIT. STAY
JIM DAVIS 4-18
© 2008 PAWS, INC. All Rights Reserved.
www.garfield.com
Distributed by Universal Press Syndicate

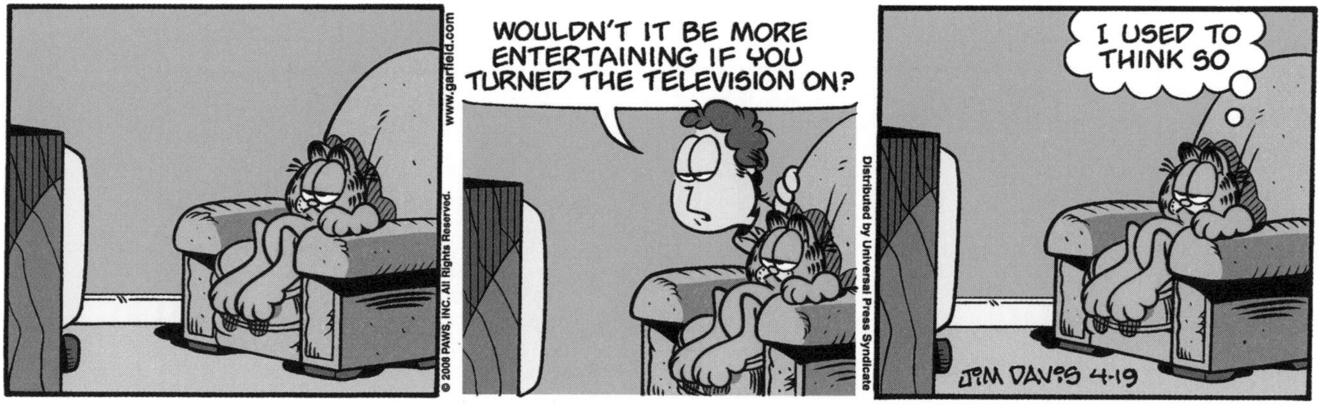
WOULDN'T IT BE MORE ENTERTAINING IF YOU TURNED THE TELEVISION ON?
I USED TO THINK SO
JIM DAVIS 4-19
© 2008 PAWS, INC. All Rights Reserved.
www.garfield.com
Distributed by Universal Press Syndicate

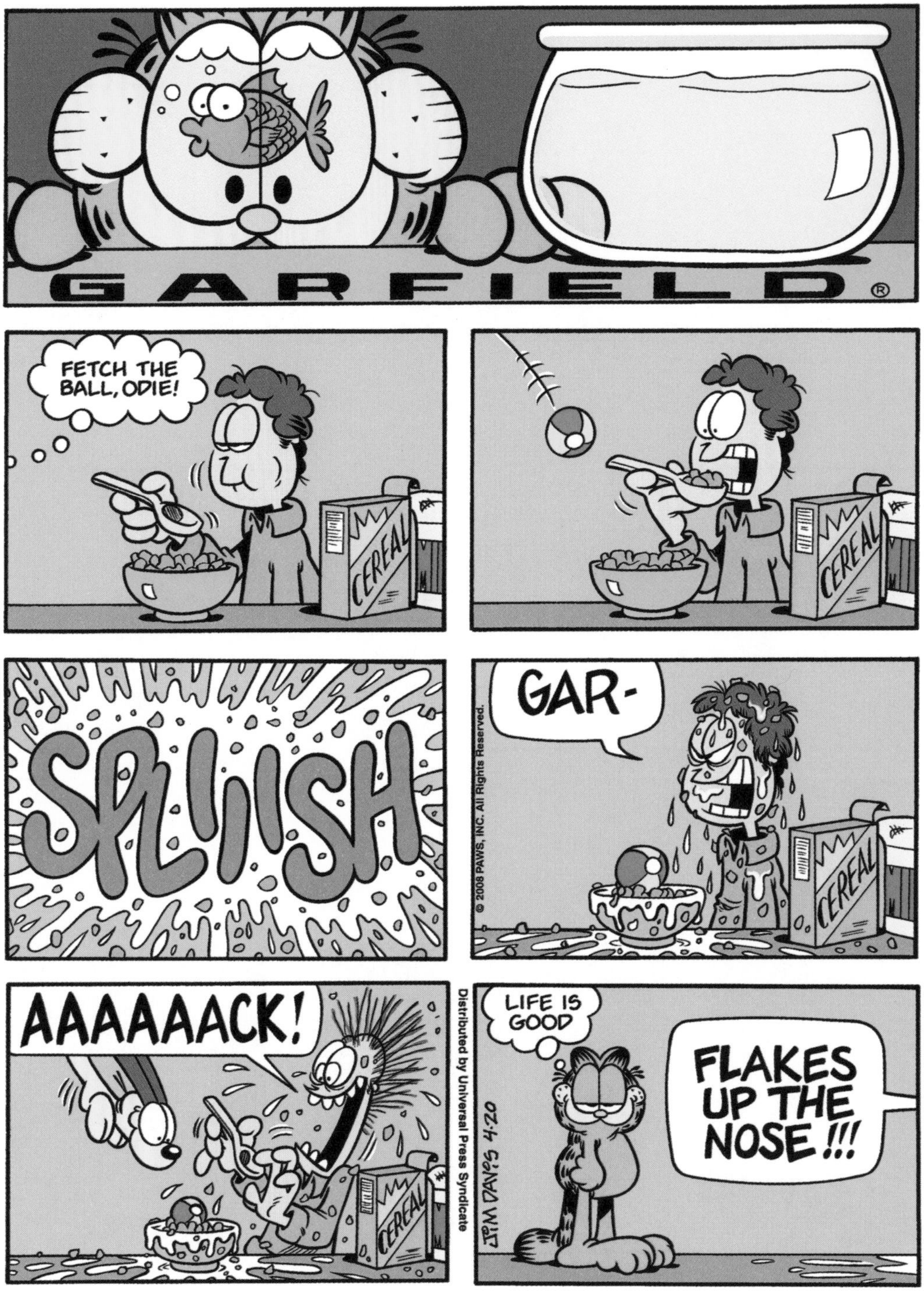

GARFIELD®
FETCH THE BALL, ODIE!
SPLISH
© 2008 PAWS, INC. All Rights Reserved.
GAR-
AAAAAACK!
Distributed by Universal Press Syndicate
JIM DAVIS 4-20
LIFE IS GOOD
FLAKES UP THE NOSE!!!

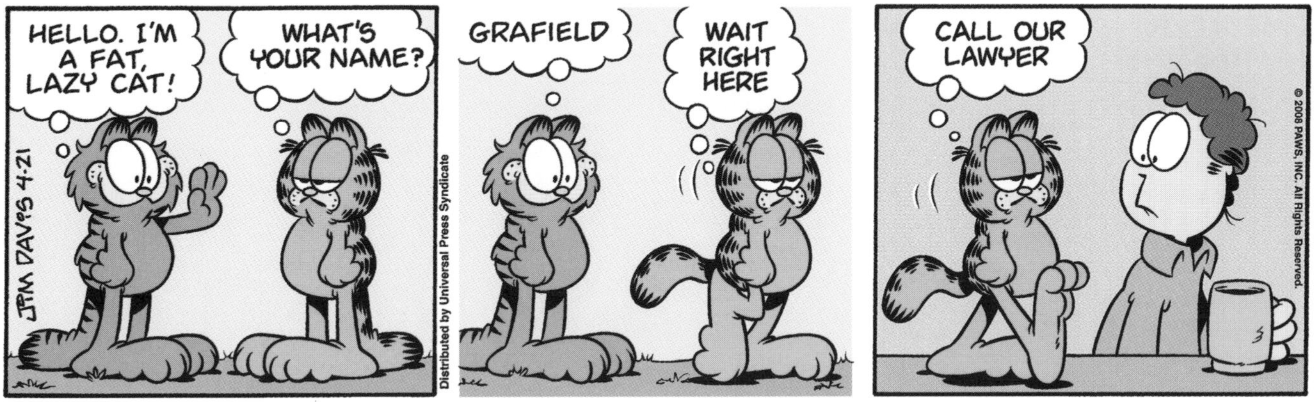
JIM DAVIS 4-21
HELLO. I'M A FAT, LAZY CAT!
WHAT'S YOUR NAME?
Distributed by Universal Press Syndicate
GRAFIELD
WAIT RIGHT HERE
CALL OUR LAWYER
© 2008 PAWS, INC. All Rights Reserved.

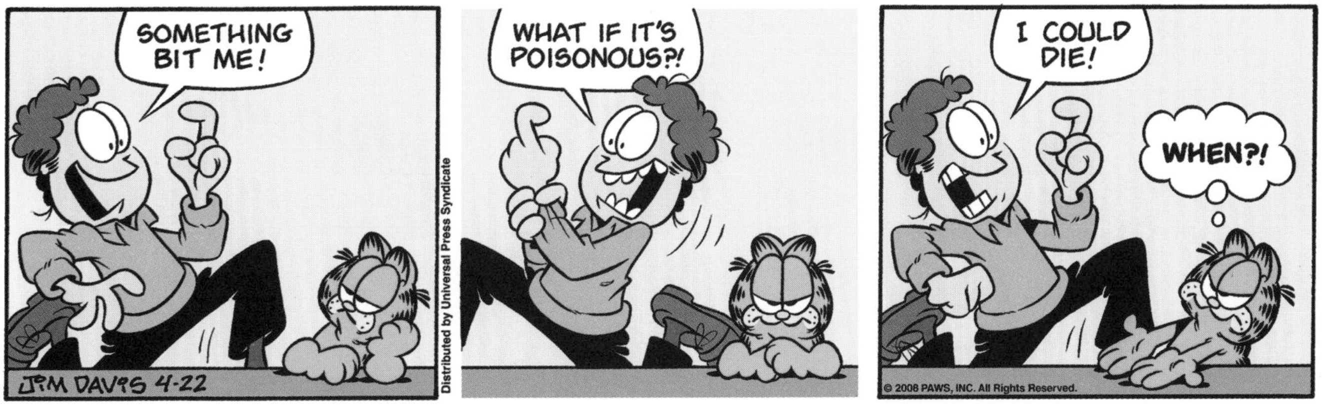
SOMETHING BIT ME!
JIM DAVIS 4-22
Distributed by Universal Press Syndicate
WHAT IF IT'S POISONOUS?!
I COULD DIE!
WHEN?!
© 2008 PAWS, INC. All Rights Reserved.

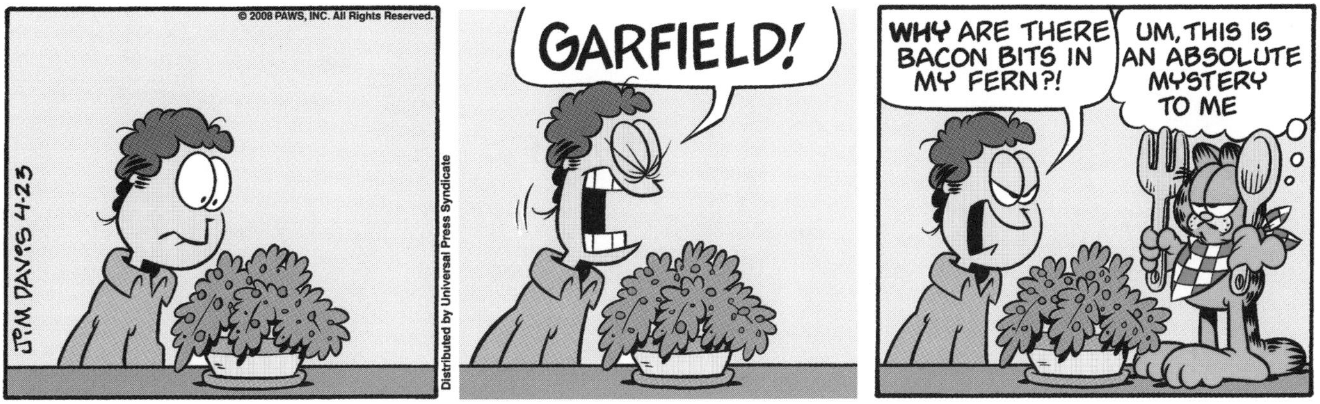
© 2008 PAWS, INC. All Rights Reserved.
JIM DAVIS 4-23
Distributed by Universal Press Syndicate
GARFIELD!
WHY ARE THERE BACON BITS IN MY FERN?!
UM, THIS IS AN ABSOLUTE MYSTERY TO ME

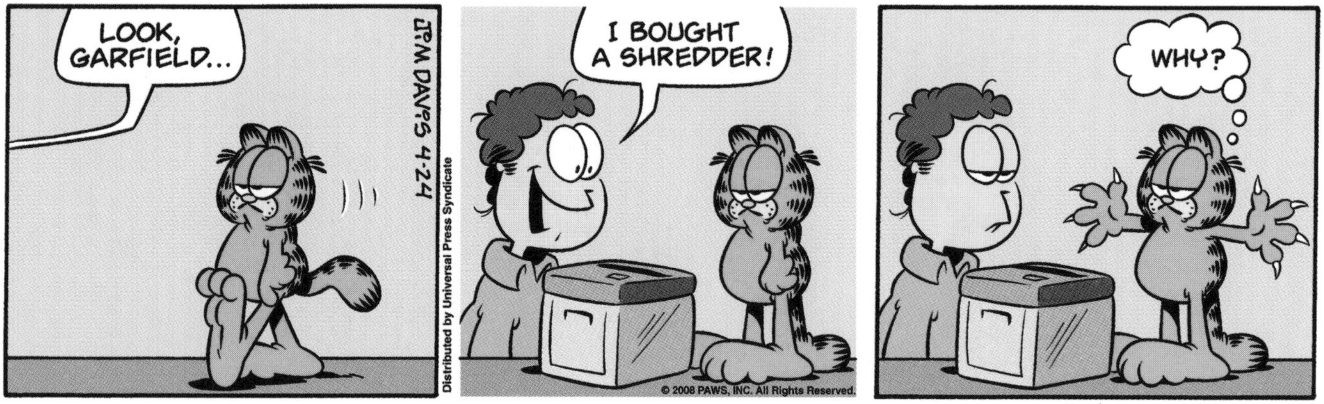
LOOK, GARFIELD...
JIM DAVIS 4-24
Distributed by Universal Press Syndicate
I BOUGHT A SHREDDER!
© 2008 PAWS, INC. All Rights Reserved.
WHY?

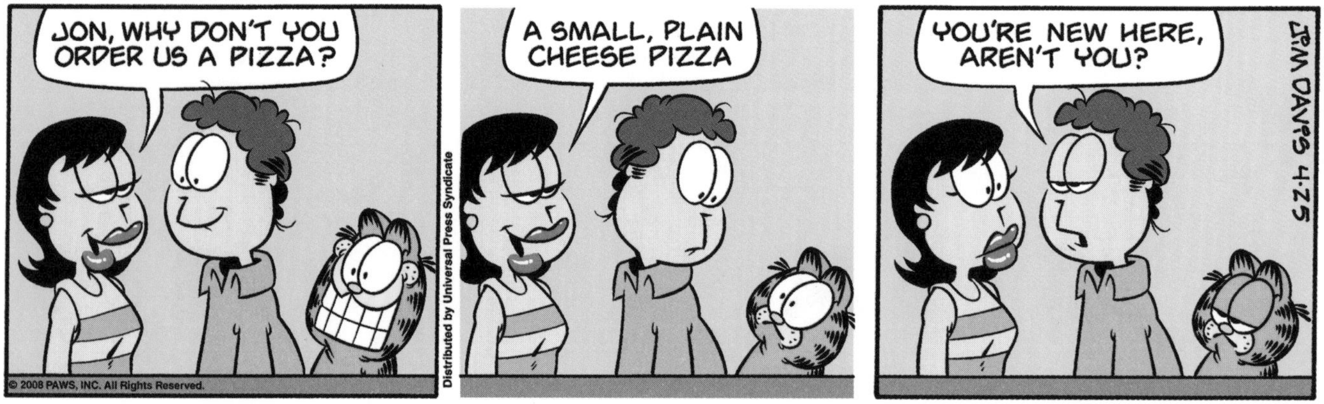
JON, WHY DON'T YOU ORDER US A PIZZA?
© 2008 PAWS, INC. All Rights Reserved.
Distributed by Universal Press Syndicate
A SMALL, PLAIN CHEESE PIZZA
YOU'RE NEW HERE, AREN'T YOU?
JIM DAVIS 4-25

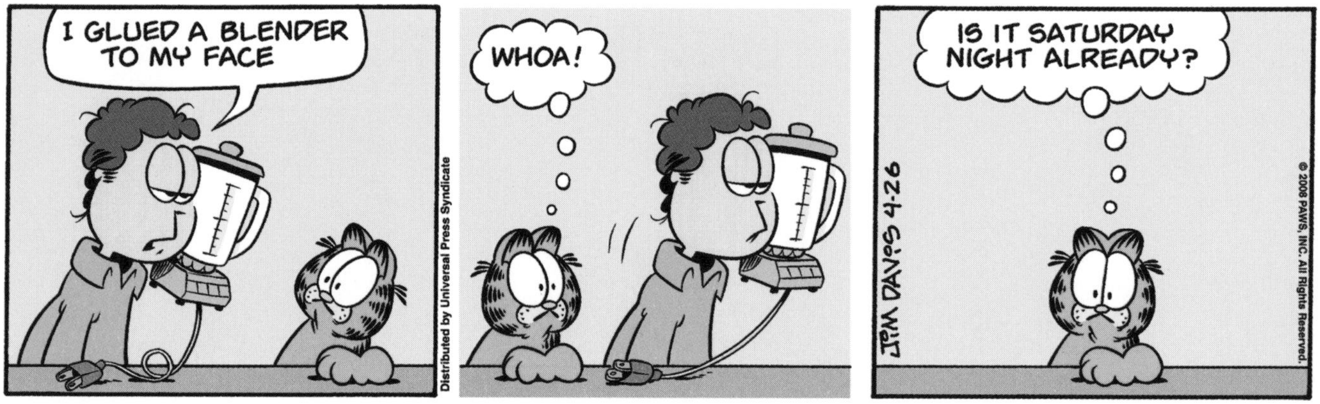
I GLUED A BLENDER TO MY FACE
Distributed by Universal Press Syndicate
WHOA!
JIM DAVIS 4-26
IS IT SATURDAY NIGHT ALREADY?
© 2008 PAWS, INC. All Rights Reserved.

Garfield's KOOKY KLASSICS

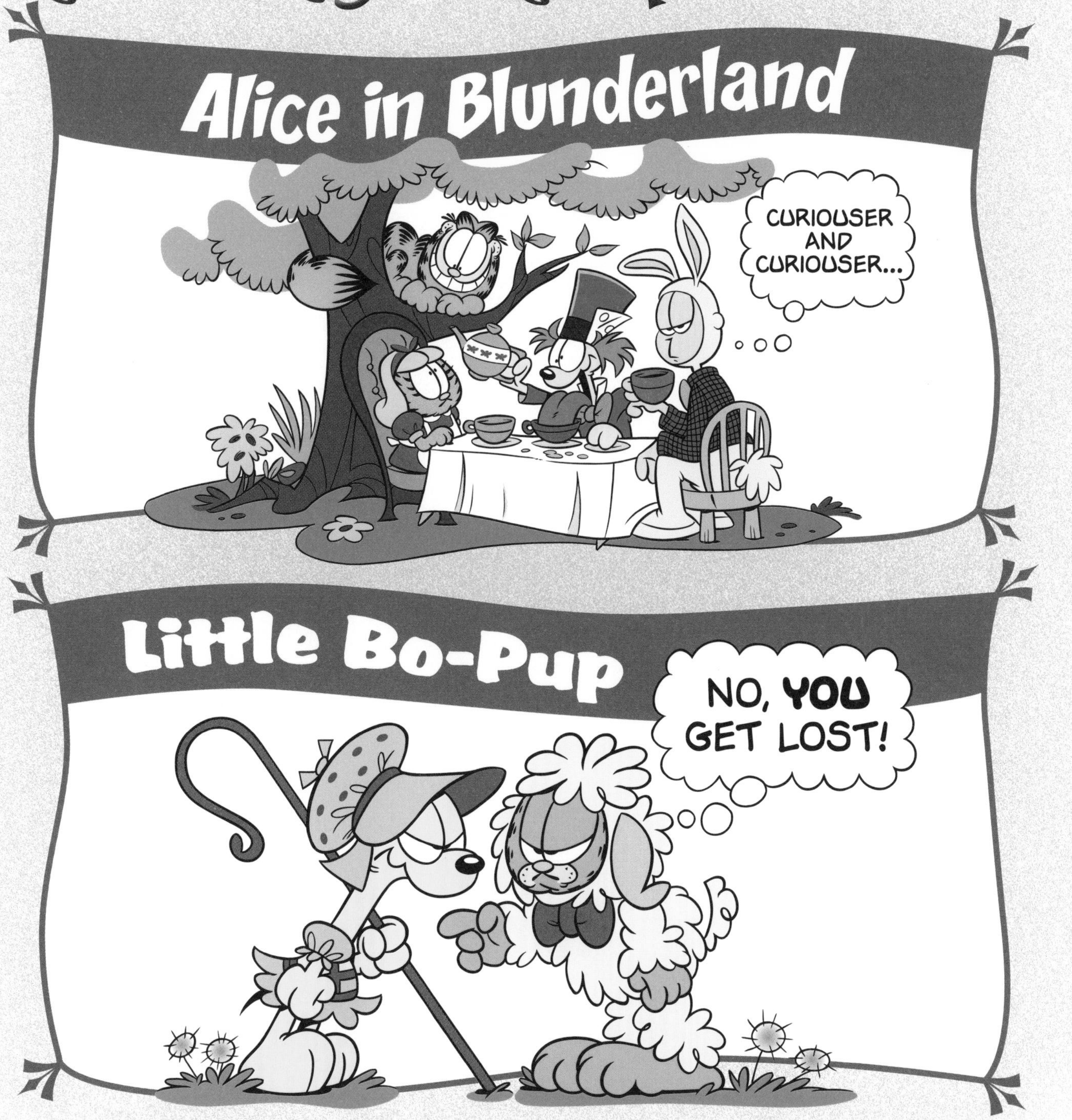
Alice in Blunderland
CURIOUSER AND CURIOUSER...
Little Bo-Pup
NO, YOU GET LOST!

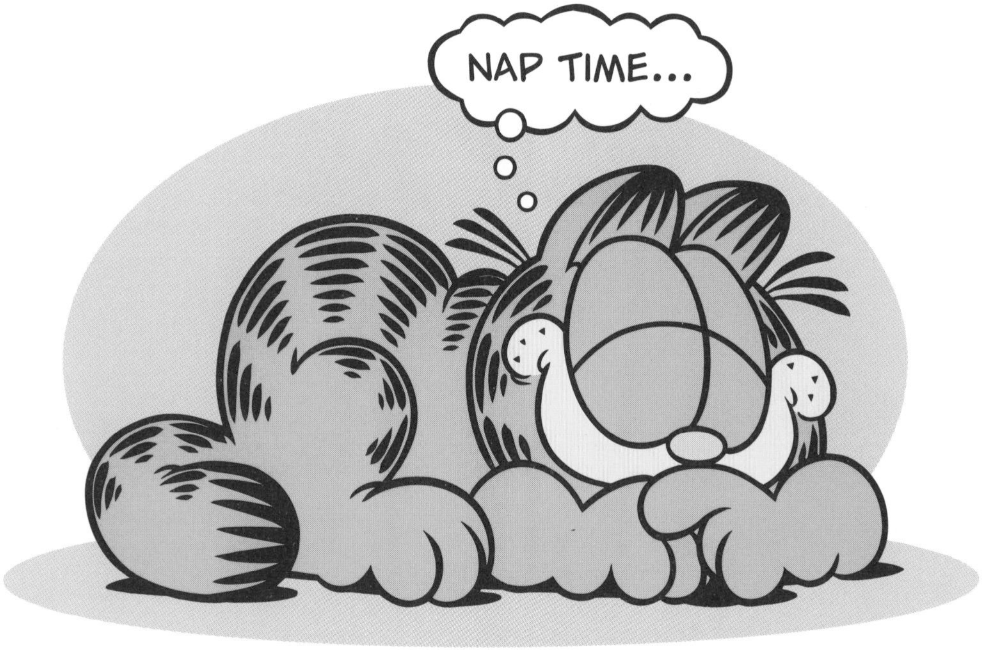
NAP TIME...